Shareholder Value –
A Business Experience

Shareholder Value –
A Business Experience

Roy E. Johnson

OXFORD AUCKLAND BOSTON JOHANNESBURG MELBOURNE NEW DELHI

Butterworth-Heinemann
Linacre House, Jordan Hill, Oxford OX2 8DP
225 Wildwood Avenue, Woburn, MA 01801-2041
A division of Reed Educational and Professional Publishing Ltd

𝓡 A member of the Reed Elsevier plc group

First published 2001

British Library Cataloguing in Publication Data

Johnson, Roy E.
    Shareholder value : a business experience. – (Quantitative
    finance series)
    1. Business enterprises – Finance   2. Corporations – Investor
    relations – Economic aspects   3. Corporate profits – Management
    I. Title
    658.1′55

Library of Congress Cataloguing in Publication Data
A catalogue record for this book is available from the Library of Congress

ISBN 0 7506 5382 5

For information on all Butterworth-Heinemann publications visit our
website at www.bh.com

Typeset by Laser Words, Madras, India
Printed and bound in Great Britain by Biddles Ltd, *www.biddles.co.uk*

Contents

Preface

Shareholder Value – A Business Experience is a book about modern corporate finance, value-based financial performance, and economic value management. It is directed toward the most important financial goal of any 'for profit' enterprise – namely, optimizing the long-term return to shareholders. This 'return' can be the increase in the common stock price, along with dividends, for a public company; or the 'warranted' equity value and/or ability to remit cash distributions for a privately owned company. While directed towards shareholder value, this book is *not* intended to be a predictor for the public stock markets in the USA or other countries. It will also *not* attempt to indicate the attractiveness of any single industry, segment, or company – in terms of *'who's hot and who's not'* at any particular time.

Rather, its purpose is to present a powerful and useful toolkit of market-based perspectives, analytic approaches, valuation techniques, and specific financial metrics – for use in everyday business life. The book is designed to help a broad spectrum of professionals and students, many of whom may not have strong financial backgrounds, better understand the salient points and real-world implications of a 'value management' movement which has taken hold in many corporations in the USA and around the world. This movement is being supported by some of the major institutional investors who influence financial markets.

One goal of the book is to help working professionals grasp the concept of value 'creators' and 'destroyers' – along with the implications. Another is to provide tools to measure the success (or failure) of major strategic and operational initiatives. Some people, in the professional workforce, may feel that they have been handed a management discipline encompassing a confusing set of new metrics, which can impact their job performance rating and compensation. The contents of the book should help corporate managers to first, *understand* how shareholder value is created and then, *direct behavior* – their own and that of others – toward 'value-based' planning and action.

For students of business and finance, the book is intended to provide a comprehensive foundation for important elements of business strategy and acquisition valuation, corporate financial analysis, capital investments, corporate financing, and economic value-based metrics. There is also an attempt to give a glimpse of the 'environment' surrounding value-based management that students may face as they embark on or pursue corporate careers.

Shareholder Value – A Business Experience is a fictional story, offering a combination of storybook reading and textbook analysis. The lead character is an experienced financial professional, whose career has been split between corporate and management consulting roles. It is a narrative of one of his last major assignments, in which he is given an opportunity to incorporate virtually all the knowledge and expertise gained during his career and assist an industrial company implement a comprehensive, value-based financial performance system. Other key characters comprise the corporate and operating management of the fictitious firm. Behavioral aspects of the effort to institute an 'economic value'-oriented financial management system, along with potential barriers to such an endeavor, are exposed through the interaction of the various characters in the story.

It is my sincere hope that no one will be offended by the character portrayals. The characters have been developed to make the story entertaining, as well as thorough. Growing older, I realize more and more that self-reflection, self-criticism, and humor are good recipes for staying productive and maintaining one's sanity. So, please don't stereotype the characters or feel offended if you occupy a position portrayed by one of the characters whom you may either not like or wish to be associated with.

In the financial markets, specific rates of return can change over time. Thus, the 'cost of capital' rates, as presented in Chapter 4 – Cost of Capital, may not be the most accurate for the reader's specific situation. For example, the 'risk-free' (long-term government bond) rate was pegged at 6.5%, a representative level at the time that the book was written. The 'market risk premium' – the excess return that the stock market has produced over time in comparison to the long-term (30-year) government bond rate – has been set at 5.0%. This rate (set to make the mathematical calculations as simple as possible) is at the low end of the relevant range for this statistic, which had been tracked for about seventy years at the time the book was written. Similarly, debt and preferred stock costs (rates) may or may not be accurate for the reader's situation and/or time frame. The reader should, therefore, make any adjustment(s) necessary to apply the material to his or her particular circumstance, if the desire is to go beyond calculations for the hypothetical firms in the book. The potential inaccuracies, regarding the cost(s) of capital, do not alter any of the underlying concepts or perceptions, but they could change the magnitude of results in the numeric examples.

In a similar vein, the Financial Accounting Standards Board (FASB) – the governing body for accounting regulations in the USA – established new rules for mergers and acquisitions that effectively eliminated 'pooling of interests' and 'goodwill amortization' at the time the book was being published. Thus, some statements about 'pooling' and 'earnings dilution' would be modified slightly with the new rules, potentially impacting a few numeric calculations in Chapter 12 – Mergers and Acquisitions. Similar to the comment in the previous paragraph about Cost of Capital, the underlying concepts or perceptions of distinguishing 'non-cash' from 'cash-based' acquisition analysis – along with justifying a merger or acquisition based on the 'economics' of the transaction – are not altered.

As the reader might imagine, my experience and views are embedded in the story. At the same time, I have attempted to be as factual and non-opinionated as my mind allows. I hope you enjoy reading this book as much as I enjoyed writing it.

I would like to express my sincere gratitude to all the people I have worked with and consulted for since 1970, when my career began. All of you have helped me, in some way, to write this book. Therefore, *Shareholder Value – A Business Experience* is dedicated to you – my colleagues and clients.

List of Exhibits

1

Getting started

The cup of early morning black coffee tasted good. "*At least we've crossed one hurdle*", sighed Jason Aradvizer, who had a lot on his mind that first day of July. His totally relaxing and satisfying, if not spectacular, golfing vacation had ended just two days ago, but the matters at hand put it in the distant past. Jason was experiencing a typical set of 'first day on the job' thoughts by wondering if he had done the right thing, even though he felt so positive about this new challenge. "*What better way*", he reminded himself, "*to conclude a corporate and consulting career than to take on this assignment as a consultant to the Chief Financial Officer of Growthstar Inc., a publicly traded industrial products and services company on the verge of a new market expansion strategy. The opportunity to utilize my thirty-something years of experience to 'reinvent' a significant segment of the corporate finance function seems almost too good to be true ... but*", as he mused to himself, "*some poor soul has to do it!*"

"*The business landscape has changed*", he thought to himself. "*Boards of Directors are paying more attention to their large institutional shareholders, and making the enhancement of shareholder wealth a 'priority' for the Chief Executive Officer (CEO). Many CEOs, in turn, are now realizing that increasing the company's stock price is not their challenge alone, and are pushing 'shareholder value creation' down to their business unit and division general managers. Even key staff members in virtually all functional disciplines and support areas are getting 'clued in' to the importance of achieving shareholder value objectives, not just growing revenue and net earnings*".

He continued talking silently to himself, as he typically did at the beginning of major work assignments ... "*Every key manager in this company, and every other 'for profit' enterprise, needs to gain an understanding of 'value-based' performance and measurement – some obviously more than others. My role is to facilitate both the accumulation and application of a 'new body of knowledge' in Finance, for execution in various parts of this company. I need to help these people think differently about the financial aspects of their business. They need to understand that there is a 'story' about shareholder value in their financials, which the traditional 'accounting-based' approach and measures will not reveal or be able to explain. With the help of the new 'economic-based' approach and measures, I can help these people uncover that message. To do this, I need to make financial theory understandable and useful to them".*

"There are also potential 'gold mines' and 'minefields' in the company's strategies, future plans, and capital investment programs which need to be evaluated. The major analytic routines and the notion of 'how' and 'where' to apply a time-tested valuation technique, as well as a couple of new ones, need to be driven into the organization".

He concluded his self-reflection with the same thought he had felt so many times. *"It's always exciting and always a challenge. Many people in business really do need a dose of 'new thinking' to an 'age-old problem' – **how to get that stock price up and sustain it**. The financial framework, approaches and measures – in and of themselves – do not contain all the answers, but they can help in 'driving' managers toward acting in the best interests of the shareholders".*

Jason then began to focus on the present situation. His former graduate school colleague, Jonathan Steadfast, had been with Growthstar for the past ten years, rising from the post of Corporate Controller and appointed as the company's CFO five years ago. Jonathan's acceptance of the new 'economic metrics' during the past year had convinced Jason that the environment at Growthstar was right for a revamping of the planning and analysis systems, plus key measurement and reporting functions, within finance.

Concerns still loomed in Jason's mind, however, as he looked over the corporate organization chart, which had his handwritten notes from conversations with Jonathan, highlighting the various personalities of the corporate vice presidents.

John (Jack) Earningsly, Corporate Controller, was going to be a 'tough sell' – a classic accountant who knew (and used) every accounting treatment to boost quarterly earnings per share (*EPS*) and often seemed to be more concerned about where an item went rather than what it meant. He scratched his head as he thought about Jonathan's comment that Jack had not ever made an incorrect accounting entry or misinterpreted a FASB ruling. The fact that Jack hung his CPA certificate above his college degree in his office was not lost on Jason. Neither was Jack's comment, in their only meeting, questioning what *a bunch of new measures* would really add to the company, except more work for an already burdened accounting staff. Last year, Jack celebrated his twentieth anniversary with Growthstar, having spent his entire career with the company in some capacity.

He joined Growthstar as Accounting Manager after five years with the company's auditing firm, having been the junior and senior auditor, then manager, for the Growthstar account. Being one of the longest-serving employees, and the longest-tenured corporate executive, he had no plans of leaving and had developed his own agenda. He also had visions of occupying the CFO's office if Jonathan decided to move on or retire.

Moving on to Earl D'Mark, Growthstar's Treasurer, Jason smiled. Earl was a fortyish 'young tiger' whom Jason had met a few years ago at a shareholder value conference. Earl had a master's degree from a rock-solid, if not overly prestigious, mid-west graduate business school, and seemed to almost worship cash flow, deriding *EPS* as far as was politically palatable in a company which had historically been 'earnings driven'. "*Jack and Earl's luncheon conversations must be interesting*", thought Jason, wishing he might be a 'fly on the wall' as he mentally compared the almost opposite views of these two key finance executives. From the time of his arrival at Growthstar three years ago, Earl had been one of the proponents of adopting more 'economic-based' ways to analyze the company's businesses and investments and, according to Jonathan, had been almost relentless in his admonitions, much to the dismay of Jack. While an experienced treasurer, Earl was a bit 'light' on some of the more technical aspects of valuation theory and its application, and welcomed an experienced outsider, to add credibility to the undertaking which Jonathan had now sponsored. To indicate his support for the endeavor, Earl had promised to make his best financial analyst available for up to 50% of his time over the next several months, to assist Jason with the 'number crunching'. Earl was, obviously, the 'coach' – a consultant's name for a key ally to get support for important findings and recommendations, especially since he had gained Jonathan's ear during the past year or so, and Jonathan was the CEO's closest confidant.

Human Resources, which Jason had called 'Personnel' until it got him in trouble several years ago with an important client, was going to be interesting. Jason gazed attentively at his notes on Florence (known to everyone as 'Flo') Withetide, realizing that he had spent virtually no time thinking about the comments that Jonathan had provided about her. Flo was a classic case of the Horatio Alger success story – a woman approaching middle age who started as an executive secretary in another company. She attended night school and earned a college degree after eight years of part-time study. She then worked her way up through compensation, recruitment and human resource administration to the position of Director for one of Growthstar's competitors. Almost everyone in Growthstar felt she was a 'steal' when she was enticed to join the company as Vice President, Human Resources to replace the retiring incumbent. For Flo, this job was the crowning achievement for a long road of hard work, so much so that she seemed unwilling to take strong positions on anything that the CEO might not agree with. To call her a 'yes' person would be unfair, but she literally calculated the impact of every comment she made to the CEO, especially on subjects he (the CEO) felt strongly about. "*She's going to be a very intriguing person to figure out*", Jason thought out loud, as he mentally progressed to the stage where his work would require changes to the compensation plan. "*Oh well*", he rationalized, "*we're a few months away from that issue*".

Valerie (Val) Performa, Vice President of Corporate Strategy and Development, was the exact opposite of Flo. Born and raised in an affluent family, she earned her bachelor's degree from a prestigious east coast college and a master's in business, concentrating in marketing, from an equally prestigious west coast university by the age of twenty-four. 'Sophisticated' was the term Jonathan had used as a 'one-word descriptor' for Val. She was also a very gracious person and, while confident of her ability, was one who listened to others and appeared to be open-minded and respectful of the opinions of others. She had moved rapidly in her twelve-year career, and was the youngest vice president ever appointed at Growthstar, having joined the company two years ago.

With a working knowledge of financial concepts, she had developed a reputation as a 'big picture' person constantly striving to be on top of – some thought ahead of – the next major strategic breakthrough in the overall global economy and Growthstar's markets. During the past year, she had formalized the strategic planning process, and the two businesses now had their 'first ever' strategies. She had collaborated with Earl D'Mark to generate 'high-level' financial expressions for these strategies, which represented a good first step in developing meaningful financial outlooks.

In terms of Corporate Communications and Investor Relations, Jonathan had managed this area himself, working closely with Val, Jack and Earl to structure the 'message' that he and the CEO took to the investors. This would soon change, as an Investor Relations Officer was about to join the company. Jonathan, while still somewhat tied to the 'old school', did believe in open and candid reporting – good or bad – to the 'street'.

Finally, the 'big man' – Ian Lord – Chairman, President and Chief Executive Officer. Ian was a striking figure. Standing 'six-foot five', he was a basketball star at a Division 1 university in his 'playing days'. Everything about him was impressive, especially his thick, silver-colored hair, and he had built a reputation over the past thirty years as a tough, yet fair, task master – one who demanded nothing short of excellence, both for himself and his subordinates. His only major shortcoming, according to Jonathan, was a predisposition to certain conclusions, even if convincing analysis demonstrated a totally different result. Ian was not irrational, as he could be swayed, but he did go into situations with at least a strong idea, if not a conviction, of what he thought the outcome should be. Ian was not fond of 'heavy' analysis. He wanted answers and decisions, not a lot of detail. Ian had the ability to get to key issues quickly, and was very decisive. He expected no less from those who worked for him. He was the quintessential executive who wanted all memos and letters to be no more than one page, with a recommended course of action supported by brief, yet compelling, rationale. *"This isn't so surprising"*, thought Jason, as Ian fitted a profile of several CEOs he had worked for and advised.

So, there they were – the executive team he would work with at the corporate level. Jonathan had given him a very condensed overview of the business unit general managers (the 'producers') which would have to be expanded in the very near future.

Jason looked at his watch. He had spent nearly an hour reviewing his notes and thinking about the corporate officers and his initial interactions with them. With his 'kick-off' meeting with Jonathan scheduled to start in less than thirty minutes, Jason turned his attention to the outline of the process he had put together three weeks ago to structure and prioritize the major work activities for the next several months.

The process Jason had developed was the culmination of his many years in consulting. Having used it with several clients during the past five years, he felt confident that it would work well at Growthstar. *"A cohesive process"*, he reminded himself, *"was so important for an undertaking of this magnitude"*. However, he also knew that Jonathan was not a process-oriented person. Jonathan would constantly have to be held in check, since he was a lot like Ian in prematurely wanting the 'answer'. The 'answer' – *"what good is it"*, Jason said to himself, *"without the rationale and supporting analysis!"*

Now, it was showtime. Jason took a left turn out of the office provided for him and strolled the short distance down the hall to Jonathan's office. Jonathan preferred a worktable with straight-back chairs to the comfortable couches that many executives, including Ian Lord, Flo Withetide and Val Performa, had in their offices. For some strange reason, Jack Earningsly and Earl D'Mark also had worktables with straight-back chairs in their offices. The two men, who had now known each other for nearly thirty-five years, extended warm greetings as Jason entered Jonathan's office. Jonathan had instructed his assistant not to stop or announce Jason, unless an important meeting or conference was going on.

"So, you're going to straighten us out financially", thundered Jonathan.

Some people felt intimidated by the volume and intensity of Jonathan's voice, but Jason was not. Besides, he had listened to that voice for so long, that its volume had lost its impact. "I'm going to give it everything I have", Jason shot back, "assuming the CFO doesn't 'stonewall' me!"

He handed Jonathan the one-page chart he had put together outlining the major tasks and approximate time frames for their completion. "First", Jason stated, "we have to get everyone on the corporate staff 'on board' with some basic definitions and perspectives as to what shareholder value is all about. Then, I explain the transition from 'accounting' to 'economics' and introduce 'value-based metrics' and 'Economic Profit' (*EP*)".

At that point, Jonathan gave Jason his first reaction. "A year ago, Jack would have tried to 'blow this apart' right from the outset. He knows that this tactic won't succeed now, because the stock market evidence is so compelling against *EPS* as a proxy for equity value, that he'll look foolish. In spite of his strong support of accounting measures as adequate for managing the company, Jack is no fool, so maybe this will not be that major an issue".

"I hope not", said Jason, "because it can sidetrack the entire process. However, even in the worst possible scenario, it will only cause a delay". Jason continued … "the next major step is to do a 'value assessment' of the company's business units (BUs). This analysis should highlight performance which creates shareholder value versus that which destroys it, and performance that is value neutral. We begin the assessment work by analyzing the Cost of Capital. As I think you know, this goes well beyond the cost of debt financing to capture the most important and expensive financing instrument used by most companies – namely, common equity. We'll want to determine if we have one cost of capital for all the businesses within Growthstar, or if there are any differences, based on business risk or financing structure".

As he was prone to do, Jonathan again interjected his thoughts. "While the assessment is obviously essential, we run the risk of making some enemies at this point. Thus, we need to inform the BU General Managers (GMs) as to where their units are in terms of their stage in the business 'life cycle' and what we expect of them now and in the next year or so. Jason, you need to meet these people, and I think a group session would be best".

Jason sighed, as he thought to himself ... "*Jonathan is getting it, and he is focused on the 'behavioral' side of this effort, as well as the 'technical'*". In a 'matter-of-fact' tone to hide his excitement, Jason replied with a simple "I agree, and the sooner, the better. Another important aspect of the assessment phase", Jason continued, "is an understanding of the underlying support measures for the aggregate metrics, which I call Financial 'Drivers'. These 'Drivers' are what the operating managers really must focus on. They establish a relatively simplistic template which, by the way, has all the substance of modern corporate finance and market valuation theory".

Jonathan responded with a smile ... "if you can give these operating people something that's simple and has integrity, you'll win them over ... and, if you win them over, Jack will come 'on board'".

"Just wait until you see how powerful and simple these 'Drivers' are", Jason retorted.

"OK", Jonathan said quickly, "let's move on".

"The next step involves progressing from 'discrete time period' metrics (*EP* and the 'Drivers') to a measure of the actual value created *over* time, which is called 'Market Value Added' (*MVA*). It's important to recognize that *EP* and its support measures give us important inputs into the 'value equation', but do not constitute 'market value *per se*'. *EP* provides a good indicator, but is usually limited to a given year or discrete time period ... and, to repeat, *EP* is *not* 'market value *per se*'. *MVA* is equivalent to the 'Net Present Value' you are familiar with and is synonymous with 'Shareholder Value impact'; that is, the value created (or destroyed) by management".

Jason paused for a moment – to gather his thoughts – because it was important that he communicate the next message clearly. "Jonathan, do you remember back in 'grad' school when we had that case study in a Business Policy course dealing with growth through acquisition or internal expansion?"

"Of course, how could I forget it", Jonathan howled, almost bursting into a fit of laughter. "You made an absolute fool of yourself by analyzing three plant expansions separately, with elaborate internal rate of return calculations, and then trying to compare each individual plant's results to an acquisition which provided the company with the overall capacity to manufacture the combined output of the three plant expansions. You got so confused and wound up in your details that you missed the 'big picture', the result being that the professor and class members (myself included) ridiculed you for weeks".

Knowing that he had communicated his point 'crystal clear', Jason began to speak again. "That ridiculing had a profound effect on me for a while, but it took years until I understood the full impact of the experience. Believe it or not, that incident, which happened so many years ago, helped me to focus on what I believe is one of the most important and misunderstood aspects of economic analysis".

"How so?" asked Jonathan.

Jason responded, "I began to realize that there is a natural 'hierarchy' for value-based analysis, and that it is vastly different from what is done here and in most other firms".

Jason could see that Jonathan was perplexed, as the CFO began to roll his eyes, and asked, "What in the world are you talking about?"

Jason, now comfortable that he had Jonathan's complete attention, spoke again ... "Let me explain the concept this way. I assume you do fairly extensive evaluations of capital investments".

"You bet", Jonathan responded (indicating a sense of pride). "We analyze all capital projects over $250,000 and nobody spends any significant amount of capital around here without justifying it with an Internal Rate of Return (*IRR*) of 15% or more and a positive Net Present Value (*NPV*). We take all projects over $500,000 to our Board of Directors".

Jason, now feeling his hook entering the fish's mouth, retorted ... "Well, isn't that just grand! Now, let me ask you a question. How do know if you should be making the investment in the first place?"

Jonathan was now getting impatient ... "Is this some type of 'intellectual game' you're playing with me?"

Jason, with the most empathetic look he could place on his face, responded by saying, "in one sense it is, but it's also a very serious problem. This is not only wasting a lot of time in corporate staff departments such as yours, but is also giving senior management and the board bad information about the return on investment of new capital. Here's the point ... I'll bet you have never done an *IRR* (or *NPV*) evaluation of a business strategy. So, how do you know that capital should be invested in a particular business in the first place? You're making the same mistake I made over thirty years ago! You're applying value-based analysis techniques at the wrong level. To say it another way, the 'project' *IRRs* and *NPVs* are meaningless, because they are done at too low a level and you can never link these 'project returns' to what is going on at the business unit level, much less at the corporate level".

Jonathan was dumbfounded, a rare feeling for him. "Oh, my God, how could I have missed this over the course of so many years? What you did as a graduate school student, I have been promoting throughout my career".

"You and many other CFOs", Jason retorted, "so don't feel too bad. The good news is that there is a solution, and it will be integrated into our Value-Based Financial Performance System".

Jonathan was not about to let this topic get away, and asked ... "OK, 'Mr Smart Guy', give me at least a 'taste' of what we're talking about here".

Jason, wanting to conclude this topic and move on, responded by saying "We apply the 'value metrics' at the corporate, business unit, strategy and major investment program levels, where we can establish a link to strategic or operational goals, but we do not evaluate individual capital projects. As you can see in the outline I gave you, there is a distinct phase in the process devoted to this subject, and we'll cover all the aspects of it at that time".

Jonathan, seeming to be satisfied, albeit still bewildered by his new realization which was now two minutes old, nodded his head and said, "You have made a startling revelation, and I withdraw my part of the ridicule which was cast upon you so long ago!"

Jason, smiling gently, responded with a simple "thanks". He then forged ahead ... "The next major task is to understand the potential market value of your business strategies and growth plans. We'll utilize the Market Value Added (*MVA*) approach that we discussed to determine how growth affects value creation. I call this the 'Magnifier Effect', and the results of the analysis are often startling".

"How so?" asked Jonathan.

"By demonstrating that not all business unit growth produces an equal impact on your stock price", Jason answered. "We'll also perform an extensive financial analysis, in terms of each major business unit's 'No Growth' and 'Growth' (or 'Strategy') values. In other words, what's the value of maintaining the status quo versus expanding? Further, we'll calculate 'Sustainable Growth', which is how fast the company can grow without the need for new equity financing. This is an important element in mapping out the company's future".

"Ian's been 'bugging' me for this type of growth and financing perspective for a long time, so we should get his attention on this point".

Jason, hoping for more, asked "Won't Ian also be concerned about the contribution of the major BUs to the company's market value?"

"To some extent, but, you have to remember that Ian believes that growth delivers stock price gains, and really doesn't understand or have a lot of patience for all this 'return on capital' and 'economic profit' stuff. Why do you think he changed the name of the company when he took over the top spot ten years ago? You do remember what we used to call this company, don't you Jason?"

"Oh yes", Jason snickered, "Q-Form Products".

At that point, Jonathan noticed his empty coffee mug and looked sheepishly at Jason, realizing that he had not offered him his favorite hot beverage. Jason quickly picked up the gesture, and said what he must have said thousands of times ... "black, no sugar".

As they both sipped a fresh cup of coffee, Jason continued ... "Merger and acquisition analysis is tackled next. We'll lay out an approach for valuing deals, to be consistent with the 'value metrics' that the group has agreed should be used in measuring the performance of the various businesses. I'm telling you right now, though, that we may dispute the notion of buying companies for the purpose of increasing earnings per share".

Jonathan leaned back and folded his arms. He was silent for a moment and then, with a very serious expression on his face almost whispered, "Well, my friend, let's just hope that my retirement portfolio is in good shape by then, and that you've collected a substantial portion of your fee".

Jason was taken back both by Jonathan's words and his expression. Then, Jonathan burst out laughing and roared ... "I got you, didn't I? I've been preparing Ian for a change in perspective on acquisitions for about six months, and he is receptive. At Earl's insistence, I have also been 'ramming' it into Jack's head for about the same time, so he knows where I'm coming from. But, it was worth at least the price of the coffee to see you tense up a bit. I'll keep it serious from now on".

Jason smiled, somewhat relieved. "You still have your sense of humor, which is good. I owe you one, now. Moving along, the internally generated investments analogous to acquisitions are called 'Value Driver Programs'. These are major strategic or operational programs, intended to support and provide 'building blocks' for your strategies and operational goals".

Jonathan leaned forward before Jason could continue and said, "That was a mouthful, so please, let's talk about it briefly".

"Value Driver Programs are an important part of strategy and value-based performance systems", Jason went on. "As I stated, they can be 'strategic' or 'operational' in nature. The key criterion is that they are significant to the business unit or the company. New product lines, alternate channels of distribution, and major manufacturing initiatives are examples. A Value Driver Program is not, however, the classical capital project, such as a machine tool, which has historically been evaluated at the expense of major programs".

Jason was 'on a roll' now. "This transitions nicely into the capital budgeting system. Based on what I've seen of your current approach, I believe a major overhaul is needed. Growthstar needs to take a more strategic perspective to its capital investments, and get a better understanding of the level of capital spending necessary to move the business in the directions you have selected. Part of this change is understanding invested capital intensity, the capital required to generate each dollar of sales. Another aspect will be fitting capital investment into a 'major program' framework, applying value-based analysis to the Hierarchy we discussed a few moments ago, and 'scrapping' the analysis of small capital projects".

"Sounds logical", Jonathan responded, "and I know that Earl is anticipating the outcome of this work, along with 'Sustainable Growth', since it affects our financing strategy and dividend policy. In fact, I now remember Earl making a comment to me several months ago about being too myopic with our capital project analysis. Unfortunately, we were in the middle of an 'earnings release' to Wall Street, and I wasn't totally focused on what Earl was saying. Now, I get it, but I have a new problem. I don't know how long I can wait, since when I get 'juiced up', I want everything yesterday. Well, you know me, 'Mr Impatient'!"

"You'll just have to be a bit patient", Jason snipped, "and we will get there. Finally, we'll review and probably revise the company's financial reporting system, based on everything we've done. Then, you'll be in a position to structure your internal communications and take the message to your investors. In conjunction, we should begin training the people. The training provides the management and staff with both a generic and company-specific perspective".

Jonathan leaned forward and took a long sip of coffee. "Before I tell you to leave my office and start working, I need to set up a meeting with our two general managers (GMs) and the corporate officers. In terms of the GMs, Larry Buildermann runs our Industrial Products business, and Peter Uppcomer is the GM of Industrial Services. I think you know that *Services* was acquired over two years ago. Larry, GM of *Products*, is a solid manager with a manufacturing background, and a bit more conservative than Ian would like. Larry has consistently delivered the 'bottom line', however, and will only pursue growth that is profitable. Peter is very aggressive with a sales and marketing background. He's probably the closest thing to a 'clone' we have for Ian, and feels strongly that *Services* growth is the key to increasing our revenue, profit and stock price over the next several years. Let me have Kay Hoppins, my Executive Assistant, set up a meeting ASAP!"

"How much of the process should I share with them?" Jason asked.

"I think", said Jonathan, "that you should concentrate on our overall objective of shifting to a cash flow-oriented economic profit and return-on-capital approach, to replace our traditional *EPS* focus, with the supporting rationale and impact for them. If they accept the concept, directional changes and rationale, they'll do whatever is required and enlist the support of their people".

"I assume", interjected Jason, "that '*simplicity with integrity*' is the message".

"You're learning fast", chuckled Jonathan. "You will also have to meet Mary Frightly, Ian's Administrative Assistant. Make sure you get on her good side. Mary only knows two types of people – friends and foes – and you don't want to be one of her foes, at least not in this company. She's followed Ian throughout most of his career, is very protective of him, and expresses her opinion of the people who are trying to influence him. And Ian listens to her. Now, as we seem to have all the necessary introductions in place, I will ask you to get out of my office and get started".

"It will be my pleasure", Jason responded with a smile, as he exited and turned back down the hall toward the office that had been provided for him.

All the corporate staff and the two GMs were prepared to meet with Jason, so scheduling a meeting with the entire group for the next day was not a problem. They all knew about the endeavor, having been prepped by Jonathan – with Ian's blessing.

Jason began delving into the pile of historical financials on the major business units. He wanted to have some background perspective for the meeting tomorrow. Jack's group had compiled the reports for Jason to begin his initial value assessments. Jack had also, at Jonathan's insistence, agreed to provide a senior accountant to answer questions and assist Jason with his historical analysis. Earl D'Mark's top analyst and most senior aide would also get involved.

Tomorrow did arrive, and Jason spent the morning preparing for the kick-off meeting scheduled for 1:30 pm. As part of his preparation, he paced around his office and kept reminding himself . . . "*simplicity with integrity – that's the message!*"

## 2

Shareholder value and sustainable value: definitions and perspectives

At 1:25, the group began arriving at the boardroom, where Jonathan had decided to hold the kick-off meeting. There was a strict rule about being on time for meetings, which Ian had instituted, when he became CEO and adhered to. Jason had arrived at 1:15 to check out the audio-visuals and Jonathan showed up 5 minutes later. As they entered the boardroom, Jonathan coordinated the introductions of the Growth-star people to Jason. Everyone gave Jason an enthusiastic handshake and greeting, except Jack Earningsly. It wasn't that Jack was cold, it was more of a 'lukewarm' reception. Jonathan, who didn't miss very much, noticed it and winked at Jason after Jack had passed by and was walking toward the coffeepot. Jason remembered his thought of yesterday morning . . . that Jack was going to be a 'tough sell'.

At exactly 1:30, everyone was seated and Jonathan stood up to address the group. "Well", he began "I believe everyone knows why we are here. For the past year, my financial staff and I have been studying value-based performance metrics and how they might apply at Growthstar. Jack, Earl and I, along with Frank Accurato, Earl's most senior level assistant, have attended a seminar on the subject of shareholder value and value-based metrics. We have, in addition, read every article on the subject that we could get our hands on. I have also had several discussions with Ian on the subject. While Ian has endorsed the approach 'in principle', he wants to learn more and see the results of our efforts over the next few months before making any decisions to formally change our financial measurement and evaluation approaches, our financial reporting systems and our incentive compensation plan. I believe everyone is clear that this effort, while heavily focused on economic-oriented 'metrics', goes well beyond and encompasses virtually everything we do in Corporate Finance and could affect the business units to a significant degree, especially the finance and planning functions".

"All of you know that we have historically been driven totally by growth in sales and earnings per share (*EPS*). Everyone in this room is paid a bonus based on *EPS* growth targets, along with key personal objectives. As a result of work done by Earl's group – specifically, Frank Accurato – I became convinced about six months ago that there was a lack of correlation between our stock price and *EPS*. In fact, research by some major institutions indicates a very low correlation for *EPS* growth as a predictor of price-to-earnings (*P/E*) ratios for the stock market as a whole. This is not new information to me. Jason Aradvizer, who is here and is going to work with us, has been pestering me with this notion for the past three years, but I did not believe it until six months ago".

Jack Earningsly started squirming in his chair. Everyone, except Jason, knew this was a signal that he had something to say. "I know the stock market research is compelling", Jack began, "but virtually all the institutional analysts who follow our company have one question on their mind – actually, two. The first is are we going to make the *EPS* number for the *quarter*, that either they have in their forecast or we've given them, and the second is will we make the *annual EPS* target? I continue to be confused as to why the analysts continue to emphasize *EPS* if there's no correlation to stock price".

Jonathan, who had been standing as he delivered his opening remarks and remained so while Jack spoke, turned to Jason and said, "Well, Jason, we might as well throw you into the pit and have you start earning your fee. While we all know Jack's reluctance to move toward economic-based measures, I think his question is legitimate".

"So do I", chimed in Larry Buildermann. "I'm new to these economic metrics, and have had the same question in my mind ever since Ian and you [Jonathan] told me we were going to seriously explore these new financial tools. It's important to me, because of the potential effect on my operation".

Peter Uppcomer leaned forward and looked toward Jonathan, indicating his desire to speak. Jonathan nodded back, and Peter stated, "I would also like to pursue this question, since I run a service business, and never felt we were very capital intensive. As a result, I would think that *Industrial Services*' value, or contribution to Growthstar's stock price, would be linked to our pretax earnings. If I were one of these Wall Street analysts, I would probably be asking the same type of questions. Besides, this is all we've been exposed to throughout our careers".

Jason rose slowly from his chair, knowing he had to get off to a good start with this group. He took a deep breath and responded, "I also think the question is both fair and relevant. Let me answer it this way. There are two aspects to the price of any stock. The first is the actual 'warranted' price (or 'fair value') over the long term, based on a company's anticipated future performance. The second is the short-term 'adjustment' (up or down) based on developments that become known to the market. The first aspect is what the research deals with, and is what Jonathan was alluding to. In other words, if you ask most institutional portfolio managers, the people who actually buy and sell your stock, you will discover that they use some type of future-oriented earnings or cash flow model to determine a 'warranted value' for an equity security. In developing their financial outlooks for a company, they incorporate the company's industry or market, its strategy, its management, its historical financial performance, and its potential to repeat or beat the past, along with any risk of not meeting past performance. These 'warranted' values are the basis for *P/Es* and other stock price ratios, and they are based on economic performance. Therefore, a company's stock price, over the long term, will reflect its ability to grow and produce an economic return above (or below) its cost of capital. Think of it in terms of your own investment portfolio or retirement fund. You want to optimize your return on investment over some time period. You invest cash and expect cash in return".

"There is also another *aspect* to stock prices, which is the daily adjustment of the long-term based values I just mentioned. The market is constantly absorbing new information about the world, countries, industries, markets, and individual companies. So, when you are being asked questions about quarterly and annual *EPS* numbers, the analysts are looking for indications as to whether you are on or off track with regard to the long-term projections which are the basis for your stock's valuation. It's also interesting to note the *way* stock prices move in response to earnings announcements. I'm sure all of you have seen a situation where a massive write-off resulted in a stock price gain. How could this happen, if the market is *EPS* driven? The rationale is that the 'market' may be seeing a permanent reduction in the company's cost structure, and factoring this into the company's long-term profit and cash flow outlook, thereby justifying a boost in the firm's 'warranted' value".

"How about another situation, where a company reports an *EPS* increase over last quarter or last year, but also states that its new order rate or its backlog has decreased, and the market 'hits' the stock for a significant price drop? The market may be forecasting a sales problem in the future, which could negatively affect profit and cash flow. So, it's not just the direction of earnings in the short term, but *why* the earnings may be moving up or down".

"To summarize", Jason continued, "long-term values are based on cash flows and economic returns. This statement is intuitively correct and supported by fact. Stock price movements in the short term are influenced by many factors, of which *EPS* is one. So, when the analysts call with the proverbial question 'what's the *EPS* number for the quarter?' remember that there are at least two possible hidden items: (1) the analyst may be feeding an input to a portfolio manager for an update to a long-term profit and cash flow forecast, to either confirm or alter a stock price, and (2) there may a 'trading' or short-term profit-taking motive which is unrelated to the long-term, or 'warranted', value of the company".

Jonathan looked around the room for reaction. He didn't have to wait long. Val Performa opened the dialogue with … "I can't comment on the integrity of the research, but I agree completely with the statement Jason made about the cash flow basis for equity valuations being 'intuitively correct' over the long term. Jonathan, you know that at the analyst meetings I have attended, after we go through the formal presentation and give our quarterly and annual *EPS* forecast, several of the analysts usually approach you and me to talk about the competition and our near- and longer-term strategy. In fact, at one meeting a group of analysts initiated a dialogue concerning how they take what we give them about our strategy, do their own analysis of our ability to execute our plans, and make an evaluation of our management, to serve as the basis for a long-term revenue, profit and cash flow forecast". Jonathan, with a slight twinkle in his eye, simply nodded in Val's direction to indicate his concurrence with her comment.

Earl D'Mark then spoke. "As you know, I spend a considerable amount of time with our investment banker on our financing instruments. During the past year, there has been a significant level of new concern (on their part) for our cash flow and capital needs, even to the extent of comparing *Products* to *Services*. We're also hearing that their equity research department (the 'sell side' of the financial market) is starting to use 'economic profit' and similar measures in their common stock recommendations".

Flo Withetide had a habit of folding her arms and slinking down ever so slightly in her chair when she wanted to say something, but wasn't certain how to say it. Jonathan picked up Flo's 'body language' and turned toward her, with a look (that only the two of them understood) indicating that he wanted her to say what was on her mind. Flo picked up the look and started to speak in her deliberate style ... "I just wanted to add to what Val said, in that during the one analyst meeting I attended during the past year, a few analysts asked me questions about our management development programs for our junior executives, the working relationship of the senior management team, and if we had any plans to change our bonus program. They indicated to me that their evaluation of our management and strategy were the most important 'non-financial' factors in recommending Growthstar as a stock to buy, hold or sell. I also overheard a conversation involving three or four analysts indicating they were starting to build new valuation models based on cash flow-based measures. Like Jack, Larry and Peter, I was having trouble translating this into their behavior, since everything I hear from Wall Street (which is admittedly not that much) is 'short-term earnings' oriented".

Jonathan looked around the room for additional reaction to Jason's comments and, sensing none, said, "OK, I think we raised an important issue, and I think Jason has provided a reasonable initial response for all of us to reflect on. We can certainly expand on what has been spoken at a later date, but I think we can move on. I have asked Jason to get us started by concentrating on our overall objective of considering a shift to a cash flow and return-on-capital approach, to replace our traditional *EPS* focus, with the supporting rationale and impact for each of the BUs. So, Jason, it's your show!"

Jason felt more comfortable with the group. While he had planned on opening up with some introductory points he had structured and rehearsed, he was actually glad that the question and dialogue had ensued, which set the stage for his formal opening.

Jason moved to the front of the conference room table. He began in a deliberate and firm tone of voice ... "Creating shareholder value is an objective for everyone in this room. In the past, the CEO bore the brunt of the challenge. Suffice it to say that Ian is still the captain of the ship and the one the shareholders ultimately look to. But, as Flo mentioned, your investors are also evaluating all of you as they compare Growthstar to other companies as investment opportunities.

Exhibit 1

*Shareholder Value is a measurement of the change in value
of the firm's investment over a period of time ....
as determined by the financial markets.*

\--

*For a Business Unit, the relevant issue is its "contribution"
to the company's value (or common stock price).*

So, let's begin with a basic definition of 'Shareholder Value'. The chart (Exhibit 1) I'm about to show gives a concise definition for both the corporation and its business units".

"It focuses on *change*, in addition to total equity market value. The stock market is concerned with what management has done (or is doing) with the capital it has been provided. As you know, the scorecard is tabulated daily in the stock tables published in virtually all the major newspapers".

Peter Uppcomer never held back when he had something to say, or if he had a question he wanted an answer to. "This daily tabulation is what I had on my mind when I spoke earlier. If what you say is true, why do we have major 'ups and downs' on such short notice, based almost solely on 'earnings' announcements?"

Jason felt the group was serious about delving into this subject, because as he looked around the room, he saw several heads nodding just as Peter was concluding his question. "I've also thought about this question a lot during the past ten years", Jason responded, "because it's so important and is in the minds of so many people. One analogy I can give is that of a family".

"How so?" Peter interjected.

"Think of it this way", Jason said. "All of us who have raised children and lived with a spouse for many years know, that on a day-to-day basis, our family relationships don't always make sense. We fight with and hate our spouse and kids one day, and the next day we love and hug them and can't get enough of them. Over the long run, though, the relationships are usually strong, especially if the family foundation is strong and the individuals are committed to making the family an important part of their lives. Strong companies, similar to solid families, have their good and bad days in the stock market. Some days will be influenced by their own performance, other days by factors beyond their control. Over time, a good company will deliver 'tangible' value to its owners, similar to a family delivering 'intangible' rewards to the members aligned to its functioning. The long-term equity markets will, therefore, provide a return to the investors commensurate with a firm's long-term performance, and will do so in an objective manner. Similar to a family, the various parts of a company have to work together for rewards to be realized. And, I think we all know the opposite side of this analogy".

"There is another aspect to the financial markets, which is called 'short-term trading'. Traders are trying to beat each other, using every bit of information that might influence a short-term stock price movement. They're not necessarily focused on the company's business or its fundamentals; rather, they're trying to exploit short-term anomalies to gain a temporary advantage. We have to be careful to distinguish 'trading' from 'investing'. The point, therefore, is that the markets don't always make sense on a short-term basis. They often seem to be irrational, which is the view that many people have. Over the long run, however, the financial markets are rational. Stock price values reflect 'real' performance. And, just as a family may have a member who is always in trouble, the markets will penalize a badly performing company or, in some cases, an entire industry (or segment within an industry) which is delivering poor returns. We can't deal with 'trading' in this endeavor, since it's short-term oriented and often arbitrary and irrational, at least on the surface. We can, however, institute systems and manage this company in a way which makes it a good long-term investment".

"This is starting to be a bit more understandable", Peter responded, "but I hope you appreciate our point of view and our feeling of confusion as to how to act in light of what we see as, basically, an irrational stock market. We're not always certain as to what we should be doing to, as you say, 'maximize shareholder value'".

Jason nodded in response ... "I appreciate and respect your comment, since I have lived and worked in this environment for a long time, and have had to respond to many people who have the same concerns, questions and frustrations as you do".

Jason then paused and looked around the room. Sensing no more questions or comments, he began a new line of discussion, albeit related to his previous comments. "We've been talking about the effect of short-term earnings on stock prices. I'd like to show you some research from a respected and well-known financial institution, which indicates that even on a long-term basis, there is no correlation between earnings per share (*EPS*) and stock prices, for the overall market. The next chart (Exhibit 2) shows the relationship of *EPS* growth and the Market-to-Book ratio. As you can see, with an R^2 of about 1%, there is no correlation. There is more research on this subject done by other, equally credible organizations, which produces approximately the same results and conclusions".

"With regard to specifics, this chart (Exhibit 2) plots *EPS* Growth for a set of companies along the horizontal axis and ratio of Market-Value-to-Invested Capital (essentially a Market-to-Book ratio) on the vertical axis. Market-to-Book (*M/B*) ratios provide one indicator of how the stock market values the job management is doing with the capital invested in the firm. The higher the vertical plot, the higher the relative value. As this analysis (along with other research) indicates, the 'market' is not using 'Earnings' as a predictor of M/B ratios, at least not in any meaningful way".

Everyone in the group took a long, hard look at this chart (Exhibit 2). Larry Buildermann was the first to speak. "While I admit to not being knowledgeable in accounting and finance, this contradicts everything I have learned on this subject. How can there be no correlation of profits and stock prices?"

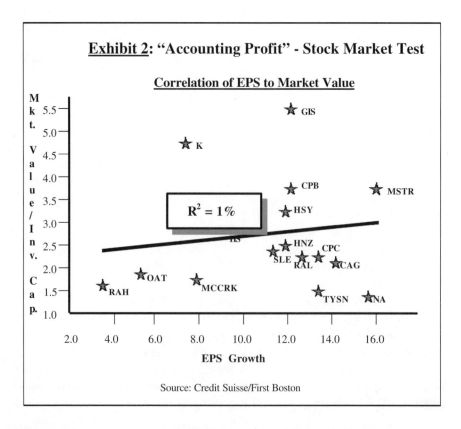

Exhibit 2: "Accounting Profit" - Stock Market Test

Source: Credit Suisse/First Boston

Flo Withetide, having recently been in a meeting with Ian and Larry, in which Ian had been 'pushing' Larry to boost his pre-tax profit margin, jumped in ... "I also have trouble believing this. It defies logic".

Peter Uppcomer scratched the side of his head and said, "I have to agree. For us non-financial folks, the notion of stock prices moving with profits is fundamental".

Jack Earningsly leaned back and smiled for the first time since the meeting began. Both Jonathan and Jason caught Jack's expression. Jason, anticipating some type of comments along these lines, responded ... "The problem is the 'accounting' definition of 'profit', which is all that most of us see". Jack's smile quickly vanished. Jason continued ... "You see, we often don't have a true indicator of 'profit' with accounting numbers". Now, Val and Earl started to smile.

"How so,?" Peter asked. "How can accounting *not* indicate profit (or loss, in the other direction)?"

Jason responded ... "Accounting numbers don't always represent cash flow, and the financial markets are ultimately concerned with a company's ability to generate cash flow-based returns for the investors. Accounting numbers don't provide good indicators of equity value creation, because that's not what they are intended to do".

Jack exploded out of his chair and shouted ... "Are you crazy? I've heard some scurrilous attacks on my profession, but this one is the most outrageous yet! How dare you say that we are misrepresenting things!"

Jonathan decided to be silent and let this debate play out, which was not easy for him.

Earl D'Mark then spoke. "Calm down Jack. Jason never said accounting wasn't any good or useful; rather, he made a very specific statement, which I believe is correct. What he said was that accounting was not intended for 'equity' (that is, 'common stock') valuation. I started out in banking and always used a borrower's audited financials for purposes of credit analysis, especially to establish net worth and loan coverage ratios. A lender's main concern is protection. With the return confined to the interest coupon, a lender needs to assess and limit his risk. Accounting numbers can be very useful for this type of analysis. The problem, however, is that when we flip the switch to the 'risk takers' (the shareholders) the game changes. Whereas accounting does a respectable job on the 'downside' (loan) analysis, it falls short on the 'upside' (equity) evaluation. The main reason is, with the accounting entries and treatments, we can lose the link to cash flow. And, as the research is showing, the stock markct is concerned with 'economics'; that is, *cash flow*".

Earl felt a compulsion to continue talking . . . "Let's not forget, either, that even within credit analysis, we often adjust accounting profits to get ratios and absolute numbers which are closer to cash flow. There is just so much in the way of 'bookkeeping' (noncash) entries which can occur between Operating Profit and Net Income that the 'net' amounts may bear little resemblance to cash flow. Reserves, restructuring charges, one-time gains or losses, etc. may have little or nothing to do with the ongoing cash flow of a business, but can have a major effect on 'earnings'".

"Oh, 'hogwash'", Jack replied. "This is just an attack on a good profession trying to present results according to a set of rules".

Now, it was Val's turn. "I don't believe that and I don't think you should take this personally. No one that I've ever heard speak on this subject has expressed a desire to 'attack' the accounting profession, *per se*. The argument has been that perhaps, as Jason stated, accounting standards are being applied to a situation where there's not a good fit – like trying to 'put a square peg into a round hole'".

Jack's expression started to soften a bit. "I can begin to accept that logic", he muttered, "but I think all of you should know that the accounting policy-makers are constantly reviewing our methods to better serve shareholders".

"I don't think anyone would argue that point", Jonathan interjected – wanting to get a thought into the dialogue after listening to the others. "It's just that there are some elements of accounting that cause problems in getting to economics and cash flow. Let's face it, accounting is not economics and it never will be. Are there any more questions?"

Peter looked at Larry and winked. "No", he said, "but it's fun to see the Economists and Accountants go at each other – similar to Manufacturing and Marketing dueling".

Jason felt it was time for him to speak again. "Now that our 'juices' are flowing, I'd like to discuss a related topic – 'Sustainable Value'. Simply stated, Sustainable Value results from a business consistently producing an economic return exceeding the cost of the capital invested in the business, while simultaneously delivering value to the customer".

Jonathan leaned forward and spoke . . . "My learned acquaintance has a habit of delivering what I call 'big mouthfuls' of information in what appear to be concise statements. So, for the benefit of the group, Mr Aradvizer, let's take this profound hypothesis and break it into digestible bits and pieces".

"You're getting to be a good 'set up man', Jonathan. I was about to do just that. The best way to frame this discussion is with a diagram (Exhibit 3)".

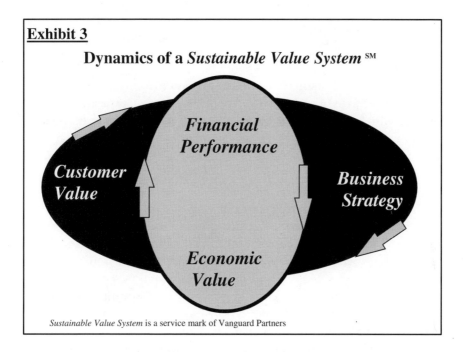

Exhibit 3

Dynamics of a *Sustainable Value System* ᴺᴹ

Financial Performance

Customer Value

Business Strategy

Economic Value

Sustainable Value System is a service mark of Vanguard Partners

"As this chart illustrates, there are always two forces at work within any business – *Customer Value* and *Economic Value*. These forces compete and, in the extreme, can oppose each other".

"Let's take *Customer Value*. I think everyone would agree that if we don't provide 'value' to our customers – in terms of products and services that fulfill their needs at a price they are willing to pay – then we'll eventually go out of business. At the same time, however, we need to address a couple of important questions, namely:

1 How much value do we need to provide to the customer?
2 What are the economic consequences of providing customer value?"

"If we pursue these questions and focus only on *maximizing customer value*, we could take actions resulting in:

• overspending on engineering and/or manufacturing to provide the 'perfect' product;
• building excess inventories, so as to never be out of stock;
• extending 'easy credit', thus lengthening the age of accounts receivable;
• granting substantial price discounts ... and, so on".

"Emphasizing *Economic Value* could lead us in a different direction and cause us to:

- cut back on essential R&D;
- reduce product or service quality to unacceptable levels;
- price too high – thus hampering sales potential ... and, so on".

"The key to success is a 'balance' of the two".

"A good way to illustrate this point is to review a mathematics concept which has been around for a long time. Some of you may remember a 'Vector Diagram' as an approach to dealing with two opposing forces. For those of you who have *not* been exposed to vectors, or whose memory may have faded, take a look at this next chart (Exhibit 4)".

"This illustration provides another way of looking at what I've been discussing, and is somewhat more precise than the previous chart (Exhibit 3). The key point is that optimizing shareholder value results from moving toward a 'balance' of customer value (CV) and economic value (EV)".

"Since the focus of our work is going to be more on the financial aspect of creating shareholder value, let me share two examples, which occurred several years ago and have had long-lasting effects. Both examples are of companies that emphasized economic value over customer value".

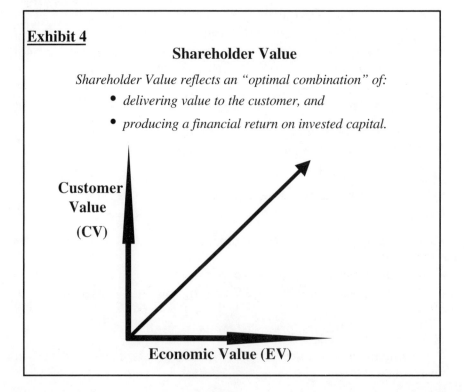

Exhibit 4

Shareholder Value

Shareholder Value reflects an "optimal combination" of:
- *delivering value to the customer, and*
- *producing a financial return on invested capital.*

Customer Value (CV)

Economic Value (EV)

"The first one is Schlitz Beer. Those of you over forty years of age may remember Schlitz as a beer with a distinct taste. You may or may not have liked it, but it was recognizable, and Schlitz had a loyal group of customers. Then, a strange thing happened. In its pursuit of higher profits, management decided to cut back on the cost of certain ingredients (I think it was the 'hops'). The result was a lower cost of goods sold and a higher gross profit margin. But, guess what happened? The customers didn't like the 'new brew' and stopped buying it. The result was that Schlitz lost a large portion of its customers and is no longer a factor in the US domestic beer market".

"The second example is General Motors, which several years ago was also in a major cost-cutting mode. GM thought it could save millions (perhaps billions) of dollars by standardizing the look and components of its major product lines. The result was that almost all of GM's sedans were very similar in appearance. It was hard to distinguish a Chevy from an Oldsmobile from a Pontiac. I heard one story (can't prove it's true, but believe it is) that one loyal 'Olds' buyer looked under the hood of a new Oldsmobile and saw a Chevy engine. You can probably guess what that customer did. Apparently, many others purchased competitor models, because GM once had 50% of the US car market and is now struggling to maintain a 30% share, with Oldsmobile disappearing".

"The message, therefore, is that while I will be emphasizing financial concepts and economic-based approaches to planning, analysis, and management, we can't forget the importance of delivering customer value, albeit in a sound financial environment. That's where you come in, Val, to help 'balance' the financial metrics with customer-focused business strategies".

"You're preaching to the choir, Mr Consultant", Val stated in her confident, yet polite, manner. "The metrics will help give us a sanity check for our strategies, and enable us to quantify our growth plans in terms of real value creation".

Larry then asked ... "Why is this going to be so much better than the two-year operating plans we've done in the past"?

Earl D'Mark had been waiting to say something and now saw his chance. "One major enhancement will be the introduction of 'balance sheet' investments – you know, little things such as buildings, equipment, inventories and receivables – into our financial outlooks, along with challenging P&L items such as pricing and cost assumptions. Further, all of this will link to your business strategy".

"Funny man", chuckled Larry, "but remember, that for me the old 'bottom line' is still sacred".

Jason now had an opening he had hoped for. "That's still relevant, but I hope to give you a new way of looking at the 'bottom line' … or, perhaps a revised definition for the 'bottom line' ".

"It better be good", Larry shot back, "because the 'old bottom line' has served me well for a long, long time".

Jonathan had rarely been silent for so long in a meeting – it must have been ten minutes or so. "I think we've had some good debate and healthy jostling back and forth. For what it's worth, I want to add a comment. In order for this approach (*creating and then sustaining shareholder value*) to be successful, we must view it as a 'system'. By that I mean we need a complete management 'system' geared toward shareholder value. Val made a good start last year in initiating a process for developing customer-focused strategies. She's close to engaging a select group of Jason's colleagues to help install a comprehensive approach for strategy development. Jason will be helping us to revamp key aspects of our financial functions. By year-end, I hope to be in a position to integrate the two, and blend them into our operations. That's what I mean by a 'system', with all the parts geared toward creating and sustaining shareholder value increases. The new financial tools should help us quantify our strategies, as Val mentioned. The strategy process provides a foundation, along with logic, for our financial projections. Larry, if this combination does *not* give us a better outlook than those two-year, trend-line forecasts we've been doing for too long now, then it's time for me to retire or move into a new line of work".

"OK", Larry sighed, "it's hard to argue with the way you've presented your case. But, as the saying goes – seeing is believing!"

Flo had her arms folded and was starting to slink in her chair. Jonathan picked it up and looked straight at her. "We will have to be careful", she stated, "that we keep this 'system' relatively simple and understandable for the 'troops'. You know that Ian does not want complexity in the way we manage the company".

Only Jonathan could have countered with … "Flo, that was not only a 'politically' correct comment; it also happens to be 'technically' correct. We must keep this new system relatively simple; but, we must not lose integrity. I'm willing to sacrifice some 'pureness', but I won't put in a 'stupidly simple' system either. Look, we walk a fine line, but this is one of the things we get paid for, and I see it as an exciting challenge. Anything else, Jason?"

"Just a couple of closing remarks", Jason responded. "Your desire for simplicity is well founded, as is Jonathan's unwillingness to install a system lacking integrity. Jonathan and I have discussed this issue, and would like to offer a phrase to set the tone for our endeavor. We call it *simplicity with integrity*".

Peter Uppcomer looked over at Jack Earningsly, then looked back to Flo and Larry, and stated emphatically, "if that truly is the message, then I propose that all of us give this effort our support". Heads nodded around the table.

"OK, then", Jonathan concluded, "let's get on with it!"

## 3

Value-based metrics: from accounting to economics

The following day, Friday, both Jonathan and Jason had been invited to a luncheon, to honor a mutual acquaintance who was retiring after a distinguished career, culminating with a position as executive vice president and chief financial officer for one of the largest publicly owned companies in the area.

As they drove to the luncheon, Jonathan commented that he was pleased with both the dialogue and outcome of the meeting the day before. He now felt the timing was right to launch into the details of the work effort through a team he had formed within the past month. Earl and Jack were designated as co-leaders. Jonathan explained, to Jason, that he wanted Jack to be an integral part of the process and did not want Jack to feel that Earl was 'taking over' such an important task for the company.

The other team members were Jill Debitson (the number two person in Corporate Accounting), Frank Accurato (Earl's most senior level direct report), and the finance directors for the two business units. Catherine (Cathy) Casher served as finance director for Industrial Products and David (Dave) Dollarby held the same position in Industrial Services. Val Performa, while not an official member of the work team, was to be brought in for all 'summary and conclusion' type meetings, and sent copies of all significant written reports.

After listening, Jason turned to Jonathan and asked, "Would you give me an overview of the backgrounds and experiences of these team members? We've talked briefly about Frank Accurato, but I know virtually nothing about the others".

"Certainly", responded Jonathan, "let's start with Jill".

"Jill Debitson graduated from a large mid-west university with a bachelor's degree in accounting. Similar to many young professionals with this educational background, she started her work career with a major accounting and auditing firm. After three years of audit work, which included earning a CPA, Jill was hired by Growthstar to fill a newly created position of corporate accounting specialist. An important part of this job was a role as Jack Earningsly's special project administrator. Jack hired Jill due to her perceived strong work ethic which, when combined with a good education and solid first job experience, made her an attractive candidate. Although young, Jill is only twenty-nine, she has impressed virtually all of Growthstar's management as the Accounting Department's most capable person supporting Jack. In fact, last year she was promoted to director of corporate accounting. While not quite as dynamic as Val Performa, she is similar in many respects, in terms of intellect and personality. Having just completed her fourth year here, she has a good grasp of the company's business and its cultural environment".

"Jill's experience has been primarily in the accounting area – auditing, operational and corporate accounting, and accounting theory – but she did work as part of a corporate finance team, led by Earl D'Mark, when the company went through a major refinancing fifteen months ago. This gave her exposure to commercial and investment banking, as well as long-range financial planning and debt/equity financing strategy. While deeply committed to the accounting profession, she understands economics and cash flow concepts. She also has recognized that some of the accounting conventions employed during the quarterly and year-end closings have no impact on the company's cash flow. To the dismay of Jack Earningsly, she has recently been proposing a serious investigation of economic-based financial performance measures. Jack has voiced some concerns to Jill (and to me) and I believe the two have had a few heated debates behind closed doors. Jill is not, however, the kind of person to back down from a position she feels strongly about, even if it means confronting her boss. It's also noteworthy that Jill attended a shareholder value conference with Frank Accurato, at my insistence and over Jack's objections. In fact, Jack, in one of his more frustrated moments, complained to me that he feels his own staff is turning against him. I don't believe this is true, but Jack has moments when he seems to feel that way".

"Moving on, Frank Accurato is Growthstar's assistant treasurer and Earl D'Mark's key aide. He graduated from a small New England college with a bachelor's degree in economics and a master's degree in business from a renowned southern university, concentrating on finance. His first job was with a major bank in the Carolinas. After four years in corporate lending, he joined a multi-billion-dollar service company as a senior treasury analyst, focusing on long-range financial planning, cash management and short-term investing policy. Immediately after Earl joined the company (three years ago) he and I collaborated on hiring Frank to 'beef up' a Treasury function that was weak and under-staffed. At the age of thirty-two, Frank is responsible for Growthstar's banking relationships, risk management and long-range financial planning. Over the past two years, he has implemented a system for enhancing the company's historical two-year budgeting and forecasting process".

"While bright and capable, Frank does not have Earl's outgoing personality. He is methodical and has established his credibility with Growthstar (and his former employer) by analysis that is so thorough that his conclusions are usually indisputable. In fact, Frank was rather shy when he joined Growthstar. Over the past two years, Earl has worked with him on his verbal skills. While still rather quiet and reserved, Frank has become very participative in meetings with the corporate and business unit officers, even when Ian Lord is involved. The officers have grown to respect Frank, because he never speaks without having evidence to support his statements. He is viewed as a 'counter-ego' to Earl, who is never lacking for opinions, even if they are 'off the top of the head' thoughts. Their strengths as a team are Earl's conceptual thinking and salesmanship supported by Frank's analysis and ability to cogently summarize key points for senior management".

"Cathy Casher resembles Flo Withetide in terms of her background and experience. She started with the company at its inception (as Q-Form Products) thirty years ago in the mailroom, after graduating from high school. Attending night school, she earned a degree in accounting from the local branch of the state university, taking eight years to complete her studies. After earning a Bachelor of Arts degree, she was offered a position as a Junior Accountant, which occurred during the time that Jack was auditing the Growthstar account. Jack was impressed with Cathy's work ethic and, soon after he joined the company, promoted her to a Senior Accountant. She rose to the position of Accounting Manager, holding that position for several years, and reported directly to Jack. With the acquisition of *Services* two years ago, and the establishment of the two business units, Cathy was promoted to Finance Director of *Products*".

"Larry Buildermann was delighted with this appointment, having known Cathy for many years and appreciating both her technical skills in finance and her dedication to the company. Cathy is Larry's type of person – hard working with a focus on the 'bottom line' – the one that Larry understands. Cathy has a strong loyalty to Jack and Larry and, while receptive to the new economic-based concepts being proposed by Earl and Val, and supported recently by me, she still has strong ties to the accounting principles she has studied and worked under for so many years".

"Dave Dollarby was brought to Growthstar by Peter Uppcomer, as part of the acquisition of *Services* from an under-performing conglomerate two years ago. Dave has worked for Peter for a total of ten years and shares many of Peter's views concerning *Services* growth being important for Growthstar's future stock price gains. Similar to most good finance professionals, he does not promote growth for its own sake, and is a strong advocate of 'profitable' growth. As a result, he is able to temper Peter's zealous pursuit of growing the business at almost any cost. Peter appreciates this characteristic of Dave, which is one reason they have worked well together during the past ten years".

"While intelligent (bachelor's and master's degrees from a West Coast university) and experienced (fifteen years total with three companies – including Growthstar) Dave has only worked in 'service' businesses, and does *not* have a strong 'balance sheet' perspective. Peter Uppcomer has never put any emphasis on a balance sheet, and neither of them has ever had their incentive pay based on any measure other than sales and profit growth. So, when Dave talks about 'profitable' growth, it is from a traditional profit and loss (that is, a 'P&L') perspective".

"So, that's a biographical sketch of these people. They are a capable and energetic group, with a desire to move the company forward in terns if being 'in tune' with the latest financial concepts. I think they all realize we need to make some changes to the way we analyze, measure, report and make key financial decisions, but they're not sure as to exactly what needs to change and how to do it. That's where you come in, Jason".

Jason had been silent during the entire time that Jonathan had been speaking. As they approached their luncheon destination, he turned to Jonathan and uttered, "I'm rather amazed at the specifics you've been able to cite about each of these people. I must say that I am impressed".

"It's part of my job to know my people", Jonathan retorted, with a slight twinkle in his eye.

The luncheon was quite a lavish and lengthy affair, lasting until nearly 3:00 in the afternoon. As they drove back to Growthstar's office, Jonathan and Jason shared some of their experiences with their colleague who had been honored.

As they entered the company's parking lot, Jonathan turned to Jason and said, "I think I told you that after our initial meeting with the corporate and operating unit officers, I would convene our work team. Before we left for the luncheon, I asked Kay to reconfirm an all-day meeting I had scheduled with the team for Monday. I'll kick it off and then let you take over".

"Terrific", Jason responded. "I'll start out with a simple example comparing accounting to economics, and then get into the specific issues and adjustments for Growthstar to consider".

"OK, see you Monday", Jonathan concluded as he parked his car and turned off the ignition.

In preparation for Monday's work session, Jason spent a part of Sunday afternoon at home reviewing his 'generic' material on transitioning from accounting to economic measurements, along with the historical and current-year financial reports for Growthstar.

At 7:55 am Monday morning, the work team members arrived at the Corporate Finance conference room. Jason and Jonathan were already inside, having arrived at 7:45. Jonathan motioned for everyone to come in and be seated.

After all the people had taken a cup of coffee or tea, Jonathan stood up and began speaking ... "I would like to welcome all of you to a very important work session. As you all know, Jack and Earl are the co-leaders of this team, which will be responsible for structuring and implementing a value-based financial performance system for our company. I have attempted to put together the best financial talent we have from both corporate and operating unit perspectives. Jason Aradvizer, who is known to some but not to all, is acting as an advisor to me and the company, and will coordinate the efforts of the work team".

Jonathan then made introductions of Jason to each of the team members, excluding Jack and Earl. Jonathan continued ... "I believe the time has come for our company to implement a comprehensive financial system encompassing planning and evaluation techniques, performance measurement and reporting. I believe, further, that this system should have a governing set of economic principles as its foundation, with a bridge to the generally accepted accounting principles (GAAP) that we utilize for external reporting to shareholders and the Securities and Exchange Commission, which we lovingly refer to as the 'SEC' ".

A few chuckles could be heard around the room, especially from the accountants who had to deal with GAAP and SEC reporting on a regular basis.

Jonathan, always one to 'read' his audience, paused and then spoke again . . . "While we need to make some changes, which could potentially be significant, I want to state emphatically that it is *not* my intention to abandon what we've been doing in Corporate Finance. Rather, I see change as an 'enhancement' – let's say an 'improvement' – to bring us into the realm of modern financial thinking and practices. Our ultimate goal should be to influence management behavior, modifying it as necessary to align our senior managers with our shareholders. As a team, our job is to provide the technical foundation for a new financial system and to develop an approach and a process that is easy to implement by those without the financial backgrounds we possess. Our theme for this endeavor is *simplicity with integrity*".

At this juncture, virtually all the people in the room leaned back and took a deep breath – for most, their first since Jonathan had begun the meeting.

Jonathan then motioned for everyone to get a cup of coffee or tea – or a refill. After everyone was settled again, he continued his introductory comments . . . "Jason Aradvizer has been hired to work with us over the next several months. His role will be to facilitate a process that will lead us through the major steps involved in implementing a value-based financial performance system – customized for our company. The end result, however, will be ours. We will take ownership of it and will likely receive our incentive bonuses according to its provisions. That's one reason why we had a kick-off meeting with the corporate and operating officers on Thursday, and it is the reason you are all here today. This effort will involve this group and the officers. As we move along, we will involve others in the company. Ian will also be apprised of our progress and findings, and will be asked to make decisions at key milestones during the process. While not completely sold on the benefits of 'value-based' management techniques (he certainly believes he is acting in the best interests of the shareholders) he realizes that more and more companies are implementing economic-based approaches and that we need to investigate them. He told me that he expects this group and the officers to think and work diligently on this effort, since we must have a system in place that will truly motivate management to create shareholder value, and compensate them accordingly".

"Well", Jonathan concluded, "that's my speech for today. I'm going to turn the meeting over to Jason, to get us started on what I hope will be the first of many productive work sessions together".

Jonathan then exited the conference room.

Jason, who moved to the front of the room as Jonathan was leaving, started to speak . . . "I would like to begin by saying that our first

---

Exhibit 5

"Accounting Profit"— Example

"Base Period"		CO. 'A'	CO. 'B'	CO. 'C'
Revenue [Sales]		$1,000	$1,000	$1,000
Net Operating Profit				
[NOP]	- $	$100	$100	$100
	- %	10%	10%	10%

The Accounting ("Earnings") model stops here. In this case, all companies are the same ... and, all are "profitable".

---

analysis will be as simple as 'A, B, C'. We'll take a look at three hypothetical firms – **'A', 'B' and 'C'** – and show how differently companies can perform from an economic perspective, while appearing to be the same on the basis of the accounting numbers".

Jason flicked on the switch of an overhead projector and placed a transparency. "Let's take a look at a simple example (Exhibit 5). *NOP* is an acronym for Net Operating Profit – on an after-tax basis".

"This exhibit reflects the traditional 'profit & loss' summary. Historically, this is what 'Wall Street' has published and what most companies have geared themselves to. The question I always ask people is ... 'what is different' about these companies and can you make any type of investment decision?"

Dave Dollarby jumped into the discussion. "You need to know something about future growth prospects to answer that question". Jason responded ... "good point ... anything else?" Dave formed a steeple with the tips of his fingers (a gesture of confidence) and retorted, "that's the major consideration – profit growth".

Jill Debitson leaned forward and said, "I would think that some risk assessment and competitive or market share analysis would be important. If one company has a stronger market position, it's probably worth more".

Cathy Casher and Frank Accurato remained quiet. Just as Jason was about to speak again, Frank said (softly) "I'm not sure you have enough information to make a stock price judgment. You're only looking at the income statement".

Jack Earningsly felt compelled to make his presence known. "I feel this is a 'setup'".

"Maybe it is", interjected Earl D'Mark.

Jack countered ... "I'll bet Jason is going to (again) attack accounting in some way. I just never know where the attack is coming from or what shape it's going to take".

"You sure are sensitive, old boy", Earl jabbed back, seeming to enjoy the 'give and take'.

Jason had been advised by Jonathan to let the personalities 'play out' and had, thus, remained quiet during these exchanges. Wanting to move ahead, however, he spoke again ... "Collectively, you have made some very relevant comments. Let me add the following inputs, by saying that we can assume there are similarities among the three companies with regard to market growth, market position, business risk and quality of management. Now, with these 'strategic' factors taken into consideration, can we distinguish among these three companies, in terms of their potential to create shareholder value?"

All the people in the room, except Earl, had puzzling looks on their faces, as they peered at the nine numbers on the exhibit, trying to see something that might be hidden. Finally, Cathy Casher stated, "there doesn't appear to be any difference at all, but I think I agree with Frank in that we don't have enough information".

"That's correct", Jason responded. "We're missing two critical factors, from a financial perspective, to begin to make shareholder value judgments. These two factors get at the heart of the shortcomings of using the traditional *Accounting Model*, based on Net Income or Earnings per Share as the key determinant for stock prices. Using 'earnings' (alone) as a proxy for 'value' misses the following:

- the *risk* of the earnings, and
- the *capital* needed to generate the earnings".

"The next chart (Exhibit 6) introduces the notion that invested capital (you know, *that 'balance sheet' thing*) and its economic cost play a role in valuing a business. As we can see in this exhibit, the three companies are *not* the same, especially in terms of the invested capital, which I sometimes refer to as '*IC*', required to generate the revenue and profit".

"So what?" Dave Dollarby asked. "I've always been told that companies exist to grow and produce profits. When we need capital, we go to the banks or the stock market. Assuming we're profitable, we should be able to get all the capital we need".

"Take a look at the next line Dave", said Earl, eager to continue the dialogue. "There's a cost for the capital invested in these companies, in this case 12%".

Exhibit 6

"Economic Profit"— Example

"Base Period"		CO. 'A'	CO. 'B'	CO. 'C'
Revenue [Sales]		$1,000	$1,000	$1,000
Net Operating Profit				
** [NOP]**	- $	$100	$100	$100
	- %	10%	10%	10%
Invested Capital [IC]		$600	$800	$1,000
Cost of Capital [CCAP]		12%	12%	12%

*The "Economic Profit" model introduces the concept of **Capital** required to produce the "Accounting Profit" and the **Cost** of this capital. We begin to see that all the companies are not the same.*

"OK, but so what?" retorted Dave. "What does this have to do with our profitability?"

It was obvious to Jason that Earl wanted his colleagues to realize he had some knowledge on this subject, so Jason remained quiet as Earl spoke again … "The 12% cost of capital, or *CCAP* as Jason refers to it, represents an important element in the 'success formula' for these companies. In essence, it's a minimum financial return requirement for management. If they don't earn at least a 12% return on total capital, they may encounter difficulty approaching the markets for new capital, especially at a reasonable cost".

"But" interjected Dave, "if the profits keep growing doesn't this take care of itself?"

"Not always", Earl responded.

"Then, please explain this to me", said Dave with a perplexed look on his face.

Earl looked over at Jason, indicating with a slight nod of his head that the consultant should take over. Jason, taking the cue, stood up and said … "let's look at the invested capital line once more before moving on. Would you agree, Dave, that Company '**A**' has the lowest amount of capital and Company '**C**' has the highest".

"Sure", Dave responded.

Jason continued, "Now, let's put *CCAP* in perspective and explain how we use it for evaluating the performance of a company or a business unit within a company. To repeat what Earl stated a moment ago, the

---

Exhibit 7

"Economic Profit" — Example

"Base Period"		CO. 'A'	CO. 'B'	CO. 'C'
Revenue [Sales]		$1,000	$1,000	$1,000
Net Operating Profit				
[NOP]	- $	$100	$100	$100
	- %	10%	10%	10%
Invested Capital [IC]		$600	$800	$1,000
Cost of Capital [CCAP]		12%	12%	12%

Economic Profit	CO. 'A'	CO. 'B'	CO. 'C'
NOP [from above]	$100	$100	$100
Capital Charge [CCAP]	(72)	(96)	(120)
Economic Profit ["EP"]	$28	$4	$(20)

---

investors in these hypothetical companies expect a rate of return on their investment. This afternoon we'll explore the cost of capital in more detail. Suffice it to say for now that this cost (assume it's 12% for all three firms) establishes a 'threshold' economic return level for these firms. It is, frankly, the best approximation of a minimum profit target that satisfies the desires of investors in the aggregate. To calculate this target, we will 'charge' these companies a cost (in this case, 12%) for the total capital they have been entrusted with by their investors".

'Now, let's see what this means, by looking at the next chart (Exhibit 7)".

"When I said that charging a cost for the capital invested in a business approximates the desires of the investors, what I mean is that this *CCAP* – 12% in our example – is the 'minimum annual return' that the investors expect from each of these three companies. So, the closest we can come to replicating the capital market perspective is to assess profitability after '*charging*' for this (minimum) return on capital requirement. Some of you may have heard the term 'hurdle rate' with respect to capital investments. *CCAP* is the 'hurdle rate' for these three firms. In this case, it is expressed as a 'dollar' amount. While not perfect, this approach captures the expectations of the financial markets".

"As we can see in this exhibit, all the firms are *not* profitable from an economic, or rate of return, perspective. In fact, only

Company '**A**' is truly profitable". As he spoke, Jason circled the *'EP'*
of $(20) – under the **Co. 'C'** column – with a *red marker*. "There are
variations on this format, in which the minimum return is expressed
as a percentage, rather than a 'dollar' amount, and the comparison
is to a percentage *CCAP*. The point for now is that, conceptually,
virtually all of the economic measures are based on the notion of
ascribing a cost (minimum rate of return) to the capital invested in a
business".

Jason paused and looked around the room for a reaction. He didn't
have to wait long.

Jill Debitson leaned forward and raised her right hand slightly, a
habit of hers indicating a desire to express an opinion. "Can't we get
an idea of this type of profit measure through the 'Interest' we pay
(and charge ourselves) on our short- and long-term debt?"

Jack, who had been slightly slumped in his chair, sat up, clenched
his fist under the conference table and uttered a *'YES'* to himself.

Dave, who liked to lean back when he spoke, started nodding his
head and said, "that's what I was thinking before, but didn't express
... that our profits should include an interest charge, and if we can
keep them positive and growing we should be OK".

Cathy now felt comfortable to say ... "That's what Larry Buildermann and I thought we should have in our 'bottom line' – a profit
after interest costs and taxes. Larry and I are 'bottom line'-oriented,
because we believe in covering all our costs. But, we don't get an
interest charge from corporate".

Now, it was time for Earl to weigh in again ... "But, folks, the
interest charges only cover the cost of one element of our invested
capital – the debt portion".

"That may be", interjected Jack, "but that's what our shareholders
are interested in – our profits available (to them) after paying our
creditors. This serves as the basis for our *Return on Equity* calculation,
as well as *EPS*, which the analysts constantly inquire about. I *tried*
to institute an inter-company interest charge, but Jonathan 'shot
me down'".

"I think we covered the analyst issue and the lack of correlation
of *EPS* with stock prices last week in the meeting with officers", Earl
retorted. "Surely, you haven't forgotten that discussion so quickly!"

Frank Accurato, as was his habit, had waited until everyone else
had spoken. He now leaned forward and said, "what I think we
have, based on the research I have done and what I learned at
the shareholder value conference I recently attended, is a cost for
our equity capital that is not recorded anywhere on our financial
statements. It's sort of a 'hidden cost' that accounting-based reporting
systems simply don't capture".

Jack, getting a little red in the face, responded by saying, "Have Jason and Earl been 'prepping' you?"

"You should know me better than that, Jack", Frank responded, looking straight at him and not noticing the smile on Earl's face, relishing Frank's willingness to stand up to Jack.

Jason knew that he had to bring the team to an appreciation of an issue that was not easily understood. This was particularly relevant for the accountants, most of whom had not been exposed to the cost of equity capital, and had spent countless hours accounting for debt financing charges. Jill had also been exposed to allocating 'inter-company' interest expense. Jason thought back to Jonathan's comments last Friday about Frank's perceptive and cogent summarization of important points. "As Frank just alluded to, *without any 'prepping'*, the debt financing charge, which we call 'Interest' expense, is only part of the cost of the capital invested in any business, and the equity cost is often hidden. And, as I mentioned a few moments ago, we're going to delve into the cost of equity capital this afternoon. So, let's assume, for the time being, that the costs of capital (*CCAPs*) are relevant for our three sample firms and that they are the same. The key point here is that we assess a charge for the total capital invested in the business. Further, if one company has more capital than another, then it will incur a greater charge, assuming (as I have in this example) that the *CCAP rates* are similar or the same".

"When we get through with all this, we get three distinct capital charges (I use the term *CCAP* both for cost of capital and capital charge) ... *and, they are different, because the invested capital levels are different for the three firms.* This is no different from the companies having different levels of overhead or selling and marketing expenses, to support businesses which all have the same gross profit margin. The difference is that the 'Accounting' model – with its focus on 'earnings' – picks up these expense (income statement) differences, whereas it doesn't typically highlight balance sheet differences".

Dave Dollarby leaned back and then forward, nodding his head. "OK, now I get it. What you're saying is that the interest cost is only part of the cost of financing a business and that the balance sheet may reveal big differences among firms that, on the surface, appear to be the same".

Jill Debitson chimed in, "and, while we produce a balance sheet every time we close the books, we really don't analyze it thoroughly".

As Jack started to squirm and Earl put his hand over his mouth and turned his head to hide a smile that was working its way from ear to ear, Jason interjected ... "Maybe I should turn the podium over to you guys, since you basically gave my speech as well as I could".

"Thanks for the compliment, Mr Consultant", Dave shot back, "but we'll keep you at the head of the class for at least a little while longer. Maybe, because of the nature of 'service' businesses, we don't appreciate the balance sheet as much as our colleagues in 'manufacturing'. We only have receivables and inventory to deal with, and we monitor them in terms of the number of days outstanding and the inventory turnover. In fact, in my last company, we were assessed a 10% charge on our monthly receivable balances over thirty days and inventory over a stipulated level. Nobody really understood it, but we factored it into our operating statements, since our bonus was based on it".

"So, you did have a working capital charge", Jason responded, "which is at least a start. I'll bet you, though, that you had other 'balance sheet' assets that you were not even aware of".

"Like what?" Dave asked.

"Like your district and regional sales offices and your vehicles and office equipment", Jason answered.

"Oh, we leased those, so they're not assets", Dave shot back.

"Not so", Earl interjected. "All you had was another form of debt financing for an asset, which didn't meet a 'capital lease' test and, therefore, wasn't recorded as an asset. This is another case of where accounting is arbitrary and doesn't reflect the economics of the business".

"Give me a break", Jack blurted out. "If we capitalized everything we'd drive ourselves crazy with balance sheet entries that probably wouldn't give us any better insights".

"I'm not so sure of that", Frank stated in a somewhat defiant tone, "because I'm guessing that one of messages Jason is implying is that these 'operating leases' may cause one business to be more capital intensive than another".

Jack couldn't come back with a rebuttal, so he just sat and stared at the exhibit on the screen again.

Jason grabbed the pause in the debate and said "As a group, you're starting to raise some very relevant issues regarding the adjustments to get from 'accounting' to 'economics'. I think we should take a short break, but before doing so, let's summarize what we have at the bottom of Exhibit 7. Company '**A**' gets a $72 million capital charge based on a 12% *CCAP* and its IC of $600 million. After this assessment, '**A**' is still 'in the black', in that it has a *positive* Economic Profit (*EP*). Company '**A**' is a *value 'creator'* if this type of performance can be sustained. Company '**B**' gets a $96 million charge, which just about wipes out its $100 million profit. I call this *value 'neutral'* since, if this is indicative of long-term performance, '**B**' will generate hardly any incremental value over and above the capital invested. In other words, the investors give this management a dollar and they get a dollar in return. Contrast this with Company '**A**', which is returning a solid 'economic' profit. Company '**C**' is a real problem, in spite of the fact that its 'P&L' looks good with a 10% margin. This company is so capital intensive that its capital charge of $120 million causes an economic 'loss' of $20 million. This 'blows people's minds' because they can't believe that a business with positive 'earnings', especially when growing, can do this. I call '**C**' companies *value 'destroyers'*. After we take a break, we'll go over the major adjustments which bridge the gap from the *Accounting* to the *Economic* model".

As the financial team returned, some filling their coffee or tea, Jason flipped on the switch to the overhead projector and placed another transparency (Exhibit 8).

"Let's take a look at the key elements of Economic Profit (or *EP* as I refer to it). The dashed line separates the income statement (or P&L) from the balance sheet, merely for clarification at this point. The great thing about *EP* is that it doesn't discriminate between the two statements. In essence, *EP* doesn't care whether an item is classified to the P&L or balance sheet. Further, the *EP* approach will provide the appropriate treatments regarding taxes and depreciation/amortization".

"Regarding the income statement, our starting point is Operating Income, either on an EBIT or EBITDA basis. In fact, we can also

---

Exhibit 8
Economic Profit — Key Elements

- **Net Operating Profit (NOP)**
  - *Operating Income (EBIT ... EBITDA)*
       times
  - *One minus the "Effective" Tax Rate (1–T)*

- **Invested Capital (*IC*)**
  - *Total (net ... gross) Assets*
       minus
  - *Non-Interest Bearing Current Liabilities*
    (essentially, Payables and Accruals)
  - **... IC includes Goodwill/Intangibles/Operating Leases**

have EBITD or EBITA, which lie in-between the two extremes (EBIT and EBITDA). So that there is no confusion with the acronyms, all of which are, in essence, *Operating Income*, they are defined as follows:

- EBIT is *earnings before interest and taxes*
- EBITD is *earnings before interest, depreciation and taxes*
- EBITA is *earnings before interest, amortization and taxes* ... and
- EBITDA is *earnings before interest, depreciation, amortization and taxes*".

"As we move from EBIT to EBITDA, we go from a definition of *Operating Profit* that is '*net of*' depreciation and amortization expense to a non-depreciated (or *pure cash flow*) definition. EBIT is, obviously, a lower amount than EBITD, EBITA or EBITDA, since the depreciation and/or amortization is added back to EBIT when calculating EBITD, EBITA or EBITDA".

"The second major element is the 'effective' tax rate. 'Effective' means the taxes that the company actually pays to the Internal Revenue Service. In essence, it's the company's 'cash' tax rate. Now, this 'effective' tax rate may *not* be the same as the tax provision on the accounting statements".

"How do you determine this?" asked Dave.

"You need to delve into the footnotes to the 'reported' financial statements", Earl chimed in, before Jason could answer.

Dave cast a look at Jack and inquired "Why do we have this situation, Jack, and how significant is it?"

Jack thought for a moment and responded, "GAAP is looking at a 'normalized' tax situation, based on statutory federal and state/local tax rates. It takes into account where we operate, especially geographically, and the source(s) of our profits".

"But", interjected Earl, "it may not coincide with how we invest and run our businesses".

"Maybe that's why I never focused on this issue", Dave continued. "We don't usually have a significant level of capital expenditures; thus, there is not much tax to 'defer' due to accelerating depreciation for tax purposes. We are, I assume, talking about deferring tax payments as a result of capital investments and using accelerated depreciation for tax purposes versus straight-line depreciation for GAAP reporting".

"We certainly are", Earl responded. "It's what we call the 'book-to-tax differential' with respect to taxes".

"In *Products*, we invest a substantial amount of fixed capital", stated Cathy.

"And you can have a tax deferral, which may be significant", quipped Earl. "Further, many manufacturing firms are in this situation, which is why the 'tax provision' we put on our financials *may not* bear any resemblance to economic reality".

"Hold on", Jack responded, his face getting red again. "We don't just pull these rates out of the air, and I object to the comments that we're out of touch with reality".

"You have got to stop taking this personally, Jack", said Earl with a slight smirk. "I simply stated that the tax provision *may not* be linked to the economics of the business".

"Well, it sounds critical and strikes me as personal", muttered Jack, "and, frankly, I'm getting annoyed with it".

"Come on, boss", said Jill, "we know there are some arbitrary aspects to our work that we can't control. Jason, Earl and Frank are just trying to point these things out for the overall understanding of the team".

Jack's face was now 'beet red', as he did not like any sort of 'push back' from his staff in front of a mixed group. His total silence indicated his high level of frustration.

Jason knew it was time for him to intervene. "I think we need to stay focused on the purpose of these key economic elements, and the reasons for making the adjustments. Ultimately, investors are interested in how much cash is *generated* by a business, as compared to the cash *invested*. Part of determining the amount of cash *generated* is to calculate the taxes actually paid. As I stated last week at the meeting with the officers, the accounting numbers don't always give us good indicators of cash flow and value creation (or destruction) because that's *not* what they were intended to do".

Jack slumped down in his chair, scowled at Jason and Earl, but remained silent.

Jason, prepared for another outburst from Jack, was not expecting the 'stone silence' that now permeated the room. Feeling at a momentary loss for words, he reverted to a habit he cultivated to gather his thoughts, which was to pause and take a sip of coffee. Turning to face first the exhibit on the screen and then back to the people in the room, he began his next dialogue ... "In a few moments, we'll explore the P&L in more depth, but let's now take a quick look at the key balance sheet elements, focusing on the bottom half of the exhibit. The basic definition of invested capital for any business (which I often call *IC*) is total assets minus non-interest bearing current liabilities, essentially payables and accruals. There is an acronym for these liabilities – NIBCLs".

"Similar to the income statement, the balance sheet can be structured on a 'net' asset (that is, 'depreciated' asset) basis or 'gross' asset (non-depreciated) basis. The point here is that the method for calculating *IC* must coincide with that for the income statement. What this means is that the proper 'connections' must be in place". As Jason spoke, he went to the flip chart and wrote:

Income Statement	**Balance Sheet**
Operating Profit = EBIT	**IC = Total assets (T/A) on a 'net' basis less NIBCLs (*)**
= EBITD	**= T/A ('gross' fixed assets… 'net' goodwill/intangibles)**
= EBITA	**= T/A ('net' fixed assets… 'gross' goodwill/intangibles)**
= EBITDA	**= T/A ('gross' fixed assets… 'gross' goodwill/intangibles)**

(*) all ICs are T/A less NIBCL's

"At this juncture, I want to stress that there is no 'perfect' Economic Profit model. Companies are different, such that a simplistic 'EBIT/ Net Asset' approach might be totally adequate for one firm, while the characteristics of another business might necessitate a more complex 'EBITDA/Gross Asset' framework. Whatever approach is selected, however, there must be consistency between the income statement and balance sheet. In essence, the definition of Operating Profit must conform to that for Invested Capital and the adjustments must link. Finally, as noted at the bottom of the exhibit, *IC* includes goodwill, intangibles and operating leases when they are significant. Any other questions, before we move on to some 'specific' adjustments?"

"I have one question, which may only be a point of clarification", interjected Jill. "You said that *IC* can be defined in different ways, depending on how we treat amortization and depreciation. I understand that. You then concluded by saying that goodwill, intangibles and operating leases are included in *IC* if they are significant. What do you mean by significant? Is it the type of 'materiality' test we use in accounting?"

"Good question", Jason responded. "*Significant* in this context means the effect on the Economic Profit (*EP*) calculation. I'm going to review this issue in more detail at a subsequent work session. For now, let me say that if moving from a simple *EP* definition to a more complex one has an impact of 10% or more, either on the Economic Profit or Return on Invested Capital calculation, then it's *significant*, and we would defer to the more complex definition. If *not*, then we can use the simpler definition and calculation. When we get to it, part of working through this issue will be what I call a 'Level 1, 2, 3' analysis, in which we'll evaluate the impact of these elements and how to make the adjustments".

"A, B, C and 1, 2, 3", chuckled Jill. "Next, we'll be going to *Romper Room* or *Mr Rogers' Neighborhood*. You're doing well on the *simplicity* aspect of our theme, Jason, so it will be interesting to see how the *integrity* piece works out".

"Gee, I can hardly wait", chortled Jack, cracking a smile for the first time all morning.

"Stay tuned and hang in there folks", Jason retorted.

With no other questions and Jack's scowl subsiding, Jason took Exhibit 8 off the projector and replaced it with another (Exhibit 9). "What I would like to do now is discuss some of the more important 'fine tuning' adjustments to transition from Accounting Profit to Economic Profit".

Jack quickly sat up in his chair and leaned forward, putting his arms and hands firmly on the top of the conference table.

Jason thought to himself that Jack might 'strike' at any moment and mentally prepared himself for this possibility. "As noted by the first 'bullet', there are at least two potential P&L adjustments related to the balance sheet. The first is the add-back of amortization expense related to goodwill or intangibles. I assume most of you know that goodwill relates primarily to acquisitions (via 'purchase' accounting)

Exhibit 9
Economic Profit — "Fine Tuning"
       (from "AP" to "EP")

Profit & Loss (P&L)
- ◆ *Related to Balance Sheet*
  - Amortization of Goodwill/Intangibles — add back
  - Interest on Operating Leases
    - *Note: Rent has 2 Components:*
      - *1) Depreciation — remains in P&L*
      - *2) Interest — add back, same as Interest on 'Debt'*
- ◆ *Taxes – "Cash" Basis ... incorporates Deferrals*
- ◆ *Other ... Add-backs*
  - Restructuring Charges (non-cash)
  - Acquisition Reserves/Write-Offs
- ◆ *R & D and/or Advertising Capitalization ... then, Amortization Expense (optional)*

in which the purchase price exceeds the 'book value' of the assets, and that intangibles often arise from things such as patents and technology-related investments". Everyone nodded.

Jason continued ... "Regarding operating leases, the rent expense has two components. The first is the *depreciation* of the asset (to the lessee) which stays on the P&L as an economic cost (to the lessee) – noting that it represents a 'return of principal' to the owner (lessor). The second is the *interest expense*, representing the lessee's cost of financing – noting that this is the economic return to the lessor. This (*interest*) expense is added back to Operating Profit, similar to interest expense on all other forms of debt financing. Please remember that we eliminate financing costs from P&L expenses, since the *capital charge (CCAP)* will incorporate the cost of both debt and equity financing. Since this issue is so important, I want to make sure that it is *absolutely* clear".

"I think so", interjected Dave, "but let's go over it one more time".

"I would also appreciate reviewing this concept again", Cathy chimed in.

"OK", Jason responded, looking over at Earl. "Would you like to comment on this, Earl?"

"I certainly would", Earl said, "but I want to ask Frank if he would like to say something first".

Frank, sensing that his speaking instead of Earl might lessen the chance of an outburst from Jack, began by saying ... "This subject of adding back *interest expense* took a while for me to grasp".

Immediately, Jill, Dave and Cathy sighed and leaned back comfortably in their chairs, each thinking that if it took Frank time to understand this concept, then they shouldn't feel bad about asking for clarification. Jack noticed the reaction of the accountants, and also leaned back a bit in his chair.

Frank continued ... "Here's the key point – we have two primary sources of capital, debt and equity. With regard to debt financing, there are two main sources. The first is what we call a 'formal' borrowing, such as a note, bond, loan, etc. This type of borrowing can be from a bank, other financial institution, or the general public, and may be secured by one or more specific assets or issued on an unsecured basis. In any case, it carries what is known as a 'coupon rate', which determines the interest expense. The second source is a lease usually secured by a specific asset or group of assets. If Jack and Jill, through their accounting tests, determine that the lease is 'capitalized', then it is set up as a fixed asset, to be depreciated over the lease term, and then as a liability, similar to a debt instrument, with a breakdown into principal and interest. The 'interest' appears in our P&L, similar to the 'interest' on our borrowings. If a lease is *not* capitalized, it is called an 'operating' lease. There is *no entry* on the balance sheet and the P&L expense is called 'rent' or 'lease' expense. Within an Economic Profit framework, we're treating *all* leases as though they were 'capitalized'. To summarize, we calculate the 'implied interest' in the operating lease and remove it from the P&L, and retain the 'depreciation' portion, just as we retain the depreciation expense on purchased fixed assets or capitalized leases".

Applause broke out from Jill, Dave and Cathy. Frank looked away, feeling embarrassed.

"You're a genius, Frank", Dave almost shouted.

Jack looked up at the ceiling and said to himself ... "*Oh, God – please help me and save me from these people*".

Jill quickly intervened with ... "We had this planned, Frank – we just didn't know exactly when it would happen".

Laughter then broke out around the table ... with the exception of Jack.

Jason seized the opportunity by shouting (over the laughter) ... "I think this is a good time for a five to ten minute 'break' ".

After everyone returned and was seated again, Jason flipped the 'on' switch to the overhead projector and began speaking ... "Frank, that was an excellent summary of the treatment for operating leases. Can I assume that everyone now understands what we do and why we do it?"

Heads nodded around the table, except for Jack, who just looked past Jason.

"As Exhibit 9 indicates, the next item is the 'cash' basis for income taxes, which I think we covered in sufficient depth a short while ago". Heads nodded again. "Oh yes", Jack interjected, "we covered that one in plenty of detail".

Jason, deciding to ignore the comment, continued ... "Companies in a restructuring mode are often required (by GAAP rules) to take charges related to their actions, especially when personnel cut-backs or lay-offs occur. In some cases, the entries can be very significant – in the extreme 'wiping out' the operating profits for the quarter or fiscal year or throwing the company into a 'loss' position. The result is often an expense reserve, offset by a liability on the balance sheet. What happens is that net earnings and *EPS* are lowered and retained earnings are also reduced through the new liability. Sometimes, these restructuring charges will be paid out over future years. When this occurs, there is *no* P&L impact, because the offset to the reduction in the *cash* account (on the balance sheet) is the *liability* (another balance sheet account). So, what you have is this potentially 'huge hit' to the P&L in one year and then a 'big benefit' in future years as the cash costs are absorbed through the balance sheet. So, the question is – what are the 'real earnings'? Because of this arbitrary type of accounting treatment, the *Economic* model suggests either adding back or amortizing the 'P&L' restructuring charges and *not* reducing the equity portion of the balance sheet with the immediate 'big hit'. Rather, reductions to 'economic' earnings are taken as the cash payments are made over the ensuing years. For companies engaged in a practice of taking regular or periodic restructuring charges, it can be difficult to track exactly what the real profit and invested capital levels are, by relying solely on the reported financial statements".

"But Mr Aradvizer", Jack chimed in immediately, "these are the costs to be incurred with a restructuring".

"Yes, that's true", Jason responded, "but the *timing* of the costs does not usually coincide with the accounting treatment of writing them off all at once".

Jill glanced warily over at Jack, her eyes suggesting that he abandon this argument.

Jason, expecting a comeback from Jack, took a sip of coffee. With nothing forthcoming, he proceeded. "Acquisitions can also create some interesting situations with the financial statements".

"Can they ever", Earl blurted out, having difficulty containing himself.

"Maybe it's time for *you* to calm down, Mr Treasurer", Jack uttered, with a tone of disdain in his voice".

"Maybe you're right, Jack", Earl retorted, "but I really get livid when I see some of the ridiculous things going on with mergers and acquisitions, which seem to be geared toward either fooling the investors or hiding something from them. Take the notion of *Pooling of Interests*, as an example. It's amazing to imagine how, when two companies come together at a merger price above the economic book value of the entities, that by some *stroke of magic* the 'premium' (that is, the actual price of the merger versus the book values) simply *goes away*. The result is an understatement of the invested capital on the new (merged) company's books and no charge to earnings for the goodwill that has been created – but, through the *accounting magic* – disappears! For those misguided people who believe that the goal of acquisitions should be to *not dilute EPS* (how's that for a 'goal setting' standard – stating it in 'negative' terms), they achieve their target, possibly at the risk of diminishing the economic profit or return on invested capital (*ROIC*) of the enterprise. Does anyone believe that the sophisticated investors, who determine the stock prices for most publicly owned companies, cannot see through this charade? In spite of this, we see a continual flow of mergers using this technique and, more disturbing, lobbying the Financial Accounting Standards Board (FASB) to continue it, in spite of substantive economic rationale to 'kill' it".

"Look who is up on the 'soapbox' now", Jack interjected, smiling for the second time this morning. "In defense of '*Pooling*', there is usually no cash exchanging hands; rather, two companies coming together and issuing new stock or additional stock of the 'surviving' company. So, in effect, we're avoiding a whole lot of confusion as to the 'real' future earnings by not assigning goodwill that will last for a long time – which, in spite of the discussion with the officers last week, is what I feel the shareholders value".

Earl was really 'revved up' now. "You're missing an important point regarding the *balance sheet*, Jack. There's a whole lot of *invested capital* that's not accounted for. It's as though you went and purchased a new auto for $30,000 and recorded $25,000. What happened to the $5,000? The fact that cash didn't exchange hands is irrelevant, because a *cash equivalent* is used in the transaction. The stock is a *cash equivalent*, because it can be bought and sold instantaneously in the public markets, and has a *market value*. What '*Pooling*' does is to arbitrarily decrease the *value* of the deal (and, thus, the ongoing invested capital) on the company's books, which then serves as the *basis* for calculating important financial performance measures. For anyone with a rudimentary knowledge of economics, this makes no sense at all. Further, as multiple deals occur over time, it can become almost impossible to determine what was actually paid for these mergers, since the 'premium' of *market value over book value* disappears".

"Well, maybe all of your '*Economics*' doesn't hang together in every situation", Jack retorted, getting agitated again.

"Give me just one example, to counter the several we've thrown at you last week and this morning", Earl replied.

Dave Dollarby, sensing another verbal jousting match between Jack and Earl, jumped into the conversation with "You two guys can really go at each other, but I think we need to move this discussion forward". Jill and Frank looked at each other, snickering slightly and sharing the thought ... "*You're just figuring this out? Welcome to our world!*"

Jason stood up and started speaking again ... "If we look again at Exhibit 9, near the bottom of the chart, there is another type of acquisition reserve – not exactly the same as that for '*Pooling*' – but with a similar impact, in that it can significantly understate a company's invested capital after an acquisition valued under *Purchase Accounting* rules. This is a 'reserve' for the write-off of goodwill or intangibles, and is particularly relevant for 'technology' deals that often have little in the way of 'tangible' assets, or in other situations where a significant 'premium' is paid for an acquisition. The technique is to use the most liberal accounting allowance for purchased research and development (R&D) which can be an immediate write-off. The result is a 'big hit' to net earnings (and *EPS*) with a lower balance sheet and higher earnings going forward, due to the elimination of future goodwill amortization. It's no wonder that many people scoff at *ROIC* calculations that are based on the published financial statements. The 'economic' profit model retains the purchased R&D on the balance sheet, treating it as a *sunk cost* – which is what it is. I guess that the best way to close out this topic is to suggest that we think in *market value terms*, regardless of the 'currency' (cash, stock, or debt/stock combination) used to consummate a transaction. If we think in terms of *market values*, we can deal with the *economics* of an investment".

"I think we get the point, Jason", Jill interrupted. "Since I have a few telephone calls I need to make, can you tell me how much more time we need, before we break for lunch".

"Just a few more minutes, to cover the last item on Exhibit 9", Jason responded. "Two of the more hotly debated elements in *EP* systems is whether or not to 'capitalize' R&D and/or Advertising Expenses – or, to conform to the traditional method of expensing them in full when calculating Net Operating Profit. Industries such as pharmaceuticals and computer hardware/software are research intensive, with R&D programs often spanning several years. The other major expense item, Advertising, is important for consumer product firms, and the notion here is that the value of Advertising campaigns does not end at the close of a fiscal year. So, the question arises as to which treatment yields a more accurate Economic Profit. This can become particularly important when incentive compensation is involved. Some people suggest always capitalizing these elements and then amortizing them into profit over some useful life. My feeling is that each company is unique, and there is no automatic answer. The analyses I have done over the years have *not* produced any conclusive findings, although in most cases accuracy was not improved by capitalizing these items. Some of the analyses have been quite involved in assessing applicable tax laws, along with cash flow implications. As far as Growthstar is concerned, we'll evaluate it, remembering that our theme is *simplicity with integrity*".

4

Cost of capital

The team returned from the luncheon break promptly at 1:30 pm. After all were seated, Jason began ... "We mentioned at least a couple of times this morning that we would discuss the cost of capital (*CCAP*) this afternoon. Others call it the 'weighted average cost of capital' (*WACC*) and there may be other terms that you may have heard or seen in the literature".

"As is the case with much of the content of value-based finance, the cost of capital is predicated on basic fundamentals from the financial markets. One of these fundamentals is that investors expect a return on their investment commensurate with the risk they are taking. Another is that owners of equities have enjoyed higher relative returns versus other types of securities over long periods of time. For many years, I have used a simple diagram (Exhibit 10) to illustrate these concepts, and I would like to share this with you now".

"As this chart indicates, cost of capital (*CCAP*) relates to the participants in the financial markets. It expresses the annual return requirements of the investors who set prices for securities in sophisticated markets such as the United States and other large, well-developed countries. Now, there has been a lot of controversy on this subject since 'value-based metrics' started to be adopted by corporations in this country and others. While I certainly don't want to minimize these conceptual issues, which are relevant in terms of the 'correctness' of an important 'benchmark' measure, I also want to point out that this is not a totally exact science and probably never will be".

"You're probably referring to 'beta' – which is being attacked and undermining the entire subject", Jack interjected just as Jason was finishing his sentence.

"That's part of it", Jason responded, "and I was planning to discuss this issue as we moved through the diagram and the various topics".

"Well, I think we should get it into it now", Jack came back, trying to seize an opportunity to mount a credible challenge. "What good is an approach when one of its major underpinnings is being challenged by some of the people (Professor Fama, for example) who invented it?"

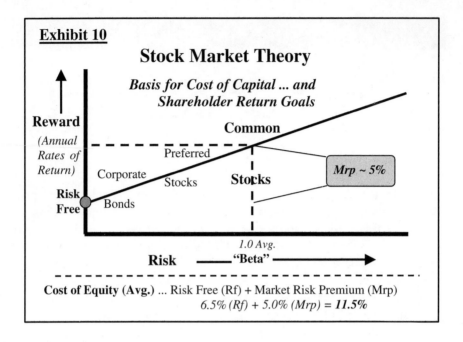

Exhibit 10

Stock Market Theory

Basis for Cost of Capital ... and Shareholder Return Goals

Reward
(Annual Rates of Return)

Common

Preferred

Corporate

Stocks

Stocks

Risk Free

Bonds

Mrp ~ 5%

1.0 Avg.

Risk ——— "Beta" ————▶

Cost of Equity (Avg.) ... Risk Free (Rf) + Market Risk Premium (Mrp)
6.5% (Rf) + 5.0% (Mrp) = 11.5%

"I'm impressed", Earl retorted, "that you've actually heard of Eugene Fama and others. While I'm sure you haven't actually read any of the classical literature on this topic, I am a bit surprised that you have become close to a subject that you are normally so distant from. Or, is this a ploy to pick up a piece of isolated knowledge in an attempt to 'derail' our effort?"

"Funny man", Jack shouted back, getting irritated. "I'm simply challenging a key element of this approach, whereby we set 'hurdle' rates based on flawed concepts".

Jason knew he had to get control of this situation, but he didn't get a chance as Dave Dollarby decided to get into the act. "Look, you guys, this is good theater, but we have some serious issues to discuss, and I'm not to going to waste a lot of my time listening to you two lob grenades at each other all day. While I'm really interested in what you've brought to the floor, Jack, I think we ought to let Jason lead us through an orderly presentation of this material. I have some things to get done today outside of this meeting, and I *would* like to go home tonight". Once again, Jill and Frank exchanged glances. Cathy fidgeted in her chair, not liking confrontations of any type, but particularly in situations where she might feel compelled to defend Jack.

Jason quickly took the opportunity to start speaking again ... "Nothing like a little sparring to brighten up a dull subject. Getting back to what I was going to discuss, let's start by looking at the vertical axis which indicates an increasing level of 'reward'. This has to be viewed in the context of the horizontal axis, which plots 'risk'. As we integrate these two axes, the message is clear – *as investors take on more risk, they expect higher returns.* This is a straightforward concept and one that most rational people would not challenge. We can continue by looking at the sloped solid line that starts on the vertical axis and moves to the right at an angle. Please note that this line starts at a point (on the vertical axis) we call the 'risk-free' rate. This is the long-term (usually thirty-year) US government bond rate, sometimes referred to as the 'long bond' rate. Typically, it's the highest of the numerous US government bond rates, since it has the longest maturity. This rate is the starting point for a corporation's cost of capital analysis, because an investor can realize this rate of return without taking any risk".

"As you can notice, I've indicated the major types of financing instruments along this sloped line. What this line is saying is that, after government bonds, corporate bonds have additional risk and, therefore command, a higher rate of return – in this case a higher interest rate versus government bonds, since both are *debt instruments.* Next, are preferred stocks, which lie in-between bonds and common stocks in terms of risk and reward. There are various types of preferred stocks – some issues carrying a fixed dividend with limited upside potential and others with provisions such as conversion privileges into common stocks. Thus, at one extreme, a preferred stock can be close to a bond and at the other extreme it can resemble a common stock. Finally, we have common stocks, which have the greatest risk (since they are the last to get paid in case of liquidation) and, thus, require the highest annual rate of return. Stocks are the vehicles generating the greatest wealth over time, but they also can produce significant financial losses, as I'm sure most of you know".

"One of the important elements in any value-based financial measurement system is the quantification of risk and return differentials, first among the different securities and then among the common stocks of different companies. This is what I believe Jack was challenging and, I should say, probably rightfully so, in light of writings and debates in some of the intellectual circles. However, before I get into the issues and potential problems concerning 'beta', let me continue with the thought process".

Jack cast ever so slight a smile at Jason, but then scowled a bit as he quickly pondered whether Jason was being genuine in his remarks, or saying some kind words to diffuse the situation and set the others up to go along with whatever he then said. Jack almost started muttering to himself, but caught himself before anyone could notice.

Jason, unaware of what was going in Jack's mind, continued ... "Common stocks have a wide range of returns with respect to individual companies, since there are thousands that are publicly owned and traded. Overall, stocks have produced an annual rate of return over the past sixty or so years that has averaged approximately five percentage points higher than the return for government bonds. This is the 'reward' that equity investors have experienced (and enjoyed) by holding on to their stocks. This is called the 'market risk premium'. Why do we use this term? The reason is that the experience of the 'market' has become a requirement for managers who have been entrusted with equity capital. This is an important point, and I plan to discuss it in more depth shortly".

"If we take all the points on this 'stock market theory' chart (Exhibit 10), we can construct the following formula to calculate the cost of equity capital for the overall stock market:

Cost of Equity equals the risk-free rate plus the market risk premium.

In our example, at the bottom of Exhibit 10, based on a government bond rate in the range of 6.5%, the return for the overall stock market is approximately 11.5%. This is the annual rate of return an investor would expect from an 'indexed' mutual fund, which represents a broad stock market average such as the Standard & Poor's (S&P) 500".

"OK, so far so good and not controversial", Jill interjected, realizing that it had been quite a while since she had spoken. "But, what about Jack's earlier comment about 'beta'?"

"We're just about there", Jason responded. While Jason spoke, Jack sat up and again placed his arms on the top of the conference table, thinking to himself ... "*maybe this will be interesting*" ... and also thinking how much he liked to have his direct reports either responding positively to or supporting his positions.

Jason, moving ahead on his own agenda, continued ... "The controversy comes in calculating an individual firm's risk, or 'beta'. So, what we're talking about is the accuracy of the cost of equity capital calculation for a company. We've established that equity capital is the most expensive form of capital, which is why we need to include it in any evaluation of management performance or in the analysis of a business strategy, new business venture or acquisition. This is what Earl, Frank and I were talking about this morning when we said that the cost of equity capital is important. This morning, we focused on the fact that this cost is not readily apparent in our financial statements;

in essence, it is 'hidden'. Now this situation is compounded by the fact that the cost of equity capital is clearly the 'most expensive', regardless of its actual cost. The argument centers on the 'beta' statistic being an accurate measure of the *volatility* for the stock price of an individual company versus the 'market' – the 'market' having a 'beta' of 1.0. Thus, the debate boils down to whether the company specific risk is, for example, 0.8 or 1.2. By working through the formula in the example on the screen (Exhibit 10) and including a factor when beta is above or below 1.0, we can analyze the results". Jason went to the flip chart and, with a black marker, wrote:

- **'Beta' = 1.0 – Cost of Equity (Ce) = 11.5% ... call this our 'base' case**
- **'Beta' = 0.8 – Cost of Equity (Ce) = 10.5% ... difference = –1.0% vs 'base'**
- **'Beta' = 0.9 – Cost of Equity (Ce) = 11.0% ... difference = –0.5% vs 'base'**
- **'Beta' = 1.1 – Cost of Equity (Ce) = 12.0% ... difference = +0.5% vs 'base'**
- **'Beta' = 1.2 – Cost of Equity (Ce) = 12.5% ... difference = +1.0% vs 'base'**

"Therefore, an error of 10% in the accuracy of the risk measure (each 0.1 of 'beta') results in an error of 4% (0.5/11.5) in the equity capital cost. However, the percentage '*points*' are more important than the percentage. By this, I mean that we should focus on the actual CCAPs (10.5%, 11.5%, and 12.5%) along with their percentage *point* differences, rather than the *percentage* comparison of error factors. These *error factor percentages* are presented to establish a frame of reference for the relative impact of an error (or inaccuracy) with the 'beta' statistic. This error will be reduced somewhat when we incorporate the cost of debt to calculate the 'weighted' cost of capital".

"Just so there is no confusion with the formula for a specific firm, it is as follows:

*Cost of Equity = Risk-Free Rate **plus** (Beta times Market Risk Premium).*

When we view the 'market' in total, the risk premium ('beta') is 1.0. Thus, the formula can be simplified to:

*Cost of Equity = Risk-Free Rate **plus** Market Risk Premium.*

Is this type of error a problem? To some, it probably is, since it is not exact. What if a risk premium is actually 1.2 instead of a published 'beta' of 1.0. That's a 20% error. The implication is an equity cost of 12.5% versus 11.5% ... one (1) percentage point (or 100 'basis' points). Personally, while I want to be correct, I'm not *too* disturbed by this degree of accuracy (or inaccuracy). After evaluating strategies, new business programs, major capital programs and acquisitions for many years, I have *not* experienced any situations where a bad analysis or poor decision was made because of a '*plus or minus 100 basis point cost of equity capital difference*'. Where the results of an analysis are so close, the investment is often marginal to begin with. The exception is for 'highly leveraged' businesses, such as leasing or other financial services, where the cost of capital is low and a small change in *CCAP* can have a significant impact on value. Recently, new models have been developed and new techniques tested which have significantly improved the accuracy and predictability of 'beta'. So, what has been a potentially harmful issue to the credibility of the movement toward economic value and value-based metrics is being defused".

Jack started squirming and Earl again placed his hand over his mouth to hide a wide grin. Dave looked over at Jack and said, "Well, Jack, you raised a potentially explosive topic a short while ago. What's your position now"?

Jill chimed in with "I must say that I'm pleasantly surprised by this new revelation. I really thought that the 'beta' issue was a serious hurdle for us to overcome, but it doesn't seem to be that way, if what you say is true, Jason".

"It makes me feel better", added Cathy. "While I know that I'm not getting *all* of this 'technical stuff', it appears that the inadequacy of *not* accounting for the cost of equity far outweighs any 'glitches' we may encounter with estimating this cost and incorporating it into our financial system".

Jack was at a total loss for words, feeling betrayed by people he once thought of as allies, and experiencing a sick feeling much like losing a game in the final seconds. His entire challenge had disintegrated in the past several moments, just as the state high school football championship had disappeared thirty years ago, when he had 'blown' his defensive pass coverage assignment, and allowed a receiver to get behind him for a forty-yard touchdown with less than a minute remaining in the game and his team ahead by three points – a memory which haunted him from time to time – and came back to him now. He walked silently over to the coffeepot, poured himself a mug, and then said, "maybe some of you might like a beverage – I see that there is a good selection".

Earl made a 'bee-line' for the coffeepot and the others followed.

Taking a sip of his coffee, Jason began speaking again ... "I would like to pick up on Cathy's comment, since I happen to share this opinion. The challenge is to utilize the most credible research and resources in calculating the cost of equity capital, not to avoid it because, as Cathy stated, there may be 'glitches'. Now, let's keep going".

"Moving up the sloped line (in Exhibit 10) the first point we arrive at is *Corporate Bonds*. The cost of this (debt) financing is the 'coupon rate' – that is, the quoted 'interest rate' – of an average (debt) instrument for the firm. While straightforward, there is one important factor that must be incorporated into the calculation, which is the interest rate environment in the financial market. What this means is that the company must determine the cost for its 'next' borrowing. When the financial market is stable, the existing debt on the balance sheet may be a good proxy for future debt financing. If not, then the company must determine its average cost of debt financing in the future".

"Are you going to discuss the *tax deductibility* of the debt financing cost?" Earl asked, as Jason took a pause for a sip of coffee.

"I was just about to do that", Jason responded, "but since I've been speaking for a while, I'd be pleased if you wish to talk about this topic".

"OK", Earl said in a deliberate tone, "let me take a 'stab' at it. Frank, please be prepared to pick up on anything I may miss". Frank nodded. "One of the reasons companies use debt financing is that it's relatively inexpensive, when compared to preferred stock and equity. Jason indicated that he was going to present examples, so I assume he will show some numbers to demonstrate this fact". Now, it was Jason's turn to nod. "The reason that debt financing is the least expensive form of financing is that companies can deduct the interest expense from their operating profit, in the same way that individuals can deduct mortgage interest from their adjusted gross income". Heads nodded around the table, except for Jack who stared at the ceiling.

"Therefore", Earl continued, "we should 'load up' on as much debt as possible, since it's the least expensive ... right? There's a complicating factor, however, in that the interest expense becomes a fixed obligation for the firm, which must be paid or risk a 'default' situation, which is something we don't want to do. Quite often, if a company has more than one debt issue, defaulting on one issue can trigger 'cross-defaults' on others. The same 'default' conditions usually exist on required 'debt principal' payments. A debt principal remittance is simply paying back a portion of what was borrowed. Since some lenders desire to have an orderly payback of the amount borrowed, there is a provision called a 'sinking fund' – another term for a principal payment. These are always specified in a loan agreement. Now, here's an interesting point ... leases also have 'default' provisions, which is another reason we consider them to be just another form of debt financing. With leases, the 'default' is usually linked to the asset(s) being financed".

Earl paused for a moment and looked over at Frank (who moved his head slightly from side to side, indicating that he had nothing to add). Earl then concluded by saying, "I know I went beyond 'tax deductibility', but the 'default' issue was on my mind and I wanted to get it on the table".

"No problem", Jason countered. "I would have covered it if you had not. To add another important element to our subject matter, please remember that for all aspects of the cost of capital, we always consider the cost of financing '*on the margin*'. That is, the cost of the *next dollar* of capital is what we're concerned with. The other key concept to keep in mind is that *all* of the component costs of capital (debt, preferred stock and equity) are 'market based'".

"The next item is preferred stock. Here, the cost can range all the way from a simple dividend rate to a cost equivalent to that for common equity, depending on the nature of the preferred stock issue. You can understand why we call preferred stock a '*hybrid*' form of financing, since it has features of both debt and equity. Preferred stock has priority over common equity in liquidation, but usually does not enjoy the level of upside potential in terms of capital gains potential. That is, unless the preferred stock is convertible into common stock or tracks in some way with the common stock".

"I think we've covered the cost of common equity adequately, with the exception of one last point. Earl talked about the fact that the interest on debt financing is tax deductible. This is *not* the case with the cost of equity, or with most types of preferred stock. Preferred stock dividends are generally *not* deductible for taxes, and the market-based returns that equity investors demand become an 'after-tax' cost to the company and its management. This is an important part of the *CCAP* 'puzzle', so I want to make sure everyone understands it". There was a pause around the table. But then, almost in unison, all but one of the heads (Jack's) started to nod, indicating that the message had registered.

Jason then looked around the room and stated ... "Unless there are any further questions, I'd like to move toward integrating these component capital costs into a 'weighted' cost of capital – first, in a generic example, and then for Growthstar".

Jack's eyes were now rolling aimlessly. He was starting to feel 'ganged up' on every point he made. He also felt that Earl and Jason might be plotting to discredit him, but realized that Jason had probably not been 'on site' long enough to orchestrate this type of effort. Regardless, he was beginning to feel discouraged and defeated, believing that the accounting concepts and principles he had embraced and practised over so many years were going to be dismantled, forcing him to adopt a new system in which he was at a disadvantage to Earl and Frank. Even Jill, he thought, might '*show me up*' in some aspects of this new economic framework. Would he also be '*shown up*' by either Dave or Cathy? No, that probably wasn't a risk. Deep down, he knew that these *economics* had *some* merit. But, he also realized that this approach, if adopted, would cut into the power base he had established through his knowledge of accounting treatments and his ability to influence the thinking of Ian and the operating heads, because of their inability to question his interpretation and presentation of the 'numbers'. To compound the situation, he was quickly coming to the realization that Jonathan was getting serious about transitioning the company to a financial framework encompassing these new *economics*. To make it even more difficult, he couldn't go after Jason, because then he had Earl to deal with, kind of a '*Mr Inside and Mr Outside*' combination. As bad as he was now feeling, he told himself that he would *not* capitulate, without at least a fight. Knowing that he had very little to say at this point, and realizing that any further challenges might be interpreted as 'cheap shots', he decided to remain silent and see if he could pick up any inconsistencies or weaknesses in either the logic or flow of the material that Jason and Earl – and even Frank – were presenting. That would be difficult with Frank, who was so darn analytical and organized. Jason, who was experienced and also had to impress Jonathan, would also be difficult to 'crack'. Perhaps, he thought, there is a chance with Earl, who is prone to talk 'off the top of his head'.

Jack's rolling eyes had caught the attention of the group and Earl turned him and said, "You seem to have something on your mind, Jack".

"No, it's nothing", Jack responded in a voice that was close to a whisper. "Let's move on. I also have other things to take care of and have plans for this evening, so I would also like to get out of here at a reasonable hour".

Jason addressed the group again ... "The generic example will be a hypothetical firm – *XYZ Industries*". Placing a new transparency (Exhibit 11) on the overhead projector, he continued by speaking to the sections of the chart ... "the capital structure of this company and the component costs of capital are outlined in Exhibit 11".

"As mentioned previously, this entire cost of capital analysis is based on 'market' values. Thus, the first set of numbers indicate the market values of this company's equity, preferred stock and debt. Next, the costs of the various components are determined, by analyzing the interest rates for the debt and equivalents, dividend rate for preferred stock (this issue has no conversion privileges – thus, the return *is* the dividend) and investor expectations for the equity through the formula we've discussed. The average debt cost is 9.3%

Exhibit 11
XYZ Industries, Inc. – Capital Structure & Costs

Millions, except 'per share' amounts and 'Betas'

Equity & Equivalent	# Shares	Price/Share	Market Value
Common Stock	100	$25.00	$2,500
Preferred Stock	30	10.00	300

Debt & Equivalent	Interest Rate (%)	Mkt. Value = Book Value
Short term	8.5%	$150
Long term (incl. Cap. Leases)	9.0	250
Operating Leases	10.0	300
Total Debt	**9.3%** (Wt. Avg. Cost)	$700

Memo: Market Value of Total Invested Capital = $3,500

Equity Cost

- **'Betas'** – Our Company (XYZ) = **1.40**

    Memo: Peer Companies:
LMN	= 1.25
QRS	= 1.50
TUV	= 1.30
Average of Peers	= 1.35

- **Cost (per Formula) … $Ce = Rf + (B * Mrp)$** … *remember these symbols!*

    $$= 6.5\% + (1.40 * 5.0\%)$$
    $$= 6.5\% + 7.0\% = \textbf{13.5\%}$$

Preferred Stock Cost

Per Share Dividend: $1.20 Dividend divided by $10.00 market price = **12%**

(pre-tax), the preferred stock carries a 12% rate which is an after-tax cost to the company, and the equity cost is 13.5%. Let's now see how these market values and component costs translate into a 'weighted' average cost of capital (*CCAP*)".

Jason actually preferred to use his personal computer to show his exhibits, and would probably do so in future meetings with the officers. However, the transparencies enabled him to 'mark up' key points with circles and underlining – which he had done throughout the day and probably would continue to do. He took Exhibit 11 off and was starting to replace it with Exhibit 12 when Cathy and Dave simultaneously broke in with, "would you put Exhibit 11 back!" They looked at each other and laughed out loud. Dave then said, "us two 'non-techies' must have the same brain waves". Cathy countered

---

Exhibit 12

XYZ Industries, Inc. – Weighted Average Cost of Capital (CCAP)

Component	Pre tax Cost	Tax Shield *	After Tax Cost	Percent of TMV **	Wt. Cost (CCAP)
Debt (total)	9.3%	35%	6.0%	20.0%	1.2%
Pref. Stock	12.0	-0-	12.0	8.6%	1.0
Equity	13.5	-0-	13.5	71.4%	9.6

Weighted Average Cost of Capital (CCAP) = 11.8%

Optional … "round off" to   12%

Notes: * Based on total 'statutory' tax rate(s) – in this example, 35%

** From Exhibit 11 – 'Component' market values as percent of Total Market Value (TMV) … with TMV = $3.5 billion

---

with, "it seems that way, because I wanted to go over the cost of equity capital formula one more time". As Jason put Exhibit 11 back on the projector, she went to the flip chart next to the screen, took a black marker and wrote:

$$Ce = Rf + (B * Mrp)$$

"I want to make sure I understand this formula", she continued. "To determine the **cost of equity (Ce)**, we begin with the **risk-free rate (Rf)** – the long-term US government bond rate, which any investor can achieve without risk and which has a 'real' return and an 'inflation' factor, similar to any other interest rate. We then" … with a momentary memory lapse, she looked over at Frank, who picked up the discussion without missing a beat … "multiply **'beta' (B)** – the index of company-specific risk relative to the entire stock market – by the **market risk premium (Mrp)** – the annual return difference of the overall equity market (for example, the *S&P 500 Index*) versus the long-term government bond rate". Cathy then recovered … "Thanks Frank. I can always count on you. We then add these two terms together to calculate the **cost of equity**".

"That-a-way, kid", Dave snickered good-naturedly at Cathy. "You get to present the next subject".

Cathy responded with "I might be willing to attempt that, assuming that Frank was there to back me up. Just kidding, Jason".

Jason smiled broadly, preferring this friendly dialogue to the 'Jack and Earl' outbursts and 'Jack attacks' on himself. Being at a slight loss for some humorous words, Jason simply said, "We're making progress when you can state the concepts in your own words. This makes me feel good, since it indicates that we're getting an understanding of some important topics and issues. May we now move on?" Heads nodded.

Jason now replaced Exhibit 11 with Exhibit 12. "As I suggested just before Cathy's and Frank's eloquent explanation of the equity cost formula, let's now see how these market values and component costs translate into a 'weighted average' cost of capital (*CCAP*)".

"As indicated by the column headings", Jason explained, "the process is to start with the pre-tax cost for each component, calculate any tax shield, which leads to an after-tax cost. Then, determine each component's market value as a percent of the total market value of the firm, remembering that this is a 'market-based' concept. Multiplying the after-tax cost of each component by its percent of total invested capital (on a market value basis) yields each component's contribution to the overall weighted average cost of capital. Adding these components yields the firm's weighted average cost of capital (CCAP). Sometimes, as I've done in this case, we 'round off' the nearest whole or one-half percent. This is basis for the 12% cost of capital in the '*A/B/C' example*".

Earl then entered the dialogue by saying "it's extremely important that we focus on the 'market value' aspect for both the costing and the weighting – and not use 'book values' from the reported financial statements".

"I think that point has been made abundantly clear", Jack retorted. Earl, deciding that another jousting match between Jack and himself was not desired by anyone, bit his tongue, looked the other way, and remained silent.

Jason had been pondering whether or not to introduce the next topic, and now decided to do so. "Since you are all becoming such experts on this subject, I want to close out the general discussion material with a technical aspect, which is probably not terribly important for your retention, but which you should probably be exposed to. It gets back to 'beta' and how sophisticated investors define risk. There are two forms of risk in the stock market. The first, which forms the basis for the 'beta', is called *systematic* – or more simply – *market risk*. What this means is that virtually *all* stocks are affected by its causes – favorable or unfavorable economic, political and/or sociological events. Adding more stocks to an investment portfolio *cannot* diversify away this risk. This is the only risk that matters from an investor's perspective, in determining the factors affecting 'beta'. The other type, called *unsystematic* (or *residual*) *risk* results from conditions or events in a particular industry or market segment. This type of risk can be diversified away in a stock portfolio. The combination of *market and residual risk* represents the total variability (that is, stock price volatility) for a specific company. However, only the *market (systematic)* risk is measured by 'beta' and, thus, only this element affects a firm's cost of capital. This whole notion of *market risk* gets into the calculation of the *standard deviation* that an individual stock has on a diversified portfolio of equity holdings, but I don't think we need to get into the actual statistics, except for one rather complicated formula".

"Do we really have to get into even one?" Dave asked, his head shaking back and forth.

"Just *one for the record*", Jason answered. "I want the group to have at least been exposed to the concept of the *financial risk premium*. A publicly owned company's cost of equity capital includes a 'premium' for financial risk whenever its capital structure includes debt of any form. The level of financial risk in a firm is a function of three variables". He went to the flip chart and below the formula that Cathy had written he wrote the following:

1 Target Debt-to-Capital Ratio, or Debt-to-Equity Ratio ... ('D/E')
2 Pre-tax cost of New Debt ... ('b')
3 Tax Rate ... ('t')

"Of these, the first – the *D/E ratio* – is the most important. The first step is to calculate a term called the *cost of equity for business risk alone*". He then wrote on the flip chart:

$$C(e - Frp)$$

"This is the symbol for the cost of equity without any debt in the capital structure. The 'dash' (–) is a 'minus' sign. Thus, the total cost of equity has to be this term plus the *financial risk premium*". He then wrote:

$$Ce = C(e - Frp) + Frp$$

"The formula gets a bit complicated at this point, so I'm just going to make notations on the flip chart and then I'll go over this in more detail with Frank, so that there will be an 'expert' in the company".

Dave, always loving a chance to throw in a 'barb' then cracked ... "Hey, Frank are you trying to buy 'job security'? How could Growthstar survive if we ever lost one of these 'grad school' formulas?"

Everyone broke out laughing, even Jack. Frank, however, could not keep up with Dave's wit, so he just kept chuckling quietly.

Jason stopped his laughing and returned to the flip chart. "You know, Dave, companies have risen and fallen on these type of things. I knew there was a reason we had to review this! Let's go back to the *cost of equity for business risk alone*". He then wrote:

$$C(e - Frp) = \frac{Ce + (1 - t) * b * (D/E)}{1 + (1 - t) * (D/E)}$$

"If we run the numbers for our hypothetical company, *XYZ Industries*, we have the following:

$$C(e - Frp) = \frac{0.135 + (1 - 0.35) * 0.093 * (0.20/0.80)}{1 + (1 - 0.35) * (0.20/0.80)}$$

$$= \frac{0.135 + 0.015}{1 + 0.163} = \frac{0.150}{1.163} = 0.129 = \underline{12.9\%}$$

Since the total cost of equity is **13.5%** for *XYZ*, their financial risk premium is **0.6%**. While this is not the most 'burning issue' for us, I have an obligation to present all the relevant information on the subject. Let me make one more comment and then we can take a short break".

Jason put Exhibit 11 back on the projector. "One item I didn't comment on was the 'peer company betas' in the Equity Cost section. This gives us a 'sanity check' on the 'beta' for a given company. This is also a useful bit of information when dealing with privately owned companies. In fact, obtaining 'betas' for comparable companies (we often call them 'proxy' companies) is typically the basis for estimating the cost of equity capital for a private firm, since there is no published 'beta'. While Growthstar is public, you may some day acquire a private firm, or a division of a public company, similar to what occurred with *Services*. This analysis of 'proxy' companies may, therefore, be the way you determine the cost of capital for the acquisition evaluation, especially if the company is 'out of the mainstream' of your main business or has a significantly different risk profile".

"I think we've now covered all the relevant points for a 'general' discussion on the cost of capital. Jonathan and Val want to participate in the analysis of Growthstar's cost of capital, so I need to call them. When we return – plan on fifteen minutes from now – we'll estimate Growthstar's cost of capital, using the techniques we've just reviewed".

Jonathan and Val joined the group fifteen minutes later, taking seats at the far end of the conference table. Jonathan, as he was prone to do, asked for a reaction to the day's activities with a general inquiry ... "So, are you all now experts on the 'basics' of economic versus accounting profit and cost of capital? I hope so, because we are going to rely on you folks after we throw Jason out of here!" Everyone laughed. The group enjoyed the lighter side of Jonathan. He was tough and demanding, but knew how to invoke humor into a situation and have some fun.

Dave was the first to respond. "This guy [Jason] along with Earl and Frank, know how to 'drain you' with their economic 'theory'. Seriously, though, I'm much more knowledgeable than I was at the beginning of the day – although that may not be saying much". They all laughed again, needing a bit of levity after a lengthy and thought-provoking session. Dave continued ... "I just hope that we can keep our calculations and estimates as simple as possible".

"Ditto", chimed in Jill and Cathy almost simultaneously.

Jack remained silent, looking at and past Jonathan, which Jonathan noticed but kept to himself. Looking back at Dave, then Jill and Cathy, Jonathan responded with "Remember our theme – *simplicity with integrity.* I'm serious about this, and so is Ian and the officer group".

Val wanted to get a pulse of the day's accomplishments, so she entered the conversation by asking "can you tell me the most significant learning from the sessions you've had so far?"

Jill gave the first answer ... "We really do some 'non-economic' things in accounting, which distort the 'cash flow' picture for our company and the businesses. Having had the chance to now sit back and reflect on what are often so many 'mechanical' transactions and entries into our financial records, I can appreciate the need to make *some* of the adjustments we talked about, especially for taxes, reserves and operating leases".

Jack slumped down in his chair.

Cathy then said, "I never appreciated how expensive the cost of equity capital is, and that we never even look at it under our traditional methods of reporting and analyzing financial results. With the help of Jason and Frank, I think I may even be able to calculate it!"

Laughter again, except for Jack, who slumped deeper into his chair.

Dave then said "I think I was probably happier before today in my naive little world of service businesses, but I recognize that 'hidden' balance sheet investments such as operating leases can be significant. I never thought of an 'operating' lease as an investment before this morning".

"Thank you", Val said. "I appreciate you sharing these comments with me. Some are the same as my 'take-away' from a seminar I attended earlier this year".

Jonathan then interceded with "Are there any more observations, or can we now discuss Growthstar's cost of capital?" Seeing that no one had any additional comments, Jonathan motioned to Jason to get 'cranked up' again.

Jason decided to sit back and speak, instead of standing up. "I'm going to ask Frank to help me estimate Growthstar's cost of capital. He's done some good analysis, which I've had a chance to review, and I'd like him to present his key findings. We will follow the approach we just completed for our hypothetical company, *XYZ Industries*. Since I don't have any 'prepared' material, we can use the flip chart, along with Exhibits 11 and 12, which I can place back on the overhead projector". Jason then stood up, placed Exhibit 11 on the projector, and moved to the flip chart. He took a marker and wrote the following:

Millions, except per share amounts and beta

Equity & Equivalent	# Shares	Price/Share	Market Value	'Beta'
Common Stock	10	$27.50	$275	1.25

"Your stock is trading around $27.50 per share. With 10 million shares outstanding, the company's common stock market value is $275 million. Since Growthstar doesn't have any preferred stock, and Jonathan has told me that he doesn't have any plans to issue any, your common stock is your total equity. Further the 'beta' of 1.25 is a *predictive factor* from a database established by a credible West Coast firm". Jason then motioned to Frank, and Frank, taking the marker from Jason, began writing on the flip chart:

Debt & Equivalent	Interest Rate	Market/Book Value
Short-term Debt	8.5%	$10
Long-term Debt	9.0	50
Operating Leases	10.0	50
Total Debt	9.4% (Wt. Avg.)	$110

'Wt. Avg.' Interest Rate computed by multiplying the 'weights' (percents to total debt) for each element of debt by their respective interest rates.

"Hey, Frank", cracked Dave, "it would help if you talk to us while you're writing, especially about the investment in operating leases. WOW, $50 million – that's as much as our long-term debt!"

Frank looked sheepishly over at Dave and said "I'll try to do it the next time. I was concentrating on getting all these numbers down correctly".

"Just kidding, pal", Dave chuckled.

"I know", Frank responded with a wide smile on his face. He did like to have fun. He had just worked so hard and diligently all his life, starting with his childhood and his job at the local grocery store in his home town, that he sometimes just plain forgot about having fun, and took people and situations he was in more seriously than he had to.

Jason thanked Frank, tore the page off the flip chart and scotch-taped it to the wall, placed Exhibit 12 on the projector, and began writing on a new flip chart page:

$$\textbf{\textit{EquityCost}} \quad \dots \textit{\textbf{Ce} = \textbf{Rf} + (\textbf{B} * \textbf{Mrp})}$$

$$\textit{\textbf{Ce} = \textbf{6.5\%} + (\textbf{1.25} * \textbf{5.0\%}) = \underline{\textbf{12.75\%}}}$$

"Would you like me to talk to you while I'm writing, Dave"? Jason asked.

Dave retorted with "maybe we should get *you* to *stop talking* so much".

"But, that's part of what I'm paid to do", Jason countered.

"OK, guys", Jonathan interjected, "this is pleasant 'banter' ... but let's get on with it. I have to see Ian in a little while".

Jason wrote:

$ Millions Component	Pre tax Cost	Tax Shield	After Tax Cost	Market Value	Percent of Total IC	Wt. Cost (CCAP)
Equity	12.75%	-0-	12.75%	$275	71.4%	9.11%
Debt	9.40%	36%	6.05%	110	28.6%	1.73
				$385	100%	

Weighted Average Cost of Capital (CCAP) = <u>10.84 %</u>

"Round Off" to .... <u>11.0 %</u>

and then stated ... "the estimate of Growthstar's *CCAP* is, there-fore, *11*%".

Jonathan then weighed in ... "The capital structure and debt costs are in line with the targets we established fifteen months ago, when we went through a major refinancing. Since the risk-free rate is just slightly under 6.5% (it's been in the 6.45% range lately) and the financial markets have remained stable during this period, I'm comfortable with these component capital costs and with the overall weighted cost. Just so we all understand, this *11% CCAP* is our 'hurdle rate' for our *return on (total) invested capital*. This is the *threshold*, not the goal, but it is the rate we'll use for the *Economic Profit* calculations and in our *Net Present Value* analysis for strategies, major investment programs and acquisitions".

"Well", Dave sighed, "I don't know about the rest of you, but I've had about enough of this for one day, maybe two or three!"

"I've had enough for a lifetime", muttered Jack, sitting up in his chair and getting ready to leave.

"Get prepared for more", countered Jonathan. "We're going to give this '*EP thing*' a big effort. I think you know our near-term schedule. Frank and Jason are going to spend the next three weeks reviewing our historical financials and building an analytic model to assess the economic profit of our two major business units and the company in total. I believe they will also be analyzing certain influencing factors as part of this effort. Is this correct, Jason?"

"That's right", Jason responded. "We'll be trying to determine what the economic profit is and what's 'driving' it. I hope it will be informative".

"I'm sure it will be, and I can't wait", snickered Jack, as he got up to leave the room.

"OK", Jonathan concluded. "We'll meet again three weeks from today at 8:00 am".

## 5

Economic profit assessment: value 'creators' and 'destroyers'

The next day, Jason began preparing the material he was going to review with Frank and Jill during the remainder of the week. They had a work session scheduled for tomorrow.

After yesterday's meeting on the cost of capital had ended, Jonathan had asked Jack if Jill was going to be involved in the initial Economic Profit (*EP*) assessments. Jack knew what the response *had* to be, so he called Jill and told her to be available upon returning to his office. Jonathan had also asked Jason to have lunch with him and Ian, so that Jason could meet the CEO.

Due partly to his late arrival because of a long-overdue dentist appointment, the morning went very quickly, and it was suddenly 12:25, five minutes before the time scheduled for the luncheon meeting. The company had a small dining room that the officers could use when, due to the nature of a meeting, they needed privacy. Jason walked the short distance to Jonathan's office, only to find that Jonathan was waiting for him. "Ian will be in a good mood today. His alma mater just recruited one of the most 'sought after' high school basketball players in the country. Ian is a big fan and booster of his old team, and their outlook for this upcoming season is very good".

Jason, himself a casual fan of most sports, responded with "It's always nice when the boss is in a good mood – helps to 'break the ice'".

As they entered the outer area of Ian's office, Mary Frightly looked up over her 'half-moon' glasses and acknowledged Jonathan with a slight smile, and then cast a suspicious look at Jason. She was one to have an immediate impression, sometimes due solely to a person's appearance. Before she could get too imbedded in her 'first impression' process, Jonathan got her attention by saying... "Mary, I want you to meet one of my most cherished colleagues and a 'trusted advisor', Jason Aradvizer". The words 'trusted advisor', when coming from someone such as Jonathan – who Mary respected because he was Ian's '*most trusted advisor*' within the company – had almost a mesmerizing effect on her. Jonathan knew this, of course, which is why he said it. Mary immediately smiled and stuck out her hand to Jason, who shook it gently. Jason had been thinking all morning about Jonathan's comment a few days ago about getting on Mary's good side, but had no clue as to how to do it. Jonathan had at least taken the first step.

Mary, in a very polite tone of voice, then said, "Mr Lord is just finishing up a conversation, I believe, and should be with you momentarily. Did you hear about the player who just committed to Mr Lord's university yesterday? Isn't it wonderful? Mr Lord is really excited. In fact, I ordered his season tickets this morning. Mrs Lord even called me to make sure I didn't forget. And, Mr Lord said I could see a game on a weekend when he has a big family affair – I think it's a wedding – and will be away".

Just as Mary was finishing, Ian appeared, having completed his phone call. He stuck out a large hand in Jason's direction and said, "You must be Jason – it's my pleasure to meet you, since Jonathan has said some nice things about you and I had a chance to read one of your articles. Welcome to Growthstar!"

Jason, pleased with the warm reception from both Mary and Ian, responded with... "Thank you, Ian" (he preferred a person's name to the term 'sir') – "I am very glad to be here and to have the opportunity to make a contribution to your company".

Ian then said, "We're looking for you to help us to fully understand and then determine how to implement these new 'economic' metrics – at least, that's my feeling".

Jonathan added, "*Implementation* – that's probably the most important element, after we work through all the techniques and customize the system for the company".

"Well, why don't we continue this conversation over lunch?" said Ian, motioning Jason and Jonathan out of the office.

Lunch was a pleasant affair, sprinkled with light conversation, including the upcoming basketball season, still several months away, at Ian's alma mater.

As the dishes were being taken away, Ian said "I want to reiterate, Jason, what I believe Jonathan has already told you. I believe there is some merit in the 'economic-based' performance metrics that are taking hold in many companies. I also understand that more and more professional money managers, on both the 'buy' and 'sell' side, are using them in their common stock valuations. I tasted a bit of this at the last annual shareholders meeting and at the last quarterly earnings session with the analysts. I am *not*, however, inclined to overhaul our financial reporting and make significant changes to our incentive compensation plan, until I am *convinced* that first, it's the right thing to do and second, that we know exactly what needs to be done at Growthstar. This means being technically correct and establishing a system that will properly motivate and reward our senior and middle managers. In other words, I'm moving toward the camp of the economists, but I'm not there yet. With all the shortcomings I read about and hear about from people such as Earl (he sent me another article last week) I have lived with the current accounting (earnings-based) system for a long time and feel it has served me well. Further, as you also probably know, I have a Controller who takes the other side and is telling Jonathan and me that all this endeavor will do is create another set of reports and add work to an already burdened accounting department. I also will have no tolerance for any new approach or technique that is so complicated that everyone in the company will need an 'MBA in Finance' to understand it. I can guarantee you that any such outcome will be 'dead on arrival' at my office and that your tenure here will be over".

Jonathan then entered the conversation with "I had mentioned most of this to Jason, but I think he also needed to hear it from you".

Jason, who had listened very attentively as the 'big man' (this was a phrase he had picked up from Earl to describe Ian) spoke, responded with... "I hear you loud and clear. In fact, I'm hoping that one of the elements I have developed over the years will work here. This is a fairly simple 'earnings' measure (I call it a *'value profit margin'*) that incorporates the key economic dynamics of the business. Starting tomorrow, Frank Accurato, Jill Debitson and I will be developing an approach with the goal of keeping it as simple as possible, but yet, as you just stated, 'technically correct'. In fact, the theme for the program that Jonathan and I have 'coined' and shared with the officers last week is *simplicity with integrity*".

"Well, you seem to be starting off appropriately", Ian stated as he rose from his chair. "Let's hope it continues and we reach an acceptable outcome. I do want to be kept informed, especially on matters discussed with the officers, and will rely on the two of you to do that. I have a meeting downtown that I have to leave for now, but I would like to get a brief recap of last week's session with the officers – nothing formal – just a verbal summary. I would like to do this at the end of the day".

"Certainly", Jonathan and Jason responded in unison.

Jason spent the remainder of the afternoon completing his preparation for tomorrow's work session with Frank and Jill. Just before 5:00, Jonathan arrived at Jason's office. They made the short walk to Ian's office, and were greeted warmly by Mary Frightly, who was getting ready to leave. "You can go in," she said... "he's alone and ready for you".

"Sit down, please", Ian motioned them to his couch and chairs. "I just want to catch up on the highlights of the meeting with the officers last week".

Jonathan had mentioned to Jason on the way to Ian's office that he would like to provide a brief overview and then let Jason talk about specifics, so he began with... "I think we (actually, Jason) emphasized that the evidence indicates the financial markets are being driven by economic, rather than accounting, factors and that 'profit' is not always what we may think it is. Further, the apparent irrationality the stock market seems to exhibit in the short run actually works itself out to be very rational over the long term. Finally, sustaining shareholder value over time results from 'balancing' the delivery of value to customers with acceptable financial performance. Jason, may be you want to add to this".

Jason, after a moment of thought, said "We also talked about how stock prices react to different *types* of earnings announcements. After we got through this issue, I gave a perspective of what shareholder value means for the corporation in total and the business units within a company".

"Talk to me about this, please", Ian interjected. Ian was very polite, but he didn't ask – he *directed* people to speak about things he wanted to hear.

"Basically, for the company as a whole, which is *your* issue, it's the change in value of the stock price over time".

"OK, I accept that, but what about the 'business units'?" Ian then inquired.

"Their issue is the 'contribution' of their business to the overall value of the corporation," Jason responded.

"I like that", Ian stated in a very firm tone of voice. "I'm tired of feeling like the 'Lone Ranger' when it comes to stock price and justifying myself to the analysts and shareholders. What was their reaction?"

Jonathan had told Jason that he would give opinions of the mood of the officers until Jason got to know Ian better, so he came back into the conversation. "I think they accept the challenge, but they were surprised and may still need some convincing that they may need to look beyond revenue and profit growth to deliver *shareholder value*".

"Hmmm", Ian mused, "they probably got that notion from me".

"I also have to admit to some past guilt in this area", Jonathan quipped.

"OK", Ian continued, "but they accept the fact that at least part of the share price is their responsibility".

Jason nodded his head as Jonathan said "That's a fair conclusion".

"OK, what else!" Again, Ian didn't ask – he *directed.*

"We emphasized", Jason said, "that any endeavor such as this one has to be viewed as a 'system' with a number of inter-related parts, and that it has to link to the company's strategy development process".

"Val must have liked this part of the dialogue", Ian chuckled. "She's been trying to get us 'good old boys' to get more sophisticated in our business planning".

"I'd say she enjoyed hearing this very much", Jonathan responded, "but Val doesn't need a heavy dose of reinforcement to validate her beliefs and research".

"That's true", Ian retorted – feeling a sense of pride that he had hired such a self-confident and capable person as his top strategic advisor inside the company.

Jonathan, feeling that this discussion had achieved its objective and that Ian was at a 'high' point, started to lean forward, indicating his intention to rise from the couch, and said, "Those are the highlights, Ian. Jason is going to begin an analysis of our 'economic' profits, in conjunction with Frank and Jill, and will be reporting to the finance team and myself in three weeks. We'll be back in touch with you after this review session".

"I'll look forward to it", the 'big man' concluded, rising out of his chair and extending his hand to both Jason and Jonathan.

Jason arrived early the next morning. Corporate Finance had a small conference room, which Jason, Frank and Jill were going to use. Just as Jason was finishing the hook-up of his personal computer, Frank and Jill arrived at the small conference room. Jason, quickly checking his watch, saw that it was 7:55. After 'good mornings' were exchanged and coffee mugs filled, Jason began... "What I would like to do is begin with *Romper Room* and then move on to *Mr Rogers' Neighborhood...* or, to say it another way, work our way through the 'Level 1, 2, 3' analysis of *Economic Profit*". After they all chuckled,

Jason continued… "I'd like to use the same hypothetical company (*XYZ Industries*) as we did the other day, which I believe will help us determine the information we need to gather and the type of analysis that will be relevant for Growthstar". Frank and Jill listened silently. They were looking for Jason to provide direction and to structure the *Economic Profit* assessment. Jason, sensing this, turned on his PC and clicked on a file containing the material he planned on using this morning.

"What we'll do is an historical analysis of first, the income statement (P&L) and then, the balance sheet for each '*level*' – explaining the major differences. Then we'll assess the impact of moving from one level to another, along with the complexity involved".

"Exhibit 13 begins the *Level 1* assessment of Economic Profit (*EP*), with a three-year historical analysis of the key 'operating' elements from the income statement (P&L)".

"As you can see, the initial focus is on revenue and major operating expense categories. An 'I' or 'C' in the farthest column to the left indicates whether an item is 'input' or 'calculated'. Next, in Exhibit 14, we capture information on interest expenses and taxes".

"My experience is that reviewing the most recent three years plus the current year (budget or forecast) usually gives an adequate, yet not excessive, amount of information to begin an assessment of *Economic Profit*. Exhibit 13 provides the starting point for the *EP* assessment – '*EBIT*'. Regardless of how a business generates it, the most important P&L element is Operating Income, which provides the first major ingredient to cash flow. 'How' a business generates its operating income will ultimately affect its valuation. At this early stage in the process, however, the concern is simply

Exhibit 13

XYZ INDUSTRIES
'Economic Profit'

($Millions) Omitted	Level '1' - reported				
History — "Actuals"	**3 Most Recent Historical Years**			**Historical**	**Current**
Profit & Loss	**Year #3**	**Year #2**	**Year #1**	**3-Yr. Avg.**	**Year Fcst.**
I Net Revenue (Sales)	$1,200	$1,500	$1,800	$1,500	$2,000
C Operating Income (EBIT)	$200	$300	$300	$267	$325
Details:					
I Cost of Sales	$550	$650	$850	$683	$925
I S G & A - excl. Interest (*net*)	450	550	650	550	750
I Other -					
C Total Operating Costs	$1,000	$1,200	$1,500	$1,233	$1,675

Exhibit 14	XYZ INDUSTRIES				
Interest, Taxes and NOP	Year #3	Year #2	Year #1	3-Yr. Avg.	Current Year Fcst.
I Memo: Interest - net	$50	$55	$60	$55	$60
I "Book" P&L Tax Rate	40.0%	35.0%	37.5%	37.5%	35.0%
Cash Tax (re: EBIT)					
I "Book" P&L Tax Provision	$60	$86	$90	$79	$93
C Tax "Shield" re: Interest - net	20	19	23	21	21
C "Book" P&L Tax Provision - re: EBIT	80	105	113	99	114
I Deferred Tax - Current Year	50	60	60	57	70
I/C Deferred Tax - Prior Year	35	50	60	48	60
C Deferred Tax – Change	15	10	-	8	10
C "Cash" Tax - Book less Def'd *	$65	$95	$113	$91	$104
C **"Cash" Tax Rate - % of EBIT**	32.5%	31.7%	37.5%	34.1%	31.9%
* *or, "Cash" taxes from Annual Report footnotes plus Interest Tax Shield*					
C **Net Operating Profit (NOP)**	$135	$ 205	$188	$176	$221

with the 'amount' of operating income, along with a perception as to whether cost of sales (also known as cost of goods sold) or selling, general and administrative expenses dominate the cost structure of the business".

Pausing for a reaction from Jill and Frank, but getting none, he continued... "Exhibit 14 takes us from 'pre-tax' operating income to 'after-tax' operating profit. Capturing 'Interest-net' is straightforward, since it is the 'net' amount charged to the income statement. Interest expense is the cost of debt financing and interest income reflects what a firm earns on the investment of any surplus cash. Note that the effective tax rate for the tax deductibility (tax 'shield') of interest-net is the 'statutory' rate, which is normally the 'book' tax rate. To get the information on deferred taxes, we usually have to analyze changes for the Deferred Tax account(s) in the liability section of the balance sheet. I'm probably not telling you anything you don't know, but so we don't have any questions when we gather information for Growthstar, I'm going to cover 'all the bases'".

"That's OK, Jason", Jill responded. "It's actually nice to have some of this relate to what I already know. It's 'brain draining' when everything is new". Frank just nodded his head, indicating that he was not having any problem so far.

Jason resumed... "The combination of the tax 'shield' resulting from Interest and the impact of deferrals on the taxes actually paid yields a 'cash' tax rate to be applied against *EBIT*. This 'effective tax' rate calculates the 'cash' tax in absolute (dollar) terms. Subtracting this 'dollar cash' tax from *EBIT* yields *Net Operating Profit (NOP)* – the operating profit for the business on an 'after-tax' basis. *NOP* is a key ingredient of *EP*, since it is the 'base' from which a capital charge will be subtracted. Any questions?"

Jill and Frank nodded their heads up and down, almost in unison, indicating they understood everything Jason had presented. As Jason had been speaking and pointing out the various items, they had taken notes (on their 'hard copies' of the exhibits) of the movements, during the years, of items such as the absolute level of revenue, expenses, interest and deferred taxes, along with changes in 'statutory' and 'cash' tax rates. The resultant pattern of *NOP* did not escape them either.

Jason pressed a key on his PC to show Exhibit 15 on the screen.

"Now, just what I know you've all been waiting for – our first look at *XYZ's* balance sheet. Invested capital (IC) can be calculated in two ways:

1 Adding all the debt financing to total stockholder's equity, and then adjusting for surplus (excess) cash, or
2 Starting with Total Assets (net of depreciation) and deducting the 'NIBCLs' – and then adjusting for surplus cash".

"Both methods produce the same result. We'll use the second, since we don't always have a specific financing structure for a business unit or a strategy. Further, since we want to focus on 'operating' results – for both the P&L and the balance sheet – the second method is preferable and more practical in most situations. The same adjustment for surplus cash is used in both methods. This

Exhibit 15		XYZ INDUSTRIES				
($Millions) Omitted		... 3 Most	Recent	Hist Yrs ...		Current
Balance Sheet - 'Beginning'		Year #3	Year #2	Year #1	3-Yr. Avg.	Year Fcst.
I	Total (net) Assets ... 'reported'	$887	$1,115	$1,373	$1,125	$1,556
	less:					
I	Cash & Equivalents	200	250	330	260	400
I	Accounts Payable	45	56	70	57	75
I	Accruals	23	28	33	28	38
I	Income Taxes Payable	15	21	23	20	23
I	Other NIBCL's	5	10	18	11	20
I	Other -					
	plus:					
2%	'Oper.'Cash @ 2% (or 1%) of Revenue	24	30	36	30	40
I	Asset Allocation(s)				-	
I	Other - Bank Overdraft				-	
I	Other -				-	
C	**Invested Capital (IC) – Level '1'**	$624	$780	$936	$780	$1,040

involves subtracting any cash accumulated in a business, except for that required to operate the business. My experience indicates that, for most businesses, a level of 'operating' cash in the range of 1% to 2% of total revenue is adequate for paying bills, etc. We don't want to 'penalize' a business that generates cash by including surplus cash in their invested capital, against which we'll charge a cost of capital. In situations where an 'overdraft' may be used, this approach will adjust for this, and calculate an appropriate level of operating cash by adding back an amount to bring the actual cash balance to 'zero' and then calculating the operating cash using the 'percent-to-revenue' formula. There are situations when a company has either an intended or unintended practise of accumulating surplus cash. When this situation exists, the actual cash is left in the invested capital. This would represent a reduction in the 'corporate' return on capital/economic profit due to the company's excess cash position. The result of all of this is the Invested Capital (*IC*) – the funds management has been entrusted with and against which we will assess a 'capital cost'. Let's now complete the puzzle by determining economic profit (*EP*), which Exhibit 16 does. Please note that the computer model 'rounds off' calculations to the nearest 'whole' number".

"I see that *CCAP* is <u>12.5%</u>", Frank commented. "We had calculated <u>12%</u> in our work session two days ago".

"You're sharp, Frank", quipped Jill. "I missed that. So, what's up, Jason?"

Jason laughed good-naturedly as he said, "You guys are fun to work with. And that is a good 'pick-up', Frank. This higher cost of capital for 'Level 1' reflects the fact that there are no operating leases in the invested capital. Thus, they are not in the financing mix of the company. If you recall that operating leases are *100% debt financing*, the proportion of debt to total invested capital is lower than it is when the operating leases are included. With a lower proportion of debt, the cost of capital (*CCAP*) is higher. In the case of *XYZ Industries*, *CCAP* is 50 basis points, or 0.5% point, higher without the operating

Exhibit 16		XYZ INDUSTRIES				
Economic Profit – Level '1'		Year #3	Year #2	Year #1	3-Yr. Avg.	Current Year Fcst.
($Millions) Omitted						
C	NOP	$135	$205	$188	$176	$221
12.5%	CCAP	(78)	(98)	(117)	(98)	(130)
C	"EP"	$57	$107	$70	$78	$91

leases than with them included. When we get to *CCAP* for 'Level 2', we'll see 12%".

"So now", Jason stated, "we're starting down the path toward the *Promised Land*, by establishing a 'base' level of economic profit. If nothing else, we've determined the 'real' taxes paid by this company and a weighted average cost of capital".

"What you call the *Promised Land* might be the *Land of the Devil*", Jill interjected, "if your name happens to be Jack Earningsly... or, if you happen to work for him".

"Whatever *Land* we may arrive at", Jason retorted, "this concludes the *EP* evaluation on a 'Level 1' basis. This is a fairly simple analysis, and is often not robust enough for many businesses. The next level (2) will bring in at least one key 'off-balance sheet' item and take a look at goodwill plus acquisition and other reserves. Please remember that in this ('Level 1') analysis and in the next analysis ('Level 2') we define fixed assets, and thus invested capital, on a basis that is '*net*' of depreciation. What this means is that 'depreciation' is considered to be an economic cost of operating the business and the invested capital will factor out the accumulated depreciation for fixed assets to determine the ('*net*') basis for assessing a capital charge".

"To begin the 'Level 2' analysis, Exhibit 17 presents the relevant data to calculate 'Operating Income' on an *EBITA* basis (similar to

Exhibit 17

XYZ INDUSTRIES

'Economic Profit'

($Millions) Omitted	Level "2" - incl. Operating Leases / Intangibles / Reserves			Historical 3-Yr. Avg.	Current Year Fcst.
History — "Actuals"	3 Most Recent Historical Years				
	Year #3	Year #2	Year #1		
Profit & Loss					
C Revenue (Sales)	$1,200	$1,500	$1,800	$1,500	$2,000
C **Operating Income (EBITA)**	$250	$314	$320	$294	$350
Details:					
C EBIT - Level 'A'	$200	$300	$300	$267	$325
C Interest Portion of Rent Expense	14	16	20	16	25
I *Memo: Interest Rate - Leases*	9.0%	9.5%	10.0%	9.5%	10.0%
C R & D Amortization **	-	-	-	-	-
I *Memo: R&D Amortiz. Factor*					
I Amortization - Goodwill / etc.	6	8	10	8	10
I Other - Reserves, etc.	30	(10)	(10)	3	(10)

*** R & D Amortization should to be evaluated re: its 'impact' on EP — not automatically included.*

Exhibit 13 defining 'Level 1' *EBIT*). As I believe we mentioned the other day, *EBITA* is the acronym for 'earnings before interest, taxes and amortization' ".

"The first adjustment", Jason noted, "is to consider operating leases and the *interest* portion of the rent (or lease) expense. This is the *financing cost* for this type of debt. Since, Frank, you covered the add-back of 'lease related' interest so eloquently the other day, I know we don't have to spend any more time on this topic".

Jill chuckled softly, as Frank looked the other way.

"Next", continued Jason, "is the issue of 'R&D Amortization'. 'Advertising' can also be included in this segment, especially for consumer product companies and other firms that spend heavily on promotion. As we noted the other day, the *theory of capitalizing* one or both of these items is that the value of R&D and/or Advertising does not go away when the fiscal year comes to a close. Thus, when done, it's a process of capitalizing (in essence, creating an asset account) and then amortizing a portion each year".

"But", interjected Jill, "I could argue the same rationale for many other expenses, particularly where salaries are paid for 'non-R&D' people with an impact on 'intellectual capital' ".

"I agree", Jason responded. "I'm *not* a strong advocate of going through all this, unless there is a *significant* impact. I would use our 'rule of thumb' for 'significance'. Further, you can experience what I call a 'roll-over' effect. That is, the amount(s) amortized in prior years start to 'roll' into subsequent years' expenses, resulting in an 'offset' of new versus old amortization. Some 'experts' say it's a good provision for compensation and reward systems, but I have a hard time justifying the additional complexity unless there's a compelling 'economic' reason – *translate into +/– 10% impact on economic profit!*"

"Should we investigate and evaluate this expense for Growthstar"? Frank asked. "I'm not opposed to doing the work, since we are spending on developing new product lines with greater 'technology' components. Advertising is, obviously, something we do, but since our customers are other industrial companies and not individual consumers, we don't invest 'heavily' in media advertising and promotion".

"We should probably look at it", Jill responded, "but try to come to a 'quick perception' on its impact before spending too much time".

"You folks are catching on fast", Jason stated... smiling. "Let's move on. Next, is the 'amortization' of goodwill and intangibles. This, again, depends on how significant a portion of a firm's asset base is composed of these items. For *XYZ*, there is enough to warrant adding back the amortization. Here, my feeling is just the opposite of R&D and/or Advertising. Unless there is virtually no goodwill or intangibles, uncommon for most technology companies and those firms growing through acquisition, I believe we should add back the amortization and calculate operating income on more of a 'cash flow' basis. This treats the goodwill (or any other intangible) as a 'sunk cost', which is what it is. It also gets around what has become a situation analogous to 'Pooling' treatments, which Earl got very emotional about the other day. In many 'technology' acquisitions, there is an allowance for a significant write-off of 'Purchased R&D' ".

"I'm quite familiar with that", quipped Jill. "We wrote off as much as we could when we acquired *Services*. The company was not having a good year, in terms of *EPS*, and Jack convinced Jonathan and Ian to take as big a 'hit' as the accounting rules would allow, to reduce the amortization charges in future years and make our *EPS* growth and Return on Equity look really good. Jack will have a 'fit' if we go back and adjust this item".

"Jack seems to have mastered the art of 'throwing fits' ", Jason retorted, "and I can't be influenced by what I think Jack's reaction might be. Frank, we need to look at it and see what the analysis reveals".

"OK", Frank responded. "It's going to be interesting to see Earl and Jack 'go at it' on this one!" Frank had a strange expression as he spoke, since he knew a 'donnybrook' would probably erupt over this issue. Not being comfortable with controversy, he never knew how to react, except to silently analyze the potential outcomes, which translated into puzzling looks, such as the one he was now revealing.

Jason wanted to proceed with the 'Level 2' analysis and resumed speaking. "Finally, 'reserves' should often be adjusted back to what the situation was before the reserve was taken and charged against earnings. Again, I would use a '*10% rule of thumb*' – in this case, the amount of the reserve(s) as a percent of 'Level 1' *EBIT*. For *XYZ*, a $40 million 'rightsizing' reserve was taken three years ago (20% of that year's 'Level 1' *EBIT*) lowering expenses by $10 million per year for four years. Its impact expires in the current year".

"May I move on to the tax and NOP related to our 'Level 2' analysis?" Both Jill and Frank nodded. "Exhibit 18 shows the 'effective' taxes on *EBITA* and the *NOP* that result. Note that the 'cash' tax rate from the 'Level 1' analysis is used here".

"This is self-explanatory", Jill commented, with Frank nodding in agreement. "Can we take a short break, before getting into the 'Level 2' balance sheet and invested capital?"

"You bet", Jason answered, wanting to take a stretch himself.

As Frank and Jill were seating themselves after returning, Jason was clicking on a new exhibit. "This next table (Exhibit 19) provides the balance sheet adjustments that generate the P&L numbers in

Exhibit 18	**XYZ INDUSTRIES**				
($Millions) Omitted *Level 2 - "Cash" Taxes & NOP*	**Year #3**	**Year #2**	**Year #1**	**3-Yr. Avg.**	**Curr Yr** **Fcst**
C "Cash" Tax Rate -- % of EBITA	32.5%	31.7%	37.5%	34.1%	31.9%
C "Cash" Tax Amount - $	$81	$99	$120	$100	$112
C **Net Operating Profit (NOP)**	**$168**	**$214**	**$200**	**$194**	**$238**

Exhibit 19	**XYZ INDUSTRIES**				
($Millions) Omitted *Balance Sheet - 'Beginning'*	**Year #3**	**Year #2**	**Year #1**	**3-Yr. Avg.**	**Current** **Year Fcst.**
C IC (Level '1')	$624	$780	$936	$780	$1,040
Operating Leases:					
I Rent Expense (Prior Year)	25	30	36	30	45
I Rent Capitalization Factor	6.0	5.5	5.5	5.7	5.5
C Capitalized Value – Operating Leases	150	165	198	171	248
R & D:					
I R & D Expense (Prior Year)				-	
I R & D Capitalization Factor				-	
C Capitalized Value - R & D	-	-	-	-	-
I Accumulated Amortization	36	42	50	43	60
I/C Other - Reserves, etc.	40	30	20	30	10
Invested Capital (IC) – C **Level '2'**	**$850**	**$1,017**	**$1,204**	**$1,024**	**$1,358**

Exhibit 17. You can see that the account descriptions are the balance sheet equivalents to those in Exhibit 17".

"In this example, *XYZ's* 'operating' leases are composed mostly of real estate leases, resulting in a relatively high rent (or lease) capitalization factor, as compared to a company with more office equipment or vehicles – having shorter lease terms and, thus, a lower lease capitalization factor. This factor is calculated by estimating the present value of the annual rent (lease) payments and then comparing this (present value) amount to the annual rent (lease) expense. This capitalization factor gives us a good 'rule of thumb' to determine the balance sheet investment (and the additional debt) for any year's rent (or lease) expense. Remember that we only account for operating leases if they are *significant*. I would suggest using a '*10% test*' to determine *significance*. If operating leases, when capitalized, comprise 10% of the 'Level 1' net invested capital in any firm, they should be accounted for in a manner similar to that shown in Exhibits 17 and 19".

"I would agree with that", said Jill.

"I'm OK with that also", Frank added.

Jason continued... "We've discussed the R&D/Advertising capitalization issue. When done, the balance sheet will reflect this capitalization, from which an annual amortization expense is calculated. I haven't included it in this example, because the calculations are specific to the company and the tax laws that apply".

"The 'Level 2' invested capital reflects the total 'sunk cost' of all 'goodwill/intangibles'. Thus, the adjustment is to add back the amount of 'accumulated' amortization shown on the reported balance sheet".

"I don't want to be the one to 'book' this one", Jill uttered, not being able to remove herself from the reaction likely to result.

Frank the chimed in, "I'll be the 'bad guy' here, because I know that I have Earl as a shield. He was not happy when he heard about the big 'write-off' for the acquisition of *Services*".

After pausing to determine if there were any other comments, and getting none, Jason said... "With 'reserves', I don't recall Growthstar having any major ones in the recent past. Do you Jill?"

"We did something either three or four years ago. I'll check and determine what it was and how significant it is, and then let you know, Frank. There has been nothing in the past two years, however".

"This takes us through invested capital for the 'Level 2' analysis", Jason continued. "What I want to show you now is the *EP* for this level and the comparison to that for 'Level 1'. Further, as a *Memo* item, I like to see what the percentage-based 'Return on Invested Capital' (*ROIC*) is, and how it compares to *CCAP* at each level".

"Exhibit 20 will provide this information".

"This summary of *EP* and comparison to the 'Level 1' numbers indicates clearly, at least to me", Jason stated, "that *XYZ Industries* needs to implement at least a 'Level 2' system. There is a *significant* difference in the *EP* and *ROIC* results between the two levels. In the analysis and discussion so far this morning, we haven't made any judgments about the 'quality' of *XYZ's* performance, since our focus is on the methodology for the *EP* 'calculation'. I am going to let you do that for yourselves. I plan to get into this aspect of the assessment when we review the historical and current year numbers for Growthstar".

"Now would be a good time to review the cost of capital for the two levels. Please note that the 'Level 2' *CCAP* will also apply to 'Level 3', since we include the operating leases at 'Level 2' and above. The approach is exactly as we discussed the other day – in fact, the numbers we discussed were those for 'Level 2' at *XYZ Industries*".

Exhibit 20	XYZ INDUSTRIES					
Level '2' EP & ROIC ... *Comparison –* ($ Millions) Omitted		Year #3	Year #2	Year #1	3-Yr. Avg.	Current Year Fcst.
	Economic Profit - Level '2'					
C	NOP	$168	$214	$200	$194	$238
12.0%	CCAP	(102)	(122)	(145)	(123)	(163)
C	Economic Profit - "EP"	$66	$92	$55	$71	$75
	"EP" Difference - '2' vs. '1'					
C	"EP" - Level '2'	$66	$92	$55	$71	$75
C	"EP" - Level '1'	57	107	70	78	91
C	EP Difference ... '2' vs. '1'	$9	$(15)	$(15)	$(7)	$(16)
	Memo:					
C	*"ROIC" (Return on Invested Capital)*					
C	"ROIC" - Level '2'	19.8%	21.1%	16.6%	19.0%	17.5%
C	"ROIC" - Level '1'	21.7%	26.3%	20.0%	22.5%	21.3%

"Exhibit 21 shows the complete set of formulas to compute *CCAP* and indicates how the 'weighting' of the components of invested capital is influenced by the exclusion or inclusion of the operating leases. I assume you remember all of this from our recent meeting with the 'team'".

"Oh, my God!" Jill shrieked, "I thought I had seen the last of this *'CCAP monster'* a couple of days ago. I don't know if I can take much more!" Frank sat motionless, with a blank look on his face, and then he suddenly moved over to comfort Jill.

Jason was quite taken back by these words and actions, and a very perplexed look came over his face. "I thought everyone, perhaps excluding Jack, was 'comfortable' with the approach and the outcome of our cost of capital session. Now, I'm confused".

"Well, maybe be you didn't exactly read the 'tea leaves' correctly", Jill retorted. When Frank jumped in with... "It *was* getting a bit 'heavy' and I sensed some discomfort by everyone except for Earl and myself"... Jason was totally dumbfounded and could not hide this feeling. His facial expression was now one of total bewilderment.

"I,... I don't know what to say", he blurted out.

"Dave didn't think you would", cracked Jill, laughing almost hysterically... "which is why he called me yesterday and made me *promise* to try to 'pull this one off' on you. I'm *not* usually good at practical jokes, but Dave is, and he rehearsed me quite well, as evidenced by your reaction".

Even Frank was laughing loudly now, which was unusual for him, and almost chortled... "Jill made me go along with the joke!"

Exhibit 21　　　　　　　　　　XYZ INDUSTRIES

Cost of Capital (CCAP) Without Operating Leases	Pre Tax Cost (Avg.)	Income Tax Shield (*)	After Tax Cost	Percent of Total IC (**)	Weighted Cost (CCAP)
C Debt	8.8%	35.0%	5.73%	12.5%	0.72%
C Preferred Stock	12.0%	0.0%	12.00%	9.4%	1.13%
C Equity	(***)	(***)	13.50%	78.1%	10.55%
I Govt. Bond - "Risk Free" (Rf)	6.50%		Weighted Average Cost (CCAP) =		**12.39%**
I Beta (B)	1.40				
I Market Risk Premium (Mrp)	5.00%		*Optional -* **Round to**		**12.5%**
With Operating Leases					
C Debt	9.3%	35.0%	6.06%	20.0%	1.21%
C Preferred Stock	12.0%	0.0%	12.00%	8.6%	1.03%
C Equity	(***)	(***)	13.50%	71.4%	9.64%
			Weighted Average Cost (CCAP) =		**11.88%**
			Optional - **Round to**		**12.0%**

(*) Debt Tax Shield @ statutory rate - use average of historical period or current/future period
(**) Capital Structure - incl. Operating Leases in Debt if *EP* analysis is at Level '2'- see below

(***) *Equity Cost Calculation- after tax —*	Risk Free Rate　*plus* [Beta　*times*　Market Risk Premium]		
In Symbols ...... Rf + [B × Mrp]	6.50%	..... plus ...... 　1.40 .... times	5.00%

Competitor / Peer Co. "Beta" Analysis		(**) "Market-Based" Capital Structure			
Company	**Beta (B)**	**Equity**	**# Shares**	**Price/Share**	**Mkt.Value**
LMN	1.25	Comm. Stock	100	$25.00	**$2,500**
QRS	1.50	Pref. Stock (*)	30	10.00	**300**
TUV	1.30	**Total**			**$2,800**
Peer Group Average	**1.35**	(*) *Preferred Stock Dividend per Share =*		*$1.20*	
				Interest Rate	**Book = Mkt. Value**
		Debt			
Notes:		Short-term		8.5%	$150
$ Millions, except Price/Share		Long-term		9.0%	250
# Shares in Millions		Sub-total (ex. Op. Lse.)		**8.8%**	**$400**
		Oper Leases		10.0%	300
		Average Interest Rate / Total Amount for Debt		**9.3%**	**$700**
		Equity + P.S. + Total Debt	w/o Oper. Leases		w/ Oper. Leases
			$3,200		**$3,500**

Jason leaned back, sighed and said... "You're sure it wasn't Jonathan who put you up to this? This would be something I'm sure he would like to do to me".

"No, it was Dave", Jill responded. "We don't have that type of relationship with Jonathan. You may, because of your former ties, but Jonathan is 'the boss' around here and, while we do have fun, he would not ask us to do this type of practical joking".

Jason started laughing. "I like this type of levity in a company. And, now I owe Dave a 'comeback'".

Jason really did enjoy practical jokes and levity. Unless he had a 'stiff' type of client, he himself always tried to make people laugh. He wasn't always sure how successful he was, but he didn't lack for trying. He took it as a positive sign when someone played a joke on him, because he felt that a 'chemistry' was developing. "*I hope I'm right*", he said to himself. Turning back to the matters at hand, he got up from his chair and spoke to Jill and Frank... "I guess it's obvious that after 'Level 2' comes 'Level 3' – at least that's what I learned in *Romper Room*".

"You're 'on top of it', Jason", quipped Jill. The 'vibes' were now good, as Jason had demonstrated he could take fun being poked at him. Jill liked that.

"The main adjustment in 'Level 3' is to add back depreciation to the P&L and balance sheet, putting the business on a 'pure cash flow' basis. There has been a lot of heated debate and dialogue by some in my profession about the treatment of depreciation, and the pros/cons of 'cash flow' return on invested capital and 'cash based' economic profit. Again, I'm not advocating one versus the other, but I do think every company needs to evaluate the impact (on its *EP*) of these alternative approaches. Exhibit 22 gets us going".

"As Exhibit 22 indicates, the major item to be adjusted on the P&L is 'depreciation' expense. If there are other items not adjusted

Exhibit 22

		XYZ INDUSTRIES				
		'Economic Profit'				
	($Millions) Omitted	Level "3" - 'Gross' Assets				
	History — "Actuals"	3 Most Recent Historical Years			Historical	Current
		Year #3	Year #2	Year #1	3-Yr. Avg.	Year Fcst.
Profit & Loss						
C	**Revenue (Sales)**	$1,200	$1,500	$1,800	$1,500	$2,000
C	**Operating Income (EBITDA)**	$280	$349	$360	$329	$400
	Details:					
C	EBITA - Level '2'	$250	$314	$320	$294	$350
I	plus: Depreciation Expense	30	35	40	35	50
I	Other -					
C	**'Cash' Tax Rate - % of EBITA**	32.5%	31.7%	37.5%	34.1%	31.9%
C	"Cash" Tax Amount - $	$91	$110	$135	$112	$128
C	**Net "Cash" Oper. Profit (NCOP)**	$189	$238	$225	$217	$272

through 'Level 2', they would be adjusted here in 'Level 3'. The result is that the operating income is *EBITDA* – 'earnings before interest, taxes, depreciation and amortization' – which some call *Cash Flow*, since it represents the cash *flowing into* a firm. On an 'after-tax' basis, net operating profit is also on a 'cash' basis, which some might call *NCOP* – net 'cash' operating profit".

"To be compatible, the balance sheet (invested capital) must also be placed on a 'gross cash' basis, in terms of the original asset values for the fixed assets; that is, before depreciation. Exhibit 23 gives the invested capital for 'Level 3' ".

"We're almost done, now, the last item being the calculation of 'Level 3' *EP*. A friend and colleague of mine coined the term *CVA* (acronym for '*Cash Value Added*') for this 'Level 3' *EP*. Then, the *EPs and ROICs* for all three levels can be summarized, and any differences determined. As you may have guessed by now, the next Exhibit (24) will provide this information. When comparisons are made, it's advisable to look at both the *absolute* amounts for all three levels (dollars for *EPs* and percents for *ROICs*) and the *comparisons* of one level against another (for example, 'Level 2' versus 'Level 1', etc.). This provides a succinct, yet comprehensive, summary of the various levels. It's important to do a thorough job at this point, because the decision as to which '*metric*' to focus on will have implications for the company and its management as the process moves ahead. The key question to be asked is '*what am I giving up by not going to the next level*'? Turning the question around, another way to phrase it is '*what price am I paying to get more accuracy*'?"

"As we review Exhibit 24, I trust you will now appreciate the theme that Jonathan and I have established ...*simplicity with integrity*".

"Amen", Jill said softly. "Let's see Exhibit 24".

"Ditto", Frank added.

As Jill and Frank studied this table and reviewed their notes on the hard copies of the other exhibits, Jason went to the coffeepot.

Exhibit 23		**XYZ INDUSTRIES**				
Balance Sheet						
($Millions) Omitted		Year #3	Year #2	Year #1	3-Yr. Avg.	Current Year Fcst.
C	IC (Level "2") .... above plus:	$850	$1,017	$1,204	$1,024	$1,358
I	Accumulated Depreciation	180	210	245	212	285
I	Other Capitalization -				-	
C	IC ("gross") - Level '3'	$1,030	$1,227	$1,449	$1,235	$1,643

Exhibit 24		**XYZ INDUSTRIES**				
Economic Profit - 'CVA'		**3 Most Recent Historical Years**			**Historical**	**Current**
($MM's)	*'Cash Value Added'*	**Year #3**	**Year #2**	**Year #1**	**3-Yr. Avg.**	**Year Fcst.**
C	NCOP	$189	$238	$225	$217	$272
12.0%	CCAP	(124)	(148)	(174)	(149)	(198)
C	"EP" .... 'CVA'	$65	$91	$51	$69	$74
	"EP" Summary					
C	Level '1' ... reported assets	$57	$107	$70	$78	$91
C	Level '2' ... Leases, G/W ++	$66	$92	$55	$71	$75
C	Level '3' ... 'Gross' Assets	$65	$91	$51	$69	$74
	"EP" Differences					
C	Difference - '2' vs. '1'	$9	$(15)	$(15)	$(7)	$(16)
C	Difference - '3' vs. '1'	$8	$(17)	$(20)	$(10)	$(16)
C	Difference - '3' vs. '2'	$(1)	$(1)	$(4)	$(2)	$(0)
Return on Invested Capital ('ROIC')						
	"ROIC" Summary					
C	"ROIC" - Level "1"	21.7%	26.3%	20.0%	22.5%	21.3%
C	"ROIC" - Level "2"	19.8%	21.1%	16.6%	19.0%	17.5%
C	"ROIC" - Level "3"	18.3%	19.4%	15.5%	17.6%	16.6%
	"ROIC" Differences (% Points)					
C	Difference - '2' vs. '1'	–1.8%	–5.2%	–3.4%	–3.6%	–3.7%
C	Difference - '3' vs. '1'	–3.3%	–6.9%	–4.5%	–5.0%	–4.7%
C	Difference - '3' vs. '2'	–1.5%	–1.7%	–1.1%	–1.4%	–1.0%

This was an extremely important aspect of their work session this morning, and he wanted to give them ample time to analyze the outcomes, at least on a preliminary basis, since over the next two weeks he would be asking them to do the same for their company. Jill and Frank went back and forth through the various exhibits that Jason had presented, poring over their notes.

After several minutes had passed, Jason asked, "So, what do you think? Even if you don't have a firm conclusion, I would be interested in getting your thoughts as to the implications of one level versus another".

This time Frank spoke first… "XYZ should go to at least 'Level 2', because there are significant differences, and the differences are not all the same. For example, the booking of the 'reserve' in year 3 (going back in time) caused the 'Level 1' economic profit to be understated in that year, in terms of the 'cash flow' performance of the firm. The subsequent years were then probably overstated. Further, the operating leases are significant and should be included in the invested capital base". Frank then paused, as was his habit, since he rarely said anything without having thought it through. He looked over at Jill, implying that she should feel free to join in the discussion.

Jill did not need much prodding. "To follow along on the operating leases, it would seem that 'Level 1' overstates the cost of capital, since there is a significant amount of this type of financing in the capital structure. Also, the amortization of the intangibles should probably be accounted for – although '*God Help Me*' if I make the same comment when we meet again with the finance team. Jack will probably 'flip out' and it's hard to predict what he may do. Oh, well, so be it... we've had a few 'lively' discussions over the past six months and I guess I'm prepared for another. The real question seems to be whether XYZ needs to go to 'Level 3'. I must admit that I don't have an answer at this point. The numbers are close, and 'Level 3' is consistently lower. But, I don't know if 'lower' means 'more accurate'".

"That's exactly the same question I had on my mind", Frank interjected.

"It also happens to be a very relevant question", Jason added.

"OK, Mr Consultant, I guess we have to succumb to your infinite wisdom, and ask you to help us make a decision with potentially far-reaching implications", Jill snapped.

"You're starting to sound more and more like Dave", quipped Jason. "Is he coaching you?"

Jill chuckled as she replied, "He may try to, but I don't think he'll be very successful. Besides, he's too smart to need any influence from me. I must admit, though, that he can make you gravitate to his style if you allow yourself too many mental lapses. Further, his style is not bad, since it forces you to think through all aspects of a situation. I guess, though, that for me it's hard to keep the 'edge' that Dave always seems to have".

"I agree with that", Frank said... "I wish sometimes that I could have about 25% of Dave's wit".

"And Dave probably wishes that he had 25% of your brain power", Jill retorted.

Frank always blushed when anyone told him how intelligent he was, and now was no exception.

Jason thoroughly enjoyed the 'banter' that Jill and Frank were engaging in. He was impressed by the combination of intellect and common sense that these two young, capable people were able to convey. He wondered, actually tried to remember, if he had this combination when he was their age. Failing to arrive at a definitive answer for himself and attributing it to a 'senior moment', he decided to give Jill and Frank the benefit of his years of experience on the subject. "You both are definitely on the right track in stating that *XYZ* should at least implement a 'Level 2' system. This is a fairly typical '*Economic Value Added*' approach, putting aside the issue of R&D/Advertising capitalization for the moment. Let me offer some thoughts that can, hopefully, lead to a good decision as to which 'level' is best for *XYZ*.

- The operating leases and resultant cost of capital implications are important. The '50 basis point' (0.5 percentage point) differential in *CCAP* is at the threshold of significance for an industrial company. For a highly leveraged bank or financial services firm, a differential of '25 basis points' can be significant. Further, from an operating perspective, managers should realize that every time they rent a building or other asset, they are making an 'investment'. This investment is no different from the capital expenditure for machinery and equipment in the factory that is recorded as a fixed asset. Thus, it helps to 'kill' a silly notion that people can 'get around' the capital appropriation system by leasing. The subject of capital spending is one that we'll spend some time on later in the process, so let's now move on to another perspective.
- The amortization of goodwill and intangibles is, I believe, getting abused due to the latitude available to controllers in US corporations. This is one of the reasons I favor treating this item as a 'sunk cost' on the balance sheet and adding back the annual amortization expense to operating income.
- I don't have the same feeling about depreciation, unless companies have let their assets deteriorate and the 'replacement' cost is completely out of line with the values reflected on the net fixed asset account on the balance sheet. Some 'old line' manufacturing companies have allowed this to occur. This is not an issue with most technology, service and distribution companies, since their fixed assets are relatively new and not heavily depreciated. Further, there is an *alternative way* to depreciate. While it requires an adjustment to the way most companies keep their books under the typical 'straight line' GAAP approach to depreciation rules, it can be done. This approach works in a way similar to that of an amortized loan. Thus, only a small amount of depreciation is recorded in the early years, with larger amounts accruing in later years. Obviously, this requires a new set of record keeping, but so does a change to a 'gross' asset metric that puts a company on a 'pure' cash flow basis.
- Tax authorities also regulate depreciation. In the United States, the governing body is the Internal Revenue Service (IRS). The way corporations pay taxes and generate cash flow is governed, in

part, by depreciation. Economic theorists have almost universally accepted the notion that fixed assets have useful lives, which can be predicted. Therefore, the cash flow of any firm is influenced by the depreciation regulations that exist".

"Taking all of this and trying to adopt the optimal 'metric' leads me to favor 'Level 2' for *XYZ Industries*. There is a significant difference in *EP* at 'Level 2' versus 'Level 1', but there is hardly any difference between 'Level 2' and 'Level 3'. *ROIC* is useful to 'round out' the analysis, but it's not the 'driver' – *EP* is! Thus, I focus on the '*EP Differentials*'. With no compelling reason to adopt 'Level 3', my choice is 'Level 2' ".

"I guess that's why you're advising us", mused Jill. "Seriously, though, I appreciate those perspectives, mainly because we just don't think about these issues in our daily routines. Do you agree, Frank, or am I just in my own little sheltered world?"

"I agree for the most part", Frank responded. "You have to make a conscious effort to take a hard look at the economic dynamics of a business. I also support your contention that adding a layer of complexity to our financial measurement system is not in the best interests of either management or the shareholders. As a result, I'm OK with 'Level 2' ".

"Well, far be it for me, a lowly accountant, to challenge the 'economic' thinking of two 'high-powered' financial pros such as you two", Jill snickered.

"You know the old saying, Jill", replied Jason… "flattery will get you everywhere! On a more serious note, I think we've 'beat' this issue of 'what's the best metric' far enough for one day. I think you have an appreciation of the information we need to gather and analyze for Growthstar, and the type of recommendation we need to make to the finance team at our next meeting. So, my next question is when should we get back together and review what the two of you are going to gather?"

"How about Friday afternoon, say at 2:00?" Frank answered. "Then, we should schedule our work over the next two weeks, in light of our other job requirements".

"Sounds good to me", Jill interjected. "Frank and I will get this effort rolling".

At 1:55 on Friday afternoon, Jill and Frank met Jason entering the small conference room, all of them carrying folders. While she was getting settled, Jill began speaking… "Did you gentlemen read about the huge merger in the oil industry?" Both Jason and Frank nodded. Since this merger – actually an acquisition of the third largest by the second largest oil company – was 'front page' and 'headline TV' business news during the past two days, it would have been almost impossible to miss it. "I noticed that the price of the *acquiring company's stock* went down immediately after the formal announcement and that it has stayed at this lower price through noon today. I was thinking about this in light of the last schedule (Exhibit 24) we reviewed on Wednesday and your comments suggesting that we independently reflect on the 'quality' of *XYZ's 'EP performance'*. I believe that there must be something from the '*EP assessment*' that we can apply to a situation such as this merger, but I'm not sure exactly what it is". As she spoke, Jill placed Exhibit 24 in front of her. Frank, seeing Jill's copy, opened his folder and did the same.

Frank, coincidentally, had just read today's article on the Internet before walking down the hall to the conference room. "There's a real issue on the 'price' paid for the deal. It's interesting to note that the seminar I attended a few months ago had a session on 'acquisition pricing'. In fact, this deal was being 'rumored' at that time and the presenter noted that the 'acquirer' had *not* earned its cost of capital for the past three years. The comment he made was that the 'new entity' would have to generate a 'return on capital' about 3 percentage points higher than its average of the last three years to justify the 'acquirer' paying a 10% 'premium' over the current market price for its 'target'. The stock price of the 'target' has been relatively 'flat' since then. With the deal being announced at a 30% 'premium', it seems logical that this type of reaction would occur in the stock market".

"OK", Jill interjected, "let's assume that the stock market is rational. Based on what you've said, Frank, it appears that it is. What I'm looking for is some type of indicator from the '*EP Assessment*' that sheds light on situations such as this one".

"Good question and good thinking", Jason responded. "To get a perspective, why don't we go back to one of the more important exhibits from our work session last week". Jason clicked to a file in his PC and found what he was looking for (Exhibit 7).

"Remember this? Please, Jill, no more 'Dave Dollarby-inspired fake outbursts' this week. There's a message in this exhibit that I was going to introduce this afternoon, so I might as well mention it now. Look at this chart (Exhibit 7) along with Exhibit 24. As I mentioned last week when we covered this material, only Company **'A'** is profitable from an 'economic' perspective. Company **'A'** is the only one with *NOP* significantly above its capital charge (or, cost of capital)".

"One of the next steps in the process is to determine the impact that the classification of a business (is it **'A'**, **'B'**, or **'C'**?) has on growth and new investment. I will demonstrate that later on, but

Exhibit 7
"Economic Profit" - Example

"Base Period"	CO. 'A'	CO. 'B'	CO. 'C'
Revenue [Sales]	$1,000	$1,000	$1,000
Net Operating Profit			
[NOP] - $	$100	$100	$100
- %	10%	10%	10%
Invested Capital [IC]	$600	$800	$1,000
Cost of Capital [CCAP]	12%	12%	12%

Economic Profit			
NOP [from above]	$100	$100	$100
Capital Charge [CCAP]	(72)	(96)	(120)
Economic Profit ["EP"]	$28	$4	$(20)

let me state for now that only **'A'**-type businesses can create value through additional growth. This is a very powerful message and one that is difficult for many people, especially 'growth-oriented' CEOs and operating heads to understand and accept, especially when their 'accounting' profits are positive and growing. I have a very compelling illustration, which I will expose you to after we complete the *EP Assessment* for Growthstar".

"Now, getting back to your question regarding this big merger of the two oil companies, what I believe the market is saying is that they don't have confidence that the combined entity can produce enough 'efficiencies' to justify the price being paid. Since the *acquiring company* is either a **weak 'B'** or a **'C'**, becoming 'more efficient' is the key issue – not getting 'bigger'. The market is indicating that a 'transfer of wealth' is occurring – **from** the *acquiring company* **to** the *target firm*, with the 'per share' price drop of the *acquiring company's* common stock indicating the magnitude of the wealth transfer. This is a very critical component of any value-based performance system – that is, the ability to measure this 'shareholder wealth impact' – and we will be giving it considerable attention in the near future. For now, though, the point I want to stress is that the *EP Assessment* provides a classification indicating whether a business is:

- a value 'creator' (**'A'**)
- a value 'destroyer' (**'C'**), or
- value 'neutral' (**'B'**).

If we return to *XYZ Industries* (Exhibit 24) we can see that the company, in total, is a solid **'A'** – regardless of which 'level' we choose – since its *EPs* are 'in the black' for every year and its *ROICs* are well above the cost of capital. If we were going to study *XYZ* further, we would 'assess' the major business units. This is what we're going to do for Growthstar and it's what we want to concentrate on – after we analyze the information that, I believe, you have assembled".

"This is starting to make some sense", Jill commented. "It's helping me to at least begin to understand the workings of the stock market and what we, as corporate managers, need to focus on. I don't understand why Jack is fighting this effort so vehemently!"

"Some people don't react well to a new way of thinking", Jason responded, "especially if it challenges the essence of their life's work and threatens their 'power base'. Putting this aside, I think we should get into Growthstar's data, since we have an important session with Jonathan, Val and the 'team' in two weeks".

Frank opened his folder. "Jill and I reviewed the financials for the past three years, along with the outlook for this year. What we have are statements ('rounded' to *millions* of dollars) for the total company – *'TOTAL CO'.*, along with *Products* and *Services*, put together in a format similar to the layout that you had for *XYZ Industries*. The first schedule (Exhibit 25) is our income statement for the total company".

As Jason studied the P&L that was on the screen, he asked... "What is your policy about allocating corporate overheads?"

"Every 'penny' is charged to the major business units", Jill responded. "That's been our policy since the acquisition of *Services*. Within the two BUs, we have some major product lines that we take to a 'contribution' level, which encompasses the expenses within the business units, but *not* corporate overheads. As you will see in a moment, we also have balance sheets for the two major business units".

"OK, so 'nothing' is left in a 'corporate expense' account".

"That's what I just said", Jill retorted.

"We also derive 'net operating profit after taxes' for each BU", Frank added. "Ian likes this because he can quickly determine the *EPS* for each BU".

"Jack has also been a proponent of this", Jill chimed in.

Exhibit 25	GROWTHSTAR INC.				

Total Company Financials

$ Millions — (as "Reported")

..... Historical Period — 3 Years .....

"TOTAL CO." Financials	FY #3	FY #2	FY #1	3-Yr Avg	Current FY Fcst.
Income Statement				*(2-Yr. for*	
Revenue:				*Svcs. Rev.)*	
Products	$220	$250	$280	$250	$300
Services	-	75	100	*88*	150
Total Revenue	220	325	380	308	450
Operating Costs and Expenses:					
Cost of Goods Sold (COGS)	130	163	190	161	219
Selling, Marketing & Service (SMS)	35	82	94	71	113
General & Administrative (G&A)	27	41	46	38	54
Research & Development (R&D)	12	16	19	16	22
Total Operating Costs and Expenses	204	302	349	285	408
Financing and Other Expenses:					
Interest Expense	2	3	4	3	5
Interest Income	(0)	0	(0)	(0)	(0)
Amortization Expense		1	1	1	1
Other - Acquisition Reserve	5			-	
Total Financing and Other Expenses	7	4	5	4	6
Net Income Before Taxes	9	19	26	19	36
Provision for Taxes	3	7	9	6	13
Net Income After Taxes	$6	$12	$17	$13	$23

"I see that all your costs and expenses are 'consolidated' on this schedule", Jason then stated.

"That's true", Jill responded, "but we have separate BU income statements which provide their specific costs and expenses, along with the allocation of corporate overheads".

"I see the acquisition reserve was booked in (historical) fiscal year #3", Jason then said.

"You would have to notice that, wouldn't you", Jill chided in a good-natured tone. "We closed this deal just prior to the end of (historical) FY #3".

"It's prominent and hard to miss!" Jason then continued by asking, "How much of the total goodwill was written off?"

"About 25%", Jill answered. "We booked $20 million of goodwill in total. If you would like to take a look at the *TOTAL CO.* balance sheet, we can show it to you".

As Jason nodded, Frank clicked on the next chart (Exhibit 26).

"We went back four years with the balance sheets", Frank stated, "because we noticed that you used 'beginning year' amounts to calculate invested capital in the *XYZ* example".

Exhibit 26	GROWTHSTAR INC.				
	Total Company Financials				
$ Millions	(as "Reported")				
	..... Historical Period — 4 Years				Current
"TOTAL CO." Financials	FY #4	FY #3	FY #2	FY #1	FY Fcst.
Balance Sheet - Year End					
Assets					
Cash	$11	$(2)	$2	$9	$24
Accounts Receivable	24	33	39	48	54
Inventory	20	31	33	40	44
Other Current Assets	5	5	5	5	5
Total Current Assets	60	67	79	102	127
Fixed Assets:					
Gross	40	65	75	85	97
Accumulated Depreciation	(14)	(20)	(23)	(28)	(34)
Goodwill, etc.					
Gross	-	20	20	20	20
Accumulated Amortization	-	(5)	(6)	(7)	(8)
Other Assets	-	1	2	2	2
Total Assets	**$86**	**$128**	**$147**	**$174**	**$204**
Liabilities & Equity					
Accounts Payable	$2	$3	$3	$3	$5
Accrued Expenses	5	7	8	6	9
Income Taxes Payable	1	2	2	2	3
Short-term Debt	25	45	45	10	10
Total Current Liabilities	33	57	59	21	27
Long-term Debt	-	-	-	50	50
Deferred Taxes	2	3	3	5	6
Other Liabilities/Reserves	-	5	5	5	5
Total Liabilities	35	65	67	81	88
Stockholders' Equity	51	63	80	93	116
Total Liabilities & Equity	**$86**	**$128**	**$147**	**$174**	**$204**

"Perfect", Jason responded. "The choice of a 'beginning' balance is often one of convenience and simplicity. Since *EP* (and value-based performance in general) is most concerned with change from an established 'base', the critical issue is to be consistent. Some firms choose to use 'average' invested capital amounts for each year – some compute two-point [beginning/year-end] averages, others do it quarterly, and still others compute twelve-month rolling averages. I have found that in most cases, a simplistic 'beginning' balance works fine and 'locks in' the invested capital for a particular year. That's what I will recommend for Growthstar, unless we uncover a problem when we evaluate forward-looking strategies and compare the results under the *EP* approach with those of the classical free cash flow method. But, that's later on. Let's keep focused on the historical financials and the translation of 'accounting' into 'economic' profit".

"Can we show you our 'reported' financials for the two major business units"? Jill asked. "As mentioned, we allocate all expenses except financing costs, and take our profits to an 'after tax' level. Our balance sheets attempt to compute the 'operating capital' in each of the two major BUs".

"Well, hallelujah!" Jason exclaimed! "I won't have to unravel an 'inter-company interest' situation, as I have had to do in several companies. I can't tell you how ridiculous and complex some of these are, with very little value added".

"We thought about it after the *Services* acquisition, but Jonathan decided against it", Frank said as he clicked on Exhibit 27 – the income statement for *Products*.

After a quick look at the P&L for *Products*, Jason spoke. "You have, I think, a Level '1' *NOP*. Oh, just a moment – I'm not sure about the taxes. Are these at 'book' rates?"

"Yes", Jill and Frank replied simultaneously.

"Then", Jason continued, "we will want to look at deferred taxes, to see if there is a difference between the 'book' and 'cash' rates".

Jill leaned back in her chair and, after a moment of thought, said, "You know, Jason, I may be getting dangerous, but I feel that some of the concepts you've been discussing are starting to 'grab hold' in my brain. Let me try this one. I have been in charge of the deferred tax accounting and have worked with Earl on this for the past three years. One of the things I noticed was that, when we closed the acquisition for *Services*, there were no deferred taxes on their books. Earl was looking for 'cash flow' items and this is one of the accounts we studied. The reason is that the type of investments made by *Services* are mostly for working capital, fixed capital with relatively

Exhibit 27	GROWTHSTAR INC.				
$ Millions	Business Unit Financials (as "Reported")				
	..... Historical Period — 3 Years				Current
"PRODUCTS" Financials	FY #3	FY #2	FY #1	3-Yr Avg	FY Fcst.
Income Statement					
Sales Revenue:					
U.S.	$180	$200	$220	$200	$225
International	40	50	60	50	75
Total Sales Revenue	220	250	280	250	300
Operating Costs and Expenses:					
Cost of Goods Sold (COGS)	130	150	168	149	177
Selling, Marketing & Service (SMS)	35	38	42	38	45
General & Administrative (G&A)	27	30	33	30	36
Research & Development (R&D)	12	12	14	13	15
Total Operating Costs and Expenses	204	230	257	230	273
Operating Income	16	20	23	20	27
Provision for Taxes	6	7	8	7	10
Net Operating Profit After Taxes	$10	$13	$15	$13	$17

short useful lives, and offices (which are mostly leased). *Products* is more fixed capital (plant, machinery and equipment) intensive and, thus, generates virtually all of the deferred taxes for the company. I'll review this in more depth, but for now I believe that *all* 'book-to-cash' tax differentials will be in *Products*".

"My, my", Jason joked, "you are getting dangerous! I'd be really careful about taking this new knowledge too far from this room. Someone might try to 'beat you up', as they've done to me over the years".

"That's very funny", Jill replied, with a slight sneer on her face. "I'm only five-foot five to begin with, so there's not too far to go".

"As you should realize by now, I'm not much taller", Jason retorted... "but I was Ian's height when I started in this profession thirty years ago".

This comment did get a laugh, albeit short-lived, from both Jill and Frank.

"Why don't we take a look at the balance sheet for *Products*?" Jason then suggested.

Frank obliged with the next schedule (Exhibit 28)

"There is no 'cash' on the balance sheets for the BUs", Jason observed.

"That's true", Frank responded. "We manage cash at the corporate level".

Exhibit 28	GROWTHSTAR INC.				
	Business Unit Financials				
$ Millions	**(as "Reported")**				
	..... Historical Period — 4 Years				**Current**
"PRODUCTS" Financials	**FY #4**	**FY #3**	**FY #2**	**FY #1**	**FY Fcst.**
Balance Sheet - Year End					
Assets					
Accounts Receivable	$24	$24	$30	$33	$36
Inventory	20	22	21	23	24
Other Current Assets	5	5	5	4	5
Total Current Assets	49	51	56	60	65
Fixed Assets:					
Gross	40	43	47	54	62
Accumulated Depreciation	(14)	(15)	(16)	(19)	(22)
Goodwill, etc.					
Gross	-	-	-	-	-
Accumulated Amortization	-	-	-	-	-
Other Assets	-	-	-	-	-
Total Assets	$75	$79	$87	$95	$105
Liabilities & Capital					
Accounts Payable	2	2	2	2	4
Accrued Expenses	5	6	6	5	7
Income Taxes Payable	1	2	2	1	2
Other	-	-	-	-	-
Operating Capital	$67	$69	$77	$87	$92

As Frank spoke, Jason spread the schedules out in front of himself. "I just noticed that on the *TOTAL CO.* balance sheet (Exhibit 26) the cash balance was 'negative' at the end of (historical) FY #3".

"That's also true", said Frank. "We had 'tapped out' our borrowing lines and had to go into an 'overdraft' position, mainly due to financing the *Services* acquisition".

"That will actually be helpful in illustrating to the 'team' the way that overdrafts (negative cash balances) are handled in the computation of invested capital", Jason noted. "It appears that *Products* had very little change in their operating capital during (historical) FY #3, but then had investment growth during the next two fiscal years".

"Yes", Frank replied. "We really 'squeezed' them in FY #3 to pay for the *Services* acquisition. What you don't see here, though, is that *Products* had built up a significant level of accounts receivable in FY #4, as compared to the previous year, which they worked off in FY #3. *Products* had also spent $10 million on new capital in FY #4 to replace and upgrade a lot of old, worn-out machinery in the plant. This program allowed us to keep the investment for new fixed capital at a relatively low level in FY #3".

Jill then chimed in, "Any other observations on *Products*?" After Jason silently indicated that he didn't have any, at least at this time, she motioned to Frank and said, "you will be able to see how we treat goodwill as we look at the historical financials for *Services*. First, the P&L" (Exhibit 29).

Jill continued... "We don't have a 'reported' income statement for *Services* for FY #3, because we closed the deal at year-end. The acquisition reserve was booked to *TOTAL CO.* (refer back to Exhibit 25)

Exhibit 29	GROWTHSTAR INC.				
$ Millions	Business Unit Financials (as "Reported")				
	..... Historical Period — 3 Years				Current
"SERVICES" Financials	**FY #3**	**FY #2**	**FY #1**	**2-Yr Avg**	**FY Fcst.**
Income Statement	**"Base"**				
Service Revenue:					
Growthstar		$75	$90	$83	$125
Other Products		-	10	5	25
Total Service Revenue	**$50**	75	100	88	150
Operating Costs and Expenses:					
Cost of Goods Sold (COGS)		13	22	17	42
Selling, Marketing & Service (SMS)		44	52	48	68
General & Administrative (G&A)		11	13	12	18
Research & Development (R&D)		4	5	5	7
Total Operating Costs and Expenses		72	92	82	135
Goodwill Amortization		1	1	1	1
Operating Income		2	7	5	14
Provision for Taxes		1	3	2	6
Net Operating Profit After Taxes	**N/A**	$1	$4	$3	$8

in FY #3, but there were no 'operating' results from *Services* in FY #3. Thus, all the historical 'averages' for this BU are for two years. I also assume that you have noticed our 'acronyms' (abbreviations) for the major cost and expense categories on our P&Ls".

"I have", Jason replied. "I have also noticed something else. The businesses have significantly different financial dynamics, with respect to the COGS and SMS expense ratios; that is, as a percent-to-revenue. I have been doing some quick calculations in my head and on the hard copies of the schedules, and the two businesses have very different ratios. *Products* (from Exhibit 27) has a relatively *high* COGS ratio and a relatively *low* SMS ratio. *Services* (from Exhibit 29) has the opposite set of ratios – *low* COGS and *high* SMS ratio".

"Very observant", countered Jill. "I had just started to notice that myself, after reviewing these financials in this format of laying the years side-by-side".

Frank then interjected, "One of the reasons behind the *Services* acquisition was to get into a higher gross profit margin business. We wanted to better 'leverage' our COGS ratio on new sales, and *Services* was seen as a way to do this".

"That's fine", Jason retorted, "but you also have to look at the rest of the income statement, and determine the ratios for the other cost and expense categories. Then, we need to look at the balance sheet, which I assume we will do now, to determine how capital intensive the two businesses are. While you have made a good start with the 'operating capital' as you calculate it, we'll need to look at the operating leases, along with any other 'off balance sheet' items that are 'investments' in the business units".

Jill was nodding her head and had a look of determination on her face. "It's starting to 'come together'. Let's look at the balance sheet for *Services* and see what 'pops out'".

Frank, as he had been doing throughout the meeting, obliged by clicking on Exhibit 30, the 'reported' balance sheet for *Services*.

"See the lower level of fixed capital versus *Products*", Jill stated, walking over to the screen and pointing to the 'Gross' Fixed Asset line (under 'Assets').

"But", Jason countered, "you need to *compare* the gross and net levels of *fixed capital* to the *revenue* for the business. This yields an important ratio called *capital intensity*. The level of *capital intensity*, which we will devote much attention to, provides a better indicator of value creation than does the *absolute level of fixed capital*. This concept also applies to the other categories of invested capital, especially working capital. Just looking quickly at the fixed asset numbers, subtracting out accumulated depreciation, and then comparing this

Exhibit 30	**GROWTHSTAR INC.**				
$ Millions	**Business Unit Financials (as "Reported")**				
		..... Historical Period — 3 Years			**Current**
"SERVICES" Financials	**FY #4**	**FY #3**	**FY #2**	**FY #1**	**FY Fcst.**
Balance Sheet - Year End					
Assets					
Accounts Receivable		$9	$9	$15	$18
Inventory		9	11	17	20
Other Current Assets		-	-	1	-
Total Current Assets		18	20	33	38
Fixed Assets:					
Gross		22	28	31	35
Accumulated. Depreciation		(5)	(7)	(9)	(12)
Goodwill, etc.					
Gross		20	20	20	20
Accumulated Amortization		(5)	(6)	(7)	(8)
Other Assets		1	2	2	2
Total Assets		$51	$58	$70	$74
Liabilities & Capital					
Accounts Payable		1	1	1	1
Accrued Expenses		1	2	2	2
Income Taxes Payable		-	1	0	1
Other		-	-	-	-
Operating Capital		**$49**	**$54**	**$67**	**$70**

'net' amount to revenue, it appears that, at least historically, *Services* may actually be *more capital intensive* than *Products*".

"Now, that's interesting", Jill came back with. "We thought we had acquired a high gross margin business with low fixed capital. This type of analysis sheds a new light on this business and, I guess, any future acquisitions we may consider. I'm not sure Jonathan appreciates this totally".

Frank then jumped in with... "Perhaps not totally, but at least partially, based on some evaluations that Earl and I have been doing recently. They (*Services*) have been purchasing a lot of personal computers, workstations and small diagnostic testing devises, which individually don't appear to be much, but when added up represent a significant investment. This has been going on ever since the acquisition. While we have a fairly rigorous capital appropriation policy for our manufacturing projects, we are somewhat lax on computers, especially since their low prices exempt them from our project authorization requirements".

"There is also another piece of the puzzle that we haven't considered yet – the operating leases. I had mentioned, Jill, that Earl and I were working these up for the BUs, but I just finished the compilations this morning and didn't get a chance to review them with you".

"Thanks a lot – just kidding", Jill chuckled. "What revelation comes from this analysis?"

"A rather interesting one", Frank replied. "When we acquired *Services* in FY #3, we took on operating lease obligations of approximately $14 million. That's the present value – the 'capitalized' value – of the future years' lease payments. During the past two years, as you know, *Services* has been opening up new offices around the country and leasing new testing equipment, as part of their strategy to service not only Growthstar's products, but also those of other targeted manufacturers. As a result, virtually all of the increase in operating lease commitments during the past two years resides with *Services*. The result has been an additional $9 million to our lease obligations since the end of FY #3, with an additional $5 million planned for this current year – all for *Services*. The only new lease obligation for *Products* during the past two years has been a $1 million commitment for a new computer system in the logistics operation. Further, no major new lease obligations are planned for this year within *Products*".

"I know, Frank, that you probably have a schedule outlining these amounts. Could we see it"? Jill asked.

"Certainly", Frank answered. "You know I would never hide anything from you". As he spoke, he clicked on a schedule (Exhibit 31).

Jason sat back and looked at the schedule, as did Jill. Jason spoke first. "As of right now, the operating lease commitments are almost the same for the two BUs. And as you stated, Frank, the recent growth has been almost entirely in *Services*".

Jill then interjected, "And if I understand this process, we add these amounts to the operating capital for each BU to determine *invested capital*".

"That's correct", Frank confirmed. "In fact, Earl and I have come to the conclusion that the company's operating leases are significant enough to be included in our invested capital, which is why I incorporated them into the cost of capital calculation that I presented to the 'team'".

Exhibit 31	**GROWTHSTAR INC.**				
$ Millions	**Business Unit Financials**				
	("Calculated")				
"OPERATING LEASES"	..... Historical Period — 4 Years				Current
	FY #4	FY #3	FY #2	FY #1	FY Fcst.
Operating Leases - 'Year-End' Values					
Products Operating Leases	$19	$26	$27	$27	$27
Services Operating Leases.	-	14	18	23	28
TOTAL CO. Operating Leases	$19	$40	$45	$50	$55
Operating Leases - 'Beginning' Values					
Products Operating Leases		$19	$26	$27	$27
Services Operating Leases.		-	14	18	23
TOTAL CO. Operating Leases		$19	$40	$45	$50

"This is a great start", Jason then said. "I think we have everything we need to begin the transition to *EP* and to formulate some initial perceptions as to *value creation*. What I will do is spend next week developing an analytic model along the lines of the *XYZ* example, and then review it with you. How about if we schedule a meeting for next Friday morning, with the understanding that I will contact you during the week with any questions or important observations".

"Sounds good to me", Jill responded. "We have a quarterly closing coming up, so I'm not going anywhere, and I should in reasonably good shape by Friday. Hopefully, I'll have some energy left".

"You're never short on energy", Frank retorted. "I'm OK with this timetable, also".

As they left the conference room, Jason thanked them again and wished each of them a good weekend.

Jason, working with the financial summaries for the total company and the business units, developed a series of analytic models for the historical analysis during the ensuing week. By Thursday, he was prepared to meet again with Jill and Frank. It was interesting for him to note that during the week he had met Jack in the hallway a couple of times, and Jack was quite cordial. He had spoken with both Jill and Frank, mainly to indicate that he was progressing, had all the information he needed, and did not have any major questions, except for deferred taxes and possible business risk differences between the two businesses. Jill, after some further investigation, confirmed that virtually all the deferred taxes were due to *Products* and that for the historical analysis, 100% should be allocated to *Products*. Frank compiled a competitor profile for the two BUs. Jason then contacted his colleagues with the financial market risk (beta) analysis model. After accessing the data on the competitors for the two BUs (one of which was the same) Jason concluded that there was not any significant 'systematic' (or, 'market') risk difference between the two BUs. After completing this study, he met with Jonathan and indicated that Growthstar had one (1) cost of capital and it applied to both business units. He also gave Jonathan a synopsis of the session with Jill and Frank, his conclusions about the information that Growthstar had on-hand, as well as the next steps. Finally, he reiterated that the next meeting with the finance team was on as scheduled.

On Friday morning, Jill, Frank and Jason, all arrived at the small conference room at the same time. Jason appreciated the fact that the people in this company were so punctual. After they greeted each other and filled their coffee mugs, Jason began with... "While I believe we are leaning toward at least a 'Level 2' methodology for Growthstar,

I think it will be useful to summarize and compare the three levels. I'm giving you hard copies of the tables and charts I expect to present to the 'team', which you can review. After our work session last week, I think you will understand the approach and calculations. Then, I want to move on to an overview of an important part of any Economic Profit or Value-Based Performance System – the support measures, or financial 'drivers' as I call them. We'll spend time with the finance team on this topic after we thoroughly review the *EP* calculations for Growthstar". He clicked on his PC and flashed a schedule (Exhibit 32). Jill and Frank began to peruse the 'hand-outs' that Jason had just given them.

"This schedule (Exhibit 32) provides the 'key' numbers for the *EP* calculations for the total company (*TOTAL CO.*). If you look at the hand-outs, which we will present to the finance team next week, you should be able to follow the derivation of these numbers. My initial conclusion confirms what we have discussed (and assumed) since we began this process – that Growthstar needs at least a 'Level 2' framework for its value-based performance system. The question is do we need to go to 'Level 3', in light of our objective – *simplicity with*

Exhibit 32	**GROWTHSTAR INC.**				
	Economic Profit - Summary				
$ Millions	**[Levels '1', '2' and '3']**				
	..... Historical Period — 3 Years				Current
"TOTAL CO."	FY #3	FY #2	FY #1	3-Yr Avg	FY Fcst.
Revenue - same for all levels	$220	$325	$380	$308	$450
Level '1'					
NOP	$8	$15	$22	$17	$28
Invested Capital (IC)	$71	$125	$139	$112	$163
CCAP - $ (@ 11.5%, w/out O. L.)	$(8)	$(14)	$(16)	$(13)	$(19)
"EP"	**$0**	**$1**	**$6**	**$4**	**$9**
"ROIC"	11.5%	12.3%	16.2%	15.0%	17.3%
Level '2'					
NOP	$13	$18	$25	$19	$31
Invested Capital (IC)	$90	$170	$190	$150	$220
CCAP - $ (@ 11.0%, with O. L.)	$(10)	$(19)	$(21)	$(16)	$(24)
"EP"	**$3**	**$(1)**	**$4**	**$3**	**$7**
"ROIC"	14.5%	10.9%	13.4%	12.7%	14.3%
Level '3'					
NOP	$17	$20	$29	$23	$35
Invested Capital (IC)	$104	$190	$213	$169	$248
CCAP - $ (@ 11.0%, with O. L.)	$(11)	$(21)	$(23)	$(19)	$(27)
"EP"	**$6**	**$(0)**	**$6**	**$4**	**$8**
"ROIC"	16.6%	10.7%	13.9%	13.6%	14.3%

Exhibit 33	**GROWTHSTAR INC.**				
	Comparisons				
$ Millions	**[Levels '1', '2' and '3']**				
	..... Historical Period — 3 Years				**Current**
"TOTAL CO."	**FY #3**	**FY #2**	**FY #1**	**3-Yr Avg**	**FY Fcst.**
"EP"					
Level '1'	$0	$1	$6	$4	$9
Level '2'	**$3**	**$(1)**	**$4**	**$3**	**$7**
Level '3'	$6	$(0)	$6	$4	$8
"ROIC"					
Level '1'	11.5%	12.3%	16.2%	15.0%	17.3%
Level '2'	**14.5%**	**10.9%**	**13.4%**	**12.7%**	**14.3%**
Level '3'	16.6%	10.7%	13.9%	13.6%	14.3%
Memo: "NOP"					
Level '1'	$8	$15	$22	$17	$28
Level '2'	**$13**	**$18**	**$25**	**$19**	**$31**
Level '3'	$17	$20	$29	$23	$35

integrity. At this point, I don't think so, but let's look at another schedule" (Exhibit 33).

"This is a better schedule to make judgments", Frank exclaimed. "The other one (Exhibit 32) was OK to see the key numbers, but this one lays out the implications".

"I agree", Jason replied, "but you can't get to this comparative summary (Exhibit 33) without the previous schedule (Exhibit 32) along with the detail that you have in your hand-out material".

"I think we understand that", Jill snipped.

"Let's look at these comparisons (in Exhibit 33) and agree on the key reasons for the differences", Jason then added, realizing that Jill might have thought he was 'talking down' to her – even though he wasn't.

Frank was in his element now – analysis where he had the facts. "The acquisition 'write-off' in FY #3 – with all due respect to Jack and his desire to 'set up' the earnings and *EPS* growth – has a major impact, not only on (historical) FY #3, but every other year. The result is that our profits and returns are understated in FY #3 and then overstated in all the other years. Earl will love this one".

"More fuel for the fire", Jill responded, "but I do see your point. The total price we paid for *Services* is somewhat hidden by the write-off".

"That's a good observation", Jason added, "and remember another thought – we're trying to approximate a 'cash flow' perspective for an acquisition or any other situation the company may engage itself in".

"OK", she resumed, "we paid $55 million in FY #3 and booked $20 million of goodwill, then wrote off $5 million of that. So, the 'net' goodwill is in the 'Level 1' *EP*, since it reflects the way we 'report' financially. With 'Level 2', you've added back all the goodwill amortization plus the write-off to both profit and invested capital".

"And the operating leases are also factored in", Jason added.

"Got it! 'Level 3' adds back depreciation to both profit and IC, and gets to 'pure' cash flow".

"That's it", Jason confirmed.

Frank then spoke again. "I think there's an issue with the 'Level 3' results in FY #3, which also relates to the acquisition. Jill, didn't we 'write up' the value of the fixed assets for *Services* and then take advantage of an accounting treatment which allowed us to take additional depreciation, thus negating a portion of the gross 'write-up' ".

"You never cease to amaze me, Frank. I had forgotten about that", Jill answered.

Frank then resumed his comments... "We also were able to take this into our tax calculations, which is why we generated a deferred tax increase of $1 million in FY #3. Recall the balance sheet for *TOTAL CO.* (Exhibit 26) which reflects the $1 million change in deferred taxes from year-end FY #4 to FY #3. So, the 'economic' impact of that transaction is already in the adjusted *NOP* and *EP*. If you compare 'Level 3' with 'Level 2' for the years after FY #3, the differences in *EP and ROIC* are not all that significant".

"I received a very clear message from both Jonathan and Ian, that we could not construct a financial system that was complex and difficult for the non-financial managers to understand", Jason commented.

"We also don't want to completely 'reinvent' our reporting system. Jack will fight it 'tooth and nail' and the accounting people might also rebel", Jill added.

Jason, wanting to conclude this portion of the meeting and move on to the next topic, then said... "At this point, I'm inclined to stick with 'Level 2'. This approach seems to make the most important 'economic' adjustments and does not require a potential adjustment to rectify a fixed asset treatment that probably adds more work than value. We'll present all of this to the team and leave it open for discussion, but are we in agreement that we favor 'Level 2'?"

"We are", Jill and Frank stated emphatically.

Jason was about to introduce one of his favorite subjects in this whole realm of value-based performance, and it was impossible for him not to smile a bit as he began speaking again... "Supporting the overall *EP* results of this company and its two businesses are a set of fundamental financial 'drivers'. These support measures are an important element of any *EP-oriented* approach and, I believe, they help in the communication and overall implementation. They are relatively simple and most people in business can understand them and learn to apply them. What I want to start with are three support metrics that I have determined, over the years, are the initial 'drivers' for management to focus on. They often lead to others". As he was speaking, he went to the flip chart and wrote:

Financial 'Drivers' – Support Measures:

– **Growth Rates ... relationship of revenue, profit and invested capital**
– **Invested Capital Intensity (ICI) ... investment per dollar of revenue**
– **Value Profit Margin (VPM™) ... minimum margin for value creation**

"The first 'driver' is focused on the *comparative* growth rates for revenue, profit and invested capital. Most people know and pay attention to the first two, but few bring the last one into the equation".

"We certainly don't", said Jill.

"The second 'driver' (*ICI*) provides an indicator of capital intensity – regardless of the size of the business. It allows us to compare any number of businesses in terms of the capital required to generate revenue. Familiar ratios such as working capital turnovers are subsets of this 'driver' ".

"We do some of the 'sub-set' ratios, but don't look at the aggregate in this fashion", Frank interjected.

"Third is *the* 'profit' measure that links with value-creation. It integrates cost of capital and investment intensity into a profit margin (pre and/or post tax) that can become a minimum performance requirement for any operating manager".

"Gee", exclaimed Jill, "if we can convert this into *EPS* we can stop right here. We might even get Jack to endorse it!"

"Believe it or not, we can – and we will – show how an entire 'value-based' financial analysis system can be structured around this 'driver'. It's very powerful and can be expressed either as a 'percentage' (typical profit margin on revenue, which is implied here) or a 'dollar' (or, other currency) measure. Any manager who can understand an income statement can understand and implement this support measure. It does require, however, adoption of the economic principles that we have been discussing".

"That we can do here", Jill retorted. "Ian and Jonathan insist that every one of our corporate and operating people, at the supervisory level and above, attend a basic 'P&L' course, which Jack and I

VPM™ is a trademark of Vanguard Partners

developed and facilitate, along with a local college professor. It goes through a fairly rigorous revenue and cost/expense example to get to the 'bottom line' – which for us is our 'net earnings'. Larry Buildermann has attended the course almost once every year, to stay 'refreshed', but I haven't seen Peter Uppcomer since his first session just after he joined the company. In fact, at that time, we put the entire *Services* management through the course and Dave Dollarby helped to facilitate".

"I'm basically done with what I wanted to review today", Jason concluded. "If you are in agreement with 'Level 1, 2, 3' analysis, then Frank and I will work through the financial 'drivers' next week in preparation for the session with the 'team' the following Monday. Jill, if you're available, we'll give you a summary of the results a week from today".

"I'll be here", she responded.

During the following week, Jason and Frank worked on the financial 'driver' portion of the analytic model, and finalized the conclusions for the historical *EP* evaluations. They met with Jill on the following Friday and briefed her on all the key findings.

Monday, the third week after the first finance team meeting arrived, and at 7:55 am, the participants, along with Jonathan, began to assemble in the large financial conference room.

Jonathan started the meeting. "I believe we have two major items to work on today. First, Jason (with any assistance he needs from Frank and Jill) will lead us through the derivation of Growthstar's 'economic profit' – for the total company and the two major BUs – with all its key details and implications".

"Hopefully, not too many details and not too alarming with respect to the implications", Dave Dollarby quipped.

"Just sufficient detail to wear you down and enough surprises to make you reflect on your business", countered Jonathan (wanting to set a tone of hard work but with some levity allowed). "Second, we are going to get an exposure to the key 'drivers' of value-based performance, which I know Jason feels very strongly about, since he's been 'bugging' me with these support measures and their importance for the past six months. After we've completed our reviews, I will want to talk about a presentation to the officers. I think we may want to include Ian in that session, since we'll be presenting some conclusions about our performance over the past three years, especially since the *Services* acquisition. Val Performa will join us later this morning. She had a prior commitment during the first part of the morning, but I know wants to be part of the session when we talk about our 'findings' with regard to *value creation or destruction*. I figure that after our 'break' she'll join us. OK, then, let's get going. Jason, carry on".

"The first item on the agenda is, as Jonathan mentioned, the determination of 'economic' profit for the total company and the major business units. Frank, Jill and I worked up the schedules that I will present from the internal reporting system. We've 'rounded' all the numbers to the nearest million (dollars). First, I'll present the total company and then *Products* and *Services*. If I need to, I will apologize in advance for the amount of 'numbers' to be presented. However, there is no way to arrive at the conclusions we're looking for without doing some comprehensive analysis".

Cathy Casher chimed in with "That's OK, Jason. As you know, *the dirt is in the details*".

Jack started to slump in his chair, since the day he had dreaded had now arrived.

Jason flicked the switch on his personal computer and, as it was warming up, passed out a package of hand-outs. The first schedule (Exhibit 34) was the 'Level 1' approach for *EP*.

"Starting from the top, we are going to walk you through a 'Level 1' *EP* for the total company. There are two adjustments to the income statement. One is the elimination of interest expense and income (we covered this at our last meeting, and indicated that our debt financing cost would be part of the cost of capital). The second is to compute a 'cash' tax rate, incorporating deferred taxes. The first one is easy – we simply eliminate the Interest. The second one is a bit more involved. We have to recalculate our 'book' taxes without Interest. Then, we determine the change, if any, in the deferred taxes on the balance sheet. Combining these two gives the 'cash' taxes paid on Operating Income, in this case, *EBIT*. The 'Level 1' invested capital makes only one adjustment of significance to your definition of 'operating' capital, which is to adjust Cash to a level just sufficient to run the business. This is 2% of revenue. Notice that in FY #3, Growthstar had $11 million in Cash, which was more than the amount needed to run the business. We subtract out the actual balance and add an amount equal to 2% of revenue. In FY #2, the opposite occurs. Here, due to the acquisition, you had a 'negative' cash balance (an 'overdraft') which is adjusted in a similar manner, except that we *add* the negative cash balance, in this case $2 million, and then add approximately $7 million more to provide for 2% of revenue. These two years are illustrative of how the 'books' can overstate and understate the real 'operating' capital in a business".

"At 'Level 1', there are no operating leases. Thus, the cost of capital (CCAP) – the basis for the capital charge against invested capital – is 11.5%. This rate is 0.5% point (50 basis points) *higher* than the CCAP

Exhibit 34	**GROWTHSTAR INC.**				
	Economic Profit				
$ Millions	[Level '1' — "Reported"]				
	..... Historical Period — 3 Years				Current
"TOTAL CO."	FY #3	FY #2	FY #1	3-Yr Avg	FY Fcst.
Income Statement					
Revenue	$220	$325	$380	$308	$450
Total Operating Costs & Expenses	204	302	349	285	408
Other Expense - Reserve	5				
Operating Income (EBIT)	**$11**	**$23**	**$31**	**$23**	**$42**
Interest, Taxes and NOP					
Memo: Interest - net	2	3	4	3	5
"Book" P&L Tax Rate	*36%*	*36%*	*36%*	*36%*	*36%*
"Book" Tax Provision	3	7	9	6	13
Tax "Shield" - Financing / Other	1	1	1	1	2
Deferred Tax	(1)	-	(2)	(1)	(1)
"Cash" Tax — $	3	8	9	7	13
"Cash" Tax — % (Rate)	*26%*	*34%*	*28%*	*28%*	*32%*
Net Operating Profit (NOP)	**$8**	**$15**	**$22**	**$17**	**$28**
Balance Sheet - "Beginning"					
Total Assets	$86	$128	$147	$120	$174
less: Cash	11	(2)	2	4	9
NIBCL's	8	12	14	11	11
plus: Operating Cash (@2%)	4	7	8	6	9
Invested Capital (IC)	**$71**	**$125**	**$139**	**$112**	**$163**
	* CCAP =				
Economic Profit - "EP"	*11.5%*				
NOP	$8	$15	$ 22	$17	$28
CCAP	*(8)*	*(14)*	*(16)*	*(13)*	*(19)*
"EP" (Level '1')	**$0**	**$1**	**$ 6**	**$4**	**$9**
* CCAP *without Operating Leases*					

presented to you three weeks ago for Growthstar, because that rate (11.0%) had the operating leases factored in. We'll see the 11.0% rate when we get to 'Level 2'. The *EP* that results shows a steady progression up from *zero* in FY #3 to an expected $9 million for the current year".

"That's in line with our 'earnings' outlook. A good, solid improvement. It's what I told Jonathan and Ian when we did the *Services* acquisition".

"Keep your shirt on, Jack", Earl D'Mark retorted. "We haven't come to the 'fun part' yet. Wait 'til you see what we do to you in 'Level 2'!"

"Jill has prepared me for a surprise. Some silly notion about reversing our acquisition reserve, which we justified and took to our board and our stockholders, based on the accepted accounting rules in effect when we did this deal".

As Jonathan cast a look at him, Jason then said... "Let's not get ahead of ourselves. We're *not* trying to do 'silly' things and we'll explain all the adjustments in depth".

"Well", Jack retorted, "if you're challenging what everyone was doing with acquisitions, then I think it's silly. We took a 'hit' and earnings have been increasing ever since".

"Any questions on 'Level 1' before we move on?" Jonathan then asked. With no responses, Jason clicked on the next schedule (Exhibit 35).

As the 'Level 2' schedule (Exhibit 35) appeared on the screen, Jack's eyes were instantly riveted on one line under the Income Statement – 'Reserves/Write-offs'. It was as though a magnet had hold of his eyes and he could see nothing else. Just as Jason was about to begin speaking, he bolted out of his chair and shouted... "Why is the acquisition reserve added back to EBIT on this schedule? Why wasn't I consulted on this? And what the *hell* do you think

Exhibit 35 — GROWTHSTAR INC.
Economic Profit

$ Millions — [Level '2' — incl. Oper. Leases, Intangibles, Reserves]

"TOTAL CO."	..... Historical Period — 3 Years				Current
	FY #3	FY #2	FY #1	3-Yr Avg	FY Fcst.
Income Statement					
Revenue	$220	$325	$380	$308	$450
Operating Income (EBIT) - Level '1'	$11	$23	$31	$23	$42
Interest — re: Operating Leases	2	4	4	3	5
Amortization Expense	-	1	1	1	1
Reserves / Write-Offs	5	-	-	-	-
Operating Income (EBITA)	**$18**	**$28**	**$36**	**$28**	**$47**
"Cash" Tax on EBIT — $	*$3*	*$8*	*$9*	*$7*	*$13*
"Book" Tax on O L. Interest — $	*1*	*1*	*2*	*1*	*2*
"Cash" Tax on Amortiz./Reserves — $	*1*	*0*	*0*	*0*	*0*
Total Taxes on EBITA — $	*$5*	*$10*	*$11*	*$8*	*$16*
Net Operating Profit (NOP)	**$13**	**$18**	**$25**	**$19**	**$31**
Balance Sheet - "Beginning"					
IC (Level '1')	$71	$125	$139	$112	$163
plus: Operating Leases - "Capitalized"	19	40	45	35	50
Accumulated Amortization	-	5	6	4	7
Other -					
Invested Capital (IC)	**$90**	**$170**	**$190**	**$150**	**$220**
Economic Profit - "EP"	** CCAP =* *11.0%*				
NOP	$13	$18	$25	$19	$31
CCAP	*(10)*	*(19)*	*(21)*	*(16)*	*(24)*
"EP" (Level '2')	**$3**	**$(1)**	**$4**	**$3**	**$7**
* CCAP with Operating Leases					

you're doing, Aradvizer, arbitrarily reversing an entry that I spent weeks working up, passed by our auditors, reviewed with Jonathan and Ian, and presented to our board of directors and then to a shareholders' meeting. Is this a deliberate attempt to undermine our accounting practises? And, what's your role in this, D'Mark?" Jack's use of surnames underscored his anger.

Jill rolled her eyes, then looked at Frank and Jason, indicating silently what she had said in one of their recent meetings – that Jack would probably 'flip out' when he saw this. She now felt compelled to speak... "Don't you want to see the outcome before 'jumping down Jason's throat'?"

"I know the outcome. It's 'trash' the accounting system and replace it with these 'new economics'. Damn it – I'm fed up with all this! You're going to destroy everything I've worked for over the past twenty years. And what's your part in this, Jill? Didn't you explain the rationale for taking the 'hit' in FY #3 when our earnings were off, based on what the rules allowed us to do, and then get the benefit of the *EPS growth* after that?"

"As a matter of fact, I did mention that point", Jill replied, in a very 'matter of fact' tone.

"So", Jack uttered – his expression approaching ugliness as he looked first at Jason and then at Earl – "you want a fight, huh? I suppose you put him up to this, D'Mark".

Then there was silence.

Jonathan knew this outburst was coming, even if Jason had not mentioned the issue of the acquisition reserve to him in their briefing on Friday. It had to. Jack was so wedded to the accounting treatments that he really believed the stock price would benefit from high *EPS* growth. In fact, it had not. Growthstar's stock price had actually grown less than its revenue and earnings over the past two years, and was only starting to show some 'spunk' recently. Jack believed this (finally) exonerated him, since Ian had been chiding both him and Jonathan until the past few months. To even consider another explanation was unthinkable. Jonathan knew, however, that he had to get beyond this situation if the 'team' was going to make progress and give the *EP* approach a 'fair shake'. Jason had also had similar experiences, although not quite as emotional as this one, and was prepared to counter this 'Jack attack'. He had indicated this to Jonathan, which is why Jonathan had remained silent through the discourse. He had his own plan if Jason could not get the meeting back on track again. Jason knew this, so after another moment of silence, he rose from his chair and looked Jack straight in the eyes and said... "Putting aside the emotions, you've made a challenge to the 'economic' approach to evaluating the performance of a business. Let me ask you a question.

I understand that you were part of a group that ultimately consummated this deal with *Services*. Is that correct?"

"Yes, it is", Jack replied, his voice at a lower volume.

"How did you justify the deal financially?"

"We did the same type of analysis that we do for a capital project".

"What's that?"

"You know darn well what it is, Mr Aradvizer. We do a rigorous financial evaluation on any investment over $250,000 and determine a net present value (supported by an internal rate of return) estimate, which becomes the basis for our offering price. We then test for earnings dilution. Without the write-off, we ran the risk of *EPS dilution* for a few years after we closed the transaction, due to the goodwill".

"But, you made your '*pricing*' decision – that is, what you were willing to *pay* – based on an economic (cash flow) analysis, taking into account appropriate risk and other factors".

"So, where is this taking us, Mr Consultant?" Jack retorted.

"Hopefully, to an understanding of why we're doing what we're doing", Jason answered.

"You're confusing me, but I guess that's one of the things that you consultants do", Jack countered.

Earl D'Mark felt like a chained animal. He wanted to unleash on Jack, but was sensible enough to let Jason 'play out' his approach. He also did not know exactly what to say.

Jason continued… "I hope that by the time we're through working together you'll consider me less confusing, but let's move on. I have just one more question, plus a follow-up. Why is the economic framework (which is what the cash flow/net present value is based on) good for the 'front' side of the deal – that is, the analysis and pricing – but not valid for the 'back' end of the same deal – that is, the performance evaluation? Further, why would you 'price' (up front) any investment or business by using one method (*economics*), but judge its contribution to the company's 'value creation' over time using another approach (*accounting*)? One message I'm trying to get across to you and the others is that we need to be *consistent* at 'both ends' of the spectrum. Another is that there is a greater correlation between 'economic' earnings and stock prices than there is between 'accounting' earnings and stock prices. This is an important part of the rationale for getting companies to implement financial systems that replicate cash flow".

Jack was dumbfounded and could not respond. He placed his head in his hands on the top of the conference table. Jonathan and Earl sat back, not trying to exploit the situation, but realizing that a piece of the finance puzzle that they sort of knew intuitively, but could not put their finger on, had all of a sudden come into focus. *Consistency of approach – how simple and logical, but so often overlooked in the day-to-day 'rat race' of finance, where measures of one sort or another just seemed to 'crop up' out of nowhere.* Dave, Cathy and Jill also leaned back, a look of tranquility on their faces – especially Jill, for whom the pieces of the puzzle had been coming together for the past two weeks.

Jonathan now knew it was his time to speak. "I think we have been given a perspective that compels us to give this economic framework a fair chance. We owe it to ourselves and our shareholders to do this".

"No argument, there", Dave commented. "Could we take a short (say, five-minute) coffee break and then come back and discuss Exhibit 35, which seems as though it's been on the screen for the entire morning?"

After the break, Jack stood up and stated... "As much as I oppose this new approach, I *cannot argue with logic and consistency.* I also know that we can't use accounting numbers alone to justify our evaluations, especially for the *NPV*-based pricing of deals such as *Services.* So, I'm willing to listen. I might even listen to you, Earl".

Jonathan sat back and beamed. It was contagious. He winked at Jason. Just at that moment, Val entered the room. "Did I miss much?" she asked. "I see that everyone is smiling. You must all be agreeing on everything".

"We're starting to come together", Jonathan replied. "You only missed a few details".

Jason, responding to the wink from Jonathan, cracked... "Remember the Exhibit (35) that Dave referred to before the break?" He clicked on it again.

"We begin by adding back the interest portion of the operating lease expense to the EBIT from 'Level 1'. For Growthstar, it's the '10% interest rate' times the 'capitalized value' of the leases – the second row in the 'Balance Sheet – Beginning' section. As an example, in FY #3, the interest portion of the operating lease expense is about $2 million (10% times the $19 million capitalized value of the leases). Next, we add back the amortization and special reserve portion of the acquisition goodwill – two entries for this line". Everyone looked at Jack as Jason made these comments, but Jack motioned with his hands to move on. Everyone sighed.

"The taxes on EBITA are a function of both the 'statutory' and 'effective' tax rates. The 'statutory' rate applies to the operating lease interest, and the 'effective' rate applies to the reserve (write-off) and goodwill amortization. You should note that not all goodwill is tax-affected. If that's the case, then there would be no tax adjustment".

"The invested capital is higher (versus 'Level 1') by the amount of the accumulated goodwill amortization and the capitalized value of the operating leases. *EP* is computed in the same way it was under 'Level 1' – that is, *NOP minus CCAP'*.

"Now, let's look at the difference in the results for *EP* and *ROIC* with the two approaches, along with the impact (on 'Level 2' results) of capitalizing and then amortizing R&D (versus expensing this item)". As he spoke, Jason showed Exhibit 36.

"Looking first at *EP*, we can see that in FY #3, the year the *Services* acquisition was closed, that a 'Level 2' economic profit of $3 million was eliminated due to the impact of the 'write-off' in 'Level 1'. In a similar vein, 'Level 1' *ROIC* is just equal to *CCAP*, which is 11.5%. This is particularly interesting since *Services*, the source of the write-off, wasn't even a part of Growthstar until almost the last day of the fiscal year. Yet, that one transaction affects and distorts the 'real' profitability of the total company for the next two years and even the current year. What this means is that *all the 'Level 1' EPs and ROICs* are 'overstated' in the years after FY #3. The annual *EP* differences of approximately $2 million and annual *ROIC* differences of 2 to 3 percentage points (between the two levels) are significant for a company such as Growthstar. This is one reason why accounting does not link to market valuation – it involves transactions that often bear no resemblance to economic reality".

Earl was beaming now and was not hiding it. Jack had a look of the 'loser' in the Super Bowl – unhappy about not winning, but satisfied to at least be in the arena. Jonathan had a look of contentment, knowing that the issues were being confronted and aired in a 'no

Exhibit 36	**"TOTAL CO."**				
	EP / ROIC Comparisons and R&D Capitalization				
$ Millions	..... Historical Period — 3 Years				Current
	FY #3	**FY #2**	**FY #1**	**3-Yr Avg**	**FY Fcst.**
"EP" Comparison:					
"EP" — Level '2'	$3	$(1)	$4	$3	$7
"EP" — Level '1'	0	1	6	4	9
"EP" Difference	$3	$(2)	$(2)	$(1)	$(2)
"ROIC" Comparison:					
"ROIC" — Level '2'	14.5%	10.9%	13.4%	12.7%	14.3%
"ROIC" — Level '1'	11.5%	12.3%	16.2%	15.0%	17.3%
"ROIC" Difference (% points)	2.9%	-1.4%	-2.8%	-2.4%	-2.9%
R&D Capitalization Impact					
Annual R&D Expense - "Actual"	$12	$16	$19		$22
** Capitalized Value - Cumulative	12	28	47		69
Annual R&D Expense - "Amortized"	4	9	16		23
*** Difference - "Actual" vs. "Amortized"	$8	$7	$3		$(1)
** *Capitalized Value is 'understated' in FY #3 and FY #2, due to 'no' consideration of R&D in prior years. In reality, there would be an amount from the two prior years to capitalize.* *** *Differences in Annual R&D Expenses are 'not significant' in the Current Year – only $(1) million.*					

nonsense' manner, with politics taking a back seat. Jill, Frank, Dave and Cathy also had looks of contentment, but more from the feeling that the major confrontation was over and the group would now focus on the merits of the remaining aspects of this endeavor.

Jack again motioned silently for Jason to continue. Jason picked up the queue and spoke again… "The R&D capitalization does not produce any clear conclusions as to whether capitalizing this item is preferable to sticking with the expensing treatment. To get a complete picture, we would have to go back beyond FY #3, but there's enough here, I believe, to make a judgment. The difference in FY #1 and the Current Year R&D is not that significant, leading me to believe that the *integrity* of our metric will not be diminished by sticking with the treatment that is now in your reporting system, and eliminates the need for additional work and calculations".

"Well, now", Jack mused. "We have finally come to an agreement on at least one issue".

"I can't tell you how delighted I am, Jack, to hear you make that comment", Jonathan interjected. "I happen to agree. This is also the type of item that Ian was cautioning us about in his desire for simplicity in the approach we recommend to him and the officers".

Jason sensed a need to get to a conclusion, so he stood up and said, "We still have one more 'level' to review for the total company, before making a decision on how we're going to structure the *EP metric*". As he spoke, he clicked on Exhibit 37.

"Do you think you could fit a few more numbers on the schedule"? Dave asked, his head shaking from side to side.

"I tried hard, but the printer held me back", Jason responded, sensing the (joking) nature of the question.

"I hope you put some of this material in 'chart form' for the officers", Dave shot back. "You will lose my boss for sure".

"Mine, too", chimed in Cathy.

"Mine, also", added Jonathan. The group broke out laughing with this comment.

"I fully understand", Jason replied. "I've done this a few times before, and I can assure you that we'll have charts. But first, us financial folks have to 'grind through' the numbers, so that there is a basis for the charts. For Growthstar, the only significant 'Level 3' adjustment is for Depreciation – adding back the annual expense to profit and the accumulated amount to invested capital. When we reviewed the 'Comparison' section (near the bottom of the schedule) on Friday, Frank mentioned and Jill confirmed that there was a 'one-time event' in FY #3 related to the *Services* acquisition. This caused a distortion in the FY #3 results. After that, the *EPs* and *ROICs* are not very different".

Exhibit 37	**GROWTHSTAR INC.**				
	Economic Profit				
$ Millions	[Level '3' "Gross" Fixed Assets]				
	..... Historical Period — 3 Years				Current
"TOTAL CO."	__FY #3__	__FY #2__	__FY #1__	__3-Yr Avg__	__FY Fcst.__
Income Statement					
Revenue	$220	$325	$380	$308	$450
Oper. Income (EBITA) - Level '2'	$18	$28	$36	$28	$47
plus: Depreciation Expense	6	3	5	5	6
Operating Income (EBITDA)	**$24**	**$31**	**$41**	**$32**	**$53**
"Cash" Tax on EBITA — $	*5*	*10*	*11*	*8*	*16*
"Cash" Tax on Depreciation — $	*2*	*1*	*1*	*1*	*2*
Total Taxes on EBITDA — $	*7*	*11*	*12*	*9*	*18*
Net Operating Profit (NOP)	**$17**	**$20**	**$29**	**$23**	**$35**
Balance Sheet – 'Beginning'					
IC (Level '2')	$90	$170	$190	$150	$220
plus: Accumulated Depreciation	14	20	23	19	28
plus/ minus: Other -					
Invested Capital (IC)	**$104**	**$190**	**$213**	**$169**	**$248**
	CCAP =				
Economic Profit - "EP"	*11.0%*				
NOP	$17	$20	$29	$23	$35
CCAP	(11)	(21)	(23)	(19)	(27)
"EP" (Level '3')	**$6**	**$(0)**	**$6**	**$4**	**$8**
* *CCAP with Operating Leases*					
"EP" Comparison:					
"EP" — Level '3'	*$6*	*$(0)*	*$6*	*$4*	*$8*
"EP" — Level '2'	*3*	*(1)*	*4*	*3*	*7*
"EP" Difference	*$3*	*$0*	*$2*	*$2*	*$1*
"ROIC" Comparison:					
"ROIC" — Level '3'	*16.6%*	*10.7%*	*13.9%*	*13.6%*	*14.3%*
"ROIC" — Level '2'	*14.5%*	*10.9%*	*13.4%*	*12.7%*	*14.3%*
"ROIC" Difference	*2.2%*	*-0.1%*	*0.4%*	*0.9%*	*-0.1%*

"I recall that", interjected Jonathan.

"Oh, yeah, so do I", added Jack.

"Well, I know how I'm voting on selecting a 'level' for our *EP metric*", Jonathan said.

"Is this a democratic election, or should we fall in behind the leader"? Jill asked, trying to hide a big grin on her face.

"You're always free to state your opinion, Jill. I just can't tell you how much weight it will carry".

Dave caught the mood and stated... "Well, I think we should go to 'Level 4'... or, maybe 'Level 5'... this approach is just too darn simple for me!"

Earl, who had been unusually quiet, joined the conversation by saying... "Why don't we just scrap the financial records entirely and run 'cash flows' – you know, 'cash in and cash out'?"

Jonathan wanted to get to a resolution, so he rose from his chair and said emphatically, "Integrating the analysis and the culture of this company, it appears to me that 'Level 2' is most appropriate for us. Any other opinions?"

Everyone in the room knew (before he said it) that 'Level 2' was the outcome Jonathan favored, and they all knew they would have come to the same conclusion if they were in his position. There just was no compelling reason to 'gross up' the assets, at least not at this time. The over-simplification and distortions with 'Level 1', though, were apparent to everyone – even to Jack, as he had been 'thinking' since the end of the morning's outburst instead of trying to find ways to subvert the process. As a result, there was no need for any discussion and the heads nodded around the table.

Jason had known for about a week or so that the 'team' would arrive at a 'Level 2' approach, and since both he and Jonathan wanted to move on to an analysis of the implications of the historical and current-year *EP* performance, he started speaking again. "We should now begin to focus on the 'meaning' of the historical trend of *EP* and, to a lesser degree, *ROIC*. We can use Exhibit 37 to get an initial perspective for the total company. Then, we'll review the *EP* performance of the two major BUs during the same time period".

Earl could not constrain himself any longer. Today was a major victory for him and he knew he could now speak without fear of a 'Jack attack'. "Jason, if you don't mind, I'd like to offer a few initial comments. Prior to the *Services* acquisition, the company was growing modestly and generating a solid level of profitability, by almost any measure. Notice the positive 'Level 2' *EP* of $3 million and *ROIC* of 14.5% (a decent 'spread' versus our *CCAP* of 11%) in FY #3. Due to the price paid for *Services* and immediate investments into that business (I'm sure we'll see some specifics in a few moments) our performance 'dipped' in (historical) fiscal years #2 and #1. We're expecting to get back to our FY #3 *ROIC* performance this year".

"Those are good observations", Jason interjected, "but let me say that the emphasis should be on the *EP* results. Notice that in the current year, you are estimating that 'Level 2' *EP* will be more that 'double' what it was in FY #3, even though the *ROIC* is about the same. The reason is that the company is getting bigger and more profitable. This should translate into a higher market capitalization, and I believe you are starting to see this happening. Growing the business while maintaining a positive 'spread' of *ROIC versus CCAP* is a formula for value creation. This should start to send a message that the goal is to optimize (some say maximize) economic profit (that is, *EP*) since this measure takes both 'size' and 'return' into account, whereas *ROIC* can be biased toward 'return'. This is why you want to put your primary emphasis on the *EP* metric, with secondary emphasis on *ROIC*".

"Is everyone comfortable with this conclusion?" Jonathan asked. "It has important ramifications for how we evaluate and invest – and, ultimately, manage".

"I like the link to size", Val answered. "It ties our growth plans to a measure of value creation".

Cathy Casher wanted to make sure she understood the impact and responded, "Isn't *EP* a revised 'bottom line'?"

"It definitely is", Earl quipped. "It is *the* 'bottom line' for financial performance evaluation".

"And assuming we implement this approach", Jonathan added, "it will affect the way you and Larry – and everyone in this room – views your business".

"With the total company as a back-drop", Jason interjected, "let's now apply the concepts and review the recent history for the two BUs. First, is *Products* (Exhibit 38)".

"Believe it or not", Jason said, "the process to establish a 'Level 2' *EP* for a BU is similar to that for the total company. FY #3 will be the same as *TOTAL CO.*, since *Products* was the only business during that year. Adding back the interest portion of operating lease expense yields EBITA. Jill has determined (I believe she has consulted with you, Earl) that all of Growthstar's deferred taxes reside with *Products*". Earl nodded in agreement. "The invested capital adds an amount for operating cash plus the capitalized value of the operating leases to the 'operating' capital you have in your existing reporting system".

"This doesn't seem to be too onerous a modification", Jonathan said as he leaned back and studied the schedule. He then looked at Jack and continued... "the operating cash is simply a percent-to-revenue and the operating leases are the present values which we report in the footnotes of the annual report. All we have to do is break them down for the two BUs. And, if we use a 'beginning' balance, the amounts go in once and stay there for the entire year. I don't see a major problem".

Jack nodded his head and replied with, "I guess you're right. It doesn't seem to involve a lot of extra work".

"*Thanks, Jonathan*", Jason said to himself. He then continued out loud with... "The resulting *EP* performance has been a steady pattern of growth until the current year, when the outlook is for about the same level as last year (FY #1). To categorize *Products*, it's a solid **'A'**

Exhibit 38	GROWTHSTAR INC.				
	Economic Profit				
$ Millions	[Level '2' — incl. Oper. Leases, Intangibles, Reserves]				
	..... Historical Period — 3 Years				Current
"PRODUCTS"	FY #3	FY #2	FY #1	3-Yr Avg	FY Fcst.
Income Statement					
Revenue	$220	$250	$280	$250	$300
Total Operating Costs & Expenses	204	230	257	230	273
Interest — Operating Leases	2	2	3	2	3
Operating Income (EBITA)	**$18**	**$23**	**$26**	**$22**	**$30**
"Book" P&L Tax Rate	*36%*	*36%*	*36%*	*36%*	*36%*
"Book" Tax Provision	6	8	9	8	11
Deferred Tax	(1)	-	(2)	(1)	(1)
"Cash" Tax — $	5	8	7	7	10
"Cash" Tax — % (Rate)	*29%*	*36%*	*28%*	*31%*	*32%*
Net Operating Profit (NOP)	**$13**	**$15**	**$19**	**$16**	**$20**
Balance Sheet - "Beginning"					
Operating Capital - 'reported'	$67	$69	$77	$71	$87
plus: Operating Cash	4	5	6	5	6
Operating Leases	19	26	27	24	27
Other -					
Invested Capital (IC)	**$90**	**$100**	**$110**	**$100**	**$120**
Economic Profit - "EP"	CCAP = 11.0%				
NOP	$13	$15	$19	$16	$20
CCAP	*(10)*	*(11)*	*(12)*	*(11)*	*(13)*
"EP" (Level '2')	**$3**	**$4**	**$7**	**$5**	**$7**
"ROIC" (Level '2')	*14.5%*	*14.7%*	*17.1%*	*15.6%*	*16.8%*

with *EP well above CCAP*. I trust you remember our **'A'**, **'B'** and **'C'** types of businesses!"

"I kind of expected this", Jonathan stated. "We've seen the market for *Products* maturing during the past couple of years".

"We're still delivering a good, solid 'bottom line', though", Cathy noted.

"Nobody said you weren't", Val interjected. "It's just that the external environment has slowed down in terms of 'demand' for our products. And, based on the work done so far on the outlook for the next three years, we have a challenge to rapidly grow *Products*".

"Good points", Jonathan the commented, "but I think we should stick with our historical profile for the moment and take a look at *Services*. Jason, if you would, please ..."

Dave perked up in his seat as Jason clicked on the next schedule – the *EP Assessment* for *Services* (Exhibit 39).

As most of the 'team' studied the schedule (Exhibit 39), they also looked at Dave, who didn't even notice the glances, since he was so

Exhibit 39	GROWTHSTAR INC.				
	Economic Profit				
$ Millions	[Level '2' — incl. Oper. Leases, Intangibles, Reserves]				
	..... Historical Period — 3 Years				Current
"SERVICES"	FY #3	FY #2	FY #1	2-Yr Avg	FY Fcst.
Income Statement	"Base"				
Revenue	$50	$75	$100	$88	$150
Total Operating Costs & Expenses		72	92	82	135
Interest — Operating Leases		1	2	2	2
Operating Income (EBITA)		$4	$10	$7	$17
"Book"P&L Tax Rate		*36%*	*36%*	*36%*	*36%*
"Book" Tax Provision		1	4	3	6
Net Operating Profit (NOP)		$3	$6	$5	$11
Balance Sheet - "Beginning"					
Operating Capital - 'reported'		$49	$54	$52	$67
plus: Operating Cash		2	2	2	3
Operating Leases		14	18	16	23
Accumul'd Amortization		5	6	6	7
Invested Capital (IC)		$70	$80	$75	$100
	CCAP =				
Economic Profit - "EP"	*11.0%*				
NOP		$3	$6	$5	$11
CCAP		(8)	(9)	(8)	(11)
"EP" (Level '2')		$(5)	$(3)	$(4)	$(0)
"ROIC" (Level '2')		*4.2%*	*7.6%*	*6.0%*	*11.0%*

intent on analyzing each row of numbers. He moved quickly through revenue, costs and operating income – he could recite the numbers in his sleep and he understood the operating lease adjustment. The tax and *NOP* lines were also no problem. He knew the business was 'profitable' – at least the way he had always defined 'profit'. His eyes then focused on the invested capital (IC) line and the amounts going across the page – $70 million in FY #2, $80 million in FY #1 (last year) and $100 million in the current year. He then scanned the *CCAP* line. These figures were all new to him. He knew that Peter Uppcomer – the person he had to answer to directly – had also never seen anything like this before, and that he (Dave) would have to explain this to Peter. Peter would give 'lip service' to Jason, but would then pull Dave aside for his explanation. It was Dave's explanation that Peter wanted... ultimately. As he then looked across the row entitled '*EP (Level '2')*' a look of alarm was apparent to everyone in the room as he saw that all the numbers were in brackets [ ] – indicating negative values, except for the current year, which was zero. "I'm a bit surprised at these numbers" was all he could utter.

"You shouldn't be", replied Earl. "It's the price of growth via acquisition! We paid $55 million for a business with $35 million of net assets 'on the books'. We also assumed $14 million of operating leases and added another $1 million of cash for operations. So, right 'out of the blocks' we have an investment of $70 million. That's what the shareholders are concerned with, since this is our 'sunk cost' for your business. We need to generate a return on *this level of IC*, plus the investments made during the past two years. As you can see, we haven't done that yet".

Dave then blurted out... "Are you telling me that *Services* is a type '**C**' business – a value 'destroyer'?"

"You bet it is... a big one", Jason shouted, to the shock and amazement of everyone – except Jill and Frank (who Jason had winked at just before making the statement) and Jonathan (who remembered that Jason had said he owed Dave a 'practical joke').

"That's too harsh of a statement", Cathy jumped in. "Perhaps there's something we overlooked".

"We haven't overlooked anything", Frank then stated coldly. Dave was speechless, a rare feeling for him. Frank turned away to hide his big grin.

"Maybe Cathy is right", Dave stammered. "Are you sure there's nothing we missed?"

"Nothing", Frank yelled, almost before Dave had finished his question.

"Seems to me, Dave, that you and Peter have a problem, especially when I report this to Ian", Jonathan then chimed in.

Jack was beginning to sense that something was up, but Earl hadn't caught on yet. In fact, Earl was not pleased with the recent impact of *Services* on the total company's 'economic' performance. He had talked to Jason about this concern after the first 'team' meeting.

Jill couldn't keep a straight face any longer and started laughing. "Oh, Dave, it's finally 'payback time'. Jason said he would get you back and I think he has". Laughter then erupted throughout the room.

Dave smiled and pointed his index finger at Jason, then gave a 'thumbs up' sign, indicating that they were now equal. "You guys had me worried for a moment".

Jonathan then spoke again... in a serious tone... "You (and Peter) should be a bit worried. Perhaps 'worried' is not the correct term. Let's say, 'concerned'. We believe we knew what we were doing when we acquired *Services* and paid a 'premium'. We expected some dilution of our 'economic' returns as we digested the business and got it on a profitable growth track. But, we also want you and Peter to be acutely aware that our investors have entrusted you with a significant amount of their capital, and they expect a return on this money. Right now, at a 'zero' *EP* estimated for the current year, *Services* is value 'neutral' – to use Jason's term. We're betting on your strategy and its results over the next few years to pull this business into the **'A'** category and truly be a 'profitable growth' business for Growthstar".

"That's a mouthful", Dave responded, "but I now understand the challenge".

"That understanding is a key first step", Jonathan replied. "I plan to 'coach' both Ian and Peter on this situation, and how acquisitions often go 'into the red' after the deal is completed, but need to get 'into the black' within a reasonable time period. I believe we have a strategy to do this. One of the things that Jason is going to help us with is 'valuing' the strategy for *Services*. This is very important, since it should be apparent that there isn't any value creation beyond our investment based on the performance to date".

"That message has come across loud and clear", Dave said softly.

"I think we've made some substantive progress this morning", Jonathan then stated. "We've 'come to grips' with the realities of our existing financial system and its shortcomings and have set the stage for what we need to communicate to the officers and Ian. After lunch, Jason is going to take us through an analysis of the key support measures – I think he likes to call them financial 'drivers' – which lie beneath economic profit and return on capital".

"That's correct", Jason said. "We'll establish a set of key support measures and track their performance, in the same way we did for *EP*. We'll then discuss how we tie *EP* and the supporting metrics into a message for Ian and the officers. See you all after lunch".

6

Financial 'drivers': support measures

As the 'team' reassembled after lunch, the mood was 'upbeat'. Even Jack seemed more relaxed, if not enthusiastic. It was almost as though a burden had been lifted from his shoulders – he didn't sense a feeling of criticism from his colleagues; rather, one of satisfaction that he was (apparently) willing to have an 'open mind' and evaluate the 'economic' framework on its merits instead of biases. *"They're not such a bad group, after all"*, he thought to himself. *"I hope they feel the same way about me"*.

Jason wanted to emphasize an important point from the *EP Assessment*, and began with ... "One of the important aspects of any 'value-based' financial system is the focus on *change*; that is, where we have been and where we are going with respect to *EP* and the support measures we are about to discuss. We've done what I think is a credible job in determining how we will construct and calculate the *EP* 'metric' for Growthstar. It may not be perfect, but it certainly is a reasonable approximation of a 'market-based' cash flow measure. I believe it is consistent with our theme of *simplicity with integrity*. So, what we've done is to '*put a stake in the ground*'. We'll measure *EP* changes and evaluate new business investments using the approach we've established. Thus, we will have consistency in 'front-end' analysis and 'back-end' reviews. We will also view the company, its business units and major new investments from the same financial perspective. This should be a major step forward and, ultimately, should enhance the quality of the financial management function".

Jonathan and the others in the room nodded in agreement. Jack gave a very slight forward nod, the first such gesture since the process had begun.

Exhibit 40

Financial "Drivers" ... Support Measures

- **Growth Rates**
- **Invested Capital Intensity**
- **Value Profit Margin**

*These **"drivers"** provide a **foundation** for the Economic Profit and Market Value Added metrics, and give managers a simple, yet powerful, template for value creation. These support measures are also the ones to focus on when evaluating business strategies and major investment programs.*

"Now", Jason continued, "I would like to move into one of the areas that I feel is very meaningful and adds substance to the effort of instilling a 'value-based' mentality. This part of the process establishes an approach to look beneath the aggregate metric *(EP)* in order to get at underlying causes and explanations for movements, trends or patterns". As he was finishing this sentence, he clicked on Exhibit 40.

"These three 'drivers' work for all the major value measurement approaches. So, whether you're at Level '1', '2', or '3', you can 'saddle up' and take a ride through these 'surrogates' which lie beneath the aggregate value metrics. The first set of 'drivers' – *Growth Rate Indicators* – establish the relationship of revenue, operating income and invested capital growth. They provide an initial input to the 'value equation'".

As he spoke, Jason went to the flip chart and wrote:

Growth Rates ...

'Relationship' of Revenue, Operating Profit and Invested Capital ... Compound Growth Rates (CGRs)

"The first one is revenue growth. Many businesses characterized by relatively small size (for their market) or high degree of operating leverage must increase the 'top line' to achieve any meaningful value enhancement. But how much growth is optimal and what level of investment is involved? What is the best mix of internal versus external (acquisition) growth?"

"The second key factor is operating profit growth, a primary and very visible value determinant. For Growthstar, we start with 'pre-tax' operating income which (under our 'Level 2' framework) we have defined as earnings before interest, taxes and amortization (*EBITA*). Since the company derives after-tax (net) operating profit for the BUs, we will focus on *NOP*. A business can increase operating profit in different ways, ranging from massive cost cutting to explosive sales growth. Such dramatically different strategies might achieve the same profit growth for a period of time, with potentially different long-term shareholder value impact. We'll cover this issue later – when we perform business unit strategy valuations as part of the corporate financial analysis".

"Therefore, the initial 'growth drivers' are revenue and net operating profit. Their comparative rates of growth are important as they begin to raise questions about sales volume, pricing and cost structure – past, present and future. You really can't go very far with value-based planning and performance evaluation until you know how much operating profit will result from the next dollar of revenue".

"Next, we get to one of my favorites – invested capital (asset) growth. As we've discussed, the element most often overlooked in traditional (earnings-oriented) measures is invested capital, which we labored with this morning. There are two important analytic aspects of invested capital. The first is its growth rate. The relationship of 'asset' to 'revenue and profit' growth provides an initial clue to the investment strategy of a business. Have earnings and returns been temporarily 'pumped up' by holding back on capital investment, or has capital spending been growing at a rate in excess of revenue/profit? If the latter pattern exists, the question of a 'pay-off' for this investment arises. I believe we saw a case of this just before lunch".

Everyone looked at Dave and snickered, who smiled back and said, "I thought, Jason, that we would leave it at being 'even' – not that you would go 'one up' on me".

"I wasn't planning on it", Jason responded, "but this one was too good to pass up. I'm sure you'll get even again before this engagement is over".

"I'll be trying to", Dave replied.

"The essential message, at this point", Jason continued, "is that growth of any one element has to be looked at in light of the other indicators. Strong revenue growth does not guarantee value creation. As we have seen, earnings growth (alone) is a poor predictor of stock price movements". Jack winced, but remained silent. "These three growth indicators work together and must be understood in terms of how they impact and relate to each other. They establish a foundation for relating the income statement to the balance sheet and provide a concise, initial expression of strategy implications".

"The second perspective on capital – and one of the more useful tools in financial analysis and planning – is the ratio of invested capital to revenue. This indicator tells how much capital is required (or expected) to generate one dollar (or other currency unit) of revenue. *Invested Capital Intensity* (*ICI*) is the inverse of the 'turnover' ratio".

Again as he was speaking, Jason went to the flip chart and wrote:

Invested Capital Intensity (ICI) ...

How much Capital to generate one dollar ($1.00) of Revenue ... in total or incremental ... encompasses working and fixed capital

"One application is to compare business units of different size on a standard basis. We'll do this for *Products* and *Services*. Another is to provide a tool to estimate capital needs for new business ventures, acquisitions, and other corporate development programs. We'll do this as we progress to future-oriented plans and programs. *ICI* is also an input to the *Value Profit Margin*, which I will present momentarily".

"As we have seen, businesses growing by acquisition need to consider goodwill and intangibles, in addition to the traditional 'hard' assets, since they can have investment implications in terms of 'sunk costs' ".

"They can also have credit rating and financing cost implications", Earl chimed in.

"Thank you for that incredibly valuable insight", Jack quipped. The 'duel' was not, apparently, completely over.

Earl smiled and shot back, "I'll make certain to keep you apprised of other insights!"

While Jonathan wanted to keep moving ahead, he knew he had to allow this 'bantering' to go on. He, therefore, just winked at Jason, indicating that Jason should not try to interrupt the 'give and take' – especially since the atmosphere was now more cordial.

Sensing that Jack and Earl were done, at least for the moment, Jason forged ahead ... "Obtaining credible *ICI* indicators involves detailed analysis. One important element of the analysis is to determine if investments move in a 'trend line' versus a 'step' (or some other) function. Further, a given investment category (such as inventory or plant machinery) may exhibit different patterns as the business moves along a growth curve (or alternatively, as it contracts). The insights derived from this type of analysis are helpful in assessing the financial impact of a past or anticipated action".

"Having highlighted growth and balance sheet 'drivers', we're getting to the heart of the operating factors with the greatest impact on value creation. Now, we need to bring it together, and provide an 'earnings performance' measure linked to value creation. If operating managers are going to have a profit target, let's give them one that correlates to value. There is a pre- and post-tax profit margin that, for any business, is a minimum requirement for the creation of shareholder value".

Jason went to the flip chart for a third time and wrote:

Value Profit Margin (VPM) ...

Minimum Profit Margin to create value for shareholders (owners)

Jack, who had experienced a momentary lapse of concentration, was suddenly 'brought back' by the words *'earnings performance'*. "Is this for real?" he asked. "You're now talking *my* language, which is something new in this endeavor".

Jonathan, who had been silent for a long time (at least in his mind) then said, "I think it would be best if *you* be the judge of this, Jack, and tell us if *you* think that this element is 'for real'".

"OK, chief, I get the message. I'll make sure I listen very attentively to this material".

"I will also pay attention", Dave interjected. "Peter is definitely going to be interested in any metric which is 'earnings' oriented".

"So will 'bottom-line' Larry", chuckled Cathy, enjoying the chance to exhibit humor.

"Now that you all know 'how great' this earnings measure is, it might make sense to explain 'what' it is", Jason stated. "The *Value Profit Margin* (*VPM*™) is derived by integrating invested capital intensity (*ICI*), cost of capital (*CCAP*), and the 'cash' tax rate. The next exhibit (41) outlines some of the key features of the *VPM*".

"We can refer back to Company '**A**' in the 'Economic Profit' Example (Exhibit 7) to illustrate the derivation of the *Value Profit Margin*. Exhibit 42 will do this for us".

"Multiplying *ICI* by the cost of capital and then dividing by 'one minus the cash tax rate' produces an operating income (in our case, *EBITA*) margin that will sustain the value of the business. On an after-tax basis, multiplying *ICI* by *CCAP* calculates the Value Profit Margin on a Net Operating Profit basis. Margins above the *VPM* will increase value, while margins below this level are destructive. Why? Because margins above *VPM* 'beat' *CCAP*, while those below *VPM* do not cover the cost for the capital employed in the business. Profit margins at the *VPM* level maintain the current level of shareholder value".

VPM™ is a trademark of Vanguard Partners.

Exhibit 41

Value Profit Margin (*VPM*™)

- **What is it?**
  - ◆ A 'minimum' profit margin ... in essence, a beginning point for value creation
  - ◆ A pre and/or post tax financial performance benchmark

- **Why use it?**
  - ◆ Allows for profitability comparisons for businesses of different size
  - ◆ Simple to calculate and easy to communicate ... especially to operating managers
  - ◆ Provides managers with a threshold ... generating a positive 'spread' creates shareholder value
  - ◆ Effective for planning ... strategies, acquisitions, major investments
  - ◆ ...And, provides an 'earnings' measure linked to value creation.

VPM™ is a trademark of Vanguard Partners

Exhibit 42

Value Profit Margin (*VPM*™) ... *continued*

- **How is it calculated?**
  - ◆ *Pre Tax Basis* — multiply *'ICI'* by *'CCAP'* ... then, divide by *'one minus the effective tax rate'*
  - ◆ *After Tax Basis* — multiply *'ICI'* by *'CCAP'*

- **Example — assume Co. 'A':**
  Revenue (Sales) = $1,000, IC = $600 [ICI = $.60]
  CCAP = 12%, and the effective tax rate = 30%
  - ◆ **VPM** — *Pre Tax Basis*
    0.60 × 12% = 7.2% / 70% = **10.3%**

  - ◆ **VPM — *After Tax Basis***
    0.60 × 12% = **7.2%** ... vs. Actual NOP = 10.0%

VPM™ is a trademark of Vanguard Partners

"Invested capital intensity has been discussed. Cost of capital is the weighted (or blended) cost of debt and equity, the basis for the capital charge in the *Economic Profit* measures. 'Cash' tax rates incorporate deferrals and, as we have noted, may differ from accounting ('book') provisions. As we have also noted, the analysis involved in calculating these capital cost and tax rates are a normal part of any 'value-based' approach to the performance evaluation of a business or company".

"One useful application of the *VPM* is to evaluate new (incremental) business. We will be doing this once we complete our historical analysis and move into the evaluation of the company's strategies and growth plans. This type of analysis enables us to cycle back to the growth indicators and invested capital intensity (*ICI*) to begin perceiving the 'value impact' of growth. Breaking down a business into its 'no growth' and 'growth' components can produce some powerful (perhaps, startling) insights. I think you will enjoy this".

"I know I will", Val said. As she spoke, she looked at Earl and Frank, who nodded – indicating they were looking forward to this phase of the process.

"I *hope* I can enjoy this", Dave quipped.

"I hope so, too", Jonathan snapped back.

Jason continued ... "We will begin by taking the relevant base points from our historical and current year assessments. Analyzing the factors presented herein can produce initial judgments as to *why* historical business growth has had a value-creating, destructive, or neutral effect, by comparing actual margin(s) to *VPM(s)*. The same can be done for operating and strategic plans, plus acquisitions and internal growth programs".

"Taken together, these financial 'drivers' represent important 'building blocks' of value-based performance. Further, due to their relative simplicity, they enable the effective implementation of value management by expressing key ingredients of value-based performance in terms that most people can easily understand. They can also serve as ingredients to incentive compensation plans, since they support the aggregate metric(s). This 'template' can, thus, be a foundation for 'driving' shareholder value into this (or any other) organization, and should be a part of the overall system".

"Let's now look at your company, in total and by BU. Since we have *Services* fresh in our minds, I'd like to start with this business".

"Is this going to be more 'Dave bashing' and, assuming so, how bad will it be?" asked the finance director of *Services*.

"It may not be as bad as you might think, Dave", answered Jason. "Let's analyze the 'drivers' in Exhibit 43".

"*Services* reflects the 'reported' revenue plus the 'restated' (to an 'economic' basis) *NOP* and invested capital, as presented this morning. Since *Services* has only two years of actual results plus the current year outlook, we'll have to analyze the growth indicators using year-to-year comparisons. *Services*' growth indicators are strong and, more importantly, are reflecting the most desirable pattern".

Several puzzled looks, one of them Jonathan's, accompanied this statement.

Exhibit 43	GROWTHSTAR INC.				
	BU Financials				
	[Restated to an 'Economic' Basis]				
	.... Historical Period — 3 Years				Current
"SERVICES"	**FY #3**	**FY #2**	**FY #1**	**2-Yr Avg**	**Yr. Fcst.**
Growth Indicators					
Revenue	----	----	33%	----	50%
NOP	----	----	100%	----	83%
Invested Capital	----	----	14%	----	25%
Invested Capital Intensity					
("ICI")	----	$0.93	$0.80	$0.86	$0.67
Value Profit Margin ("VPM")					
Actual NOP Margin (%)	----	4.0%	6.0%	5.1%	7.3%
Value Profit Margin ("VPM")	----	10.3%	8.8%	9.4%	7.3%
"Spread" - Actual NOP %					
versus VPM	----	–6.3%	–2.8%	–4.3%	0.0%

"I see the 'strength', but please help me with the 'desirable pattern' part of this", Jonathan interjected.

"You must have been reading my mind", Dave added. "I like the words, but I can't visualize the message from what's on this schedule".

"Maybe a picture would help", Jason replied. As he spoke, he clicked on a graph (Exhibit 44).

"Aha", uttered Jonathan.

"I get it", Dave exclaimed. "You want the 'gray' middle bar *(NOP)* to have the highest growth rate, followed by Revenue (the 'white' bar on the left). That leaves Invested Capital (the 'black' bar on the right) with the lowest rate of growth".

"But do you know *why* this pattern is the most desirable one over time?" asked Earl. Everyone, including Jason, looked at Earl as if to query him with "*how would you know why?*" They didn't realize that Earl had read about this concept in one of Jason's published articles. After a moment of bewilderment, Jason then remembered that he had given Earl a package of reading material after the first meeting with the officers. Earl repeated the question ... "Do you know *why* this pattern is the most desirable over time?"

"No", Dave stammered, "do you?"

"I think so", Earl replied. "May I offer an explanation?" As he was speaking, he cast a look at Jason, requesting permission to continue.

"Be my guest", Jason responded.

"Think about the 'cash flow' implications of this pattern over the long term". Earl's 'juices' were really flowing, since he cherished any opportunity to display his knowledge of subjects in corporate finance. "If *NOP* grows faster than revenue, then profit margin should increase. If revenue grows faster than invested capital, then *ICI*

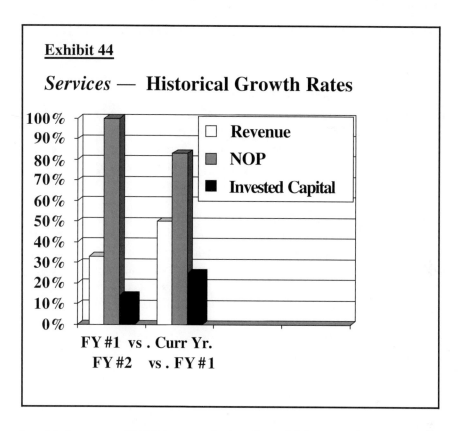

Exhibit 44

Services — **Historical Growth Rates**

should decrease. If *NOP* grows faster than *IC* (invested capital), then *NOP* should increase by more than *CCAP*. If *NOP* exceeds *CCAP* and is increasing at a higher rate, then *EP* should grow. When *EP* grows, additional shareholder value is created".

Applause erupted, even a little from Jack, similar to when Frank gave the explanation on adding back the interest portion of annual operating lease (rent) expense.

"I'm impressed", Jonathan stated. "You must be reading more than you've let on to me".

Earl looked at Jason and winked. "I've been exposed to some good source material" was all that he said. Val picked up Earl's wink to Jason and smiled slightly, feeling that the stage was being set for some robust financial evaluation of the business unit strategies.

Jason knew he had to pick up the discussion at this point, so he said, "Look at the *ICI* row of numbers that are underlined in the middle of Exhibit 43. It should be evident that, after the adjustment for all the goodwill associated with the acquisition, invested capital intensity has been decreasing during the past two years. This means that less capital is required on an 'operating' basis to sustain and grow the *Services* business".

Dave had learned enough to realize this was a good trend, so his look of confidence reappeared. The others nodded, indicating that they understood the 'message' regarding *ICI* from the row of numbers in Exhibit 43.

"The result on the Value Profit Margin *(VPM)* and the 'spread' versus the actual *NOP* margin is shown in the last three rows of Exhibit 43. As you can see, the trend is good, even if the absolute numbers are not".

Dave leaned forward with his hands on the top of the conference table and his fingers pointing upward as a 'steeple', a sign of confidence. A broad smile covered his face, which was noticed by everyone.

Jonathan then said, "While the trend is favorable and *Services* is moving in the right direction, at least financially, let us *not* forget that we are just getting to a type '**B**' business category, which is 'value neutral'. We need to assess the strategy for *Services* to determine if the outlook over the next few years justifies the price that we paid for the acquisition. As we sit here now, with the 'economic' performance that we expect for the current year, we essentially 'got what we paid for'. Obviously, we want to do better and demonstrate that this business has the potential for shareholder value creation".

Dave's smile disappeared, but the look of seriousness was also one that reflected an understanding of where *Services* had come from and where it had progressed. He also knew that planning under the proposed 'economic' framework would be different from what it had been in the past. It would more demanding and would require thoughtful analysis and a blending of strategic actions and financial implications. The days of simple 'trend line' analysis were over.

Val nodded approvingly, because developing a value-creating strategy was one of her key objectives for this year and an effort she was in the midst of, along with the management of *Services*.

"Are there any other questions regarding the financial 'drivers' for *Services*?" Jonathan then asked the group.

Cathy leaned forward and asked, "If we are going to grow by acquisition, should we assume that negative *VPM* 'spreads' will occur?"

"That's a common occurrence", Jason responded, "but the *magnitude and duration* of such an indicator is dependent on factors such as the amount of goodwill plus the inherent *ICI* and profit margin of the business acquired, to name just a couple".

Jonathan looked around the room again and asked, "Any other questions?" With no response from the group, he motioned to Jason to continue.

"I would now like to review the same set of 'drivers' for *Products*, which portray a somewhat different situation". As Jason spoke, he clicked on Exhibit 45.

Exhibit 45	**GROWTHSTAR INC.**				
	BU Financials				
	[Restated to an 'Economic' Basis]				
	.... Historical Period — 3 Years				**Current**
"PRODUCTS"	**FY #3**	**FY #2**	**FY #1**		**Yr. Fcst**
Growth Indicators				**2-Yr CGR**	
Revenue	----	*14%*	*12%*	*13%*	*7%*
NOP	----	*15%*	*27%*	*21%*	*5%*
Invested Capital	----	*11%*	*10%*	*11%*	*9%*
				3-Yr Avg	
Invested Capital Intensity *("ICI")*	*$0.41*	*$0.40*	*$0.39*	*$0.40*	*$0.40*
Value Profit Margin ("VPM")				**3-Yr Avg**	
Actual NOP Margin (%)	*5.9%*	*6.0%*	*6.8%*	*6.3%*	*6.7%*
Value Profit Margin ("VPM")	*4.5%*	*4.4%*	*4.3%*	*4.4%*	*4.4%*
"Spread" - Actual NOP % versus VPM	*1.4%*	*1.6%*	*2.5%*	*1.9%*	*2.3%*

"Notice that the growth of revenue and profit is fairly stable for the historical years, but is slowing down in the current year. Further, *NOP* increased at a higher rate historically, but the pattern is changing in the current year. Invested capital, which grew at the lowest rate during the historical years, is projected to grow faster than both revenue and *NOP* in the current year. Finally, *all* growth rates are below 10% – a reduction versus the past".

All eyes were now on Cathy. "You're not going to start 'picking on me', are you?" she asked sheepishly. "Maybe we should go back to the 'old ways' of doing things".

Jonathan responded with, "Everyone has to put their feet to the fire. Jason, can we see a 'picture' of the growth indicators for *Products*, similar to what we saw for *Services*?"

"I thought you might want this", Jason replied, as he clicked on Exhibit 46.

"This is quite a change in the current year", Earl exclaimed. "Let's take the logic trail I laid out a few moments ago and apply it to the current year for *Products*. If *NOP* grows slower than revenue, then profit margin should decrease (which has occurred, albeit very slightly). If revenue grows slower than invested capital, then *ICI* should increase (which it has, if only slightly). If *NOP* grows slower than *IC* (invested capital), then *NOP* should increase by less than *CCAP*, causing *EP* growth to slow down or cease. When *EP* growth slows or stops, less shareholder value is created. Referring back to this morning's analysis (Exhibit 38) the 'Level 2' *EP* for the current year is projected to be the same ($7 million) as the *EP* for last year (FY #1). *Products* generated two years (FY #2 and #1) of stellar

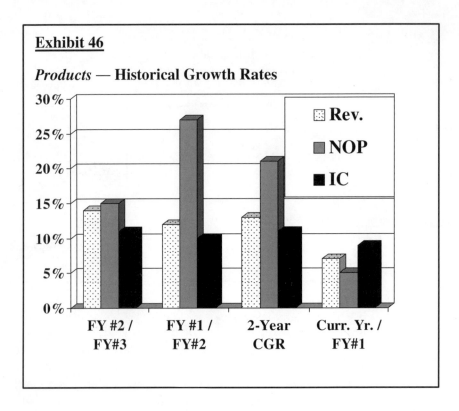

Exhibit 46

Products — **Historical Growth Rates**

performance, but has reached a 'plateau' based on the current year forecast".

"That's an interesting observation", Jonathan said as he sat back and folded his arms, a gesture he made when he was in a very serious situation or troubled by something. "I hope it's not ominous".

Val then entered the conversation. "We've been anticipating a slow-down in *Products* for some time now. The indicators that we monitor have been signaling some 'softness' in a couple of the key market segments. This trend should improve somewhat next year, but not much. So, we are faced with a maturing market for *Products*, based on our current line of product offerings".

Cathy chimed in with "Our strategy is to market more technolog-ically advanced products to penetrate one or more new segments, in order to grow faster than the current market segments where we participate. We have one major new product close to completion and it will be rolled out next year. Others are in the 'pipeline'".

Val came back with "I'm aware of that, since I'm involved with the strategy. It's going to be interesting to see the 'growth relationships' of this strategy – for *all three elements*".

As much as he wanted to pursue all relevant aspects of the discus-sion, Jason also wanted to complete the historical profile of the financial 'drivers' for *Products*. "*ICI*, as indicated by the underlined row of numbers in the middle of Exhibit 45, has been fairly stable in the '*$0.40 range*'. Thus, it takes about forty cents of invested capital to generate one dollar of revenue for *Products*. As Val implied, we will want to see what the strategy will require in terms of new capital to support the revenue growth you just mentioned, Cathy".

"I'm taking notes", Cathy replied, "since I don't have a clue as to the invested capital requirements". She looked at Jack and shrugged her shoulders as she spoke, causing Jack to slump down slightly in his chair.

"I'm privy to the pricing and cost assumptions", Val interjected, "which seem to be predicting that we can maintain (but probably not increase) our current margins, but I haven't heard any mention yet of the capital required to carry out the plans for *Products*".

"You will now", Earl stated triumphantly.

While he appreciated his enthusiasm, Jason didn't want Earl to get too carried away, so he quickly began speaking again ... "The *VPM* and 'spread' versus the actual *NOP* margin also shows an interesting pattern, if we can all look at the bottom of Exhibit 45. The 'spread' increased in each of the historical years. In the current year, we still have a solid 'spread' of 2.3 percentage points, but it's expected to be down slightly versus last year (FY #1). If what Val and Cathy are saying (about profit margins remaining at their current level) turns out to be true, then the *ICI and revenue growth* will be critical factors in terms of the shareholder value impact of the strategy. Are you beginning to see how these support measures, in conjunction with *EP*, can be used to discuss the business in financial terms and develop a 'value-based' assessment?"

Heads nodded.

"Now", Jason continued, "let's look at the total company in the same format". He clicked on Exhibit 47.

The 'message' was starting to take hold. Jason felt that by taking the 'team' through the BUs first, and then reviewing the total company, a shareholder value 'story' would start to unfold. The 'experience' would not be complete until Market Value Added (*MVA*), the 'Magnifier' concept, strategy valuations, free cash flow analysis, plus the internal and external investment program evaluations were incorporated, but a story was starting to take form. More importantly, the 'team' was starting to grasp it. He could sense it as he looked around the conference table and saw expressions that had changed from ones of puzzlement to comprehension. "*This process really works*", Jason thought to himself.

Frank was the first to speak about the *TOTAL CO.* results in Exhibit 47. "Contrary to what many people around here thought, the

Exhibit 47		**GROWTHSTAR INC.**				
		Total Company Financials				
		[Restated to an "Economic" Basis]				
		... Historical Period — 3 Years ...				**Current**
"TOTAL CO."		**FY #3**	**FY #2**	**FY #1**		**Yr. Fcst.**
Growth Indicators					**2-Yr. CGR**	
Revenue		----	48%	17%	*31%*	*18%*
NOP		----	38%	39%	*39%*	*24%*
Invested Capital		----	89%	12%	*45%*	*16%*
					3-Yr. Avg.	
Invested Capital Intensity						
("ICI")		*$0.41*	*$0.52*	*$0.50*	*$0.49*	*$0.49*
Value Profit Margin ("VPM")					**3-Yr. Avg.**	
Actual NOP Margin (%)		5.9%	5.5%	6.6%	*6.1%*	*6.9%*
Value Profit Margin ("VPM")		4.5%	5.8%	5.5%	*5.3%*	*5.4%*
"Spread" – Actual NOP %						
versus VPM		*1.4%*	*–0.2%*	*1.1%*	*0.7%*	*1.5%*

Services acquisition added more to invested capital than anything else during the two most recent historical years". Jack leaned forward and Jonathan sat back with his arms folded, but neither said anything. "This is not necessarily bad, it's simply a fact. It's the price of an acquisition".

Jill had been quiet for most of the meeting, but now felt compelled to speak. "I must echo that comment. In one of the sessions we had in preparation for this meeting, I made a point of how we felt we were buying a business with a lower fixed capital content than we had with *Products*. Jason, to my dismay at that time, pointed out that we actually increased our total capital intensity when we factored in all the 'economic' investments that we incurred with this deal. I agree with Frank that this is not bad, but it casts a completely different light on acquisitions and on what we perceive as 'performance'. Look at the numbers ... our revenue and *NOP* have grown at compound rates of 31% and 39%, respectively, over the most recent two-year period, putting us in a 'star' category for growth in a traditional sense. But, look at the growth in *IC*. At a 45% compound growth rate during the past two years, it far outpaces our growth in revenue and earnings. We never even thought of this before accessing the 'economic' model. Our capital intensity, which is the real issue when analyzing the balance sheet, has increased from forty-one cents for each dollar of revenue to around fifty cents, due to the price we paid and the goodwill we incurred for *Services*. If you think about this in 'relative' terms, it's a 25% increase (say, ten cents on forty cents). That, I believe, is significant! Looking at the *VPMs* and the 'spreads', we took a 'hit' for the two years following the acquisition and are now back at where we were in FY #3, with a positive 1.5 percentage point 'spread'. But, look at FY #2, when we went 'into the red' (at −0.2%). I guess my feeling is that, having been educated and spending my entire career in the 'accounting' side of corporate life, there is a perspective that the 'accounting' model doesn't capture. I could never have articulated this 'story' without adopting the concepts that we have been discussing during the past few weeks. So, while we need the 'GAAP' rules and discipline to 'report' our financial performance in a way that the world supposedly understands, I believe we also need this 'economic' framework to complete the task of measuring the value delivered to our shareholders".

Jason clicked on Exhibit 48, a graphic portrayal of the growth indicators in Exhibit 47, but it was an anti-climatic event to the message that Jill had just delivered.

"I think the 'message' is clear", stated Jonathan. "I have been truly affected by the comments that all of you have made today. Growthstar is, I believe, moving in the right direction, at least from a

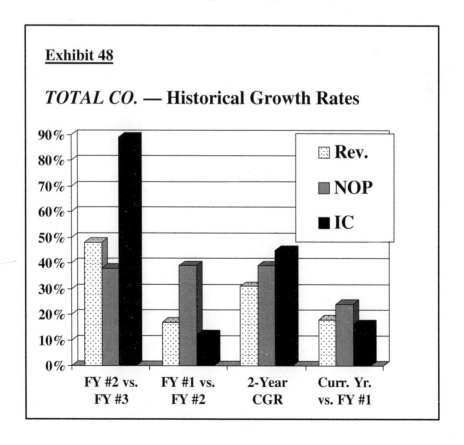

Exhibit 48

TOTAL CO. — **Historical Growth Rates**

Legend: Rev., NOP, IC

X-axis categories: FY #2 vs. FY #3, FY #1 vs. FY #2, 2-Year CGR, Curr. Yr. vs. FY #1 financial perspective, even though we have had a few 'bumps' along the way. I am encouraged by the shape of the bars (in Exhibit 48) for the current year. If I match the bars on the graph for the current year to the numbers in the table (Exhibit 47) we have year-to-year growth rates of 18% for revenue, 24% for *NOP*, and 16% for invested capital. That's the 'most desirable' pattern over the long term and the amounts are respectable. I, too, want to see the results of the BU strategy valuations".

The impact of Jonathan's words permeated the room. Jason sighed a bit, feeling that the first stage of the process had proven itself worthy. There was still a long way to go, but he felt good that there was 'buy-in' from the group and that the 'tale' was starting to take form. He followed up on Jonathan's comments with ... "I believe the financial 'drivers' help us to focus on key elements of the financial structure of the company and the BUs. As we will see in a while, the *VPM* technique will enable us to build an alternative valuation methodology with a link to the Economic Profit *(EP)* and Free Cash Flow *(FCF)* approaches".

"This I want to see", exclaimed Val.

Even Jack's curiosity was evident. "You may have a chance, Jason, if you can build a valuation methodology based on an 'earnings' formula".

Jonathan smiled and leaned forward, remembering his first conversation with Jason and the recent meeting with Ian, in which Jason had alluded to this subject.

"Stay tuned folks, the best is yet to come", Jason replied. "And, before we adjourn, I want to mention that the financial 'drivers' can lead to and spawn a host of more detailed support measures, many of which you are familiar with. As an example, P&L ratios such as gross margins and various expense ratios, and working capital ratios such as inventory turnover and days outstanding for accounts receivable are known to most people, especially those in finance. We can look at the 'intensity' of fixed capital alone and, now, we can do the same for operating leases and/or intangibles. It might be interesting, for instance, to compute how much goodwill – on a 'cents per sales dollar' basis – is incurred for the revenue stream purchased in a 'technology' acquisition. So, the list can go on and on. The 'template' we have established today helps to prioritize the effort of digging into the details of a business to determine the underlying causes of either an absolute level of performance, or a change in financial results. The unique aspect of this approach is that it pursues the '*drivers of shareholder value*'".

After looking around the room to ensure that there was no additional commentary from anyone on the 'team', Jonathan spoke again.

"I'm going to schedule a meeting with the officers either at the end of this week or the beginning of next week, depending on the schedules of the people involved. I've had Kay do some initial checking with Mary Frightly and the assistants to Larry Buildermann and Peter Uppcomer, so I know that one of these times will work. I'll let you know – Val, Jack and Earl – when I get a firm date and time".

"Do it in the morning, if possible", suggested Earl. "We want them 'fresh'".

"Amen", added Val.

"I'll try", Jonathan concluded, as he rose and walked out of the room, followed by the others.

## 7

Market value added (MVA): 'magnifier' concept

The next day arrived with Jason reviewing the highlights of the previous day's session and starting to prepare for the upcoming meeting with the officers. As he and Jonathan had walked back to their offices, Jason had mentioned that it would be advisable to spend about thirty minutes with the 'team' prior to the meeting with Ian and the officers. At that time, he would provide them with the conceptual underpinning for Market Value Added (*MVA*) and how it progresses from Economic Profit (*EP*). Jason and Jonathan agreed that it would be beneficial to take the '**A**', '**B**', '**C**' example to the next step with the 'team' and have them versed in the basic elements of *MVA* before exposing it to the officers. This preparation would be particularly useful for Cathy and Dave, in case Larry or Peter had questions.

The telephone then rang. It was Kay Hoppins, Jonathan's administrative assistant. She was calling to inform Jason that the meeting would be next Tuesday morning, a week from today. The 'team' would meet at 8:00 am and the officers would join them at 8:30.

The agenda for the meeting would be a review of *EP* and the Financial 'Drivers' and then the concept and application of *MVA*. The week went by quickly, and Jason finished his preparation on Friday.

On Tuesday, as the finance team was getting settled for the day's session, Jonathan began speaking... "Today should be an important one for us in our attempt to give the value-based financial performance concept a fair hearing with our officer group. Jason wanted to give you an exposure to the underpinning for the concept and application of 'Market Value Added' – known as *MVA* – in preparation for the meeting with Ian and the officers. I agreed that we should do this, which is why we're meeting in advance of the main session today. So, Jason, can you get us started, please".

"We need to refer back to one of our basic definitions", Jason began. "Market Value Added – or *MVA* – is essentially the same as enhancing shareholder value. What I want to show you is how we measure it in a very simplistic sense. As we progress through the day, we'll show Ian and the officers a graphic example of how *EP* is, literally, 'magnified' into *MVA*, based on the category ('**A**', '**B**' or '**C**') that a business falls into and its anticipated growth rate. Let's start with the definition of *MVA*. The first exhibit we showed the officers, at our initial meeting with them, gave a definition of 'shareholder value'. Since this definition applies to *MVA*, I'm going to begin with it". Jason then clicked on Exhibit 49 (a duplicate of Exhibit 1).

"Larry gave me his hand-outs from that meeting, so I remember this chart", Cathy said.

"Peter didn't give me his, so I don't remember", Dave quipped.

"But", Earl interjected, "you received your own copy, because I had Kay distribute all the hand-outs provided to the officers".

"Oh", Dave said very quietly. "That must be that envelope that's been (unopened) on my worktable for a while".

"Like almost a month", Earl retorted.

"OK, I apologize", Dave responded.

"I guess I should do the same", Cathy said, "because I don't remember seeing my copy".

Jonathan then interrupted with … "We'll forgive the 'lapse' – let's move on, since our main audience will be here shortly. Are there any questions with this definition?" Heads moved from side to side,

---

Exhibit 49

Shareholder Value is a measurement of the change in value
of the firm's investment over a period of time ....
as determined by the financial markets.

For a Business Unit, the relevant issue is its "contribution"
to the company's value (or common stock price).

indicating 'no questions'. "*MVA* will be the ultimate measurement of value 'created' or 'destroyed' by a business. Jason, please continue".

Jason picked up the dialogue ... "Shareholder value is all about determining what management has done, or is expected to do, with the capital they have been entrusted. One of our important objectives is to do exactly that – measure the 'value impact' of our past and present financial performance, along with our strategies and future investment programs. We've taken the first step with *EP* and the Financial 'Drivers' we reviewed last week. Now, we're going to take these indicators to the next level. To do this, I'm going to refer back to the '*EP* Example' for the '**A**', '**B**' and '**C**' companies, which you're all now familiar with". He showed Exhibit 50 as he was speaking.

"This is a duplicate of Exhibit 7", Jason noted, "which we covered in our first session on transitioning from 'accounting' to 'economics'".

"I feel as though it has been etched in my brain forever", snapped Dave.

"Maybe that's good" ! Jonathan shot back. "I want you to be thinking in terms of *EP*, especially as you 'load up' my balance sheet with goodwill and operating leases".

Jack turned the other way and Dave could only muster a slight grimace.

Jonathan nodded at Jason, who continued ... "The *EP* status of a business positions it as a value 'creator' or 'destroyer' – or, as with **Co. 'B'**, being value 'neutral'. This has major implications for what

---

Exhibit 50

"Economic Profit" - Example

"Base Period"	CO. 'A'	CO. 'B'	CO. 'C'
Revenue [Sales]	$1,000	$1,000	$1,000
Net Operating Profit [NOP] - $	$100	$100	$100
- %	10%	10%	10%
Invested Capital [IC]	$600	$800	$1,000
Cost of Capital [CCAP]	12%	12%	12%
Economic Profit			
NOP [from above]	$100	$100	$100
Capital Charge [CCAP]	(72)	(96)	(120)
Economic Profit ["EP"]	$28	$4	$(20)

Exhibit 51

"Market Value Added" - Example

Valuation Summary ... Assumptions
1. All companies maintain same invested capital to revenue ratio.
2. All companies continue to earn same profit margin on revenue.
3. All companies increase revenue by 10% per year, for 4 years.

'growth' will produce in terms of shareholder value – or *MVA*. If we apply a growth scenario, with a very limited number of assumptions, to the three firms ('**A**', '**B**' and '**C**') we can begin to get an appreciation of why *EP* is so important in the value creation process. Exhibit 51 will provide the foundation. Later on, when we meet with the officers, I'll show some graphic illustrations".

"These assumptions, while simple and few in number, are representative of a forward-looking valuation model, which investors use to value companies and businesses within companies. It's also indicative of the type of thinking we'll get into when we value Growthstar's BU strategies. Obviously, we could expand these assumptions into a more robust scenario, but the above ones will suffice to illustrate the concept. Let's move on to a numeric expression of these assumptions for our three companies – '**A**', '**B**' and '**C**' – in the next Exhibit (52)".

Exhibit 52

"Market Value Added" - Example

Pro Forma	CO. 'A'	CO. 'B'	CO. 'C'
"EP" - Value Impact			
Year # - 1	$31	$4	$(22)
2	34	5	(24)
3	37	5	(27)
4	41	6	(29)
Sub-total: 4 Years	143	20	(102)
Years 5 on ... Residual	342	50	(242)
Market Value Added [MVA]			
Sum of EPs + Residual	$485	$70	$(344)
before discounting			

"**Co. 'A'** increases its *EP* throughout the forecast period – in this case, four years. If you think about the consistency of performance implied in the assumptions (which, again, are probably over-simplified) you should understand the *EP* forecast results for **Co. 'A'** – *EP* increases each year at the 10% growth rate for revenue – $31 million in future year #1 to $41 million in future year #4. The 'year 5 on residual' is the typical way that the years after the forecast horizon are treated, which 'capitalizes' the year 4 *EP* at the *CCAP* rate (in this case, 12%). This assumes that the plan can produce *no incremental EP* even if the business continues to grow, which is equivalent to saying that, after year 4, the company will just earn its cost of capital on new investment. The *MVA* for this growth scenario is the sum of the *EPs* for the four-year growth period plus the residual value".

"This example is over-simplified, at this point, in that it doesn't (yet) account for *discounting* of the future values. However, it does show that **Co. 'A'** is creating shareholder value with its growth plan. Therefore, the total 'warranted' market value of **Co. 'A'** (again, *before discounting* the future year *EPs*) is the 'base' period *IC* of $600 million (from Exhibit 50) plus the above *MVA* of $485 – for a total of nearly $1.1 billion. Obviously, the 'real' *MVA* and total warranted value for **Co. 'A'** will be less when we apply the 12% discount rate to future year *EP* and residual values, but for now we can see that **Co. 'A'** should command a 'premium' over its invested capital when 'valued' in the financial markets. Why? Because management is earning more than the cost of capital and is growing the business. You should be able to visualize that if **Co. 'A'** can increase its revenue growth, then it will generate more *MVA* – and, thus, should experience a greater 'warranted' total market value".

"One of the interesting features of this analysis is that we get approx-imately the same *MVA* result as we would with the traditional 'free cash flow' (*FCF*) approach. I hope you all now understand that once we factor in an appropriate discount rate – which we will do after we get through with this 'non-discounted' example – *MVA* (under the *EP* approach) is *about the same* as the Net Present Value (*NPV*) calculated using the *FCF* technique. One reason that the *EP* model is receiving widespread application in corporations and the financial institutions that invest large sums in the equity markets is that it is the concep-tual equivalent to the *FCF* approach, with the result (*MVA*) equal or very close to the *NPV*. You'll have to accept my word for now, but we will demonstrate this equivalency later on. Further, with the *EP* approach, we can determine meaningful 'period-by-period' financial results – indicative of value creation, destruction or neutrality – which is usually *not* possible with the free cash flow technique. The *FCF* model provides a value-based 'end result', but is *not* typically very useful in assessing value creation 'progress along the way' ".

As Jason paused, he noticed all of the heads – even Jack's, albeit it ever so slightly – nod forward around the table, indicating an understanding and acceptance of what was being said. He took a sip of coffee before continuing.

"Company '**B**' presents a somewhat different scenario. Even though it grows and maintains its 10% after-tax profit margin, the company does not produce any significant future year *EPs*. By now, this should be apparent, since **Co. 'B'** just earns its *CCAP*. **Co. 'B'** may get bigger, but it doesn't get much better, at least in terms of shareholder value creation. Notice the very modest $70 million *MVA*, which is less than 10% of its $800 million invested capital. This is noteworthy, because it indicates that **'B'-type** companies should be valued (in the financial markets) fairly close to their 'economic book' value. They simply don't return much more to the shareholders than what was invested in the first place".

"Company '**C**' is truly a problem. It *cannot grow* out of its dilemma of earning a return *below* the cost of capital, without radically changing the way it conducts its business. Yet, the business world is 'littered' with **'C'-type** companies and businesses, thinking that they can grow and be successful without changing their fundamental structure. This is a very serious situation in 'Corporate America' since a significant percentage (20% or more according to some research) of publicly traded companies in the United States fall into the '**C**' category. Whatever assumptions we may make, the impact is clear – growth 'destroys' shareholder value for **'C'-types** – and more growth means more destruction!"

There was silence in the room. Jonathan looked at his watch and noticed it was 8:24. Ian and the other officers would arrive in approximately one minute. "Are there any questions?" Even though he would have cut them off due to the next meeting starting in five minutes, the looks of comprehension told him that the 'message' had sunk in to all the members of the finance team.

Right on schedule, Ian and the officers arrived just one minute later. As Ian entered the boardroom, everyone rose from their chairs. "*Now, here's a CEO who commands respect*", Jason thought to himself as he watched the finance team members nervously utter their 'good mornings' to Ian. He was an imposing figure – and he knew it. The other officers were just a few steps behind Ian, and at exactly 8:30 all the coffee mugs were filled, greetings and pleasantries were being concluded, and Jonathan rose to begin the meeting.

"I want to welcome you and thank you all for coming this morning. As you all know, we formally began a process of investigating the concept of 'value-based' financial performance about one month ago.

We have had an initial meeting with the officers, a brief meeting with Ian, and some intensive/thought-provoking sessions with the 'work team' composed of corporate and business unit financial managers. I am personally pleased with the progress to date. We have far to go, but I think we have made a good start. Today, we want to present to you and discuss with you several key topics:

- The transition from accounting to economic metrics, resulting in Economic Profit, which we call '*EP*';
- Supporting measures, known as Financial 'Drivers', of which three will occupy our focus initially; and
- Market Value Added, shortened to the acronym '*MVA*', which is equivalent to the concept of Shareholder Value discussed at our initial officers' meeting about a month ago. A part of this topic will be the 'Magnifier' Effect on shareholder value, resulting from the *EP* of a business".

Ian then leaned forward in his chair, placed his large hands on the boardroom table and spoke. "I also want to thank all of you for the effort you have made to date. I have been keeping track of the highlights of work to date, through conversations with Jonathan and Jason. I'm not committed to any particular approach, but am here to listen with an open mind. For those of you who know me well, and most of you do, that's not always one of my great qualities". Nervous laughter broke out with this comment, especially from the non-officer members of the finance team, whose exposure to Ian in the context of today's type of meeting was limited. "We need to be certain that whatever we do is correct from an outsider's perspective and, at the same time, easily manageable internally. Jonathan and Jason have both been informed that any overly complex, unmanageable system will have a very short life, along with its architects". Jack smiled, Earl winced, Peter and Larry leaned back with looks of contentment, and the others just sat there expressionless. "Well, those are my remarks for the moment. Jason, I believe you wish to get started". As was his habit, Ian's last remark was a 'directive'.

Jason rose and addressed the group. "To reiterate the agenda that Jonathan just outlined, we are going to cover three important topics today". As he spoke, he walked over to a flip chart and wrote in large letters:

- **Economic Profit – 'EP'**
- **Financial 'Drivers' – Support Measures**
- **Market Value Added (MVA) and the 'Magnifier' Concept**

"An initial step in the process is to make the transition from 'accounting' to 'economics', retaining what is based on cash flow concepts and modifying what is not. Let's begin with the traditional

---

Exhibit 53

"Accounting Profit" - Example

"Base Period"	**CO. 'A'**	**CO. 'B'**	**CO. 'C'**
Revenue [Sales]	**$1,000**	**$1,000**	**$1,000**
Net Operating Profit			
[NOP] - $	**$100**	**$100**	**$100**
- %	**10%**	**10%**	**10%**

The Accounting ("Earnings") model stops here. In this case, all companies are the same ... and, all are "profitable".

'accounting' model". As he spoke, he clicked on Exhibit 53 (a duplicate of Exhibit 5).

"I believe you are all familiar with this 'earnings-based' approach to measuring financial performance, since it is what presently is in use here. In this example, all the companies have the same performance and they all are 'profitable'. If we make some qualifying assumptions, they would appear to have the same, or very similar, 'value propositions'".

"That's what we've grown up on", stated Larry Buildermann ... "the 'bottom line'".

"It's been my 'yardstick' also", added Peter Uppcomer. "Account for all the costs down through the P&L".

Earl then entered the discussion with ... "The problem, however, is that the 'accounting' model does *not* contain *all* the costs. In fact, it misses a very important one". Cathy and Dave sat forward, knowing that at any time their bosses might ask a question and look for them to assist with the answer.

Val Performa felt that she should 'weigh in' and said, "what Earl says is true and it has 'strategic' implications". Larry and Peter 'perked up' at this comment. Their strategies were on their minds, since they were about to embark on their business planning process.

Earl, knowing what the next chart was, glanced at Jason, who responded by showing Exhibit 54 (a duplicate of Exhibit 6).

"As Earl alluded to", Jason stated, "the 'cost' for the *total* capital invested in the business has not been included in the 'earnings' model".

Exhibit 54

"Economic Profit" - Example

"Base Period"		CO. 'A'	CO. 'B'	CO. 'C'
Revenue [Sales]		$1,000	$1,000	$1,000
Net Operating Profit				
[NOP]	- $	$100	$100	$100
	- %	10%	10%	10%

Invested Capital [IC]		$600	$800	$1,000
Cost of Capital [CCAP]		12%	12%	12%

*The "Economic Profit" model introduces the concept of **Capital** required to produce the "Accounting Profit" and the **Cost** of this capital. We begin to see that all the companies are not the same.*

"Hold on", interjected the 'big man'. "While we only report 'operating profit' for the business units, we go 'all the way' for the total company and include our interest expense". Jack leaned back and smiled.

Cathy looked at Jonathan and Jason, paused for a brief moment, and then blurted out ... "But, Ian, there is a 'hidden' cost – the cost of our 'equity' capital – which is *not* recorded anywhere on our 'accounting' statements". Jack leaned forward, the smile disappearing.

Ian cast a hard look at Jack and then simply said, "I see. Go on".

Jack was about to speak, when Ian looked at him again, saying ... "Let Jason continue".

Jason then clicked on Exhibit 55 (a duplicate of Exhibits 7 and 50) and said, "this next schedule reflects the impact of imposing a 'capital charge'. As you see, the results can be dramatic".

Peter looked over at Dave and Larry at Cathy, since they had no clue as to how interpret this table of numbers. Peter then looked at Larry. As he was prone to do, Peter spoke ... "Can someone tell me how to 'read' the numbers in the box at the bottom of this table. I see amounts ranging from a 'positive' $28 (millions, I presume) for **Co. 'A'** to a 'negative' $(20) for **Co. 'C'**. I guess that's what you mean by 'dramatic'. I can't argue, but how do we go from the profit (*NOP*) of $100 million to these numbers?"

Dave felt he should put his newly found knowledge to work, so before anyone else could say anything, he spoke ... "Here's how it

---

Exhibit 55

"Economic Profit" - Example

"Base Period"	CO. 'A'	CO. 'B'	CO. 'C'
Revenue [Sales]	$1,000	$1,000	$1,000
Net Operating Profit			
[NOP] - $	$100	$100	$100
- %	10%	10%	10%
Invested Capital [IC]	$600	$800	$1,000
Cost of Capital [CCAP]	12%	12%	12%

Economic Profit			
NOP [from above]	$100	$100	$100
Capital Charge [CCAP]	(72)	(96)	(120)
Economic Profit ["EP"]	$28	$4	$(20)

---

works, Peter. The investors are looking for a 12% return on their investment. See the Cost of Capital (*CCAP*) line – 12% for all companies?"

"OK", Peter responded.

"Without worrying about the details for now, assume that the investors in each company want a 12% return on their capital. What we do to replicate that situation and approximate what it means for management is to 'multiply' *CCAP* (12%) by the amount of invested capital (*IC*) – which the investors have provided. On a periodic basis, this provides a 'dollar' return that is a minimum requirement for the investors in total. The impact is that the more 'capital-intensive' firm ('**C**') must 'return' more in terms of profit (*NOP*) dollars in order to satisfy the investors. This requirement is due to the higher level of capital that '**C**' has taken to run its business, versus the other two companies. Now, here's the 'kicker' – if you divide the $100 million *NOP* for **Co. 'C'** by its $1 billion ($1,000 million) *IC*, you'll get a percentage return on invested capital of 10%". Dave then went to the flip chart and wrote:

$$\$100\ NOP/\$1,000\ IC = 10\%\ ROIC$$

"But", Dave continued, "the investors want a 12% return, so there's a 'shortfall'. The business is *not* performing up to the expectations of the investors. The Economic Profit (*EP*) – 'negative' $20 million for **Co. 'C'** – is the 'dollar' equivalent of a two (2) percentage point 'shortfall'

(10% actual versus 12% requirement) for the return on invested capital. Jason calls this type of company a value 'destroyer' ".

"That's my financial guy", Peter retorted as he looked first at Jonathan and then at Ian ... "always leading with the 'negative'. Why didn't you talk about Company '**A**' which is probably a 'good news' story?"

Everyone knew that Peter was just 'jabbing' at Dave and was actually very proud that he had stepped up and had the courage to offer an explanation in front of Ian and the other officers.

Dave knew this also and was never afraid of invoking humor, even in Ian's presence. "Gotta give you the bad news first, boss, because then the good news sounds even better. And, be prepared for some surprises in *our* business!"

Jonathan then felt he should 'wrap up' this issue and stated emphatically, "This example illustrates the three major categories of businesses, from the perspective of judging financial performance and its potential impact on value creation. A business with sustainable net operating profit well above its cost of capital is an '**A**' and is called a value 'creator'. A business that just earns its cost of capital (perhaps slightly above or below) is a '**B**' and is value 'neutral'. It gives back approximately one dollar for every dollar invested. The 'problem' of the business world is category '**C**'. While often 'profitable' in a traditional sense (notice that **Co. 'C'** in this example enjoys a 10% after–tax profit margin) a '**C'-type** business actually 'destroys' value, because it does not earn an adequate return on its invested capital. The 'accounting' model misses this, which is why many companies are using the 'economic profit' approach".

Ian leaned back and scratched his head. This initial aspect of a shareholder value 'experience' had taken hold of him. He looked at Jonathan and asked, "Is there any other way to get at this result?"

Jonathan replied with "Except for a 'value profit' metric that Jason will introduce in the next segment of today's session, there is nothing that is any more straightforward or simpler, in terms of evaluating the performance of a business on a year-by-year basis. We can use one or more techniques to evaluate major investments and acquisitions, but they 'drive off' the conceptual base that is illustrated in this example".

"OK", Ian countered ... "is this example the essence of what 'Economic Value Added' is all about?" This was a question.

"That's correct", Jonathan responded.

Dave wanted to conclude his comments and added, "Here's the second 'kicker' – which really 'floored' me when I first heard it". Ian was looking at Dave very attentively as he spoke. "Companies in the '**C**' category *cannot grow* their way out of their problems without altering their operating cost or investment structure".

"That's a mouthful, young man" ! Ian thundered.

Dave was taken back somewhat by the tone of Ian's remark, so Jonathan jumped in with "It may be a mouthful, but it happens to be true".

"I'm listening", the 'big man' concluded, motioning for Jason to move on to a new topic.

Jason, who had enjoyed the dialogue of the people in the meeting, began speaking again. "Larry, do you remember that I told you I would suggest a *new definition* for the 'bottom line'? Well, this is it!" Larry just sat there, motionless and expressionless. He was telling himself that he still had to be convinced.

"With the '**A**', '**B**', '**C**' example as a 'back-drop', we'll now take you through an historical summary of the *EP* performance of Growthstar (in total) and the two major business units – *Products* and *Services*. To review this historical performance, we've looked at the past three fiscal years plus the current year. The members of the finance team have pored over the 'numbers' and have worked with me to make the necessary adjustments to transition from 'accounting' to 'economics'. We have considered the assets we lease and all the goodwill incurred in the acquisition of *Services* to be in our invested capital base".

As he heard this comment, Peter looked first at Jack and then at Dave. Jack turned and looked away, but Dave smiled back at Peter and gave him a wink – indicating that he was 'on board' with what was about to be shown.

Larry looked over at Cathy, who nodded forward slightly, her signal of approval as to the upcoming material.

Val, Earl, Jill and Frank all leaned forward, anxious to get started. Jack slumped down slightly. Flo Withetide sat with a look of concern – looking first at Ian, then at Jonathan.

Jason, catching part, but not all, of the 'body language' around the table, forged ahead ... "We'll analyze the historical and current 'economic' profit performance for the total company first, using Exhibit 56".

"What we have plotted (in Exhibit 56) are the three most recent historical fiscal years, an average for those (three) years and the current year outlook. For each year, there are *three vertical bars*. *NOP* is the striped bar on the left pointing upward, *CCAP* is the gray-colored middle bar pointing downward, and *EP* is the black bar on the right of each set".

"The 'ideal' pattern is to have the '*EP bars*' – the black ones on the right of each set – increasing steadily in an upward direction. As you can see, that is *not* the pattern for the total company. As we will see shortly, the acquisition of *Services* – completed just prior to the beginning of FY #2 – had an effect, particularly in FY #2 when all the

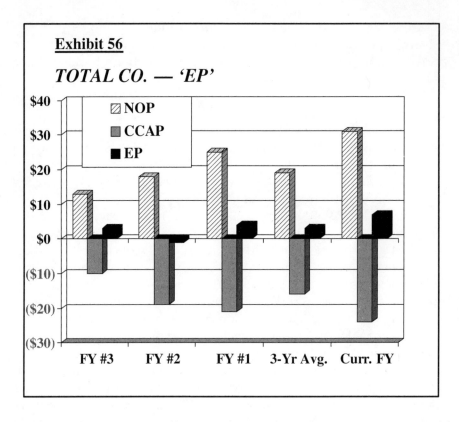

Exhibit 56

TOTAL CO. — 'EP'

acquisition investment 'hit the books'. So, in spite of the fact that *NOP* has been rising steadily, *EP* has not. The capital charge (*CCAP*) in FY #2 'wiped out' all of the *NOP*. The last two fiscal years have seen a recovery. This is a typical pattern for firms growing by acquisition, as capital is added in large 'chunks'. While not a *bad* pattern, it does require attention, to assure that the low *EP* just following the acquisition is brought back to being 'in the black' at a reasonable time after the completion of the acquisition or merger".

Ian leaned forward and said, "So, the steadily growing 'earnings' and *EPS* trend that we have generated, partly due to writing off a portion of the goodwill in FY #3, just before year-end, has *not* been reflected in our 'economic' profits".

Jonathan responded ... "The 'profit' (*NOP*) part has increased steadily, but we have *invested* a significant amount of capital, resulting in a larger 'capital charge'. Please remember, Ian, that we have included 'leased' assets here, which are *not* on our 'reported' balance sheet, as well as *all* of the *Services* acquisition goodwill".

"I remember", was all that Ian replied.

As Ian looked at him, Jack was wishing that he could be on a beach somewhere in the South Pacific, or anywhere except the boardroom of Growthstar Inc., at this moment. Ian continued to look in his direction, and Jack had to muster all his inner strength to not look away, as he had done with Peter. People who tried that with Ian usually paid a heavy price. Ian, scratching his chin, glanced again at the chart and then back at Jack. He also looked at Jonathan, who returned the gesture with a steady gaze of his own. While Jack was concerned about 'covering his tracks' and justifying his bookkeeping entries, Jonathan was not. Jonathan was comfortable in knowing that he always did what he felt was appropriate at the time. If later on, he was proven wrong or if he realized that he had made an honest mistake, he accepted it and filed it away for future reference. Jack was different. He constantly feared making mistakes, especially in front of his superiors, and shuddered at the thought of incurring criticism from Ian. Fortunately for Jack, Ian was, at least for now, just 'thinking' and said nothing. Ian motioned for Jason to continue.

"If we turn to *Services*, we can see a visualization of what Jonathan just stated". As he spoke, Jason clicked on Exhibit 57.

"A picture certainly does tell a story, doesn't it", Ian exclaimed. "Look at all the 'black' *EP* bars pointing downward. I don't see an *EP* bar for the current year, so I guess that we got back to 'zero'. What a story to tell to our shareholders. We're maximizing *CCAP*. I

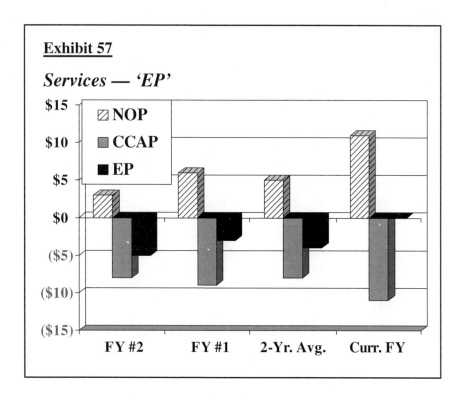

wonder what type of 'multiple' we get for that! Did we buy a **'C'-type** business?" As he spoke, he looked first at Jonathan, then at Peter, and finally at Jack.

Jack wanted to crawl into a hole. Realizing that he had no hope of finding one, he quietly walked to the coffeepot to refill his mug. Peter was gazing very attentively at the chart before him, almost in the same way that Dave had gazed at the 'table version' of this *EP* portrayal for *Services*. Peter then looked over at Dave and uttered, "Can you explain this?"

"Probably", Dave replied, "since it was made clear to me about a week ago. Growthstar transferred some wealth to our former owners when they bought our business and paid more than the 'book value' of our assets. Further, we have a lot of money tied up in operating leases. Until very recently, our finance team meetings to be precise, I never realized that all the offices we rent and testing equipment we lease are actually 'assets'. While I didn't understand it at first, I now appreciate the fact that we 'invest' much like *Products*. We just invest in different things. Up until recently, I thought our only 'investments' were for inventory and receivables".

"As one of the 'bad guys' in this story", Earl chimed in, "let me 'temper' the message and offer a perspective. The goal is not to 'maximize' *EP* every year. It usually isn't possible. What this *EP Assessment* has done for us is to indicate that the 'accounting' results don't tell the whole story – in fact, they can mis-represent the story of what is happening from an 'economic' perspective. It is true that we paid a full price for *Services*. I'm not saying that we overpaid, but we did incur goodwill. Further, that goodwill – *all of it* – is a 'sunk' cost and you need to earn a return on it, along with all the other capital invested in *Services*. The 'good news' is that the 'trend' for *EP* is favorable. Remember, this concept is about *change*. Peter, you and your managers have taken *Services* from a 'negative' *EP* of $(5) million in FY #2 to a 'break-even' forecasted for the current year. That's improvement!"

Val then added, "based on what I've seen so far in the future outlook for the business, I believe we should be able to move *EP* 'into the black' soon with some solid growth. Earl and I will be working with Dave and others in *Services* to provide a realistic financial outlook for the next few years, linked to the business plan you'll be developing, with my assistance".

Ian continued to look at the graph and scratch his chin. Flo Withetide remained silent and motionless in her chair. She had no idea what was going on in Ian's mind and didn't want to speculate. True to her nature, she wouldn't utter a word until she could determine what Ian's position was.

Peter was impressed by what Earl and Val had just said. Throughout his career, he felt disdain for corporate staffs – he had never worked in a corporate staff position, having always been in marketing or operations at a business unit. *"This corporate group is different"*, he thought to himself. *"They're smart, and they can convey a message that's relevant and perceptive … and which I really need to focus on. Maybe this 'economic' stuff can have some benefit to me and how I manage my operation"*. Peter then spoke out loud … "I think what you're telling me is that the shareholders have entrusted me with a significant amount of their money – more than I ever realized. For the past two years and including this year, I've been paying back this 'excess'. Now, it's time for me to 'deliver'!"

Ian smiled for the first time. "Peter, you took the words out of my mouth. I have felt that *Services* is an attractive business and it has strong growth potential. What I need to see are the results of your strategy and the upcoming year's operating plan, and then some tangible evidence of execution".

"You'll get it", Peter replied confidently.

Flo then smiled for the first time and said, "We've got a new management development program scheduled to 'kick off' later this year. Perhaps we should include a segment on the key aspects of *EP* – keeping it really simple, of course".

"That may be a good idea", Ian stated. "Let's talk about that after today, Flo".

Flo's smile grew to a wide grin. Jonathan looked at her and winked. Flo then sighed, with a look of relief on her face.

Jonathan, reading Ian's mind then looked at Jason, silently motioning for him to move on to the *EP Assessment* for *Products*.

Jason obliged by clicking on Exhibit 58.

"I guess it's my turn, now", Larry quipped. "Let's see how this *new* 'bottom line' looks. Cathy, I'm sure you've seen the numbers. Any conclusions?"

Cathy Casher had prepared herself for this meeting. After all, it wasn't every day that she had the opportunity to sit 'face-to-face' with the 'big man' and all the officers. "*Products* has had a steady increase in both *NOP* and *EP* through last year (FY #1). During the past two years, our *EP* has more than doubled, from $3 million in FY #3 to $7 million last year (FY #1). We have reached a temporary 'plateau', however, due to conditions in our market that we are aware of and are addressing. Thus, the outlook for the current year is to maintain *EP* at the same ($7 million) level that was achieved last year".

Ian then commented … "We've been talking about this slowdown, Larry, but this chart puts it in perspective. Your net operating profit is up slightly, but *EP* is 'flat'".

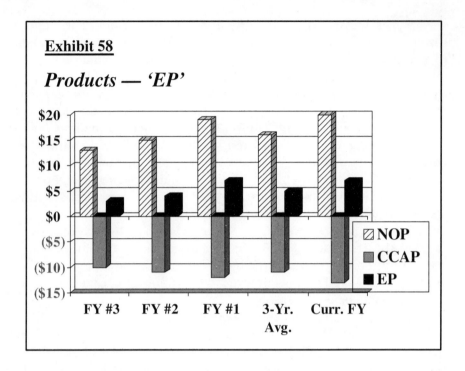

Exhibit 58

Products — 'EP'

Val then said, "we have some significant 'strategic' issues with a couple of key market segments, which need to be addressed in the business plan".

"We're aware of these issues and the challenges they pose for us", Larry countered, "and will be dealing with them. However, I thought that we at least had *some* growth in our 'bottom line' this year, until this 'economic' stuff came along".

"So did I", responded Cathy, "but I believe there is merit in this 'economic' perspective".

"We'll see" was all that Larry could mutter ... quietly.

Jonathan, sensing a bit of restlessness in the group, stood up and said ... "The coffee is unusually tasty this morning. Why don't we take a ten-minute break. We'll get into the Financial 'Drivers' when we return".

After everyone was seated again, Jason stood up and said, "the Financial 'Drivers' are key support measures that lie beneath and help explain *EP* – in terms of its absolute level and its change". He then clicked on Exhibit 59 (a duplicate of Exhibit 40).

"These three 'drivers' provide a simple, yet effective, 'template' for operating management focus. They encompass growth indicators, capital intensity and an 'earnings' target geared toward value creation". Ian and the two BU general managers 'perked up' when

---

Exhibit 59

Financial "Drivers" ... Support Measures

- **Growth Rates**
- **Invested Capital Intensity**
- **Value Profit Margin**

*These **"drivers"** provide a **foundation** for the Economic Profit and Market Value Added metrics, and give managers a simple, yet powerful, template for value creation. These support measures are also the ones to focus on when evaluating business strategies and major investment programs.*

Exhibit 60

Financial "Drivers" ... continued

- **Growth Rates**
  - *"Relationship" of Revenue, Operating Profit and Invested Capital Growth .... CGRs*

- **Invested Capital Intensity**
  - *How much Capital to Generate One Dollar ($1.00) of Revenue (Sales) .... in total or incremental .... encompasses working and fixed capital*

- **Value Profit Margin**
  - *Minimum Profit Margin to Create Value for Shareholders (Owners)*

---

they heard the word 'earnings'. Jason had guessed that they would, which is why he chose to use this word. Jack noticed this reaction and smiled slightly. Sensing that Ian, Larry and Peter – they were now his audience – grasped the 'message', Jason clicked on the next Exhibit (60).

"We've spent quite a bit of time with the finance team discussing these 'drivers' and how they interact. Is this exhibit (60) clear and understandable?" Jason looked at Ian, Larry and Peter as he asked the question.

Ian leaned forward and responded ... "It's clear to me".

Larry and Peter nodded their heads forward, indicating they 'got it'.

"OK", Jason came back with. "Now, I'm going to show you these indicators, for each BU and the total company, for the same historical and current period used to assess *EP*. Let's start with *Products*". He clicked on Exhibit 61.

"At our 'team' meeting last week, Dave and Earl provided an eloquent explanation of how the first set of 'drivers' – the growth rates – contain a 'story', so I'm going to ask them to speak. Dave, would you give the overview and Earl the specifics for *Products*?"

Dave was enjoying the 'air time' he was getting and noticed that Peter reacted with a look of satisfaction every time that he spoke in front of Ian. "Over time, you want the 'gray' middle bar (*NOP*) – to have the highest growth rate, followed by Revenue (the 'white' bar on the left). That leaves Invested Capital (the 'black' bar on the right) with the lowest rate of growth. This is the most desirable pattern over the long term, but it doesn't always happen every year, especially if you're investing for future growth".

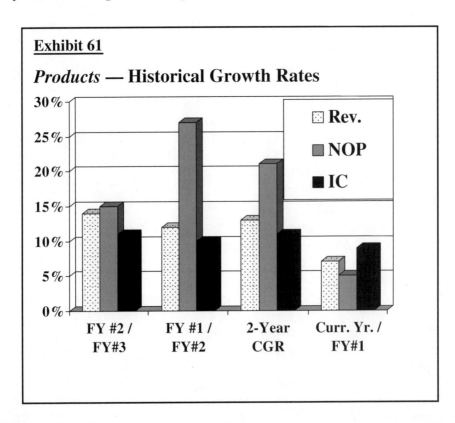

Exhibit 61

Products — **Historical Growth Rates**

Larry had an ability to quickly grasp the message with graphs, even though he struggled with numeric tables, and interjected ... "We achieved the 'most desirable' pattern for the entire historical period".

"That's true", Cathy responded, "but we're seeing a change in the 'pattern' in the current year outlook".

"You would to have to 'temper' the situation", Larry muttered.

"Let's look at this a little closer, Larry", Earl then stated. "If *NOP* grows faster than revenue, then profit margin should increase. If revenue grows faster than invested capital, then *ICI* should decrease. If *NOP* grows faster than *IC* (invested capital), then *NOP* should increase by more than *CCAP*. If *NOP* exceeds *CCAP* and is increasing at a higher rate, then *EP* should grow. When *EP* grows, additional shareholder value is created. As you correctly assessed, this is what happened in the historical period".

"We can take this same logic trail and apply it to the current year for *Products*. If *NOP* grows slower than revenue, then profit margin should decrease (which has occurred, albeit only slightly). If revenue grows slower than invested capital, then *ICI* should increase (which it has, if only slightly). If *NOP* grows slower than *IC* (invested capital), then *NOP* should increase by less than *CCAP*, causing *EP* growth to slow down or cease. When *EP* growth slows or stops, less shareholder value is created. Referring back to the *EP Assessment*, the Economic Profit for *Products* in the current year is projected to be at about the same level ($7 million) as the *EP* for last year (FY #1)".

"Can you see a 'story' starting to unfold?" Jonathan then asked, looking at Ian, Larry and Peter. They all nodded. "OK, Jason, please move on to Invested Capital Intensity or, as you like to call it, *ICI*".

Jason responded by clicking on Exhibit 62 and stating emphatically, "This 'driver' provides the starting point for the key balance sheet ratios and enables us to assess different businesses, such as *Products and Services*, on a common basis. In addition to being useful in analyzing history, it should be very helpful in assessing the future years' investment implications for your strategies".

"As I think you can see on this graph (Exhibit 62) the *ICI for Products* has been fairly steady in the $0.40 range. This means that about *forty cents of invested capital* (you know, that 'balance sheet' thing) *has been required to produce one dollar of revenue*. This is a 'reasonable' level of capital intensity for a manufacturing firm, recognizing that there is no 'standard' or 'correct' level. As we'll see shortly, the 'drivers' taken together determine value creation or destruction".

"This is getting interesting", Ian noted. "What's next?" That was a signal to move to the next topic (or chart, in this case). Jonathan knew all of Ian's 'signals' and gave a silent nod for Jason to continue. Besides, Jonathan wanted to get to the 'Value Profit Margin' as much

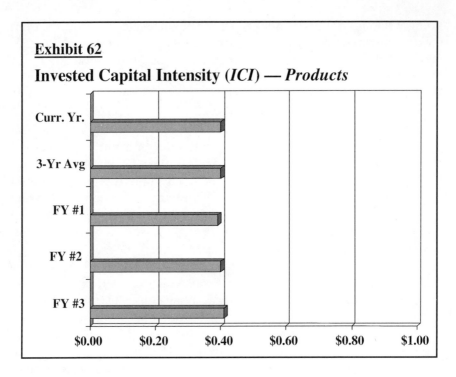

Exhibit 62

Invested Capital Intensity (*ICI*) — *Products*

as Jason did. Since Ian got the message about the *ICI* for *Products*, it was time to move on.

Jason obliged by clicking on Exhibit 63 as he said, "The *Value Profit Margin* – which our firm has 'trademarked' as *VPM*™ – pulls *CCAP* and *ICI* together to provide a profit margin, in this case an 'after-tax' (*NOP*) margin, which is the starting point for value creation. It's a minimum profit margin requirement, based on the risk and capital intensity inherent in a business. The objective is to generate a positive 'spread' for the actual profit margin when compared to the *VPM*. We'll look at the historical *VPM* profile for *Products*, similar to what we've done for the other 'drivers'".

"Looks like a 'pretty picture' to me", Larry stated, as he quickly noticed the 'black' bars on the right side of each set pointing upward, indicating a positive 'spread' for *VPM*".

"It is a good picture", Cathy responded. "We increased our 'spread' of *VPM* versus our actual *NOP* margin last year (FY #1). The question is, *where do we go from here?*"

"That is a key question for me", Ian said. "Where are we going with *Products*?"

"It's a major issue", chimed in Val ... "one that the strategy for *Products* has to address".

VPM™ is a trademark of Vanguard Partners

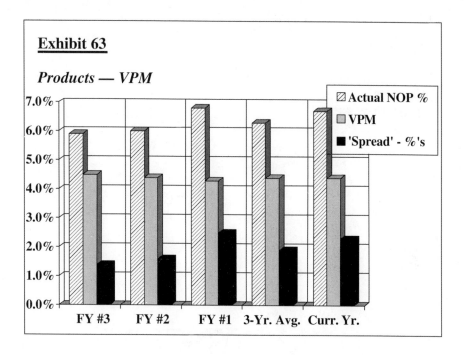

Exhibit 63

Products — VPM

Legend:
- ☑ Actual NOP %
- ☐ VPM
- ■ 'Spread' - %'s

"We know that and we are going to address it", Larry replied ... "and, Val, I know that you are going to help us". Val smiled back at Larry. She would help. The plan for *Products* was a key objective for her.

"Next, we'll analyze the financial 'drivers' for *Services*", Jason stated, as he clicked on Exhibit 64.

"Since *Services* has only been operating as a business unit of Growthstar for two full years, we are limited to year-over-year growth rate comparisons – for last year (FY #1 versus FY #2) and the current year (versus last year). As you can all see by the 'bars' on this graph, the indicators are showing the 'most desirable' pattern. The significant growth in *NOP* is noteworthy. *NOP* has been growing rapidly during the past two years, but remember that the 'base' level (FY #2) was low. This factor is just the opposite with the growth rates for *IC*, which started at a high level – which we'll see in a moment. The key point, though, is the indicators are moving in the right direction at a significant pace. This pattern is what was necessary to justify the price paid for the acquisition. Please remember that this 'economic value' approach is focused on 'change' as well as 'absolutes'".

Peter looked at Ian, then at Dave, then at Jonathan, then at Jason and said ... "This truly is getting interesting. Are you saying, Jason, that I'm now 'creating' shareholder value?"

"What I'm saying – actually, what the chart (Exhibit 64) is saying – is that while your *actual EP* has been negative historically and is now

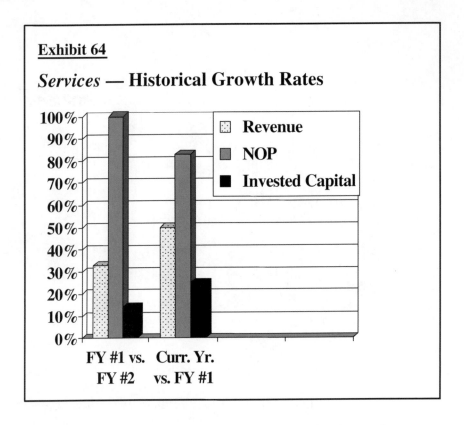

Exhibit 64

Services — **Historical Growth Rates**

projected to be zero, indicating 'value neutrality' for the total company, your growth indicators are showing a positive and desirable pattern. If this can be sustained in the future, then you will definitely be 'creating' value as time moves forward".

"So", Peter continued, "the 'story' is that we're starting to come 'out of the hole' – excuse my words, Ian, but they're the ones that came to mind – and our challenge is to continue this 'growth rate' pattern".

"I think you're grasping the message very nicely", Earl interjected. "If you follow the 'logic trail' I just described, you can start to formulate a perception on value creation". Peter nodded approvingly.

Ian then said, "OK, I think we have the 'picture' on *Services* growth – let's move on".

Jason obliged by showing Exhibit 65. As he was doing so, he said, "The acquisition of *Services*, as Frank noted to the finance team last week, involved a significant amount of invested capital, especially in relation to the existing revenue base at the time of the acquisition. Starting at the bottom of this chart and moving to the top, we see that *ICI* is significant, in absolute terms, but is *decreasing* at about 'thirteen cents per year' – from a level of $0.93 in FY #2, to $.80 in FY #1, to $.67 expected for the current year".

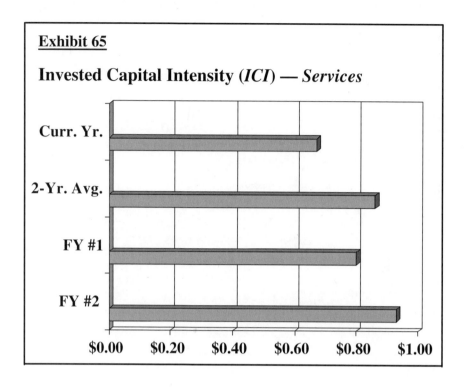

Exhibit 65

Invested Capital Intensity (*ICI*) — *Services*

"I guess this 'tempers' my enthusiasm for the previous chart", Peter stated. "You financial guys know how to 'rain on a person's parade' – isn't that true, Dave?" Peter chuckled slightly, knowing that he wasn't the only person responsible for the *ICI*.

"Perhaps", Dave responded, "but don't underestimate what Jason is talking about when he states that *ICI* has gone down by 'thirteen cents' each year for the past two years. I'll bet that on an 'incremental' basis our capital intensity is improving – that is, it's *lower*".

"My, my", Jason countered – "you have been paying attention. The next chart shows the 'incremental' *ICI* for *Services*. This *ICI* is '*net new investment divided by new revenue*', which is the analytic approach we'll use in our strategy work". He clicked on Exhibit 66.

"I like this current year!" Peter exclaimed, almost jumping out of his chair. "We're now *much* less capital intensive than *Products* on an 'incremental' basis".

Jonathan replied with "You may finally be getting there, Peter – but look at the 'new' cash invested, translated into *ICI*, to get to this position – 'sixty cents on average' for the past two years. If I'm reading the graph correctly, the second bar from the top ('2-Yr. Avg.') gives this amount; and this is *after* the $55 million invested to 'acquire' *Services*".

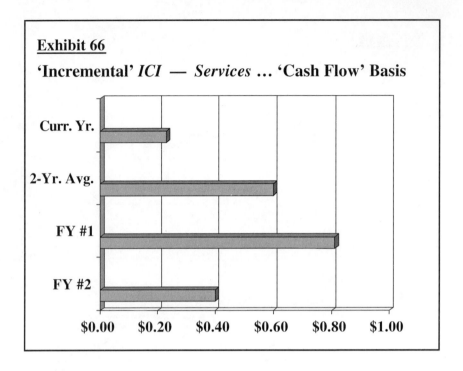

Exhibit 66

'Incremental' *ICI* — *Services* ... 'Cash Flow' Basis

Ian then entered the discussion by saying, "I think we can all see clearly the results of this analysis. Jonathan, why haven't we seen this kind of information before?"

"Neither you nor I have been that receptive to it, until recently", Jonathan responded coolly. "Nor has it been 'pushed' on us by anyone except Earl – and Jason, of course".

"I guess you're right", replied the 'big man'. He started to look toward Jack, but then turned his head back toward the exhibit (66) on the screen.

Jack wanted to find a 'huge' hole and disappear. Knowing that this wasn't possible, he simply stared, pretending to study the chart, even though he understood what it implied, along with all the other charts that had been presented.

Jonathan then looked at Jason and said, "I think we should 'wrap up' the analysis of the support measures for *Services*, so that we can move on to the total company review. Jason, let's show the *VPM* analysis for *Services*".

Jason clicked on Exhibit 67 ... and then spoke ... "There are two important points with respect to Exhibit 67. The first is that the *VPM* for *Services* has been reduced from 10.3% in FY #2 to 7.3% in the current year – a three (3) percentage point drop – due to the decrease in *ICI*. Secondly, *Services* has now reached a 'break-even' for *VPM*, which equates to a 'zero' *EP*".

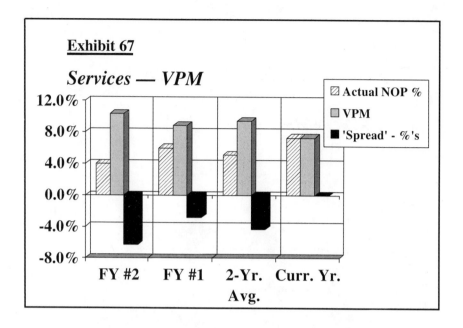

Exhibit 67

Services — VPM

Legend:
- ▨ Actual NOP %
- ▢ VPM
- ■ 'Spread' - %'s

Heads, even Ian's, were nodding around the table. Jason and Jonathan both noticed this, as did Earl. Jonathan had a look of satisfaction on his face. He also knew that he and Jason had to keep moving, first through the financial 'drivers' for the total company and then on to *MVA*. He, therefore, leaned forward and said, "What Jason is going to do now is quickly to take us through the same type of presentation for the total company. Then, I would suggest a short break before we delve into our final topic for the day".

With the room silent, Jason clicked on Exhibit 68, the growth rates for the total company.

"The 'huge' rise of invested capital in FY #2, related to the *Services* acquisition, should no longer be a surprise". It wasn't. With no response, Jason then stated ... "The two-year compound growth rates reflect the fact that *IC* growth still outpaced *Revenue and NOP*, but the gap was narrowed. Finally, the current year is showing the 'desirable' pattern".

"Last week, at our finance team session, I commented on this last point", Jonathan interjected. "What I said then, and what I would like to say again now, is that our company is, I believe, moving in the right direction, at least from a financial perspective, even though we have had a few 'bumps' along the way. I am encouraged by the 'pattern' of the bars (in Exhibit 68) for the current year. The 'current year' bars on the graph (the set on the far right side of the chart) reflect 'year-to-year' growth rates of 18% for revenue, 24% for *NOP*, and 16% for invested capital. As we've noted, that's the 'most desirable'

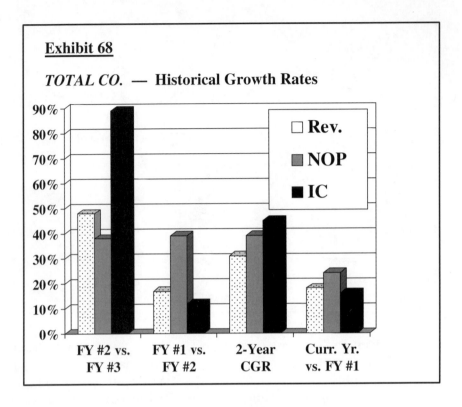

Exhibit 68

TOTAL CO. — **Historical Growth Rates**

pattern over the long term and the amounts are respectable. I'm very interested to learn what our strategies for the business units are going to tell us about the future".

"I must say that I am also becoming very interested in this issue", Ian added. "Val and Earl . . . and Jason . . . it looks as though you have your work cut out for you". Val and Earl nodded. Jason smiled. "Next chart", the 'big man' directed.

Jason clicked on Exhibit 69, the *ICI* for *TOTAL CO.*

Ian then spoke up. "Let me see if I understand the implications here. It appears that the *Services* acquisition increased our capital intensity – our *ICI* – by about 'ten cents' for each revenue dollar, from roughly '40 cents' prior to the acquisition (FY #3) to the '50-cent' range now. On a 'base' of forty cents, a 'ten-cent' increase is significant".

"That's it", Jonathan responded. He liked to answer Ian directly. "We now need to see what the BU strategies are going to produce in the way of invested capital requirements. My hunch is that we should be 'in the range' of the 'historical' *ICIs* for *Products* and the 'incremental' *ICIs* for *Services*. As you just noted, our work is 'cut out for us' to forecast our balance sheet investments".

Ian simply nodded. Peter and Larry took note of this gesture.

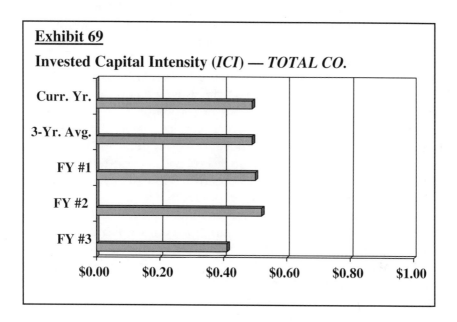

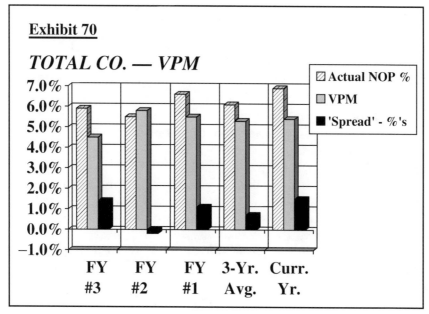

"We can conclude this portion of the meeting with the following illustration of the *VPM* for the total company", Jason then stated, as he clicked on Exhibit 70.

"This exhibit shows an interesting movement in the actual *NOP* margin and *VPM*. If we focus on the most distant and most recent years (FY #3 and the current year, respectively) notice that the actual *NOP* and *VPM* have increased by about one (1) percentage point.

Each of the two major BUs has enjoyed a rising *NOP* margin during the past two historical years and into the current year. *Products* has benefited recently from strength in maturing market segments that are issues, however, with respect to future growth prospects. *Services* is starting to reap higher margins from growing its base business and penetrating a new market (servicing other company products) – thus, leveraging its Selling, Marketing & Service (SMS) Expense over a larger revenue base. Offsetting these benefits, your 'total cost' of doing business – including 'balance sheet'-related costs – has increased. This is reflected in the total company's *VPM*, which has risen by one (1) percentage point. The *VPM* 'driver' is, I believe, vastly superior to the traditional earnings target in that it establishes a threshold for value creation in terms that most of you are familiar with – an after-tax profit margin. Without this type of analytic perspective, it would be impossible to know that the profit margin 'requirement' has increased, basically offsetting the improved operating performance. This can be seen in the 'spread', which is about the same (1.5%) in the current year as it was in FY #3. If you continue this analysis, you'll find that your return on invested capital (*ROIC*) is at the same (14%) level in the current year that it was in FY #3. This is after 'dropping' in FY #2 due to the *Services* acquisition and starting to recover last year (FY #1)".

"How did you get to that conclusion"? Larry asked, looking very puzzled.

"Divide the *NOP* margin by *ICT*', Jason answered.

"Is this why our stock price didn't respond more to the higher net earnings and *EPS* we generated in the past two years?" Ian asked, as he cast a look at Jack.

"It could be", Jason replied, "since more and more institutional investors are using the 'economic' metrics in their stock selection and pricing. How could you expect your 'multiple' or 'market-to-book ratio' to *increase* if your *ROIC* was *decreasing*?"

For one of the very few times in his career, Ian was silent and had no rebuttal, nor could he question the comment. Jason had made a calculated gamble that the 'big man' had to be confronted on this issue, regardless of what the consequences might be. Feeling that his 'gamble' had paid off, he continued ... "There is one other calculation that is relevant for this analysis. If we multiply the 'spread' (actual *NOP* margin versus *VPM*) by the annual revenue, does anyone know what we obtain?"

The blank looks around the table indicated that nobody knew – except for one person. Earl had given Frank Accurato Jason's articles and Frank recalled the one on this subject. The link to the most prominent metric they had discussed all morning suddenly became apparent. In his deliberate style, he said ... "I believe that calculation gets you to *EP*".

"Did everyone hear what Frank said?" Jason asked. "If you multiply the current year outlook for total revenue ($450 million) by the 1.5% 'spread', you will calculate the current year *EP* of $7 million. This is the 'link' of *VPM* to *EP*! We can close out this discussion by stating that 'economic profit' and 'valuation' models can be constructed based on this *VPM* concept. We'll demonstrate this and show an example when we get to the 'Valuation Methodology' phase of the process. I hope that you all now understand that we can provide you with a value-based 'earnings' target to strive for, encompassing the risk and investment dynamics of your business".

Jack had slumped down in his chair, staring blankly at the exhibit on the screen, when Jason had made the comment on Growthstar's stock price. But, as if given a reprieve, he quickly recovered as Jason made his last statement.

Broad smiles broke out on the faces of Larry and Peter. As they noticed it, Dave and Cathy also smiled. Ian looked around the room and silently took note of the reactions. Val, Earl, Frank and Jill looked at each other and exchanged glances of satisfaction. Jonathan leaned backward and looked upward, as if to be giving recognition to a higher authority.

Jonathan wanted to bring the Financial 'Drivers' to a 'crescendo-type' of ending, to set the stage for a vibrant session on the implications for Market Value Added (*MVA*) and the 'Magnifier' Concept. As Jason completed his comments on Exhibit 70, Jonathan rose and began to speak. "I feel that we are now beginning to 'experience' some realistic perceptions of shareholder value for Growthstar Inc. We have looked at our company and its two major business units from a number of 'value-oriented' perspectives, comparing this framework to our traditional 'accounting-oriented' system. The implications are 'thought provoking' in that they force us to look at our total company and our business units in ways that are different from what we are accustomed to. The financial markets are moving in this direction. While history can be 'thought provoking', the future can be truly 'dynamic', if we choose to pursue it in this fashion. What Jason will present after we return from a short break is a very powerful analytic concept. He will demonstrate, using the '**A**', '**B**', '**C**' example we've now become very familiar with, that the *EP* category of a business has a major impact on its value-creating potential. My exposure to this concept has been enlightening. 'Freshen up' your coffee or tea and return with an 'open mind'!"

As the group reassembled, Ian spoke before taking his seat. "I must say, that I did not expect that the economic framework and these supporting metrics could form the basis of a 'story' regarding our financial performance and its potential implications for our stock price. I am eager to explore the next topic and hope that all of you share my enthusiasm".

The group didn't need any more stimulus that that. They all leaned forward in their chairs to listen.

"Thank you for those words of encouragement, Ian", Jason began. "We've been at this for a while now, so I'll try to keep the last segment of this morning's sermon succinct. As Jonathan mentioned just before the break, the future can be 'dynamic'. However, it's the job of management to make sure the future is dynamic in a 'positive' sense. In this segment of today's session, the word 'positive' will imply 'creating shareholder value'. During the thirty minutes prior to our main session this morning, the finance team was exposed to the concept of Market Value Added and its acronym – *MVA*. Market Value Added is consistent with Shareholder Value. In fact, *MVA* measures the *amount* of shareholder value created, due to historical or anticipated future performance ... or both. So far, we've concentrated on the past. Now, we want to look toward the future. To begin this future outlook, however, we need to revisit a 'base' period to establish a frame of reference for *EP* performance. We'll refer back to Exhibit 55 and use the **'A', 'B', 'C'** example that Dave has come to simply adore as a starting point". Jason and Dave winked at each other as Jason uttered this comment and scanned back in his file to Exhibit 55.

Exhibit 55
"Economic Profit" — Example

"Base Period"		CO. 'A'	CO. 'B'	CO. 'C'
Revenue [Sales]		$1,000	$1,000	$1,000
Net Operating Profit				
[NOP]	- $	$100	$100	$100
	- %	10%	10%	10%
Invested Capital [IC]		$600	$800	$1,000
Cost of Capital [CCAP]		12%	12%	12%
Economic Profit				
NOP [from above]		**$100**	**$100**	**$100**
Capital Charge [CCAP]		**(72)**	**(96)**	**(120)**
Economic Profit ["EP"]		**$28**	**$4**	**$(20)**

"I use the term 'Base Period' to initially convey, for a company or business, a level of performance experienced for some relevant time period. In the **'A'**, **'B'**, **'C'** example, this will translate into a future expectation for two (2) elements – *NOP* margin and *ICI*. The assumption, therefore, will be for each firm to maintain its profit margin and its level of invested capital intensity. We will assess the impact of revenue growth on the value-creating potential for each company. Our focus will be on **Co. 'A'** and **Co. 'C'**, since we have already demonstrated that 'value neutral' firms, such as **Co. 'B'**, essentially 'run in place' and really *don't go anywhere* from a shareholder value perspective. The point to be illustrated is that the *EP* position of a business helps to dictate what its future actions should be . . . if the objective is to create shareholder value. Hopefully, that *is* the goal".

"Company '**A**' has a positive *EP*. If we calculate *VPM* and *ROIC*, which we have done with the finance team, we have positive 'spreads' – comparing the actual *NOP* margin to *VPM* and *ROIC* to *CCAP*, respectively. So, every indicator is looking good. The following exhibit (71) gives an overview of what **Co. 'A'** should do".

"This exhibit 'says a lot'. I know that 'growth' is what *your company* wants. You just have to make sure that the businesses are in an '**A**' category in terms of their 'sustainable' economic profit. If they are *not* there now, as is the case of *Services*, then the near- and longer-term strategy has to get them into an '**A**' position".

"Keeping in mind the 'balance' of customer value and economic value", Val interjected, "which we covered in our initial meeting on this subject".

Exhibit 71

How to Increase Shareholder Value

Company 'A'

Invest capital in growth-oriented strategies / programs ... with high return potential
- ✦ *"Go for Growth"* — *instill growth as a driving force throughout the organization*
- ✦ *Emphasize staying close to existing margins and capital intensity, with room for some deterioration if the opportunity is significant*

... Growth adds value — "Bigger is Better" !

"Good point", Jonathan added, looking at Ian as if to remind him of their first conversation on this subject. Ian picked up the gesture and nodded to Jonathan. Ian also had a look of extreme satisfaction on his face. Growth was his 'hot button' and Jason had struck a cord. Further, Ian was beginning to envision a framework to help him determine 'where' and 'how' to grow.

Jason, sensing that Ian and the two general managers wanted to see something tangible, picked up the discussion with ... "The potential for shareholder value creation of this 'go for growth' objective for Company '**A**' can be illustrated in the next exhibit (72)".

Jason felt, from past experience, that this chart needed careful explanation, and the facial expressions around the table confirmed this feeling.

"Let's start with the 'horizontal' axis, which plots annual compound growth rates for revenue and net earnings – which are the same, since we're assuming a steady profit margin (10%). I've constructed growth rate scenarios, over a four-year future time horizon, in 'increments' of five (5) percentage points ... from 'zero' (or, 'no growth') to 20%. Again, these are annual CGR's. OK so far?" Heads nodded around the table.

"Next, the 'vertical' axis plots *MVA* in millions of dollars. The *MVA* is the 'net present value' (*NPV*) of the various growth scenarios, based

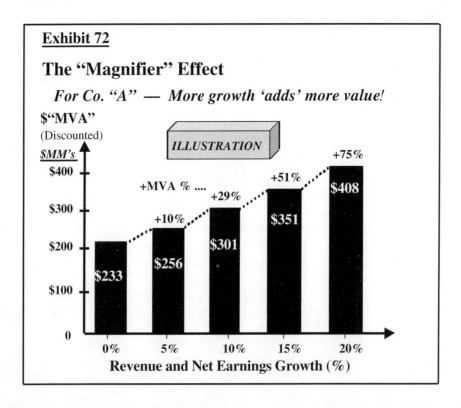

Exhibit 72

The "Magnifier" Effect

For Co. "A" — More growth 'adds' more value!

$"MVA"
(Discounted)

$MM's

ILLUSTRATION

+75%

$400

+MVA % ....   +51%

+29% $408

$300   +10%

$351

$301

$200

$256

$233

$100

0

0%   5%   10%   15%   20%

Revenue and Net Earnings Growth (%)

on the assumptions for *ICI* and *NOP* margin. Again, *MVA* measures the shareholder value created – it's the *NPV* for each growth plan. OK?" Heads nodded again.

"The 'Magnifier' Effect is the 'impact' on *MVA* (shareholder value) for the selected revenue growth rates. Starting with the 'no-growth' (0%) scenario, if the business stays at its 'base period' level of revenue and earnings, it will create $233 million of *MVA*. This results from the company ('**A**') generating an economic profit (*EP*) of $28 million. Under a 'no-growth' scenario, this level of *EP* would continue forever. The *MVA* (or shareholder value) is simply the *EP* 'capitalized' at the 12% cost of capital. $28 million divided by 12% is approximately $233 million. What this means is that management has created a 'warranted' *MVA* of $233 million. This is the amount of 'shareholder' value that management has added to the 'economic book' value of $600 million – remember the *IC* for **'Co. 'A'**?" Heads nodded again. "So, if management decides to 'go fishing', its *MVA* would be limited to what it has produced to date".

"Now, let's assume that a '5%' growth plan is communicated to the investors. With the assumptions we have made, this 5% growth in revenue and earnings translates into a 10% increase in *MVA*. In essence, revenue and earnings growth is 'magnified' into increasingly higher growth rates for *MVA*. As we continue along the horizontal axis, to higher growth rates for revenue and earnings, look at what happens to the height of the (vertical) *MVA* bars. They rise at even higher rates – again, in a 'magnifying' fashion. At the peak of this example, a 20% CGR for sales and earnings over a four-year future time period produces a 75% increase in shareholder value. Extending the time horizon or further increasing the growth rate would 'magnify' the situation even further".

"My goodness", exclaimed Ian. "I have had this intuitive feeling for my entire career about the impact of growth. All of you know this. It's the reason I renamed the company – to focus on growing our business. But, I always thought it was driven by *EPS*". Ian glared at Jack as he spoke, and Jack shuddered to himself. "Based on this example, value creation is dependent on *EP* (drop the 'S' from *EPS*) and strategic growth".

"Amen", Val whispered, saying the word just loud enough so everyone heard.

Earl was not about to let this moment pass and he stated emphatically … "That's why some of the 'great names' we know in business continue to produce incredible gains in their stock prices. They produce positive 'economic' profit – which translates into a high return on their invested capital (well in excess of their cost of capital) – and they grow rapidly!"

"That's the formula I want for this company!" Ian thundered, as he looked at Jonathan, Val, Flo, Larry and Peter. "And, I want people who think this way! Earl, I want to commend you for being so diligent in pursuing this approach, in spite of the 'roadblocks' that may have been thrown in your way".

Earl was so excited that he almost spit the coffee that he had just sipped onto the boardroom table. Gasping, he simply nodded in Ian's direction. Jonathan chuckled to himself, knowing that Earl had, for quite some time, been looking for this type of reaction from the 'big man' (Earl's nickname for Ian) and would have liked to have been able to respond verbally. "*Oh well*", Jonathan thought to himself, "*at least Earl got the recognition he was looking for*".

Jack was really feeling lost now, and quietly walked to the coffeepot for a refill.

Except for Jack, the atmosphere was the vibrant one that Jonathan had hoped for. Even Flo had a very enthusiastic expression on her face, obviously influenced by Ian's comment about 'people'.

"A picture is really worth a thousand words", Jonathan then commented. "This is what I meant by saying that while history is 'thought provoking', the future can be 'dynamic' – if we choose to make it so".

Jason wanted to keep the meeting rolling, because in spite of the energy, he knew that the group would soon start to 'wear down' from all the new concepts presented and discussed. "Let's quickly look at the situation for Company '**B**' ", he said as he clicked on Exhibit 73.

"Company '**B**' needs to become 'more efficient' – not bigger", Jason continued. "Their predicament is rather straightforward. Many of the conglomerates are in the '**B**' category. They buy firms that

---

Exhibit 73

How to Increase Shareholder Value
Company 'B'

Earn more operating profit with the same capital
  ✦ *Squeeze additional profit from existing capital base*
        .... Selective pricing and/or cost cutting
  ✦ *Emphasize margin improvement*

... Growth is secondary — adds minimal value !

are sometimes in different businesses, with very little in the way of common marketing, distribution, or other functions. They are running what amounts to a 'portfolio' of companies – in essence, a miniature mutual fund. What they fail to realize are some important shortcomings. First, most institutional investors want to construct their own portfolios, not one that a CEO or management group has chosen. Second, 'focus' – *not* 'diversification' – has produced the highest total shareholder returns (TSRs) in the stock market. This is partly due to the management complexity that conglomerates or diversified companies are subject to. It's very difficult to be an 'expert' at everything! Finally, growth by acquisition alone creates obstacles to value creation in that it's hard to avoid the 'transfer of wealth' phenomenon – the payment of a 'premium' to gain control of another company through a purchase. Unless an acquisition target has been mis-managed and a 'turn-around' opportunity exists, or a truly synergistic combination can be implemented, or the seller is not very astute (a rare situation today with the involvement of boards of directors and shareholder activists) it is hard to 'hit a home run' with acquisitions. Companies usually do much better with internally developed products and/or services, new marketing channels, distribution methods, manufacturing techniques, etc. I don't want to 'belabor' this point, except to conclude this discussion by saying that without greater efficiency (thus, higher *EP*) **'B'-type** firms will continue to 'tread water'. They may get 'bigger', but they won't get any 'better' if they don't become more efficient with the capital they currently employ".

"Here's the real challenge", Jason stated firmly, as he clicked on Exhibit 74.

Exhibit 74

How to Increase Shareholder Value

Company 'C'

Reduce the level of capital employed
+ *Streamline / re-engineer / re-structure operations*
+ *Validate capital invested in major lines of business*

... Growth 'destroys' value !

"'**'C'-type**' firms or businesses *cannot* grow and create value, without a fundamental – perhaps radical – change in the way they manage their invested capital. The points in the exhibit (74) are clear. These '**C**' businesses are those where major restructuring or re-engineering efforts can have a big pay-off. Let's quantify the impact in Exhibit 75".

"Does this illustration convey the message?" Jason asked.

Jonathan responded with ... "I'm sure, Jason, that everyone can see the 'negative' implications of the bars pointing downward, but the structure of this chart is somewhat different from the 'Magnifier' Effect for Company '**A**', so I think you should give an explanation".

"You're right, Jonathan. Sometimes I get so immersed in the 'message' – having presented this example so many times – that I forget to describe all the elements".

"As Jonathan noted, this chart is somewhat different in its structure. The growth rate scenarios for revenue *and* net earnings are

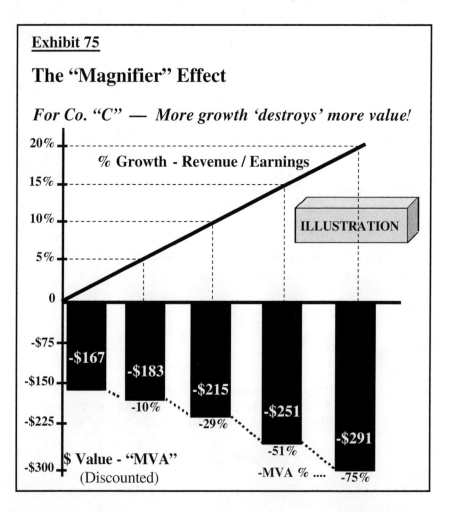

plotted in an 'upward' direction on the top portion of the 'vertical' axis. The 'diagonally sloped' line with points of intersection at '5% growth rate increments' represent the traditional picture of rising revenue and earnings, the implication being that shareholder value and stock prices rise accordingly".

"That's always been my view", Larry quipped ... "until this morning, that is".

Jack slumped down. He had consumed enough coffee and had nowhere to go. He felt a sense of being surrounded by unknown forces. Unlike his reaction at the 'team' meeting last week – when he felt some 'relief' – today he felt great discomfort in the presence of Larry, Peter and, especially, Ian. "*This is absolutely one of the worst meetings I have ever had with the officers and the CEO*", he said silently to himself. "*Even Larry, my close ally, is starting to question the 'old bottom line'. But, I've got to get through it ... somehow*". His mood was not helped as Cathy nodded, indicating her understanding.

"You're not alone, Larry", Jason replied. "This 'earnings growth' model has driven many valuations, or at least valuation 'perceptions' for a long time. However, as the bottom portion of the chart indicates, this is *not* the case. What's happening is that every percent of compound growth will cost **Co. 'C'** more in *CCAP* than it will produce in *EP*. This is in spite of the fact that Company '**C**' is generating a 'profit' – at least in the traditional method of calculating profit. As we saw in Exhibit 55, however, **Co. 'C'** is actually producing an 'economic loss'. If firms with this performance characteristic signal to the 'financial markets' that this pattern (that is, too much capital) will continue, then the 'markets' should, in theory, respond with valuations that would follow the progression of the *MVA* bars in the lower portion of the graph".

"Let's take them one at a time. In the 'no-growth' scenario, the 'negative' *EP* of $20 million (remember that number from Exhibit 55?) would be 'capitalized' at 'negative' $167 million. That's −$20 million divided by 12% (*CCAP*). This management has got some 'fixing' to do before they 'go fishing'. You may have seen some firms that have actually contracted (gotten smaller) and created value. Well, this is why!"

"Now, assume that management communicates a 5% growth plan to its investors, maintaining the same *NOP* margin and *ICI* as in the 'base period'. The investors should respond by shaving an additional $16 million from the firm's 'economic book value'. Thus, 'negative' *MVA* 'grows' (how's *that* for misuse of a word?) by 10% to −$183 million. The dash sign (−) in front of the dollar sign indicates a 'negative' value. The 'Magnifier' Effect is now working in reverse".

"Follow the *Yellow Brick Road* to the 20% growth level for revenue and earnings. *MVA* (shareholder value) has been 'destroyed' by 75%. Now, I hope the message is clear – that, regardless of 'accounting' earnings, **'C'-type** businesses will destroy value as they grow, and the more they grow, the more value they will destroy!"

The others in the room had never witnessed the looks of astonishment on the faces of Ian, Peter and Larry. Ian just sat there, scratching his chin. Peter and Larry imitated the gesture. Flo even got into the act, and she *never* scratched her chin.

Ian, however, did not sit still for long, nor did he dwell on any 'negatives' for very long. He didn't rise to a CEO position without being able to handle just about any situation. This was no different. With a wry smile on his face, he said, "Life is a never-ending journey of learning from past mistakes and benefiting from new knowledge and experience. Today has been a good example of both. We may have inadvertently made some mistakes in our understanding of what really 'drives' shareholder value. I'm sure we're not alone. We've also been educated on some new concepts that can, and probably should, be applied here at Growthstar. Finally, I feel good about the experience, since I think we all understand our company more than when we entered this room earlier today. Jason, do you have anything else? Or does anyone else have a question?"

"I have one", Peter responded. "How do you categorize 'start-ups'?"

"That's an excellent question", Jason replied. "I generally put them in a special category (**'A-Prime'**). They may 'technically' be a **'C'**, based on 'start-up losses', but the expectation is to become an **'A'**. These (start-up) businesses have to be valued totally on future prospects with an attempt made to establish a 'base level' *EP* and set of 'Drivers' ".

With no more questions from anyone, Jason said, "I would like to summarize what we've covered today. As Jonathan stated when we began, we had three main agenda items:

- The transition from accounting to economic metrics, resulting in Economic Profit, which we call '*EP*';
- Supporting measures, known as Financial 'Drivers', of which three will occupy our focus initially; and
- Market Value Added, shortened to the acronym '*MVA*' and the 'Magnifier' Effect on shareholder value, resulting from the *EP* of a business.

This next, and I promise, last exhibit – at least for today – summarizes these three topics. I now give you Exhibit 76".

Exhibit 76

SUMMARY — *EP*, Financial 'Drivers', *MVA*

- Economic Profit incorporates income statement performance, balance sheet investments and a capital cost ... making it more robust than "earnings".
- Operating managers can "drive" value creation by focusing on three key financial items:
  - The relationship of revenue, profit and invested capital growth
  - The amount of capital needed to generate one dollar of revenue
  - Margins (before and/or after tax) above a minimum level required for value enhancement.
- The economic profit approach and supporting financial "drivers" provide a template to assess progress toward shareholder value goals.
- Economic Profit translates into Market Value Added through a future outlook.
- Businesses can be broken down into existing ('no growth') and strategy ('growth') elements, with market values attributable to each through application of the economic metrics.
- Growth "magnifies" value creation (positively or negatively) depending on whether economic returns are above or below the cost of capital.

Jonathan then leaned forward and said, "I believe this exhibit provides a good synopsis of what we've learned and worked on today. I appreciate all your inputs, since it makes me feel that, at least up to this point, our historical and current year analysis of the 'economic value'-based approach and metrics has been worth while. We haven't done the 'future-oriented' *MVA* analysis yet for Growthstar, but we will as we evaluate our strategic plans. At least you all know what is coming".

"I'm glad you said that", Ian interjected, "because my next question was going to be ... *where do we go from here*? Can you elaborate, please". This was a *directive*.

"Certainly", Jason responded. "Our most immediate task will be to work with the finance team to review the major valuation methodologies in conjunction with 'where' and 'how' they are applied. We'll then use the methodologies to 'value' the strategies for the business units within Growthstar. This should coincide with the development of the BU strategies. Next, we will apply the approach and metrics to major internal and external investments, along with the company's process for capital planning, evaluation and control. We'll complete the effort with revisions and/or enhancements to your financial reporting and communications. Finally, we'll educate and train people within the company".

"As you can see, we have a way to go", Jonathan stated.

"That's true", Ian said as he rose to adjourn the meeting, "but we've made a good start".

When Ian rose from his chair, meetings were over. Today was no different, and everyone followed the CEO out of the boardroom.

Value-based analysis: valuation hierarchy

Both Jonathan and Jason had commitments for the remainder of the week, so they decided to meet again the following Monday morning.

Jonathan walked into Jason's office at 9:00 am the following Monday. "I just saw Ian, and he reiterated his satisfaction with the work done to date and the perceptions that have surfaced. He seemed to be particularly pleased that Peter is starting to 'latch on' to the concepts, that Dave and Cathy are making some very good observations, and that Larry is at least receptive to 'considering' new ways of analyzing his business".

"That's good", Jason responded. "I guess I 'have a life' for at least a little while longer".

"At least for a while", Jonathan chuckled. "Let's get some coffee". Jason did not have to be asked twice.

As they sipped their coffee, Jason began to describe the next step. "Remember the first day in your office, when we recalled the 'blunder' I made in graduate school about being too myopic in my analytic perspective on capital investments, and then how you've been too narrow in your approach here at Growthstar?"

"How could I forget", Jonathan replied.

"Well, that's our next topic. We need to cover this with the 'team' before delving into any future-oriented 'value analysis'. We don't have to get the officers involved, except to summarize our conclusions. This 'Valuation Hierarchy' sets the stage for where we apply the economic metrics and exactly what type of evaluation is done and which metric(s) are emphasized. It sets a framework for the 'strategic' and 'investment' driven evaluations that we will undertake, as we strive to assess the 'value impact' of your critical future endeavors".

"So, specifically what do we do"? Jonathan asked.

"Arrange a 'team' meeting as soon as possible. I have almost everything prepared".

"Wednesday is the best day this week for me. I'll have Kay set it up for the afternoon – right after lunch. I have a meeting with one of our bankers in the morning".

On Wednesday at 1:30 pm, the finance team assembled in the corporate finance conference room.

After all were seated, Jonathan began with ... "We're entering the next phase of our value-based performance effort. Jason wants to introduce us to an analytic perspective for applying the 'economic' metrics that we've been immersing ourselves in. The objective is to determine 'where' (specifically) to apply the measures". Jonathan then motioned to Jason to get started.

"I would like to use an example to help convey this message. Let me start, however, by explaining *what the message is*. This message is, essentially, an attack on traditional 'project-oriented' applications of the discounted cash flow-based measures, which are the foundation for the *EP* and related metrics we're pursuing for potential implementation here at Growthstar. Specifically, I'm going to attack the evaluation of 'capital projects' and try to demonstrate the futility of applying value-based analysis at a level which is too low in the 'hierarchy' to benefit from the rigor of the evaluation".

"Great day in the morning", Dave exclaimed. "Is this my reward for all the 'Dave bashing' I've endured recently? I have never been able to understand, at any company I've worked for, the incredible amount of time and effort that is spent on capital projects. I feel lucky that most of the testing equipment we either purchase or lease is below the capital authorization limits imposed by corporate, and that our office leases have not been subjected to the capital budgeting process".

"We're very much aware of that", Jonathan grimaced.

"I can't believe this", Cathy chimed in. "It seems that I spend half of my professional life filling out capital project forms and justifying every capital expenditure over $250,000". She looked inquisitively at Jack, who could only shrug his shoulders. "I've been bothered by this for some time, now, but just assumed it was part of a finance person's job. There doesn't seem to be any 'connection' among all these capital projects, and we're constantly factoring in various things when the numbers don't look attractive. Larry asked me, about three months ago, what our objective was with this year's capital budget, and I could *not* give him a credible answer. There are just so many 'projects' floating around, that I don't know what they're accomplishing. Further, there's no way to go back and intelligently 'track' the internal rate of return (*IRR*) or the net present value (*NPV*) for a specific project".

"I'm becoming 'painfully aware' that we may have made some mistakes over the years in the area of capital investment evaluations", Jonathan replied. "I'm going to try to take solace in Ian's comment last week about *life being a never-ending journey of learning from past mistakes and benefiting from new knowledge and experience.* With this as a 'backdrop', I would like Jason to take us through his example and then provide us with what he calls a 'Valuation Hierarchy'".

Jason did not expect the comments from Dave and Cathy, which he interpreted as positive toward his position, and he began speaking enthusiastically. "In the world of corporate finance, few activities are more entrenched than capital project evaluations. This focus on individual projects often comes at the expense of identifying and analyzing major programs, the building blocks of a strategy. Valuing the strategy itself, the ultimate indicator of future business success, can also be overlooked in the pursuit of net present value (*NPV*) or internal rate of return (*IRR*) calculations for 'individual' capital investments. 'Project' analysis keeps countless financial analysts and managers (à la Cathy) hard at work ... I also have vivid memories of my early years in finance ... and consumes a significant amount of time for corporate managers and directors – and vice presidents". Jason winked at Jonathan as he made this last comment, which Earl noticed. "A review of project analysis and what it accomplishes, in light of what is really going on in any business, can be revealing. In this appraisal, we all must be willing to raise some candid questions about certain 'traditions' in finance".

"Let's pursue this topic with a hypothetical, yet realistic, example for a company that is similar to *XYZ Industries*, the fictitious firm that we used to understand the basics of economic profit, and potentially analogous to your own company. Do we really need to be assured that, say, a $750,000 machining center for a manufacturing company with $3 billion in sales is economically viable? Or that a $300,000 CAD/CAM system for the engineering department will have a payoff? When such small investments are put in their proper context, capital project evaluations can appear virtually meaningless – as, in reality, they usually are".

Cathy rolled her eyes, first shaking her head from side to side and then looking at Jack and Jonathan and saying to herself ... "*What have you guys been putting me through?*" Frank felt empathy toward Cathy, but could only look in her direction to indicate that he understood her frustration, even though he had supported Earl's efforts to ease the analytic burden for capital projects, which Jack had fought against, citing 'loss of control' as a risk. Jonathan had simply not given the matter any attention, in spite of Earl's prodding, due to his other 'priorities'. Jack tensed up. He could sense another 'battle' brewing, and he still had not fully recovered from the trauma he experienced at last week's meeting with Ian and the officers. Jill wasn't that involved in capital projects, so she just sat and observed the 'body language' of her colleagues.

"Is this an exaggerated claim?" Jason asked . . . continuing on. "Let's assume that our (hypothetical) $3 billion company has three business units (BUs), each with roughly $1 billion of sales. Further, assume that the machining center and CAD/CAM projects are in BU 1, which has a strategy of growing at 15% per year by offering a combination of high product quality and competitive cost. BU 1, therefore, plans to grow sales by approximately $150 million next year. Its current year balance sheet reflects the following amounts for fixed assets, which I will write on the flip chart". He went to the chart and wrote:

> **Gross fixed assets $300 million**
> **Accumulated depreciation ($100) million**
> **Net fixed assets $200 million**

"Comparing the gross fixed assets (GFA) and net fixed assets (NFA) amounts to sales, we can calculate *ICI* ratios for each". He wrote on the flip chart:

> **GFA – $300 million (assets) divided by $1 billion (sales) equals $0.30, or 30%**
> **NFA – $200 million (assets) divided by $1 billion (sales) equals $0.20, or 20%**

"The GFA and NFA ratios reflect capital intensity, which you all now know is the level of capital required to generate each dollar of sales. If we were to determine that the growth strategy will be in line with past experience in terms of *ICI*, then BU 1 will need to invest about $45 million next year – 30% of its 'new' sales. After depreciation, the 'net' new fixed capital investment will be approximately $30 million (20% of $150 million) if the strategy replicates recent investment patterns".

"Even if the strategy can 'leverage' the existing assets and require less new capital, on a relative basis, we're still dealing with annual investments of many millions of dollars to support the strategy.

Since strategies usually require more than one year to execute, the aggregate amount of new capital over the next few years, necessary for BU 1 to grow and prosper, could be $100 million or more".

"So what is the point of financially justifying the investment in the machining center or the CAD/CAM system? Why drive people crazy by requiring elaborate evaluations on relatively small projects that have no purpose or life of their own, and are only pieces of a much larger puzzle?"

"The job of management is to put the puzzle together, not to place each piece under the microscope. I'll bet that many companies, similar to yours, that perform extensive capital project evaluations have not quantified the shareholder value impact (that is, the *MVA* – or *NPV/IRR*) of their overall strategy. The key points are, if a strategy has value, then the individual projects should have value, since they are part of the strategy; further, these projects cannot, and should not, be separated out for purposes of analysis. That's why you've been hearing me, along with Val, Earl and Jonathan, say – several times – that our next major action is to assess the value creation for the BU 'strategies'".

"The purpose of 'value-based analysis', regardless of which metric you may prefer, since they are all an extension of *NPV/IRR*, is to determine value at appropriate levels in the 'corporate' hierarchy – the company, business unit, strategy, and major program. The major program (for example, an important operational or strategic initiative) is the *absolute lowest level for which value-based analysis should be performed*".

Cathy shook her head again and looked upward. Dave smirked. "*I won't have to succumb to this 'analysis paralysis' after all*", he thought to himself. Earl smiled and looked at Jack, who scowled.

"The 'strategy' for BU 1 may encompass *growth via high quality and competitive cost*. A supporting 'program' might be one to *enhance product quality and*, at the same time, *contain or reduce costs*. This type of initiative would seem logical – in fact, it may be an 'essential' program. Let's assume that this 'program' encompasses ten machining centers averaging $1 million each plus a CAD/CAM system. At this level, 'value analysis' can be meaningful, as it may well represent a building block of the strategy or operating plan, or both. As we present a numerical example, we will highlight the impact of focusing on the 'program' versus the ten individual machining center 'projects'. It is my belief that too many companies still concentrate on the individual investments, rather than grasping the larger, and more important, link to either the strategy or operational objective". Jason looked at Earl and Frank as he made this last comment.

Jason continued. "A 'walk through the numbers' can demonstrate the 'Valuation Hierarchy'. Let's start with the project. Assume the $750,000 machining center, mentioned earlier, reduces cost, but does not have the throughput capability to increase sales beyond the current level. Therefore, this 'project' is presented as a classical cost reduction investment. Due to this myopic perspective, we miss the point that the strategy is for growth, through enhanced product quality features, along with competitive cost. Exhibit 77 illustrates a typical cost savings analysis to justify spending $750,000. If we take this approach to a ridiculous extreme, we could conceivably have ten (10) separate evaluations, some growth, some cost reduction, and some maybe combining the two. What a potential nightmare! For some companies, though, this is their analytic world".

"I sometimes feel that this is *my* 'analytic world' and that I'm *stuck in it*", Cathy snipped. "I've done this type of analysis so many times, I could 'lead' the discussion".

"Would you like to do that"? Jason asked.

Exhibit 77
"Project" Analysis

Invest in a $750,000 N/C Machine Center to Save Costs [$000's Omitted]	Rates/ Factor		Year 1	Year 2	Year 3	Year 4	Year 5
Capital Investment (outlay)		$	(750)				
Annual Cost Savings (pre tax)		$	150	200	200	200	200
Taxes @ Corp. Tax Rate =	33%	$	(50)	(67)	(67)	(67)	(67)
Tax Shield re: Depreciation:							
Annual Deprec. — Life (years) =	10	$	75	75	75	75	75
Tax Shield @ Rate =	33%	$	25	25	25	25	25
Free Cash Flow/Profit After Tax [*FCF/PAT*]		$	(625)	158	158	158	158

	Rates/ Factors		Year 6	Year 7	Year 8	Year 9	Year 10
Annual Cost Savings (pre tax)		$	200	200	200	200	200
Taxes @ Corp. Tax Rate =	33%	$	(67)	(67)	(67)	(67)	(67)
Tax Shield re: Depreciation:							
Annual Deprec. — Life (years) =	10	$	75	75	75	75	75
Tax Shield @ Rate =	33%	$	25	25	25	25	25
Free Cash Flow/Profit After Tax [FCF/PAT]		$	158	158	158	158	158

Cost of Capital (CCAP) = | 11% | .... Weighted cost of equity and debt

Net Present Value
... of 10-year FCF/PAT minus
    Initial Cash Outlay | **$227**

Internal Rate of Return (IRR) | **21%**

"Sure, why not", Cathy replied, "maybe I can 'vent my frustration' and 'sound smart' at the same time. As Jason indicated, this 'project' is a classical cost reduction. In this case, by looking at the second row of numbers, we can see that the investment is expected to generate cost savings of $200,000 annually for ten years. Apparently, the first year savings are only $150,000 – probably due to start-up inefficiencies. The next three rows compute the tax implications of the 'project'. The analysis – done under the 'free cash flow' (*FCF*) approach – yields a positive net present value (*NPV*) of $227,000 and an internal rate of return (*IRR*) of 21%, a ten (10) percentage-point 'spread' over *CCAP*".

"So what", Earl cracked, glaring at Jack. "How can anyone seriously get excited by an *NPV* of $227,000 in a billion dollar business? Is this what we want management and the board to concentrate on? Or, is there something more important, in terms of achieving the primary goal of any 'for profit' enterprise – that is, to execute the strategy in order to maximize the value of the investments that the shareholders have made, and will continue to make, in the business. By the way, in at least one research study of institutional investors, strategy development and execution was one of the most important factors in their investment decision for a particular company; and, 'strategy value' is *one or two levels* above 'project returns'".

"How do you know that", Jack scowled.

"I cheated", Earl chortled. "Jason showed me the 'wrap-up' chart in his office yesterday".

The 'team' broke out in laughter – except for Jack, who continued to scowl. Earl once commented that Jack could 'hold a scowl' for longer than anyone he had ever known.

Jason then picked up the dialogue ... "when we elevate our analysis to the 'program' level, we can begin to grasp the strategy for this business. The capital investment 'program' alluded to previously is evaluated in Exhibit 78, again using the *FCF* method".

"The highlights of this program are as follows:

- Ten machining centers are to be purchased over a two-year investment period.
- The average investment per machine is $1 million.
- The machining centers each have an average useful life of ten years.
- CAD/CAM systems are to be purchased in years 1 and 6, noting that these systems have a useful life of five years. The first CAD/CAM costs $300,000 and the second is estimated to cost $500,000 in year 6.
- The investment 'program' generates cost savings plus the capability to produce new sales, albeit at a lower 'throughput ratio'.

Exhibit 78
"Program" Analysis

Invest in a $10.8 million "Cost Savings/Quality" Program [$000's Omitted]	Rates/ Factors		Year 1	Year 2	Year 3	Year 4	Year 5
Average Cost per N/C Machine Center		$	1,000	1,000	1,000	1,000	1,000
Number of N/C Machine Ctrs.			5	5	-	-	-
Total Capital Investment (outlay) including 1 CAD/CAM in Year 1		$	(5,300)	(5,000)	-	-	-
Incremental Sales - resulting in	$1,500	$	-	7,500	15,000	15,000	15,000
Incremental Profit @ Margin =	12%	$	-	900	1,800	1,800	1,800
Cost Savings (use 'per Machine' Impact from Exhibit 1)		$	750	1,750	2,000	2,000	2,000
Total Profit Impact		$	750	2,650	3,800	3,800	3,800
Depreciation — N/C Machines	10	$	(500)	(1,000)	(1,000)	(1,000)	(1,000)
(# years) CAD/CAM	5	$	(60)	(60)	(60)	(60)	(60)
"Net Taxes" @ Rate =	33%	$	(63)	(529)	(912)	(912)	(912)
Free Cash Flow/Profit After Tax [FCF/PAT]		$	(4,613)	(2,879)	2,888	2,888	2,888

			Year 6	Year 7	Year 8	Year 9	Year 10
Free Cash Flow/Profit After Tax [FCF/PAT] Year 5 "Steady State" — Adjusted for:		$	2,888	2,888	2,888	2,888	2,888
Additional CAD/CAM in Year 6		$	(500)				
Free Cash Flow/Profit After Tax [FCF/PAT]		$	2,388	2,888	2,888	2,888	2,888

Net Present Value — of 10-year FCF/PAT
...net of Initial Cash Outlays | $5,300 | ... the 'Program' has a present value of $5+ million
[No Residual — terminated > Year 10]

Internal Rate of Return (IRR) | 28% |

BU 1 generates about $3.00 of sales for each $1.00 of gross fixed asset. This equipment reduces manufacturing cost and generates 50% of the overall asset base 'throughput ratio' – or, $1.50 of sales for each $1.00 of new capital".

Earl was not to be restrained. "Is there any question as to what is the *more relevant* 'net present value' for senior management and the board – the 'program' value (*NPV*) of $5.3 million, or the 'project' value of $227,000? How about *ten* 'project values' of $227,000 each? That ought to really confuse them! The 'project' is narrow in scope and presents only a very limited perspective of the goals for the business. The 'program' gets closer to the strategic intent for the business". The glaring and scowling between Earl and Jack continued. The others took note and chuckled to themselves – except for Jonathan.

Jason then spoke again. "To appreciate the *real* 'value potential' for the business, the analysis has to be elevated to a higher level – that of the business strategy itself. This evaluation level is one of the most productive (also, one of the most difficult) for management to work through, because it forces managers to think about their most critical financial 'drivers', and rationalize why they will stay the same or change, based on the strategy. These 'drivers', in addition to providing insights into historical and current performance (as we've seen), help determine the value potential for the strategy and, ultimately, the entire business".

"Exhibit 79 gives an example of financial expectations for BU 1's strategy. It assumes:

- The business will grow by 15% annually for the next four years, maintaining its recent 'pre-tax' operating profit margin of 12%.
- The historical capital intensity ratio will be reduced, from $0.30 'gross' and $0.20 'net' to $0.27 and $0.17, respectively, as a ratio to sales, due to the ability to 'leverage' prior years' investment in plant and equipment.

We'll also assume that detailed assumptions for volume, pricing and cost structure are imbedded in the summary results".

As the 'team' members were viewing Exhibit 79, Jason made a comment. "If you add up the 'net' new fixed capital investments ('after' depreciation) anticipated for the next four years to execute the strategy, you will calculate an amount of slightly over $125 million. How can anyone focus their attention on *analyzing* each 'million-dollar project' when the business unit may need to invest $125 million ('net') over the next four years? That's not to say we shouldn't *control the expenditures* for the capital 'projects', but we need to move away from *evaluating* them, because the 'projects' do not provide a mean-ingful basis or perspective for value analysis. 'Control' systems can, and should be, detailed and specific, but 'evaluation' systems need to be focused at a higher level. *To repeat, the 'major program' is the absolute 'lowest' level for value analysis, and the major emphasis should be on the value creation for the 'business strategy'* ".

Earl wanted one 'last shot' at this topic, and nobody – especially his 'buddy' Jack – was surprised when he launched into another dialogue. "Look at what we miss if our attention is at the 'project' versus the 'program' and 'strategy' level. BU 1 appears to have a strategy with a very strong value-creating potential, 'to the tune' of over $40 million of *NPV* and a total business return (*TBR*, which is similar to *IRR*, since it's the 'internal rate of return' for the entire strategy) of 24%. And we should be 'losing sleep' over a $750,000

Exhibit 79
"Strategy" Analysis

Enhance Product Quality and Control Costs to Grow Sales and Maintain Margins	*Rates/ Factors* ... also,	Year 1	Year 2	Year 3	Year 4	Residual
[$ Millions, except Ratios]	"Base" #'s					
Sales — Total	1,000	$ 1,150	1,323	1,521	1,749	
"New" Sales @ Annual Growth =	*15%*	$ 150	323	521	749	
"New" Operating Profit (pre tax)	120	$ 18	39	63	90	
... @ O. P. Margin =	*12%*					
"New" Taxes @ Rate =	*33%*	$ (6)	(13)	(21)	(30)	
"New" Net Operating Profit (NOP)		$ 12	26	42	60	254
"Net New" Fixed Investment						
... @ Capital Intensity Ratio =	*$0.17*	$ (26)	(29)	(34)	(39)	
"New" Working Capital @ Ratio =	*$0.20*	$ (30)	(35)	(40)	(46)	
Free Cash Flow - for 'Strategy'		$ (43)	(38)	(32)	(24)	254
Net Present Value — 4-yr. FCF ...plus 'Residual' Value	$41	... *'Strategy' has a present value of $41 million*				
		['Residual' continues Yr. 4 NOP thru Yr. 10]				
Total Business Return (TBR)	24%	... *equivalent to IRR — for the 'Strategy'*				

Memo: 'Cumulative' (4-year total) Net New Fixed Capital Investment = $127million

machining center to help execute a major cost containment objective? At Growthstar, we're going to the board with capital project *IRRs*, but *not* with the 'value analysis' for our strategies? What management and the board *really* need to know is the contribution of our strategies to the overall value (stock price) of the enterprise, and then what the key building blocks (the 'programs') of the strategies are".

Jason could see that Earl was 'running out of steam', so he jumped in with ... "Major programs are necessary to ensure that the strategy has substance. They also provide a mechanism to prioritize investments and track progress toward achieving key success elements of a strategy. 'Projects' are a basis for cash and expenditure control, but provide no foundation for meaningful valuation analysis. Further, 'project analysis' can actually *confuse* people as to what is really going on in the business, and can actually lead to *inappropriate* or *wrong* decisions about investing. Therefore, *project 'evaluations' should be scrapped and replaced with value 'analysis' focused at the level where value 'creation' occurs!*"

"Hurrah", shouted Earl, again glaring at Jack.

"OK, Earl, I think we all understand that you want to abandon 'project' evaluations and have been speaking to a couple of 'deaf ears' around here", Jonathan interrupted, before Earl could start another dialogue. "The ears are opening and starting to listen. To demonstrate this, I want to share with you all a quote from one of the most respected experts on corporate management in the twentieth century. Most of you, I assume, have heard of Peter Drucker". Heads nodded around the conference table. "This quote is from one of his books[1] (which I was reading recently) and I had Kay type it up". Jonathan flicked the switch of the overhead projector to show Exhibit 80.

"I think there is a message in this quote", Jonathan continued, "that applies to what Jason and Earl have been speaking about, and what Cathy and Dave have alluded to, in terms of their frustration or inability to comprehend the need for 'project' analysis. Drucker talks about 'interdependence' and 'performance of the whole' as key to the functioning of any system. Since our financial approaches need to support our overall business system, I am now coming to grips with the notion that financial evaluations have to be done at a level that encompasses the important interdependencies that exist in our businesses. I translate Drucker's comment about the 'performance' of the whole to 'shareholder value' of the whole, in terms of what we are trying to accomplish with value-based analysis and performance. What I now realize and want to make sure all of you understand is that we can do a great job of selecting an overall 'metric' such as *EP* and all the supporting financial 'drivers' – and totally 'botch' the implementation through misapplication. I had *not* thought seriously

---

Exhibit 80 — *Quote from Peter F. Drucker*

There is one fundamental insight underlying all management science. It is that the business enterprise is a system of the highest order. And one thing characterizes all genuine systems, whether they be mechanical like the control of a missile, biological like a tree, or social like the business enterprise: it is **interdependence**. *The whole of a system is not necessarily improved if one particular function or part is improved or made more efficient. In fact, the system may well be damaged thereby, or even destroyed. In some cases, the best way to strengthen the system may be to weaken a part – to make it less precise or less efficient. For* **what matters in any system is the performance of the whole;** *this is the result of growth and dynamic balance, adjustment and integration rather than of mere technical efficiency.*[1]

---

[1] Peter F. Drucker, *Management: Tasks, Responsibilities, Practises*, p. 508.

about this issue until Jason and I had our first meeting on the day he started with us, but I have given it a considerable amount of personal attention since then. We *must* perform 'value analysis' in a logical 'hierarchy' that fits with the way that value is actually 'created' in our company. I, like Earl, have also 'cheated' a bit, since I am privy to the 'wrap-up' chart".

"Well then", Jason quipped, "we can adjourn the meeting now, since so many know what's in the 'wrap-up' chart".

"Not so fast", Dave snapped, "I haven't seen it, nor have some of the other 'underprivileged' members of our 'team'".

Jason looked at Earl and Jonathan. "I guess we'll have to show it".

"Maybe we can charge an admission fee to see it", Earl joked.

Jack was rolling his eyes now, a look of frustration on his face, as he muttered, "I hope you're all getting your 'jollies'. Could we please end this – I *do* have some other work I need to get done ... like the 'quarterly earnings' release".

"We certainly don't want to miss *that*", Earl retorted, his glare replaced with a wry smile.

"You're right", Jonathan stated in a very serious tone ... "we don't ... we still *do* report *EPS* ... and *some* people pay attention to it ... in spite of the 'new economics'".

Exhibit 81

Value-Based Analysis ... Valuation Hierarchy

• Total Company/Operating Units and/or Strategic Business Units ... Analysis 'over time'	**Full Value Analysis**: - *EP* * / *MVA*** - Financial 'Drivers' ***
• Business Strategies/Plans • (Annual) Operating Plans	*MVA*** / Financial 'Drivers' *** *EP** / Financial 'Drivers' ***
• Major Programs – Strategic – Operational	*MVA*** (linked to a strategy, over an appropriate life cycle) Financial 'Drivers' ***

• *Capital Projects*	*No Value Analysis — focus is on 'control' of appropriations and/or expenditures — part of a program*

Notes: * *EP* — **Economic Profit** (similar to Economic Value Added) ... focus on historical versus future patterns and progression

** *MVA* — **Market Value Added** (consistent with Shareholder Value) ... focus on an appropriate future growth time horizon

*** **Financial 'Drivers'** — support (underlying) metrics for *EP* and *MVA*

"Thank you", Jack replied, "for at least some small measure of vindication".

Jason felt that it was time to 'wrap up' this session. "We can conclude this meeting with an exhibit that presents a summary of which metric(s) to apply at the various levels in the 'hierarchy'". He clicked on Exhibit 81.

"This basically 'says it all' in terms of application", stated Jill Debitson, who had been silent so far. "This is an 'eye opener' and fits in another piece of the puzzle for me".

"It's an 'Amen' for me", said Dave, a look of seriousness on his face.

"I'm OK", added Frank, who had understood everything that was presented.

After Cathy nodded, Jonathan rose to close the meeting. Jack was silent, rose and left the conference room ahead of all the others.

9

Valuation methodologies

Jaonathan and Jason walked back to Jonathan's office together after the 'team' members had left the finance conference room. As they seated themselves in Jonathan's office, the CFO folded his arms – a sign of concern – and said, "I didn't realize that Cathy had such strong feelings on capital project evaluations. She has never indicated – or maybe I wasn't listening if she ever did express – her frustration with this aspect of her job. Frankly, I had expected that this was going to be a 'mind blower' to Cathy, in that I thought she might oppose elevating the level of analysis, because of her closeness to Jack and her past inclination of following, almost blindly, Jack's positions and directions. I figured that Dave would welcome anything that entailed less work, but I was surprised at the level of understanding that I thought was implied in his comments. Once you 'cut through' his style, Dave seems to be more insightful on the subject than I have given him credit for. I knew that Jill would have no real input, since she has not had any exposure to this area of finance, and that Frank would comprehend everything. Earl was totally predictable in his 'soapbox' dialogues. Jack's negativeness – reflected in his continuous scowling – was a bit more than I had expected, and bothers me, because I had thought he would be more 'open-minded' based on his comment at our last 'team' meeting".

"He had what I believe was a 'bad time' at the officers' meeting", Jason responded. "I observed him and he seemed almost 'devastated' on a couple of occasions".

"I hadn't really noticed that", Jonathan retorted. "I know he was very quiet, but I was so concerned with Ian, Larry and Peter, that I didn't think much about Jack, especially since he said at the last 'team' meeting that he would listen and react with a more open mind".

Jason came back with . . . "If I know anything about 'body language', then Jack was really disturbed – I'd say almost frightened, especially when Ian cast a couple of 'hard' glances at him. Based on the officers' meeting and today, we may be back to 'square one' with Jack".

"Well, isn't that just great", Jonathan sighed, his arms tightening as they remained folded.

"I think we need to 'give' Jack something", Jason then stated. "In spite of our comments about 'enhancing' the finance function with this new 'economic' approach, he has expressed the point that we have been 'attacking' the accounting disciplines and rules that he stands for. Further, he may feel that his power base in the company is being stripped away from him. You know that the person controlling and interpreting the numbers has a significant level of power and influence. He may be thinking, especially after Ian's comments last week, that his star is fading and Earl's is rising".

"So, what do you think we can do" ? Jonathan asked.

"Probably nothing immediately", Jason replied, "but as we move forward into the subject of 'Valuation Methodologies', perhaps the *Value Profit Margin* approach might be a 'winner' for Jack. He seemed to react favorably when we introduced *VPM* and called it an 'earnings' target".

Jason continued speaking ... "I want to give you a *white paper* on the subject of *present value* that we should distribute to everyone – including the officers. Then, we should have a meeting with the 'team' to review the three major valuation methodologies, as preparation for launching into the corporate and business unit valuations related to the strategies that are being developed".

"Do you have the *white paper*"? Jonathan asked.

"Yes, it's in my briefcase".

"Let me have a copy. I'll read it and then distribute it to the 'team' and the officers. I'll have Kay set up meetings for next week. As this is moving forward, I'd like you to contact Val and Earl, and join them to sit in on the business unit strategy setting sessions and help with the development of the BU strategic financial outlooks. I've mentioned this to both of them and they're expecting you to contact them".

"My pleasure", Jason replied, as he handed Jonathan the *white paper* (Exhibit 82).

Early Friday morning, Kay Hoppins called Jason to inform him that a meeting with the 'team' would be held next Thursday morning, with the subject being 'Valuation Methodologies'. After Jason finished talking with Kay, he left for an 'all-day' strategy session with *Products*. On Monday, he would attend another session with *Products*, and on Tuesday and Wednesday he would be included in similar work sessions for *Services*. *"This is getting interesting"*, he thought to himself as he walked to the session with *Products*.

Exhibit 82

p. 1 of 3

'Present Value'

To begin a discussion of valuation metrics, it is important to explain the concept of **'present value'**. *When a supplier of capital is making an investment decision, especially where risk is involved, the focus is on what the investment will produce in terms of future profit and cash flow. Since the benefits of virtually all investments will occur in the future, the desire of the investor is to determine how the anticipated future results can be expressed in terms of the funds to be invested* **now**. *That is, assuming risk and some level of inflation (which reduces future purchasing power) exist, the investor wants to know the implications of making an investment in terms of* **today's values**. *For example, if an investor contemplates investing say, $10 million, will the future returns produce a value above or below the $10 million ... when expressed in terms of* **today's purchasing power**?*

A technique has been devised to calculate these **'present values'**. *It is called* **'discounting'**. *To understand* **'discounting'** *we need to first understand* **'compounding'**. *To understand the theory of* **'compound values'**, *we need go no further than a standard bank savings account or a series 'E' government bond. In the first case, a bank depositor can leave a sum of money in a savings account and watch it increase in value over time. The bank is* **'compounding'** *the value of the initial investment by paying interest on the total amount invested. The federal government does essentially the same thing on money it borrows from the general public by guaranteeing a future value greater than the amount invested. The actual amount depends on the interest (compounding) rate, along with the timing of the investment – that is, how long the government has use of the investor's money. The same situation exists with the bank. Similarly, investors purchase common stocks and other more risky investments with the hope that they will be worth more in the future than they are today. Thus, the first challenge is to determine how much the investment will* **'compound'** *as time goes on.*

While **'compounding'** *can calculate a future position and make judgments regarding the potential future worth of an investment, it does not give a perspective of whether one will be 'better off' with the investment, in terms of the risk involved coupled with a basic loss of purchasing power over time. To answer this question, we need to* **reverse** *the* **'compounding'** *process.* **Reversing** *this process is* **'discounting'** *a future value back to its* **'present value'**.*

On the following Thursday morning, the 'team' gathered for the scheduled meeting. Jonathan had a conflict and, since he was familiar with present value concepts and the basics of the valuation methodologies, decided not to attend the meeting. Thus, it was the 'team' – Jack, Earl, Frank, Jill, Cathy and Dave – in attendance. Val Performa decided that it would be a good 'refresher' for her,

Exhibit 82 (continued)

p. 2 of 3

'Present Value' (continued)

The two most well known valuation metrics – **Internal Rate of Return ('IRR')** *and* **Net Present Value ('NPV')** *– perform this function. Some firms refer to the* **'IRR'** *as* **'ROI'**. *The* **'IRR'** *expresses its result as a percentage, which is then compared to a 'hurdle' rate (a minimally acceptable rate of return) to make an accept/reject decision. That is, does the investment meet or exceed a minimum requirement for this type of investment, taking into account all relevant risk and timing factors. The* **'IRR'** *is solving for a percentage result, based on the cash outflows and inflows over the total time period for the investment. The* **'NPV'** *expresses its result as an absolute amount – dollars or other relevant currency. This metric employs a similar technique of evaluating cash outflows and inflows over a time horizon, but differs (from* **'IRR'**) *in that it utilizes a pre-determined rate (called the 'cost of capital') to discount future values to* **'present value'**. *Any* **'NPV'** *result above zero signals that the future returns (inflow/s) are greater than the investment (outflow/s), thus indicating an acceptable return, since the investor establishes what the 'hurdle' rate is through the cost of capital. The higher the* **'NPV'**, *the higher the* **'present value'** *created. A zero* **'NPV'** *indicates just earning the cost of capital – thus, indifference, since 'real' value is neither created nor destroyed.* **'NPV'** *below zero signals an unacceptable investment, since the investor is worse off in terms of* **today's value** *by making the investment than by not making it.*

Examples of this concept can be found in publications such as **The Wall Street Journal** *and* **FORTUNE**. *Articles abound on situations where the stock price of one company has either remained flat or has fallen after the announcement of an acquisition. The reason is that the shareholders are not expecting the future return/s (cash inflow/s) from the target company to be sufficient to justify the price being paid (the investment). In other words, they are either indifferent or disappointed.*

Thus, the **'NPV'** *– in these cases, judged to be zero (at best) or negative – is factored into the* **present market value** *of the company. In theory, any company making an investment with a negative* **'NPV'** *(or an* **'IRR'** *below the hurdle rate) will detract from its* **current value**, *whether it is publicly or privately owned. A zero* **'NPV'** *is usually a waste of time, since much effort and money can be expended for no reward above a bare minimum standard.*

especially since she had not been able to attend last week's session on the 'Valuation Hierarchy', so she also showed up at the corporate finance conference room at 8:25 for the 8:30 meeting.

Jonathan had instructed Jason to run the meeting by himself, so he began … "We are going to explore three (3) valuation methodologies today". He walked over to the flip chart and wrote:

Exhibit 82 (continued)

'Present Value' (continued)

At the other extreme, articles in these publications have applauded mergers with significant strategic implications, in which the combined entities are expected to perform better than they would separately. Public companies are the easiest to observe and analyze, due to the daily publication of their stock prices, but the concept applies to privately held firms, since all 'for profit' entities should have a goal of increasing their **warranted value**. *The term* **'warranted value'** *means a realistic value for a business based on its anticipated cash flows over time in relationship to the capital invested in the business. It establishes a value for a business based on its existing level of operations and future outlook.*

'Present value' *concepts, techniques and metrics are useful in evaluating investments where an 'accept/reject' decision is necessary.* **'Present value'** *analyses – resulting in the* **'IRR'** *and* **'NPV'** *metrics – are, therefore, primarily used for growth-oriented strategies, new internal business programs and mergers/acquisitions. The reason is that something new or different is contemplated. To apply the approach to situations where you are basically trying to retain what you have or make only marginal improvements to an existing operation is not the primary intent of this type of analysis. This type of situation is essentially one of 'no growth' and the determination of* **'net present value'** *is accomplished by 'capitalizing' an existing level of net operating profit (after tax). In a 'no growth' situation, the net operating profit (NOP) should be close to or equal to the free cash flow (FCF), since there is usually no 'incremental' investment beyond the amount of fixed capital that is depreciated annually. 'Capitalizing' is accomplished by dividing the NOP by the cost of capital.*

Valuation methodologies:

1. **Free Cash Flow (FCF)**
2. **Economic Profit (EP) ... [Economic Value Added]**
3. **Value Profit Margin (VPM™)**

"The first one has been around 'forever' – at least it seems that ever since finance courses have been taught in graduate schools and corporate finance departments have existed that the *FCF* method has been there. The reason is simple – it's still the best for 'forward-looking' evaluations. The problem with the *FCF* method is that it can't look 'backward' very well and it is often not useful at making 'performance' judgments for the individual years within a strategic planning time horizon. For example, the question ... *'How are we*

VPM™ is a trademark of Vanguard Partners

doing in year 3 – of, say, a seven-year planning (or investment) time period can often *not* be answered with the *FCF* method".

"The second method – *EP* – is a 'cousin' to *FCF*. It works off the same conceptual base, which is that both future *EPs* and *FCFs* can be discounted back to a net present value (*NPV*), indicating the 'shareholder value' impact of a strategy, financial plan, or major investment. In most cases, the results will be close, if not exactly the same. The *EP* approach adds the capability to make judgments about 'periodic' (annual, etc.) results".

"The third method – *VPM* – is an 'offshoot' of *EP*. What I found was that some companies either felt that *EP* was too much of a change from a traditional 'earnings'-driven approach, or that it was too complicated for widespread application. At the same time, they wanted an 'economic-based' method for performance evaluation and, possibly, incentive compensation. As I worked through this dilemma, *VPM* became a viable option. So, *VPM* – via the 'spread' of the actual or forecasted profit margin versus the *VPM* – can be structured as a 'support' measure (as we've discussed to date) or it can serve as the 'primary' metric with a comprehensive valuation routine connected to it".

"What I would like to do – with your 'blessing' of course, Dave – is to take these three methodologies one at a time using our now 'infamous' example with the **'A', 'B', 'C'** companies".

Dave looked at Jason and the group and said … "This **'A', 'B', 'C'** thing is going to become so planted in my psyche that maybe I should get it 'tattooed' on my arm".

"But, then you would have to wear short-sleeve shirts all the time so that people could see it", Earl joked. "That might be a problem in the winter".

"Maybe we could get **'A', 'B', 'C'** tee-shirts and sweatshirts for you, Dave", chimed in Jill. "That way you could have a constant reminder, be a walking advertisement for the **'A', 'B', 'C' Example**, and be comfortable during all of the seasons".

"Tee-shirts and sweatshirts", Dave mused … "that's a clever idea, Jill. Would we 'capitalize' them on the balance sheet or 'expense' them through the P&L?"

"With *EP*, it doesn't matter", Frank snipped, enjoying the banter and wanting to join in.

Even Jack managed a smile, as he observed the fun that the 'team' was having.

Jason knew that the mood might be a bit 'lighter' without Jonathan present. That was OK, as long as the group stayed 'on track'. In fact, Jonathan had said (to Jason) the other day that he hoped that a 'light' mood would exist in the meeting. He wanted the 'team' to have some fun with the value-based performance concept and the work.

As the 'team' was enjoying the 'give and take', Jason 'booted up' his computer. He then began to speak again. "We're going to keep the numbers really simple for now and analyze the '20%' and '15%' growth plans for **Company 'A'**. We'll also keep the same assumptions used to illustrate the 'Magnifier' Effect that growth has on shareholder value (*MVA*) creation. As a reminder, we assumed that the 'base' period profit margin and capital intensity would remain constant during the four-year growth horizon".

"Since the 'mother' of all value-based analysis is the Free Cash Flow (*FCF*) approach, let's explore this method first. Then, we'll evaluate the selected scenarios for **Co. 'A'** under the Economic Profit (*EP*) and Value Profit Margin (*VPM*) methodologies".

"The *FCF* method first computes a net operating profit (*NOP*). This step may be fairly simple for some businesses and very complex for others. This is similar to what we do for the *EP* approach. In fact, the '*NOP*' for the *FCF* and *EP* valuation methods should be the same. The *FCF* approach then determines 'net new investment' – the change in Invested Capital (*IC*) each year. This can be done in one of two ways:

1 Evaluate the 'incremental' working, fixed and other capital elements associated with the 'new' revenue (sales). The 'new' investment(s) – either the absolute amount(s) or the *ICI* ratio(s) – may or may not be the same as those for the 'base level' revenue (sales). The major elements within working capital are receivables, inventories, and accruals/payables. Fixed capital encompasses all depreciable items, such as building/plant, machinery, equipment and fixtures. Other capital includes goodwill and intangibles. Under this approach, the 'base' level of revenue (sales) is expected to continue with *no* 'net' new investment beyond what is depreciated annually.

2 Analyze the balance sheet investments for working, fixed and other capital for the business as a whole ('base' plus 'growth') – either year by year, or over the entire planning horizon with estimates for the individual years. The annual change in total (net) invested capital (*IC*) is the 'new' investment. Sometimes, the capital letter '*I*' is used to abbreviate 'new' investment, similar to using '*IC*' to represent 'invested capital' – however it is defined".

"Once '*NOP*' and '*I*' have been determined, **FCF** can be calculated as **'NOP minus I'**. The free cash flows for the years during the plan are discounted to present value using the cost of capital (*CCAP*) rate. Finally, the 'residual value' for the period beyond the forecast (or planning) horizon is typically assumed to be the present value of the final year's *NOP* capitalized at the *CCAP* rate. This assumption implies that management will *not* be able to add further shareholder value without a change to the plan (or strategy), but will be able to 'maintain' the level of operations as of the final year, with *no* further 'net new investment' beyond the annual depreciation of the final year. The sum of the 'discounted' *FCFs* and the *Residual Value* (also referred to as the *Terminal Value*) is the *NPV*/*MVA*/shareholder value impact for the business based on the growth plan. Let's illustrate the *FCF* valuation for the '20%' plan with Exhibit 83".

Exhibit 83

Valuation via Free Cash Flow (*FCF*)

Company 'A'

[$ Millions, except 'ICI']	"Base"	Year 1	Year 2	Year 3	Year 4	Residual
Assumptions:						
Annual Growth Rate (CGR) =	*20%*					
Annual Profit (NOP) Margin =	*10%*					
Invest. Capital Intensity (ICI) =	*$0.60*					
Cost of Capital (CCAP) =	*12%*					
Revenue	1,000	1,200	1,440	1,728	2,074	
Invested Capital (IC)	600	720	864	1,037	1,244	
Free Cash Flow (*FCF*)						
NOP	100	120	144	173	207	
'Net' New Investment		(120)	(144)	(173)	(207)	
Free Cash Flow (*FCF*)		-	-	-	-	207

Valuation	Total Mkt. Value *	"Base" IC	MVA... Base + Growth
Net Present Value (NPV)	**981**	**600**	**381**

* 'Discounted' values (FCFs + Residual)

"Let me see if I get this", Jill interjected. "My puzzle continues to come together and I get intrigued with the new pieces. The firm has a 'warranted' market value of close to $1 billion (actually, $981 million). Since there is $600 million invested – in essence a 'liquidation' value – management is contributing $381 million of value".

"But", added Cathy, "the annual free cash flows are 'zero' throughout the plan period, so all the 'value creation' – the *MVA* – is dependent on the *residual value*. That's kind of interesting".

"That's also a very good observation", Jason chimed in, "and it illustrates two important points. First, high growth requires capital for new investment. Second, the *FCF* method is not always useful to determine progress toward a goal or objective, as I mentioned previously. Let me show you what I mean, by taking the '15% growth plan' for **Co. 'A'**. I'm going to do exactly the same type of *FCF* analysis, but this time the annual compound growth will be 15% instead of 20%. Exhibit 84 will illustrate this analysis".

Exhibit 84

Valuation via Free Cash Flow (*FCF*)

Company 'A'

[$ Millions, except 'ICI']	"Base"	Year 1	Year 2	Year 3	Year 4	Residual
Assumptions:						
Annual Growth Rate (CGR) =	*15%*					
Annual Profit (NOP) Margin =	*10%*					
Invest. Capital Intensity (ICI) =	*$0.60*					
Cost of Capital (CCAP) =	*12%*					
Revenue	1,000	1,150	1,323	1,521	1,749	
Invested Capital (*IC*)	600	690	794	913	1049	
Free Cash Flow (*FCF*)						
NOP	100	115	132	152	175	
'Net' New Investment		(90)	(104)	(119)	(137)	
Free Cash Flow (*FCF*)		25	29	33	38	175

Valuation	Total Mkt. Value *	"Base" IC	MVA... Base + Growth
Net Present Value (*NPV*)	920	600	320

* '*Discounted*' values (FCFs +Residual)

"Well, will you look at that!" Dave exclaimed. "This is interesting". Even Jack raised his eyebrows a bit.

"These annual free cash flows in the '15%' growth scenario are 'higher' – that is, more positive – than those in the '20%' growth plan", Cathy jumped in. "But, we know intuitively that the '20%' plan adds more shareholder value – since we're dealing with **Co. 'A'** – based on the 'Magnifier' Effect".

"Now, do you see what I meant when I said that growth requires capital and the *FCF* method, while getting to the correct *NPV* (or *MVA*) answer, doesn't always accurately assess progress along the way?"

Heads nodded.

"OK", Jason continued, 'let's now evaluate the '20% growth' scenario for **Co. 'A'** under the Economic Profit (*EP*) approach, using Exhibit 85".

"With this (*EP*) approach, the total 'warranted' market value and *MVA* for the firm are slightly higher, which sometimes happens when comparing the two methods. In my opinion, the results are reasonably close – within 3% or so. If, however, I really want to be 'precise' on the *NPV* over the entire planning (or strategic) horizon, I will rely on the *FCF* method. I usually utilize both methods to determine if there

Exhibit 85

Valuation via Economic Profit (*EP*)

Company 'A'

[$ Millions, except 'ICI']	"Base"	Year 1	Year 2	Year 3	Year 4	Residual
Assumptions:						
Annual Growth Rate (CGR) =	20%					
Annual Profit (NOP) Margin =	10%					
Invest. Capital Intensity (ICI) =	$0.60					
Cost of Capital (CCAP) =	12%					
Revenue	1,000	1,200	1,440	1,728	2,074	
Invested Capital (*IC*)	600	720	864	1,037	1,244	
Economic Profit (*EP*)						
NOP	100	120	144	173	207	
Capital Charge (*CCAP*)	(72)	(86)	(104)	(124)	(149)	
Economic Profit (*EP*)	**28**	**34**	**40**	**48**	**58**	**58**

Valuation	Total Mkt. Value	"Base" IC	MVA... Base + Growth*
Net Present Value (*NPV*)	**1,008**	**600**	**408**

* 'Discounted' values (EPs +Residual)

are differences. If I'm 'selling' I'll go with the 'higher' value and if I'm 'buying' I'll go with the 'lower' *NPV*". Muted laughter broke out. "Notice how *EP* progresses from $28 million in the 'Base' to $58 million by year 4, in line with revenue growth. Now, I'm going to show the '15%' growth scenario under the *EP* methodology. Cast your eyes on Exhibit 86".

"As you can see in Exhibit 86, *EP* growth tracks with the overall growth scenario and the annual *EPs* are lower in the '15%' growth plan than they are in the '20%' growth plan. The 'warranted' total market value (*TMV*) of $951 million under the *EP* method is within 3% of the $920 million *TMV* using the *FCF* approach. Let's now take a short break".

As the 'team' went to the coffee and tea pots, Jason went to the flip chart. With a black marker, he wrote:

Method/Plan	Year 1	Year 2	Year 3	Year 4	Residual (***)	TMV
FCF/'20%' (*)	-0-	-0-	-0-	-0-	207	981
FCF/'15%' (**)	25	29	33	38	175	920
EP/'20%' (*)	34	40	48	58	58	1008
EP/'15%' (**)	32	37	43	49	49	951

(*) **'20%' Growth Scenario**
(**) **'15%' Growth Scenario**
(***) **Residual = 'NOP' under the FCF Methodology**
'EP' under the EP Methodology

Exhibit 86

Valuation via Economic Profit (*EP*)

Company 'A'

[$ Millions, except 'ICI']	"Base"	Year 1	Year 2	Year 3	Year 4	Residual
Assumptions:						
Annual Growth Rate (CGR) =	*15%*					
Annual Profit (NOP) Margin =	*10%*					
Invest. Capital Intensity (ICI) =	*$0.60*					
Cost of Capital (CCAP) =	*12%*					
Revenue	1,000	1,150	1,323	1,521	1,749	
Invested Capital (*IC*)	600	690	794	913	1,049	
Economic Profit (*EP*)						
NOP	100	115	132	152	175	
Capital Charge (*CCAP*)	(72)	(83)	(95)	(110)	(126)	
Economic Profit (*EP*)	28	32	37	43	49	49

Valuation	Total Mkt. Value	"Base" IC	MVA... Base + Growth *
Net Present Value (*NPV*)	951	600	351

* 'Discounted' values (EPs + Residual)

"I did not go through the calculation of *EP*, since we have spent so much time on it".

"That's OK, Jason", Cathy uttered, "since we're all 'experts' on *EP*", winking at Dave as she spoke. Dave laughed and gave her a 'thumbs up' sign.

"What I want to point out are the features and differences between these two valuation methodologies", Jason continued. "If we start with the *FCF* approach, the '20%' case 'consumes' the same amount of cash as it 'generates'. As a sideline, if the growth rate was *more than* 20% (say, *25%*) the annual *FCF*s would *all* be 'negative' and the Total Market Value (*TMV*) and Market Value Added (*MVA*) would be higher than the '20%' case – based on the assumptions in the example that produce a higher final-year *NOP/Residual Value*. You can run your own numbers to prove this fact. Or, you can ask me for them, and if you treat me nicely I'll give them to you. Getting back to the scenarios that we have analyzed and that I've summarized on the flip chart, it should be evident that the higher the growth rate, the higher the cash consumption and the more reliance on the 'residual' for shareholder value creation. This is a fundamental fact for all growth businesses evaluated using the *FCF* method".

"The '15%' scenario, when first viewed, appears to be 'counter-intuitive' with the *FCF* methodology, until you understand how it works. Notice that there *appears* to be more value (via the 'positive' free cash flows) during the plan period. However, there is less 'residual' value due to the slower growth of *NOP* versus the '20%'case. If we were to compensate the management of **Company 'A'**, how could we do it within the *FCF* framework? I certainly don't know how, and I doubt that any of you do either. We could *not* do it based on the *FCFs* during the (four-year) plan period, because the incentive would be to cut back on growth, which is exactly the opposite of what the share-holders want management to do with this firm. If forced to use this (*FCF*) approach, we would have to construct one or more 'surrogates' or 'proxies' for value creation".

Earl then jumped into the dialogue with ... "This issue of the 'free cash flow' becomes a treasury challenge, in terms of 'financing' the growth plan. It's my job, and that of *all* corporate treasurers, to assure that the funds are available at reasonable cost to fund value-creating strategies and plans".

"That's a good comment", Jason added, "and we will be covering this issue in a separate topic – called 'Sustainable Growth'. We'll be doing this analysis as the last element of our corporate financial analysis, after we complete the work on business unit valuations and cash flows".

"If we can now return to the flip chart and the '*EP*' Methodology, we can begin to envision a way to maintain the integrity of cash flow-based valuation while instituting an approach that better assesses progress toward the objective of creating shareholder value. The *EP* method usually comes close to the 'answer' derived via the *FCF* approach and provides annual (or periodic) measures that people *can be* compensated on. This is a reason why more and more compa-nies – of all type and sizes – are adopting the '*EP*' methodology for implementation across their operations. The major type of firm where it doesn't work well is the 'start-up' – in which there are often *no* profits, especially when a capital charge is assessed. In these cases, 'proxy' measures need to be developed, some of which may be 'non-financial'. Some or all of the financial 'drivers' we have discussed may be useful in this type of situation".

"Are you saying that established companies such as ours should only have 'financial' measures for evaluating people?" Dave asked, with a curious look on his face.

"Certainly not", Jason replied. "I'm only pointing out, at this point, the differences between the *FCF* and *EP* methodologies and the difficulty in using the *FCF* framework for anything other than forward-looking 'analysis'. There is also another issue, or problem, with the *FCF* approach, in that it does *not* allow you to assess 'historical' performance very well. Try to do the assessments for Growthstar's businesses during the past three years under the *FCF* method". Except for Earl, Val and Frank, there were puzzled looks around the table. Then, as Jill, Cathy, Dave ... and, even Jack ... looked through the historical *EP Assessments* that had been covered in previous meetings, and made some calculations on their notepads, the heads started to nod, as they realized the inability to make judgments based on historical free cash flows. Jason went to the coffeepot to 'freshen up' his mug while this activity was going on.

As the pencils were placed back on the conference table and the heads turned up again, Jason said deliberately... "There is another noteworthy element in reviewing and comparing these two important valuation methodologies, indicated by an 'asterisk' (*) in the exhibits. The *FCF* method, by discounting the free cash flows and then capitalizing/discounting the final year's *NOP*, determines the Total Market Value (*TMV*) for the business. Then, the 'base' period invested capital (*IC*) is subtracted to calculate Market Value Added (*MVA*) – which we all know is equivalent to shareholder value creation. The *EP* method, through its discounting of the future economic profits and then capitalizing/discounting the final year's *EP*, determines the *MVA*. Then, the *IC* is added to calculate *TMV* – which we know is the Net Present Value (*NPV*) for the entire business, 'base' plus 'growth'. The *EP* method, thus, provides a more direct route to *MVA*. So, while the two methodologies arrive at approximately the same result, they go about it in slightly different ways".

"Hey, Jack", Jill then stated ... "this is 'pretty cool' stuff, don't you think!"

Jack shuddered, shook his head, but remained silent – rising to make another visit to the coffeepot, as he thought to himself ... *"Am I going to 'lose' Jill to this 'new' world of finance? Will Cathy be next?"* Jack's head was shaking visibly as walked back to his chair.

Jason, Val and Earl noticed Jack's body language, but said nothing.

Frank, who been his usual quiet self, was anxious to 'get into' the Value Profit Margin (*VPM*) methodology that Jason had alluded to and asked ... "Have we 'covered off' on the *FCF* and *EP* methodologies?"

"Let's ask your colleagues", Jason responded. "Are there any other questions or comments on the first two approaches?"

"Probably", replied Dave, "but since I can't think of any at the moment, let's move on. I'll let you know if I think of something we haven't covered".

"I'm sure you will", Jack interjected, realizing that he had been totally silent for the entire meeting and felt a need to say something or become a 'non-entity' in these sessions. Dave gave Jack a strange look. Dave had never been close to Jack. In fact, he wasn't that close to *any* of the finance people in the company ... at least not yet.

"As you all know by now, I've been in the consulting profession for a long time. I have also worked for major corporations that were very 'earnings' oriented, and cashed a few bonus checks that were based on either pre- or post-tax earnings". Jason was looking directly at Jack as he spoke. Jack looked back at Jason almost inquisitively. "Over the years it has become apparent to me that some companies are 'ripe' for major changes, but others are not. Even though the 'economic' way of thinking and measuring has taken hold in many companies, there are still many hard-working and well-meaning managers who don't adapt as quickly to new methods. For others, there can be an issue of not understanding the new methods. As I pondered these potential impediments to the goal of a broader adoption of the 'economic' framework for performance measurement and management behavior, I realized that the *VPM* financial 'driver' could be expanded, in some cases, to a 'full-blown' valuation methodology and as a way to implement *EP*".

Jack spoke again. "As I stated in a previous meeting, if this can be done, then I may be able to 'get on the bandwagon'. We've got a lot of history in this company that needs to be considered before 'tossing everything overboard', even though you have presented some compelling examples and analysis for instituting some type of change". All the heads perked up. This was Jack speaking, and his words did carry weight, since he was considered to be the 'number two' person in corporate finance, due mainly to his length of employment, even though Earl was highly regarded.

"Well then", Jason jumped back in, "let's get on with it. As we've seen, *VPM* represents a minimum pre- or post-tax profit margin for the initiation of value creation. In the case of Growthstar, we're going to take the 'post-tax' approach, since you take your profits down through taxes, and understand the deferred taxes. We've also seen that when we multiply the 'spread' (of the actual *NOP* margin versus the *VPM*) by revenue, the result is *EP*. Let's now apply the *VPM* concept to a valuation of the '20%' case, with Exhibit 87".

"With the *VPM* approach, the result is going to be the same as with the *EP* method, since we 'wind up' with *EP*, albeit through an alternative calculation. As I have mentioned before, the focus for 'operating' managers is with growth and profit margin – financial elements they are familiar with. However, the finance people have to perform the same type of robust *NOP* and *IC* analysis that is done with the other two methodologies. This is necessary in order to obtain 'forecasted' *NOP* margins supported by pricing strategies and cost structures that are consistent with the strategy or growth plan. These 'forecasted' margins become the basis for computing the 'spread' versus the *VPM*. Credible *ICI* indicators must be established, since they are key ingredients to the *VPM*. This can be done either by analysing the 'year-by-year' dynamics of a plan, or gaining an

Exhibit 87

Valuation via Value Profit Margin (*VPM*)

Company 'A'

[*$ Millions, except 'ICI'*]	"Base"	Year 1	Year 2	Year 3	Year 4	Residual
Assumptions:						
Annual Growth Rate (*CGR*) =	*20%*					
Invest. Capital Intensity (*ICI*) =	*$0.60*					
Cost of Capital (*CCAP*) =	*12%*					
Revenue	1,000	1,200	1,440	1,728	2,074	
Invested Capital (*IC*)	600	720	864	1,037	1,244	
Net Operating Profit (*NOP*)	100	120	144	173	207	
Value Profit Margin (*VPM*)						
Actual *NOP* Margin	10.0%	10.0%	10.0%	10.0%	10.0%	
"VPM" 'ICI' times 'CCAP'	7.2%	7.2%	7.2%	7.2%	7.2%	
'Spread' = "VPM" vs. Actual	**2.8%**	**2.8%**	**2.8%**	**2.8%**	**2.8%**	
Economic Profit (*EP*)	28	34	40	48	58	58

Valuation	Total Mkt. Value	"Base" IC	MVA... Base + Growth*	
Net Present Value (*NPV*)	**1,008**	**600**	**408**	* 'Discounted' values (EPs + Residual)

understanding of the implications of a strategy over an appropriate time horizon and 'normalizing' the pattern(s) for all the years in the plan period. In our example, the financial dynamics have been 'normalized'. While *CCAP* is an ingredient to *VPM*, we'll assume for now that our cost of capital analysis has yielded a *CCAP* that will 'stand up' through the planning period".

"In the **Co. 'A'** example, the assumptions were over-simplified to illustrate a concept. In the 'real world', the dynamics of a business – both P&L and balance sheet – must be carefully evaluated to gain credible indicators. The operating people should be involved in the planning, and provide input on items such as volume/pricing trade-off, all major cost and expense areas, inventory turnover, accounts receivable policy, capital spending plans related to growth objectives, and R&D programs. At the end of all this, however, they only need to focus on two elements – **revenue growth and *NOP* margin**. So, by involving them in areas they are already familiar with, we can 'turn them loose' to grow and generate a 'bottom line' in terms they are comfortable with – while, at the same time, acting in the best interests of the shareholders. Why? Because the *VPM* – the benchmark for performance – has the appropriate risk and capital requirements imbedded into it".

"That's a mouthful", Dave blurted out.

"It's also an approach I may be able to support", Jack stated. "It retains the 'bottom line' orientation that I have advocated and that most of our people have lived by for many years. If we're talking about basically a 'one-time' effort for our planning and budgeting – to really understand the specifics of our P&L and balance sheet – I can probably live with that. I may also be able to live with the 'economic' adjustments to the P&L".

"I thought you would finally 'come around' when you saw this", Earl snickered. "It's an *'accountant-turned-economist's dream'*. You can still preach the virtues of 'earnings' and know that this 'earnings' measure is supported by economic principles linked to shareholder value creation".

"I said I *might* support it, not that I *would* support it", Jack retorted. "And I'm *not* ready to turn into an economist just yet. I've got a few more 'debits and credits' to process before I make that transition. And, by the way, 'GAAP' still means *'God Almighty Applied Principles'* for me". The smile accompanying the remark, however, indicated that Jack had come a 'long way' in his attitude toward the 'economic' approach. Most of the group felt he was now groping for a way to implement it in a 'face-saving' manner.

In fact, Jill was thinking to herself that this was one of the very few times that Jack had smiled – *really smiled* – during this process to date. *"There has to be something in it for him"*, she thought to herself. *"And I may have to contribute to that outcome"*.

"So, where do we go from here?" Dave asked, a look of sincere interest on his face.

"Oh, I don't know", Earl responded ... "how about to the tennis court? I'll serve up *CCAP* and you can return with *ICI!"*

"Funny, funny man", Dave chuckled. "How can a person who deals with bankers and interest rates all day long have such a good sense of humor?"

"I've often wondered about that myself", Earl replied jokingly. "But, if you'd like to point this out to Jonathan, I would certainly be appreciative ... especially, if you put a 'positive spin' on it".

"Maybe this is a good time to adjourn", Jason interjected, "before this situation gets to be totally ridiculous".

"I agree", Jack added, "but let's first discuss our next steps – after the 'tennis match', of course". Again, everyone 'perked up' at Jack's first definitive statement about 'moving forward' with the process.

"We now have the foundation", Jason said, "to move forward with our corporate financial analysis, which includes the business unit valuations (broken down into 'no growth' and 'growth' values), BU contributions to the company's total market value and shareholder value, cash flow analysis and sustainable growth perceptions".

Val, who had been 'listening' during the meeting, then stated ... "I have spent the past four days participating in planning sessions for

Products and *Services*. There's some progress being made, but there's more in the way of understanding the Selling, Marketing & Service (SMS) expense outlook for *Services*, especially for the new business segment, along with the impact on inventory turnover and fixed capital requirements (including 'leased' assets) for *Services*' overall growth strategy. With regard to *Products*, one key issue is the impact on Gross Profit Margin (taking both price and manufacturing cost into account) for the new products intended to 'counter' the maturing of two key market segments. Fixed capital is almost always a concern for a manufacturing business, and the situation is no different here. Additionally, it seems that R&D is another area deserving attention, with regard to how much spending will be required to produce the company's next generation of products. Finally, the 'future growth' opportunity for *Products* needs some more work. Once this is accomplished, Cathy and Dave should be in a position to produce credible financial outlooks for the next three years that can then be a foundation for 'valuing' the business units and then the total company. This work should 'position' us to evaluate internal investment programs and acquisitions in support of our strategies".

"I guess that means we're making progress, but we're not there yet", Dave chimed in.

"I think you've got the message and understand the challenges ahead of us", Jason responded. "And, I think this meeting can now be adjourned".

## 10

Corporate financial analysis

Jason met with Jonathan the following day to summarize the session on 'Valuation Methodologies'. Jonathan was pleased that Jack had responded positively to the *VPM* approach and might be starting to think of how it might be adopted within the company. Jason also apprised the CFO of his thoughts on the planning process, based on the four days of strategy sessions he had attended prior to the finance team meeting yesterday. His thoughts echoed Val's in terms of what needed attention and more work in order to develop credible financial outlooks.

The annual summer plant shutdown, during which most of the workers and staff took vacation, was about to begin. Jason knew about the shutdown and planned to take the time off. His golf clubs had been relatively idle during the time since he had begun this engagement, and the family wanted its normal vacation at the beach.

After the shutdown was over, the planning sessions resumed. As part of his role, Jason introduced the participants to the concept of 'value driver' programs that would support the business strategies and to which the valuation methodologies could later be applied.

The summer and the planning process were both now drawing to a close, and the people within *Products* and *Services* – with the help of Val, Earl, Frank ... and Jason – had addressed the issues that Val had raised at the conclusion of the finance team meeting on 'Valuation Methodologies'. In fact, Cathy and Dave had taken it upon themselves to 'lead the charge' to develop resolutions and assumptions for inclusion in the financial expressions of the BU plans. Ian and Jonathan had been kept abreast, mostly by Val and Earl, of important developments, and seemed satisfied with the quality of the effort and also with the fact that Larry Buildermann and Peter Uppcomer had been involved, along with their 'direct reports'.

The stage had, thus, been set for the development of the financial outlooks for the two major business units, which would serve as the basis for the business unit valuations and other aspects of the corporate financial analysis. The two businesses had operated independently since the acquisition, except for the joint marketing of 'bundled' product and service offerings to customers, integration of R&D to the extent possible, and some shared financial and administrative tasks. Ian had, however, attempted to instill a 'Growthstar' philosophy of aggressive penetration of new market opportunities and defense of existing positions of strength through a 'corporate' vision of a comprehensive and coordinated product/service capability. Ian wanted Larry and Peter to run *Products* and *Services* as 'businesses', but he also wanted a 'corporate' sense of 'community', so that the people in the BUs would feel they belonged to a larger enterprise. Jonathan reinforced the sense of 'corporate community' by continually reminding people in the business units that they all worked for a corporation with a 'common' group of shareholders and other stakeholders.

Ian and Jonathan had made a decision, earlier in the year, to reinforce the communication of a corporate message and expand the company's coverage in the investment community by hiring a person at the corporate vice-president level, reporting to Ian, to manage corporate communications and investor relations. Both Ian and Jonathan knew that the company was growing to a level where Jonathan could no longer handle these functions on a part-time basis. A four-month search had, thus, resulted in the hiring of Amanda (Mandy) Bettertalk as Vice-President, Investor Relations. While not formally in her title, the responsibility for corporate communications was an important responsibility. Ian was just not one for long titles. In fact, he refused to allow them. It was also clearly understood that, while Mandy would report to Ian, Jonathan would still be involved and Mandy would review important issues and announcements with Jonathan as well as Ian.

Mandy Bettertalk had an interesting background. She had never before worked in an industrial corporation, but rather had spent her entire career on the 'other side' of the investor relations, public affairs and corporate communications arena. After graduating from a small college in the Southwest, she went to work for a large public relations firm in that region of the country. She spent ten years with this firm and then moved to one of the premier investor relation organizations in New York City, with an office in the 'Wall Street' area. This job brought her into close contact with the 'goings on' of the financial markets, which had been one of her goals. She worked for a broad range of companies in terms of size and industry, representing large firms and coordinating investor relation functions for a select group of small- to-mid sized companies. Having now spent eight years in this environment, she wanted to experience a 'corporate' role as the chief contact person with shareholders and key stakeholders. Polished, well spoken, and armed with an enviable list of contacts in the investment community, she was a very credible candidate for the position. In fact, she was far ahead of the person considered to be the next most qualified. After Ian and Jonathan got over their 'sticker shock' from Mandy's compensation demands, they reached an agreement for her to begin working after the plant shutdown. She attended most of the planning sessions and gave valuable insight regarding what the professional investors were looking for and questions they were likely to ask. Val and Earl were delighted to have her 'on board.' Jack was non-committal.

In spite of this 'corporate' perspective, everyone at Growthstar knew that 'shareholder value creation' would result from the execution of the strategies and the achievement of the future financial outlooks for the two business units – *Products* and *Services* – along with any other corporate development initiatives that might occur. As a result, this year's planning outlook would treat Growthstar as the 'sum of the parts'; that is, *Products* plus *Services* equals *TOTAL CO.* To deal with synergistic opportunities between the two BUs, Cathy and Dave – along with Val, Earl, and Frank – had attended every planning session where the financial implications of the BU strategies were discussed or analyzed. The benefits from *Products* and *Services* being part of the corporation had, thus, been factored into the financial outlooks for the two business units, to be consistent with the actual reporting of results. All corporate overheads were allocated to the business units.

As the cooler temperature of autumn began to replace the warmth of summer, the final review session for the financial outlooks also began – as usual, promptly at 8:30 on a beautiful fall morning. After the typical comments were exchanged about how everyone would rather be somewhere else on such a gorgeous day and the members of the finance team plus Val, Mandy and Jason had 'loaded up' on coffee or tea, Jonathan rose to start the meeting. "It's been quite an experience to witness our most comprehensive strategic financial planning effort since I've been with the company. I'm sure it's been all of that, and perhaps more, for those of you who have actually done the work. If nothing else, I'm grateful for the diligence and dedication to the task. I can assure you that Ian, Larry and Peter share this feeling, based on my recent discussions with them – individually and collectively. As I understand the process for today, Cathy and Dave will lead the sessions for their respective businesses (*Products* and *Services*), with Frank providing the consolidation and others available for assistance. Cathy, I guess it's 'your nickel' ".

For Cathy, leading this type of session, which went beyond the reporting of actual results to looking into the future, was almost beyond comprehension for her. She had, frankly, never thought of this role as part of her responsibility. While 'deep down' she relished the opportunity, she was quite nervous as she stood up to address the group. "We should probably have let Dave start off, since I'm the shy person and he's the outgoing type … but, let's 'jump into the pool' with our financial outlook over the next three years for *Products*. I just hope I can 'swim' in these waters which are new to me".

"You'll do fine", Dave quipped, "and you'll probably be a hard act to follow". Dave had come to respect Cathy during this process, as he realized she had entered into what had been 'uncharted' territory until recently. "*Who am I kidding*", he thought to himself … "*I'm in the same situation as she is. This is a bit 'nerve wracking' – to have to lead a session on 'planning'. OK, Cathy – go for it!*"

Unaware of what Dave was thinking, Cathy began, but only after looking at Frank to make sure he was there. Frank's slight nod indicated that he would be there to assist her as necessary. "It seems as though we've been climbing a big mountain with unexpected crevices and surprises along the way. However, this has been one of the positive aspects of this planning process, in that we've been able to work our way through the various issues that have 'cropped up' along the way. For someone 'steeped' in accounting, this has been quite a learning experience. Before I present the results of our efforts and our financial outlook for the next three years, I want to thank the corporate people – you know who you are – and say that we wouldn't have been where we are today without you. Larry wanted me to say how appreciative he is of everyone's efforts, even though there were times when he wondered what we were all doing. He certainly had never experienced a work effort such as this one, nor the type of questions that were raised".

Cathy continued with … "We've prepared three summary schedules in a format that we all concurred represents the financial output of our plan. I believe that Dave will present *Services* in the same format and Frank will do the same for the total company". Both Dave and Frank nodded in agreement as Cathy turned on her first schedule (Exhibit 88).

Exhibit 88	GROWTHSTAR INC.					
	Business Unit Financials					
	Next 3 Years - Growth Plan					
"PRODUCTS" Financials						
[$ Millions (MM's) except Per Share	Current FY Fcst.		Future Outlook -- Next 3 Years			*CGR /*
and Capital Intensity Amounts]	**$MM's**	*% Rev.*	**Yr. #1**	**Yr. #2**	**Yr. #3**	*Avg. Ratio*
Income Statement						
Sales Revenue:						*CGR*
U.S.	$225	*75%*	$253	$285	$320	*12.5%*
International	75	*25%*	90	108	130	*20.0%*
Total Sales Revenue	**$300**	*100%*	**$343**	**$393**	**$450**	*14.5%*
Operating Costs and Expenses:						*Avg. Ratio*
Cost of Goods Sold (COGS)	177	*59%*	195	216	247	*55%*
Selling/Marketing/Service (SMS)	45	*15%*	60	79	90	*20%*
General & Administrative (G&A)	36	*12%*	37	39	45	*10%*
Research & Development (R&D)	15	*5%*	21	24	27	*6%*
Total Operating Costs/Expenses	273	*91%*	312	357	409	*91%*
Operating Income	27	*9%*	31	35	40	*9%*
Interest — Operating Leases	3	*1%*	3	3	4	*1%*
EBITA	30	*10%*	34	39	44	*10%*
"Effective" Tax Rate	32%		32%	32%	32%	
Tax on EBITA	10		11	13	14	
Net Operating Profit (NOP)	**$20**	*6.7%*	**$23**	**$26**	**$30**	*6.7%*
'Growth Plan' - Cumulative						
Sales Revenue - $			*$43*	*$93*	*$150*	
NOP - $			*$3*	*$6*	*$10*	
NOP Margin - %			*6.7%*	*6.7%*	*6.7%*	

"This exhibit summarizes our key income statement elements, set up in a format that will accommodate the Economic Profit calculations. Structurally, the columns provide the current year forecast – dollars and percents-to-revenue – and then the outlook for the next three years based on our strategy. The last column indicates either compound growth rate (CGR) or average ratio assumptions arrived at after considerable analysis. At the bottom of the schedule, the last three rows – the cumulative impact for the 'growth plan' – highlight revenue, net operating profit (*NOP*) and *NOP* margin".

Cathy's confidence was building, as she felt she had 'survived' the initial portion of her presentation. "As you all know, one of the issues raised by Val at our last 'team' meeting was our 'future growth' opportunity. We need to look at growth domestically and internationally. In the US, our markets are maturing somewhat. With a new generation of products, we believe we can achieve 'real' growth of 10% annually. With pricing potential limited to the anticipated inflation rate of about 2.5% annually, we expect to achieve 'top line' growth of 12.5% per year for the next three years. We believe our international growth opportunity to be significantly higher, in that a maturing product line in the US is still very viable overseas, especially in the Asia–Pacific region. Our new generation of products has received excellent reviews in Europe, as well as in the US. Thus, we feel we should be able to grow our international business by 20% per year, most of which is 'real' growth. We're assuming relatively stable currency relationships over this period. The result is a total growth rate for *Products* of 14.5% annually".

"Regarding our costs and expenses, we believe that a shift will occur with respect to COGS and SMS. The new generation of products is being produced with lower cost materials, which will result in a higher gross margin. Our international expansion will offset this benefit, however, and increase our SMS cost ratio, as we spend to further penetrate the European and Pacific Rim markets. Another issue is our spending on R&D, which will increase in both absolute and relative terms – increasing from 5% to 6% of total revenue. G&A efficiencies should enable us to maintain our current year *NOP* margin at 6.7% throughout the plan period. Obviously, there could be a 'blip' in any one of the future years, but for the plan period, we are confident that we can 'maintain' our current year net operating profit margin".

"You don't, however, see any possibility of 'increasing' the *NOP* margin", Jonathan interjected. He wanted it to be a question, but he knew otherwise.

"We really don't", Cathy replied. "And you know who we work for – Mr 'Bottom Line' himself. We have spent countless hours on this subject, and it's *not* merely a coincidence that our margins are forecasted to be the same as they are now. In support of this statement, we analyzed the annual growth rates for our major cost and expense categories, and compared them to our overall revenue growth. The patterns link to our strategy of lowering COGS as a percent-to-sales ratio through our 'materials' program, spending on SMS for the European and Pacific Rim expansion, leveraging our existing G&A infrastructure and increasing our R&D expenditures faster than we grow our sales revenue for the 'next generation' of products. Exhibit 89 provides a summary of this 'compound growth rate' analysis".

"I'm not surprised", Jonathan responded. "Let's see what the balance sheet looks like".

Cathy responded with Exhibit 90.

"During our review of the current year forecast, we discovered some interesting developments", Cathy continued. "We are going to give extended payment terms to sell off some of our 'old' product line, which will temporarily increase accounts receivable, but will significantly reduce finished goods inventory. This is reflected in

Exhibit 89	GROWTHSTAR INC.	
	Business Unit Financials	
	Next 3 Years - Growth Plan	
"PRODUCTS" Financials	***'Compound Growth Rates'***	
	Future Outlook — Next 3 Years	
Income Statement	***CGR***	***+ / – vs. Revenue***
Total Sales Revenue	14.5%	—
Operating Costs and Expenses:		
Cost of Goods Sold (COGS)	11.8%	–2.7%
Selling/Marketing/Service (SMS)	26.0%	11.5%
General & Administrative (G&A)	7.7%	–6.8%
Research & Development (R&D)	21.6%	7.1%
Total Operating Costs / Expenses	14.5%	0.0%

the 'high' *ICI* ($0.17) for receivables and the 'low' *ICI* for inventory ($0.06). Neither is reflective of a long-term ratio. Our average period for receivables is about 40 days, which translates into an *ICI* of $0.11. On a 'COGS' basis, our plan is for inventory turnover of 4 to 5 times (annually). That translates into a 'sales' turnover of about 8 and an *ICI* of $0.13. We've been spending heavily on plant machinery and equipment for the past two years, to gear up for the 'Next Generation' – as most of you know. This two-year capital program will total $15 million. We should realize the benefits, in terms of a lower requirement for fixed capital over the next three years, at least in 'relative' terms. We'll probably spend close to what we've been experiencing in the recent past on an 'aggregate' basis, but when we spread this fixed capital spending on our higher future revenues, our *ICI* for fixed capital ('net' of depreciation) should be in the $0.10 range. Finally, we only need a modest amount for new operating lease – $1.5 to $2 million per year – which results in an *ICI* of $0.03. The result of this analysis is a net invested capital intensity in the $0.40 range, which is in line with our history. Again, this is not just a coincidence, but represents our best thinking of what is needed over the next three years to support our domestic and international strategies". Then, with a look

Exhibit 90	GROWTHSTAR INC.			
	Business Unit Financials			

Next 3 Years - Growth Plan

"PRODUCTS" Financials

[$Millions (MM's) except P/Share and Capital Intensity Amounts]	Current FY Fcst.		Future Outlook — Next 3 Years			CGR/
			Yr. #1	Yr. #2	Yr. #3	*Avg. 'ICI'*
	$MM's	CGR	$MM's	$MM's	$MM's	CGR
Total Revenue	$300		$343	$393	$450	
Revenue Growth — Annual	$20	7%	$43	$50	$57	*14.5%*
Revenue Growth — Cumul.			$43	$93	$150	
New Investment	**$MM's**	***'ICI'***	**$MM's**	**$MM's**	**$MM's**	***'ICI'***
Cash	$0.4	*$0.02*	$0.9	$1.0	$1.1	*$0.02*
Accounts Receivable	3.4	*0.17*	4.8	5.5	6.4	*0.11*
Inventory (net of A/P's in Plan)	1.3	*0.06*	5.4	6.2	7.1	*0.13*
Other Current Assets	1.0	*0.05*	0.5	0.6	0.7	*0.01*
Total Current Assets	6.1	*0.30*	11.6	13.3	15.4	*0.27*
Fixed Assets (net)	5.0	*0.25*	4.1	5.0	5.6	*0.10*
Operating Leases	-	-	1.5	1.5	2.0	*0.03*
Goodwill/Other	-	-	-	-	-	-
Net New Investment ('I')	**$11.1**	***$0.55***	**$17.2**	**$19.8**	**$23.0**	***$0.40***
Cumulative 'I' — Plan			**$17.2**	**$37.0**	**$60.0**	***$0.40***
Beginning IC	**$120**	***$0.40***	**$131**	**$148**	**$168**	***$0.37***
Ending IC	**$131**	***$0.44***	**$148**	**$168**	**$191**	***$0.42***

of relief on her face, Cathy concluded with … "Gee whiz, I actually got through it".

"In a very professional and thorough manner", Jonathan commented, with a look of satisfaction on *his* face. He, too, was impressed with the way that Cathy had stepped up to this new challenge.

"See", Dave chimed in, "I told you that you'd be OK. Now, I have to sound as though I know what I'm talking about".

"That could be a challenge for you", Earl chortled.

"There's the funny man again", Dave shot back. "On a more serious note, I would also like to begin by expressing my appreciation for the help from the corporate finance people – even you, Earl. You were all a constant source of support for me. Peter, my boss, shares Larry's feelings and wanted me to make the same type of comment that Cathy made earlier".

"This is, without question, the most comprehensive financial planning process that I have ever been through, and the first time that I have ever linked all the major elements of a balance sheet to a growth strategy. While frustrating at times, I can say that I now appreciate the rationale for the process and have a much clearer understanding of the financial elements that should 'drive' our future financial performance. So, similar to what Cathy presented, let me review our key 'P&L' factors with my first exhibit (91)".

Exhibit 91	GROWTHSTAR INC.					
	Business Unit Financials					
	Next 3 Years - Growth Plan					
"SERVICES" Financials						
[$ Millions (MM's) except Per Share	Current FY Fcst.		Future Outlook — Next 3 Years			CGR/
and Capital Intensity Amounts]	**$MM's**	*% Rev.*	**Yr. #1**	**Yr. #2**	**Yr. #3**	*Avg. Ratio*
Income Statement						
Service Revenue:						*CGR*
Growthstar	$125	*83%*	$153	$187	$228	*22%*
Other Products	25	*17%*	40	64	102	*60%*
Total Service Revenue	**$150**	*100%*	**$193**	**$251**	**$330**	*30%*
Operating Costs and Expenses:						*Avg. Ratio*
Cost of Goods Sold (COGS)	42	*28%*	63	80	106	*32%*
Selling/Marketing/Service (SMS)	68	*46%*	81	105	139	*42%*
General & Administrative (G&A)	18	*12%*	19	25	33	*10%*
Research & Development (R&D)	7	*5%*	9	12	16	*5%*
Total Operating Costs/Expenses	135	*90%*	173	223	294	*89%*
Operating Income	15	*10%*	20	28	36	*11%*
Interest — Operating Leases	2	*1%*	2	2	3	*1%*
EBITA	17	*11%*	22	30	39	*12%*
"Effective" Tax Rate	36%		36%	36%	36%	
Tax on EBITA	6		8	11	14	
Net Operating Profit (NOP)	**$11**	*7.3%*	**$14**	**$19**	**$25**	*7.6%*
'Growth Plan' - Cumulative						
Service Revenue - $			*$43*	*$101*	*$180*	
NOP - $			*$3*	*$8*	*$14*	
NOP Margin - %			*7.3%*	*7.9%*	*7.8%*	

"We break out our *Services* revenue into two primary components – 'Growthstar' and 'Other Companies' products that we provide repair and maintenance services for. As you can see on the first two lines of this schedule (Exhibit 91), we are planning for a decent rate of growth (22%) for the Growthstar component and an explosive growth rate (60%) for Other Products. The fact that we have such a small current base of Other revenue has an effect on its projected growth rate, but the dollars are also significant. Our strategy should produce over $100 million in growth for the Growthstar component and over $75 million of new revenue for the Other component during the next three years".

"Our cost and expense ratios are expected to change, but it's just the opposite of what's anticipated for *Products* with respect to COGS and SMS. The Other Products component is being aggressively priced to increase our market penetration. The result is that our overall COGS ratio (to revenue) should increase by about four (4) percentage points during the plan period – from 28% to 32%. Later on, we'll see a big benefit with inventory. But, sticking with costs and expenses, we should be able to reduce our SMS and G&A ratios. We have 'loaded up' on service technicians and computer software since the acquisition. Jack and Jill have 'hammered' me during the past two years on these expenses – perhaps with good reason – since it has affected our net earnings".

"We have been focused on that, I will admit", Jill responded.

"Well", Dave replied back, "we may be near a 'payoff'. We have the staffing necessary to significantly expand our coverage. Thus, we now can take on more service contracts with a very low incremental cost for salaries and related items. We have also built up our administrative function to a point where we can realize the benefits of our infrastructure. We expect, therefore, to offset the four percentage point increase in our COGS ratio with a corresponding reduction in our SMS expense ratio, and to generate a 2% reduction in G&A as a percent-to-revenue. We'll be increasing the 'dollars' for these categories, but when spread over our significantly higher revenues, the ratios are expected to decrease. Finally, we will more than double our annual R&D expenditures by the third year of this plan period. As a percent-to-revenue, R&D expense should remain close to 5%. The 'net' result is an improvement in our *NOP* margin from 7.3% in the current year to 7.6% by year 3 of the plan period".

"The very bottom of the schedule (Exhibit 91) shows the cumulative impact of the strategy. We expect to generate $180 million of new *Service* revenue, contributing $14 million in incremental profit (*NOP*), which is a 7.8% margin on the strategy's revenue. Are there any questions before I move on to my greatest challenge – trying intelligently to rationalize a balance sheet outlook?"

"This is incredibly coherent", Earl replied. "I was armed with a 'bunch' of questions, but you seem to have covered most, if not, all of the 'bases' with regard to the P&L".

"Well, satisfying you is certainly gratifying", Dave retorted.

"Explaining and justifying your future years' balance sheet investments will, I am sure, be even more gratifying", interjected Jonathan. His desire to move forward was evident.

"I had that same feeling", Dave responded, "and I will do just that … after I give you the same input on the 'compound growth rates' that Cathy just provided". As he was speaking, Dave clicked on Exhibit 92.

"As this schedule shows", Dave continued, "we'll be incurring significantly higher expenses, but at a slightly lower rate – in total – than our aggregate revenues. COGS and R&D will increase at rates greater than revenue, while SMS and G&A will increase at rates lower than the compound rate of growth for revenue".

"I can't argue with the logic and the linkage to the strategy", Jonathan commented. "These are two good summaries of the 'income statement' portion of the outlook".

Exhibit 92	GROWTHSTAR INC.	
	Business Unit Financials	
	Next 3 Years - Growth Plan	
"SERVICES" Financials	***'Compound Growth Rates'***	
	Future Outlook — Next 3 Years	
Income Statement	**CGR**	**+ / – vs. Revenue**
Total Service Revenue	30.1%	—
Operating Costs and Expenses:		
Cost of Goods Sold (COGS)	35.7%	5.6%
Selling/Marketing/Service (SMS)	26.7%	–3.4%
General & Administrative (G&A)	22.5%	–7.6%
Research & Development (R&D)	32.3%	2.2%
Total Operating Costs / Expenses	29.5%	–0.6%

"With this as a foundation", Dave then stated, "I can now move on to our outlook for invested capital and its key elements". Exhibit 93 was flashed on the screen.

"I must say that the invested capital is now on my 'radar screen'", Dave continued. "I'm also pleased to report that I believe *Services* has a powerful story with respect to our balance sheet, which Frank has really helped me to understand during the past several weeks. So, please, Frank, fill in any 'gaps' if I 'miss' something important". Frank nodded. While shy, he really did appreciate the recognition. He could not, however, bring himself to do anything more than nod or utter a simple 'thank you'. He wished he could be more outgoing, but it just wasn't his nature.

Dave knew that he was 'on stage' now, and he paused for a moment before launching into his next dialogue. He had observed Jason pause on several occasions before an important topic, and figured out the technique to gather your thoughts before speaking. "Let me start with our expected overall result, and then work back through the details and rationale. If you look at the 'third line from the bottom' of Exhibit 93 – *Cumulative 'I'* – you will see that we expect to invest $60 million of 'net' new capital, equating to an invested capital intensity (*ICI*) of $0.33. This is the 'net new investment'

Exhibit 93	**GROWTHSTAR INC.**				
	Business Unit Financials				
	Next 3 Years - Growth Plan				
"SERVICES" Financials					
[$ Millions (MM's) except P/Share	**Current FY Fcst.**		**Future Outlook — Next 3 Years**		*CGR /*
and Capital Intensity Amounts]			**Yr. #1**	**Yr. #2**	**Yr. #3**	*Avg. 'ICI'*
	$MM's	*CGR*	**$MM's**	**$MM's**	**$MM's**	*CGR*
Total Revenue	$150		$193	$251	$330	
Revenue Growth — Annual	$50	*50%*	$43	$58	$79	*30%*
Revenue Growth — Cumul.			$43	$101	$180	
New Investment	**$MM's**	*'ICI'*	**$MM's**	**$MM's**	**$MM's**	*'ICI'*
Cash	$1.0	*$0.02*	$0.9	$1.2	$1.6	*$0.02*
Accounts Receivable	3.0	*0.06*	5.0	6.8	9.3	*0.12*
Inventory (net of A/P's in Plan)	2.5	*0.05*	2.7	3.6	5.2	*0.06*
Other Current Assets	(1.0)	*(0.02)*	-	-	-	-
Total Current Assets	5.5	*0.11*	8.5	11.5	16.0	*0.20*
Fixed Assets (net)	1.0	*0.02*	3.6	4.8	6.5	*0.08*
Operating Leases	5.0	*0.10*	2.0	3.0	4.0	*0.05*
Goodwill/Other	-	-	-	-	-	-
Net New Investment ('I')	**$11.5**	*$0.23*	**$14.1**	**$19.4**	**$26.5**	*$0.33*
Cumulative 'I' — Plan			**$14.1**	**$33.5**	**$60.0**	*$0.33*
Beginning IC	**$100**	*$0.67*	**$112**	**$126**	**$145**	*$0.44*
Ending IC	**$112**	*$0.74*	**$126**	**$145**	**$172**	*$0.52*

we will need to generate our incremental revenue of $180 million over the next three years. Let me now provide our support for this outlook".

"This year, we 'tightened up' on our collections, which will produce an unrealistically low incremental *ICI* for the current year. On an ongoing basis, we will officially have payment terms of 'net 30 days', but realistically should collect in about 40 days. We've added a 'cushion' and are assuming 43 to 44 days in our outlook, equating to an *ICI* of $0.12 for each new revenue dollar. We'll bring the 'hammer' down on accounts over 45 days. The next item – Inventory – is where we expect to continue a trend that began this year. On *virtually all* of our 'Other Products' business, we have negotiated for the manufacturing companies to carry the spare parts inventories and ship directly to the customers – who they sold in the first place. It's actually easy for them to do this, since most of the companies have new inventory control systems installed. So, they bill us and ship the parts to the customer. We eliminate a significant spare parts inventory, which is reflected in the *ICI* of only $0.06. Historically, we invested $0.10 and $0.14 per revenue dollar for 'purchased' and 'leased' fixed assets, respectively – a total of $0.24 in total for the 'fixed capital' base in our business. Before this exercise, I hardly looked at the 'purchased' assets, and never had a 'clue' as to the 'leased' assets".

"As I have mentioned to you previously", Jonathan stated – as he leaned back and folded his arms – "we are 'painfully' aware of that fact. We are also delighted that the 'light bulb' is, apparently, now lit with regard to understanding the total capital invested in the *Services* business unit".

"Indeed this 'light bulb' has been turned on, which is why we probably spent so much time and effort on this element of our plan. While we have, admittedly, spent considerably on our regional and district service facilities, we now have 'state of the art' operations that can propel us and enable us to achieve our strategic objectives. We were, just this month, awarded three new contracts and two of the customers stated that it was because of our network of facilities and our modern testing equipment. The point is that the 'facility' investment has, essentially, been made and we can grow the business without nearly the level of fixed capital investment we have required in the past. In fact, we feel strongly that our *ICI* for the strategy (that is, new fixed capital related to new revenue) will be roughly half of what it was historically. This translates into an *ICI* of $0.08 ('net' of depreciation) for 'purchased' fixed assets and $0.05 for 'leased' assets. We plan to continue our historical practises of what we purchase and what we lease, especially since it will now all be accounted for in our total invested capital".

"This lower 'incremental' capital requirement is reflected in the last two rows of the schedule (Exhibit 93) – noting the *ICI* for 'Beginning' IC (the 'next to last' row and the basis for our *EP* calculation) will fall steadily from the $0.67 level in the current year to an *ICI* of $0.44 by year 3".

Dave suddenly realized that he had been on 'auto pilot' for the past several minutes, and that he had completed his 'message'. He couldn't contain himself and blurted out … "I think I did it! I actually explained the development of a 'balance sheet' outlook in terms of 'net new investment'".

"In a very professional and thorough manner", Jonathan commented, in exactly the same tone that he had used with Cathy. Similar to his feeling for Cathy, he was impressed with the way that Dave had stepped up to this new challenge. Jonathan also knew that Dave's enthusiasm would have an impact on Peter. Dave was a 'politically savvy' person and Jonathan knew that Peter would quickly realize that Dave was not simply 'blowing smoke' with his recently discovered attention for invested capital and its link to the strategy for Services. *"This is starting to 'play out' nicely"*, he thought to himself. *"Now, if we can get Jack to 'come on board'"*.

Val and Earl were very pleased and sat with looks of satisfaction on their faces, which all the participants could detect. Jill had been constantly nodding her head and making notes during the presentations by Cathy and Dave, and it was obvious that her 'puzzle' was continuing to come together. Jack had been silent, but had not scowled at all so far.

Earl wanted to 'get into the act' but couldn't add much to what Cathy, Dave and Jonathan had already said. That never stopped him, however, and he spoke. "This has been an enlightening and meaningful summary of a lot of hard work. It's been a pleasure for me to see our Finance Directors in the two BUs 'coming to grips' with the 'economics' of their businesses, distinguishing the future from the past, and reconciling the 'numbers' with the 'strategies'. Frank, I think it's our turn to present the total company outlook".

Frank nodded and clicked on Exhibit 94.

Frank then began speaking deliberately. "This schedule (Exhibit 94) is the 'sum' of the income statement outlooks for *Products* and *Services*. At this point, there is nothing in our corporate strategy for any other business venture – either internal or external. This could change as we move forward, but this is where we are at this point in time".

Exhibit 94 — GROWTHSTAR INC.
Total Company Financials
Next 3 Years - Growth Plan

"TOTAL CO." Financials

[$ Millions (MM's) except Per Share and Capital Intensity Amounts]	Current FY Fcst. $MM's	% Rev.	Yr. #1	Yr. #2	Yr. #3	CGR / Avg. Ratio
Income Statement						
Revenue:						CGR
Products	$300	67%	$343	$393	$450	14.5%
Services	150	33%	193	251	330	30.1%
Total Revenue	**$450**	**100%**	**$536**	**$643**	**$780**	**20.1%**
Operating Costs and Expenses:						Avg. Ratio
Cost of Goods Sold (COGS)	219	49%	257	296	353	45%
Selling/Marketing/Service (SMS)	113	25%	141	184	229	29%
General & Administrative (G&A)	54	12%	57	64	78	10%
Research & Development (R&D)	22	5%	30	36	43	6%
Total Operating Costs / Expenses	408	91%	485	580	704	90%
Operating Income	42	9%	51	63	77	10%
Interest — Operating Leases	5	1%	5	6	7	1%
EBITA	47	10%	56	69	84	11%
"Effective" Tax Rate	32%		34%	34%	34%	
Tax on EBITA	16		19	24	29	
Net Operating Profit (NOP)	**$31**	**6.9%**	**$37**	**$45**	**$55**	**7.1%**
'Growth Plan' - Cumulative						
Total Revenue - $			$86	$193	$330	
NOP - $			$6	$14	$24	
NOP Margin - %			7.0%	7.3%	7.3%	

"Our BU strategies are expected to position us as a company with close to $800 million in total revenue by the end of year 3 – the 'target setting' date for this year's strategic plan. Our overall growth rate for this period is projected at 20% per year. If you recall the BU summaries, the total incremental revenue impact for the 3-year period is $330 million. This number is found near the bottom of the schedule – 'third line up from the bottom'".

"A four percentage points 'swing' is expected for our two most significant cost and expense categories. COGS will go down due to the lower material costs in *Products*, along with the impact of *Services* which has a lower COGS ratio versus *Products*. The reverse is expected for SMS, as the expansion of *Products* in Europe and Asia-Pacific is combined with the impact of a rapidly growing *Services* business incorporating an inherently higher SMS ratio-to-revenue. We've discussed the anticipated 'leveraging' of our G&A infrastructure and the need to spend for R&D, so these results should not be surprising".

"The net result is a slight improvement in the outlook for *NOP* margin – rising from 6.9% forecasted for this year to 7.1% for the final year (# 3) of the plan. The 'strategies' are expected to generate an 'incremental' $24 million of *NOP*, which is a margin of 7.3% on the 'growth' revenue of $330 million forecasted over the next three years".

"If we accept the BU numbers, we have to accept the consolidated results", interjected Earl, "since we have 'allocated' all our overheads into the BU expense outlooks".

"I see ... and I agree", Jonathan said slowly, recognizing that this consolidation could *not* be challenged without going back to the 'sources' – the business unit strategies. "OK, let's keep going".

Frank responded with the 'compound growth rate' analysis (Exhibit 95).

"This schedule (Exhibit 95) shows the (combined) compound growth rates for the major expense categories as compared to overall revenue growth. In the aggregate, the three-year compound growth rate for costs and expenses will almost equal that for total revenue. I think we've had a good explanation of the specifics through the presentations made by Cathy and Dave". Everyone nodded in agreement with Frank's comments.

"The investment scenarios", Earl jumped in, "have been most interesting and lay out some changing indicators that will impact our cash flow analyses, which will follow later. If you recall the estimates and rationale provided by the two BU's, the internal growth strategy for *Services* is actually 'less' capital intensive than the growth plan for *Products*. As I'm sure you all appreciate, this is a departure from the past. The next schedule, which Frank will talk to,

Exhibit 95	GROWTHSTAR INC.	
	Total Company Financials	
	Next 3 Years - Growth Plan	
"TOTAL CO." Financials	***'Compound Growth Rates'***	
	Future Outlook — Next 3 Years	
Income Statement	***CGR***	***+ / - vs. Revenue***
Total Revenue	20.1%	—
Operating Costs and Expenses:		
Cost of Goods Sold (COGS)	17.2%	–2.9%
Selling/Marketing/Service (SMS)	26.4%	6.3%
General & Administrative (G&A)	13.1%	–7.0%
Research & Development (R&D)	25.2%	5.1%
Total Operating Costs / Expenses	19.9%	–0.2%

summarizes the 'corporate' outlook for net new investment, *ICI* and total invested capital. Frank, can you 'wrap this up' and then we'll take a break – assuming this is OK with you, Jonathan?"

"It's fine with me", Jonathan replied. "I'm just about ready for a break".

Frank clicked on Exhibit 96.

"As you might expect", Frank said, "*TOTAL CO.* lies in between *Products* and *Services*, in terms of the invested capital intensity for the plan period. This schedule also points out some interesting movements in the *ICI* numbers and perceptions about the impact of the strategies for the two BUs and the resultant total balance sheet amounts. If we take these 'one at a time', I think you will see what I am talking about. I would like to start at the 'bottom' of the schedule (Exhibit 96) and focus on the last four lines. Starting with the fourth and third lines 'from the bottom' – the year-by year and cumulative 'net new investment' dollar amounts and *ICIs* are shown, respectively. The 'incremental' *ICI* of $0.36 for *TOTAL CO.* is the weighted average for the BU investments – $0.40 for *Products* and $0.33 for *Services*. As Dave just discussed, the strategy for *Services* is expected to result in a much lower capital intensity than our historical experience, although we are seeing the trend in the current year. So, on an 'incremental' (or,

Exhibit 96	**GROWTHSTAR INC.** Total Company Financials					

Next 3 Years - Growth Plan

"TOTAL CO." Financials

[$ Millions (MM's) except P/Share	Current FY Fcst.		Future Outlook -- Next 3 Years			CGR /
and Capital Intensity Amounts]			Yr. #1	Yr. #2	Yr. #3	*Avg. 'ICI'*
	$MM's	**CGR**	**$MM's**	**$MM's**	**$MM's**	**CGR**
Total Revenue	$450		$536	$643	$780	
Revenue Growth — Annual	$70	*18%*	$86	$108	$137	*20%*
Revenue Growth — Cumul.			$86	$193	$330	
New Investment	**$MM's**	**'ICI'**	**$MM's**	**$MM's**	**$MM's**	**'ICI'**
Cash	$1.4	*$0.02*	$1.7	$2.2	$2.7	*$0.02*
Accounts Receivable	6.4	*0.09*	9.8	12.3	15.6	*0.11*
Inventory (net of A/P's in Plan)	3.9	*0.06*	8.1	9.8	12.3	*0.09*
Other Current Assets	-	-	0.5	0.6	0.7	*0.01*
Total Current Assets	11.7	*0.17*	20.1	24.9	31.4	*0.23*
Fixed Assets (net)	6.0	*0.09*	7.7	9.8	12.1	*0.09*
Operating Leases	5.0	*0.07*	3.5	4.5	6.0	*0.04*
Goodwill/Other	-	-	-	-	-	
Net New Investment ('I')	**$22.7**	**$0.32**	**$31.3**	**$39.1**	**$49.5**	**$0.36**
Cumulative 'I' — Plan			**$31.3**	**$70.5**	**$120.0**	**$0.36**
Beginning IC	**$220**	**$0.49**	**$242**	**$274**	**$313**	**$0.40**
Ending IC	**$243**	**$0.54**	**$274**	**$313**	**$363**	**$0.46**

'strategic') basis, *Services* will be less capital intensive than *Products*. Each BU anticipates *investing* the same 'net' amount ($60 million), but *Services* expects to generate $180 million of new revenue versus the $150 million of incremental revenue forecasted for *Products*".

Frank continued by saying ... "Dave also pointed out that – and now I'm referring to the last two lines, especially the second line 'up from the bottom' (in Exhibit 96) – the 'Beginning' *ICI* on the balance sheet would decrease significantly for *Services* by year 3 of the plan period. This impact is reflected in the 'Beginning' *ICI* for *TOTAL CO.* falling from $0.49 in the current year to $0.40 by year 3. The 'Ending' *ICI* should also drop from the current year to year 3 in the future, as shown in the very last line of Exhibit 96".

"This schedule is telling us that the internal growth strategies for the two BUs will require significantly less capital on a 'relative' basis than has been our experience with the acquisition of *Services* and the build-up of its infrastructure. The details, under the 'New Investment' heading in the main body of the schedule, provide the same type of information that you have reviewed for the two BUs and support the conclusions".

"I guess that tells us something about growing internally versus by acquisition", Jonathan exclaimed, looking at Jason with an expression that indicated he now understood clearly what Jason had been telling him – that acquisition growth is usually very costly in terms of the investment and that the 'pay-off' needs to be significant. "I also believe we have also reached a point where we can take a much-needed break. Let's reconvene in fifteen minutes".

Upon the return of the group, Jason stood up. "This is probably the 'most silent' that I've been since we started this process, and I'm sure that did not offend anyone. On a serious note, I'm extremely pleased at the way you folks have grasped the concepts that were so well presented this morning. It's always gratifying when the knowledge transfer occurs and the client's people can articulate a 'tale' about the 'economics' of their businesses".

"As we discussed at our last two planning sessions", Jason continued, "these financial outlooks will be the basis for various analyses, including economic profit, cash flow and valuation. When we perform valuations, we begin – but don't always end – with the time frame for the plans, in this case three (3) years. The time period for projecting a financial outlook for a business does not always coincide with its 'strategic' time frame. What we're concerned with in this 'strategic' context is the ability of a business to 'grow profitably' – that is, increase revenue and earn an economic return above the cost of capital. Specifically, *how long* the business will be able to perform in this manner. This time horizon affects the 'warranted value ' for the business, and is often a very important factor for 'growth-oriented' firms".

"When 'valuing' a strategy, there are two basic treatments for the time period beyond the planning horizon, which in our case is three years. The first treatment assumes that the business can *no longer* produce an economic return above the cost of capital, which puts the business in a 'no-growth' mode at that time. There is a distinct way to 'value' the 'no-growth' scenario, which I have presented to you and which we will discuss momentarily. An option is to project a time period, rate of growth and economic return for the business beyond the end of the planning period. This should be based on the 'market' that the firm or business participates in, as well as the firm's position in the market *vis-à-vis* its competitors. It may not be overly detailed in its analytic rigor, but should be defensible. Sometimes, the stock price of the firm itself or its competitors will provide clues as to the time period for profitable growth. If growth, profitability and cost of capital factors are known, the future time period for 'profitable growth' can be solved mathematically".

"When we discussed and analyzed this topic in recent planning sessions, we came to some conclusions, which I would like to summarize on the flip chart and get the final concurrence of the 'team' ".

"This is something that Ian is going to be particularly interested in", Jonathan stated, "so I want to make sure I understand the conclusions and the supporting rationale".

"We all figured that you would", Jason countered, "and we reviewed the topic with Larry and Peter, for their respective businesses. What follows, therefore, is a consensus which I am going to ask Earl to explain". As he spoke, Jason walked to the flip chart and wrote:

Business Unit	+Growth Years	Growth Rate	NOP Margin	ICI
Products	*+2 to 3*	*12%*	*6.7%*	*$0.40*
– *US*	*same*	*10%*	*lower*	*lower*
– *Int'l*	*same*	*15%*	*higher*	*higher*
Services	*+ 4*	*25%*	*7.3%*	*$0.40*
– *Growthstar*	*same*	*21%*	*higher*	*higher*
– *Other*	*same*	*33%*	*lower*	*lower*

Earl had been anticipating this segment of the meeting with a more 'proactive' role for himself and launched into his prepared remarks. "*Products* is in a situation where the 'Next Generation' that is now under development will have a five to six-year 'window'. This should add two to three years of 'profitable growth' to the three-year plan period. This additional 'growth' period should encompass somewhat *slower* growth, along with approximately the same *NOP* margin and *ICI* as forecasted for the 'growth plan'. The income statement and balance sheet dynamics are relatively stable, and there is nothing envisioned over the next five to six years that significantly changes these relationships".

"*Services* represents a different scenario for the period beyond the next three years. This BU, based on the size and growth of its 'market' and its status within this market, can realistically envision continued future growth for another four years beyond the end of the plan period. At that point, which is 'seven years out', there will probably be major changes that would entail a new strategy and a new set of financial 'drivers'. Technology forecasts and the environmental trends for 'outsourcing' support this perception. While the business has an extended growth period, it will probably not be able to grow as fast or maintain the *NOP* margin and *ICI* forecasted for the next three years. This is due to competitive pricing, the need to 'staff up' after three years and the requirement to invest fixed capital in the operations at a more rapid rate than required during the next three years. The results are the numbers that Jason has noted on the flip chart – a 'slowdown' in growth, a decline in profit margin and an increase in capital intensity".

"So, let me make sure I understand all of this", Jonathan inter-jected. "*Products* can grow for an additional two to three years beyond the plan period with stable ratios. *Services* can execute its strategy for an additional four years, albeit at slightly deteriorated ratios".

Exhibit 97	GROWTHSTAR INC.		

'Base' Period Financials	**Valuation Highlights** *Current Year — 'No Growth' Value*		
[$ Millions]	*Products*	*Services*	*TOTAL CO.*
Income Statement			
Revenue	$300	$150	$450
Net Operating Profit (*NOP*)	$20	$11	$31
Balance Sheet			
Invested Capital (*IC*)	$120	$100	$220

"That's it, boss!" Earl responded.

Jason began speaking again. "We've run the strategy valuations under these scenarios – first, assuming 'no growth' beyond the plan period and second, under the assumptions just outlined for the 'post-plan' years. So, if everyone is ready for the 'ride' into the world of 'warranted value analysis', I will begin".

"We're as ready as we're ever going to be, so let's 'get on' with it", Jonathan responded.

"We begin with our 'no-growth' values", Jason stated as he got ready to show a set of exhibits. "The next schedule (Exhibit 97) summarizes the key financial valuation indicators for the current year – the basis for the 'no-growth' evaluation".

"In a 'no-growth' situation, the total 'warranted value' for each business is the capitalized value for the current year's *NOP*".

"We can illustrate this with the all the valuation approaches and we will do just that. The Free Cash Flow (*FCF*) methodology will be shown first, using Exhibit 98. In a 'no-growth' scenario, the Total Market Value (*TMV*) is calculated – by 'capitalizing' the Net Operating Profit (*NOP*). Then, the Invested Capital (*IC*) is subtracted to determine the Market Value Added (*MVA*)".

"We can also arrive at a similar result using the Economic Profit (*EP*) approach. Here, the 'capitalized value' of the current year *EP* equals the *MVA*. The *IC* is then added to *MVA* to calculate *TMV*. The result of these approaches is as follows", Jason stated, as he went to the flip chart and wrote:

$Millions	NOP	EP	TMV (*)	MVA
Products	20	7	182	62
Services	11	-0-	100	-0-
TOTAL CO.	31	7	282	62

(*) TMV is the 'warranted' market value of equity (common stock) plus debt.

Exhibit 98	GROWTHSTAR INC.		

Valuation Highlights

'Base' Period Financials — *Current Year — 'No Growth' Value*

[$ Millions]	Products	Services	TOTAL CO.
Valuation - 'FCF' Approach			
Net Operating Profit (NOP)	$20	$11	$31
Cost of Capital (CCAP)	11%	11%	11%
Total Market Value (TMV)	**$182**	**$100**	**$282**
Total Market Value (TMV)	$182	$100	$282
less IC	(120)	(100)	(220)
Market Value Added (MVA)	**$62**	**$(0)**	**$62**

Exhibit 99	GROWTHSTAR INC.		

Valuation Highlights

'Base' Period Financials — *Current Year — 'No Growth' Value*

[$ Millions]	Products	Services	TOTAL CO.
Valuation - 'EP' Approach			
Net Operating Profit (NOP)	$20	$11	$31
Capital Charge (CCAP) — @ 11%	(13)	(11)	(24)
Economic Profit ('EP')	$7	$(0)	$7
'EP' / CCAP = 'MVA' (*)	$62	$(0)	$62
plus IC	120	100	220
Total Market Value (TMV)	**$182**	**$100**	**$282**

(*) 'MVA' — Market Value Added

"Exhibit 99 illustrates the Economic Profit (EP) methodology".

"And, as I have shown you, the *VPM* method is an alternative to the *EP* approach, as Exhibit 100 shows".

"So, can everyone see what the company and the two major BUs are worth without any future growth?"

"Loud and clear", Jonathan responded. "I assume that if we subtract the 'No Growth' portion of *TMV* from our overall Total Market Value – that is, the sum of our equity and debt values, we can determine the 'warranted' total market value of our 'growth'".

"Indeed you can", Earl jumped in, before Jason could speak. "Our debt is currently $110 million. If I add this amount to the $275 million equity value of our common stock (10 million shares at $27.50 per share) our overall *TMV* is $385 million. Subtracting the 'No

Exhibit 100	GROWTHSTAR INC.		
	Valuation Highlights		
'Base' Period Financials	*Current Year — 'No Growth'Value*		
$Millions, except 'ICI"	*Products*	*Services*	*TOTAL CO.*
Valuation - 'VPM' Approach **Ratios:**			
Invested Capital Intensity ("ICI")	*$0.40*	*$0.67*	*$0.49*
Value Profit Margin ("VPM")			
Actual NOP Margin (%)	*6.7%*	*7.3%*	*6.9%*
Value Profit Margin ("VPM")	*4.4%*	*7.3%*	*5.4%*
"Spread" - Actual NOP% vs.VPM	*2.3%*	*0.0%*	*1.5%*
Valuation:			
Revenue	$300	$150	$450
VPM "Spread" - %	2.3%	0.0%	1.5%
VPM "Spread" - $	$7	$(0)	$7
"Spread" / CCAP = 'MVA'	$62	$(0)	$62
plus IC	120	100	220
Total Market Value (TMV)	**$182**	**$100**	**$282**

Growth' value of $282 million leaves a 'value' for our future growth of $103 million. This is what the financial markets seem to be telling us at this time. To state it another way, our current level of performance accounts for nearly 75% of our total market value, with our future growth prospects comprising the remaining 25% or so".

"What we're going to be doing shortly", Jason added "is to determine the 'warranted' value of the company's growth plan and then the total market and equity values as compared to the actual values in the stock market. This will help direct your investor relations efforts". Jason looked at Mandy as he made this last statement.

"I can assure you all that this topic will be a 'hot button' for Ian", Mandy responded, "and it will, thus, be important for all of us". As she spoke, Mandy looked over at Jonathan, who nodded in agreement.

Jonathan then added … "Anything that we can do to give Ian a credible valuation of our growth plans will be a very important piece of information. As you know, he looks at the 'net earnings' now and puts a simple 'multiple' to get his 'home-spun' value estimates".

As he uttered this last comment, Jonathan looked over at Jack, who only shrugged his shoulders. Jack had been silent, but very attentive. He had reconciled himself to the fact that *some type* of change would be forthcoming. His hope now was that it would *not* be *too* dramatic and could fit reasonably within the existing reporting structure and would not completely 'overthrow' the system he had built so diligently over the years.

Jason had another perception to present on 'market value' and began to speak again ... "I want to introduce two indicators of 'value creation' – the Market Value Index (*MVI*) and the Market-to-Book (*M/B*) Ratio. Both provide 'relative' indicators of value creation and can be very useful, especially when making comparisons of value creation – either actual through past/current performance, or potential through the attractiveness of a strategy. Exhibit 101 gives an illustration of these two indicators".

"*MVI* tells us how much 'value' is created for each dollar of investment – a 'return' index. The way to interpret this 'value indicator' is to view it as an 'incremental' return above and beyond what has been invested in the business. For *Products*, the business – with *no* future growth – has returned 'fifty-two cents' for every 'dollar' that has been invested. In other words, the business has been a good performer. As we have also noted, the issue for *Products* is 'where is it going'? *Services*, as we have discussed at length, has generated no 'excess' return – at least at this point in time – beyond what has been invested. In essence, through the current year, the shareholders have invested a 'dollar' and have received a 'dollar' in return. Thus, *MVI* is 'zero'. For *Services*, 'shareholder value' is totally dependent on the future strategy and growth potential".

"The 'Market-to-Book' (*M/B*) ratio provides an indicator of how the 'market' should value the company in relation to its invested capital.

Exhibit 101	**GROWTHSTAR INC.**		
'Base' Period Financials	**Valuation Highlights** *Current Year* — *'No Growth' Value*		
$Millions, except MVI	*Products*	*Services*	*TOTAL CO.*
Market Value Index ('MVI')			
'Base' ('No Growth')			
Market Value Added (MVA)	$62	$(0)	$62
Invested Capital	$120	$100	$220
MVI .... Additional MVA for			
each Investment Dollar	*$0.52*	*$(0.00)*	*$0.28*
'MVI' reflects the 'warranted' MVA for the business as a ratio of invested capital.			
Market-to-Book ('M/B') Ratio			
(re: "Total" Market Value ..... 'Base')			
Total Market Value (TMV)	$182	$100	$282
Economic Book Value	$120	$100	$220
Ratio: Market-to-Book Value	*1.52*	*1.00*	*1.28*
M/B Ratio reflects the 'warranted' TMV for the business versus the economic book value.			

It's a 'report card' on the job that management has done with the capital that it has been entrusted with, and is another way to view the *MVI*. Essentially, if you add 1.0 to the *MVI*, you will arrive at the *M/B* ratio in a 'no-growth' scenario. In theory, then, *Products* would be valued at about 1.5 times its economic book value, *Services* would be valued at exactly book value and *TOTAL CO.* at nearly 1.3 times book value ... in a 'no-growth' mode".

"To summarize, *MVI* provides a 'relative' indicator for *MVA* and *M/B* gives a 'relative' indicator for *TMV*. We'll be calculating these ratios for the strategies of the two BUs and the total company when we evaluate the future outlooks. The 'no-growth' valuation is important because it provides an indicator of what a business or a company is worth based on the level of performance built up through the present. It also provides insight as to how the 'market' may be viewing the future prospects for growth and profit. In the case of Growthstar, there's about a '75/25 split' in terms of the present and future performance contributing to the firm's market value. What our strategy valuation work will do is to confirm this perception or uncover a potential 'disconnect' between what we may feel is a 'warranted' value and the actual value of the company in the financial market".

Mandy Bettertalk had been listening attentively to the presentation on the 'no-growth' value analysis. She felt genuinely good about the exercise that the company was going through and said, "the investors look at this historical – 'no-growth' as we are calling it – perspective as a basis of making their own projections about the future. They may or may not break it down as we are doing, but they certainly do look at the recent past and the present as a benchmark to either determine their own forecasts or make judgments regarding what we may tell them about our view of the future".

Jonathan came back into the discussion by stating ... "I feel intuitively – without seeing the numbers – that our CEO would probably wish to see a greater percentage of our stock price linked to our future growth and profit. He's also been asking Mandy and me almost daily, if we're fairly valued in the stock market ... you can probably guess his feeling on this subject ... so I'm very anxious about this next exercise. Can we begin the 'value assessment' of our strategies and get at this issue?"

"Unless anyone has any questions on the 'no-growth' valuation and its implications", Jason responded.

All the 'team' members understood the 'no-growth' valuation and the conclusions. Even if they didn't, none of them would have restrained Jonathan from moving forward. While he was a reasonable person, there were times when Jonathan did not want to be held back. This was one of those times and everyone in the room sensed it.

Exhibit 102	GROWTHSTAR INC.			
"PRODUCTS" Financials	**Valuation Highlights** BU 'Strategy' Financials			
$Millions, except Per Share and Index/Ratio Amounts	*Future 3 Yrs. - 'Business Strategy'Value*			
	Year 1	*Year 2*	*Year 3*	*Residual*
Free Cash Flow Approach				Year 3 'NOP' cap'd at CCAP 11%
Net Operating Profit (NOP) *	$2.9	$6.2	$10.0	
Net New Investment (I)	(17.2)	(19.8)	(23.0)	
Free Cash Flow (FCF) - 'Strategy'	$(14.3)	$(13.6)	$(13.0)	$91.2
Net Present Value (NPV) - Strategy	$27			

[* 'Incremental' NOP vs. Current Year 'Base']

Jason, therefore, did not want to take a formal break, but instead motioned to the coffee and teapots, indicating that anyone who wanted a refill should get up and get one. He then began speaking again. "I believe that we have a credible set of financial outlooks for the two business units, for the three-year plan period and the post-planning period. What I am going to do, therefore, is to present the valuations that Frank, Earl and I have developed based on these outlooks and employing the three valuation techniques that we have presented to you – Free Cash Flow (*FCF*), Economic Profit (*EP*) and Value Profit Margin (*VPM*). Let's start with the outlook for *Products*. Exhibit 102 presents a summary of the *FCF* valuation for *Products*, based on the assumption that no further growth will occur beyond the plan period. Exhibits 103 and 104 will provide the same type of valuation summary for the *EP* and *VPM* methods. What we are doing in these analyses is to view the 'growth plan' as an independent endeavor, in order to determine its contribution to the total value of the company. This is important, because it provides a basis for making investment decisions and a mechanism to test and compare the perception of the financial markets to our internal outlook".

Jack focused his eyes on Exhibit 104, the *VPM* approach. He knew that the method had integrity and that he could probably salvage an 'earnings' metric if he threw his support behind this approach. He, therefore, leaned forward and spoke . . . "I would like to put myself in the position of discussing a strategically based set of financials with Larry Buildermann – with your involvement, Cathy. What I'm hearing is that the strategy for *Products* results in revenue growth of 14.5% and an *NOP* margin of 6.7%. If these are acceptable from a 'value enhancement' perspective, or if it's all that we can reasonably expect from *Products* over the next few years, then I'm comfortable with stipulating financial

Exhibit 103

GROWTHSTAR INC.
Valuation Highlights

"PRODUCTS" Financials   BU 'Strategy' Financials

$Millions, except Per Share and Index/Ratio Amounts	*Future 3 Yrs. - 'Business Strategy' Value*			
	Year 1	*Year 2*	*Year 3*	*Residual*
				Year 3 'EP' cap'd at CCAP 11%
Economic Profit Approach				
Net New Investment - 'Cumulative'	$17.2	$37.0	$60.0	
Net Operating Profit (NOP) *	$2.9	$6.2	$10.0	
Capital Charge (CCAP) -- @ 11%	(1.9)	(4.1)	(6.6)	
Economic Profit ('EP')	$1.0	$2.1	$3.4	$31.2
Net Present Value (NPV) - Strategy	**$26**			
Strategy ROIC — Return on 'Incremental' Net New Investment	16.8%	16.8%	16.7%	

[* 'Incremental' NOP vs. Current Year 'Base']

Exhibit 104

GROWTHSTAR INC.
Valuation Highlights

"PRODUCTS" Financials   BU 'Strategy' Financials

$Millions, except Per Share and Index/Ratio Amounts	*Future 3 Yrs. - 'Business Strategy' Value*			
	Year 1	*Year 2*	*Year 3*	*Residual*
				Year 3 'EP' cap'd at CCAP 11%
Value Profit Margin (VPM) Approach				
Ratios:				
Invested Capital Intensity ("ICI")	*$0.40*	*$0.40*	*$0.40*	
Value Profit Margin ("VPM")				
Actual NOP Margin (%)	*6.7%*	*6.7%*	*6.7%*	
Value Profit Margin ("VPM")	*4.4%*	*4.4%*	*4.4%*	
"Spread" - Actual NOP% vs. VPM	*2.3%*	*2.3%*	*2.3%*	
Valuation:				
Revenue	$43	$93	$150	
VPM "Spread"- %	2.3%	2.3%	2.3%	
VPM "Spread" - $(equals 'EP')	$1.0	$2.1	$3.4	$31.2
Net Present Value (NPV) - Strategy	**$26**			

objectives in this context. Corporate Accounting can provide support to calculate the capital intensity element and P&L adjustments to implement the approach". As he spoke, he looked at Jill, who nodded in approval and also at Jonathan, who gave a slight nod.

"That's all fine and good", Earl interjected, "but let's also focus on the 'value creation' impact of the strategy for *Products*".

"That's not a bad idea", Jonathan added, "since that's what I thought this meeting was all about. We may want to *implement* the 'economic' metrics with the *VPM* approach, but let's hold off on that for now and focus on the 'value implications' of our strategies, as expressed in the financial outlooks. What you are showing us is a business with a 'warranted' *TMV* of $182 million based on the current level of performance plus $26 or $27 million based on a '3-year' profitable growth horizon for the business. It's obvious that the vast majority of the 'present market value' in *Products* is predicated on our current level of operations – including the invested capital – if we accept this scenario".

"I just wanted to make the point that I'm starting to see a way of implementing the 'economics' that you all seem to be so enamored with in a practical manner, that allows the operating people – Larry and Peter in particular – to execute what may be desirable from a corporate finance perspective without totally turning their lives 'upside down'".

"Without upsetting yours either", Earl retorted.

"OK guys", Jonathan jumped in, "let's keep moving *forward*".

"Try to remember two things, Jonathan", Val commented. "First, we don't know if this '3-year' profitable growth period is what the 'market' is estimating in its valuation. Second, we're not sure if the growth rates, *ICI* and profit margins are the same as what the 'market' is using in its valuation of our company. We'll test this shortly. However, this *relatively* high value contribution for the 'no-growth' portion is *not exactly typical* for 'growth' companies".

"That's one of the reasons we've addressed the time period *beyond* the three-year plan", Jason added, as Earl nodded his head vigorously. "My suggestion is to next present the values for the 'plan period' for *Services* and then *TOTAL CO*. This will give us a 'base line' for the 'strategy' valuation. After that, we can delve into the impact of extending the 'post-planning' time horizons for the two BUs. The next three exhibits (105, 106 and 107) will provide the same type of valuation summary for *Services* as we just saw for *Products*".

Dave Dollarby almost jumped out of his chair when he saw that the 'strategy' value for *Services* was in the range of 56 to 57 million dollars – more than double that for *Products* – and the 'incremental' *ROIC* exceeded 20%. "Will you look at that", was all he could say. "Does this mean we're entering the exalted realm of an **'A'-type** business?"

"It sure does", Jason replied, feeling compelled to give a positive response. Jason sensed that Dave finally felt vindicated for the 'abuse' taken during the historical assessments, and also for the hard work he had put in to develop a credible financial outlook linked to the business strategy for *Services*.

Exhibit 105	GROWTHSTAR INC.			
	Valuation Highlights			
"SERVICES" Financials	**BU 'Strategy' Financials**			
$Millions, except Per Share	*Future 3 Yrs. - 'Business Strategy' Value*			
and Index/Ratio Amounts	*Year 1*	*Year 2*	*Year 3*	*Residual*
				Year 3 'NOP'
Free Cash Flow Approach				cap'd at CCAP
				11%
Net Operating Profit (NOP) *	$3.0	$8.2	$14.2	
Net New Investment (I)	(14.1)	(19.4)	(26.5)	
Free Cash Flow (FCF) -				
'Strategy'	$(11.1)	$(11.1)	$(12.3)	$128.9
Net Present Value (NPV) -				
Strategy	**$57**			
[* 'Incremental' NOP vs. Current Year 'Base']				

Exhibit 106	GROWTHSTAR INC.			
	Valuation Highlights			
"SERVICES" Financials	**BU 'Strategy' Financials**			
$Millions, except Per Share	*Future 3 Yrs. - 'Business Strategy' Value*			
and Index/Ratio Amounts	*Year 1*	*Year 2*	*Year 3*	*Residual*
				Year 3 'EP'
Economic Profit Approach				cap'd at CCAP
				11%
Net New Investment -				
'Cumulative'	$14.1	$33.5	$60.0	
Net Operating Profit (NOP) *	$3.0	$8.2	$14.2	
Capital Charge (CCAP) @ 11%	(1.6)	(3.7)	(6.6)	
Economic Profit ('EP')	$1.5	$4.6	$7.6	$68.9
Net Present Value (NPV) -				
Strategy	**$56**			
Strategy ROIC — Return on				
'Incremental' Net New				
Investment	21.3%	24.6%	23.6%	
[* 'Incremental' NOP vs. Current Year 'Base']				

"Let me gather my thoughts", Dave stated, pausing for a moment. "This 'value' doesn't take into account the *additional* years of profitable growth that we have forecast, does it?"

"No it doesn't", Jason answered. "We'll be presenting this impact shortly".

"Well now, this is getting interesting and will definitely get Peter's attention", Dave exclaimed. "You know, Jonathan, this 'economic

Exhibit 107	GROWTHSTAR INC.			
	Valuation Highlights			
"SERVICES" Financials	**BU 'Strategy' Financials**			
$Millions, except Per Share and Index/Ratio Amounts	*Future 3 Yrs. - 'Business Strategy' Value*			
	Year 1	*Year 2*	*Year 3*	*Residual*
				Year 3 'EP' cap'd at CCAP 11%
Value Profit Margin (VPM) Approach				
Ratios:				
Invested Capital Intensity ("ICI")	*$0.33*	*$0.33*	*$0.33*	
Value Profit Margin ("VPM")				
Actual NOP Margin (%)	*7.1%*	*8.2%*	*7.9%*	
Value Profit Margin ("VPM")	*3.6%*	*3.7%*	*3.7%*	
"Spread" - Actual NOP% vs.VPM	*3.4%*	*4.5%*	*4.2%*	
Valuation:				
Revenue	$43	$101	$180	
VPM "Spread" - %	3.4%	4.5%	4.2%	
VPM "Spread" - $(equals 'EP')	$1.5	$4.6	$7.6	$68.9
Net Present Value (NPV) - Strategy	**$56**			

value' stuff does have a nice 'ring' to it". Dave snickered at Jack as he spoke.

Jonathan responded with ... "It's amazing how one's perception is influenced by the direction and magnitude of the numbers. I seem to remember that the shareholder value contribution of *Services* is 'zero' based on the current level of performance. One way to look at this situation is to recognize that there's no way to go but up. You know, Dave, maybe we should keep *Services* on the 'old accounting' system. All of this 'balance sheet' and 'cost of capital' stuff may be too much for you and Peter".

"Hold on there, Chief", Dave retorted. "We must look to the future, not the past. Further, are you forgetting the eloquent dissertation that I just gave on 'ICI' and the other 'growth drivers'?"

"How could I", Jonathan chuckled. "OK, we'll let you come to the 'economic value' party".

Jack was rolling his eyes and thinking to himself ... "*I have to get 'VPM' installed, or these people may go 'crazy' with a completely new economic-based performance and reporting system, with Earl and Frank 'coaching the team' and Dave coming 'on board' as their 'cheerleader'. Jill and Cathy may also support a completely new system*".

"Well, it's always nice to get a 'convert' to come to the party", interjected Earl, feeling a sense of accomplishment. "It will be interesting to see if any other 'converts' are out there", he snapped ... casting a glaring look at Jack, who glared right back at him.

Exhibit 108

GROWTHSTAR INC.
Valuation Highlights

"TOTAL CO." Financials   'Strategy' Financials

$Millions, except Per Share and Index/Ratio Amounts — *Future 3 Yrs. - 'Business Strategy' Value*

	Year 1	Year 2	Year 3	Residual
				Year 3 'NOP' cap'd at CCAP 11%
Free Cash Flow Approach				
Net Operating Profit (NOP) *	$5.9	$14.5	$24.2	
Net New Investment (I)	(31.3)	(39.1)	(49.5)	
Free Cash Flow (FCF) - 'Strategy'	$(25.4)	$(24.7)	$(25.3)	$220.1

Net Present Value (NPV) - Strategy	$84

[* 'Incremental' NOP vs. Current Year 'Base]

Exhibit 109

GROWTHSTAR INC.
Valuation Highlights

"TOTAL CO." Financials   'Strategy' Financials

$Millions, except Per Share and Index/Ratio Amounts — *Future 3 Yrs. - 'Business Strategy' Value*

	Year 1	Year 2	Year 3	Residual
				Year 3 'EP' cap'd at CCAP 11%
Economic Profit Approach				
Net New Investment - 'Cumulative'	$31.3	$70.5	$120.0	
Net Operating Profit (NOP) *	$5.9	$14.5	$24.2	
Capital Charge (CCAP) @ 11%	(3.4)	(7.8)	(13.2)	
Economic Profit ('EP')	$2.5	$6.7	$11.0	$100.1

Net Present Value (NPV) - Strategy	$82

Strategy ROIC — Return on 'Incremental' Net New Investment	18.8%	20.5%	20.2%	

[* 'Incremental' NOP vs. Current Year 'Base']

"Maybe we ought to take a look at the results of the 'plan' on the total company", Jason countered, not wanting to have Earl and Jack engage in a confrontation at this time.

Jonathan gave Jason a nod to continue, which he did.

"The next three exhibits (108, 109 and 110) will provide the 'plan only' valuation summaries for *TOTAL CO.* As you can surmize, they're the sum of the two BUs".

Mandy Bettertalk had been listening very attentively and had mentioned to Jason, prior to the meeting, that she wanted to offer a 'financial market' perspective. "There are two important perceptions

Exhibit 110	GROWTHSTAR INC.			
	Valuation Highlights			
"TOTAL CO." Financials	**'Strategy' Financials**			
$Millions, except Per Share	***Future 3 Yrs. - 'Business Strategy' Value***			
and Index/Ratio Amounts	*Year 1*	*Year 2*	*Year 3*	*Residual*
				Year 3 'EP'
Value Profit Margin (VPM) Approach				cap'd at CCAP
Ratios:				11%
Invested Capital Intensity ("ICI")	$0.36	$0.36	$0.36	
Value Profit Margin ("VPM")				
Actual NOP Margin (%)	6.9%	7.5%	7.3%	
Value Profit Margin ("VPM")	4.0%	4.0%	4.0%	
"Spread" - Actual NOP% vs.VPM	2.9%	3.5%	3.3%	
Valuation:				
Revenue	$86	$193	$330	
VPM "Spread" - %	2.9%	3.5%	3.3%	
VPM "Spread" - $ (equals 'EP')	$2.5	$6.7	$11.0	$100.1
Net Present Value (NPV) -				
Strategy	**$82**			

from the analysis of the 'plan' period. The first one will be reflected in the shareholder value contribution for these next three years, which is in the $82 to $84 million range. In a moment, Jason will show us how this 'tracks' with the company's value in the financial markets. The other perspective is one that is becoming increasingly important to the investment community – especially to some of the 'leading edge' firms on the 'sell side' – that is, those making recommendations to 'buy or sell' a company. This perspective is the return on incremental capital ('incremental' *ROIC*) which is the last row in Exhibit 109. The total company is forecasting an 'incremental' *ROIC* of 20%, driven by *Services*. This is a very strong level, considering that *CCAP* is 11%. This (*ROIC*) metric gives an indication of the financial attractiveness of the strategy, in 'relative' terms. With a 900 basis point (9 percentage point) 'spread' versus *CCAP*, we have a 'margin of error' in terms of profitable growth. This is a good position to be in with the investors, particularly when presenting a strategy or growth plan to the 'Wall Street' crowd. The more they can see in 'downside protection', the better the scenario is from a credibility perspective".

"Very well put", Jonathan commented.

Jason then re-entered the discussion with ... "As Mandy mentioned, we have compared the 'plan only' valuation to Growthstar's current market value. As Exhibit 111 will show, the market expects a higher level of performance from us, either in an extended growth horizon or better performance during the next three years. If we 'cut off' profitable growth after the next three years, then the equity has a warranted value of approximately $25.50, versus its current value of $27.50. In absolute dollars, this $2.00 per share

Exhibit 111	GROWTHSTAR INC.			
	Valuation Highlights			**Current**
$Millions, except 'per share'	*'No Growth' plus Next 3 Yrs. Growth Plan*			
Valuation - 'FCF' Approach	**'No Growth'**	**'Strategy'**	**'Total'**	**Mkt. Value**
Products	$182	$27	$209	
Services	100	56	156	
TOTAL CO.	$282	$83	$365	$385
less: Total Debt			(110)	(110)
Equity Value			**$255**	**$275**
# Shares (millions)			*10*	*10*
Per Share Value			***$25.50***	***$27.50***

difference is worth $20 million, based on ten (10) million common shares".

"So, we're expected to do a bit better than our plan for the next three years", Jonathan interjected.

"That's one way to state it", responded Mandy. "Another is to say that the financial market forecast of our 'profitable growth horizon' – or 'competitive advantage period' ('CAP') – is longer than three years, but not too much longer. This 'flies in the face' of our CEO's outlook for the company. Ian's vision is for high growth well into the future".

"Mine also", chimed in Jonathan.

Mandy continued ... "Frank, Earl, Val, Jason and I have been evaluating some potential scenarios based on our press releases and analyst meetings this year. Perhaps it would make sense for Earl to review a scenario which seems to explain our stock price, and then present the results of taking our growth, profit and investment projections beyond the end of the three-year planning period".

"By all means", thundered Jonathan. "I want to see this!"

Jason clicked on Exhibit 112, as Earl prepared to speak.

"We've given some signals and produced results during the year that could be leading the major analysts and portfolio managers following our stock to forecast a revenue growth rate of 18%, an *NOP* margin of 7.0% and *ICI* of $0.40 per new revenue dollar". Earl continued by saying, "If we take these assumptions and impose a profitable growth time horizon of 5 years, we come almost 'dead on' our stock price. Jason, I believe you and Frank have analyzed this scenario under both the *FCF* and *EP* methodologies".

"That's right", Jason responded. "Exhibit 113 will provide the key inputs and results for the Free Cash Flow (*FCF*) approach, which Frank will review".

Frank pointed to Exhibit 113 and said, "This *FCF* evaluation looks at the next five years for the total company. *NOP* is estimated from the

Exhibit 112

GROWTHSTAR INC.
Valuation Input

"TOTAL CO." Financials   **Strategy Financials - 'Investor Scenario'**

$Millions, except Per Share and Index/Ratio Amounts	*Future Years - Plan Period (3 Yrs.) + 2 Add'l Years*				
	Year 1	*Year 2*	*Year 3*	*Year 4*	*Year 5*
Assumptions					
Revenue - % Growth	*18%*	*18%*	*18%*	*18%*	*18%*
Total Revenue $	533	631	747	885	1,048
Incremental $ - Annual	83	98	116	138	163
Incremental $ - Cumul.*	83	181	297	435	598
NOP - % Margin	*7.0%*	*7.0%*	*7.0%*	*7.0%*	*7.0%*
Total NOP $	37	44	52	62	74
Incremental $ - Annual	6	7	8	10	11
Incremental $ - Cumul.*	6	13	21	31	42
Net New Investment ('I') - "ICI"	*$0.40*	*$0.40*	*$0.40*	*$0.40*	*$0.40*
Total $ - Annual	33	39	46	55	65
Total $ - Cumul.*	33	72	119	174	239

[* 'Cumulative' Amounts are versus Current Year 'Base']

Exhibit 113

GROWTHSTAR INC.
Valuation

"TOTAL CO." Financials   **Future Outlook - Investor Scenario**

$Millions, except Per Share and Index/Ratio Amounts	*Year 1*	*Year 2*	*Year 3*	*Year 4*	*Year 5*	*Resid.*
						Yr. 3 'NOP' cap'd @ 11%
Free Cash Flow Approach						
Net Operating Profit (NOP)	$37.4	$44.3	$52.5	$62.2	$73.6	
Net New Investment (I)	(33.2)	(39.3)	(46.5)	(55.1)	(65.2)	
Free Cash Flow (FCF) – 'No Growth' plus 'Strategy'	$4.2	$5.0	$6.0	$7.1	$8.4	$669

Net Present Value (NPV) - Total Co. =	$380

7% margin and the growth in total revenue. As an example, *NOP* for future year #1 ($37 million) is calculated by multiplying the revenue of $533 million (from Exhibit 112) times the margin estimate of 7.0%. Net new investment of $33 million is calculated by multiplying the *ICI* of $.40 times the change in revenue ($83 million ... $533 million minus $450 million in the current year). The difference between *NOP* and I is approximately $4 million, which is the Free Cash Flow (*FCF*) for future year #1. The process continues for the remaining years in the analysis, and then the year 5 *NOP* is capitalized to calculate the residual value. This analysis combines the 'no growth' and 'strategy' elements into an 'aggregate' valuation. The Net Present Value (NPV)

Exhibit 114

GROWTHSTAR INC.
Valuation
"TOTAL CO." Financials   **Future Outlook - Investor Scenario**

$Millions, except Per Share and Index/Ratio Amounts

	Year 1	Year 2	Year 3	Year 4	Year 5	Resid.
Economic Profit Approach						Yr. 3 'NOP' cap'd @ 11%
Growth NPV + 'No' Growth TMV						
Net New Investment - 'Cumulative'	$33	$72	$119	$174	$239	
Net Operating Profit (NOP) *	6.3	13.2	21.3	31.0	42.5	
Capital Charge (CCAP) @ 11%	(3.6)	(8.0)	(13.1)	(19.1)	(26.3)	
Economic Profit ('EP')	$2.7	$5.2	$8.2	$11.9	$16.2	$147

Net Present Value (NPV) - 'Growth' = $108
'No Growth' Total Market Value =   282
Total Market Value (TMV) - Total Co. = $390

Strategy ROIC — Return on 'Incremental' Net New Investment	18.9%	18.2%	17.9%	17.8%	17.7%

[* 'Incremental' NOP vs. Current Year 'Base']

of $380 million represents the Total Market Value (*TMV*) – that is, the value of the debt plus equity – for the company".

Jason then clicked on Exhibit 114.

After everyone had looked at Exhibit 114 for a moment, Frank continued ... "We can also perform the valuation for what we're calling the 'Investor Scenario' using the *EP* approach, in a similar fashion to what we've done for the BU strategies. We begin with the cumulative net new investment for each year, which is the last row of numbers in Exhibit 112. The *NOP* is the incremental amount versus the current year 'base' and is also found in Exhibit 112. *CCAP* is applied to the cumulative net new investment and *EP* is, as you know, *NOP* minus *CCAP*. Total market value (*TMV*) is slightly higher ($10 million, or 2.5%) at $390 million than the $380 million calculated using the *FCF* approach, but well within a range of acceptability. Notice the last row in Exhibit 114 – the 'incremental' *ROICs*. As Mandy noted, this is a metric that investors are focusing on, as they strive to determine what level of 'economic return' management is earning on new capital. Their expectation for us, in this case, is in the 18% range".

Earl jumped back into the dialogue. "We have summarized this 'Investor Scenario' evaluation by 'averaging' the two methods for *TMV* to determine the equity value. This is reflected in the next exhibit (115) which I know Jason is just 'itching' to show".

Jason obliged by clicking on Exhibit 115.

Exhibit 115	GROWTHSTAR INC. 'Investor Scenario' Valuation Highlights			
$Millions, except 'per share'	**'No Growth' + Growth Plan + 2 Add'l Yrs.***			**Current**
Valuation	**'No Growth'**	**'Strategy'**	**'Total'**	**Market Value**
Average of 'FCF' and 'EP' Approaches				
TOTAL CO.	$282	$103	$385	$385
less: Total Debt			(110)	(110)
Equity Value			$275	$275
# Shares (millions)			10	10
Per Share Value			**$27.50**	**$27.50**
	* Five (5) years of growth in total			

Earl was not finished, and he spoke again. "We don't know if this scenario is what the investors have in their valuation models for us, but it may be close to their thinking. As Mandy mentioned, our performance along with remarks made this year could lead one in this direction. While the result could be coincidental, I doubt it. We haven't given any concrete evidence that we can grow profitably beyond a five-year time horizon, and Jack, Jonathan and I have given references to our '7%' profit margin expectation for the company this year. Those who choose to review our balance sheet – and my feeling is that more and more people on both the 'buy' and the 'sell' side are doing this – can derive an 'incremental' *ICI* in the $0.40 range. Dividing a 7% *NOP* margin by an *ICI* of $0.40 yields an *ROIC* of 18%. So, based on published information and our external communication, one could arrive at the forecast and valuation in the 'Investor Scenario'". Mandy then added to the commentary by saying ... "We need to get out and determine if these assumptions are in the valuation models of a significant number of the professionals who either follow/recommend our company or own shares. We also need to find out if this is the perception of investors who do *not* own our stock, but who would appear to be 'targets' for investing in Growthstar".

"Now, that's a good observation", Jonathan snapped, "and I hope it's an area that you can help us with, Mandy. Goodness knows, we haven't even begun to penetrate this subject. I like the progress we're making and the perceptions that are resulting from this work. It would now seem prudent to pursue our own analysis of the impact of growing profitably beyond the three-year plan period".

Val Performa looked toward Jason. She had become quite enamored with the 'relative' indicators of value creation – the Market Value Index (*MVI*) and Market-to-Book (*M/B*) Ratio – because she felt they were so applicable to Growthstar's two business units, as well as the total company. She thought that Jason was going to cover them, but wanted to make sure. Therefore, she said, "before we leave the 'plan only' growth analysis and the 'Investor Scenario', I'm hoping that we can see their impact on the *MVI* and *M/B Ratio*, to compare them to the result of the 'no-growth' evaluation. These two 'relative' indicators of value creation present a powerful summary of the results of our market opportunities and strategic efforts. I'm also sure they are looked at carefully by our shareholders – actual and prospective".

Mandy nodded at Val, indicating her concurrence.

Jason had planned to present these indices, so the comments by Val provided a good 'lead-in'. "It just so happens that I have an exhibit – or two or three – on this subject".

"I really want to see these 'market' indices and how they relate to our 'book' value", Jack quipped. All the heads snapped around the table. The thought was pervasive throughout the room ... "*Jack made a comment that was positive! Except for his brief remark earlier in the session, Jack had been silent and reclusive for so long, that we were all starting to be concerned. Perhaps this is the 'breakthrough' we're all looking for*".

Jill Debitson, who continued to take notes and focus so attentively that she started to experience a slight headache, was particularly moved by Jack's comment. She took her glasses off and wiped her eyes with a tissue, saying to herself, "*Please, boss, 'come on board' and 'join the party'*".

Jason was taken back for a moment, but he had trained himself over the years for the unexpected. He never knew what it would be, but he knew that 'something' would usually occur in a meeting or presentation that could *not* be anticipated. He, therefore, in a 'matter of fact' manner, said ... "let's illustrate what Val is alluding to with three Exhibits (116, 117 and 118). Exhibit 116 will provide the Market Value Index (*MVI*) for the 'Plan' and compare it to the 'no-growth' scenario. Exhibit 117 will do the same for the Market-to-Book (*M/B*) Ratio. Exhibit 118 provides the *MVI* and *M/B* analysis for the 'Investor Scenario' in a format similar to the way we viewed the 'No-growth' scenario for the company, the exception being that there is no detail for the business units in the 'Investor Scenario'. Let's start with Exhibit 116 and move right through the next two".

Jason began his commentary on the exhibits with ... "Based on what we've seen so far regarding the outlooks for the next three years, the *MVI* in Exhibit 116 should not be startling. The (three-year) 'plan' *MVI* ($0.55) for *Products* is close to that for its 'no-growth' *MVI*. That's not surprising since, as Cathy has explained, the future ratios for *Products* are in line with those for the current year. The dramatic surge in the 'plan' *MVI* for *Services* is the result of its aggressive

Exhibit 116	GROWTHSTAR INC.		
	Valuation Highlights		
'Plan Period' Financials	*Next 3 Years - 'Growth' Period*		
[$Millions, except MVI]	*Products*	*Services*	*TOTAL CO.*
Market Value Index ('MVI')			
(re: '3-Year Growth' Plan)			
Market Value Added (MVA)	$27	$56	$83
Net New Investment - 'Discounted'	$48	$48	$96
MVI .... Additional MVA for			
each Investment Dollar	*$0.55*	*$1.17*	*$0.86*

'MVI' reflects the 'warranted' MVA for the strategy as a ratio of 'discounted' net new investment.

Market Value Index ('MVI')			
(re: 'No Growth')	*$0.52*	*$(0.00)*	*$0.28*
"MVI' Difference	*$0.03*	*$1.17*	*$0.58*

Exhibit 117	GROWTHSTAR INC.		
	Valuation Highlights		
'Plan Period' Financials	*Next 3 Years - 'Growth' Period*		
[$Millions]	*Products*	*Services*	*TOTAL CO.*
Market-to-Book ('M/B') Ratio			
(re: Total Market Value ... **"No Growth' plus 'Strategy')**			
Total Market Value (TMV)	$209	$156	$365
Economic Book Value	$131	$112	$243
(Current Year - Ending)			
Ratio: Market-to-Book Value	*1.60*	*1.39*	*1.50*
Market-to-Book ('M/B') Ratio			
(re: Total Market Value ... **"No Growth' only)**			
Total Market Value (TMV)	$182	$100	$282
Economic Book Value	$120	$100	$220
(Current Year - Beginning)			
Ratio: Market-to-Book Value	*1.52*	*1.00*	*1.28*

M/B Ratio reflects the 'warranted' TMV for the business versus the economic book value.

outlook, with *TOTAL CO.* reflecting the combined impact of the two BUs – that is, eighty-six cents of 'excess' return for each dollar of new investment, on a 'discounted' basis".

"Exhibit 117 presents an interesting 'message'. In spite of the significantly higher 'value contribution' of its strategy, *Services* still has a lower warranted *M/B* ratio if growth were 'capped' at the 'plan' level and 'profitable growth' ceased after three years. With improvement in both business units, the warranted *M/B* ratio for *TOTAL CO.* increases from a 'no-growth' level of 1.28 to a 'plan' level of 1.50".

Exhibit 118	GROWTHSTAR INC.		
	Valuation Highlights		
'Future 5-Year' Financials	*'Investor Scenario'*		
$Millions, except MVI	*Products*	*Services*	*TOTAL CO.*
Market Value Index ('MVI')			
('5-Year Growth')			
Market Value Added (MVA)			$108
Net New Investment - 'Discounted'			$171
MVI .... Additional MVA for			
each Investment Dollar			*$0.63*
'MVI' reflects 'warranted' MVA for the business as a ratio of 'discounted' net new investment.			
Market-to-Book ('M/B') Ratio			
(re: "Total" Market Value ..... 'Base' + 'Growth')			
Total Market Value (TMV)			$385
Economic Book Value			$243
Ratio: Market-to-Book Value			*1.59*
M/B Ratio reflects the 'warranted' TMV for the business versus the economic book value.			

"Exhibit 118 yields a couple of interesting perceptions. First, the *MVI* of $0.63 for the 'Investor Scenario' growth plan is *less* than the *MVI* for the 'internal' growth plan. This results from the following relationships, which I'll write on the flip chart".

	Revenue Growth	**NOP**	**'ICI'**
Internal Plan (*)	20%	7.1%	$0.36
Investor Scenario	18%	7.0%	$0.40
Difference	2% pts.	0.1 % pt.	$(0.04)

(*) for TOTAL CO. – weighted average of Products and Services

"So, on a 'relative' *MVA* – that is, an *MVI* – basis, the return for the 'Investor Scenario' is lower. On a *M/B* ratio basis – which reflects *TMV* related to the current economic book value – the 'Investor Scenario' is higher (1.59 versus 1.50). This might seem to be contradictory, but if you think through the financial dynamics, you should determine that the growth of the business over five years produces a higher *TMV*. This higher *TMV* for the 'Investor Scenario' ($385 million versus $365 million *TMV* for the 'plan') drives the *M/B* ratio higher".

Jonathan, getting a signal from his stomach, began to rise from his chair and said, "Do we need any more explanation of these three exhibits? As Mandy stated, the 'financial market' may be imputing a lower growth rate and higher capital intensity over a somewhat longer time horizon versus what we've incorporated into our three-year plan".

With Val providing a 'thumbs up' sign and no further reaction from the group, Jonathan began to motion toward the door and said ... "I think we could all use a 'lunch break'. I know I could". The 'message' in Exhibits 116, 117 and 118 was clear, the concepts were understood, and no one argued the need to 'break' for lunch.

After the lunch break, the group reassembled to work on three topics:

1 The 'valuation' of incorporating the additional growth period beyond the three-year 'plan' horizon;
2 The integration of valuation with cash flow; and
3 sustainable revenue growth.

Jason had arrived back at the conference room and was writing these topics on the flip chart as the other people took their seats around the conference table. After everyone was seated, he began to speak. "This morning, we covered the key inputs and outputs for the three-year financial plans, worked through the 'no-growth' valuations, and 'valued' the three-year plans along with a potential 'Investor Scenario'. We also established a set of assumptions for the 'post-planning' period, which we will now translate into a valuation for the BUs and the total company".

Jonathan leaned forward as Jason finished the last sentence, since he knew this was an important part of 'a shareholder value tale' that had to be communicated, first to Ian and then to the major investors.

"After we complete this valuation", Jason continued, "we will 'integrate' our valuation results with the cash flow implications of the BU strategies. Finally, we'll complete our corporate financial analysis by determining the company's 'sustainable growth' – the maximum level of revenue growth that can be afforded – given the company's financing policy and the assumptions imbedded into the plans for the business units. While not 'value *per se*' this topic is important, as it relates to the financing of the company in the future".

"To begin the evaluation of the post-planning period, let's first get a consensus on the only questionable area of the assumptions we established". As Jason spoke he went to the flip chart and 'flipped' to the sheet with the assumptions for the post-planning period.

Business Unit	+ Growth Years	Growth Rate	NOP Margin	ICI
Products	+2 to 3	12%	6.7%	$0.40
– US	same	10%	lower	lower
– Int'l	same	15%	higher	higher
Services	+ 4	25%	7.3%	$0.40
– Growthstar	same	21%	higher	higher
– Other	same	33%	lower	lower

"We need to set the 'plus growth years' for *Products* at either two or three years. We've run the valuation under both assumptions, but we should settle on whether it's 'two' or 'three' years of additional 'profitable' growth and move on. Cathy, what are your thoughts?"

Cathy had thought about this issue ever since it was raised, and was prepared to answer Jason's question. "I think that we may get another three years, but it's a 'stretch'. If this is going to be communicated inside and outside the company, then I would take the conservative approach and go with 'two' years of additional growth. Larry and I have confidence in this assumption".

"I would agree", chimed in Val. "If alternative technology develops at the fastest rate possible, then the two-year time frame is safe, but the three-year period is in jeopardy".

"OK, then", interjected Jonathan, "let's go with the 'two-year' assumption for *Products*. We're sticking with the 'plus four years' assumption for *Services*, aren't we?" As Jonathan asked this question, he looked at Dave Dollarby.

"By all means", Dave answered. "Our business is 'on a roll' ".

Jonathan and the others smiled at Dave, whom they knew was finally starting to enjoy the 'economic value' process.

"If that's the decision, then Exhibits 119 and 120 provide the valuation inputs for *Products* and *Services*, respectively", Jason stated.

"We've *shaded* the 'Year 3' column in Exhibit 119, so ignore it", Jason noted.

Jason commented, "we set up the 'assumption model' for five years, so please ignore the 'year 5' column in Exhibit 120. These two

Exhibit 119 "PRODUCTS" Financials	**GROWTHSTAR INC.** Valuation Highlights BU 'Strategy' Financials				
$Millions, except Per Share and Index/Ratio Amounts	*Future Years — Beyond the End of Plan Period*				
	Year 1	Year 2	Year 3	Year 4	Year 5
Assumptions					
Revenue — % Growth	12%	12%	12%		
Total Revenue $	504	564	632		
Incremental $ - Annual	54	60	68		
Incremental $ - Cumul.*	204	264	332		
NOP — % Margin	6.7%	6.7%	6.7%		
Total NOP $	33.8	37.8	42.4		
Incremental $ - Annual	3.6	4.1	4.5		
Incremental $ - Cumul.*	13.7	17.7	22.3		
New Invest. ('I') — "ICI"	$0.40	$0.40	$0.40		
Total $ - Annual	21.6	24.2	27.1		
Total $ - Cumul.*	81.6	105.8	132.9		

[* 'Cumulative' Amounts are versus Current Year 'Base']

Exhibit 120

GROWTHSTAR INC.
Valuation
Highlights

"SERVICES" Financials

BU 'Strategy' Financials

$Millions, except Per Share and Index/Ratio Amounts	*Future Years - Beyond the End of Plan Period*				
	Year 1	*Year 2*	*Year 3*	*Year 4*	*Year 5*
Assumptions					
Revenue — % Growth	*25%*	*25%*	*25%*	*25%*	
Total Revenue $	413	516	646	807	
Incremental $ - Annual	83	103	129	161	
Incremental $ - Cumul.*	263	366	496	657	
NOP — % Margin	*7.3%*	*7.3%*	*7.3%*	*7.3%*	
Total $	30	38	47	59	
Incremental $ - Annual	5	8	9	12	
Incremental $ - Cumul.*	19	27	36	48	
New Invest. ('I') — "ICI"	*$0.40*	*$0.40*	*$0.40*	*$0.40*	
Total $ - Annual	33	41	52	65	
Total $ - Cumul.*	93	134	186	251	

[* 'Cumulative' Amounts are versus Current Year 'Base']

Exhibit 121

GROWTHSTAR INC.
Valuation
Highlights

"PRODUCTS" Financials

BU 'Strategy' Financials

$Millions, except Per Share and Index/Ratio Amounts	*'Business Strategy' Value - 2 Years Beyond Plan*					
	Year 1	*Year 2*	*Year 3*	*Year 4*	*Year 5*	*Residual*
						Yr. 3 'NOP' cap'd @ 11%
Free Cash Flow Approach						
Net Operating Profit (NOP) *	$2.9	$6.2	$10.0	$13.7	$17.7	
Net New Investment (I)	(17.2)	(19.8)	(23.0)	(21.6)	(24.2)	
Free Cash Flow (FCF) - 'Strategy'	$(14.3)	$(13.6)	$(13.0)	$(7.9)	$(6.5)	$161

Net Present Value (NPV) - Strategy =	**$44**

Memo: Value / Add'l Growth Yrs. =	*$17*

[* 'Incremental' NOP vs. Current Year 'Base']

exhibits (119 and 120) provide the inputs for the valuation, which is summarized in Exhibits 121, 122 and 123".

"Oh, my", exclaimed Jonathan. "This is getting to be intriguing".

"I should say so", chimed in Val and Earl (who knew the outcome) simultaneously.

"The *Services* 'strategy impact' is 'dynamite' ... wow, $121 million for the 'seven' years and $65 million for the 'post-plan' growth period all by itself ... wait 'til Peter sees this. **'A-type'** business, here we come!" Dave shouted, unable to constrain himself.

"We're also making a contribution with *Products*", Cathy stated with a sense of pride. "And, remember, *Products* still has the

Exhibit 122

GROWTHSTAR INC.
Valuation
Highlights

"SERVICES" Financials   BU 'Strategy' Fin'ls

$ Millions, except Per Share and Index/Ratio Amounts	'Business Strategy' Value - 4 Yrs. Beyond Plan							
	Yr. 1	*Yr. 2*	*Yr. 3*	*Yr. 4*	*Yr. 5*	*Yr. 6*	*Yr. 7*	*Resid.*
Economic Profit Approach								Yr. 3 'EP' cap'd @ 11%
Net New Investment - 'Cumulative'	$14.1	$33.5	$60.0	$93.0	$134.4	$186.0	$250.6	
Net Operating Profit (NOP) *	$3.0	$8.2	$14.2	$19.1	$26.6	$36.0	$47.8	
Capital Charge (CCAP) @11%	(1.6)	(3.7)	(6.6)	(10.2)	(14.8)	(20.5)	(27.6)	
Economic Profit ('EP')	$1.5	$4.6	$7.6	$8.8	$11.8	$15.6	$20.3	$184

Net Present Value (NPV) - Strategy = $121

				Memo: Value of Add'l Growth Yrs. = $65			
Strategy ROIC — Return on 'Incremental' Net New Investment	*Yr. 1*	*Yr. 2*	*Yr. 3*	*Yr. 4*	*Yr. 5*	*Yr. 6*	*Yr. 7*
	21.3%	24.6%	23.6%	20.5%	19.8%	19.4%	19.1%

[* 'Incremental' NOP vs. Current Year 'Base']

Exhibit 123

GROWTHSTAR INC.

Valuation Highlights

$ Millions, except 'per share'	Plan + 2 Yrs. (Products) and 4 Yrs. (Services)			Current
Valuation - 'FCF' and 'EP' (*)	'No Growth'	'Strategy'	'Total' Value	Market Value
Products	$182	$44	$226	
Services	100	121	221	
TOTAL CO.	$282	$165	$447	$385
less: Total Debt			(110)	(110)
Equity Value			**$337**	**$275**
# Shares (millions)			*10*	*10*
Per Share Value			*$33.70*	*$27.50*

(*) 'FCF' Approach for Products and 'EP' Approach for Services

greatest 'total' value at $226 million, even with a shorter growth time horizon".

"It is certainly interesting and potentially exciting", interjected Mandy ... "but, we have to get the 'message' – that we're worth at least $6.00 per share (over 20%) more than our current market value – to the shareholders ... and, then, get them to believe it".

"Amen", said Jason softly.

"So, what do we do with this"? asked Jonathan.

"Start working on our next quarterly presentation to the analysts ... or, think about scheduling a special meeting focused on our strategy and future growth and profitability outlook", Mandy responded. She was enjoying the dynamics of a corporate role, which was entirely new for her. The fact that there appeared to be a 'real' shareholder value opportunity at Growthstar added to her feeling of enthusiasm. She also had enhanced her knowledge of valuation techniques through the 'learning' that had taken place during the past few weeks and in today's meeting.

"A special presentation", mused Jonathan. "That's something we should talk about, Mandy, and then discuss with Ian".

"I have been thinking about this myself", Mandy replied. "Let's 'sleep on it' tonight and discuss the 'pros and cons' tomorrow – in advance of the meeting with Ian and the general mangers the day after tomorrow".

"That's a good idea", responded Jonathan. "We need to be prepared to discuss this topic at the next meeting. With everything that's going on, I had almost forgotten about this session".

Jason had a few comments that he wanted to make before moving to the next topic. "Please notice that the valuation (in Exhibit 121) for *Products* was based on the *FCF* approach. The 'post-plan' *NOP* margin, *ICI*, and *ROIC* are equal to or very close to those for the 'plan' period. For *Services*, the valuation in Exhibit 122 was done using the *EP* approach, to reflect the drop in 'incremental' *ROIC* as the business moves into the 'post-plan' years. This is still solid performance, in that the 'return' is above *CCAP*, but the lower *NOP* margin combined with a higher *ICI* results in a lower 'incremental' *ROIC* versus the three years in the 'plan' period. This highlights one of the reasons for using *EP* and *NPV/MVA* as the metrics for decision-making, since significant shareholder value is created even though the percentage-based returns are declining somewhat. *NPV/MVA* (thus, shareholder value) will continue to increase as long as growth is complemented by a 'return' (*ROIC*) above *CCAP*. The level of *MVA* is dependent on the rate of revenue growth, along with the *NOP* margin and *ICI* ratio. Finally, as Exhibit 123 indicates, this scenario estimates a 'growth' value for the total company in the range of 35% to 40% of 'total' value (*TMV*) – that is, $165 million of 'strategy' value for *TOTAL CO.* out of the $447 million 'total' value (*TMV*). This appears to be more in line with the vision and outlook that most of you have for Growthstar".

"That is definitely more in line with our thinking", Jonathan responded, adding his 'stamp of approval' to this aspect of the work session.

Jack had been quiet, since his comment that had 'silently rocked' the conference room before lunch. He had, however, been carefully studying the various exhibits and valuations, especially the 'investor' and the 'post-plan' growth scenarios. He was now even more convinced that the *VPM* approach could work – to preserve a simplistic 'earnings' framework that he was comfortable with and that Ian, Larry and Peter could understand and manage. "*Growth and value profit margin – that's the way to proceed*", he thought to himself. "*It's manageable, and, it captures the key 'economic' dynamics that 'cash flow' Earl and his cohorts want*". Jack, while 'steeped' in traditional accounting, was a very intelligent and capable professional who knew that the world was changing and that he had to change with it. He also knew that Growthstar was run by a capable group of operating managers who had good business acumen, but were *not* very sophisticated financially. While resistant to some of Jason's concepts, Jack was grateful that Jason had introduced the company to *VPM* – since it provided a vehicle for him to be supportive of the effort. At the same time, Jack felt that he could administer a fairly straightforward financial performance system with all the 'economic ingredients' that Val, Earl and the 'sophisticated' investors were, apparently, looking for.

Jack, like Val, had also become 'enamored' with the two 'relative' value indicators – *MVI* and *M/B* ratio – especially the market-to-book ratio. Similar to his desire to maintain a metric expressed in terms of 'earnings', he had long been an advocate of 'book' value as an indicator of financial solvency and strength. He quickly grasped onto the natural linkage to value creation and the expression of 'shareholder' value and 'total market' value in terms of its relationship to 'book' value. He had, since his ascendancy to the position of corporate controller, supported the reporting of 'Return on Equity' (*ROE*) in addition to Earnings per Share (*EPS*) and *EPS* growth. Jonathan had been the 'driving force' behind reporting the company's *ROE*, since he believed strongly in a 'return' measure that was visible to the shareholders. Jack was now seeing the 'tide' turning to incorporating 'all' of the company's capital in its financial performance system and to making the 'economic' adjustments that had been proposed and analyzed during the past few months. Earl had been successful in getting Ian's attention and Jack knew that the final outcome would be very close to what was being proposed, with respect to *IC* and *ROIC*. Fighting this would be a futile effort, and potentially more damaging to his career at Growthstar than accepting the changes and proactively suggesting an emphasis on one or two of the metrics that were most palatable to him. If he could get a focus on the *M/B* ratio, along with an 'earnings-oriented' metric (i.e. *VPM*) and the company's commitment to revenue growth (which Ian would never change), he felt that he could 'live' with a new system. Thus, he had established the rationale for his comment earlier in the day and the one he was about to make.

Exhibit 124	GROWTHSTAR INC.		

Valuation Highlights

'Future' Period Financials — 'Plan' + 2 Yrs. (Products) and 4 Yrs. (Services)

$ Millions, except MVI	Products	Services	TOTAL CO.
Market Value Index ('MVI')			
('Plan' + 'Post-Plan' Growth)			
Market Value Added (MVA)	$44	$121	$165
Net New Investment (discounted)	$77	$153	$230
MVI .... Additional MVA for			
each Investment Dollar	$0.57	$0.79	$0.72

'MVI' reflects 'warranted' MVA for the business as a ratio of 'discounted' net new investment.

Market-to-Book ('M/B') Ratio	Products	Services	TOTAL CO.
(re: "Total" Market Value ..... 'Base')			
Total Market Value (TMV)	$226	$221	$447
Economic Book Value	$131	$112	$243
Ratio: Market-to-Book Value	1.73	1.98	1.84

M/B Ratio reflects the 'warranted' TMV for the business versus the economic book value.

"Jason, this morning, before we broke for lunch, you showed us the implications on the market-to-book ratio for two scenarios – our internal 'plan' and the 'investor scenario'. I believe the exhibits were 117 and 118. I found them to be useful in giving guidance to our operating managers and also from the standpoint of analyzing the 'corporate' value creation potential for our future investments. Do you have a similar evaluation for the scenario incorporating the 'post-plan' period growth?" Again, the heads 'snapped' around the table. "*Could it really be*", the others thought to themselves, "*that Jack is 'coming around' ... or, does he have 'something up his sleeve'?*"

Jason responded with, "I was waiting for that question, Jack, and I'm delighted it came from you". Jason quickly clicked on Exhibit 124.

"Well, will you just look at that", Dave chortled – he was really enjoying these exhibits. "The *Services* business continues to 'rock on' in terms of value creation. We do it in both 'absolute' and 'relative' terms".

"That's very informative", Jack snipped, as he steered a wary glance at Dave. "But, I wanted to take a serious look at these ratios and see what we've learned and what we need to reflect on for the meeting with the officers the day after tomorrow". Everyone, including Jonathan, leaned forward, in anticipation of Jack's next comment. He continued to surprise them when he walked over to the flip chart, took a marker and began to speak. "Let's summarize the 'value indicators' for the scenarios we have reviewed today". Jack then began to write on the flip chart.

Market-to-Book Ratios	Products	Services	TOTAL CO.
'No Growth' (Exh. 101)	1.52	1.00	1.28
'Plan' – 3 Yrs (Exh. 117)	1.60	1.39	1.50
'Investor Scenario' – 5 Yrs (Exh. 118)	–	–	1.59
'Plan + Post-Plan' – 3 +2/4 Yrs (Exh. 124)	1.73	1.98	1.84

Revenue Growth Rates (*)	Products	Services	TOTAL CO.
'Plan' – 3 Yrs (Exhibits 89/92/95)	14.5%	30%	20%
'Investor Scenario' – 5 Yrs (Exh. 112)	–	–	18%
'Plan + Post-Plan' – 3 + 2/4 Yrs (calculated)	13.5%	27%	19% (**)

(*)   'Average' for the <u>total</u> 'growth period'
(**) incl. Products growth at <u>12%</u> for years 6 & 7

VPM – Average 'Spreads'	Products	Services	TOTAL CO.
'Plan' – 3 Yrs (Exhibits 104/107/110)	2.3%	4.2%	3.3% ... yr.3 = Avg.
'Investor Scenario' – 5 Yrs (calc'd from Exh. 112)	–	–	2.6% ... (7.0% – 4.4%)
'Plan + Post-Plan' – 3 + 2/4Yrs (calculated)	2.3% (same)	3.5% (est.)	2.9% (est.) Avg. of Prod's & Svcs

After he had finished writing on the flip chart, Jack started speaking again. "With all due respect to the need to determine and understand the 'value creation' of the strategies in comparison to our 'no-growth' situation, I also want to suggest a 'template' for communication to our operating general managers and our investors. I'm not going to delve into each number – you all can read them – but I would like to highlight the ones I feel are the most important. Jonathan, you have always been an advocate of *ROE* and our *M/B* ratio on an 'equity' basis". Jonathan nodded in agreement and Jack continued ... "Thus, the first set of numbers that I wrote on the flip chart compare the *M/B* ratios for the scenarios we have evaluated today. They can be easily translated into a stock price. Our people are interested in this. Based on which set of assumptions you want to believe about our future, we're worth 1.5 to 1.8 times the capital invested in the company. I'm willing to *live* with the 'total' invested capital as opposed the traditional 'equity' capital if that's what proves to be the best measure".

"After we've established a 'total value' metric, I believe we can – and should – transmit the results of our plans in a simplistic 'revenue growth' and 'NOP margin' format. As you can see, we're in a range of 18% to 20% for revenue growth. I've written the *VPM* 'spreads' on the flip chart to provide the basis and support for the *NOP* margin. The relevant range for the *VPM* 'spread' is 2.5 to over 3 percentage points. These two performance measures – '*growth and margin*' – can become the *objectives* for the operating GMs. Regarding the *VPM* and its 'spread', we can tell Ian, Larry and Peter what the *VPM* is in 'general' terms. They really don't care that much about *ICI* and *CCAP*, and would just as soon be given a 'target' that they know is well researched and understood by us in finance. If we tell them that revenue growth of '*x*' and *NOP* margin of '*y*' will result in a *M/B* ratio of '*z*', they'll 'run with it', especially if we then tell them what it's worth in terms of our stock price – say, going from $27.50 to $33 or $34 per share, or whatever level we feel is justified. With the institutional shareholders, we can get more involved with *ICI* and *CCAP*. Those who are using the 'economic' framework will test it out, and those who are using the traditional 'earnings' models should be 'OK' with the *NOP* margin metric and should *not* feel as though we are turning their world 'upside down'. And yes, Earl, it also preserves part of my world!"

There were 'sighs' all around the room. Jason noticed it and also had a realization that Jack must have been giving this subject a lot of thought and consideration during the past several weeks. Jonathan leaned back, then forward, and then got up and paced back and forth behind his chair. "You know, Jack, you may have something here". Jonathan looked at Earl as he was speaking. Earl was leaning back in his chair with a look on his face that indicated satisfaction with the 'thought process' that Jack must have gone through to make his comments. Mandy also had a look indicating an appreciation of the analysis that Jack must have put himself through. Jill was so exuberant that she had to turn her back to the group, faking a cough. Cathy did the same. Dave sat with a smirk on his face, still relishing the 'value creation' numbers for *Services*. Frank smiled quietly.

Val then spoke. "I'm quite intrigued and interested in this outcome. This could very well be a way to begin 'crossing the bridge' into the world of 'economics' in a way that is non-threatening to many of the people – internal managers and external stakeholders – who are either not capable of fully understanding the entire world of 'economic metrics' or not ready to make the 'jump' ". Val was always diplomatic, but never complimentary for its sake alone. Thus, everyone – even Dave – listened carefully to what Val said. She continued ... "I would like to include the *MVI*, at least for this group, in the measures we focus on, since it is a powerful return metric. However, I also understand that some people may have difficulty with the concept of '*net present value compared to discounted net new investment*'. So, maybe we need to keep *MVI* in a 'corporate valuation' setting, as long as we realize that it's an extremely important measure to gauge the success of our strategies".

"I can live with that", Jack replied.

"So can I", Jonathan stated.

The astonishment at the developments had a 'silencing' effect. Thus, no one else said anything. Even Earl felt restrained from speaking, a most unusual feeling for him. Sensing this, Jonathan said, "this would seem to be a good time to take a short break. Please be back here in fifteen minutes".

Jason spoke briefly to Jack during the break, indicating that he also thought that Jack's conclusions and perceptions had merit, and warranted serious attention as a way to begin implementing the concepts. Jack's 'thank you' seemed to be genuine, and Jason sensed an atmosphere of conciliation that he had not yet felt.

After everyone in the group was seated again, Jason spoke, deciding to stay seated himself for at least a few moments or until he had to show an exhibit or use the flip chart. "The next challenge is to combine the BU valuations with the impact of the growth plans on cash flow. We'll do this in tabular form today, and we'll have an interesting graphic for the operating officers meeting in a couple of days. Since we have all the inputs, let's 'get on with it' ... we should be able to get through this analysis fairly quickly. Let me, first, show

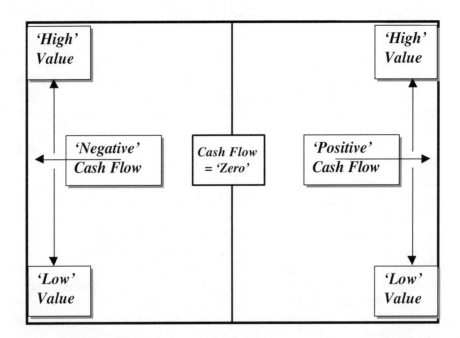

you how we'll portray this for the meeting with the operating officers, and then I'll give you the relevant numbers for the analysis". Jason didn't stay seated for very long and went to the flip chart to draw a diagram.

"Can everyone understand what I've drawn and its implications"? Jason asked.

"Not exactly", Jill, Cathy and Dave said instantly ... almost in unison.

"OK, then, let me explain", Jason countered. "*Value* – either *MVA, TMV*, or equity value per share – is reflected vertically ... the higher the 'vertical plot', the higher the 'value' ".

"Got it", they said in unison.

"*Cash flow* – that is, a business 'generating' or 'using' cash –is plotted horizontally ... 'positive' cash flow to the 'right' of the center dividing line (which indicates cash flow equal to 'zero') and 'negative' cash flow to the 'left' of the center dividing line".

"Got it again", they said in unison, with Dave adding ... "we're getting dangerously smart about these topics ... watch out, Jason, you may have some competition".

"I'll try to *keep my edge*", Jason responded ... chuckling.

"I don't think you're at great risk, Jason", Jack chortled, looking and laughing first at Dave, and then at Jill and Cathy. "Besides, who would be left to work here?"

Jill and Cathy were so ecstatic about Jack's apparent positive attitude that they just sat still in their chairs and laughed along with him. "*This sudden change in attitude is almost bizarre*", they were thinking to themselves, but they also realized that Jack's mind must have been thinking through these issues for some time, now. Jack was just not the type of person to 'turn on a dime' in the opposite direction.

Dave wanted to keep the 'banter' going, but a stern look from Jonathan told him otherwise. Jonathan then said, "let's get the cash flow impact of our strategies 'on the table'. I've been focusing so much on the 'value' aspects and, now, Jack's suggestion on how to implement, that I almost forgot about Mr D'Mark's area of responsibility".

Jonathan and Earl looked at each other.

"Exhibit 125 will give us the information we need", Jason responded.

"The top portion of Exhibit 125 summarizes the annual free cash flows for the business units and the total company, based on the plans that have been developed and reviewed. As you can see, *Products* generates 'positive' free cash flow in each year of the 'plan' period. This result should not be surprising, given the moderate growth for this BU. As a reminder, 'free' cash flow does *not* include any financing

Exhibit 125	**GROWTHSTAR INC.**					

Cash Flow Highlights

'Future' Period Financials	*Next 3 Years - 'Growth Plan'*					
$ Millions		*Products*		*Services*		*TOTAL CO.*
Annual Free Cash Flow ('FCF')						
Year 1		$5.7		$(0.1)		$5.6
Year 2		6.4		(0.1)		6.3
Year 3		7.0		(1.4)		5.6
Total 3 Years		**$19.1**		**$(1.6)**		**$17.5**

Valuation Highlights

$ Millions	*'Plan' plus 2 Yrs. (Products) and 4 Yrs. (Services)*					
Valuation - 'FCF' and 'EP' (*)		*Products*		*Services*		*TOTAL CO.*
'No Growth' Value		*$182*		*$100*		*$282*
'Strategy' Value		*44*		*121*		*165*
'Total' Value		*$226*		*$221*		*$447*

(*) 'FCF' Approach for Products and 'EP' Approach for Services

costs – interest expense, debt principal repayments, or stock dividends. As a further note, when we're analyzing cash flow, we usually do so within the time period of the 'financial plan' – in this case, three years. *Services* is projected to 'consume' cash, but not that significant an amount, in light of their aggressive growth plan. A higher 'incremental' *NOP* margin combined with a lower *ICI* have a positive impact on cash flow consumption. The result is that the two BUs combined are expected to be 'cash positive' in each year of the 'plan'. This implies that the 'plan' can be financed from internal sources – thus, no need for outside financing – unless interest expenses plus dividends and debt principal repayments would be greater than the free cash flow for *TOTAL CO.* in any year. My conversations with Earl and Jonathan on this topic indicated that such is not the case. Earl, can you confirm this?"

"That's basically true", Earl answered. "We don't start debt principal repayments until *after* the three-year plan period. Our interest payments and common stock dividends should just about be covered with the 'free' cash flow we expect to generate from the execution of our strategies. Thus, any financing needs would probably be modest and covered within our credit line. We'll give everyone the 'net' cash flow outlook, including all financing charges, as part of the 'Sustainable Growth' analysis, which is our next topic".

Jack could not hold back, looked over at Earl and said, "maybe we could do away with the treasurer's position, since we appear to be able to finance ourselves internally. Had any good job offers lately, Earl?"

"Now, look who's trying to be 'Mr Funny'. You must be trying to take over Dave's role", Earl retorted. Jill and Cathy did think the comment was funny and started to laugh. Earl sneered at them. Even Frank smiled a bit, but turned away from Earl as he did so.

Jonathan then jumped into the conversation. "We may have some other growth initiatives, such as another acquisition, which could require a need for financing, so maybe we'll keep you, Earl". Earl knew that Jonathan was 'playing' with him and Jack was not really serious, so he simply smiled at Jonathan and casually pointed his index finger at Jack, indicating a small victory (for Jack). Earl tried to make it a point of only speaking when he was on the 'offensive' and keeping quiet when he felt he was on the 'defensive'. Jonathan then motioned for Jason to continue.

"The bottom portion of the schedule (Exhibit 125) recasts the valuation that we agreed is representative of the 'future opportunity' for the company – with a *TMV* of nearly $450 million that translates into a stock price of $33 to $34 per share. We'll present this 'message' graphically to Ian and the operating officers when we meet, but I think you get the point. The company has a 'warranted' value greater than its current price in the stock market and should be able to finance its plans for at least the next three years almost entirely from internal sources. I'll write and 'circle' the cash flow position of each business unit on the diagram, to give you an idea of where they are. We'll spend more time on this the day after tomorrow and show the plots of cash flow integrated with the 'components' of warranted market value – 'no growth', 'strategy' and 'total'".

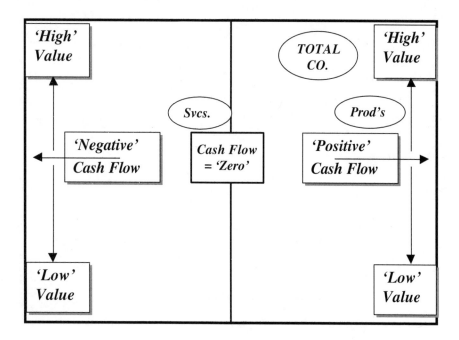

Seeing the heads nod around the conference table, Jason stated, "if there are no further questions or discussion on this topic, I would now like to move on to our last topic for the day – 'Sustainable Revenue Growth'. I don't think we need a break, but this would be a good time to stretch and get a soft drink, water, coffee or tea".

After everyone was settled again, Earl rose and spoke. "Jonathan and Jason asked me to give a brief introduction to our next topic. Hopefully, this will enable me to keep my job". Earl glanced at Jack and continued … "The rate at which we can 'afford' to grow our businesses and the company in total is one of great importance to any treasurer. I have had some exposure to the subject, and Jason has helped me to 'complete the cycle' in terms of factoring in the financing aspect of it. He's also given me some of his charts to help explain the concept, which I would like to now share with all of you. The first chart (Exhibit 126) presents a graphic illustration of the

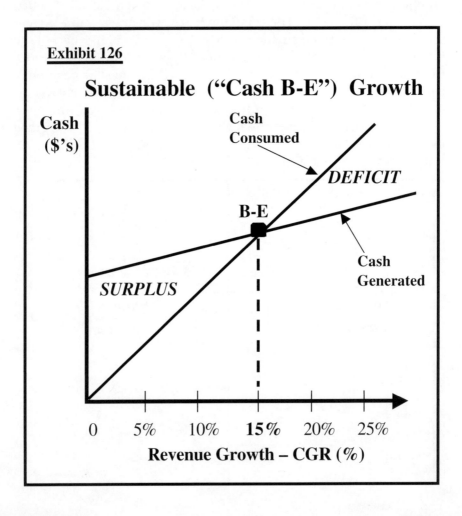

Exhibit 126

Sustainable ("Cash B-E") Growth

basic notion of 'sustainable' – or, 'cash break-even' as some people call it – revenue growth".

"Most 'profitable' businesses are characterized by this diagram with respect to cash flow. What this means is that at low rates of growth, net cash flow is usually positive, resulting in a cash 'surplus'. At some rate of growth (15% in this 'hypothetical' example) cash generated equals cash consumed. Please note that these numbers and their implications are *not* indicative of our firm – they're merely used to illustrate a concept. Does everyone understand this point?" Heads nodded. "Beyond the 'break-even' point, as the rate of growth increases, cash is consumed, reflecting the need for new financing. Normally, we're evaluating the need for new 'equity' financing and determining how fast the company can grow its revenue before it needs to issue new stock (if it's a public company) or seek new equity investment (if it's a private firm). One assumption is that the company will maintain a debt-to-equity ratio consistent with its financing policy".

"If everyone is 'in tune' with the conceptual framework, I would like to next show how operating and financial management participate in the 'growth and cash' arena. Exhibit 127 provides an overview of these roles".

"As you might expect, operating managers have the greatest impact on net cash flow, just as they do for value creation. Their ability to generate profit – the 'source' of cash flow – and their need to

---

Exhibit 127

Growth and Cash

Operating Management:

Profit Margin
Investment ... Total IC and "ICI"

Financial Management:

Retained Earnings
Debt-to-Equity (Leverage) Ratio

invest – the 'use' of cash – far outweighs anything we, as corporate folks, do. That does *not* mean, however, that the corporate role is insignificant. The setting of dividend (retained earnings) policy and the ability to provide capital at a reasonable cost through our debt-to-equity capitalization (leverage) program, contributes to the goal of profitably growing the company".

"The next Exhibit (128) outlines the formulas used in the calcu-lation of 'cash generated' and 'cash consumed'. The deviation from the 'free' cash flow model is in the 'cash generated' formula – with the incorporation of first, a factor reflecting our financing policy and second, the inclusion of interest expense to calculate 'net' (income after tax) profit margin. We have, as you know, excluded all interest expense in our calculation of net operating profit (*NOP*) – dollars and margin – for economic profit and valuation analysis. The 'cash consumed' formula is the same one used for 'incremental' net new investment ('I') in our 'strategy' models". Earl clicked on Exhibit 128 as he spoke.

"I also want to mention that the analysis and determination of 'sustainable' revenue growth is done at the 'corporate' level. We use the inputs from the businesses, as we have done in our 'strategic' financial planning and evaluation work. We then impose

---

Exhibit 128

Growth and Cash

Cash Generated:	**Cash Consumed (Used):**
$\dfrac{\text{Retained Earnings Ratio}}{\text{Debt/Equity Factor}}$	Invested Capital Intensity ("ICI")
times	
Net Profit Margin	*times*
times	
Last Year's Revenue (Sales) + Growth	Revenue (Sales) Growth

our corporate financing assumptions and translate these inputs into an evaluation of how fast the 'total company' can grow. Our goal, thus, is to determine 'sustainable growth' for Growthstar Inc". Earl looked around the room for reactions. He didn't have to wait long.

Dave leaned forward and said, "So, now that we've conquered 'value analysis', you want us to become 'corporate' finance experts. Are we going to get big pay raises after we become so knowledgeable and accomplished?" He had a 'twinkle' in his eye and a broad grin on his face as he looked over at Cathy and Jill.

"We thought we'd make this a technical requirement to *maintain* your 'grossly excessive' salary level", Jonathan retorted, with a bigger and broader grin on his face.

Dave, as Earl had done a few moments ago, responded with a casual pointing of the index finger in Jonathan's direction. He also pulled out his neatly pressed white handkerchief, unfolded it, and then waved it gently in the air. The rest of the group quietly broke out in laughter, appreciating both Dave's humor and Jonathan's desire to 'join in the levity' and 'have some fun'.

Earl was grateful for the reaction and took a sip of his water. He then turned to Frank and said ... "My trustworthy associate has worked with Jason on the 'sustainable growth' calculations for our company, and I would like to now turn the meeting over to him. Jason, is this OK with you, or is there something you want to go over before Frank presents this analysis?"

"That's fine", Jason replied. "Your overview was thorough and we're ready for the specifics for Growthstar. Go to it, Frank".

In his deliberate style, Frank began speaking. "As Jason and Earl have noted, this analysis comprises two components – cash 'generated' and cash 'consumed'. Cash 'generated' by a company is the after tax earnings, less dividends paid to shareholders, plus any additional debt allowable under the firm's financing policy. Cash 'consumed' is dependent on the level (or rate) of growth and the investment in working and fixed capital to support that growth. As you know, we have probably spent more time and effort on this aspect of our business than we have ever done in the past. The following two exhibits (129 and 130) will present the key 'inputs' (Exhibit 129) and the 'analysis' (Exhibit 130) for our sustainable growth over the next three years. We will analyze 'sustainable growth' on a 'dollar' and 'percentage' basis and compare it to our 'plan' ".

Frank then clicked on Exhibit 129.

"Does everyone understand what we're doing here"? Frank asked.

"I'm with you except for the last three rows", Jill answered. "I know we've talked about these ratios and factors on occasion, but the numbers are *not* quite clear".

Exhibit 129	**GROWTHSTAR INC.**			
	Total Company Financials			
'Future' 3-Year Financials	**'Sustainable Growth' - Inputs**			
$Millions, except 'ICI'	*Next 3 Years - Growth Plan*			
				Effective Rates
	Year 1	*Year 2*	*Year 3*	
Income Statement				*CGR*
Revenue – Prior Year	$450	$536	$643	*20.1%*
Net Income (After Taxes)				
EBITA – Prior Year	48	56	69	*Interest Rates*
Interest - Operating Leases	(5)	(5)	(6)	10.0%
Interest - Total Debt	(5)	(5)	(5)	8.9%
Pre Tax Income	38	46	58	*Tax Rate*
Taxes (@ 'Effective Rate')	(13)	(16)	(20)	34%
Net Income (Cash-Based)	**$25**	**$30**	**$38**	
				Avg. N. I. %
Net Income Margin (%)	**5.6%**	**5.6%**	**5.9%**	**5.7%**
Balance Sheet Invest's				*Total 'I'*
Net New Investment ("I")	$31	$39	$50	$120
				Avg. 'ICI'
Invest. Cap. Intensity ("ICI")	**$0.36**	**$0.36**	**$0.36**	*$0.36*
Financing				*Avg. Ratios*
Earnings Retention Ratio	90%	90%	90%	*90%*
Leverage (Equity/Debt) Factor (*)	50%	50%	50%	*50%*
Financing Factor	**1.80**	**1.80**	**1.80**	*1.80*
(*) Inverse of D/TC ratio				

"Let's take the 'earnings retention ratio' first. Our historical practise is to pay out roughly 10% of our 'trailing' net earnings to the common shareholders as a dividend".

"Is this a policy?" Jill queried.

"No, but it has been our 'practise' to do so", Frank replied, "and there is nothing that Earl or I am aware of that would change this 'practise' in the future. Ian seems to favor a pay-out in the range of 10% of net income". An expressionless look on Jonathan's face indicated that he could *not* add anything definitive to Frank's comment. Thus, Frank continued ... "If we pay out 10% of net income, then the inverse (90%) is our 'earnings retention ratio'. OK?" Jill's nod indicated that she understood. Cathy and Dave, along with Val and Mandy, also nodded. "The 'leverage factor' indicates our ability to finance the company with additional debt – in this case, 'real' debt and operating leases. If you recall the current year's beginning invested capital (from Exhibit 96) of $220 million and our existing total debt (including operating leases) of $110 million, the ratio of 'debt-to-total capital' is 50%. In the 'sustainable growth' formula, we *reverse the terms* and compute an '*equity-to-capital*' ratio. Since ours is 50%, the reversal of the terms does not change the factor.

Exhibit 130	**GROWTHSTAR INC.**		
	Total Company Financials		
'Future' 3-Year Financials	**'Sustainable Growth' - Analysis**		
$Millions, except 'ICI'	*Next 3 Years - Growth Plan*		

		Year 1	*Year 2*	*Year 3*
"Sustainable Growth"				
Absolute Dollar Growth				
Formula:		[(Net Income %) times (Revenue)] times [Financing Factor]		
		[ICI minus (Net Income % times Financing Factor)]		
		Year 1	*Year 2*	*Year 3*
Equals:		$44	$54	$69
		0.266	0.263	0.256
Equals:		**$166**	**$207**	**$268**

Comparison to Plan:					*Total 3 Years*
Sustainable' Growth		*$166*	*$207*	*$268*	*$641*
'Plan' Growth		*86*	*108*	*137*	*330*
Excess / (Deficit)		**$80**	**$99**	**$132**	**$311**

Percentage Growth				
Formula:		[Net Income % times Financing Factor]		
		[ICI minus (N. I. % times Financing Factor)]		
		Year 1	*Year 2*	*Year 3*
Equals:		0.098	0.101	0.107
		0.266	0.263	0.256

					Avg. for 3 Yrs.
Equals:		**37%**	**39%**	**42%**	39%
				versus 'Plan'	
				CGR ...	20%

If we were to change our 'leverage' policy and target, then the factor would change also. The 'financing factor' is the earnings retention ratio (90%) divided by the leverage factor (50%) which equals 1.80. What this means is that every dollar of net income can be 'leveraged' by 1.8 times, providing additional cash to 'fuel' our future growth". As usual, Frank's presentation was thorough and technically correct. He had studied the formulas that Jason had taught him until he knew them 'cold' and had spoken to the exhibit (129) without any notes.

"The next aspect of this analysis", Frank stated, "is to determine the 'revenue growth' that can be 'sustained' under the assumptions and factors outlined in Exhibit 129. Sustainable growth can be viewed from two perspectives. The first is the 'absolute' (say, aggregate dollar – or other currency) level of growth and the second is the sustainable, or affordable, 'rate' of revenue growth – again, without the need for new equity financing. When evaluating the 'absolute level' of sustainable growth, we can do so either on a year-by-year basis, or an aggregate amount over a future time horizon – in our case, the three-year 'plan' period. The cash break-even (or sustainable) 'percentage rate' of growth is often viewed over a multi-year (e.g.

three-year) time period, but it can also be analyzed on a year-by-year basis. Let's take a look at Exhibit 130 to see *our* results".

Before Frank could start explaining Exhibit 130, Jonathan pounded his fist on the conference table, in reaction to the two numbers in the very bottom-right corner of the schedule – the 39% 'sustainable' growth rate versus the 20% 'plan' rate of growth for the total company. "Am I really seeing what I think I'm seeing", he thundered.

"You are, boss", interjected Earl, unable to hide his enthusiasm. "By 'fully leveraging' the firm, we can almost *double* the growth in the 'plan'".

"What are we waiting for ... let's all go down and 'camp out' at Ian's office! Just kidding, but this is terrific! This is one of the key conclusions that Ian is looking for. I can see his 'juices' flowing when he sees this!"

Jonathan then gathered himself and said to Frank, "I'm sorry, Frank, to have interrupted your presentation, but I was so excited that I couldn't contain myself. Are there any comments you want to make?"

"Not much that you haven't already figured out", Frank replied, with a grin on his face. Frank, like all the others, enjoyed the moments when Jonathan got excited. "The numbers reflect the inputs and the formulas we have reviewed. The company, if it 'leverages' itself to the maximum extent allowed by our lenders ... and, ourselves ... has an appetite for an additional $300 million or so of revenue growth beyond the $330 million forecasted in our 'plan'".

Earl responded with ... "That is a 'big number' and one we need to give consideration to, but we also need to be aware of the debt that we would take on to accommodate these 'sustainable' growth levels. I'm not saying that we can't do it, but there is a degree of 'risk' involved that *everyone*, including Ian, needs to be comfortable with".

"That's a point well taken", Mandy stated. "The shareholders would have to be comfortable with this additional debt and, perhaps more importantly, our ability to 'manage' a much larger company than we currently have or are expecting with our 'plan' for internal growth only. They will scrutinize our skills and our depth in terms of running a much larger enterprise than we now have. It's an exciting challenge, but one that we can't take lightly".

Val then spoke up. "There's also the issue of whether our 'markets' and the businesses we participate in can accommodate this level of growth. By that, I mean that the competitive landscape needs to be evaluated in terms of things such as the 'market share' we might command if we were to grow to the level that can be 'afforded' over the next few years. Further, the issue of how much growth we could achieve through 'organic' (internal) sources versus the need to 'acquire' a business or another company needs to be evaluated. So, what may be a fairly simplistic financial projection, may be much more complicated in its strategic execution. However, as Mandy states, it is an exciting situation to be faced with, and one that we should start exploring".

"All of these reactions and comments are excellent", interjected Jonathan. "We need to make sure that Ian, Larry and Peter appreciate these issues when we meet with them. So, what's next?"

Jason responded with, "We need to present the 'net' cash flow for the 'Plan' to see what our projected cash position will be over the next three years. Earl, I believe you're going to cover this topic".

"Right on", Earl replied. "And, I'm going to cover the topic quickly, as I can see that everyone is starting to get a bit weary from all that we've been through today".

"Thank you, Mr Treasurer", Dave quipped.

"You're quite welcome. We don't want to 'over-burden' our 'over-paid' BU finance director", Earl snickered at Dave. "I have to stand slightly corrected in my previous statement about our internal financing capability. When we add our common stock dividends, we go 'into the red' on a 'net cash flow' basis. This means that we'll have to tap our $30 million credit line for about $4 to $5 million per year. To date, we've used $10 million, so we have an adequate 'cushion' to fund our three-year 'plan'. Exhibit 131 provides the specifics".

"As you can all see, we're a bit 'cash negative' on a 'net' basis. *Before* common stock dividends we're about 'cash neutral' – in other words, *cash 'inflow' is close to 'outflow'*".

Jonathan felt incredibly good about the day's accomplishments, but he also knew that it was time to adjourn, if for no other reason than fatigue. He was feeling tired, and knew that the others must be feeling the same. He rose from his chair and stood in back of it, with his hands resting on its top. "Well, this certainly has been quite a day, in several respects. We seem to have convinced ourselves that our stock price should be higher than its current level in the 'financial market'.

Exhibit 131	**GROWTHSTAR INC.**			
	Total Company Financials			
'Future' 3-Year Financials	**Cash Flow Highlights**			
$ Millions	*Next 3 Years - Growth Plan*			
	Year 1	*Year 2*	*Year 3*	*Total 3 Years*
"Net Cash Flow"				
Free Cash Flow	$5.6	$6.3	$5.6	$17.5
Interest - Debt + Oper. Leases	(10.4)	(10.2)	(11.1)	(31.7)
Interest Tax Shield @ 34%	3.5	3.5	3.8	10.8
Common Stock Dividends	(2.5)	(3.0)	(3.8)	(9.3)
Net Cash Flow	**$(3.8)**	**$(3.4)**	**$(5.5)**	**$(12.7)**

We're starting to see a real 'value contribution' from *Services*, which confirms the expectations we had when we made the acquisition. *Products*, while not as spectacular in terms of future growth, is still a solid performer with a respectable outlook for the future. The 'accounting folks' seem to be getting quite knowledgeable and proficient regarding the 'economics' of the business, in terms of our current performance and future opportunities. Dave and Cathy, your ability to articulate the concepts was very impressive. Val and Mandy gave us valuable insights from strategic and investor perspectives, and Jack has made a very sensible and practical suggestion as to how to initiate and implement a change in our financial mindsets and behavior, which should be very palatable to the operating officers. Jill is starting to 'put the puzzle together', and Earl and Frank provided thorough and professional analysis. And, finally, we seem to have the financing to explore some 'breathtaking' – almost 'scary' – growth prospects. So it's been a productive day, and we get to do at least part of it again the day after tomorrow. Jason, I assume you'll cover the 'highlights' in graphic format, similar to our last meeting with Ian, Larry and Peter".

"We will do just that", Jason responded.

"OK, then, this meeting is concluded … we'll see you all soon", Jonathan stated as he rose to leave the conference room.

Jonathan and Mandy met the next day, and decided to recommend (to Ian) a separate meeting with the 'analysts' and 'institutional' shareholders to discuss the business strategies and financial outlooks. Jonathan apprised Val, Earl and Jack of this decision. Jason spent most of the day preparing his charts and presentation for tomorrow's meeting. He had been surprised by a visit from Jack to talk about *VPM* and requesting a spot on the agenda tomorrow to present his recommendation for 'implementing' value-based financial performance via the *VPM* approach. Jason agreed and then left a voice message for Jonathan informing him of this development.

At 8:29 the following morning, Ian, Mandy and Jonathan arrived at the boardroom. The finance team, Val, Peter and Larry had arrived a few minutes before and were getting coffee and tea. Mandy and Jonathan had visited with Ian to apprise him of their suggestion to hold a 'special' meeting with the stock market research analysts following the company and institutional portfolio managers – those owning and any not owning but 'targeted' as prospective owners. Ian, after filling a mug and taking his seat at the head of the large table, addressed the group. "I've been receiving input from various sources about all the hard work going on during the past couple of months in terms of our strategies and financial outlooks for our businesses. I am personally grateful for what appears to be a sincere and diligent effort to chart a future course for our internal growth and translate these plans into a forward-looking financial outlook. While they seemed exasperated at times, both Larry and Peter have indicated that the work has been useful and productive in better understanding where we have been and where we are going. Val has given me comfort with regard to the 'strategic' underpinnings for our outlook over the next three years, which is something I was looking for. Just this morning, Jonathan was very positive regarding his appraisal of the finance team meeting held two days ago and the accomplishments made during this year's planning process. So, I'm eager to listen to the 'story' you have prepared and suggest we get started. Jonathan, do you have any opening comments?"

"No, and I'm going to let Jason facilitate today's meeting", Jonathan responded. "The members of our 'team', along with Val and Mandy will, I am sure, be contributing. Jason, get us going, please".

As Jonathan was completing his brief remark, Jason passed a set of handouts around the table and went to the flip chart, where he had written the meeting agenda, while Mandy and Jonathan were meeting with Ian. "We have a number of topics to cover today, most of which will be a summary of the meeting two days ago. The agenda on the flip chart is also the first page of your handout". As Jason spoke, the people in the boardroom looked at the flip chart and their handout.

Corporate Financial Analysis – Discussion Topics

- **Growth Plan – Financial Summary and 'Drivers'**
- **Valuation – 'No Growth' and 'Strategy' Values**
- **Valuation – 'Magnifier' Effect**
- **Cash Flow – Integration with Value**
- **'Sustainable' Revenue Growth**
- **Value-Based Performance Implementation – Issues and Thoughts**

"Regarding our first topic, Cathy and Dave did an outstanding job, the other day, of presenting and justifying the financial outlooks for *Products* and *Services*. I am going to let them summarize these outlooks for you. Frank will present the total company's outlook, essentially a consolidation of the two BUs. I will then review the financial 'drivers' that result from the plans".

Cathy, always nervous when speaking to Ian, but confident based on her experience two days ago, began. "I'm going to summarize the P&L and balance sheet impact of our planning efforts for *Products*,

Exhibit 132	GROWTHSTAR INC.			
	Business Unit Financials			
	Next 3 Years - Growth Plan			
"PRODUCTS" Financials	Current	Future Outlook	*Change / Impact*	*'Plan'*
[$ Millions (MM's) except Per Share and Capital Intensity Amounts]	**FY Fcst.**	**Year 3**	*of 'Plan'*	*CGR / Ratio*
Sales Revenue:				
U.S.	$225	$320	*$95*	*12.5%*
International	75	130	*55*	*20.0%*
Total Sales Revenue	$300	$450	*$150*	*14.5%*
Net Operating Profit ('NOP') — $	$20	$30	*$10*	*14.5%*
— %	6.7%	6.7%	*0.0%*	*6.7%*
			'I'	*'ICI'*
Invested Capital (IC) - 'Ending'	$131	$191	*$60*	*$0.40*

which the finance team reviewed in detail two days ago. The next page in your handout (Exhibit 132) will provide the inputs for the financial 'drivers' that Jason will discuss shortly. We expect to increase our domestic (US) sales by 12.5% per year–10% from 'unit' growth and 2.5% from 'pricing' which is our inflation estimate for the next three years. Our international growth rate should be higher, as indicated by our planned growth rate of 20% per year. This combination results in our forecasted growth of 14.5% for the overall business".

"Are you going to show the exhibit on the screen?" Larry Buildermann asked.

Jason blushed a bit and said, "Sorry, that's supposed to be my job", as he flashed Exhibit 132 on the screen.

Cathy then continued ... "Our *NOP* margin is expected to remain at about the same level as it is now. As I explained to the finance team, this is the result of *lower* anticipated ratios (to sales) for *COGS and G&A*, offset by *higher* forecasted ratios for *SMS and R&D*. Our *ICI* is expected to remain in the range of $0.40, and we should invest approximately $60 million of 'net' new capital to generate $150 million of incremental revenue over the next three years".

The 'message' was not surprising to either Ian or Larry and, of course, the others had been through this analysis only two days ago. Ian nodded his head in understanding.

Dave then stood up and spoke. "With regard to *Services*, we feel that our outlook provides a 'pay-off' for the investment made to acquire and develop this business".

Jason clicked on Exhibit 133 as Dave was speaking.

"In support of that statement, we expect to produce high growth – 22% per year for the Growthstar segment and 60% for the smaller Other Products portion of our business. Thus, we are forecasting

Exhibit 133	**GROWTHSTAR INC.**			
	Business Unit Financials			
	Next 3 Years - Growth Plan			
"SERVICES" Financials	Current	Future Outlook	*Change / Impact*	*'Plan'*
[$ Millions (MM's) except Per Share and Capital Intensity Amounts]	**FY Fcst.**	**Year 3**	*of 'Plan'*	*CGR / Ratio*
Service Revenue:				
Growthstar	$125	$228	*$103*	*22%*
Other Products	25	102	*77*	*60%*
Total Service Revenue	$150	$330	*$180*	*30%*
Net Operating Profit ('NOP') — $	$11	$25	*$14*	*32%*
— %	7.3%	7.6%	*0.3%*	*7.8%*
			'I'	*'ICI'*
Invested Capital (IC) - 'Ending'	$112	$172	*$60*	*$0.33*

overall growth of 30% per year. With our operating leverage and infrastructure in place, we expect to be more profitable on a 'ratio to revenue' basis. Our *NOP* margin on total revenue should increase by 'three-tenths of a percent', reaching a level of 7.6% by the end of the three-year 'plan' period. Our *NOP* margin on the 'strategy' revenue is forecasted at 7.8%. We calculate this ratio by dividing $14 million of incremental *NOP* (over the 'plan' period) by $180 million of 'strategy' revenue. We plan to invest $60 million of net new capital, an *ICI* of $0.33 on our incremental revenue".

"Hmmm, this is quite interesting", Ian stated, a quizzical look on his face. "This outlook is quite contrary to what we reviewed as the historical assessment".

"This is what Dave meant when he spoke about the 'pay-off' for the investments made to date", Peter interjected, feeling *very* good about the future prospects for his business. He had been apprised yesterday (by Dave) of the key dynamics and the reaction from Jonathan at the finance team meeting the other day.

"OK, let's see what our 'total company' looks like", Ian directed.

Frank responded by motioning for Jason to show Exhibit 134.

"*TOTAL CO.* is the 'sum' of the two business units", Frank stated. "The results of the 'plans' are a corporate revenue growth rate of 20%, slight increase in *NOP* margin, *ICI* of $0.36, and net new investment of $120 million – $60 million for each BU. There's not much that I can add to what Cathy and Dave have presented".

"We're getting within 'striking distance' of my goal to be a 'billion-dollar' company", exclaimed Ian. "If we take this 'plan' out another year or so, we're just about there".

Jason looked the other way as Ian made that comment. "*I've got to get this CEO focused on how much his 'market value' should be, not on how 'big' the company is in terms of revenue*", Jason thought to

Exhibit 134

GROWTHSTAR INC.
Total Company Financials
Next 3 Years - Growth Plan

"TOTAL CO." Financials	Current	Future Outlook	Change / Impact	'Plan'
[$ Millions (MM's) except Per Share and Capital Intensity Amounts]	FY Fcst.	Year 3	of 'Plan'	CGR / Ratio
Revenue:				
Products	$300	$450	$150	14%
Services	150	330	180	30%
Total Revenue	$450	$780	$330	20%
Net Operating Profit ('NOP') — $	$31	$55	$24	21%
— %	6.9%	7.1%	0.2%	7.3%
			'I'	'ICI'
Invested Capital (IC) - 'Ending'	$243	$363	$120	$0.36

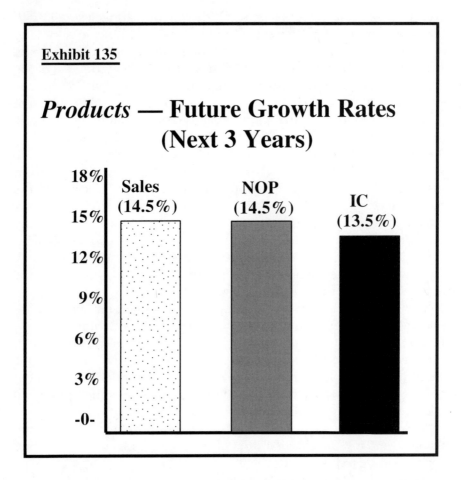

Exhibit 135

Products — Future Growth Rates (Next 3 Years)

Sales (14.5%)   NOP (14.5%)   IC (13.5%)

himself. He looked over at Jonathan and gave a slight shrug of his shoulders. Jonathan picked up the gesture and its meaning.

"That's a good point, Ian", Jonathan stated, "and we're going to enhance this perspective by looking at the implications of our future growth and profitability on our stock price".

"That subject is 'near and dear to my heart', also", the 'big man' responded.

Jason sighed, and said to himself ... "*Thank you, Mr Steadfast*". Jason then rose and said to the group ... "The next set of exhibits will illustrate the financial 'drivers' that we exposed you to during the historical assessment phase of our work. First, we'll review the future growth rates for revenue, net operating profit and invested capital. *Products* will be shown in Exhibit 135, *Services* in Exhibit 136 and *TOTAL CO.* in Exhibit 137".

"*Products* is expected to increase its revenue, profit and invested capital at almost identical rates, as Cathy has alluded to in her comments. Exhibit 135 illustrates these relationships. Next, Exhibit 136 will show quite a different pattern for the growth rates incorporated into the 'plan' for *Services*. Here, the 'most desirable' long-term relationships exist. We must remember, though, that the company paid a 'price' for this outcome when it acquired *Services*. That 'price' appears to have been justified".

"As this chart (Exhibit 136) shows, the most significant financial aspect of the 'plan' for *Services* is the ability to grow rapidly with a relatively low investment requirement. Growthstar has never had a business with an *ICI* of only $0.33. We need to remember, however, that the company has 'invested' for this leverage during the past three years".

"It is nice, though, to see the benefits", Dave interjected, looking at Peter as he spoke.

"Indeed it is", Peter added.

"To 'wrap up' the analysis of the growth rate 'drivers', Exhibit 137 will give us the profile for the total company", Jason continued, appreciating the enthusiasm of Peter and Dave, but wanting to move ahead.

Ian leaned back and said, "If I remember the comments and dialogue from this analysis of our recent history, the 'shapes' of these bars, at least for *Services* and *TOTAL CO.*, represent the 'optimal' long-term pattern. That's no criticism on you, Larry, since your 'plan' is in line with our perceptions for the next three years. It does put some pressure on you, Peter, to execute your strategy in the manner illustrated in Exhibit 136".

"We understand and are prepared to achieve these forecasted numbers", Peter replied.

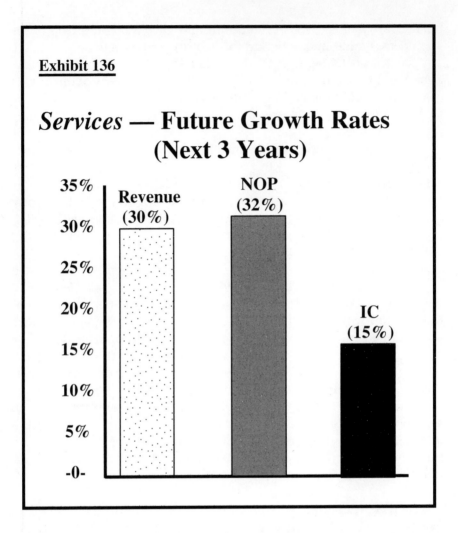

Exhibit 136

Services — **Future Growth Rates (Next 3 Years)**

"In that case, I'm satisfied and we can move to our next topic", Ian stated emphatically.

"That topic would be Invested Capital Intensity, or *ICI*", Jason responded. "The next chart, Exhibit 138, provides a graphic summary of the capital intensity forecasted for the two BUs and the total company over the next three years".

"As this exhibit (138) shows, the *Services BU* is forecasted to be less capital intensive than *Products* during the 'plan' period. The trend started this year, with an 'incremental' *ICI* of only 'twenty-three cents' (see Exhibit 93) when calculated on the basis of *new capital invest-ment versus new revenue*. There is a one-time accounts receivable benefit that affects this year's 'incremental' *ICI*. The rationale for the '33-cent' *ICI* is that the 'infrastructure' has been put in place to move this business forward".

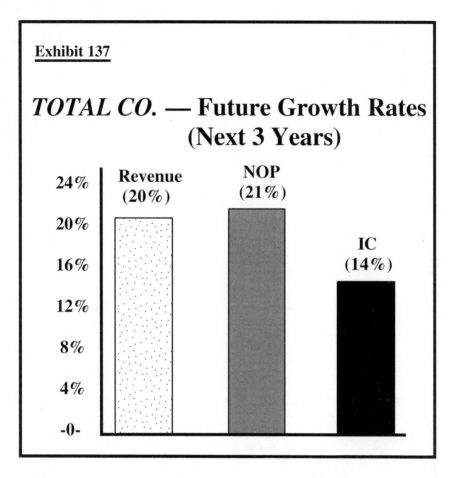

Exhibit 137

TOTAL CO. — Future Growth Rates (Next 3 Years)

"That's correct", Peter interjected. "Our investment in 'state-of the-art' facilities and equipment since the acquisition has positioned us well for the next few years". Peter looked at Dave as he spoke and Dave nodded vigorously. Ian picked up the gesture.

Jason continued with "*Products* is expected to remain at about the same level for *ICI* as its recent history. *TOTAL CO.* is then, the 'weighted average' of the two BUs".

Jonathan then stated "A considerable amount of time and effort has gone into the investment requirements to support our growth plans. I have reviewed these, along with Earl, Jack, Frank, Jill and Jason, and endorse what you are now seeing". Ian nodded.

"The last financial 'driver' is the Value Profit Margin (*VPM*). As Exhibit 139 will show", Jason commented, "the 'plan' for both BUs generates a positive 'spread' – that is, the 'actual' *NOP* margin is expected to be above the *VPM*. This relationship indicates that 'value creating' growth plans have been developed. We'll indicate 'how much' value shortly. As you can see, *Services* is expecting to 'leverage' its

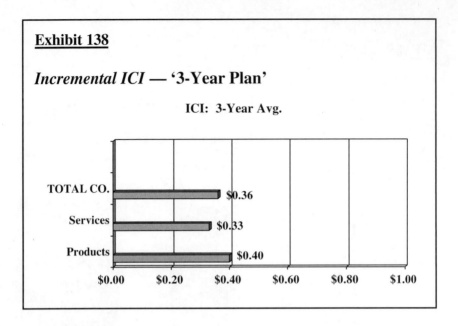

Exhibit 138

Incremental ICI — '3-Year Plan'

ICI: 3-Year Avg.

- TOTAL CO.: $0.36
- Services: $0.33
- Products: $0.40

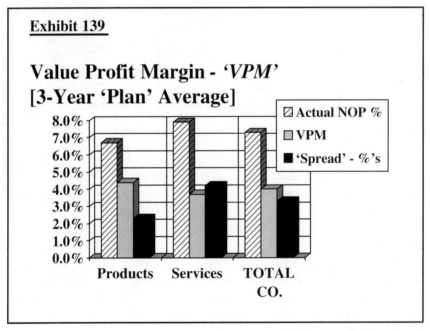

Exhibit 139

**Value Profit Margin - *'VPM'*
[3-Year 'Plan' Average]**

Legend:
- Actual NOP %
- VPM
- 'Spread' - %'s

Categories: Products, Services, TOTAL CO.

infrastructure. Recall that *Services* just reached a 'break-even' point this year for *VPM* (and *EP*), so this improvement is quite significant. *Products* is forecasting a 'spread' in line with its recent history, which should not be surprising based on what you have heard so far".

Dave, still feeling his exuberance and always loaded with enthusiasm, wanted to make sure that Peter and Ian understood the implications of the 'plan' for *Services*. "The execution of our plan and delivery of the results imbedded into the plan should place *Services* solidly into the **'A-type'** business category".

Peter immediately leaned forward and peered at the chart. Larry did the same. "You mean to tell me", Peter asked, "that if I can achieve anything above a 4% *NOP* margin, I'm creating value for the shareholders?"

Jack perked up and saw an opening. "That's correct", he exclaimed. "And, Jason, Frank and Earl can tell you 'how much' value based on the revenue growth".

"Well, now", Peter countered, "that's a simplistic set of metrics that I can certainly live with". Jack smiled broadly. Everyone in the room noticed, which caused silence for a moment.

Larry then spoke. "Let me visualize my situation. It appears that my *VPM* is a bit over 4%. Is that correct, Cathy?"

"4.4%, to be precise", Cathy replied. "Say, 4.5% to be 'safe', which is what our historical level has been".

Larry looked first at Peter, then at Ian, then at Jonathan and Jack and stated, "Well, I can certainly live with a system of *NOP* margin and sales growth. That's what I've lived by since I began running this business. Cathy, you and Dave and the corporate finance people can worry about all the *ICI* and cost of capital issues. Ian, how do you feel about this?"

"My feeling is that if we can adopt a financial performance system that enables us to create value for our shareholders by focusing on sales growth and a net profit margin, then I'm starting to feel very positive about this endeavor".

"That's what can happen", Jack blurted out. "With relatively minor modifications to what you're doing now, we can install a 'value-based' financial performance system".

Jonathan leaned back and thought to himself ... "*What a fascinating turn of events*", as he recalled his first meeting with Jason. "*I initially thought that if we could get the GMs to go along with a system that achieved our goal of 'simplicity with integrity', that Jack could be brought 'on board'. Now, Jack is actually 'selling' the VPM concept as if he suggested it*". Jonathan looked at Jason as he was thinking to himself. While not aware of exactly what was going through Jonathan's mind, Jason could tell that Jonathan was thinking to himself and guessed that it had something to do with Jack's comments. Earl and Val exchanged glances, as did Frank and Jill.

Jonathan then felt compelled to speak. "I support the comments from the three of you – Ian, Larry and Peter. Let me say, however, that just because we may want to implement a very simplistic system – which may well be the best way for us to get started – no one should think for a moment that the emphasis on invested capital and the cost of capital is in any way diminished".

"That's a very important point", Earl said defiantly. "This is still a 'cash flow' oriented system with an emphasis on 'economic' returns. It's just that we have a method for implementation that allows the operating heads to concentrate on two major metrics".

"That's exactly what I like about this approach", Larry retorted. "Heck, I know that fixed and working capital are important, even though I can't understand all these calculations. But, for the first time since this whole process began, I can see a way that *I* can deal effectively with the challenge that Ian is throwing at me, and let Cathy tell me if I'm 'on track' with the elements beyond 'growth and margin'".

"That's very well, put", Peter said, "and I would 'echo' those thoughts".

Ian got the 'message'. He also knew there were other agenda items that needed to be dealt with, and that this meeting could not go on all day. He, therefore, said ... "I think we should file this for now and move on to our next topic". That was all that needed to be stated.

Jason took the cue and said ... "Our next topic is the 'valuation' of the BUs and the total company". Everyone glanced at the flip chart and saw that this was the second major agenda item.

"We spent a considerable amount of time the other day on this topic. I will show you the results of a comprehensive financial planning effort, but first let's understand what the company is worth ... or should be worth ... based on the 'existing' performance of the businesses. This is called the 'no growth' value. A table (Exhibit 140) will highlight the 'warranted' value of Growthstar without any future growth".

"Most of the 'no-growth' total market value (*TMV*) and all of the market value added (*MVA*) resides with *Products*. Based on the historical assessment that you all endured, this should not be a surprising revelation". Ian, Larry and Peter nodded, indicating their understanding and concurrence. "The term '*TMV*' expresses what each business and *TOTAL CO.* should be worth based on the level of net operating profit expected for this year. *MVA* indicates how much 'shareholder value' has been created, beyond the aggregate investment in the business. As we know, with *Services* just beginning to earn its cost of capital (*CCAP*) this year, 'no' shareholder value has

```
┌─────────────────────────────────────────────────────────────────────────┐
│ Exhibit 140                    GROWTHSTAR  INC.                           │
│                                                                           │
│                              Valuation Highlights                         │
│  'Base' Period Financials    Current Year — 'No Growth' Value             │
│      $ Millions                 Products      Services      TOTAL CO.     │
│                                                                           │
│  Valuation - 'No Growth'                                                  │
│  Net Operating Profit (NOP)       $20           $11            $31        │
│  Cost of Capital (CCAP)           11%           11%            11%        │
│  Total Market Value (TMV)        $182          $100           $282        │
│                                                                           │
│  Total Market Value (TMV)        $182          $100           $282        │
│  less IC                         (120)         (100)          (220)       │
│     Market Value Added (MVA)      $62           $(0)           $62        │
│                                                                           │
└─────────────────────────────────────────────────────────────────────────┘
```

been created based on performance to date". All the heads nodded again.

Jason then went to the flip chart and wrote:

[$ Millions except per share]	Market Values
Current Stock Price per share	**$27.50**
times # shares (millions)	**10**
equals Equity Market Value	**$275**
plus Debt/Leases	**110**
equals Total Market Value (TMV)	**$385**
... versus 'No Growth' TMV	**282 ... 73% of TMV**
Difference ('Growth')	**$103 ... 27% of TMV**

"Here's one financial market perspective", Jason stated. "What it says is that the firm's current year performance level accounts for nearly three-fourths of the company's total market value".

Ian stared at the flip chart, a look of concern and dismay on his face. "This is not the perspective that I have for this company", he muttered.

"We didn't think that it was", Mandy responded, "but this is the reality of the situation".

"Now I understand why you want a 'special' meeting with the analysts and our major investors", Ian stated. "We need to get our 'story' out to them".

"We all agree", Mandy came back, "so why don't we see what that 'story' is".

"Do it", Ian directed.

Jason motioned to Earl to pick up the commentary, since Earl had wanted to have a role in the strategy valuations. Earl rose and stated "We have three 'future years' scenarios to present. The first is our 'plan' with 'profitable growth' through the end of the three-year planning period, but none after that. The second is a 'potential' outlook in the minds of the investors, based on 'piecing together' information we have communicated to them. The third is a plausible case for us, in which we see growth opportunities in both businesses beyond the end of the planning period".

"I would certainly hope so", Ian exclaimed. "This company is about 'growth'".

"Let's take a look at the 'plan' scenario first. As I mentioned, we grow profitably for three years, based on the factors you reviewed in the Exhibits (132 through 137) shown at the outset of the meeting. Exhibit 141 provides a summary of this valuation scenario".

"Please look at the third column", Earl admonished the group. "This column summarizes the 'strategy' values – in essence, the values for our growth plans. Notice that the 'strategy' value for *Services* is approximately twice that for *Products*. This is a reversal of what we've seen in our historical assessments". As Earl spoke and they gazed at the exhibit (141), wide smiles broke out on the faces of Peter and Dave. Larry and Cathy looked at each other, with expressions of seriousness. They knew that their growth prospects were not as exciting as those for *Services*, but they also felt that their BU was the 'heart and soul' of the company – at least it had been up until now.

Earl continued ... "The fourth column provides the 'total' market value – the sum of the 'no growth' and 'strategy' values. At the bottom of this column is the stock price that relates to these values – about $2.00 (7%) *below* the current price in the stock market".

"If this is the case", Ian snapped, then the 'market' expects us to grow more than our 'plan' indicates".

"Either grow faster over the next three years, or grow profitably at a rate, which could be at or below the 'plan' rate, for a longer period

Exhibit 141	**GROWTHSTAR INC.**			
	Valuation Highlights			
$ Millions, except 'per share'	*'No Growth' plus Next 3 Yrs. Growth Plan*			Current
Valuation	'No Growth'	'Strategy'	'Total'	Mkt. Value
Products	$182	$27	$209	
Services	100	56	156	
TOTAL CO.	$282	$83	$365	$385
Less: Total Debt			(110)	(110)
Equity Value			**$255**	**$275**
# Shares (millions)			*10*	*10*
Per Share Value			*$25.50*	*$27.50*

of time", Val retorted. "Some investors call this a 'profitable growth horizon' or 'competitive advantage period'".

"OK, I understand", Ian shot back.

"The next scenario", Earl said as he reassumed the 'lead role' in the dialogue, "is a potential 'investor' scenario, based on information we have released publicly. As you will see, it links almost perfectly to our stock price". As he spoke, he went to the flip chart, turned over the page Jason had just written on and wrote:

	'Investor Scenario'	Growthstar *'Plan'*
Revenue Growth Rate		
–'TOTAL CO.'	*18%*	*20%*
NOP Margin	*7.0%*	*7.3%*
ICI	*$.40*	*$.36*
'Growth' Period	*5 years*	*3 years*

"In this 'investor scenario', the growth rate is lower than our 'plan' by two percentage points (18% versus 20%). The profit margin is also lower and the capital intensity is higher. The only factor more favorable than our plan is the period for profitable growth – five years versus three years. This longer time horizon outweighs the lower assumptions for the key 'drivers' and produces a market valuation higher than that for our 'plan' and equal to our valuation in the stock market. Exhibit 142 provides a summary of the results".

"Next, is the scenario that the finance team, along with Val and Mandy, feel is most representative of our future potential".

"Peter, you remember, don't you, the meeting we had when we discussed our growth *beyond* the three-year 'plan' period", Dave quipped, looking at Peter.

"Oh, yes, now I do", Peter replied.

Exhibit 142	**GROWTHSTAR INC.**			
	'Investor Scenario'			
	Valuation Highlights			
$ Millions, except 'per share'	*'No Growth' + Growth Plan + 2 Add'l Yrs.**			**Current**
Valuation	**'No Growth'**	**'Strategy'**	**'Total'**	**Market Value**
TOTAL CO.	$282	$103	$385	$385
less: Total Debt			(110)	(110)
Equity Value			**$275**	**$275**
# Shares (millions)			*10*	*10*
Per Share Value			*$27.50*	*$27.50*
	Five (5) years of growth in total			

Larry looked over at Cathy and asked, "We analyzed this also, didn't we, Cathy? I remember assigning some people to review our technology and the engineering aspects of our business".

"We sure did", Cathy answered, "and we even did a bit of market research, using our customer survey profiles".

"That's right", Larry mused. "We figured we could grow profitably with the 'Next Generation' for two to three years beyond the end of the 'plan' period".

"Ours was four years, if my recollection is correct", Peter interjected.

"It is", Dave replied.

Earl wanted to move on, so he said ... "Jason, did you bring the 'flip chart' page from the meeting the other day?"

"I just happen to have that", Jason responded. As he spoke, Jason taped the page to the wall, so that everyone could see the page from two days ago along with the one with the notations about the 'investor scenario' and 'plan' assumptions.

Business Unit	+ Growth Years	Growth Rate	NOP Margin	ICI
Products	+2 to 3	12%	6.7%	$0.40
–US	same	10%	lower	lower
–Int'l	same	15%	higher	higher
Services	+4	25%	7.3%	$0.40
–Growthstar	same	21%	higher	higher
–Other	same	33%	lower	lower

"Here are the conclusions we came to", Earl stated, a sense of determination evident in his voice. "We decided on the lower end of the 'time horizon' for *Products* – thus, two years of profitable growth after the end of the 'plan' period. *Products* should grow slower, 12% versus 14.5% in the 'plan' and maintain its *NOP* margin and *ICI*. *Services* is forecasted to slow down somewhat (25% versus 30% growth in the 'plan') and also see its key 'drivers' deteriorate a bit. This deterioration, however, does not inhibit our 'value potential', as you will see in Exhibit 143. Jason, do we have this one ready?"

"I think I can handle that", Jason replied. "For those of you at the meeting the other day, this exhibit (143) is the same as Exhibit 123".

Jill pored through her material from the meeting two days ago, and sighed when she found it. Cathy also found the schedule in her package. Dave was too enamored with the day's developments to bother looking. Nor did Frank, since he had it memorized.

"Now, that's more like it", Ian said excitedly, rising from his chair and pacing a bit back and forth. "The assumptions on these flip chart pages are my 'minimum' targets – take note, Larry and Peter – and they don't include any corporate development activities, which could

Exhibit 143	GROWTHSTAR INC.			

Valuation Highlights

$ Millions, except 'per share'	Plan + 2 Yrs. (Products) and 4 Yrs. (Services)			Current
Valuation - 'FCF' and 'EP' (*)	**'No Growth'**	**'Strategy'**	**'Total' Value**	**Market Value**
Products	$182	$44	$226	
Services	100	121	221	
TOTAL CO.	$282	$165	$447	$385
less: Total Debt			(110)	(110)
Equity Value			**$337**	**$275**
# Shares (millions)			*10*	*10*
Per Share Value			**$33.70**	**$27.50**

(*) 'FCF' Approach for Products and 'EP' Approach for Services

result in another acquisition or two during this 'plan' period, and certainly if we go beyond the next three years. Let's see, $33.70 versus $27.50 ... that's a 'premium' of over 20%. I assume, Mandy and Jonathan, that this is what you were referring to this morning, when you suggested a 'special' meeting with the analysts and major investors".

"That's it, along with the 'story' behind the numbers", Mandy and Jonathan said in unison.

"OK, I'm in agreement with this recommendation and with the stock price resulting from this scenario. We can even start dropping some hints before a formal meeting, as long as the message is coordinated and consistent. Mandy, you should control this and keep Jonathan informed. For the rest of you, let Mandy, Jonathan and me handle this for now. We'll get you involved when the entire 'shareholder value tale' – which is now coming together for me – is put in a format for public disclosure and dissemination. This is really exciting! I knew our stock is worth more than its current price level. I just could never get my arms wrapped around *why*. This analysis puts the pieces of the puzzle together!"

"Let me put another piece in it for you", Jason chimed in. "Remember the 'magnifier' effect?"

"I do, now that you've reminded me", Ian answered. Peter and Larry also nodded, as did Flo Withetide.

Flo had been listening attentively all morning, but had been so silent that you would never had known she was there. She had also been relatively quiet at the first meeting of the officers, making only a comment about including an 'economic profit segment' in a new management development program that she was structuring. Now that Ian had made his commitment, she said, "I find this concept to be particularly interesting in terms of its potential to influence the behavior of the 'direct reports' for Larry and Peter". Larry and Peter turned toward Flo, surprised to hear her speaking.

"How so"? asked Peter.

"I'm not sure exactly how to do it, but the notion that a sales increase, or cost efficiency program, or a combination of the two, can 'magnify' value creation is something that I want to give some consideration to in our management development and training. I'll get back to you when I have something more solid, which will be sooner rather than later". Larry and Peter looked at each other, but said nothing.

Jonathan wanted to get into the 'magnifier' charts, so he said ... "I'm intrigued by what you are saying, Flo. Why don't we discuss this over lunch next week?" Flo nodded. Jonathan then motioned toward Jason.

Jason took the cue and said, "Shortly, I'm going to show a chart for *TOTAL CO.*, as one of the key points you will want to share with the investors. First, though, *Services* deserves attention. With a 'no-growth' *MVA* of 'zero', the 'magnifier' for *Services* can *not* be calculated in *percentage* terms, since you get an 'infinite' result when you divide by 'zero'. Suffice it to say, though, that the impact is significant. If you refer to Exhibit 141 (the 'strategy' value column for *Services*), the *MVA* for the 30% growth rate over three years is $56 million. One way to express the 'magnifier' is that every 1% of revenue growth in the 'plan' translates into nearly $2 million of shareholder value. You can prove this 'rule of thumb' by running selected growth scenarios using the 'plan' assumptions for *NOP* margin and *ICI*. For the 'most likely' case that Ian just endorsed and that you may communicate at your 'investor' meeting, the 'rule of thumb' is that for every 1% of *Services* growth, $4.5 million of *MVA* (or, shareholder value) is created".

"Now you've really got my attention", Ian said excitedly, his tone of voice very evident to everyone in the room. "How can this be?" This comment was a *directive*, rather than a question.

"Let me try to explain the 'Magnifier' Effect for *Services* with a schedule (Exhibit 144)", Jason responded.

"This 'Magnifier' is a function of time, growth and profitability – with profitability expressed in terms of 'economic returns'. While growth and profitability are, obviously, important, so is the ability to develop and execute strategies that can be sustained for long periods of time. All the stock market 'performers' – those firms with constantly increasing share prices – typically have these characteristics. In the case of *Services*, sustaining 'value creating' performance for an additional four years – albeit at rates and ratios that are slightly below those in the three-year 'plan' – has a dramatic 'magnifying' impact. In fact, extending the time horizon for profitable growth is more critical

Exhibit 144	GROWTHSTAR INC.			
	Business Unit Financials			
	'Magnifier' Effect			
"SERVICES" Financials	Final Year	Growth Rate	*NPV/*	*NPV/MVA for*
$ Millions	Revenue	(CGR)	*MVA*	*each 1% Growth*
'Plan' — 3-year growth horizon	$330	30%	$56	**$1.9**
'Most Likely' — 7-year horizon	$807	27%	$121	**$4.5**
Memo: Current Year Revenue	*$150*			

to your stock price than the higher returns during the 'plan' period. So, now you've seen an illustration of a 'rule of thumb' for *MVA* to complement the 'percentage' relationships we analyzed as part of the historical assessments. Depending on the circumstances, you can express the 'Magnifier' either as a 'percentage' or an 'absolute' change in shareholder value related to a growth rate for revenue".

Ian was silent and speechless for one of those rare moments. He leaned back in his chair with a look of total satisfaction on his face. All the people in the boardroom knew to keep silent and wait for the 'big man' to say the next words. It didn't take him long. "I have never in my life seen so powerful, yet simple, a concept as this. This is the 'answer' that I have been searching for. We truly do have a shareholder value story to tell, and we're going to 'package' it and then communicate it to the financial world. Jonathan, this is outstanding! Can we see the 'Magnifier' for *TOTAL CO.*?" This was a question.

"By all means", Jason replied. "Let's start with Exhibit 145, reflecting the 'plan'".

"Wow – look at the third bar!" exclaimed Dave, knowing that *Services* was a major contributor to the 'Magnifier' for the total company. "OOPS, I'm sorry", he said, realizing that he had blurted out his feelings in somewhat of an unprofessional manner.

"That's OK", uttered Ian and Peter almost in unison. "I was thinking the same thing", Peter then said.

"This is 'dynamite stuff' isn't it?" Earl piped in. "Our 'plan' – without any further growth beyond the third (final) year – produces a 'warranted' shareholder value increase of 134% on a 'compounded' 20% revenue growth. As the third bar shows, $145 million is $83 million of *MVA* attributable to the BU strategies (refer to Exhibit 141 – third column) added to the 'no-growth' *MVA* of $62 million (refer to Exhibit 140 – last column)".

"What's the 'Magnifier' for the 'Most Likely' Scenario"? asked Jonathan.

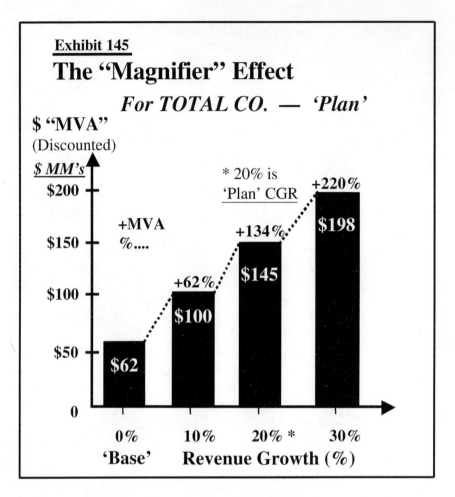

Exhibit 145

The "Magnifier" Effect

For TOTAL CO. — 'Plan'

"Take a look at Exhibit 146", Jason answered.

"This is pretty amazing", Ian said rather softly. He didn't need to express any more enthusiasm. He felt that everyone knew he was excited about the prospects that his 'dream' of translating growth into real value creation was within his grasp. "Look at what might happen if we could grow by 30% for seven years".

"Grow 'profitably' ... maintaining the level of *NOP* margin and *ICI* that we believe we can achieve in a '17% to 19% growth' scenario", Jonathan was quick to add.

"OK, I get the point", the 'big man' retorted. "It's not just by 'magic' and by making another acquisition. Although, if we can acquire another *Services-type* company or business and develop a solid strategy, maybe we can get close. We've got an interesting challenge", he concluded, looking at Val.

Larry had been attentive during the discussion on the 'Magnifier' Effect. He could visualize the 'message' from the charts, but was

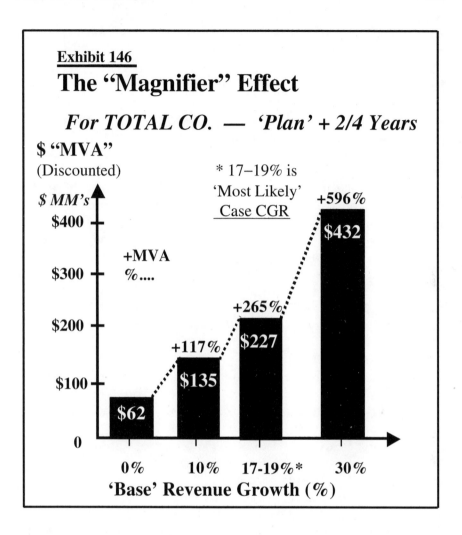

Exhibit 146

The "Magnifier" Effect

For TOTAL CO. — 'Plan' + 2/4 Years

$ "MVA"
(Discounted)

* 17–19% is
'Most Likely'
<u>Case CGR</u>

'missing' something. Thus, he asked, "Before we leave this topic, could you explain the 'percentage' increases in shareholder value that are printed above the tops of the bars in Exhibits 145 and 146?"

Jason answered with "Look at the first and third set of bars in each exhibit. Take Exhibit 145 first. The first bar plots the *MVA* for the 'no-growth' situation'. If you refer back to Exhibit 140, you will find this as the last number on the schedule under the *TOTAL CO.*' column. The 'plan' results in a 20% revenue growth rate, which is the third bar. If you now refer back to Exhibit 141 and look at the third column, you'll see that the third column provides the 'strategy' values (*MVAs*). Notice that the *TOTAL CO.* amount is $83 million. If you add $83 million (the 'plan') and $62 million ('no growth') the result is $145 million ('no growth' plus 'plan'). To calculate the percentage change in shareholder value (*MVA*), divide $83 million (the 'value' created by the 'plan') by

$62 million ('no-growth' *MVA*). The result is 134%, the percentage increase in *MVA* related to a 20% compound growth rate for revenue. Thus, there is a 'magnified' impact on shareholder value due to the fact that Growthstar is an '**A-type**' company".

"If you perform the same analysis for the 'Plan + 2/4 Years' (of growth) – which we're calling a 'most likely' case – there is an additional 'magnifying' effect due to the longer time period for 'profitable' growth, even though the 'rate' of growth slows somewhat. Now, look at the first and third bars in Exhibit 146. The first bar is the same as the one in Exhibit 145 and plots the 'no-growth' *MVA* of $62 million. The third bar plots *MVA* for a growth rate of 17% to 19% per year for the 'seven-year' time horizon. Go to Exhibit 143 and see that, in the third column, $165 million of shareholder value is created from the 'strategy' ('growth') portion of this scenario. Dividing this amount by the $62 million of 'no growth' *MVA* equates to a 265% (rounded) increase in shareholder value (*MVA*). Adding the 'no growth' *MVA* of $62 million to the 'growth' *MVA* of $165 million results in $227 million of 'total' *MVA*, which is plotted as the height of the bar".

"Got it", replied Larry.

Val then chimed in with "There is one more aspect to this discussion, which we can cover quickly. Jason, can you show the exhibit on the market value index (*MVI*) and market-to-book (*M/B*) ratio resulting from what we're calling a 'Most Likely' case?"

"Oh, I think I can handle that", Jason answered. "For the finance team, that was Exhibit 124 from our meeting the other day. I've renumbered this schedule Exhibit 147".

Peter, not to be outdone by Larry, with respect to asking a question on a topic that he intuitively understood but had difficulty with the specifics, inserted himself back into the conversation. "I've been exposed to the Market-to-Book (*M/B*) ratio, and happen to believe it is a good indicator of management performance with respect to the 'capital' that has been invested in a business. I believe it's the market price of our stock divided by our 'book' value. In this case, market prices in the range of '1.7 to 2 times' the value we record for equity in the books of account".

"That's correct", Earl responded, wanting every opportunity to express his knowledge, "with two caveats. First, this calculation is not our 'equity' value, but rather our 'total' market value ... in essence, our equity plus debt. Thus, we can determine 'value creation' for the BUs on a 'relative' basis. Second, we calculate our 'economic' book value, to get this analysis closer to 'cash flow'. In this analysis, we're using our 'year-end' invested capital, since we are approaching the end of our fiscal year".

```
Exhibit 147                    GROWTHSTAR  INC.

                               Valuation Highlights
'Future' Period Financials     'Plan' + 2 Yrs. (Products) and 4 Yrs. (Services)
$ Millions, except MVI         Products      Services       TOTAL CO.

Market Value Index ('MVI')
('Plan' + 'Post-Plan' Growth)
  Market Value Added (MVA)        $44          $121            $165
  Net New Investment (discounted) $77          $153            $230
  MVI .... Additional MVA for
    each Investment Dollar       $0.57         $0.79           $0.72
```

'MVI' reflects 'warranted' MVA for the business as a ratio to 'discounted' net new investment.

```
Market-to-Book ('M/B') Ratio  | Products |   Services        TOTAL CO.
(re: "Total" Market Value ..... 'Base')
  Total Market Value (TMV)       $226         $221            $447
  Economic Book Value            $131         $112            $243

Ratio:  Market-to-Book Value     1.73         1.98            1.84
```

M/B Ratio reflects the 'warranted' TMV for the business versus the economic book value.

"Thank you for the clarification", Peter responded. "Now, help me with the Market Value Index (*MVI*). This is a 'new' metric for me".

"It's new for a lot of people", Earl retorted, "and it may be best for Jason to explain this metric, so that we get it correct".

Jason, realizing that the 'technical' aspects were his responsibility, said "Think of the *MVI*, Peter, as though you were the investor. One of your requirements should be to determine what your 'return' is for each dollar that you are investing. Over a seven-year time horizon for the scenario we are calling the 'Most Likely' case for the company, the net new investment to support the growth is approximately $350 million. When we 'discount' this net new investment to present value, the amount is $230 million. As an investor, you are going to invest a considerable sum of money in this company. What are you going to get in return? One measure, the *MVI*, says that for each 'discounted' dollar of total investment you (the investor) will receive the following returns".

As Jason uttered the last sentence, he walked over to the flip chart and wrote the following:

	Products	Services	TOTAL CO.
MVA	$44	$121	$165
IC ('Economic')	$77	$153	$230
MVI	$0.57	$0.79	$0.72

"This is the 'top' portion of Exhibit 147. The 'strategic' outlook says that you, as an investor, will receive '72 cents' of 'excess return' for each 'net' new dollar invested in Growthstar. With 'profitable growth' prospects greater for *Services* than for *Products*, the 'relative' return is greater for *Services* – in this case, '79 cents' for each 'discounted' dollar of investment – versus '57 cents' of return for each dollar invested in *Products*".

"OK, OK!" Peter responded. "You finance guys are like the 'clock maker', who when you ask him '*what time is it*'? responds with '*how a clock is built*'".

"But, that's the nature of what we have to do", Jonathan replied, knowing that he had to 'stand up' for corporate finance … their role and their responsibility. "We are the 'last resort' for technical input to the economic value-based performance measures that may be implemented in the company".

Peter nodded at Jonathan, indicating both in understanding and appreciation of corporate finance's role.

Jonathan could sense a 'crescendo' in the mood – particularly from Ian – which usually signaled a good time for a break. He, therefore, suggested a fifteen-minute break, which no one objected to.

Upon the return of the meeting participants after the break, Jason went to the flip chart and turned to the sheet with the discussion topics. "We've covered the first three (3) item – the financial summary and 'drivers' for the growth plan, the valuation of the company and the BUs under 'no-growth' and 'growth' scenarios, and the 'magnifier' effect. Earl did a good job the other day explaining the integration of cash flow with value, and Frank did the same with 'sustainable' revenue. So, I'm going to ask them to summarize these topics today. Then, our last item will be 'implementation'. Jack has given you his thoughts, and I know that Jonathan has something to say on this subject".

Earl rose and began to speak. "We have analyzed our cash flow over the next three years from two (2) perspectives – 'free' cash flow and 'net' cash flow. The difference between the two is the financing charges we incur on a corporate basis. 'Free' cash flow (*FCF*) is defined as net operating profit (*NOP*) minus net new investment (*I*). 'Net' cash flow (*NCF*) is *FCF* minus interest charges/principal repayments on debt and dividends on common/preferred stock. What we're going to do on the next chart (Exhibit 148) is to integrate the 'values' you have just reviewed with the impact on cash flow".

"Earl, this looks very interesting", the 'big man' stated, "but I think you have some explaining to do".

"We have Jason to blame for this", Earl chuckled. "I'm just following his instructions".

"My guess is that we have Jason to blame for just about *all* we've seen today", Ian shot back, casting a wry smile first at Jason, then at Jonathan, and then at Earl".

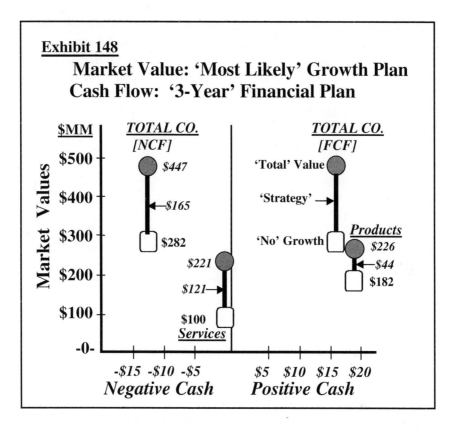

Exhibit 148

Market Value: 'Most Likely' Growth Plan
Cash Flow: '3-Year' Financial Plan

"Guilty as charged", Jason quipped.

"OK, getting serious, now", Earl came back ... "Market values are plotted 'vertically' and cash flows 'horizontally'. Thus, the higher the vertical plot, the higher the market value. These 'market value' plots also conform to the way we've looked at the BUs and the total company. The 'warranted' market values reflect the 'no-growth' and 'strategy' (or, 'growth') values – adding to the 'total' market values, based on current plus anticipated future financial performance. The 'squares' at the 'bottom' of each plot reflect the 'no-growth' values. The height of the 'vertical lines' indicates the value created by the strategies ('growth plans'). The 'circles' at the top reflect the 'total' warranted present values for the BU's and the total company. Notice that there are two (2) sets of 'plots' for *TOTAL CO.* The plot to the 'right' indicates the cash flow of the company under a 'free' cash flow approach. That is, we should be 'cash positive' before financing charges. This results from strong 'positive' free cash flow generation from *Products* and a slightly 'negative' free cash flow from *Services*. When we add back our mandated interest payments on debt and forecasted dividends on common stock, we have a 'net cash use' (i.e. negative net cash flow) of about $13 million for the total company.

We have a $30 million credit line, of which we've used $10 million. Thus, we have $20 million of debt financing available, which should be sufficient to support our 'plan' for the next three years, and enable us to continue the practise of paying out 10% or our 'net earnings' to the shareholders".

"Now, that clears it up for me", Ian responded. "Does everyone understand this?"

Earl's explanation had been concise and thorough, and all the heads nodded.

Jonathan then stated, "I believe this type of work and result takes Corporate Financial Analysis to a new level, one that will become increasingly important for us as we grow".

"I agree, and it's been a revelation for me", Ian beamed.

Earl, feeling as good as he had felt since the process started months ago, then turned to his assistant and said, "Frank, can you 'wrap up' the session – before we discuss near-term implementation – with 'sustainable revenue growth'?"

Frank felt pleased that he had been chosen to present the final 'formal' topic on the agenda, and began speaking deliberately. "As the last chart (Exhibit 148) alluded to, growth requires cash for invest-ment. Growth also produces cash from the profit that is generated. The relationship of the two indicates whether a business generates positive or negative cash flow. As we've seen with our company, *TOTAL CO.* is expected to be a 'cash user' during the next three years. This is a 'net' result of cash generated from profit, and cash used to invest in the businesses and cover our financing charges. When we look at 'sustainable' revenue, we do so from the perspective of determining how fast we can grow before the need to issue new equity. When making this determination, we add one factor to what we have discussed so far – the capability to take on additional debt (beyond our 'credit line') to maintain what we call a 'target' debt-to-total capital ratio. In our case, this ratio can go up to 50%. It's simply our total debt (including operating leases) divided by total (net) invested capital. This is a maximum 'debt leverage' point for us as a company. The impact is to enable the funding of additional growth through this additional borrowing capacity".

"Doesn't this get risky"? asked Larry.

"It can", Frank answered, "but countering that risk is the fact that the company is bigger with more revenue and profit – depending on the 'profitability' of the new revenue. The key point about 'sustainable growth' is that it tells us what we 'could' do, not necessarily what we 'should' do".

"Got it", Larry shot back. He always seemed to use that phrase when his questions were answered to his satisfaction.

"If everyone is OK with this explanation, let me illustrate the 'sustainable growth' for Growthstar with Exhibit 149. We're going to show this in two ways – first, in terms of the 'absolute' amount of 'cumulative' revenue growth that is sustainable over the three-year 'plan' period, and then the 'percentage' growth rate that is sustainable. In each case, we'll compare the 'sustainable' level to the level forecasted in the 'plan'. We use the 'plan' period (next three years) for this analysis, since we're interested in 'financing' capacity, not value creation". Jason clicked on Exhibit 149 as Frank was speaking.

"This graph shows clearly", Frank continued, "that there is ample room for growth beyond what we've forecasted in our 'internal plan' for the next three years".

Ian looked at Jonathan and Val. "As I stated earlier", the 'big man' thundered, "we have some exciting challenges here at Growthstar. It's all now very clear to me. This puts the last piece in the puzzle. I would suggest a brief 'stand-up break' before we conclude our session today with a discussion of 'implementation issues and thoughts' ".

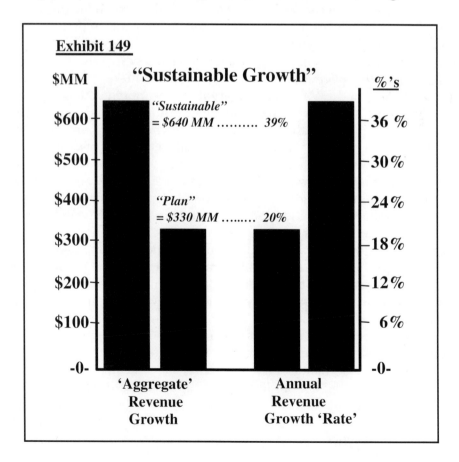

After mugs and cups had been refreshed, Jonathan stood up to address the group. He had told Ian that he wanted to lead this last portion of the meeting, since how the company began its implementation was a matter he felt compelled to coordinate. Ian had agreed with him. Jonathan began with ... "I feel we all are in agreement that we need to do 'something' to change the way we analyze our business and measure financial performance. I also feel that, in spite of your individual concerns about certain 'technical' elements of economic value analysis, you all believe the overall concept is sound. Moving toward an economic value framework would, therefore, seem to be in the best interests of everyone who works for this company, as well as the various corporate stakeholders – shareholders and others". All the heads nodded around the boardroom table – even Jack's, albeit ever so slightly.

"So far, we've concentrated on proving the viability of an economic-based approach, the key elements that impact a company such as ours, and an evaluation of our past, present and future performance under this type of framework. We've also highlighted metrics that support the overall concept. Now, it's time for us to begin making decisions on the specifics of how we are going to apply this approach here at Growthstar. We need to balance *simplicity with integrity*, which has been our goal since we started this process a few months ago. Jack Earningsly has offered a suggestion for implementation. Jack seems to be in favor of the 'Value Profit Margin' (*VPM*) approach to Economic Profit. Peter and Larry have reacted favorably to this suggestion. Under this approach, the corporate and business unit finance staffs perform all the necessary background analysis on cost of capital and invested capital requirements for our businesses. We then hold the operating heads responsible for a growth rate for revenue and *NOP* profit margin that generates an acceptable 'spread' above the *VPM*. This 'combination' should produce a 'warranted' market value added (*MVA*), market-to-book (*M/B*) ratio and market value index (*MVI*) that are in line with corporate objectives for shareholder value".

"I have to say that I think this framework makes a lot of sense for me personally", Peter interjected. "I'm getting more knowledgeable with every session, but I am by no means any type of an 'expert' on these financial concepts. This keeps me close to my 'comfort zone' and also gives me a realization that Dave will keep me 'honest' with regard to cost of capital and investment considerations".

"I would 'echo' those comments", Larry chimed in. "I can see the relationship to the 'bottom line' that I have managed by for so long now, and the institution of a 'growth factor' won't allow anyone to 'cut back' and be successful. I may be able to take on the 'full platter' of economic concepts over time, but taking it all on at the outset might be too much of a challenge. I don't want any new financial system to interfere with the time I have to spend on 'running the business'. My 'direct reports' can take on the *VPM* with some basic training, and Cathy can keep an eye on some of the more involved aspects, similar to what Dave can do in *Services*".

Ian had wanted to hear the comments from his two general managers before speaking. He had made his decision, but wanted to hear what Peter and Larry had to say. "I think we should 'start' with '*VPM* and growth' as our key financial metrics. Let's give this a year, and see how it works. We can then enhance our measurement system if we see fit to do so. As far as communicating to the investment community, we can say that we're adopting 'economic value' principles to help us better govern and manage the company. We can also tell them that we have constructed a system 'customized' for our needs and our capability to take on a change in how we evaluate our performance. I also believe we should prepare to fold the '*VPM spread*' and 'growth targets' into our incentive bonus program. Flo, I'm going to want to talk to you about this matter, and then get back to all of you. Jason, I believe you said you work with a compensation consulting firm. I want to get their name so that Flo can talk to them". Jason nodded toward Ian. "Finally, I want to thank everyone for their participation and for all the hard work that has gone into this effort so far. This new financial performance system should be very useful in helping us achieve and sustain increases in shareholder value".

Jack sighed deeply. He felt that while not victorious, he had at least avoided defeat.

11

Value driver programs: major internal investments

After the meeting, Jonathan and Jason walked back to Jonathan's office together. As they sat down in Jonathan's office, the CFO looked Jason 'straight in the eye'. "I don't know what else to say, except that the 'big man' is sold on implementing an 'economic value-based' framework. I guess that means you're accomplishing your task".

Jason responded with ... "It's gratifying to hear you say that. I'm convinced that a shareholder value 'experience' is taking place here. The remaining elements will be 'icing on the cake'. That doesn't mean, though, that they are not important. On the contrary, the remaining tasks are essential to solidify the accomplishments that have been made. Since most cakes taste better *with* the 'icing' than *without* it, we should meet as soon as possible to briefly discuss them one-by-one and then agree on an action plan".

Jonathan nodded his head and said "Let's do it tomorrow, after lunch. Earl and I have to meet with our insurance carrier regarding some business interruption insurance and other risk management issues in the morning. Now that Jack has 'come around' – at least to the 'Value Profit Margin' – I would like to have him and Earl involved in this meeting. What about Val?"

"In light of the fact that we're going to outline 'strategic' investments as part of our session, I would say she should also be a participant".

"Kay", Jonathan said, rising and walking toward the administrative assistant's area of his office suite, "would you please contact Val

Performa and invite her to a meeting in my office tomorrow after lunch – say, at 1:30".

Jason rose and as he left said, "I'm pleased with the way most of the people here have adapted to the 'economic' way of thinking about finance. See you tomorrow".

At 1:30 the following day, Earl, Jack and Val joined Jason and Jonathan in the CFO's office. Jonathan had a 'white board' in his office, and Jason had arrived a few minutes early to write down the remaining tasks. Thus, as everyone took their seats around Jonathan's worktable, they could read the following:

Remaining tasks:

- **Value Driver Programs ... Major Internal Investments**
- **Mergers & Acquisitions ... Major External Investments**
- **Capital Investments ... Planning, Evaluation and Control**
- **Financial Reporting & Communication ... Traditional / Modification / New**

Val started speaking. "I was quite impressed with the openness and receptiveness of Larry and Peter to initiating some change in our financial performance measurements".

Jack chimed in with "I felt that they would be receptive to the 'value profit margin and growth' metrics".

Earl retorted by saying "You almost sound as though *you* initiated the concept of *VPM*".

Jason remained silent. The positive response and the initiation of change were enough for him at this point.

Earl, however, was not through talking. "Just because we may emphasize the two metrics that you just noted, Jack, in terms of focusing the attention of the two GMs, we shouldn't forget the other financial 'drivers' – the comparison of revenue, *NOP* and *IC* growth and the invested capital intensity of the BUs, on a total and incremental basis".

"I agree with that, Earl", Jonathan added ... looking at Jack as he spoke ... "and we *will* incorporate these into our revised financial reporting system. I believe that now we want to talk about the remaining tasks necessary to complete our overall work in this area. Jason, would you please discuss the agenda for today's meeting".

"As you can see on the 'white board', there are four remaining tasks. Value Driver Programs can entail significant internal investments and represent key building blocks for business unit strategies or operational objectives".

"How are they different from strategies?" Val asked.

"That's a good question", Jason answered. "Let's start 'from the top' and review a key point from the Valuation Hierarchy segment of our meeting on Value-Based Analysis. Value 'analysis' should follow value 'creation'. To make this happen, value 'analysis' (i.e. the application of valuation metrics and techniques) should follow a logical hierarchy. This hierarchy works from the 'top down'. I'm sure that you all remember Exhibit 81, which concluded that meeting and for which Earl thought about charging an admission fee".

"How could we forget another 'Mr Funny' attempt to get attention", Jack snickered, although not in his customary 'nasty' tone.

As Jack was snickering, Jason passed out copies of excerpts from Exhibit 81 (Value-Based Analysis ... Valuation Hierarchy).

Jason continued his comments with ... "Shareholder value creation is a process of first setting a vision and strategy for a company and its major business units, and then establishing major business programs to execute the strategy. Within this framework, there is sometimes a 'fine line' between a strategy and a business program. What one person may call a *strategy*, another might call a *program* and vice versa. So, by evaluating *programs* we are often getting very close to

---

Exhibit 81

Value-Based Analysis ... Valuation Hierarchy

• Total Company/Operating Units and/or Strategic Business Units ... Analysis 'over time'	**Full Value Analysis**: - *EP * / MVA*** - Financial 'Drivers' ***
• Business Strategies/Plans	*MVA*** / Financial 'Drivers' ***
• Major Programs – Strategic – Operational	*MVA*** (linked to a strategy, over an appropriate life cycle) Financial 'Drivers' ***

• *Capital Projects*	*No Value Analysis* — *focus is on 'control' of appropriations and/or expenditures — part of a program*

Notes: * *EP* — **Economic Profit** (similar to Economic Value Added) ... focus on historical versus future patterns and progression
** *MVA* — **Market Value Added** (Consistent with Shareholder Value) ... focus on an appropriate future growth time horizon
*** **Financial 'Drivers'** — support (underlying) metrics for *EP* and *MVA*

strategies. In some cases, we actually get there. So, Val, the answer to your question is that sometimes there is *no* difference, while at other times a Value Driver Program may be a supporting element of a strategy. A good working definition of a Value Driver Program is that it's *an initiative, in support of an important strategic or operational goal, with value-creating potential*. Much of the time, Value Driver Programs are related to 'internal' growth or efficiency objectives, but they can also be acquisitions".

"There are two of these that I believe we identified for evaluation as part of this process", Val countered. "The first is the '*NG Euro*' program, a code name for 'Next Generation' products for the European market, which we believe can also be sold in Japan, if not all of the Asia–Pacific region of the world".

Earl nodded in agreement and said, "this is an example of an important element of a strategy to further grow the European market. '*NG Euro*' is a product line designed for some unique dynamics related to the new European economic integration and standards for industrial products. It's judged to be a critical component for successful execution of the European strategy within *Products*".

"That makes sense", Val responded. "The next one selected for evaluation is the 'Other Company' strategy for *Services* in the United States. There is a 'business model' for this strategy, which can be run through the economic profit and valuation process. Before you comment, Earl, let me guess that this a case of where a 'program' is essentially the same as a 'strategy'".

Earl nodded, as did Jason.

"What's the schedule for evaluating these two programs"? Jonathan asked.

"Immediately", Earl answered.

"Is there are any more that we need to say about Value Driver Programs before we move to our next topic?"

With no further questions or comments, Jason placed a 'check mark' next to the first topic. "Mergers and acquisitions are an extension of the 'internal' evaluations. Here, though, we do get into a situation where we often have to pay a 'premium for control' – which is why *acquisitions* can be more challenging than *internal* Value Driver Programs in terms of generating a high Return on (Incremental) Invested Capital (*Incremental ROIC*) and/or Market Value Index (*MVI*)". Jason looked over at Val, who nodded to indicate her understanding. "Val, do you want to talk briefly about the two 'targets' you have on your 'platter'?"

"Certainly", she replied. "The first is a division of an equipment leasing company that has been handling the vast majority of our customer financing programs. Ian has been interested in the 'leasing profit' that he believes exists on financing our products ... and potentially other industrial products".

"I would offer two comments on this proposal", Jason interjected. "First, you should evaluate the possibility of building this type of business internally. Second, I'd be careful as to 'how far' you stray from your own products and how much capital you commit to this type of 'financing' business. We can talk more about these issues when we evaluate a specific 'deal', but I offer these comments as 'food for thought' for the time being".

"Any other comments?" Val asked. With no further input from the group, she continued ... "The other 'deal' we're looking at involves acquiring a European *Services* company, which is viewed as the most logical way to enter this market for servicing industrial products – ours and those manufactured by other companies".

"We knew this one was coming", Earl stated. "With the outlook for the *Services* business unit here in the US, I know that Peter will be 'pushing' this one – to a potentially very receptive CEO, I might add ... again, based on what both Peter and Ian have just seen as the plan and valuation for *Services*".

Jonathan, who was sitting closest to the 'white board', placed a 'check mark' next to the second item and motioned to Jason to continue.

Jason responded with "While I don't have any specific changes to recommend at this time, I think it's safe to say that the area of capital appropriations needs some work and overhaul".

Earl jumped into the conversation by saying "One change, for sure, will be to elevate our 'value analysis' to the 'program' level".

Jonathan glanced at Jason and Earl, and simply nodded in agreement. He then said, "I don't think there is any argument with that comment, Earl. We need to put *all* of our heads together on this subject, however, since it has far-reaching implications throughout the organization".

"When are we going to make these changes?" Jack inquired.

"I think we should have something for next year's capital budget", Jonathan replied.

"Then", Jack responded, "we need to work on this topic as soon as possible, since we will be issuing budgeting guidelines within the next two weeks".

Earl then said, "I think we should insert a section in the guidelines on 'programs'. I'll ask Frank to 'draft' something on this, give it to Jason for his review, and then review it with this group by, say, the middle of next week". Everyone nodded in agreement, and Jonathan placed a 'check mark' next to the third item on the 'white board'.

Jonathan then spoke. "We will, obviously, make some modifications to our financial reporting and communication. Earl made a comment a few moments ago, which is relevant and Jack, Earl and I will take on this responsibility. I think we now have a framework and know what the key elements are. We need to 'codify' it and put it into our financial system. This will get done. Jack, Earl and I will meet next week to 'get the ball rolling' on this matter". As he was speaking, he 'checked' the last item on the board.

Jason then spoke again. "Val, we should assemble work teams in *Products* and *Services* to evaluate the two Value Driver Programs, with you and Frank representing *Corporate*".

"I agree", Val responded, "since these two programs are integral to the strategies for the business units, and we need to finalize these evaluations as soon as possible. What are your suggestions as to the composition of the work teams?"

"They should be 'cross-functional' to the extent possible", Jason answered. "In this way, we'll have a comprehensive set of inputs, and the people will get a good 'hands-on' exposure to important aspects of value-based financial performance".

"How many people, specifically, do you envision on these work teams?" Jonathan queried.

"I would say, four to five from each BU – including Dave or Cathy – plus Val, Frank and myself as an advisor", Jason replied. "We should have representation from Sales and Marketing, Manufacturing (for *Products*) and Operations (for *Services*), plus R&D".

"I'll call Larry, Peter, Dave and Cathy tomorrow, to get this rolling", Jonathan stated.

"Dave and Cathy are aware of this part of the process and will be prepared to coordinate the work teams for their BUs", Earl interjected. "We've discussed the concept of a Value Driver Program and the two specific initiatives with them. In fact each is aware of not only their own, but of the other's. Further, both Cathy and Dave have told me that they communicated this to Larry and Peter, so no one will be surprised".

"Well, in that case, the calls to Larry and Peter will be 'courtesy' in nature. I'll apprise them that we're going to get started on the Value Driver Program evaluations. The calls to Cathy and Dave will be to tell them what my expectations are and ask them what they may be looking for, in terms of direction and support, from *Corporate*".

Cathy was the coordinator and team leader for the '*NG Euro*' program and rose to begin speaking at the team's first meeting. As Jason had suggested, the heads of sales and marketing, manufacturing, and R&D were on the team, along with Val and Frank from *Corporate*.

Jason was an advisor to the group. "I keep getting 'thrown into' situations for which I thought I wasn't qualified, but I must admit that it is challenging and fun. As most of you know, the '*NG Euro*' program is critical to our growth and profitability in Europe and Asia during the next five years. The purpose of this work effort is to quantify what many of us in *Products* believe is a potentially valuable endeavor for the company. Jason, Frank and I will conduct an orientation session on the 'value-based performance' metrics for the operating people on the team in the next few days, when we can get the three of you back together again. This meeting will give you an overview of what we're going to measure, and the 'strategic' information developed so far on this program. To get started, I'm going to ask Val to review the '*NG Euro*' information developed as part of our planning work that was recently concluded. Then I'll ask Jason to discuss the type of work we're going to be doing over the next several weeks".

Val began by saying "As Cathy mentioned, much of the 'strategic' work for this program has been done, and you people have participated, through your efforts in developing the strategy for *Products*. Everyone here was a part of the business strategy development process. What we're going to do now is to put an important part of the 'Europe' strategy for *Products* through a valuation process. Since the '*NG Euro*' product line should represent over one-fourth of *Products'* International revenue in two to three years, we're going to evaluate this program. Many of the inputs have been developed, so we'll be reviewing and 'fine tuning' work that has already been done".

Val continued ... "Today, I'm going to concentrate on the overall market potential for this 'Next Generation' line of products, along with the '*NG Euro*' sales forecast and gross profit margin outlook. The first two exhibits are a tabular summary of the 'unit' and 'dollar' market analysis reflecting the 'size' of the market. As you all know, we conducted a considerable amount of research leading to the results summarized in the next two exhibits". Val turned on the personal computer and clicked on Exhibit 150.

"Exhibit 151 expresses market potential (for equipment and related sales) in 'dollars' ".

"Graphically, the overall market potential (in 'percent-to-total dollar' terms) by type of sale can be portrayed as follows", Val stated as she clicked on Exhibit 152.

"While I believe all of you know this material", Val continued, "let's do a 'quick review'. We divide our European market into three major geographic regions – the British Isles, the European Continent and Scandinavia. Within the Continent, we break down our sales potential within Germany and all other countries on the Continent. We have three types of sale for our products – new equipment

Exhibit 150

'NG EURO'
UNITS - EQPT. SALES
MARKET POTENTIAL - YEAR 3 (*)

(*) Year 3 judged to be 'representative'

# Units	G. B.	Cont. - Germ.	Cont. - Other	Scand.	Total
New Eqpt.	700	1,900	2,900	1,000	6,500
Retrofit	20	4,100	50	5,000	9,170
Conversion	2,000	270	490	—	2,760

Exhibit 151

'NG EURO'
MARKET POTENTIAL – YR. 3

$ Millions	G. B.	Cont. - Germ.	Cont. - Other	Scand.	Total
New Eqpt.	$13.9	$16.4	$47.0	$16.4	$93.7
Retrofit	0.4	9.6	0.2	16.4	26.6
Conversion	4.8	0.4	0.6	—	5.8
Total	$19.1	$26.4	$47.8	$32.8	$126.1

sales, retrofits of existing equipment and conversions of older to new models. Year 3 – the 'target' year for our 'growth plan' – should have a market potential of roughly $125 million in total sales. Our forecast for the 'Next Generation' is based on this potential and our company's estimated market share".

"Our sales forecast is based on a study of our historical share of this market, along with our current competitive positioning and our future positioning with the 'NG Euro' line of products. The next two charts – Exhibits 153 and 154 – reflect a summary of the market

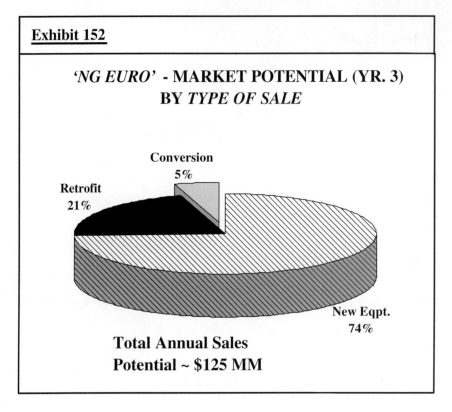

Exhibit 152

'NG EURO' - MARKET POTENTIAL (YR. 3)
BY TYPE OF SALE

Conversion
5%

Retrofit
21%

New Eqpt.
74%

Total Annual Sales
Potential ~ $125 MM

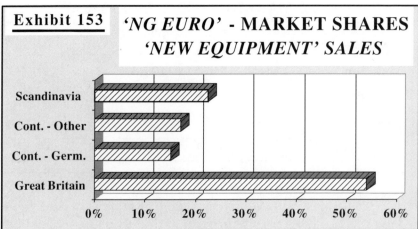

Exhibit 153   **'NG EURO' - MARKET SHARES**
'NEW EQUIPMENT' SALES

Scandinavia

Cont. - Other

Cont. - Germ.

Great Britain

0%   10%   20%   30%   40%   50%   60%

share analysis for the two types of sale where 'share' is the key sales forecasting technique. Conversions are forecasted using a different approach".

"The above analysis/estimates, along with our outlook for Conversions, results in the sales forecast for the 'plan' period and also the two-year 'post plan' period. This sales forecast is shown graphically

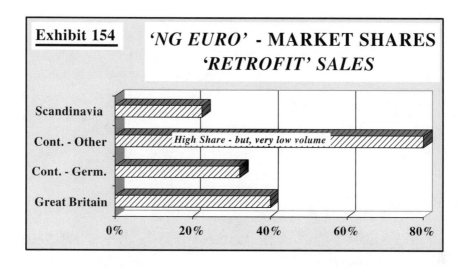

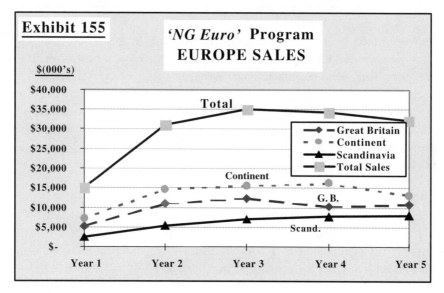

in Exhibit 155. As you can see, we expect to achieve 'peak' sales in the $35 million range in year 3".

"This chart (Exhibit 155) shows the European sales forecast for *Products* in 'thousands' of dollars. Overall, in Europe, we're estimating a market share in the range of 25-30% for this 'Next Generation' line of products. You can calculate this market share – which actually is 28% – by comparing our sales forecast of $35 million in year 3 to the overall market size of $126 million".

"I'm going to show one chart summarizing our outlook for gross margin, and then I'll defer to Cathy, Frank and Jason for the remainder of the financial discussion – either today or at a subsequent meeting.

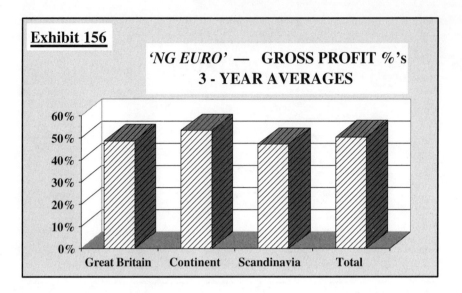

As was mentioned at the last meeting with Ian and the operating officers, we expect a lower cost of sales, mainly due to new materials in the 'NG Euro' line. This translates into a higher gross margin than we have ever experienced in *Products*, which is illustrated in the following chart (Exhibit 156). We have some pricing differences in the three geographic regions, which are also reflected in the gross margin estimates. These gross margins are the 'averages' for the 3-year 'plan' period. The sales, cost of goods sold and gross margin estimates set the stage for the rest of the financial outlook for this program".

Val then turned to Cathy and said "I've gone about as far with this program as I'm capable of . . . now, I'll place it in your good hands".

The operating managers were familiar with the market information and had a grasp of the rationale underlying the cost of goods sold and gross profit margin outlook, so there were no questions.

Cathy then stood up and said . . . "We have discussed this program in the context of our strategy for Europe and the overall business. What we need to do is to meet with the operating people in a separate session, introduce you to the key elements of economic profit and its surrogate measures, and then apply them to this program".

There was nothing additional to discuss, so the group adjourned, with an agreement that they would meet within the next three days to hear the overview on the value-based performance approach and begin to finalize a financial forecast for the 'NG Euro' program, based on analysis done to-date and any new developments for this market.

As Cathy had indicated, she arranged an orientation session with the operating people within *Products*. Jason, Frank and Cathy each took a role in providing an overview of value-based performance, tailored to the needs and understanding of the three functional heads within this BU.

A completion date and final review session was then set for four weeks from the date of the orientation session. During this period, the group met to 'fine tune' the market data, delve into the various financial 'drivers' and develop a complete financial outlook and valuation for the '*NG Euro*' program. Cathy grabbed hold of this effort. With guidance from Jason and analytic support from Frank, she ran the meetings and took responsibility for the outcomes.

Four weeks later, the 'team' assembled in the large conference room in the *Products* wing of Growthstar's headquarters to present their findings and conclusions to Larry and Jonathan. Earl and Jack were also invited to attend, along with Val, Frank and Jason. Cathy was starting to get much more comfortable coordinating work sessions and meetings, and was proving to be effective in this new role. Reports of her performance were starting to circulate around the company. After everyone was seated, she began speaking.

"We've conducted a comprehensive evaluation of our '*NG Euro*' program and will today present the results of our team's efforts over the past several weeks. Jason and Frank have graciously offered to help me articulate the key financial elements and shareholder value impact of this important building block to our global strategy".

"Larry, I know that you're familiar with the market and sales information that Val Performa presented at our first meeting. Jonathan, I believe you have seen the material and have spoken to Val about it". Both Larry and Jonathan nodded, indicating that there was no need to again review this information.

"With the 'strategic' aspects covered, I would like to now present our financial outlook for this program, along with its contribution to the company's shareholder value. The first element (Exhibit 157) is the profit and loss (P&L) outlook for the program".

"We've analyzed our volume, pricing, cost of goods and expense structure in detail. In fact, programs such as '*NG Euro*' are the 'building blocks' of our strategy for the business. Val has reviewed the sales and gross profit elements. Our selling, marketing and service (SMS) expenses should be in the 25% (percent-to-revenue) range for the first two years, then decrease to about 22.5% in years 3 and 4 and to 20% by year 5, when the program is winding down. There is a big promotional effort for about two years, which can be leveraged by year 3 – the 'peak' year for sales and profitability – and into year 4, before product sales start to 'tail off' in the fifth year. G&A and R&D are in line with the ratios for the overall business unit. In fact, programs such as this one are the 'drivers' for overall R&D spending.

Exhibit 157

	Growthstar - *Products* BU			*'NG Euro'*	
	Market - *Europe*			Region - *All*	

Profit & Loss Summary

($000's Omitted)	F U T U R E		Y E A R S		
	Year 1	Year 2	Year 3	Year 4	Year 5
P&L Statement					
Net Sales					
Great Britain	$5,280	$11,048	$12,310	$10,284	$10,778
Continent	7,179	14,758	15,558	16,225	13,196
Scandinavia	2,574	5,324	7,084	7,684	8,084
Net Sales	$15,033	$31,130	$34,952	$34,193	$32,058
Cost of Goods Sold (*)					
F & D %					
10% Great Britain	$2,542	$5,409	$6,199	$5,555	$5,881
10% Continent	3,195	6,650	7,170	7,398	6,890
10% Scandinavia	1,358	2,692	3,632	4,176	4,416
Total COGS	$7,095	$14,751	$17,001	$17,129	$17,187
(*) COGS includes Freight & Duty (F&D)					
Gross Profit					
Great Britain	$2,738	$5,639	$6,111	$4,729	$4,897
Continent	3,984	8,108	8,388	8,827	6,306
Scandinavia	1,216	2,632	3,452	3,508	3,668
Total Gross Profit	$7,937	$16,379	$17,950	$17,064	$14,871
Operating Expenses					
25% 20% Selling/Mktg./Service	$3,758	$7,782	$8,301	$7,979	$6,412
10% 10% General & Admin.	1,503	3,113	3,495	3,419	3,206
7% 6% Research & Development	1,052	2,179	2,447	2,223	1,923
Total OPEX	$6,314	$13,075	$14,243	$13,621	$11,541
Operating Income (EBIT)	$1,623	$3,304	$3,707	$3,444	$3,330
9% Interest – Oper. Leases	28	59	59	59	59
EBIT/A	$1,651	$3,364	$3,767	$3,503	$3,389
32.0% Taxes	528	1,076	1,205	1,121	1,085
Net Operating Profit (NOP)	$1,123	$2,287	$2,562	$2,382	$2,305

We think the profit outlook is good, and Exhibit 158 provides the key profit ratios – on a percent-to-revenue basis".

"The gross profit margins are just about the highest we've ever seen in *Products*, due to the new materials that, by now, we've bored you with. But, as you can see, they are significant. They also perform well operationally and entail lower costs".

Cathy continued by stating "We have also taken a 'hard look' at the capital investments (working and fixed) that are necessary to execute this program, and can illustrate them in Exhibits 159 and 160. Exhibit 159 provides a summary of the outlook for working capital investments, and Exhibit 160 does the same for fixed capital. Please note that, similar to Exhibit 157, these schedules are in *thousands* of US dollars".

Exhibit 158			*Products 'NG Euro'*			
Ratios		**Year 1**	**Year 2**	**Year 3**	**Year 4**	**Year 5**
Gross Profit %						
	Great Britain	*51.9%*	*51.0%*	*49.6%*	*46.0%*	*45.4%*
	Continent	*55.5%*	*54.9%*	*53.9%*	*54.4%*	*47.8%*
	Scandinavia	*47.2%*	*49.4%*	*48.7%*	*45.7%*	*45.4%*
	Total Gross Profit %	*52.8%*	*52.6%*	*51.4%*	*49.9%*	*46.4%*
EBIT/A % -	***Total Program***	*11.0%*	*10.8%*	*10.8%*	*10.2%*	*10.6%*
NOP % -	***Total Program***	*7.5%*	*7.3%*	*7.3%*	*7.0%*	*7.2%*

Exhibit 159 **Growthstar Inc. - *Products 'NG Euro'***

Market - *Europe* **Region- *All***

INVESTED CAPITAL

($000's Omitted ... except "per unit" or "ratios")		"BASE"	FUTURE YEARS Year 1	Year 2	Year 3	Year 4	Year 5
REFERENCE DATA							
Net Sales			$15,033	$31,130	$34,952	$34,193	$32,058
COGS (excl. F & D)			$6,450	$13,410	$15,456	$15,572	$15,625
WORKING CAPITAL							
Accounts Receivable							
Est. A/R "DSO"		42	42	42	42	42	42
"DSO" as % to Annual Revenue ... #DSO / 360		12%	12%	12%	12%	12%	12%
A/R estimate			$1,754	$3,632	$4,078	$3,989	$3,740
Inventory - Fin. Goods							
est. Months of Supply	*Avg. ICI [Inven./ Sales] $0.11*	3	3	3	3	3	3
"MOS" as % to Annual COGS ... #MOS / 12		25%	25%	25%	25%	25%	25%
Inventory estimate			$1,613	$3,352	$3,864	$3,893	$3,906
Operating Cash — @							
% of Revenue	*2%*		$301	$623	$699	$684	$641
Other Working Capital							
(*) Payables	*-10%*		$(161)	$(335)	$(386)	$(389)	$(391)
Total "Other" W/C			$(161)	$(335)	$(386)	$(389)	$(391)
(*) Payables as % of Inventory							
Net Working Capital			$3,506	$7,272	**$8,254**	$8,177	$7,897
"ICI" ... NWC			*$0.23*	*$0.23*	***$0.24***	*$0.24*	*$0.25*

Jonathan nodded in approval at Cathy as she was clicking on to Exhibit 159, and then looked at Larry and the two exchanged looks indicating satisfaction with Cathy's statement about taking a 'hard look' at capital investments.

Cathy was 'on a roll' now and starting to enjoy the situation. "As we presented during our strategy review session, our average collection period for accounts receivable is about forty days overall. Europe tends to run a bit more than the United States and, thus, is in the range of 42 days – resulting in an *ICI* of approximately $0.12 for each new revenue dollar. We expect a three-month supply of inventory on average. This translates into an inventory turnover of 4.0 on a COGS basis and about 9.0 on a net sales basis, producing an *ICI* of

$0.11. Adding in operating cash at 2% of sales and subtracting 10% of inventory for accounts payable results in an *ICI* for net working capital in the $0.23 to $0.25 range".

"Let's now take a look at Exhibit 160, to get a summary of the outlook for fixed capital".

"We have just started the building renovations to our factory in Europe, in order to accommodate the '*NG Euro*' and will complete them before the middle of next year – at a cost of $2 million. Even though about one-third of this capital will be expended by the end of this fiscal year, we've put it all in year 1 for purposes of analysis". Cathy paused and looked around the room for a reaction. With Jonathan nodding his head in approval, she continued. "We'll spend $5.5 million in total for machinery, equipment and tooling, plus an additional $150,000 for office equipment. A mainframe computer system will be leased in two stages for nearly $700,000 in total capitalized value. The impact of all of these capital investments is over $8 million of 'gross' fixed capital investment and about $6.5 million 'net of depreciation' by year 3. Adding net working and fixed capital, the 'peak' level of invested capital approaches $15 million in year 3 – the 'target' year for sales and profit performance. The fixed capital *ICI* for this program is significantly higher than for the *Products* business overall, due mostly to the building expansion".

Larry then commented ... "This enhancement to our European factory will, however, set us up for continued growth beyond this program. We have been experiencing space constraints for the past two years and must do something. With US manufacturing now

($000's) **Exhibit 160**		Growthstar Inc. - *Products 'NG Euro'*					
Except "ICI" **Market - *Europe***				**Region - *All***			
FIXED CAPITAL		F U T U R E		Y E A R S			
Total	**Gross Investment (new)**	**"BASE"**	**Year 1**	**Year 2**	**Year 3**	**Year 4**	**Year 5**
$2,000	Building		$2,000	$ -	$ -	$ -	$ -
4,500	Machinery & Equipment		2,000	1,500	1,000	-	-
1,000	Tooling		250	500	250	-	-
150	Office Equipment, etc.		50	50	50	-	-
661	*1%* Operating Leases		311	350	-	-	-
$8311	**Sub-total**	$ -	$4,611	$2,400	$1,300	$ -	$ -
	"ICI"		$0.31	$0.08	$0.04	$ -	$ -
# Yrs.	***Accum. Depreciation***						
20	*Building*	$ -	*$100*	*$200*	*$300*	*$400*	*$500*
8	*Machinery & Equipment*	-	*250*	*688*	*1,250*	*1,813*	*2,375*
8	*Tooling*	-	*31*	*125*	*250*	*375*	*500*
4	*Office Equipment, etc.*	-	*13*	*38*	*75*	*113*	*150*
	Operating Leases						
	Sub-total	*$ -*	*$394*	*$1,050*	*$1,875*	*$2,700*	*$3,525*
	Net Fixed Capital	$ -	$4,218	$5,961	**$6,436**	$5,611	$4,786
	"ICI" ... NFC		*$0.28*	*$0.19*	*$0.18*	*$0.16*	*$0.15*
	INVESTED CAPITAL (IC)	$ -	$7,723	$13,232	**$14,690**	$13,788	$12,683
	"I" = Change from Prior Year		*$7,723*	*$5,509*	*$1,458*	*$(903)*	*$(1,105)*

nearing its capacity, we have to expand our European plant to handle the growth we are forecasting".

Jonathan, Val, Jack, Earl and Frank were aware of all the rationale behind the European plant expansion, so they nodded in understanding toward Larry. Larry then motioned toward Cathy to continue.

Cathy looked over at Jason and said, "I'll get this next topic started, but may ask Jason to help me finish it". Jason smiled and nodded to Cathy as she clicked on Exhibit 161.

"This exhibit (161) reflects the Economic Profit (*EP*) generated by 'NG Euro', along with the three key financial 'drivers' – comparative growth rates, *ICI* and *VPM*. *EP* follows a pattern for this program, rising from roughly $275,000 in year 1 to a 'peak' of nearly $950,000 in year 3, before starting to decline in year 4 and 5. The growth rates for net sales and *NOP* have been calculated using a three-year time horizon, with year 1 as the 'base' and year 4 as the 'final' year. After year 4, the program starts to 'wind down'. Sales and profit (*NOP*) are expected to increase at fairly comparable rates – averaging close to 30% for the 3-year period". Cathy then motioned to Jason and said … "I'm going to ask our advisor to comment on the invested capital aspects of this program".

Exhibit 161		**Growthstar Inc.** - *Products 'NG Euro'*				
Market - *Europe*				**Region** - *All*		
'EP' ... 'Drivers'						
($000's Omitted ... except		**F U T U R E**		**Y E A R S**		
"per unit" or "ratios")	**"BASE"**	**Year 1**	**Year 2**	**Year 3**	**Year 4**	**Year 5**
ECONOMIC PROFIT						
Net Operating Profit		$1,123	$2,287	$2,562	$2,382	$2,305
11% Capital Charge (CCAP)		(850)	(1,456)	(1,616)	(1,517)	(1,395)
Economic Profit (EP)	$ -	$273	$832	$946	$865	$910
FINANCIAL 'DRIVERS'	**3-Year**					
GROWTH RATES — %'s	**CGR(*)**					
Net Sales	31.5%	----	107.1%	12.3%	–2.2%	–6.2%
NOP	28.5%	----	103.7%	12.0%	–7.0%	–3.2%
Invested Capital	N/A	----	71.3%	11.0%	–6.1%	–8.0%
(*) Year 1 - 4 ... Sales/profit decline in year 5						
INVESTED CAPITAL INTENSITY	**AVG.**					
"ICI"	**$0.42**	$0.51	$0.43	$0.42	$0.40	$0.40
VALUE PROFIT MARGIN (NOP)	**AVG.**					
Actual Margin	**7.3%**	7.5%	7.3%	7.3%	7.0%	7.2%
Value Margin (VPM)	**4.7%**	5.7%	4.7%	4.6%	4.4%	4.4%
"Spread"	**2.5%**	1.8%	2.7%	2.7%	2.5%	2.8%

Jason responded with "The growth rate for invested capital (*IC*) is not as relevant as it normally is, due to the heavy capital expenditures in the first two years. We've focused, therefore, on invested capital intensity (*ICI*) for the total program and its relationship to the *ICI* for the overall business, as forecasted in the 'growth plan'. The average *ICI* for '*NG Euro*' is expected to be around $0.42 (for each dollar of sales) – slightly higher than the $0.40 *ICI* estimated for the overall *Products* business over the next five years. This higher *ICI* will cause the value profit margin to be in the 4.7% range (versus 4.4% for the *Products* BU in total). Offsetting this, the *NOP* margin is expected to be 0.6% ('six-tenths of a percentage point') higher than that for the overall BU (7.3% versus 6.7%) due mainly to lower material costs and their proportion of the cost structure for this program. The net result is a *VPM* 'spread' of about 2.5%, slightly higher than the 2.3% 'spread' in the outlook for *Products*. These differences are relatively minor, and I think it's fair to say that this program does not represent a major departure from the overall business".

"We've moved along fairly quickly", Jonathan interjected, "so let me ask you to pause for a moment. We have a business program with annual revenue and profit potential of $35 million and $2.6 million, respectively, referring back to Exhibit 157. We'll invest approximately $16.5 million by year 3, almost evenly split between net working capital and gross fixed capital (about $8.3 million each)".

Earl then jumped in with … "This is a good example of economically justifying major 'programs' and committing to the total investment necessary to initiate and execute the 'program'. Breaking apart the aggregate investment (over the next three years) would be meaningless, in terms of 'evaluating' shareholder value creation, since all the individual projects need to work together for the program to be successful".

Jack reacted, but with an expression of inquisitiveness, not a scowl. "What about capital expenditure control?"

Jason answered … "Spending control should be at a level appropriate for the company and its systems – typically at the 'project' level. Evaluation, as Earl has noted, should be done at a 'total program' level".

For Jonathan, the point came through loud and clear, especially as he had to acknowledge Cathy's stare. "I now know, Cathy, that you've been burdened with far too many disjointed analyses of capital expenditures. As of right now, this will change. We've inserted a section in the capital budgeting guidelines (that I will give you all a copy of) elevating our analysis to the 'major program' level, and I will personally take this message to the appropriate people in the company. Jack and Larry, you're the first two key people".

"Thanks", Cathy said softly. "You've lifted a huge burden from me".

Jack knew this was coming and simply nodded toward Jonathan, indicating his understanding and acceptance of the new rule of analysis.

Larry responded with ... "I must admit that I never understood why we evaluated almost every capital project over a certain dollar limit. I must also admit to some 'project splitting' to avoid doing the analysis. I just assumed that this was part of the way things were done in Corporate Finance". As Larry spoke, he looked over at Jack, who simply shrugged his shoulders. "I think this type of analysis that I'm seeing here today makes a lot of sense, since it breaks the business down into meaningful and manageable components. I can look around the room to the people in manufacturing, marketing and R&D and ask some intelligent questions about various aspects of this program, along with other initiatives that we need to execute over the planning horizon. So, Jonathan, you have my support".

"I appreciate these comments, Larry", Jonathan replied. "Let me continue with my 'summary' of the '*NG Euro*' strategic program. We have an average *ICI* of $0.42 – slightly higher than our history and the outlook in the *Products* growth plan – and a 'spread' of 2.5 percentage points over the *VPM*, essentially in line with *VPM* 'spread' forecasted in the growth plan".

"That is a concise and accurate summary", Cathy replied.

"So now", Jonathan continued, "I guess we need to see what this program is worth".

"Right again", Cathy responded, looking at Jason.

Jason, taking the cue, rose and said "We've summarized the valuation in Exhibit 162. We've evaluated this program using the *EP* and *VPM* approaches, since we calculated these metrics as part of the program analysis". Jason clicked on Exhibit 162.

"The *MVA* for '*NG Euro*' is approximately $9.5 million, equivalent to 22% of the overall 'strategy' value for *Products* – using the 5-year 'profitable growth' time horizon and then liquidating the (net) invested capital in year 6. This is an alternative residual value approach to the 'perpetuity' concept (employed in the 'strategy' valuations) of capitalizing the final-year *NOP*, and can be used for 'programs' that end after a discrete time period. The Market Value Index (*MVI*) is $0.85 – on a 'discounted' basis".

"Based on this analysis, this 'strategic' program should be funded and executed", Larry exclaimed.

"I would agree", Jonathan replied. "Thanks to all of you who participated in this effort. Larry, you and I need to summarize this program and recommend its approval to Ian. Earl, we need to prepare a written summary for our next Finance Committee and Board of

Exhibit 162		Growthstar Inc. - *Products 'NG Euro'*				
Market - *Europe*				**Region -** *All*		

VALUATION — Market Value Added ("MVA") *

($000's)

			F U T U R E Y E A R S			
EP Approach		**Year 1**	**Year 2**	**Year 3**	**Year 4**	**Year 5**
Annual EP's (from Exh. 161)		$273	$832	$946	$865	$910
+ Residual - *IC* Liquidation	$12,683					

	NPV	
MVA = Discounted EP's (000)	**$9,503**	* *MVA is the increase in Total Market Value*

	Equivalent to	**22%**	*of Products 'strategy' value re: 5-year growth*
			[Note: Products 'strategy' value is $44 million]

VPM Approach

NOP "Spread"		1.8%	2.7%	2.7%	2.5%	2.8%
Annual EP = "Spread" times Net Sales		$273	$832	$946	$865	$910

	NPV	
MVA = Discounted EP's (000)	**$9,503**	* *MVA is the increase in Total Market Value*

($000's Omitted ... except ratio)

MVI = *MVA* as a ratio to *NPV* of *IC* = $9,503 divided by $11,245   *equals $0.85*

Directors meetings. This can be a 'test case' for 'program' evaluation and approval". Jonathan rose as he concluded his remarks and exchanged pleasantries with everyone as he left the room.

During the time that the '*NG Euro*' program was being evaluated, a separate team in the *Services* business unit – with Dave Dollarby serving as the coordinator – was embarked on a similar effort for the 'Other Company' strategy (code-named '*OCS*'). They had set a time frame for their work to coincide with '*NG Euro*'. As such, this team was now in the process of concluding its work and a meeting was scheduled for the following week.

As the '*OCS*' team, along with Peter Uppcomer, Jonathan, Jason and the corporate staff that had been part of the '*NG Euro*' review session assembled in the *Services* conference room, Jonathan rose to begin the meeting. "Last week, we had our first glimpse of how we will be developing and evaluating Value Driver Programs. I am looking forward to the same type of perspective for the '*OCS*' initiative within *Services*".

Peter, the General Manager of *Services*, had been energized by the 'value contribution' of the strategy for *Services*. Recognizing the reaction of Ian to the strategy valuation and the emphasis that Jonathan was placing on value-based performance, Peter became actively involved in the '*OCS*' Value Driver Program. He attended and participated in most of the work sessions, along with his heads of operations, marketing/sales and R&D. He had also spent time privately with Dave to 'get up to speed' on the essentials of the value-based performance metrics. For a person with a sales, marketing and operations back-ground and a general feeling of disdain for corporate finance, this was quite an undertaking. But, seeing the 'handwriting on the wall', he knew that he had to have at least a working knowledge of the basic elements of value-based performance. As he spent more time with Dave – who, himself, had progressed rapidly in his knowledge and understanding of the concepts – Peter began feeling that the 'economic' framework was fairly straightforward and made intuitive sense. "*Getting to a 'cash-based' return (on investment) is a logical way to look at any business*", he concluded to himself. He had actually called Jonathan a few weeks ago, after the strategy review session, to thank him for the 'new exposure', an action he never thought he would consider. "*Cash is King*", he reconciled to himself, "*and the closer we can come to judging performance in 'economic' terms, the better off everyone would be. Besides*", he finally decided, "*I have never understood accounting ... and the financial 'drivers' supporting the 'EP' metric are easier to comprehend than most of the accounting-driven measures I've been exposed to and have usually ignored*".

Therefore, after Jonathan had made his opening remark, Peter said ... "The past couple of months have been enlightening beyond anything I have ever experienced in the financial arena. For the first time in my career, I can appreciate the fact that Corporate Finance is more than a 'numbers exercise' and actually has a purpose. As I have now seen financial analysis integrated with business strategy, the implications are truly powerful. For most of my career, the term 'shareholder value' has been one to give 'lip service' to, but not much else. The effort we've embarked upon here at Growthstar has been an 'eye opener' in revealing how I, along with my co-workers, can focus our efforts in a way that is in the best interest of our shareholders. Dave Dollarby and I are taking this 'value-based' performance initia-tive seriously, and Dave will lead us through a presentation of how our *Other Company Strategy* ('*OCS*') contributes to corporate value. Dave, it's your show".

As Peter was concluding his remarks, Jason, Jonathan, Val and Earl looked at each other and smiled. Jack noticed the gesture and sat up abruptly in his chair, indicating a sense of attentiveness. "*I know where this is going*", he muttered to himself.

Dave, like Cathy Casher, was getting more comfortable with his expanded role as a leader and coordinator of 'value driver' initiatives within *Services*. His exposure to Ian and the corporate officers had also given him more confidence in speaking to groups of people. With this new sense of composure, and a feeling of enthusiasm about the *Services* business, he rose and began speaking ... "Our strategy for *Services* is, essentially, the combined impact of the two business strategies – for the Growthstar element (our mainstay) and the emerging 'Other (Company) Products' segment. The 'Other (Company) Products' segment is expected to grow rapidly and comprise a larger percentage of our revenue by the end or year 3 (the 'target' year for our plan period). Currently, this segment represents approximately 17% of revenue – $25 million put of a total $150 million forecasted for this (current) year. By year 3, we expect the 'Other Products' segment to produce over $100 million in revenue – growing at 60% annually – which equates to just over 30% of our anticipated $330 million in *Services* revenue".

"As we have come to realize over the past few months, there is more to life than just revenue", Dave continued. "However, we do need to start there, so let's look at our 'top line' outlook by major customer, using Exhibit 163".

"After year 3", Dave continued, "the revenue growth rate is expected to decline to approximately 33% per year for the ensuing four years. Thus, by year 7, '*Other*' revenue should exceed $300 million and, if you recall our strategic outlook for *Services* overall revenue, comprise 40% of *Services* $800 million total revenue (by year 7). That's a solid level of annual growth and makes this segment a significant contributor to our business".

Peter, genuinely enthused about the prospects for '*OCS*', interjected ... "If you calculate the growth rate that's incorporated into this seven-year outlook, it's 44%". All the heads snapped around the table. Usually Peter relied on Dave to offer anything of a numeric nature, so there was some element of surprise for most of the people in the room. Peter winked at Jonathan as he made his comment.

Dave picked up the dialogue by saying ... "As I mentioned, there's more to life than revenue growth, so let's take a look at the costs and expenses and the resultant net operating profit outlook for '*OCS*' – as reflected in Exhibit 164".

Exhibit 163 *[$ Millions except Per Share & Capital Intensity Amounts]*	**GROWTHSTAR INC.** '*OCS*' Financials '*Strategy*': 3-Year Plan + 4 Additional Years							
SERVICES Financials	*'Base'*	*Yr. 1*	*Yr. 2*	*Yr. 3*	*Yr. 4*	*Yr. 5*	*Yr. 6*	*Yr. 7*
Service Revenue:								
Company 'X'	$10	$15	$23	$34	$44	$57	$74	$96
Company 'Y'	9	13	20	30	38	50	65	84
Company 'Z'	6	9	14	21	27	36	46	60
New Customers (5 to 6)	-	3	8	18	27	41	57	79
'*OCS*' Total	$25	$40	$64	$102	$137	$183	$242	$320
'*OCS*' Growth ($)	----	$15	$24	$38	$34	$46	$59	$78
'*OCS*' Growth Rate (%)	----	60%	60%	60%	34%	34%	32%	32%

Exhibit 164 **GROWTHSTAR INC.**								
[$ Millions except Per Share & Capital Intensity Amounts] **Other Co. Strategy ('OCS') Financials** *'Business Strategy': 3-Year Plan + 4 Additional Years*								
SERVICES Financials	*Avg. Ratio*	*Yr. 1*	*Yr. 2*	*Yr. 3*	*Yr. 4*	*Yr. 5*	*Yr. 6*	*Yr. 7*
Operating Costs/Expenses:								
Cost of Goods Sold (COGS)	32%	$13	$20	$33	$44	$59	$77	$103
Selling/Mktg./Service (SMS)	45%	18	29	46	62	82	109	144
General & Admin. (G&A)	10%	4	6	10	14	18	24	32
Research & Devel. (R&D)	5%	2	3	5	7	9	12	16
Total Oper. Costs/Expenses	**92%**	**37**	**59**	**94**	**126**	**168**	**223**	**295**
Operating Income	8%	3	5	8	11	15	20	26
Interest — Operating Leases	1%	1	1	1	1	2	2	3
EBITA	9%	4	6	9	12	17	22	29
"Effective" Tax Rate	36%	36%	36%	36%	36%	36%	36%	36%
Tax on EBITA	—	1	2	3	4	6	8	10
Net Operating Profit (NOP)	—	**$2**	**$4**	**$6**	**$8**	**$11**	**$14**	**$19**

"In terms of Operating Costs and Expenses for '*OCS*', COGS, G&A, and R&D should follow the pattern of our overall *Services* business, with ratios-to-revenue of 32%, 10%, and 5%, respectively. We expect to spend significantly more for SMS in order to penetrate this market, with the result that SMS expenses should average 45% as a ratio-to-revenue. This is higher than the 42% ratio forecasted for *Services* overall and, by deduction, significantly higher than the *Growthstar* segment's SMS ratio, which will benefit from the spending and infrastructure build-up during the past two years. Even though we have held the G&A ratio at 10% (of revenue) we hope to experience some G&A efficiencies with less administrative follow-up and lower transaction costs, due to not having spare parts inventories to purchase, warehouse and deliver to customer locations. We'll explain this when we get to the discussion on working capital".

"The NOP results are highlighted at the bottom of Exhibit 164 and in Exhibit 165".

"As you can see in Exhibit 165, the average profit (*NOP*) margin for '*OCS*' will be nearly two (2) percentage points – 5.9% versus 7.6% – lower than the margin for the overall *Services* strategy. Again by deduction, the *NOP* margin for '*OCS*' will be significantly lower than the margin for the *Growthstar* segment's strategy".

Exhibit 165 **GROWTHSTAR INC.**								
[$ Millions except Per Share & Capital Intensity Amounts] **Other Co. Strategy ('OCS') Financials** *'Business Strategy': 3-Year Plan + 4 Additional Years*								
SERVICES Financials	*7 Years*	*Yr. 1*	*Yr. 2*	*Yr. 3*	*Yr. 4*	*Yr. 5*	*Yr. 6*	*Yr. 7*
Net Operating Profit (NOP)								
Amount ($) - "rounded"	**$64**	$2	$4	$6	$8	$11	$14	$19
Ratio-to-Revenue (%)	**5.9%**	6.1%	6.0%	5.9%	5.9%	5.9%	5.8%	5.8%
Annual Growth Rate (%)	**39%**	—	57%	58%	33%	33%	32%	32%

Jonathan, who had been quiet so far, then said ... "I didn't realize that there was such a margin disparity between the two strategies of *Services* – *'OCS'* versus *Growthstar*. This is enlightening, but now I'm concerned about the 'value creation' implications".

"That's a legitimate comment, Jonathan", Dave responded. "Shortly, we'll take a look at the other part of the 'value equation' – the invested capital requirements for *'OCS'*".

"OK", Jonathan replied, "I'll hold off for now".

Peter, getting a taste of how the 'value equation' worked – at least conceptually – then stated ... "I think you'll be pleased with the 'invested capital' dynamics for *'OCS'*". Again, heads snapped ... *"Peter talking about the 'balance sheet' ... things really are changing"*, thought Earl ... and some of the others in the room.

Dave picked up quickly on the comment from his boss and the reaction of the group. "We'll work our way through the working and fixed capital investments anticipated for *'OCS'* and then conclude with the 'shareholder value' implications. Let's start with Exhibit 166 – Invested Capital".

"In terms of working capital, *'OCS'* and the *Growthstar* segment have the same requirements for operating cash and accounts receivable – *ICI's* of $0.02 and $0.12, respectively. As I mentioned in our strategy review session a month ago, we have negotiated for the 'other' manufacturing companies to carry spare parts inventory and ship directly to customers. The new computerized inventory control

Exhibit 166				**GROWTHSTAR INC.**				
[$ Millions except Per Share & Capital Intensity Amounts]				**Other Co. Strategy ('OCS') Financials** *'Business Strategy': 3-Year Plan + 4 Additional Years*				
'SERVICES' Financials	*Avg.*	*Yr. 1*	*Yr. 2*	*Yr. 3*	*Yr. 4*	*Yr. 5*	*Yr. 6*	*Yr. 7*
Invested Capital	*'ICI'*							
Working Capital								
Operating Cash	$0.02	$0.3	$0.5	$0.8	$0.7	$0.9	$1.2	$1.6
Accounts Receivable	0.12	1.8	2.8	4.5	4.0	5.4	6.9	9.1
Inventory (*)	0.01	0.2	0.2	0.4	0.3	0.5	0.6	0.8
Other	-			-		-	-	-
Net Working Capital	**$0.15**	**$2.2**	**$ 3.5**	**$5.6**	**$5.0**	**$6.8**	**$8.7**	**$11.5**
Fixed Capital								
Fixed Assets (**)	$0.06	$0.8	$1.3	$2.1	$1.9	$2.6	$3.3	$4.4
Operating Leases (**)	0.03	0.5	0.8	1.3	1.1	1.5	2.0	2.6
Goodwill/Other	-		-	-	-	-	-	-
Net Fixed Capital	**$0.09**	**$1.3**	**$2.1**	**$3.4**	**$3.1**	**$4.1**	**$ 5.3**	**$7.0**
Net New Investment	**$0.24**	**$3.5**	**$5.7**	**$9.0**	**$8.1**	**$10.9**	**$13.9**	**$18.5**
	$MM's							**$MM's**
Invested Capital - 3 Years =	**$18**			**Invested Capital ... 7-Year Total =**				**$70**

(*) Inventory – Equipment Vendors will ship 'directly' to *Services* customers.

(**) Fixed Capital *ICI* at roughly '2/3' that for *Services* overall, due to no warehouses.

systems in place in almost all companies today facilitate this method of delivering spare parts to customers. The manufacturing companies are charging a higher price for the parts – reflected in our COGS ratio – to compensate them for this service. As you saw in our P&L, the COGS ratio is forecasted to average 32% (as a percent of revenue) during the 'plan' period and beyond, versus 28% for the current year. The benefit is in the Inventory *ICI*, which should be 'zero'. We've put in a 'penny' ($0.01) to be conservative, but we do not expect to have any inventory for the '*OCS*' program. The result is an *ICI* (for working capital) of $0.15 ('fifteen cents') versus $0.20 ('twenty cents') for *Services* overall. By deduction, '*OCS*' is significantly lower than the *Growthstar* segment strategy, in terms of working capital intensity".

Dave paused for a drink of water. With no comments from the group, he continued. "We should also experience a lower *ICI* for fixed capital, mainly due to a much lower facility requirement for warehousing inventories. Our estimate is that the '*OCS*' program will only require two-thirds of the fixed capital – on a 'relative' basis – that is anticipated for *Services* overall. This translates into *ICI*'s of $0.06 and $0.03 for fixed assets and operating leases, respectively – $0.09 in total for fixed capital – versus $0.13 for *Services* overall".

"Therefore, our total (or, net) *ICI* for this program is in the $0.24 range. This results in about $18 million of net new capital during the next three years and approximately $70 million over the total seven-year outlook period".

Jason leaned back in his chair, looked at Jonathan and grinned. *"This type of articulate presentation – from a person who only a few months ago didn't even give much attention to the balance sheet – makes all the hard work worthwhile"*, Jason thought to himself. As he looked at Jonathan, Jason knew that the CFO could read his mind. Jonathan smiled back.

Peter, always observant, picked up the gestures and said, "It seems that we have a program that has a respectable level of profit margin and a low capital intensity".

Jonathan, sensing that a little levity might be in order, responded with, "Peter, if you keep this up, we're going to offer you a position in Corporate Finance". Peter looked back at Jonathan, a twinkle in his eye. Jack slumped in his chair and looked up at the ceiling. Earl gave a 'thumbs up' sign to Dave and then glanced over at Val.

For Dave, the feeling was exhilarating. He, therefore, said in a confident tone ... "We now need to 'wrap up' this presentation with an analysis of what the '*OCS*' program is potentially worth to the shareholders. Exhibit 167 provides this information".

Exhibit 167		**GROWTHSTAR INC.**						
[$ Millions except Per Share & Capital Intensity Amounts]		**Other Co. Strategy ('*OCS*') Financials** *'Business Strategy': 3-Year Plan + 4 Additional Years*						

'SERVICES' Financials	*Yr. 1*	*Yr. 2*	*Yr. 3*	*Yr. 4*	*Yr. 5*	*Yr. 6*	*Yr. 7*	*Resid.*
Valuation								Yr. 7 '*NOP*'
Free Cash Flow (FCF)								cap'd @
								11%
Net Operating Profit (NOP)	$2.4	$3.8	$6.0	$8.0	$10.7	$14.1	$18.7	
Net New Investment (I)	3.5	5.7	9.0	8.1	10.9	13.9	18.5	
Free Cash Flow (FCF)	$(1.1)	$(1.8)	$(3.0)	$(0.1)	$(0.2)	$0.2	$0.2	$170

'*OCS*' Net Present Value (NPV) =	**$69**							

Economic Profit (EP) Approach								*Resid.*
Net New Investment - 'Cumul.'	$3.5	$9.2	$8.2	$26.3	$37.3	$51.2	$69.6	Yr. 7 '*EP*'
								cap'd @
Net Operating Profit (NOP)	$2.4	$3.8	$6.0	$8.0	$10.7	$14.1	$18.7	11%
Capital Charge (CCAP) – 11%	(0.4)	(1.0)	(2.0)	(2.9)	(4.1)	(5.6)	(7.7)	
Economic Profit ('EP')	$2.1	$2.8	$4.0	$5.1	$6.6	$8.5	$11.0	$100

'*OCS*' Net Present Value (NPV) =		**$68**	... *say,*	**$68.5**	*Services Strategy Value =*			**$121**
			...*or,*	**56%**	*of 'Svcs.' Strategy Value*			*Avg ROIC*
'OCS' Program Annual ROIC	69.1%	41.7%	33.2%	30.5%	28.8%	27.6%	26.8%	**29.7%**

Peter leaned back in his chair. A wide grin covered his face. He looked at Jonathan and said ... "This strategy appears to be a 'winner', at least by any calculation I'm capable of making".

"I have to agree ... wholeheartedly", Jonathan replied. "Let's see ... a $68 million shareholder value contribution, and a return on capital of close to 30% over the life of the program".

"Jason, is this the type of analysis and result we're looking for in the analysis of Value Driver Programs?"

"It certainly is", Jason answered, "and '*OCS*' provides a good example of the power of working capital management – in this case inventory turnover".

"How so?" Peter asked ... his curiosity showing.

"Let's get into the numbers", Jason responded. "As Exhibit 165 shows, the *NOP* margin is below that for the *Growthstar* segment and for the *Services* business unit in total. This 'margin differential' is significant – 5.9% *NOP* margin for '*OCS*' versus 7.6% for the overall *Services* strategy. If we focused on the traditional 'earnings' measure, we might view '*OCS*' with skepticism. But, look at how the balance sheet is impacted by the virtual 'non-existence' of inventory. Working capital *ICI* is $0.15 ('fifteen cents') versus $0.20 ('twenty cents') for the *Services* strategy. That's a 25% improvement. The lower inventory requirement also affects the need for the facilities portion of new fixed capital investment – purchased *plus* leased assets – in this case $0.09 ('nine cents') for '*OCS*' versus $0.13 ('thirteen cents') for *Services* in total. That's a 31% positive impact".

"When all of this is put together, the 'net' result is a program with great value creation potential. This 'value potential' is evidenced by the high ROIC and the fact that '*OCS*' has a market value added (*MVA*) – '*NPV*' – comprising 56% of the overall *Services* strategy value, even though '*OCS*' generates only 31% of total *Services* revenue by year 3 ($102 out of $330 million) and 40% by year 7 ($320 out of approximately $800 million). This is probably as good an example as we could envision as to why *all* the 'economic value' principles are so important in assessing shareholder value creation".

Earl, sensing an opportunity to emphasize one of his 'pet' objectives, chimed in with ... "This Value Driver Program is also a great example of investing in a 'strategy' and not a 'project'. Referring back to Exhibit 166, we're looking at a commitment of $18 million over the next three years. If there's anyone left in this room who still feels that individual projects should still be evaluated and approved for funding, I hope that this program will dispel any of these lingering beliefs. The entire $18 million needs to be committed to, with appropriate controls and checkpoints regarding the actual expenditure of capital funds, based on progress toward revenue and other goals that we may establish for this strategy".

Earl cast looks at both Jonathan and Jack as he concluded his remarks. Jonathan nodded in agreement, himself casting a glance at Jason. Jack shrugged his shoulders and nodded his head gently, indicating his affirmation of Earl's statement. Dave was beaming, because this meant no capital project evaluations, with only a 'repackaging' (for the Board of Directors) of the material that had just been presented. Peter noticed Dave's reaction and smiled to himself, his look of confidence apparent to anyone in the room who chose to glance in his direction.

Jason looked over at Jonathan, indicating that it was time to end the meeting and the Value Driver Program evaluations. Jonathan took the cue and said ... "We now have driven the concept of Value Driver Programs into both business units. I am pleased with the outcomes, especially the quantification of what many of us felt intuitively. Both the '*NG Euro*' and '*OCS*' programs will be presented at the next Finance Committee and full Board meetings for approval – and yes, Earl, for the entire amounts of required invested capital. We'll request $34.5 million (say, $35 million) to be spent during the next three years – $16.5 million for '*NG Euro*' and $18 million for '*OCS*'. The evaluations given to the Board will be those presented at the two review meetings, perhaps condensed. No individual project evaluations will be done on these programs. Annual capital plans will outline and detail the expenditures for the ensuing year, along with

any revision(s) to the timing and/or amount of expenditures estimated in the Value Driver Program analyses. So, that should just
about do it. Thank you again, everyone, for all your hard work and
your insights into these two exciting initiatives".

With the meeting concluded, everyone left the conference room to
return to their offices.

## 12

Mergers and acquisitions: major external investments

"*Acquisitions ... an aphrodisiac for so many*", Jason thought to himself as he sat in his office. It had been almost a week since the '*OCS*' Value Driver Program review meeting. Now, the attention had moved to the two acquisitions that Val had mentioned over a month ago. These 'deals' had been moving along and economic evaluations needed to be done. As Jason continued to ponder, he was almost speaking (softly) to himself ... "*How amazing it is that so many companies underestimate the challenges in creating value through either merging with other firms or acquiring companies in part or whole. The ones that are successful have the merger and acquisition process down to a 'science' – with knowledgeable people dedicated to the various aspects of the M&A process. Now that 'Services' is moving into the 'A' category – generating returns above the cost of capital – Growthstar can at least move forward in pursuit of external growth. Their strategies seem to be reasonably well thought out and documented. Depending on the nature of the 'Leasing' proposal, the two deals 'on the table' can, possibly, be rationalized within the context of the corporation's direction. With the Services acquisition starting to 'pay off', this business unit may be able to create additional value for shareholders through another acquisition in the near future. It's going to be difficult, though, to match the returns for the 'NG Euro' and 'OCS' programs. Well, tomorrow we'll begin to see what we have*", he concluded – thinking about the kick-off meetings scheduled for the next day on the '*Leasing*' company deal and the day after tomorrow on the *European Services* company (code-named '*EuroServ*').

As it always does, tomorrow did arrive and a small group assembled in the Corporate Finance conference room. Val Performa was there, along with Earl D'Mark, Mandy Bettertalk and Jack Earningsly. Val was responsible for corporate development and was always the team leader for acquisitions. Earl was personally handling the financial evaluation of the '*Leasing*' deal, due to his banking and financial services experience. He had assigned Frank Accurato to evaluate '*EuroServ*'. Mandy had been asked to be a team member on all acquisitions, to provide guidance for investor relations. Jack also participated in all acquisitions, to address the corporate accounting and reporting issues. Jason had been asked to coordinate the application of value-based metrics to the acquisitions, similar to his role in the Value Driver Programs.

  Val, feeling that an informal meeting was in order, remained seated as she began to speak. "Earlier this fiscal year, we were approached by a company that has been offering customer financing – essentially, leasing programs – for our products for the past several years. This firm is going to exit the financing segment into which our products fit as part of a strategic redirection they are taking. They have also contacted the other three vendors who lease our products. All the others are financial services firms. Ian thinks that there may be financing profits we are missing, and that we should perhaps be offering a 'bundled' package of *product/service/financing*. We have had several discussions on this subject during the year, without reaching any clear conclusions. Further, we have *just* recently devoted – as all of you know – a significant amount of time to the (internal) Value Driver Program initiatives and, thus, have not spent too much time during the past month or so on this potential deal. Earl and I resumed our analysis on this transaction during this past week, and want to share our initial findings with you. Then, we need to 'map out' a plan to carry this through to a final analysis and recommendation to Ian and Jonathan. Earl, can you show us the results of what we have so far".

  "It would be my pleasure to do so", the treasurer responded. "All we have so far is an historical assessment, based on information provided to us by the seller. Thus, this meeting will be brief. We will be receiving a future outlook in a couple of days and, Jason, I will then want to get together with you to evaluate these projections". Jason nodded to Earl, since he had expected this comment.

  Earl continued ... "I have three exhibits to share with you today. The first is an income statement. The second is a balance sheet, and the

Exhibit 168	GROWTHSTAR INC.				
$ Millions	**Acquisition Target Financials** **(as "Reported")**				**Current**
	..... Historical Period — 3 Years				
"Leasing" Financials	**FY #3**	**FY #2**	**FY #1**	**3-Yr Avg**	**FY Fcst.**
Income Statement					
Leasing Revenue:					
Growthstar	$18	$20	$22	$20	$24
Other Products	7	10	13	10	16
Total Leasing Revenue	25	30	35	30	40
Operating Costs and Expenses:					
Cost of Leasing Revenue (COLR)	6	8	9	8	10
Selling & Marketing (S&M)	1	2	2	2	3
General& Administrative (G&A)	1	1	1	1	1
Total Operating Costs & Expenses	8	11	12	10	14
Operating Income	17	20	24	20	26
Interest Expense	8	9	11	9	12
Income before Taxes (IBT)	9	10	13	11	14
Provision for Taxes	3	3	4	3	4
Net Income After Taxes (NI)	$6	$7	$9	$7	$10

third is a summary of supporting data and an initial set of ratios. We have put the seller's financials in a format similar to that done for our own *Products* and *Services* historical assessment. Remember, though, that this is a 'financing' business – not an industrial operation". Earl clicked on Exhibit 168.

"As this schedule shows, our ('Growthstar') percentage of their total revenue base has declined from 72% three years ago to 60% today. There was a conscious effort to diversify the firm's lease portfolio and not be so reliant on our company – remembering that three other firms finance our products. They're expecting to make a 'net profit' of $10 million this year, up about 11% from $9 million last year (FY #1). Their operating costs and expenses seem to be under control – based upon my experience in this type of business – and are in the range of 32% to 36% as a percentage of lease revenue. As in all finance businesses, Interest expense is significant due to the heavy use of debt financing".

"Their 'net margin' of 25% is pretty solid", Jack remarked – as he mentally computed the $10 million of net income divided by $40 million of lease revenue for the current year.

"It needs to be high, to justify the investment in the leasing business", Jason responded.

"Thank you for that 'lead in' to their balance sheet", Earl chuckled as he clicked on Exhibit 169. "By the way, all numbers are 'rounded' to the nearest million dollars".

Exhibit 169	**GROWTHSTAR INC.**				
	Acquisition Target Financials				
$ Millions	**(as "Reported")**				
	..... Historical Period — 4 Years				Current
"Leasing" Financials	**FY #4**	**FY #3**	**FY #2**	**FY #1**	**FY Fcst.**
Balance Sheet - Year End					
Assets					
Cash	$1	$1	$1	$1	$1
Finance Receivables - Short term	*92*	*113*	*133*	*150*	*158*
Other Current Assets	1	1	1	1	2
Total Current Assets	94	114	134	152	160
Fixed Assets:					
Gross	10	11	12	12	14
Accumulated Depreciation	(4)	(5)	(6)	(7)	(8)
Goodwill, etc.					
Gross	-	-	-	-	-
Accumulated Amortization	-	-	-	-	-
Finance Receivables - Long term	*55*	*68*	*80*	*90*	*95*
Other Assets	1	1	1	2	2
Total Assets	**$156**	**$189**	**$221**	**$249**	**$263**
Liabilities & Equity					
Accounts Payable	$1	$1	$1	$1	$1
Accrued Expenses	1	1	1	1	1
Income Taxes Payable	1	1	1	1	1
Short-term Debt	*65*	*79*	*93*	*105*	*110*
Total Current Liabilities	67	81	96	108	113
Long-term Debt	*42*	*51*	*60*	*68*	*71*
Deferred Taxes	1	2	3	4	5
Other Liabil's/Reserves	-	-	-	-	-
Total Liabilities	109	134	158	180	189
Stockholders' Equity	47	55	63	69	74
Total Liabilities & Equity	**$156**	**$189**	**$221**	**$249**	**$263**

"As you can see", Earl continued, "the two main assets are the short and long-term finance receivables. Finance companies purchase equipment and then lease them out to customers over varying time periods. This firm uses a five-year time frame as the determinant of a short versus long term lease. On the liability side, a combination of short-term and long-term debt is employed, consistent with the asset base mix".

"The next exhibit (170) provides a very preliminary set of ratios based on the information we have received so far".

Jason leaned forward in his chair, looking at the exhibit on the screen and the 'hard copy' of Exhibit 170 that Earl had provided. As he did so, Earl began to speak again.

"I've tried to capture a few key ratios that are relevant for finance companies, based on the limited information that has been provided to us. The first set of data (in Exhibit 170) relates to whether or not dividends are being 'upstreamed' to the parent company or new equity is being infused. Generally speaking, the use of new 'equity' capital is *not* desirable for financing this type of business. There are always exceptions, but leasing (and financing in general) is mostly about using

Exhibit 170	**GROWTHSTAR INC.**				
	Acquisition Target Financials				
$ Millions, except Capital Intensity	**(as "Reported")**				
"Leasing" Financials					
Supporting Data & Ratios	..... Historical Period — 3 / 4 Years				
				Memo:	**Current**
Net Income vs. Ret. Earnings	**FY #3**	**FY #2**	**FY #1**	**3-YrAvg**	**FY Fcst.**
Net Income	$6	$7	$9	$7	$10
Ret. Earnings Change	8	8	6	7	5
Diff. = Dividends /(New Equity)	$(2)	$(1)	$3	$(0)	$5
Dividend Pay-out (%)			29%		52%
Debt-to-Total Capital Ratio	**FY #4**	**FY #3**	**FY #2**	**FY #1**	**CFY Fcst.**
Debt (Ending)	*$106*	*$129*	*$153*	*$173*	*$181*
Equity (Ending)	*$47*	*$55*	*$63*	*$69*	*$74*
Ratio (D/TC)	*69%*	*70%*	*71%*	*71%*	*71%*
Return-on-Equity	**FY #3**	**FY #2**	**FY #1**	**3-Yr Avg**	**CFY Fcst.**
NI	*$6*	*$7*	*$9*	*$7*	*$10*
Equity (Beginning)	*$47*	*$55*	*$63*	*$55*	*$69*
Ratio (ROE) *	*13.2%*	*13.0%*	*14.0%*	*13.3%*	*13.8%*
* Before impact of Deferred Taxes					
Return-on-Invested Capital	**FY #3**	**FY #2**	**FY #1**	**3-Yr Avg**	**CFY Fcst.**
NOP	*$12*	*$14*	*$16*	*$14*	*$18*
IC (Beginning)	*$154*	*$186*	*$218*	*$186*	*$246*
Ratio (ROIC) *	*7.5%*	*7.3%*	*7.6%*	*7.5%*	*7.4%*
Invested Capital Intensity ('ICI')	**FY #3**	**FY #2**	**FY #1**	**3-Yr Avg**	**CFY Fcst.**
IC (Beginning)	*$154*	*$186*	*$218*	*$186*	*$246*
Revenue	*$25*	*$30*	*$35*	*$30*	*$40*
ICI	*$6.25*	*$6.20*	*$6.17*	*$6.20*	*$6.14*
Equity Capital Intensity ('ECI')	**FY #3**	**FY #2**	**FY #1**	**3-Yr Avg**	**CFY Fcst.**
EC (Beginning)	*$47*	*$55*	*$63*	*$55*	*$69*
Revenue	*$25*	*$30*	*$35*	*$30*	*$40*
ECI	*$1.90*	*$1.82*	*$1.77*	*$1.82*	*$1.73*

'other people's money' and lending it out at a 'spread' above its cost. The greater the spread, the greater the profitability – that is, a higher return on investment, or a higher economic profit. Obviously, some equity is required as a support to the debt financing, but it should be as little as possible – consistent with the risk of the asset(s) that are being financed. As the first set of numbers in Exhibit 170 shows, the three-year historical result is no new 'net' equity over the three years, even though equity was infused during FY #3 and FY #2 and, a dividend was remitted in FY #1 – basically, a 'wash'. A dividend of approximately 50% of Net Income is expected for the current fiscal year".

Earl looked in Jack's direction and, seeing that Jack was looking intently at Exhibit 170, asked … "Do you have anything that you want to say, Jack?"

"Nothing more than there seems to be steady growth in earnings during the past three fiscal years, extending into the current year",

Jack responded. "Net Income has grown by \$1 to \$2 million per year in each of the fiscal years".

"So noted", Earl replied. "Anything else?" With no further comment, Earl moved on. "Next, we reviewed this firm's capital structure in terms of its 'Debt-to-Total Capital' (*D/TC*) ratio. Their *D/TC* ratio has been fairly steady around 70% – indicating that about 'seventy cents' out of every 'one dollar' of capital is debt financing, which is typical for finance companies. Some are more and some are less, but this is in the range of what we would expect. So, there's nothing out of the ordinary with respect to capital structure".

"We then looked at 'profitability' in two ways – first, the Return on Equity (*ROE*) and then the Return on Invested Capital (*ROIC*). As Jason and I have discussed privately, *ROE* is very often a good metric for finance companies, due to the significant amount of Interest expense in the P&L – related to the Debt financing – and the fact that the balance sheet is usually stated in 'current' terms. By that, I mean that there are usually no inventories and a relatively low level of fixed assets in relation to the total asset base. For the most part, 'P&L' expenses are 'cash outflow' in nature and follow the 'cash inflow' nature of lease revenues. Further, from a practical standpoint, many people in the finance business have difficulty envisioning an income statement *without* Interest expense, since it is usually a very significant expense. *ROIC* is also relevant, since it provides insight into the 'return' on the overall lease portfolio. In most cases, it should be an indicator of the Internal Rate of Return (*IRR*) of all the individual leases or other transactions in the corporate portfolio. You need to keep in mind, however, that the *ROICs* are usually going to be lower than those for an industrial business. This is due to the competitiveness of the finance business, the absence of significant barriers to entry, and the fact that the heavy use of debt financing reduces the cost of capital, thus lowering the requirement for successful financial performance – remembering that 'success' is beating the cost of capital".

Jason then asked ... "Have you calculated the cost of equity (*Ce*) and the weighted average cost of capital (*CCAP*) for this firm?"

"Not yet", Earl answered. "I thought we would calculate *Ce* and *CCAP* when we meet to evaluate the future projections".

"Fair enough", Jason replied. "At this point, then, we can *not* make any definitive 'value judgments', except to state that the three-year historical averages for *ROE* and *ROIC* are probably at or slightly above what would seem to be reasonable costs of equity and total capital. But, let's not get ahead of ourselves – especially since, as indicated by your footnote in Exhibit 170, we don't yet have any impact of deferred taxes on these ratios".

"Finally", Earl continued, "we looked at capital intensity, since some people do not understand just how 'capital intensive' the leasing business is. The last two sets of numbers indicate the capital intensity, first for total invested capital (*ICI*) and then for equity capital (*ECI*). If the capital intensity of the finance business is not understood, these ratios should provide a clue. We're looking at an *ICI* of more than $6.00 ('six dollars') for every dollar of annual lease revenue for this company's business portfolio. On an 'equity' capital basis, with a heavy dose of debt financing, this firm still invests about $1.80 to generate one dollar of lease revenue. If you compare the *ICI*, in particular, to that for our company's *Products* business, it's higher by a factor of more than *15 times* (that is, the average $6.20 *ICI* for this finance company versus approximately $0.40 *ICI* for *Products*). If we compare this finance firm's average *ICI* ($6.20) to the highest level ever for *Services* ($0.93 in FY #2 just after the acquisition and then $0.80 in FY #1) you can see that this finance company's *ICI* is higher by a factor of about *7 to 8 times*".

"This perception is enlightening", Val interjected. "I never really understood this aspect of the finance business".

Jason then stated ... "This, by itself, is not bad – it's simply reality. The leasing business, in particular, is *very* capital intensive, even though the asset is only a 'piece of paper' – that is, a lease receivable. That's why, Jack, the profit margins need to be high – to cover the high level of invested capital. There's another perception, Val, that you might also find enlightening. The whole notion of a finance business is about earning an 'economic' profit – or return on invested capital for each transaction. Most leasing and other finance deals are priced on a 'spread versus cost of money' basis to yield a positive net present value or an acceptable internal rate of return".

"I sort of knew this", Val responded, "but thank you for solidifying this point".

"I knew about the capital intensity", Jack muttered, "but didn't realize it was so high. I guess the 'earnings' model wouldn't work too well in evaluating a finance business, even though I hate to admit it".

"Great day in the morning", Earl exclaimed. "Please let this dialogue continue".

"Stay calm, Earl", Jack retorted, "and don't flaunt the fact that your economic arguments are, apparently 'winning the day' ".

"OK", Earl responded. "Is there any other point to be made today?"

"Just a follow-up to the comment on capital intensity", Jason replied. "Let's focus on the Invested Capital (*IC*) and Equity Capital (*EC*) amounts for current fiscal year – which are last year's ending amounts. The *IC* is close to $250 million ($246 million to be exact).

This *IC* produces an annual revenue stream of $40 million. Growth-star (as a total company) had $220 million of *IC* at the end of last year, producing revenue of $450 million (refer to Exhibit 32 and others). Thus, this *Leasing* business has more invested capital (over $25 million) than your entire company. Again, this is not necessarily bad, but it does point out the extremely high levels of invested capital that finance companies carry with them. The issue for Growth-star is the balance sheet taking on characteristics of a finance company – that is, high levels of invested capital and debt – if this deal were to be done. You need to 'think through' whether or not this is what you want for your company. Finally, look at Stockholders' Equity Capital (*EC*). Even with the high 'leverage' (debt) there is *EC* (albeit on a 'book' basis) of $69 million in the current year for '*Leasing*', versus $93 million for Growthstar (refer to Exhibit 26). I'm not going to say anything further at this point, but everyone needs to be aware of the implications that this deal entails".

"Sounds to me as though you're trying to 'squelch' the '*Leasing*' acquisition", Jack retorted, a sense of disdain evident in his tone of voice.

"Not really", Jason countered. "I just want to make sure that all of you know what you are getting into by *financing* your products and, possibly, those of other manufacturers".

"It's called *making an informed decision*", Earl snapped, as he snickered at Jack – who returned the look with a cold stare. Maybe the 'battle' wasn't completely over.

"I think that's enough material to review and discuss for today", Val interjected in a polite tone, sensing that it was time for this meeting to end. "We'll get back to everyone by the end of the week as to our schedule for evaluating this acquisition further".

The following day, Val, Mandy, Jack, Frank Accurato, Dave Dollarby and Jason met in the same conference room, to begin the evaluation of the proposed acquisition for *Services* – code-named '*EuroServ*'.

Dave was moving from one person to the next, chatting about anything and everything, as the group filled their coffee and tea mugs before getting started with the meeting. The past month or so had been a 'coming out party' for him. Not only had the *Services* BU been cast in a 'value-creating' light, but he had really started to get to know people in the company that, previously, he had known only casually or not at all. Peter had also been praising his accomplishments privately and that always made him feel good. In fact, Peter had wanted to attend today's meeting, but was on his way to Europe to meet with the principals of the company being discussed for acquisition. Val had met them earlier this year, but Peter had not and he had a family vacation tied into the trip. Thus, he decided to keep his appointment in Europe and attend one of the next meetings to be scheduled on this deal.

Val, as she had done the day before, began this meeting by speaking from her seat at the conference table. "It's been a long time – at least twenty hours or so – since some of us last met", she joked ... referencing yesterday's meeting on the '*Leasing*' acquisition. "Today, we're going to get back to our industrial world – at least the 'service' aspect of it – and take our first 'hard look' at acquiring a company in Europe, which this company has never done before. Most of you are familiar with the origin of this deal, which goes back to the beginning of this fiscal year. As we discussed the potential for expanding our *Services* business beyond North America, it became apparent that Europe was the most logical geographic region and that we could not effectively 'build' a service operation at a reasonable cost and within a reasonable time frame. There are barriers, especially within one major country on the continent of Europe, that make an internal growth strategy almost too challenging. Marketing, infrastructure build-up and business licensing regulations are among the more important hurdles, but there are others, also".

"On a positive note", Dave chimed in, "if we can replicate what we've done here in the United States – recognizing that *Services* was Growthstar's first major acquisition – we may be able to produce another success story".

"I think we're all hoping – and planning – for that outcome", Jack shot back. "In fact, I doubt we would bother to investigate this transaction unless that were our objective".

Jason then asked ... "Mandy, what do you think are the important investor perceptions for this deal?"

"Thank you for asking that question", Mandy responded. "I think that the investors first need to hear the 'shareholder value tale' for *Services* in the United States. I'm working on a 'special' meeting (call it a 'road show' type of presentation) with our institutional shareholders and the key sell-side analysts that follow our stock. The focus of this presentation will be the recent performance of *Services*, along with the strategic outlooks for the business units. Peter and Dave will participate, so that the portfolio managers and analysts can get to know them better. Jonathan and Ian will conclude with a 'corporate' perspective and outlook, the implied message being the higher 'warranted' stock price that we all believe is more realistic than our actual market valuation over the last several months".

Mandy continued ... "We need to give the investors some idea of our performance for the two major business units, since they have not yet been provided with any information beyond our consolidated results and overall growth objectives".

"That's always been Ian's tactic for dealing with the 'Street' – sales and earnings growth during the year and a realistic growth objective that we can meet", Jack interjected.

"I can't argue with that comment", Mandy replied, "but I think that – after what he's experienced during the past few months – Ian realizes that we need to provide a more 'strategic' perspective. He's heard it from some key institutional investors and analysts and he's now hearing it from Val and me".

"Jonathan is definitely 'on board' with this perspective, also", Jason added.

"Don't I know that all too well", Jack muttered. "He's putting pressure on Jill and me to get this 'value-based' financial reporting system up and running by the start of the next fiscal year. After we get through these two acquisitions, that's my next priority".

"Well", Frank stated, "for Earl and me, it's the capital planning, evaluation and control process, so we each have one more major task on our platter".

"I think this has been a healthy dialogue", Val said politely, "but could we now 'wrap up' any additional investor perceptions and get into the '*EuroServ*' deal?"

"We should do that", Mandy responded, "but – if I may – let me add just one more point about our upcoming meeting with the major institutional investors and analysts. If they are convinced that we are now about to create 'real value' in the *Services* business unit, they should be very receptive to another acquisition. If they are not, then we may be wasting our time!"

"So noted", Val sighed. She understood the importance of the session that Mandy was preparing – with her assistance. "We're going to 'knock their socks off' and show them the potential for our company", she stated confidently, looking first at Dave and then at Frank ... and, finally, casting a glance at Jack to make him feel that he was a part of this effort.

Jack returned the look with one of his own, indicating his appreciation of the fact that the corporate strategy officer hadn't abandoned him, in spite of the objections he had initially raised to the 'economic value' approach that he knew Val supported. "*Val has class*", Jack said silently to himself. "*Perhaps some day I'll say the same about Earl*", he thought – having difficulty eliminating his adversarial relationship with the treasurer, but realizing that things would have to change in the future.

"We're going to take a similar approach to what we did yesterday", Val said, "with Frank giving us an historical perspective on the 'target' company. Then, we'll adjourn this meeting and get back to you with our schedule to move forward with our evaluation. Before Frank begins, let me comment about a few unique features of this company. First, when you see the historical income statements, you will notice that they are barely profitable, from a 'traditional P&L' perspective. One major factor here is the very high compensation to the owners, which extends to two European families. Frank will show the 'reported' numbers and then present a 'breakout' of the executive and owner compensation structure, along with other items of interest and importance to our economic analysis".

"Ah shucks"! Dave blurted out. "Peter and I thought we might put some of this 'excess cash' in *our* pockets".

The group burst into laughter, even Jack who chuckled and said, "well, it's entertaining to have a replacement for 'Mr Funny' – otherwise known as Earl D'Mark – being that he's not here".

"I just want to make sure we have a little humor in the midst of all the serious analysis", Dave shot back.

"Oh, you're good at that", Jack chided.

Jason looked over at Val and winked. They shared a thought – actually, a hope – that "*perhaps (finally) Jack was ready to 'come on board' and end his resistance to value-based economics*".

Val then resumed her commentary. "Frank will also highlight some other financial indicators that we have uncovered in our initial due diligence analysis, with respect to gross margins and selected invest-ment – by that, I mean balance sheet – items. Peter will be discussing some of these issues with the owners this week during his visit to the company. So, Frank, I think this sets the stage for what you're going to present to us".

Frank began by looking at Dave and saying with a very serious expression on his face ... "I thought, Dave, that we had agreed to '*my cut*' of the excess owners' compensation. It sounds as though you and Peter have '*cut me out*' ".

Muted laughter broke out, which brought a smile to Frank's face. He was trying so hard to become more 'loose' in his personality and style and was always gratified at the least bit of acceptance of such from his peers. They knew he was trying to combine his incredible intellect with a more 'easygoing' style and wanted to help him.

Frank then launched into a summary of the analysis he had performed. "The Europeans have a few nuances to their financial reporting which we had to deal with. I must say, though, that my counterpart on their side has been most cooperative and has been instructed by the owners to be very responsive to our requests for information and to answer our questions candidly – unless, of course,

Exhibit 171	**GROWTHSTAR INC.**				
	Acquisition Target Financials				
$ Millions	(as "Reported")				
		Historical Period — 2 Years			Current
"EuroServ" Financials	FY #3	FY #2	FY #1	2-Yr Avg	FY Fcst.
Income Statement	("Base")				
Service Revenue:					
Growthstar		$26	$35	$31	$45
Other Products		9	12	10	15
Total Service Revenue	$25	$35	$47	$41	$60
Operating Costs and Expenses:	% to Rev.				
Cost of Goods Sold (COGS)	20%	7	9	8	12
Selling, Marketing & Service (SMS)	45%	16	21	18	27
General & Administrative (G&A)	(*)see note	8	12	10	16
Research & Development (R&D)	3%	1	1	1	2
Total Oper. Costs & Expenses	Avg. Int. Rate	32	44	38	57
Interest Expense	10.1%	0	1	1	1
Income Before Taxes		3	2	2	2
Provision for Taxes	40%	1	1	1	1
Net Income After Taxes		$2	$1	$1	$1

(*) Includes excess owners' compensation and rent/operating lease expense.

he just can't do so. As Val mentioned, we're going to present their Profit & Loss (P&L) statements as they have been 'reported' and then show separately the 'excess' compensation to the owners. We've also done a preliminary analysis of the tax situation and have calculated a 'normalized' tax rate for this deal. We don't expect any significant deferred taxes, and will be conservative on our estimate of an effective tax rate. If we do wind up paying lower taxes than we have estimated, we'll consider this to be a 'windfall' in terms of cash flow and shareholder value creation. We're confident that we will not pay taxes higher than what we have estimated. Let's begin, then, with Exhibit 171".

Jack gazed at the historical income statements for '*EuroServ*', his mind instantly computing profit margins at the various levels of the P&L. "I see what you mean by this company being barely profitable. I hope the owners are taking some sizable bonuses out of the business".

"Be assured that they are", Frank responded. "We'll show the amounts in a separate schedule".

"Why do you think that we wanted a *piece of the action?*" Dave cracked. "These people are paying themselves handsomely".

"That often is the case in privately owned companies", Jason quipped, "since they only have to justify their pay packages to themselves".

Val then said … "the topic of executive pay is 'near and dear to our hearts', but I think that we should have Frank point out the important operating features of this company".

Frank took the cue and stated … "We have similar information to that for our own *Services* BU. By that, I mean we have a two-year historical profile and a forecast for the current fiscal year. Being that we're in the fourth quarter, this forecast is based on three quarters of actual results, so it should be a good forecast of how the current year will turn out".

"As you can see, revenue has grown from $25 million three years ago to $60 million this year. Thus, '*EuroServ*' has about 40% of the revenue of our *Services* BU – noting that we'll do about $150 million this year. They have a larger percentage of 'Other' – 25% ($15 out of $60 million) versus 17% ($25 out of $150 million) for our *Services* BU. Further, they have had this percentage throughout the historical period, versus our *Services* BU just starting to 'ramp up' this segment of the business. The significance is that an '*OCS*' for Europe comes with this acquisition, since '*EuroServ*' has always had it! If you wish to reference the historical numbers for our *Services* BU, you can go back to Exhibit 29 of your file".

"This is a very appealing aspect of this deal", Dave chimed in, "at least for Peter and me".

"I also like this '*OCS*' element", Val interjected. "We should be able to learn from each other with regard to '*OCS*'. By that, I mean we are planning to do some innovative things for this business segment that may be transferable to Europe. On the other side, this firm has always had an '*OCS*' as part of their business model, and they can, hopefully, provide insight to us as we attempt to rapidly grow this area of our company".

"The investors should also like it", Mandy stated, "especially after they see the impact of our overall *Services* BU strategy and the '*OCS*' Value Driver Program. I, too, hope there are synergies between the two major segments – our mainstay 'Growthstar' business and '*OCS*' ".

"That 'investor' perspective is going to be a 'key' one", Jason added.

"That's why Mandy is here", Val retorted.

Frank then went back to the contents of Exhibit 171 by stating ... "The *COGS* ratio in Europe is lower than that in the US. Customers seem to be willing to pay for good service, and our 'target' company for acquisition has an excellent reputation. As a comparison, our *COGS* ratio for our *Services* BU will be about 28% this year – $42 million *COGS* on a revenue base of $150 million. The *COGS* ratio for '*EuroServ*' will be about 20% – $12 million *COGS* on a revenue of $60 million. The *SMS* ratio-to-revenue (45%) for '*EuroServ*' is about the same as the ratio our *Services* business unit in the US. G&A is affected by owner compensation, which I will review shortly, so let's hold off on this item for now. R&D is lower than we experience in our US *Services* BU, at 3% (for '*EuroServ*') versus 5% for *Services*. The Interest expense is based on their current borrowing. I mentioned that we have made a conservative estimate for an effective tax rate for all of this business

Exhibit 172		GROWTHSTAR INC.			
$ Millions, except Ratios		**Acquisition Target Financials** (as "Reported")			
"EuroServ" Financials	**"Base"**	**Historical Period — 3 Years**			**Current**
Balance Sheet - Year End	**(Ratios /**	**FY #3**	**FY #2**	**FY #1**	**FY Fcst.**
Assets	Percents)				
Cash	**$0.05**	$2	$2	$2	$3
Accounts Receivable	**$0.17**	6	6	8	10
Inventory	**$0.10**	4	4	5	6
Other Current Assets		-	-	-	-
Total Current Assets		11	11	15	19
Fixed Assets:					
Gross		5	6	6	7
Accumulated Depreciation		(2)	(2)	(3)	(3)
Goodwill, etc.					
Gross		-	-	-	-
Accumulated Amortization		-	-	-	-
Other Assets		1	1	1	-
Total Assets		$15	$15	$19	$23
Liabilities & Equity					
Accounts Payable		$0	$0	$0	$1
Accrued Expenses		1	2	2	2
Other Current Liabilities		-	-	-	-
Short-term Debt	**9.0%**	2	3	3	4
Total Current Liabilities		4	5	6	7
Long-term Debt	**11.0%**	3	4	5	6
Deferred Taxes		-	-	-	-
Other Liabil's/Reserves		-	-	-	-
Total Liabilities		6	9	11	13
Stockholders' Equity		9	7	8	**10**
Total Liabilities & Equity		$15	$15	$19	$23

in Europe, which is 40%. It won't be any higher, and if it turns out to be lower, we'll have a 'windfall'. Any questions?"

As usual, Frank's analysis was complete and his explanation understandable, so no one had any questions, beyond those already raised about the owners' compensation.

After looking around the room, Frank spoke again. "Exhibit 172 provides 'year-end' balance sheets for the past three years, along with the expectation for the end of the current fiscal year".

"If we look at the major accounts, we first queried them on the level of 'operating cash' needed to operate the business. 'EuroServ' manages cash based on this concept, so this issue was straightforward. Because of the number of countries they operate in, they use a 5% factor (of total revenue) as a required level of cash, which is higher than the 2% level we believe is necessary for our operations at Growthstar. We'll probably be able to manage at our (lower) level, but for the analysis we stuck with their input. Receivables tend to be higher in Europe than in the US and their experience across Europe is a 'days outstanding' level of about 60 days, which translates into an *ICI* of $0.17. We'll try to improve this ratio should we acquire this business, but we're sticking with their input to evaluate the deal. Inventory experiences a 'turnover' (or, alternatively, 'months of supply') which is in line with our existing *Services* business unit. Due to the higher pricing mark-up, however, the 'capital intensity' is lower – about $0.10 for '*EuroServ*' versus an historical range of $0.13 to $0.17 for *Services*. Fixed assets, 'as reported', are low because this firm leases much of its equipment and almost all of its requirement for facilities".

"Moving to the 'liability' side of the balance sheet, '*EuroServ*' finances approximately 50% of its 'book' invested capital with a combination of short-and long-term debt. The respective interest rates are shown in the column entitled 'Base'. We'll take a closer look at Stockholders' Equity in a moment".

In a very serious tone, Frank then said, "You can verify all of the comparisons to our existing *Services* BU by referring back to Exhibits 29 and 30 in your file".

Just about everyone broke out in laughter after this statement, with Dave laughing the loudest and the longest. No one was about to even think about questioning Frank's comparative analysis, knowing that he calculated each ratio after a very careful review of the numbers for *Services*. Frank didn't expect this reaction, although he probably should have, and blushed. Even Mandy chuckled softly, having now been exposed to Frank's analytic prowess and comprehending the reaction of the others. Frank was lost as to what to say next.

Val, sensing this, jumped in and said, "Now, I think we're ready to review G&A ... that is, the owners' compensation ... in more detail, along with Stockholders' Equity".

This brief interlude allowed Frank to quickly gather his thoughts and he added, "we have two additional items to cover – first, rent expense for facilities and operating lease costs for equipment and second, a loan to a shareholder".

"OK, I stand corrected", Val responded.

"I've placed all of these items into Exhibit 173 – *Supporting Data & Ratios*", Frank stated as he clicked on the schedule.

All eyes were riveted on the fifth row of numbers – account # 7005. "Oh my", Jack exclaimed ... "these pay-outs are a bit more than what I'm accustomed to".

"More than most of us are familiar with", Val countered – mentally calculating her annual bonus, "but, as Jason mentioned, it's not uncommon with privately held firms. If we can get past the 'gawking' at the size of the numbers, let's let Frank explain what we do with this type of extraordinary pay-out".

"When we develop our 'economic' analysis, we'll adjust the G&A for the entire amounts, or a percentage of the amounts, in account

Exhibit 173		GROWTHSTAR INC.			
$ Millions, except Ratios "EuroServ" Financials Supporting Data & Ratios		Acquisition Target Financials (as "Reported")			

Income Statement

G & A Detail:	Account #	Historical Period — 2 Years			Current
		FY #2	FY #1	2-Yr Avg	FY Fcst.
Admin. Salary - Clerical	7001	$1.2	$1.8	$1.5	$2.4
Admin. Salary - Supervisor	7002	0.8	1.2	1.0	1.6
Admin. Salary - Executive	7003	1.2	1.8	1.5	2.4
Executive Bonus	7004	0.8	1.2	1.0	1.6
Owner Bonus	7005	*2.0*	*3.0*	*2.5*	*4.0*
Telephone & Utilities	7006	0.4	0.6	0.5	0.8
Office Rent	7007	*0.8*	*1.2*	*1.0*	*1.6*
Equipment Lease	7008	*0.4*	*0.6*	*0.5*	*0.8*
Office Supplies & Other	7009	0.4	0.6	0.5	0.8
Total G & A		$8.0	$12.0	$10.0	$16.0

Balance Sheet

Other Assets Detail	Historical Period — 3 Years			Current
Shareholder Loan:	FY #3	FY #2	FY #1	FY Fcst.
Opening Balance	$-	$1.0	$1.0	$1.0
New Borrowing/(Payment)	1.0	-	-	(1.0)
Closing Balance	$1.0	$1.0	$1.0	$ -

				Current
Stockholders' Equity Detail	FY #3	FY #2	FY #1	FY Fcst.
Opening Balance	$7.8	$8.8	$6.6	$8.0
Net Income	1.0	1.6	1.4	1.4
(Dividend) / New Capital	(0.0)	(3.8)	(0.0)	0.2
Closing Balance	$8.8	$6.6	$8.0	$9.6

#7005. We need to look at the two accounts (#7003 and 7004) Executive Salary and Bonus, to determine if they are indicative of what capable senior managers need to be paid to run this business. We'll analyze the overall executive compensation program for our next meeting".

"Moving on to office rent and equipment lease expense (accounts #7007 and 7008) these will be 'capitalized' and incorporated into invested capital". As he spoke, Frank went to the flip chart and wrote:

Capitalized Value – Operating Leases

$ Millions	Annual Expense (*)	Factor	Cap'd Value
Facilities	$1.6	6.0	$9.6
Equipment, etc.	0.8	2.0	1.6
Total (IC)	$2.4	4.67(**)	$11.2

(*) per Current Year
(**) $11.2 divided by $2.4 ... say, '4.5' as an 'average' capitalization factor

"The average facility lease runs about twelve years for 'EuroServ'. This considers renewal options and terms. At any point in time, this firm is roughly 50% into the obligation, which leads to the 'factor' of 6.0. For equipment and vehicles, the average lease term is four years, with a remaining obligation of two years. '*EuroServ*' leases all of its vehicles, virtually all facilities, and a significant portion of its testing equipment".

"So", Jack interjected, "you'll compute an 'interest' component and factor that out of the P&L, similar to what has been done for *Products* and *Services*?" Jack's tone was inquisitive, not confrontational. Everyone, especially Val, picked this up. She turned and smiled to herself. Jason noticed this, but did not respond outwardly. He did register the gestures inwardly, though.

"Exactly", Frank answered. "As part of our 'economic' analysis, we'll portray the adjustments to the P&L and the balance sheet in the same manner as done for our existing BU's and the total company".

"OK, got it!" Jack shot back.

"The next item has now become a 'non-issue', but we're showing it to explain the 'Other Asset' account on the balance sheet. One of the shareholders took out a loan from the company about three years ago. The loan has just recently been paid off. We're showing this to indicate that these transactions can occur with privately owned companies and need to be included in the 'due diligence'. The last section of Exhibit 173 provides an explanation of changes in Stockholders' Equity ('reported' book value) which has been one of the factors used by the lenders to '*EuroServ*'. In (historical) fiscal year #2, the shareholders paid out a dividend of $3.8 million – in addition to the $2 million owners' bonus. They have since ceased dividend payments, opting instead for higher annual owner bonuses. There may be some personal tax implications for the two forms of compensation, but we are not aware of them and the owners of '*EuroServ*' do not want to discuss them. They have provided us with all the relevant information to make the adjustments to their 'reported' financials, but will not discuss the rationale for their specific forms of compensation. They have signed representations and warranties, however, that everything they have done is perfectly legal and has been done for what they call 'personal' family considerations. To support this argument, Earl has indicated to me that he thought that in one or more European countries there have been new tax laws enacted during the past two years, with respect to corporate dividends".

"Again", Jason piped in, "this is not that unusual with a private company. The 'legal' issue is important, however, since I believe that the owners want to sell the business on an 'equity' – not an 'asset' – basis. Any violation of tax or other law could cause problems for the purchaser – in this case, Growthstar".

"We're aware of that issue", Val quipped, "but thank you for reminding us. That's about it for today, unless there are any questions on what has been presented and discussed".

With no further reaction from the group, they adjourned the meeting, with the understanding that Val would communicate the next steps and timetable within a few days. Dave, Val and Mandy walked down the hall together, talking about the upcoming meeting with the major Growthstar shareholders and sell-side analysts. Dave was visibly animated about the prospects for his first contact with the 'Street'.

Val had sent a memorandum indicating the schedule for further work sessions and meetings for the proposed '*Leasing*' acquisition. After a conversation with Earl and Jason, she outlined the next steps as follows:

1 Establish an 'economic' basis for the historical financials.
2 Identify the most critical issues – now and in the future.
3 Analyze the future outlook to be provided by the acquisition 'target'.
4 Develop an 'economic'-based future outlook.
5 Value the deal.
6 Prepare a recommendation – '*go/no go*' ... or *an 'alternative' scenario.*

Jason and Earl were sitting down in Earl's office to begin working on the first step when Jack burst in and shouted ... "So, you two are going to leave me 'out of the loop' on this deal. That's a nice way of saying 'thanks' for my starting to lean toward your 'economic' performance metrics and modifying my 'accounting' perspectives".

Earl and Jason looked at each other with totally dumbfounded expressions on their faces. They thought that Val had clearly asked them to prepare the economic-based financials, meet with Jack and then reconvene the 'team'. Earl thus stammered ... "I thought" ... but before he could continue Jack *screamed* at him ... "You *don't* always think, D'Mark, which is one of your *major* problems. So, consider us to again be '*at war*'!"

Earl and Jason were so taken back by this 'Jack attack' that they just sat speechless for a moment. This gave Jack the time he needed to, first burst out laughing and then chortle ... "Chalk up another practical joke for Dave Dollarby. He suggested this at the end of our meeting on the '*EuroServ*' deal. Dave said that this 'scare tactic' worked so well on Jason that you should also share in the experience, Earl. As for you, Jason, he said the 'score is now even'". He then went over to Earl, put his hand on the treasurer's shoulder and quipped

... "No hard feelings, I hope ... just having a little fun, Mr Funny! I'll be interested in the results of your work today. Let me know when you want to meet. I'll make time in my schedule".

Earl was equally dumbfounded by this gesture. Desperately grasping for something to say, but finding nothing, he simply shook his head from side to side. He finally gathered himself and muttered, "This is one of the best things that's happened since this process began. Thank you ... and thank Dave ... I mean it!"

Jack had made his point and left Earl's office as quickly as he had entered it. Jason and Earl continued to look at each other, but a grin began to appear on Jason's face. "We've got him convinced ... he's 'on board' now".

Earl smiled back and said, "I think you're right ... finally!"

The two of them sat for at least five more minutes, each thinking about all that had transpired during the past several months, and the 'mountain' that they felt they'd been climbing to enlist Jack's support for the 'value-based performance' endeavor. They both wanted to savor the moment of reaching the 'peak' by engaging in silent reflection, especially since neither of them had any words that would convey their feelings.

Earl broke the silence by saying ... "I never cease to be amazed by the 'goings on' in corporate life. Well, *my* attitude is 'pretty good' for moving ahead with our work".

Jason nodded. "So is *mine*", he responded. "Let's get started with figuring out what the cost of capital is for '*Leasing*'".

"We need to evaluate the major *CCAP* elements", Earl said. "First, in terms of the cost of equity (Ce) we need to determine a risk factor (*Beta*). If I've been paying attention, we should have a different cost of capital for '*Leasing*'".

"Absolutely", Jason replied, "particularly with regard to the financial leverage (that is, the high level of debt financing). But, you're correct in saying that we need to look at the *Beta* factor for '*Leasing*' to determine if it's different from Growthstar's 'mainstream' businesses. In fact, I think I have the answer".

"What do you mean?"

"I've accessed the *Beta* factor for the parent company of '*Leasing*' along with two other firms that appear to be comparable".

"So, Mr Consultant, what's the result"?

"As I suspected, the *Betas* fall within a range close to 1.10. The 'parent' is at 1.10. The others are at 1.02 and 1.15. Thus, I would suggest using 1.10. This level is consistent with other financial service evaluations I have been involved with, albeit slightly higher".

"OK, I buy into that", Earl responded. "And, it's *less than* the *Beta* of 1.25 that we've established for Growthstar. The rationale must be that '*Leasing*' has a lower 'business' risk due to the presence of an asset (the lease receivable) supported by the equipment being financed – thus, providing collateral for the revenue and income stream – somewhat offset by a higher 'financial' risk premium due to the leverage. What's next?"

We already have a 'risk-free' (long-term government bond) rate and market risk premium from the cost of capital analysis we did for Growthstar and the business units. They don't change. The risk-free rate (Rf) we're using is 6.5% and the market risk premium (Mrp) is 5.0%".

"OK, that should leave the cost of debt and the 'weighting' of the equity and debt".

"The debt costs (interest rates) are the ones that you produced as part of the historical analysis".

"The short-term debt rate is 7.0% and the long-term rate is 7.5%. Further, the effective tax rate for purposes of determining the 'tax shield' is 30%. What we need to do now is to translate this information into a schedule".

"That's true", Jason replied. "In this cost of capital analysis, however, we're going to highlight the cost of equity, as well as the weighted average cost of capital, since my guess is that we'll probably calculate Economic Profit (*EP*) on both bases".

"OK with me", Earl responded. "Let me see, what exhibit are we on now?"

Jason looked in his file and answered, "Exhibit 174".

Earl, with Jason looking over his shoulder and providing a bit of guidance, then produced Exhibit 174 on his computer.

As Earl completed the schedule and printed it, he exclaimed ... "the weighted average cost of capital (*CCAP*) for '*Leasing*' is just about 7% and the cost of equity (*Ce*) is 12%. You said that we would use both and, possibly, wind up analyzing this business on an 'equity' basis".

"I think so", Jason replied. "My experience with financial service businesses is that *Return on Equity* is a relevant measure and people who work in financial services often have difficulty judging performance when Interest Expense is not explicitly accounted for".

"I can relate to that comment based on the time I spent in banking and, also, since the 'debt-to-total capital' ratio is 71% – at least on a standard 'book' basis. That really has an impact on *CCAP* – 7% for '*Leasing*' versus 11% for our industrial businesses. Their cost of equity is much closer to ours (12% versus 12.75%), the difference in the *Betas* accounting for the difference in *Ce*".

"Well", Jason reiterated, "that's what financial services is all about ... earning a 'spread' on a low cost of capital through 'leveraging' the

Exhibit 174		**GROWTHSTAR INC.**			
		Acquisition Target Financials			
		Cost of Capital (CCAP)			
"Leasing" Financials					

Cost of Capital (CCAP) Without Operating Leases	Pre Tax Cost (Avg.)	Tax Shield (*)	After Tax Cost	Percent of Total IC (**)	Wt. Cost (CCAP)
Debt — see *'Memo'* for Interest Rates	7.2%	30.0%	5.04%	71.1%	3.58%
Preferred Stock		0.0%	0.00%	0.0%	0.00%
Equity	(***)	(***)	12.00%	28.9%	3.47%

Govt. Bond - "Risk Free" (*Rf*)	6.50%	**Weighted Average Cost (CCAP) =**	**7.05%**
Beta (B) - Parent Co. of 'Leasing'	1.10		
Market Risk Premium (*Mrp*)	5.00%	*CCAP - Round to ....*	*7.0%*

'Memo' - Interest Rate Detail:			
Short-term Debt	7.00%	**Cost of Equity (Ce) =**	12.00%
Long-term Debt	7.50%		
		Ce - Round to	*12.0%*

Notes:
(*) Debt Tax Shield @ statutory rate - use historical average

(**) Capital Structure - no Operating Leases ('not material') ... Book value is equivalent to Market Value

(***) *Equity Cost Calculation- after tax ....*	Risk Free Rate plus [Beta times Market Risk Premium]		
In Symbols .... Rf + [B x Mrp]	6.50% .... plus	1.10 .... times	5.00%

"Beta" Analysis ... Target Firm's stock trades at "predictive" beta of 1.10

(**) **Debt/Equity – 'Book' Basis ~ 'Market'**	Amount - ($Millions)		Percent of Total IC	
[Note: Operating Leases are 'not material']	Prior Year Actual	Current Yr. Forecast	Prior Year Actual	Current Yr. Forecast
Debt	$173	$181	71%	71%
Equity	69	74	29%	29%
Total	$242	$255	100%	100%

business. The important point is that '*Leasing*' clearly has its own cost of capital, whether it's *CCAP* or *Ce*. Let's move on".

"I think", Earl then stated, "that I can prepare the 'economic' analysis for the historical period. The main adjustments revolve around the impact of deferred taxes. As I see it, there are two adjustments. First is the 'cash' tax rate to calculate *NOP* and an 'economic based' Net Income (*NI*) After Taxes – based on *changes* in deferred taxes. Second is an Equity Capital (*EC*) that includes the deferred taxes on the balance sheet, since it represents a form of retained earnings. Operating leases are not 'material' and there is no goodwill on their books".

"OK, send me a copy when you're done".

"On the issue of the future outlook, I received their projections and, after I prepare the historical economic analysis, I should be able to do the same for the future outlook. Let me quickly show you what they've sent me", Earl said as he handed Jason copies of two financial schedules – Exhibits 175 and 176.

Jason reacted to the projected Income Statement by saying, "there's something that I'm concerned about with this deal".

"What's that?"

"When we look at what Growthstar should be willing to 'pay' for this business, I start to wonder if the future growth that the management of '*Leasing*' is forecasting – especially for 'Other Products' – is all that meaningful for *you*".

"I don't understand what you're saying. You've been *indoctrinating* us with the notion that the 'total present value' of a business is the sum of its 'no-growth' plus 'growth' components. Why wouldn't this logic hold true for an acquisition?"

"Normally it does. For example, when Frank, Dave and I 'value' the '*EuroServ*' deal, I believe the future outlook will have an impact on the price that we're going to pay".

"So, then, why wouldn't the same logic apply here?"

"Because, the future growth rate that the management of '*Leasing*' is forecasting – especially for the 'non-Growthstar' portion of the lease

Exhibit 175	**GROWTHSTAR INC.**				
$ Millions	Acquisition Target Financials (as "Reported")				
	.... Future Outlook Period — 5 Years				
"LEASING" Financials	Yr. #1	Yr. #2	Yr. #3	Yr. #4	Yr. #5
Income Statement					
Leasing Revenue:					
Growthstar Segment					
- *Growth Rate (%)*	*12.5%*	*12.5%*	*12.0%*	*11.0%*	*10.0%*
- $ Millions	$27	$30	$34	$38	$42
Other Products					
- *Growth Rate (%)*	*18.8%*	*18.8%*	*18.0%*	*16.5%*	*15.0%*
- $ Millions	$19	$23	$27	$31	$36
Total Leasing Revenue					
- **$ Millions**	**$46**	**$53**	**$61**	**$69**	**$77**
- *Revenue Growth Rate (%)*	*15.0%*	*15.1%*	*14.6%*	*13.4%*	*12.3%*
Operating Costs and Expenses:					
Cost of Leasing Revenue (COLR)	13	15	16	18	19
Selling & Marketing (S&M)	3	4	5	5	6
General & Administrative (G&A)	1	1	2	2	2
Total Operating Costs / Expenses	17	20	22	25	27
Operating Income	29	33	39	44	50
Interest Expense	13	15	17	20	23
Income before Taxes (IBT)	**16**	**18**	**21**	**24**	**28**
Provision for Taxes	5	5	6	7	8
Net Income After Taxes (NI)	**$11**	**$13**	**$15**	**$17**	**$19**
- *NI Growth Rate (%)*	*13.5%*	*12.5%*	*15.5%*	*11.1%*	*13.3%*

Exhibit 176	GROWTHSTAR INC.				
	Acquisition Target Financials				
$ Millions	(as "Reported")				
	.... Future Outlook Period — 5 Years				
"Leasing" Financials	**Yr. #1**	**Yr. #2**	**Yr. #3**	**Yr. #4**	**Yr. #5**
Balance Sheet - Beginning					
Assets					
Cash	$1	$1	$1	$1	$2
Finance Receivables - Short term	*158*	*190*	*218*	*250*	*284*
Other Current Assets	2	2	2	2	2
Total Current Assets	160	193	222	254	287
Fixed Assets:					
Gross	14	16	18	21	23
Accumulated Depreciation	(8)	(9)	(11)	(12)	(13)
Goodwill, etc.					
Gross	-	-	-	-	-
Accumulated Amortization	-	-	-	-	-
Finance Receivables - Long term	*95*	*104*	*119*	*136*	*155*
Other Assets	2	2	2	2	2
Total Assets	**$263**	**$305**	**$351**	**$401**	**$454**
Liabilities & Equity					
Accounts Payable	$1	$1	$1	$2	$2
Accrued Expenses	1	1	1	1	2
Income Taxes Payable	1	1	1	2	2
Short-term Debt	*110*	*133*	*153*	*175*	*199*
Total Current Liabilities	113	136	157	180	204
Long-term Debt	*71*	*78*	*89*	*102*	*116*
Deferred Taxes	5	6	7	8	9
Other Liabil's/Reserves	-	-	-	-	-
Total Liabilities	189	220	253	290	329
Stockholders' Equity	74	85	97	111	125
Total Liabilities & Equity	**$263**	**$305**	**$351**	**$401**	**$454**

portfolio – may not be what is in the best interests of Growthstar's shareholders. By that, I mean the investment of new capital into lease receivables for products manufactured by other companies. This type of investment – to diversify the lease portfolio – may be a 'winner' for the other firms (all of which are financial services companies) evaluating this deal, but may not have the greatest value creation potential for Growthstar's shareholders. This was the case with an industrial company that I worked for, early in my career, that diversified into financial services. Over a period of several years, they built up a large lease portfolio of 'other company' products. After finally realizing that this portfolio was not as profitable as the lease portfolio containing their own products, they sold off a significant portion of it".

"So, then, what are you saying ... that we should only be willing to pay for the 'run-off' of existing leases – the 'no-growth' component?"

"Perhaps", Jason answered. "This deal is a bit puzzling. You may remember when Val first mentioned the '*Leasing*' acquisition in the meeting we had in Jonathan's office, I suggested that one option would be to initiate this type of business within Growthstar as an 'internal' new business venture, which we could consider as a Value Driver Program. The company – the one I just mentioned – that I worked for earlier in my career took this approach. Their diversification came after a 'base' leasing business had been established. I need to think about this some more, but this 'make versus buy' decision is one of the critical issues that we need to discuss at our next meeting. Another issue is whether Growthstar should go beyond financing its own products, if we decide that venturing into the 'finance' business is the right thing to do in the first place. Getting into the 'finance' business entails a redefinition of the company's business, and needs to be given very serious thought. As you've seen, it produces a new cost of capital, a totally different financing policy, and potentially different valuation dynamics – for example, a different (probably lower) Market-to-Book (M/B) Ratio – versus what you're accustomed to with an industrial company. So, the issue may be ... does Growthstar believe it can potentially enhance its competitive position in the market by offering its own financing and 'bundling' a combination of sales, services and financing ... or does the company feel that it should diversify into a totally new business".

"That's an enlightening perception", Earl responded, "and I will think about it as I work through the analysis. There may be more to this deal than we've envisioned. Let's take a quick look at the balance sheet projections (Exhibit 176) and then adjourn this session".

"Lease receivables and debt seem to be increasing in line with the growth of the business. We'll analyze invested capital intensity and other key aspects of the balance sheet as we do the economic analysis".

Jason then asked, "has the parent company of '*Leasing*' put a price on the business?"

"I was going to mention that to you, since it was in the package of material that just arrived. They're asking $125 million (for the equity) plus the assumption of all the debt".

"OK", Jason replied. "At least we have something to compare your valuation to. When do you want to get together again?"

"Let's plan for the end of next week. Then, I'll schedule a meeting for the full team for a few days later. I'll inform Val and Jack of this timetable", Earl said – a twinkle appearing in his eye as he said Jack's name. "Do you really think Jack is 'on board'?"

"I do", Jason stated as he rose and left Earl's office.

Peter Uppcomer sent a message to Val Performa from Europe, while he was visiting with the owners and managers of '*EuroServ*', requesting a meeting as soon as possible after his return to the office. He wanted to provide a recap of his trip and was interested in the results of the initial meeting that was held while he was en-route to Europe. He also indicated that '*EuroServ*' did *not* have a long-range strategic or financial plan. They had just completed their annual 'operating plan' for the upcoming fiscal year and a copy was being sent along with Peter's message.

Val had been structuring a work schedule for '*EuroServ*' similar to the one that she had prepared for '*Leasing*', so the receipt of this message from Peter was helpful to her in establishing a timetable for the work needed for the review meeting upon Peter's return to the United States. Val, therefore, communicated the following to the 'team' members in terms of the next steps for '*EuroServ*':

1 Establish an 'economic' basis for the historical financials ... to include a 'pro forma' incorporating the 'adjustments'
2 Develop a realistic set of assumptions for a future outlook, working with the historical information and the 'operating plan' for the upcoming fiscal year
3 Translate these assumption (from #2) into an 'economic'-based future outlook
4 Identify critical issues and/or success factors
5 Value the proposed acquisition
6 Recommend what action(s) should be taken.

Peter's message put a heightened sense of urgency on the first three tasks. As a result, Dave and Frank cleared their calendars and scheduled a meeting for the next day. As Dave, Frank and Jason sat at the table in *Services*' conference room, Dave quipped ... "These people at '*EuroServ*' operate the same way we used to before being acquired by Growthstar. We *never* did any planning beyond 'next year' and the only goal we had was to increase revenue and pre tax profit over the prior year".

"Amazingly, there are still many companies that operate this way", Jason snapped back. "With technology advancing, certain markets getting more competitive and barriers to entry being reduced, and the globalization of business, there's probably a *greater need* for strategic and financial planning than ever before".

"So", Frank then said, "*we* have to construct the financial outlook and value the deal, with very little input from the 'target' company".

"That's the situation", Dave cracked ... "but, with our newly found knowledge about financial 'drivers', it should be a 'piece of cake'". Frank laughed at Dave's comment.

"First, though", Jason interjected, "we need to finalize the historical financials on a 'pro forma' basis for Growthstar and then put them

Exhibit 177		**GROWTHSTAR INC.**			
		Acquisition Target Financials			
$ Millions		("Economic" Basis)			
		Historical Period — 2 Years			Current
"EuroServ" Financials		**FY #2**	**FY #1**	**2-Yr Avg**	**FY Fcst.**
Income Statement Adjustments					
General & Administrative (G&A)	Acct. #				
Admin. Salary - Executive	7003	$1.2	$1.8	$1.5	$2.4
Executive Bonus	7004	0.8	1.2	1.0	1.6
Sub-total		**$2.0**	**$3.0**	**$2.5**	**$4.0**
Owner Bonus	7005	*$(2.0)*	*$(3.0)*	*$(2.5)*	*$(4.0)*
Operating Leases:					
Office Rent	7007	$0.8	$1.2	$1.0	$1.6
Equipment Lease	7008	0.4	0.6	0.5	0.8
Total		$1.2	$1.8	$1.5	$2.4
Capitalized Value	@ Factor =				
[add to Balance Sheet - IC]	*4.5*	*$5.4*	*$8.1*	*$6.8*	*$10.8*
	@ Rate =				
Interest Expense	*10.00%*	*$(0.5)*	*$(0.8)*	*$(0.7)*	*$(1.1)*
G&A Adjustments:					
Owner Bonus		*$(2.0)*	*$(3.0)*	*$(2.5)*	*$(4.0)*
Interest Expense		*(0.5)*	*(0.8)*	*(0.7)*	*(1.1)*
Total G&A Adjustments		*$(2.5)*	*$(3.8)*	*$(3.2)*	*$(5.1)*

into our economic format. Then, we'll be in a position to structure a set of assumptions about the future and develop an outlook".

"Fair enough", Dave countered. "Let's get started with finalizing the 'adjustments' and getting '*EuroServ*' on a 'pro forma' consistent with what we would expect if this business were part of Growthstar. I've thought about this situation and believe the answer is fairly straightforward". As he spoke, he handed copies of Exhibit 177 to Frank and Jason and said ... "Frank, I prepared this schedule from the material you provided at our first meeting – Exhibit 173 and the 'flip chart' data for operating leases".

"I believe", Dave continued, "that we can have a competitive pay plan for Europe by simply *eliminating* the 'owner bonus'. I've researched our executive pay levels – salary and incentive pay, and compared them to the sub-total for accounts 7003 and 7004 – Executive Salary and Executive Bonus, and feel that they are comparable based on the relative size and dynamics of the respective businesses. Further, the 'family' will be 'taken out' of the business with the acquisition, so they're no longer a factor".

"So", Frank mused, "we can eliminate $2 million of G&A expense in (historical) FY #2, $3 million in FY #1 and $4 million in the Current Year".

"As usual, Frank, you've got it! Moving right along ... I calculated the imputed Interest Expense for operating leases based on the capitalization factor of '4.5' and the interest rate we're using for our own operating leases".

"Sounds reasonable", Jason said.

"The impact of the '*Total G&A Adjustments*' is $2.5 million in FY #2, increasing steadily to about $5 million in the Current Year", Dave concluded. "Now, we can develop an 'economic' analysis on a basis compatible with our business".

"Let's do it", Frank stated emphatically. "Who's at the computer, Dave, you or me?"

"I need the practise more than you", Dave answered, "so let me construct the information with you two looking over my shoulder. Help me, guys ... what do I need to do?"

Frank responded with ... "First, determine Economic Profit (*EP*), then the Value Profit Margin (*VPM*) and then a 'No Growth' valuation".

"You *do* 'catch on fast', Frank", Jason quipped. "Go to it, Dave".

The three of them then collaborated to produce the following:

    Exhibit 178 – *Economic Profit*
    Exhibit 179 – *Value Profit Margin*
    Exhibit 180 – *Valuation- 'No Growth'*

"'*EuroServ*' is profitable economically and earns a very respectable return on its invested capital", Frank said as looked at the bottom two rows of numbers in Exhibit 178".

"The 'adjustments' change the whole profitability picture", Jason commented. "Jack will be interested in this".

"Did you say Jack?" Frank stammered.

"Yes, I said *Jack*", Jason repeated, winking at Dave. "And we *are* even, Dave".

"What's going on"? Frank asked sheepishly.

"Two good things", Dave replied. "First, the 'joke on Earl' obviously worked ... but, more importantly, Jack made his overture and has now come 'on board'. He told me this after our last meeting, which is why I put him up to the 'scare tactic' prank with Earl".

"Are you serious?" Frank said inquisitively ... having a hard time believing what he was hearing about Jack coming 'on board' with the 'economic-based' approach to financial performance.

"We are", Dave and Jason responded together.

Since nothing more needed to be said, they all looked at Exhibit 179.

"'*EuroServ*' has a larger *VPM* 'spread' and a higher *ROIC* than we do", Dave exclaimed.

"Yes", Jason responded, "but they're not carrying the 'goodwill' burden that you are".

"I think it's good that we've done the Value Profit Margin analysis on both a 'pre-' and 'post-tax' basis", Frank interjected. "I know we're

Exhibit 178

GROWTHSTAR INC.

Acquisition Target Financials

$ Millions

("Economic" Basis)

"EuroServ" Financials
Economic Profit

	"Base"	Historical Period — 2 Years			Current
		FY #2	FY #1	2-Yr Avg	FY Fcst.
Income Statement	"Base"				
Revenue	$25	$35	$47	$41	$60
Total Operating Costs & Expenses		32	44	38	57
G&A Adjustments		(3)	(4)	(3)	(5)
Operating Income (EBIT/A)		**6**	**7**	**6**	**8**
"Book" P&L Tax Rate		40%	40%	40%	40%
"Book" Tax Provision		2	3	2	3
Net Operating Profit (NOP)		**3**	**4**	**4**	**5**
Balance Sheet - "Beginning"					
Operating Capital - 'reported'		$13	$13	$13	$17
plus: Operating Cash	incl. @5%	-	-	-	-
Operating Leases		5	8	7	11
Invested Capital (IC)		**$19**	**$21**	**$20**	**$27**
Economic Profit - "EP"	* CCAP = 11.0%				
NOP		$3	$4	$4	$5
CCAP		(2)	(2)	(2)	(3)
"EP" (Level '2')		**$1**	**$2**	**$2**	**$2**
* CCAP same as Growthstar					
"ROIC" (Level '2')		**18.2%**	**18.8%**	**18.5%**	**18.4%**

Exhibit 179

GROWTHSTAR INC.

Acquisition Target Financials

$ Millions, except "ICI"

("Economic" Basis)

"EuroServ" Financials
Value Profit Margin

	Historical Period — 2 Years			Current
	FY #2	FY #1	2-Yr Avg	FY Fcst.
Revenue	$35	$47	$41	$60
Invested Capital	$19	$21	$20	$27
Invested Capital Intensity ("ICI")	*$0.54*	*$0.46*	*$0.49*	*$0.45*
Value Profit Margin ("VPM")				
- EBIT/A Basis				
Actual EBIT/A Margin (%)	*16.4%*	*14.4%*	*15.3%*	*13.9%*
Value Profit Margin ("VPM")	*9.9%*	*8.4%*	*9.1%*	*8.3%*
"Spread"– Act. EBIT/A % vs. VPM	**6.5%**	**6.0%**	**6.2%**	**5.6%**
- NOP Basis				
Actual NOP Margin (%)	*9.8%*	*8.6%*	*9.2%*	*8.3%*
Value Profit Margin ("VPM")	*5.9%*	*5.1%*	*5.4%*	*5.0%*
"Spread"– Actual NOP% vs. VPM	**3.9%**	**3.6%**	**3.7%**	**3.3%**
Verify 'VPM' to 'ROIC' (NOP Basis)				
Actual NOP Margin (%)	*9.8%*	*8.6%*	*9.2%*	*8.3%*
Invested Capital Intensity ("ICI")	*$0.54*	*$0.46*	*$0.49*	*$0.45*
"ROIC" (Level '2')	18.2%	18.8%	18.5%	18.4%

focused on 'after-tax' results, but it's also nice to see these numbers on a 'pre-tax' basis".

"I agree", Dave added, "and Peter likes to view 'pre-tax' results, also. So, what is this firm worth, based on the existing level of revenue and profitability?" As Dave was speaking, they all looked at Exhibit 180.

"Hmmm" ... Jason muttered as he focused on the 'far right' column of the last section (*Warranted 'Equity' Value*) ... "$45 million of Total Market Value (*TMV*) and $35 million of Equity Value with 'no' future growth. Do we have any idea of what the owners are asking for this business and whether they want to sell stock or assets?"

"*Yes and yes*", Dave answered. "While it's not in writing, we believe that a price of $75 million for 100% of the equity in the company plus the assumption of debt is the 'asking price' and that the owners are definitely selling their equity (that is, their common stock). Val said this was communicated to her verbally on her visit earlier this year. Peter will be confirming this price and deal structure, but he has said nothing in his recent message, so he probably hadn't discussed this subject when he sent his message".

"OK", Jason responded, "we've completed the historical analysis. Dave, you have an 'operating plan' for the upcoming fiscal year. Let's see what they're projecting. Then let's prepare a schedule of growth

Exhibit 180		**GROWTHSTAR INC.**			
		Acquisition Target Financials			
$ Millions		**Valuation Highlights**			
		Historical Period — 2 Years			Current
"EuroServ" Financials		FY #2	FY #1	2-Yr Avg	FY Fcst.
Valuation - "No Growth"		*["Warranted" Value ... for each year's "Economic" Results]*			
'FCF' Approach					
Net Operating Profit (NOP)		$3	$4	$4	$5
Cost of Capital (CCAP)		11.0%	11.0%	11.0%	11.0%
Total Market Value (TMV)		**$31**	**$37**	**$34**	**$45**
Total Market Value (TMV)		$31	$37	$34	$45
less IC		19	21	20	27
Market Value Added (MVA)		*$12*	*$15*	*$14*	*$18*
'EP' Approach					
Net Operating Profit (NOP)		$3	$4	$4	$5
Capital Charge (CCAP) @ ...	*11.0%*	(2)	(2)	(2)	(3)
Economic Profit ("EP")		$1	$2	$2	$2
"EP" / CCAP = 'MVA' (*)		*$12*	*$15*	*$14*	*$18*
plus IC		19	21	20	27
Total Market Value (TMV)		**$31**	**$37**	**$34**	**$45**
(*) 'MVA' — Market Value Added					
Warranted "Equity" Value					
Total Market Value (TMV)		$31	$37	$34	$45
less: Total Debt		(7)	(8)	(7)	(10)
Equity Value		**$25**	**$28**	**$26**	**$35**

factors, along with the other financial 'drivers' to help us in developing an outlook for the future. Without a strategy, this is going to be a bit of a 'guess', but we can at least make an effort. Let me start the financial 'driver' analysis with the following, which captures some of the dynamics of the past two to three years". Jason then went to the computer and prepared Exhibit 181.

"I don't know how much help this information will be, but it folds in the 'incremental' performance indicators – *ICI* and *VPM* – as well as the key growth rates. Revenue is increasing very fast (31% per year over the past 2 years) with profit (*NOP*) and invested capital (*IC*) growing at about 20% per year during the same period. This explains the fact that both *ICI* and *EBIT/A* margins are lower, on an incremental basis. The 'net' result is that the *VPM* 'spread' is lower on an 'incremental' basis – versus the *VPM* 'spread' on a 'total revenue' basis – but it's still positive. We can use these indicators to calculate 'incremental *ROIC*'. Dave, perhaps you can do this and incorporate into the forecast for next year".

"I just may be able to do that", Dave snickered.

"We've probably gone about as far as we can today", Jason concluded. "We should get together with Val in a few more days and include Jack in our session. Jack possesses a wealth of knowledge and a keen financial mind, which can now be channeled in an 'economic' direction. Assuming that he's really 'on board', Jack can help us develop a future outlook for this business. Then, we should

---

Exhibit 181

GROWTHSTAR INC.
Acquisition Target Financials
Financial 'Drivers'

$ Millions, except "ICI"

"EuroServ" Financials	Historical Period FY #2	Historical Period FY #1	Current FY Fcst.	2-Yr Avg (FY#1/CFY)
Growth Rates				
Revenue	40%	33%	30%	31%
Net Operating Profit (NOP)		17%	25%	21%
Invested Capital (IC)		13%	28%	20%

Invested Capital Intensity ("ICI")	Historical Period — 2 Years FY #2	FY #1	2-Yr Avg	Current FY Fcst.
Total Invested Capital (IC)	$0.54	$0.46	$0.49	$0.45
Incremental IC ("I")		$0.21		$0.43

Value Profit Margin ("VPM")	Historical Period — 2 Years FY #2	FY #1	2-Yr Avg	Current FY Fcst.
- EBIT/A Basis ... Total				
Actual EBIT/A Margin (%)	16.4%	14.4%	15.3%	13.9%
Value Profit Margin ("VPM")	9.9%	8.4%	9.1%	8.3%
"Spread" - Actual EBIT/A % vs. VPM	6.5%	6.0%	6.2%	5.6%
- EBIT/A Basis ... Incremental				
Actual EBIT/A Margin (%)		8.4%		12.1%
Value Profit Margin ("VPM")		3.9%		8.0%
"Spread" - Actual EBIT/A % vs. VPM		4.4%		4.2%

be ready to meet with Peter, get his input and finalize our projections and the valuation for this acquisition".

"Sounds good to me", Dave responded. Frank smiled and nodded his head.

Earl, Jack and Jason met as scheduled to review the highlights for the cost of capital analysis and the outlook submitted by '*Leasing*'. After Jack had a chance to review Exhibits 174, 175 and 176, they delved into the translation of the 'reported' financials into a set of 'economic'-based financials – historical and future. Earl then contacted Val and Jonathan, gave them a synopsis of their progress and results of their work, and suggested a meeting date for the '*Leasing*' team. Jonathan indicated that he wanted to be part of this next session, which would be comprehensive and thought provoking, and establish the framework for a review meeting with Ian.

As the 'team' gathered in the Corporate Finance conference room, Jonathan 'made the rounds' to thank everyone for their inputs and to indicate that Earl and Val had kept him abreast of the status of this acquisition. Val maintained her informal style of running these meetings by greeting everyone, including Jonathan, while remaining seated. "We should probably start by listing the key issues that have surfaced since our last 'team' meeting". She got up, went to the flip chart, and wrote:

ISSUES – RE: 'LEASING'

- **Diversification – into a new line of business ... extending to financing other company products, in addition to Growthstar's**
- **The value of 'their' growth plan to 'our' shareholders ... what is it worth?**
- **Entry into a financing business via acquisition versus internal development**

"These are the 'most critical' issues that have surfaced. Are there any others?"

Jonathan thought for a moment and then said ... "Based on my conversations with Earl, I would say that the level of 'debt financing' – that is, the financial leverage that comes along with the finance business – and its impact on our overall capital structure (that is, our consolidated debt-to-total capital ratio) could be an issue, especially for our lenders".

Mandy Bettertalk jumped into the discussion with ... "The management time and effort entailed with this deal could be an issue for the major shareholders, especially if they perceive a distraction – especially on the part of Ian and Jonathan – to executing the plans that we've been analyzing during the past couple of months. This is relevant, since we're about to have a 'special' meeting to tout our future plans for *Products* and *Services*".

"Any other issues?" Val asked. With no more input, she went to the flip chart and wrote, beneath the first three issues:

- **Financial Leverage – 'consolidated' D/TC ratio**
- **Management Attention – potential for 'distraction'...** **shareholder views**

"Earl, Jack and Jason have constructed a set of 'economic'-based financials from the information supplied by the management of '*Leasing*'. They will lead us first through an historical analysis and then a future outlook, essentially taking the 'as reported' information and transforming it into 'economics' for this type of business. Gentlemen, it's your show!"

Earl, taking a cue from Val, remained seated in his chair and said ... "At our last session, you were given the 'reported' historical *Income Statement* (Exhibit 168), *Balance Sheet* (Exhibit 169) and a schedule entitled *Supporting Data & Ratios* (Exhibit 170). We've calculated what we believe to be appropriate costs of capital for '*Leasing*', noting that they are different from our existing industrial businesses". Earl then walked over to the flip chart, and on a new sheet, wrote:

Cost of Capital	Cost of Equity (Ce)	Cost of Capital (CCAP)
Growthstar	12.75%	11.0%
'Leasing'	12.0%	7.0%

Financial Leverage	D/TC Ratio	E/TC Ratio
Growthstar	29%	71%
'Leasing'	71%	29%

"Now, isn't that interesting", Jonathan quipped. "The financial leverage for '*Leasing*' is the 'reverse' of our existing businesses. Earl, how much debt does '*Leasing*' have?"

"$173 million at the end of last year (historical FY #1) and around $180 million by the end of the current year, as compared to our total debt levels (including operating leases) of $110 million at the end of last year and $115 million forecasted for the end of this year. This is somewhat of an 'apples to oranges' comparison, as you know, since the finance business is highly leveraged as compared to an industrial business".

"I'm aware of that", Jonathan countered. "I just wanted to get a 'feel' of the 'numbers'".

"Based on what I've been exposed to over the past few months, their *CCAP* is incredibly low", Jack interjected.

"As we discussed, that's the nature of the finance business", Jason replied.

"We need to keep moving", chimed in Earl, "so let's all realize the completely different financing and cost of capital structure associated with '*Leasing*', versus what we have been accustomed to".

"Next, we have developed an 'economic' based historical profile for '*Leasing*' – as indicated by Exhibits 182 and 183. Exhibit 182 is the 'economic' based Income Statement, which we've entitled *Profit & Loss* – with the dollars 'rounded'".

"The only adjustment of significance is Deferred Taxes, which does have an impact on the 'effective' tax rate. As you can see by looking at the bottom row of numbers, the impact is about $1 million per year of additional Net Income (*NI*). You will also notice that we've analyzed the 'economics' on a 'Net Income' basis – *including* Interest Expense. Jack, Jason and I have deliberated on this subject. Finance businesses can be evaluated 'economically' either on a total invested capital or equity capital basis. Since it's easier to do the analysis leaving in the Interest Expense and since there are no operating leases of significance, our ultimate 'valuation' of this business will be on an 'equity' capital basis. We'll derive an Economic Profit (*EP*) using the cost of equity (*Ce*), as well as the weighted average cost of capital (*CCAP*). We will, thus, show the analysis both ways and then move forward to our valuation using the 'equity' capital approach.

Exhibit 182	GROWTHSTAR INC.				
	Acquisition Target Financials				
$ Millions	("Economic" Basis)				
	..... Historical Period — 3 Years				Current
"LEASING" Financials	FY #3	FY #2	FY #1	3-Yr Avg	FY Fcst.
Profit & Loss					
Total Leasing Revenue	$25	$30	$35	$30	$40
Total OPEX	8	11	12	10	14
Operating Income	17	20	24	20	26
Interest Expense	8	9	11	9	12
Income before Taxes (IBT)	9	10	13	11	14
Provision for Taxes	3	3	4	3	4
Deferred Taxes:					
Current Year	2	3	4		5
Prior Year	1	2	3		4
Change	1	1	1		1
"Cash" Taxes	2	2	3	2	3
[Book less Deferred]					
"Cash" Tax Rate (%)	18.8%	20.2%	22.0%	20.5%	22.6%
Net Income After Taxes (NI)	$7	$8	$10	$9	$11
vs. "Reported" NI	$6	$7	$9	$7	$10
Difference	$1	$1	$1	$1	$1

Exhibit 183	GROWTHSTAR INC.				
	Acquisition Target Financials				
$ Millions	("Economic" Basis)				
	..... Historical Period — 3 Years				Current
"LEASING" Financials	FY #3	FY #2	FY #1	3-Yr Avg	FY Fcst.
Invested Capital (IC)	$154	$186	$218	$186	$246
Equity Capital (EC)					
"As Reported"	$47	$55	$63	$55	$69
plus Deferred Taxes	1	2	3	2	4
"Economic" Basis	$48	$57	$66	$57	$73
Economic Profit ("IC" Basis)					
Operating Income	$17	$20	$4	$20	$26
"Cash" Tax Rate	18.8%	20.2%	22.0%	20.5%	22.6%
Net Operating Profit (NOP)	$13	$16	$18	$16	$20
Cost of Capital (CCAP) - %	*7.0%*	*7.0%*	*7.0%*	*7.0%*	*7.0%*
Capital Charge (CCAP) - $	(11)	(13)	(15)	(13)	(17)
Economic Profit ("EP")	**$2**	**$2**	**$3**	**$3**	**$3**
Economic Profit ("EC" Basis)					
Net Income - "Economic"	$7	$8	$10	$9	$11
Cost of Equity (Ce) - %	*12.0%*	*12.0%*	*12.0%*	*12.0%*	*12.0%*
Capital Charge (Ce) - $	(6)	(7)	(8)	(7)	(9)
Economic Profit ("EP")	**$1**	**$1**	**$2**	**$2**	**$2**
"Economic" ROIC	*8.7%*	*8.4%*	*8.4%*	*8.5%*	*8.2%*
"Economic" ROE	*15.1%*	*14.3%*	*14.9%*	*15.1%*	*14.4%*

The historical *EP*, Return on Invested Capital (*ROIC*) and Return on Equity (*ROE*) are all shown in Exhibit 183".

Earl continued by saying ... "As I believe is evident, '*Leasing*' has been and is currently profitable by almost any measure. They are generating returns above both their *CCAP* and *Ce*, respectively, as indicated by the bottom two rows – 'Economic' *ROIC* and *ROE*. Economic Profits are also positive in all years. So, the initial reaction is ... *hey*, this looks 'pretty good' ... and it is. However, we have this 'consultant' who is challenging us as to the rationale for being in this business and, if we decide to enter the finance business, how far should we go. Jason, do you want to say anything?"

"Not yet, except to pay close attention to the 'no-growth' value, when we get there. You and Val have articulated my issues up to this point. We should continue with the future outlook, but think about whether we need to acquire '*Leasing*' to generate the future revenue and income stream – again, assuming you want to be in the finance business – or whether you could build this up on your own. The future is mainly about hiring people, installing systems, selling to customers who are yours to begin with, and accessing debt capital, which you can do. The revenue and income stream from leases already 'out there' is something you would have to acquire".

Exhibit 184	GROWTHSTAR INC.				
$ Millions	**Acquisition Target Financials** ("Economic" Basis)				
	.... Future Outlook Period — 5 Years				
"Leasing" Financials	Yr. #1	Yr. #2	Yr. #3	Yr. #4	Yr. #5
Profit & Loss					
Total Leasing Revenue	$46	$53	$61	$69	$77
Total OPEX	17	20	22	25	27
Operating Income	29	33	39	44	50
Interest Expense	13	15	17	20	23
Income before Taxes (IBT)	16	18	21	24	28
Provision for Taxes	5	5	6	7	8
Deferred Taxes:					[est.]
Current Year	6	7	8	9	10
Prior Year	5	6	7	8	9
Change	1	1	1	1	1
"Cash" Taxes	4	4	5	6	7
[Book less Deferred]					
"Cash" Tax Rate (%)	23.6%	24.4%	25.3%	25.8%	26.4%
Net Income After Taxes (NI)	**$12**	**$14**	**$16**	**$18**	**$20**
vs. "Reported" NI	$11	$13	$15	$17	$19
Difference	$1	$1	$1	$1	$1

Earl then picked up the dialogue. "We now want to view the future for *'Leasing'*, at least the way that their management sees it. Exhibit 184 provides the *Profit & Loss* outlook".

"The management of *'Leasing'* is forecasting a nice, steady increase in the 'top' and 'bottom' lines. Gee, what a surprise!" Muted laughter ensued. "However, there is a substantial new capital investment required to execute this growth plan. After we look at Exhibit 185, I'll show you the implications. First, though we need to see what the future aggregate levels of total capital and equity capital are estimated to be, along with the *EP*, *ROIC*, and *ROE*, as reflected in Exhibit 185".

"The economic profits and returns (on total and equity capital) are continuing the historical patterns. Gee, another surprise! But, so are the capital intensities, which should be expected, as indicated by the bottom two rows – *ICI* and *ECI*. The impact on new investment 'dollars' is as follows", Earl stated as he walked over to the flip chart and, on a new sheet, wrote:

New Investment – 'Leasing'	**Yr #1**	**Yr #2**	**Yr #3**	**Yr #4**	**Yr #5**
Annual Total – $ Millions	**$14**	**$42**	**$44**	**$50**	**$53**
5-Year Total – $203 million					

"Even though *'Leasing'* will earn a return above its cost of capital, according to this outlook, Growthstar is looking at a future scenario in which $200 million or so of 'new' capital will be invested at a return in the range of 8.2% to 8.5% – a 'spread of 1.2 to 1.5 percentage

Exhibit 185	**GROWTHSTAR INC.**				
	Acquisition Target Financials				
$ Millions, except	("Economic" Basis)				
Capital Intensity	.... Future Outlook Period — 5 Years				
"Leasing" Financials	**Yr. #1**	**Yr. #2**	**Yr. #3**	**Yr. #4**	**Yr. #5**
Invested Capital (IC)	$260	$302	$346	$396	$449
Equity Capital (EC)					
"As Reported"	74	85	97	111	125
plus Deferred Taxes	5	6	7	8	9
"Economic" Basis	$79	$91	$104	$119	$134
Economic Profit ("IC" Basis)					
Operating Income	$29	$33	$39	$44	$50
"Cash" Tax Rate	23.6%	24.4%	25.3%	25.8%	26.4%
Net Operating Profit (NOP)	$22	$25	$29	$33	$37
Cost of Capital (CCAP) - %	7.0%	7.0%	7.0%	7.0%	7.0%
Capital Charge (CCAP) - $	(18)	(21)	(24)	(28)	(32)
Economic Profit ("EP")	$4	$4	$4	$4	$5
Economic Profit ("EC" Basis)					
Net Income - "Economic"	$12	$14	$16	$18	$20
Cost of Equity (Ce) - %	12.0%	12.0%	12.0%	12.0%	12.0%
Capital Charge (Ce) - $	(9)	(11)	(13)	(14)	(16)
Economic Profit ("EP")	$3	$3	$3	$3	$4
"Economic" ROIC	8.5%	8.3%	8.3%	8.2%	8.2%
"Economic" ROE	15.3%	14.9%	15.2%	14.9%	15.1%
Memo: Capital Intensity					
"ICI"	$5.65	$5.70	$5.71	$5.76	$5.81
"ECI"	$1.71	$1.72	$1.72	$1.73	$1.74

points above *CCAP*. We need to contrast these with the expected future 'returns' and 'spreads' of our *Products* and *Services* business units. As we've seen in their plans, *Products* is anticipating a return on new capital ('incremental' *ROIC*) in the 17% range – consistent with its historical performance. *Services* is planning for high returns of 20% or more on its 'strategic' investments over the next few years. As you all know, part of my job is to find the capital to fund *all* value-creating investment, and I'm prepared to do that. However, everyone involved in the decision on this deal needs to be aware of the implications. As most of you also know, I am certainly *not* opposed to entering the finance business, if it can create economic value commensurate with the investment. I come from a banking background and think I understand 'lending' – which is what we're talking about with this deal. We need to be certain that it's a good strategic fit and an economically viable investment for Growthstar".

"This last statement, along with the one on the *ROIC* for '*Leasing*' versus that for *Products* and *Services*, are particularly relevant for the shareholders", Mandy interjected. "Our business definition and direction has to be clear to them, to enable them to do their own valuations of our common stock, based on our present performance and future opportunities".

"I'm starting to get a grasp of the issues . . . and they are significant", Jonathan added.

"Let me try to 'close the loop' on the invested capital aspect of this deal with a comparison of the new investments for our various plans", Earl then stated. "I'll use a five-year future time frame to be consistent. What I'll write on the flip chart are the five-year aggregate net new investments for '*Leasing*', *Products* and *Services*".

5-Year Change in Invested Capital	$Millions
'*Leasing*'	$203
Products	$106
Services	$134

"I think the implications are clear. The finance business is very capital intensive. Again, this is not bad, it's just a fact. We're now in a position to review the equity valuation for this deal. As I've done before, I'm going to ask Jason to lead us through this final topic".

"This deal certainly presents an interesting set of dynamics", Jason began. "On the one hand, we have a potentially powerful 'instant' strategic move into the bundling of product sales, service and financing. On the other hand, we may be paying for future revenue streams with questionable value to Growthstar's share-holders, compounded by the possibility of creating the most relevant part of these streams internally. Next, as Earl and Mandy have pointed out, is the issue of 'perception' in the investment commu-nity as to 'what type of company' Growthstar is and the implica-tion on *Market-to-Book* and other valuation ratios. So, as we view Exhibit 186 – *Valuation*, we need to do so with the realization that the equity values that 'fall out' from the plan submitted to us by '*Leasing*' may not be what Growthstar should be paying. Growth-star's 'price' may be different from that of another financial services firm that is already in the 'finance' business and for whom this deal may provide a good entry into a market deemed to be attractive. With all these caveats, let's take a look at the final result of what we have been working on – the 'no-growth', 'growth' and 'total' equity values for '*Leasing*' ".

"Just a reminder", Earl interjected, "that all the values are for the 'equity' of the business, and entail the assumption of all the debt, which will be approximately $180 million. Further, these 'equity' values need to be compared to the 'asking price' of $125 million".

Exhibit 186	GROWTHSTAR INC.				
	Acquisition Target Financials				
$ Millions	**Valuation Highlights**				
	Valuation re: Current Year & Future Outlook / 5 Years				
"Leasing" Financials					
Valuation - "No Growth"	**Current FY**				
"EP" / Equity Capital Approach					
Current FY "EP"	$1.7				
Cost of Equity Capital (Ce)	*12.0%*				
MVA = Current FY "EP" capitalized	$14				
plus: EC ("Economic" Book Value)	$79				
Equity Value - "Market"	**$93**				
Market-to-Book (M/B) Ratio	1.18				
Valuation - "Growth"	**Yr. #1**	**Yr. #2**	**Yr. #3**	**Yr. #4**	**Yr. #5**
Net New Equity - 'Cumulative'	$5	$18	$31	$46	$61
Net Income (NI) - "Economic"	$1.5	$3.1	$5.4	$7.2	$9.8
Equity Charge (Ce) — @ 12%	(0.7)	(2.2)	(3.7)	(5.5)	(7.3)
Economic Profit ('EP')	$0.8	$0.9	$1.6	$1.7	$2.5
					Residual Year 5 'EP' cap'd at Ce 12.0%
Net Present Value (NPV) - "Growth"	**$16**				$20.5
"Growth" ROE — Return on 'Incremental' New Equity	**Yr. #1** 27.2%	**Yr. #2** *16.9%*	**Yr. #3** *17.2%*	**Yr. #4** *15.8%*	**Yr. #5** *16.0%*
Valuation - "Total" ["No Growth + Growth"]	**$109**				

"I've been listening very attentively to just about everything that's been said", Jack said as he surveyed the 'next to the last row' of numbers – 'Growth' ROE – "and I must say that these 'incremental' ROEs look mighty attractive".

"They do indeed", Jonathan added. "In fact, most of the 'numbers' for this deal appear to be 'attractive'. The 'issues' are the potential stumbling blocks. I think we've seen a very thorough analysis today, which is certainly thought provoking. Any other comments?"

Jack was coming 'on board' and had studied all the exhibits and, also, gone back to his notes from the previous 'team' meeting. "If we compare the 'total' equity value of $109 million in Exhibit 186 to the 'asking price' of $125 million, we're about $16 million 'short' – or, to say it another way, they want $16 million more than what we say it's worth 'on paper'. I suppose we could negotiate some of this difference, but if a bidding situation ensues, this might not be possible. Looking at their forecasted balance sheet for the end of this current year, the 'reported' stockholders equity is $74 million, and our 'economic' figure – adding in $5 million of deferred taxes – is $79 million. So, depending on which 'book' value you choose, the *M/B* ratio is in the

1.6 to 1.7 range – dividing the $125 million 'asking price' by the 'book' value. Is this reasonable?"

"It may be a bit high, but isn't 'out-of-line' for banking and financial service company acquisitions", Earl answered. "However, that's the case when one finance firm buys or merges with another, especially to 'gain control'. The issues get back to what Jason has stated ... is the *price* – 'asking' or 'warranted' – relevant for our company? Should we even consider paying more than the 'no-growth' value – in this case, $93 million? Do we want a 'run-off' stream of lease revenue and income from 'Other' products? While it's part of the $93 million 'no-growth' equity value, what is it really worth to us? How 'attractive' is their growth plan? The incremental revenues over the next five years for '*Leasing*' are almost evenly split between 'Growthstar' and 'Other'. This diversification may be an ideal scenario for another financial services firm, but is it what *we* want? Further, how 'valuable' is the growth plan that we would acquire, since it contributes only 15% ($16 out of $109 million) of the total warranted equity value? Could we build a comparable growth scenario for less than $16 million? I still don't have the answers, but the fact that these questions keep 'popping up' is starting to send me a message".

"Which is ...?" Jonathan said inquisitively.

"That entering the finance business via the *acquisition* route may *not* be in the best interests of our shareholders".

Val then chimed in with ... "I'm not convinced that being in the finance business is critical for our competitive positioning, either. It's important for our customers to have financing available at what they would consider a reasonable cost. Now, they have it – via '*Leasing*' and the other finance firms providing customer financing and considering the acquisition of '*Leasing*'. We haven't seen any of our competitors offer 'bundling' ... at least not yet. This may be a trend in the future, but we didn't see it as an immediate threat in this year's strategic plan. 'Bundling' of product sales, service and financing may be the 'wave' of the future, but it will have to be at a competitive cost. Our customers will only go so far to get the convenience of 'bundling'. And, as has been stated, we could conceivably build a leasing business for our products *internally*".

"Well", Jonathan exclaimed, "I'm delighted that this deal is so 'crystal clear' in terms of the message we need to take to Ian". Everyone broke out laughing with this comment.

Mandy jumped in with ... "That's we get paid for – to sort out complex issues, structure the analysis, and help our CEO make decisions to enhance shareholder value".

"Amen", Jonathan sighed. "Well, we've 'beaten this horse' enough today. *Our* CEO is going to have to sift through these issues as we've done and 'weigh in' with his perspective. We'll need to present these financial schedules in 'chart form' for Ian".

"We've started", Earl replied, "and will have them completed in a day or so".

"Val, let's get on Ian's calendar within the next few days. We need to reach a decision on this deal – and we need to do it soon. I assume that '*Leasing*' wants a response of some sort".

"You must be reading my mind, Jonathan", Val responded. "I just got a call yesterday indicating that the first round of bids must be submitted within the next ten days. Further, there's no provision in their documents for 'pulling apart' the deal or buying a portion of the lease portfolio. They want to sell and exit this business in its entirety".

As Dave, Frank, Val, Jack and Jason were gathering around the *Services* conference table, Dave noted that the entire 'team' was present except for Mandy. "Jonathan may 'pop in' at some point", Val said", since he hasn't yet participated in a session on '*EuroServ*'. That is, assuming his mind is clear from the issues on the '*Leasing*' deal. We can get started, however".

Dave had a perspective on the way to get started on a future outlook and wanted to get it 'on the table'. "I've reflected on the process that we used to develop our growth plan for *Services*, in light of the situation we face with having to develop an outlook for '*EuroServ*'. There are forecasting methods and inputs that we used to develop our financial plan, which should be appropriate for '*EuroServ*'. After all, the two businesses are basically the same. Specifically, I think the areas that have comparability are as follows", he said excitedly as he went to the flip chart and wrote:

'*EuroServ*' Outlook

1. **Revenue Growth ... 'Growthstar' – relate to sales for Products-Europe**
2. **Revenue Growth ... 'Other' – relate to US, but lower rate of growth**
3. **COGS and SMS ... ratio to revenue – use historical ratios**
4. **G&A and R&D ... inflationary increases to Current Year forecast – US will handle any 'growth oriented' requirements ... these are two (2) 'operating leverage' points for this deal**
5. **Operating Cash, Receivables and Inventory ... use 'Intensity' (ICI) – they will increase at the growth rate of Total Revenue**
6. **Fixed Capital and Operating Leases ...??**

With grins on their faces, all the others observed Dave and his gestures as he wrote on the flip chart.

"So", Jack snickered good-naturedly, "this is the guy who had never done a 'long-range' plan before coming to Growthstar and who never did much work on a balance sheet. Is this a 'boy genius' teaching us how to do financial planning? Jason, you can probably do your 'exit routine' – since we now have 'Dave the Planner' working for us".

"Amen", Jason reacted, "I'll clean out my desk, load up my briefcase, and be 'out of here'! Before I leave, though, let me commend you, Dave, on the simplicity and reasonableness of what you've outlined".

Val then logged in with ... "Before you leave, Jason, please keep your seat for a while longer and, along with our new 'boy genius', guide us through this financial outlook and valuation for '*EuroServ*'".

"I don't know if we *need* Jason any longer, Val. Dave seems to have 'caught on' to planning really fast". Jack was, for the first time, *really* feeling part of the group and enjoying the banter.

"Now, look who's trying to be 'Mr Funny' and get the laughs", Dave quipped.

"Well", Val responded, "I guess we can sit here and see who has the most clever 'one-liners' ... or, we can mix in a little work with our humor".

Dave retorted with ... "I'll vote for the 'mix' – just as long as it's only a 'little' work ... just kidding! On a more serious note, I don't have a good 'feel' for the fixed capital element of this deal. I really don't know what they have or what they need. Peter knows about this issue, however, and assured me that he would return with enough information to prepare a credible capital expenditure outlook".

"In that case", Jason interjected, "I would suggest that we use your 'planning template', Dave, and forecast all the other elements – completing the capital expenditure portion when Peter returns and meets with us".

"Does everyone agree with this approach?" Val asked. Jack and Frank nodded. "OK, then, let's get started by developing an outlook for the *Growthstar* segment revenue".

"That's always the hard part", Dave responded. "Getting started on this effort is even more difficult, at least for me, because I have virtually no knowledge on the '*NG Euro*' program, which provides a foundation for the revenue forecast for our *Growthstar* segment in Europe. The only perspective that I can offer here is from the discussion we had during our planning session. If I go back to our plan for *Services* – essentially a US plan – you may recall the growth rates we all agreed on". Dave then walked over to the flip chart and wrote:

Services (US) – *Future Revenue Growth Rates*

Growth Rates	'Plan' (3 Years)	'Post Plan' (+4 Years)
Growthstar Segment	22%	21%
Other Products ('OCS')	60%	33%

"Perhaps I can add to this", Frank stated, as he opened his file on *'NG Euro'* and pulled out the information. "Dave, for your information, we said that the revenues for the 'Next Generation' (of *Products*) for Europe – code-named *'NG Euro'* – would account for over one-fourth of *Products'* International sales by Year #2 or #3 of our 'Plan', and approximately one-third of the sales for *Products-Europe*. For Year 3 – our 'target' – we've estimated *'NG Euro'* sales at about $35 million, *Products-Europe* sales at $110 million, and sales for *Products* overall International operations at $130 million". Frank then went to the flip chart and, underneath what Dave had written, he wrote:

'Products-Europe' Future Sales Outlook – per 'Plan'

$Millions	Year 1	Year 2	Year 3	Year 4	Year 5
Sales	$81	$95	$110	$125	$140
Growth %	16%	17%	16%	13%	13%
Memo:					
'NG Euro' Sales	$15	$31	$35 ... then, <u>decline</u> in years 4 & 5		

"So, now what?" Dave asked.

Jason answered ... "this becomes a 'puzzle' where we need to fit the various 'pieces'. To do this, we need to identify all the 'pieces'. One factor that may be relevant is the ratio of *Services-to-Products* revenue". He went to the flip chart and wrote:

Services (US) – *'Growth Plan'* ... % to Products Revenue (*)

$Millions	Curr. Yr.	Yr. 1	Yr. 2	Yr. 3	Yr.4	Yr. 5
Services – $	125	153	187	228	275	333
Products – $	225	253	285	320	352	388
Services – %	56%	60%	66%	71%	78%	85%

(*) Note: for 'US' revenue – per 'Plan' growth rates

"Are you saying, Jason", Dave said inquisitively, that we should forecast our revenue for *'EuroServ'* using a ratio of our US *Services* revenue to that of *Products*?"

"I *think* what Jason is saying is that this ratio is one 'piece' of information that should be considered as we develop the *'EuroServ'* outlook", Jack interjected. "It's part of the 'puzzle', as I see it".

"You're seeing it correctly", Jason replied – enjoying Jack's new role as an 'ally'.

"Well then", Jack responded, "let *me* add a 'piece' of information".

'EuroServ' – History ... % to 'Products-Europe' Revenue

$Millions	FY #2	FY #1	Current Year
'EuroServ' – $	26	35	45
Products – $	48	57	70
'EuroServ' – %	55%	61%	65%

"I went back into our historical accounting records", Jack continued, "and found the actual revenue for the European segment of *Products*. Historically, between 95% and 100% of *Products*' International revenue has been generated in Europe. As we have begun a more aggressive expansion in Asia–Pacific, this will go down somewhat this year, but Europe will still account for over 90% of the overall International Sales for *Products* in the current year".

"By the end of the '3-year' plan period, with a more rapid growth rate in the Asia–Pacific region, Europe will still account for 85% of *Products*' International sales", Val added.

"OK, I'm starting to get it!" Dave exclaimed. "Here's a 'piece' of information from what you just wrote down, Jack. It appears that '*EuroServ*' has a greater percentage of *Products* sales revenue than we do here in the US".

"Now it's *your* turn to explain", Val chimed in.

Dave went to the flip chart and wrote:

Services Revenue as a % to Products Sales – Current Year

	Services Revenue	Products Sales	%
'EuroServ'	$45	$70	65%
Services – US	$125	$225	56%

As he finished writing, Dave said, "I see some relationships, but I still need help in determining what to do with them".

"We'll get there", Val said ... looking over at Jason.

"Let's take the current year sales, the operating plan for next year (future year #1) and see if we can develop a couple of scenarios", Jason suggested. "Dave, can you show on the screen the Operating Plan for next year that was provided by '*EuroServ*'?"

"Certainly", Dave replied. "Exhibit 187 summarizes their 'plan' for the upcoming year. They look at year-to-year growth and margins as a basis for developing objectives and, then, their operating plan ... and, they only prepare an income statement. Can you imagine that", he chuckled. "I wanted to send a message to them indicating how *un*sophisticated they are, but I thought it would be more appropriate to keep quiet for the time being".

"You're getting smarter by the minute", Jack snipped, as Dave clicked on Exhibit 187.

Exhibit 187

GROWTHSTAR INC.

Acquisition Target Financials

$ Millions

(as "Reported")

"EuroServ" Financials	Current FY Forecast		Next Year's Operating Plan		
	$ ' s	% to Rev.	% Growth	% to Rev.	$ ' s
Income Statement					
Service Revenue:					
Growthstar	$45	75%	20%	72%	$54
Other Products	15	25%	40%	28%	21
Total Service Revenue	$60	100%	25%	100%	$75
			[calculated]		
Operating Costs and Expenses:					
Cost of Goods Sold (COGS)	12	20%	25%	20%	15
Selling, Marketing & Service (SMS)	27	45%	22%	44%	33
General & Administrative (G&A)	16		25%		20
Research & Development (R&D)	2	3%	67%	4%	3
Total Operating Costs & Expenses	57		25%		71
Interest Expense	1				1
Income Before Taxes	2				3
Provision for Taxes	1				1
Net Income After Taxes	$1				$2

Jack focused his attention on the very top line and said, "'*EuroServ*' is projecting a 20% growth in its 'Growthstar' segment for next year. If you analyze their 'Growthstar' segment revenue growth during the past two years, it's 30% per year. So, I would hope that 20% is achievable. Further, this (20%) growth rate is in line with the 22% rate of growth in the 3-year plan and the 21% rate in the '4-plus' years for *Services* in the US. What I would suggest is to run a scenario at 20% annual growth for five years, and then a 'downside' scenario at 15% annual growth for the 'Growthstar' segment".

"I agree", Dave responded. "Peter won't even consider this deal unless it can grow at 20% or more. He's never run a business that didn't grow at this level".

"Our CEO would also view '15% growth' as a 'worst case' scenario", Val added.

"We should then calculate the '*EuroServ*' revenue as a percent to the sales outlook for *Products-Europe* as a 'test of reasonableness' for each scenario", Jason chimed in.

"Agreed", said Val. "Let's move on to 'Other Products' (or, '*OCS-Europe*') revenue".

Dave then asked ... "Jack, do you have the same comparative growth rates for '*OCS-Europe*' as you have for the 'Growthstar' segment?"

"Thought you'd never ask", Jack answered. "During the past two years, the 'Other' segment has grown at the same 30% rate as the 'Growthstar' segment. If we look at the second row in Exhibit 187, they're planning for growth of 40% next year. I'm not sure that this is realistic – going from 30% to 40%".

"You need to look at the 'dollars' as well as the 'percentages'", Dave retorted. "Based on what I've seen, increasing revenue for this segment by $6 million should be achievable. I can say that if we owned '*EuroServ*', Peter would deliver on this level of growth, just as he'll deliver $15 million of new revenue in the US for '*OCS*'. You've seen our customer profile and targets for doing this as part of the '*OCS*' Value Driver Program, and we know there is the same 'relative' type of opportunity available in Europe".

"I would concur with that outlook for next year", Val said confidently. "My question is the compound rate of revenue growth over the longer term. I discussed this subject with the owners of '*EuroServ*' earlier this year, and I'm 'comfortable with an annual growth rate of at least 30% – but *not* the 60% rate of growth that we have in the 'plan' for *Services* (in the US) for the next three years. This is in line with what you wrote on the flip chart as your 'second bullet' at the beginning of this session".

"I think I'm 'comfortable' with a 40% growth rate – or two-thirds of the rate we've planned for in the US". Dave countered. "Let's see ... if we grow the 'Other Products' segment of '*EuroServ*' at 40% off a base of $21 million ... that's about $8 to $12 million per year for another two years. We should be able to do that, based on our 'track record'. We're capable of adding $10 million per year in a market such as Europe".

"You've proven your ability to grow", Jack interjected. "It's just that we 'corporate' folks tend to be a bit conservative when doing these type of future projections".

Dave then said ... "I would suggest that we view a '40% growth per year' as one scenario, and then have a 'downside' of $8 million per year for the next two years (#2 and #3) and then $10 million per year for the ensuing two years (#4 and #5)".

"That sounds reasonable", Val responded. "Any other opinions or thoughts?"

"I think this is a good start and a good foundation on which to build the outlook", Jason replied.

"I'm OK with these two scenarios", Jack added.

"Me, too", Frank said.

"OK", Val said, "why don't we take a short coffee and tea break and resume working (and having fun, Dave) in about ten minutes".

As the group returned to their seats, Jonathan walked into the room.

"Perfect timing", Dave quipped, "we've just completed the difficult work".

"That's why we hire competent people such as you", Jonathan snapped back, "so that I can simply 'show up' and be handed the results to give a 'blessing' to".

Val laughed softly and then said, "we've outlined an approach and a set of assumptions to develop two 'revenue scenarios' for '*EuroServ*'. We all believe they provide a realistic 'target' and a 'downside' to develop valuations for. Now, we're going to get into the 'expenses' and then 'working capital'". As she spoke, Val went to the flip chart and turned back to the first sheet, so that Jonathan could view the process that Dave had outlined at the beginning of the session.

"So, you've completed #1 and #2, and are starting on #3 – *COGS and SMS*".

"That's right", Val responded. "Dave feels that these two expense categories are straightforward and can be forecasted on a 'ratio-to-revenue' basis".

"I would agree", stated the CFO, "based on our experience with *Services* in the US".

"If you look at the 'plan' that '*EuroServ*' has submitted for next year", Dave said as he clicked back on Exhibit 187, "you will notice that the *COGS* ratio is consistent at 20%. I've analyzed their history and current year, along with the 'plan' for next year, and see no reason why this ratio won't continue for the foreseeable future. So, we can use 20% in the outlook for years #1 and #2. To be on the 'safe side', however, let's assume that the 'market' becomes more competitive and the *COGS* ratio increases by 10% to a ratio of 22% (of revenue) for the last three years. Their *SMS* ratio is expected to decrease by one (1) percentage point next year, from 45% to 44%. This makes a lot of sense, since they should be able to 'leverage' their revenue growth and achieve a lower *SMS* ratio. As I think all of you know, our *SMS* ratio for *Services* (here in the US) is currently 46% and is projected to decrease to 42% during the next three years, as we 'leverage' this expense. So, I think their somewhat lower rate of improvement for this ratio is reasonable in terms of developing an outlook for the purpose of assessing the 'value' for this business".

"You're getting quite proficient at this 'art' of financial planning", Jonathan snipped.

"I said the same thing just a while ago", Jack chimed in.

"And I'm just about ready to 'pack my bags' and leave this outlook in Dave's hands", Jason joked.

"And I'm going to contact 'Comedy Central' to get this act on stage", Val retorted. "However, I also agree with this approach and the assumptions. Can we move on to the next item (#4) – *G&A* and *R&D*?"

With all the heads nodding, Dave looked over at Frank and motioned for him to pick up the dialogue. Frank responded by saying ... deliberately ... "You've all seen the adjustments we have made to the *G&A* expense category. For those of you who have lost track of the exhibit numbers, the major accounts for *G&A* were provided in Exhibit 173, and the 'adjustments' were specified in Exhibit 177". As the group shuffled through their papers to locate these exhibits, Frank continued ... "We eliminated the 'Owner Bonus' and adjusted for 'Operating Leases' by factoring out the 'Interest' portion of expenses for office rent and equipment leases". As he was speaking, Frank went to the flip chart and on a new page, wrote:

'EuroServ' ... G&A Expense – 'Adjusted' for Growthstar

$Millions	Hist. FY #2	Hist. FY #1	Curr. Year	Next Year
'EuroServ'	$8.0	$12.0	$16.0	$20.0
Total Adjustments	−2.5	−3.8	−5.1	est. −7.5
Under 'Growthstar'	$5.5	$8.2	$10.9	est.$12.5
% Change (Growth)				
'Adjusted' G&A	–	49%	33%	15%
Revenue	–	33%	30%	25%

"Well, now, isn't this interesting!" Jonathan exclaimed. "'*EuroServ*' has been growing G&A faster than revenue, at least through the current year, even when we eliminate the excessive compensation to the owners".

Frank countered with ... "'*EuroServ*' has been building an infrastructure and a management group to accommodate their existing and anticipated growth. This will be basically completed by the end of this year. Val has indicated that, per her discussions, the owners are 'pressured' to add $2 million every year to the 'family take' from the business. I was informed that they have one or two major leases to take on next year, which should add nearly $1 million to office rent and equipment leases combined. If you apply our capitalization factor and interest rate, you'll be able to calculate the $7.5 million 'adjustment' to *their* G&A for next year. That is, take the $5.1 million 'adjustment' for the current year. Add $2 million for the 'Owner Bonus'. Then, capitalize $1 million at 4.5 and take 10% of that amount, which works out to about $400,000. This is how we arrive at the estimate of a $2.4 million 'addition' to the $5.1 million 'adjustment' for the current year – resulting in an estimate of $7.5 million 'total adjustment' for next year. The 'adjusted' G&A of $12.5 million is 15% higher than the 'adjusted' $10.9 million forecasted for this year".

"Taking this a step further", Dave said, "the 15% increase in G&A is 'sixty percent' of the 25% growth rate for revenue (15% versus

25%). I believe this is a good relationship for the ensuing years. To provide a comparison, our (*Services*) G&A is expected to increase at annual rate of 22.5% over the next three years, versus annual revenue growth of 30% overall. That's a 'factor' of '75%'. If you wish to reference this relationship, you can refer back to Exhibit 92. I believe that, should we own '*EuroServ*', a number of administrative tasks can be performed in the US, thus taking a burden away from '*EuroServ*'. As a 'downside' scenario, assume that the 'factor' of G&A-to- Revenue growth will be 'in-between' these two extremes – that is, '67%'".

"That's a reasonable set of assumptions", Jonathan replied. "I'm satisfied with this approach. What's next?"

"R&D is the next item", Val answered, pointing to the second notation under item #4 on the first page of the flip chart. "You noted, Dave, that this expense could be 'leveraged' – along with G&A".

"That's correct. Similar to administrative tasks, there is work going on in this area that is directly transferable to Europe. In fact, I would go so far as to say that, after next year, R&D for '*EuroServ*' can return to its historical level of '3% of Revenue' if we don't allocate expenses for work that we're going to do (anyhow) in *Services* to '*EuroServ*'. There is a project (within '*EuroServ*') scheduled for completion next year that we're aware of. We're not going to 'tinker' with next year's operating plan. Since almost all the increased expense next year is for 'outside' research work, I think that my formula will work for the outlook beyond next year. The 'downside' here would be to calculate an annual R&D expense based on our 'most likely' scenario for '*EuroServ*' revenue, and then hold constant the R&D expense, which is really a conservative assumption".

"Remember that you're working with 'conservative' finance people", Jack snickered.

"Speak for yourself", Val retorted good-naturedly.

"I'm comfortable with this assumption", Jonathan added. "Let's move on".

Val looked over the flip chart and said ... "The next discussion item (#5) is Working Capital – essentially operating cash, receivables and inventory (net of payables, I assume)".

"Right on", Dave responded, "and these are totally in line with the 'intensities' that we've established".

"I'm OK with this", Jonathan stated ... looking at Frank, Jack and Jason for a reaction ... for which there was none, since they all agreed with this approach. "I'm also aware that Peter will be delving into the 'fixed capital' situation – item #6 on your list – during his visit with the owners of '*EuroServ*'. So, what's our schedule for finalizing the outlook and the valuation for this deal and taking it to Ian?"

"We should be ready to meet with Ian within two weeks", Dave answered, looking at Frank for concurrence. Frank nodded, knowing that he could do the work at-hand in a couple of days of concentrated effort, especially with Dave and Jason – and now, Jack – to call on for assistance. With Peter due to return with inputs on capital expenditures at the very beginning of next week, that would provide ample time to complete the analysis.

"That includes charts", Jonathan reminded them.

"We know that", Dave and Frank said in unison.

"OK, then", the CFO stated, "we'll reconvene this group in about a week or so, and I'll schedule a session with Ian for as close to two weeks from tomorrow as I can".

"I think we can adjourn", Val concluded.

Ian's presence always evoked a reaction and today was no different. As the '*Leasing*' acquisition team gathered in the Boardroom to meet with the CEO, Jason thought to himself ... "*This man makes his presence known and commands attention.*"

Ian greeted everyone and took his customary seat at the head of the table. He opened the meeting by turning to Val and asking (actually, 'directing') ... "Val, I assume you are going to conduct today's session, with assistance from your colleagues".

"That's correct", she replied. "We have captured the highlights of this proposed deal to acquire a division of a major financial services firm that currently provides customer financing for our products, along with those of other manufacturers. We also have uncovered a number of major issues that need to be discussed. Let me begin by summarizing the proposed transaction and listing the key issues". As she was finishing this last sentence, Val clicked on Exhibit 188.

"I'm aware of the 'basics' of this deal", Ian stated, "through our discussions, Val, and also from talks I've had with Jonathan and Mandy. I need to focus on the 'specifics' that you've outlined". It didn't take Ian long to react. "So, we have to purchase the business in total, similar to purchasing an entire company. If we combine the equity and debt, we're looking at a 'total consideration' of $305 million – that is, assuming that we met the 'asking price'. This is the largest deal we've ever considered. What did we pay for *Services* – $50 million?"

"$55 million, to be exact", Earl replied.

"This puts us into a 'new league'", the CEO continued. "We get an income stream through the 'take-over' of the existing lease portfolio. Does this come close to justifying the 'asking price'?"

"It comes within about 75%", Earl answered.

Exhibit 188

'Leasing' Acquisition – Highlights / Issues

Highlights:

- Purchase of 'Equity' for $125 million – 'Asking Price'
- Assumption of Total Debt – approximately $180 million
- Transfer of existing lease portfolio
- Three other firms (all in financial services) are being given an opportunity to bid.

Issues:

- Diversification – into a new line of business … extending to financing other company products, in addition to Growthstar's
- Value of 'their' growth plan to 'our' shareholders … what is it worth?
- Entry into a financing business via acquisition versus internal start-up
- Financial Leverage – 'consolidated' Debt-to-Total-Capital ratio
- Management Attention – potential for 'distraction'… shareholder views

---

"So, the 'existing' business is worth 75% of the 'total value' of the firm. That only leaves 25% for the 'growth' value". As he spoke, he looked at Jason and, with a wry smile on his face said … "You see, Jason, I'm starting to speak *your language*".

Jason reacted with his own wry smile, saying … "And doing a commendable job of it".

Ian picked up the dialogue again. "This is similar to the 'problem' we had with our plans for *Products* and *Services* – not enough value from 'growth' – until we lengthened the 'growth horizon'. What are we using in this analysis as a 'growth horizon'?"

"Five years", Val replied, "and we're using the 'plan' developed by *'Leasing'* ".

"Have we developed our *own* plan for this business?"

Before responding to this question that Ian raised, Val looked over at Earl, who looked at Jason and said … "Jason, do *you* want to get into this issue, or should *I* do it?"

Jason replied by saying … "You've thought this through. I think you can handle it".

Earl paused for a brief moment, took a sip of coffee, and then began speaking. "We have a situation unlike any I have ever dealt with in my career in finance".

"How so"? Ian said inquisitively.

Earl looked over at Val and motioned for her to set the stage for presenting the analysis that had been prepared for Ian. Val reacted by saying … "What Earl is alluding to gets into the first two issues in Exhibit 188. It may *not matter* what type of growth we achieve beyond that for our own (Growthstar) portfolio of products – in terms of 'value' for our shareholders. This statement may sound strange and, on the surface, not make much sense. Let me suggest taking you through the highlights of our evaluation of this deal and then coming back to what has just been said. I think you'll understand the implications, and be armed with the relevant factors involved with this acquisition".

"Fair enough", Ian responded ... nodding his head. "Proceed".

Earl then said ... "We've analyzed '*Leasing*' from an 'accounting' and an 'economic' perspective. Everyone on the 'team' has been involved". Earl looked at Jack and Mandy as he made this statement. Both Jack and Mandy nodded to Ian to indicate their concurrence with what Earl was saying. "Let's start with the most 'basic' information – Revenue and Net Income – which is summarized, both in terms of history and a future outlook, in Exhibit 189. We'll then move on to a set of 'economic' indicators and wind up with a 'valuation' for this deal".

Jonathan, who had been silent so far, then entered the discussion. "Ian, you are going to see a 'profitable' business portrayed before you – one that has very attractive earnings, both historically and for

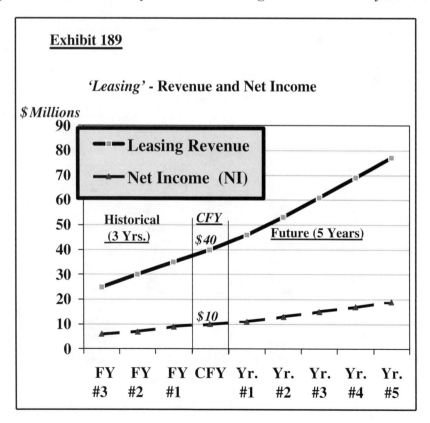

the future (assuming the plan submitted to us by the management of '*Leasing*' is credible). You need to keep in mind, however, that there will also be capital requirements significantly different from what we're accustomed to with our industrial businesses".

"Sounds like an interesting show", the 'big man' retorted ... "let's get on with it!"

"For the current year", Earl stated, "'*Leasing*' net earnings will be $10 million, on revenue of $40 million. As you can see on the chart, lease revenue is expected to grow to over $75 million and net income to nearly $20 million. Call it a 'doubling' of the business over the next five years. The next chart, Exhibit 190, provides the annual percentage growth rates for Lease Revenue and Net Income (*NI*) over the 5-year future outlook period. The lighter-colored (gray) bar plots Revenue growth and the darker (black) bar plots *NI* growth, on a 'percent increase over prior year' basis".

Ian's normal reaction would be to comment on the 'earnings growth' without regard to much else. The experience of the past few months, along with Jonathan's earlier comment, caused him to remain silent, however. He understood the numbers in both charts (Exhibits 189 and 190), and realized there was more to come.

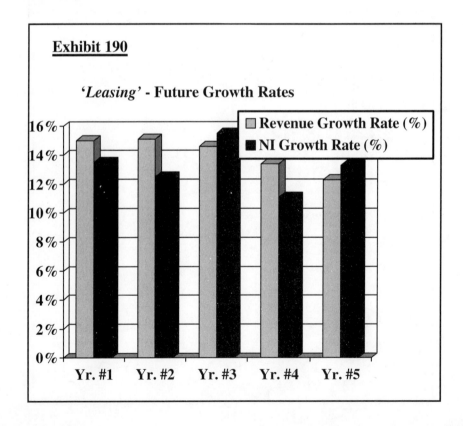

With no outward reaction from Ian, Earl continued. "The next two items are the 'economic returns'. First, we'll review the Return on Invested Capital (*ROIC*) that you've been exposed to through our economic evaluations for *Products*, *Services*, and *TOTAL CO*. Then we'll take a look at Return on Equity (*ROE*) and explain why we use this metric for finance companies. Exhibit 191 provides the *ROIC* profile for '*Leasing*' ".

Now Ian did react. "Is this the 'sucker punch'? Are we saying that in spite of the solid earnings, the *ROIC* is so low that it's unacceptable? Didn't we have *ROICs* for *Products* and *Services* in the 17% to 20% range for the 'plan'? And, weren't the *ROICs* for the two Value Driver Programs also high – around 18% for '*NG Euro*' and close to 30% for '*OCS*'?" The 'big man' was now scratching his chin gently – with a look of frustration appearing on his face.

Jonathan then spoke. "Ian, there's more to this than the 'absolute' level of *ROIC* ... and, this is *not* a 'sucker punch'. What this chart

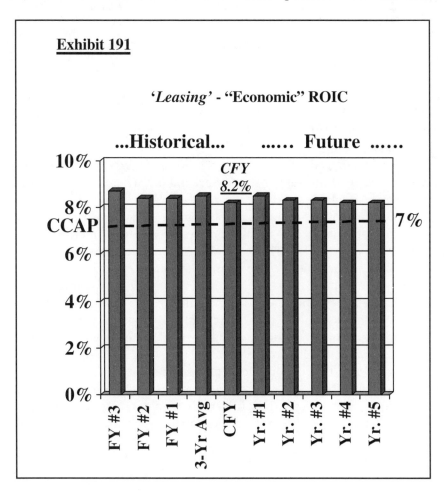

(Exhibit 191) indicates is that the 'risk/return' profile for a finance business is inherently and significantly different from an industrial business. Further, it starts to introduce the notion of the capital intensity for the leasing business, a topic we will cover in more depth. First, though, I want to make certain that you don't get a 'negative perception' from a 'positive situation'. When reviewing and analyzing this chart (Exhibit 191) focus on the 'dashed' horizontal line labeled '*CCAP*', as well as the height of the bars. The cost of capital for a finance business is usually much lower than *CCAP* for an industrial firm. If it's not, then the finance business is, as you just postulated, not earning an acceptable return. Let me explain". Jonathan then went over to the flip chart and wrote ... as he said ... "The way a *finance* business is *financed* establishes a totally new framework for measuring returns".

Cost of Capital	Cost of Equity (Ce)	Weighted Average Cost of Capital (CCAP)
Growthstar	12.75%	11.0%
'Leasing'	12.0%	7.0%
Financial Leverage	**D/TC Ratio**	**E/TC Ratio**
Growthstar	29%	71%
'Leasing'	71%	29%

"In case you're wondering at my newly found aptitude on this subject, I copied this from a 'flip chart' presentation that Earl made at our last meeting on '*Leasing*' ".

Ian chuckled and said ... "I was thinking to myself that you must have stayed up 'half the night' memorizing an article on this subject. I appreciate the honesty".

"Here's the point", Jonathan shot back. "This (finance) business has a capital structure opposite from ours, resulting in a much lower *CCAP* – 7% versus 11%. Thus, the *ROIC*, which is fairly stable in the 8% to 8.5% range, needs to be compared to the 7% *CCAP*".

"OK, I understand now. But, it's still a low *ROIC* by comparison to our existing lines of business ... and, the 'spread' of *ROIC* over *CCAP* is lower. Mandy, what's your reaction and how do you think our major institutional shareholders might react to Growthstar taking on a business with this level of return?"

"That's a good question, which we've spent time discussing in our 'team' meetings. One perception is that we'd still be 'beating' our cost of capital and that this deal would create value for our shareholders – depending, of course, on the price we paid to make the acquisition".

"What about the reaction on the 'Street' to the $125 million 'asking price'?"

"That could be a 'transfer of wealth' problem, as you will see shortly. Another perception, however, gets to the 'image' that the 'Street' has of our company. By that, I mean ... is Growthstar a growth-oriented company *focused* on industrial businesses, or is it a *diversified* growth company? The answer could have an impact on who may want to own the stock and also on how it may be valued. Often, valuation ratios such as Market-to-Book (*M/B*) are different for the two types of business".

"I hear you and you've got me thinking, but I still am enamored by the prospect of additional leasing 'profits' and annoyed by the fact that we don't currently have them in our business portfolio".

"That's why we're going through all this analysis and discussion, boss", Val interjected. "We all see the steady stream of income and a return in excess of the cost of capital. But, it's really different from our 'mainline' operations, which is part of the reason that all of us involved with this deal have so many questions. Part of it is a learning process. Before we commit to $300 million, though, we've got to get these questions answered and these issues resolved".

"I fully respect that comment and sincerely appreciate all the hard work and creative thinking that has, obviously, gone into your due diligence on this deal", Ian said empathetically. "Let's keep going ... this is truly an interesting and challenging situation".

Earl responded with ... "Next, we want to examine Return on Equity (*ROE*) which we can do with Exhibit 192".

"Similar to the *ROIC* chart, you need to focus on the height of the *ROE* bars versus the 12% cost of equity (*Ce*)".

"The message has been received 'loud and clear' ... and 'registered' ..." the CEO stated. "I notice that the word 'economic' is on both Exhibit 191 and 192. Should I assume that you have gone through a process of *adjusting* the 'as reported' financials for '*Leasing*'?"

"Yes", Earl replied, "but the only significant adjustment is for Deferred Taxes, which lowers the 'effective' tax rate and increases the equity capital on the 'books'".

"OK. You also said that *ROE* is a relevant metric to use for a finance company. Can you explain, please".

"Return on Equity (*ROE*) is a good metric for many finance companies, because the financial statements are, for the most part, on a 'current' basis. By that, I mean that the largest assets are the leases – or customer receivables. Normally, you don't have a large base of 'fixed' assets, which may be understated in terms of their 'depreciated' values. In the case of '*Leasing*' there is *no* goodwill. Therefore, the expenses generally follow the flow of revenue, and the balance sheet is – except for the one item I just mentioned – already stated in 'economic' terms. Further, Interest Expense is such a major

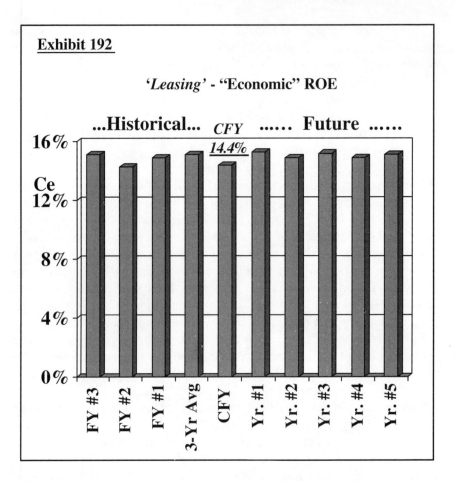

Exhibit 192

'*Leasing*' - "Economic" ROE

...Historical...　*CFY*　...... Future ......

cost item that many (probably most) people in the finance business have difficulty measuring performance without considering this expense – which is directly related to the 'debt' financing. As Jonathan just mentioned, debt is the primary form of 'financing' for a 'finance' business. Finally, we can construct a valuation model using the 'Equity Capital' *vis-à-vis* 'Cost of Equity' approach. We'll go over this shortly. Is that clear, Ian, as to why we're introducing *ROE*?"

"Crystal clear", Ian replied. "Please go on".

"As Jonathan alluded to earlier in the meeting, the leasing business has not only a radically different financing structure and cost of capital from a traditional industrial business, but also a much higher level of capital intensity. If you recall our analysis of financial 'drivers' for *Products* and *Services*, the capital intensities are in the range of 'thirty-to-forty' cents, in terms of what it takes to generate one dollar of revenue. When we factor in the goodwill associated with the acquisition of *Services*, the amounts are obviously higher".

"I most certainly do recall these financial indicators", Ian shot back. "In fact, I've even started to quote these figures in discussions with 'sell-side' analysts and portfolio managers at some of the mutual funds that own our stock".

"Well", Earl then stated ... with a 'twinkle' in his eye ... " 'hold onto you hat', because you are now going to enter a 'new world' of capital!" As he concluded this statement, Earl clicked on Exhibit 193.

"Are you serious", Ian exclaimed. "Over 'six dollars' of *ICI*!"

"I'm afraid we are", Val jumped in. "I was surprised the first time that I saw these numbers".

"Let me interject, if I may", Jason said, "that there is nothing inherently 'wrong' or 'value destructive' about these indicators. As I have repeatedly said in our 'team' meetings, this high level of capital intensity is simply a 'fact of life' with the leasing business. It provides the basis (collateral, if you will) for the debt financing. The competitiveness of the finance business drives down the 'return' to

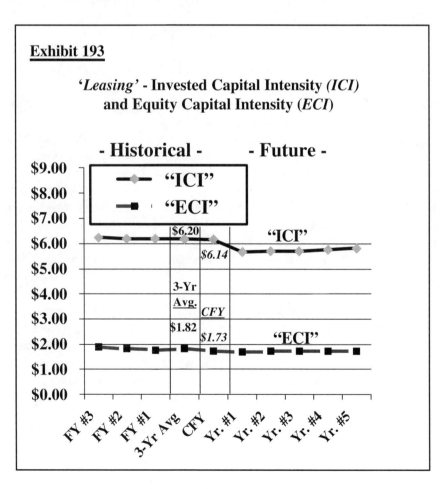

where you can't generate the 'relative' amount of revenue that you get with an industrial business. On the other hand, the high level of debt financing allows for success to be achieved at a lower 'return', since the cost of capital is lower. So, it all 'hangs together'. The issue here is that if you proceed with this deal to acquire '*Leasing*', then you *must* be willing to accept the capital intensity that will naturally follow".

"You sure know how to spoil my parties, Jason", Ian scowled. But, then the wry smile appeared and he said, "but I do honestly appreciate the forthright nature of your input". The CEO then sighed, leaned back in his chair, and said … "I need a 'break' and I certainly need another cup of coffee. We've got a lot to think about with this deal, and I understand we're on a 'short time fuse' to make a decision. Let's reconvene in fifteen minutes".

After the break, Ian picked up the dialogue. "*How much* capital and new investment are we talking about with this '*Leasing*' deal … *after* we purchase the business?"

"According to *their* outlook, about $200 million over five years", Jonathan answered.

"What's the amount for our 'internal' plans for *Products* and *Services*?"

Jonathan looked over at Earl, who replied … "Around $240 million for the two BUs combined".

"Hmmm", the CEO mused, as he again scratched his chin and looked up at the ceiling – a habit of his when he knew he had a major decision on his hands and had to enlist his most creative thinking. The room remained silent (almost eerily so) while Ian continued to ponder the issues before him. He closed his eyes momentarily, then opened them and looked first at Val and then at Jonathan. Both of them knew that the CEO was starting to put his thoughts in order and build his 'logic trail' to get to a decision. He then leaned forward and with his characteristic wry smile said, "Can't you bring me an 'easy' deal?"

The room broke up in laughter. Ian had a knack of knowing when, in the midst of a most difficult and critical decision-making process, to make the people feel at ease – especially when he knew that everyone on the 'team' was being totally objective, had identified and begun to think through the critical issues, and had presented him with the most relevant information to help him make a decision that was in the best interests of the shareholders.

"I sense that there's more – so let's continue", Ian then directed.

"Exhibit 194 illustrates the Economic Profit (*EP*) – historically and for the future".

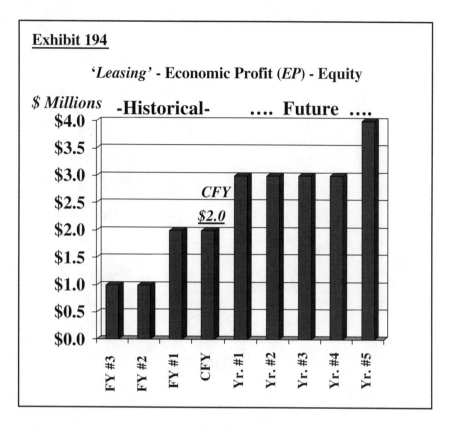

Exhibit 194

'*Leasing*' - Economic Profit (*EP*) - Equity

Before Ian could react to this chart, Earl said ... "The 'pattern' of the bars is affected by the fact that we've rounded the information supplied to us by '*Leasing*' to the nearest 'whole' million dollar. If we had rounded to 'thousands' (of dollars), the height of the bars would portray a more gradual slope upward".

"I get the picture", Ian responded, "that *EP* is positive – in line with the positive 'spreads' for *ROIC* and *ROE*".

"That's the conclusion", Earl replied back, "and we can leave it there. Finally, all of these financials have been integrated into a valuation for the equity in this business. Exhibit 195 gives a summary of this valuation".

"So, these are the numbers supporting the comment made earlier that the 'no-growth' value – essentially, the existing level of customer receivables and revenue/profit – comprises about 75% of the 'asking price' for the equity", Ian commented. "How about that, Jason", the 'big man' chided, "I'm *really* getting into your jargon".

Jason smiled and nodded his head. There wasn't anything he could say as a 'comeback'.

Ian continued ... "So, we have a deal that *we* value at $109 million – say, $110 million if we 'stretch' a bit. *They* want $125 million. So,

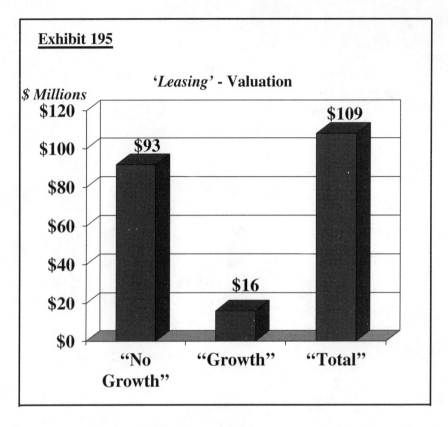

Exhibit 195

'*Leasing*' - Valuation

we're approximately $15 million apart. I'm assuming, at least for the moment, that their 'plan' is realistic in terms of future opportunity. As I said previously, I'm concerned about the relatively low value attributable to the 'growth plan'".

"I also want to follow up on two comments that were made earlier. Mandy, you said there was a 'transfer of wealth' problem. I understand conceptually what you're saying, but let's make sure. Can you elaborate, please".

"It's actually quite simple. If we pay more than $109 million, under the scenario that we've evaluated, then we (Growthstar) are 'transferring' wealth to the parent company shareholders of '*Leasing*'. This conclusion also assumes that *this scenario* is what our shareholders would incorporate into their valuation models. If we extend the time period for growth beyond five years or can grow more rapidly during the next five years, then we might close or eliminate this 'value gap'. Unless a lower price can be negotiated, however, there is probably no significant 'value creation' to *our* shareholders from making this acquisition, regardless of what type of 'plan' we formulate. The relatively low 'value contribution' of the 'growth' portion of the scenario indicates a relatively low level of 'sensitivity' to growth. Contrast this situation to that for our *Services* BU, where extending the time horizon for their 'growth plan' had a significant and very positive impact on shareholder value. Did I say that correctly, Jason?"

"Perfectly".

Ian nodded his head, indicating his understanding and then turned to Val. "You made a comment, Val, that ... and I quote ... *'It may not matter what type of growth we achieve beyond that for our own (Growthstar) portfolio of products – in terms of 'value' for our shareholders'*. Can you, or someone else, please expound on this statement".

Earl, Jonathan and Val looked at each other, and then all of them looked at Jason.

Ian picked up the gestures and, looking at Jason, snapped ... "Are *you* the 'poison'?"

"Probably", Jason responded, looking Ian straight in the eye. "But, hopefully, for some credible reasons. Perhaps the best way to rationalize the statement that Val made – but, that I admit to first suggesting, is to go back to the issues outlined on our first chart (Exhibit 188). 'Diversification' is a thorny topic – with a wide range of opinions in the business community. Some believe it's the way to increasing stock prices through 'spreading' risk around a corporate business portfolio. Others believe diversification steals focus away from what you're really good at – the 'core competency' that built a company to where it is – and, therefore, that diversification can be 'value destructive'. Let's put the general philosophy aside and look at it very specifically for your company. Unless you truly want to diversify into 'financial' services, it's my opinion that the income stream from the 'non-Growthstar' lease portfolio is of questionable value to *your* shareholders. Think of it this way. If we could find a marketable security that yielded more than the cost of money we had to borrow to purchase the security, then we should do that, also. Because, that's what you have with the 'non-Growthstar' leases – customer receivables that provide a 'yield' – period!"

Val then jumped into the dialogue with ... "I doubt that our competitive position in our 'mainstream' businesses will be improved by acquiring and growing a lease portfolio collateralized by 'non-Growthstar' products. In fact, we might 'trigger' a reaction that could put our *competitors* in the financing business – potentially jeopardizing the future outlook for the 'non-Growthstar' leases that *'Leasing'* is incorporating into their 'plan'. Now, let me get into the financing of our own products. This may well be an action that we may *want* to take – or may *have* to take – particularly if we think that the 'bundling' of product sales, services and financing becomes a competitive positioning issue. Our research this year indicated that while the *availability* of financing was important to the customer, the *source* of financing was not – as long as the cost was reasonable. The *convenience* of paying for everything in one invoice was *not* a critical issue in terms of selecting a vendor for the product sale".

Ian nodded his head and then glanced briefly up at the ceiling. "But, what if when we do our strategic assessment next year, the customers tell us that they *want* 'bundling'?"

Val responded with ... "Through prodding by the man who keeps 'spoiling your parties', we are thinking that we may be able to develop this type of financing business internally. That's the third issue in Exhibit 188. Jason is suggesting that developing a finance business for *our products alone* is mainly about hiring people, installing systems, developing leasing programs and selling them to customers who are ours to begin with, and gaining access to debt capital – which we should be able to do. This type of initiative would be a Value Driver Program, perhaps similar to the '*NG Euro*' and '*OCS*' programs that we recently evaluated and approved for funding".

"That's an interesting thought", the CEO said softly, his eyes looking toward the ceiling again. "We might be able to get the leasing profits on *our own* products and *not* have to purchase the others. If we don't pursue this deal, let's put the analysis of this option on our agenda for early next year. Hmmm ... I'm intrigued by this possibility. Jason, maybe there's hope for you after all" ... the wry smile reappearing, as the CEO began to envision a potential solution to the dilemma he had felt entrapped in a few moments ago.

"This option would also result in a reduced debt burden", Jonathan interjected.

"That's true", Earl added, "especially since we would be 'building' financial leverage, not taking it all on in 'one fell swoop'".

Ian was scanning the issues in Exhibit 188. He leaned forward, folded his hands on the top of the table, and said ... "I guess, Mandy, that this option of building a finance business internally sometime after this year would 'put off' any investor concerns about us being 'distracted' from executing our growth plans for *Products* and *Services*".

"That's probably an accurate assessment. I certainly wouldn't say anything at the upcoming 'special' meeting that, as you know, is scheduled for three weeks from today. We may, however, want to send a signal early next year when we give them our outlook for the upcoming fiscal year, along with strategic perspectives about our future".

"I knew there was a reason we hired you", Ian fired back. "Seriously, though, you're probably correct ... I just want to think about this a bit more".

"So, let's see where that leaves us. We have a deal for which we're having difficulty justifying the 'asking price' based on actual performance and *their* outlook for the next five years. Of the value that we've calculated, most is for the 'no-growth' element of the business. That conflicts with one of my basic tenets for this company – that a significant portion of our stock price should come from the 'warranted' value of our growth opportunities. Our customers are not yet demanding that we provide 'bundling' and be the source of financing. The returns, while steady and in excess of the costs of both equity and total capital, do not provide as high a 'spread' as our existing BUs. Further, they're well below the 'absolute' returns of *Products* and *Services*. While not bad, this could cause some confusion – hopefully, only temporary – for our investors, especially when combined with a reversal in our debt-to-capital ratio, causing us to suddenly become a highly leveraged firm. Further, the returns on the 'non-Growthstar' portion of the lease portfolio may be of questionable value to our shareholders, since they relate to financing activities outside our mainstream businesses. These are, essentially, financial transactions, and I'm not interested in creating a bank or a financial institution. The issue of diversification is unclear, in terms of the potential for long-term value creation. Finally, we could be accused of becoming distracted from a 'plan' that we're going to promote at a 'special' analyst and investor session, making a case that we believe there is 'value' in our company that is not being fully reflected in our current stock price".

Ian looked around the room for a reaction. There was none. The CEO knew when he had all the issues 'on the table' – as did the others in the room. "This decision is easier than I expected. Val, tell your contact at '*Leasing*' that, while all of us at Growthstar are very appreciative of the opportunity to bid on this deal, we will 'pass'. If he (or she) would like an explanation of our decision, please refer that person to *me*. Thank you all for your insightful inputs. I'm proud to be associated with you. Meeting is adjourned!"

Peter Uppcomer had returned from Europe with the information necessary to prepare a capital expenditure outlook for '*EuroServ*'. Peter had held a meeting with the owners specifically on this subject and had, also, visited most of the company's major sites and discussed the subject of fixed capital on one or two other occasions during his visit. He had briefed Dave on all the specifics, from which Dave had prepared a summary schedule. Peter would attend the next 'team' meeting and be able to answer any questions that might arise on the subject of capital expenditures (CAPEXs).

Frank, Jack, Dave and Jason gathered in the *Services* conference room to develop the future financial outlook for '*EuroServ*', based on the assumptions that had been agreed to at the previous meeting and the input from Peter on capital expenditures. They laid out a work plan that called for them to structure the 'Most Likely' Scenario and a 'Downside' Case. From this work, presentations for the 'team' and CFO/CEO would be developed.

Dave had taken on the role of coordinator in Val's absence. Jason was pleased to see the 'proactive' attitude that Dave had assumed. Everyone else in the company could see it, also, and Jason felt that Dave's attitude had influenced Jack. Dave opened with … "I met with Peter upon his return from Europe and then apprised Frank of the key points regarding this meeting, along with providing Frank a copy of the schedule that I'm about to show you all. OK, Frank?"

Frank nodded. He wanted to say something, but couldn't think of anything that he thought would be noteworthy – so he remained silent.

Dave, enjoying his role as spokesperson, then said … "What I've done is to construct Exhibit 196, a summary schedule of estimated capital expenditures (CAPEXs) for the next five years, based on the inputs provided to Peter in Europe and then by Peter to me".

"This family-owned European firm", Dave continued, "has three major fixed asset categories. They lease all their facilities, so they don't even have a 'land & buildings' category. Peter actually was given quite a bit of detail supporting these numbers. One of the most noteworthy items is the level of 'leaseholds' needed next year. They occupy a couple of older buildings that are in desperate need of renovation. Peter noticed this condition during his visits to the

Exhibit 196	**GROWTHSTAR INC.** Acquisition Target Financials ("Economic" Basis)				
	.... **Future Outlook Period — 5 Years**				
"EuroServ" Financials	**Yr. #1**	**Yr. #2**	**Yr. #3**	**Yr. #4**	**Yr. #5**
Capital Expenditures -					
Summary ($000's –thousands)					
Leasehold Improvements	$750	$2,000	$1,200	$800	$800
Furniture & Fixtures	500	500	300	300	300
Testing Equipment	750	1,500	1,500	1,900	1,900
Total CAPEX's	**$2,000**	**$4,000**	**$3,000**	**$3,000**	**$3,000**
CAPEX ... ICI - "Most Likely'					
{$ Millions, except "ICI")					
Total CAPEX's (above)	*$2*	*$4*	*$3*	*$3*	*$3*
Revenue - Current Year	$75	$95	$119	$152	$194
Revenue - Prior Year	60	75	95	119	152
Revenue - Change	$15	$19	$25	$32	$42
"ICI"	*$0.13*	*$0.21*	*$0.12*	*$0.09*	*$0.07*

company's various sites, and the owners (reluctantly) agreed that they needed to make up for several years of 'neglect' of their field facilities. The ensuing years (#3 through #5) reflect a continued requirement for new investment in leaseholds, although not at the level of year #2. This work really should have been moved up a year, but with the current ownership, that will not happen. The result is a 'bubble' in year #2, in which $4 million of 'gross' new investment will be made. Without this investment, the facilities are 'risky' in terms of functionality. They're *not* at any risk of falling down, however".

This schedule (Exhibit 196) was straightforward and, since Frank had seen and reviewed it, none of the others felt a need to comment or ask questions. This capital expenditure forecast would be taken at 'face value', for the 'Most Likely' and 'Downside' analyses.

Dave looked over at Jason. While he had come a long way, he had not ever been through an economic evaluation of an acquisition. Neither had any of the others, including Jack – the most experienced member of the 'team' – who (heretofore) had concentrated mostly on the 'accounting' aspects of mergers and acquisitions. Jason picked up the cue and, as he rose and began to speak, walked over to the flip chart. "We developed all the major assumptions for a future outlook at our last meeting. Now, with the capital expenditure requirements in Exhibit 196, we're ready to construct the 'Most Likely' Scenario and a 'Downside' Case. This analysis will give us a range of 'warranted values' for 'EuroServ' that we can compare to the 'asking price'". Jason then wrote on the flip chart:

'EuroServ' – Most Likely Scenario and Downside Case

- *Revenue*
- *Profit and Loss*
- *Invested Capital – 'New'... 'Balance Sheet'*
- *'EP' and 'VPM'*
- *Valuation – 'FCF' and 'EP' Approaches*

"This outline looks familiar", Dave quipped. "I could probably have written this".

"I would hope so", Jason snapped back. "For each scenario (or case) we need to develop a schedule for each of these items".

Dave chimed back in with ... "Val, Mandy, Peter and Jonathan will join us when we've prepared these exhibits, our objective being to get a consensus on the 'economics' of this transaction and to then structure a presentation for Ian".

Jack shrugged his shoulders, but didn't say anything. He knew that Ian and Jonathan would also want to know the 'earnings per share' impact of the proposed acquisition, which he could easily do once the future outlook and deal structure were established. Sensing the need, at least for the time being, to focus on the 'economics' of the transaction, Jack decided to remain silent.

Dave, who had his personal computer with him, said ... "I'll do the financial modeling. We can all participate in developing the inputs and formulae, and then viewing the output on the screen. After we're in agreement, I'll call Val to arrange the 'expanded' session".

Dave, Frank, Jack and Jason proceeded to work through all the assumptions agreed to at the most recent meeting, and to translate these assumptions into a set of exhibits. Just before lunch, they finished. Dave contacted Val, who indicated that the 'expanded' session would convene at 1:30 pm.

As the 'team' plus Val, Mandy, Peter and Jonathan ... plus Earl ... gathered in the *Services* conference room, Jonathan said ... "Well, we managed to 'kill' one deal ('*Leasing*') in a session similar to this one, so I'll be interested in what the 'fearsome foursome' has come up with for '*EuroServ*'. I've invited Earl to join us, since he'll have to finance this deal if we go through with it".

Dave retorted by saying ... "I wasn't part of that 'killing' – Earl was". He snickered at Earl, who returned the look. "Val, how do you want to run this session?"

"You should coordinate, Dave, with help from your esteemed colleagues", Val answered.

"That's fine", Dave replied. He then looked at Peter, Jonathan, Mandy and Earl and said, "we'll present our 'Most Likely' Scenario first and then the 'Downside' Case".

Dave went to the flip chart and gave a brief overview, referring to the elements that Jason outlined earlier. "We spent the morning working on an outlook for Revenue, Profit & Loss, Invested Capital, Economic Profit, Value Profit Margin, and a Valuation for the 'Most Likely' Scenario and the 'Downside' Case. To get this analysis started, Exhibit 197 summarizes our ' Most Likely' outlook for Revenue, incorporating the assumptions and rationale that we agreed to at our last meeting on this subject. The other exhibits will follow a similar pattern".

Peter, Jonathan, Val and Mandy peered at Exhibit 197.

Val opened the dialogue by saying ... "So, our assumptions of 20% compound annual growth for the 'Growthstar' segment and 40% for 'Other' results in overall '*EuroServ*' revenue increasing from $60 million in the current year, to $75 million next year (#1) and to nearly $200 million by year #5".

<u>**Exhibit 197**</u>	**GROWTHSTAR INC.**				
	Acquisition Target Financials				
$ Millions	("Economic" Basis)				
	.... "Most Likely" Future Outlook — 5 Years				
"EuroServ" Financials	**Yr. #1**	**Yr. #2**	**Yr. #3**	**Yr. #4**	**Yr. #5**
"Most Likely" Scenario -	[AOP]				
Revenue					
'EuroServ' Revenue					
Growthstar - % Growth	*20%*	*20%*	*20%*	*20%*	*20%*
- $ Millions	$54	$65	$78	$94	$113
Other Products - % Growth	*40%*	*40%*	*40%*	*40%*	*40%*
Other Products - $ Millions	$21	$30	$41	$58	$81
'EuroServ' Revenue - $	**$75**	**$95**	**$119**	**$152**	**$194**
Revenue "Tests"					
Growthstar Segment:					
Europe:					
Growthstar - 'EuroServ'	$54	$65	$78	$94	$113
Products-Europe Sales	$81	$95	$110	$125	$140
'EuroServ' - %	67%	69%	71%	75%	80%
U.S.:					
Services - Revenue	$153	$187	$228	$275	$333
Products - U. S. Sales	$253	$285	$320	$352	$388
Services - % of Products	60%	66%	71%	78%	86%
Total Service Revenue - $					
Growth Rates:					
Europe - 'EuroServ'	*25%*	*26%*	*26%*	*27%*	*28%*
U. S. - Services BU	*29%*	*30%*	*32%*	*25%*	*25%*
Difference	*-4%*	*-4%*	*-6%*	*2%*	*3%*

"That's a healthy outlook, and one that I can live with ... at least for the 'top line' ..." Peter chimed in.

Jonathan added ... "The 'test' of the 'Growthstar' segment's *Services-to-Products* revenue indicates that, while 'EuroServ' is ahead of *Services* (US) for years #1 and #2, they're equal (at 71%) in year #3. Then, 'EuroServ' lags behind in years #4 and #5. I suppose this is a reasonable assumption in terms of us not wanting to *overstate* revenue potential and inflate the 'value' that would result". He glanced at Jason and Earl, who both nodded in agreement. Continuing, the CFO said ... "it also appears that the revenue outlook for 'EuroServ' entails lower percentage growth for years #1 through #3 versus *Services* in the US, so that would seem to be reasonable. Years #4 and #5 reflect higher growth rates for 'EuroServ'. Hmmm?"

"I've looked at this briefly", Peter interjected, "and the lower 'absolute' revenue base for 'EuroServ' provides an opportunity for a higher growth rate. As I stated before, I'm confident that I can 'deliver' this outlook. Remember, also, that 'EuroServ' will benefit from marketing and research efforts that should be well underway by this time frame".

Frank, who had been so intimately involved in the evaluation of 'EuroServ' and quiet so far, stated ... "Based on our company's 'plan' for *Services*, the 'OCS' Value Driver Program analysis, and the most recent financial performance for *Services*, I believe that this revenue outlook is 'within the realm of reason'".

Dave smiled and looked at Peter. Peter nodded back. Dave felt that Frank was speaking objectively and that he must have thought through the assumptions and results before making such a statement. Everyone else in the room shared this feeling. Dave looked around the room for a reaction. There was none.

"Next, is the *Profit & Loss* outlook. The assumptions we made about the four major cost and expense categories are reflected here; that is, in Exhibit 198. In case anyone has forgotten, we established the following assumptions, which I'll write on the flip chart".

'EuroServ' – Most Likely Scenario Assumptions

- **COGS – 20% for 2 years, then 22% for years #3–5 (ratio-to-revenue)**
- **SMS – 44% (ratio-to-revenue) for all 5 years**
- **G&A – increase at '60%' of the annual revenue growth rate**
- **R&D – Year #1 AOP, then 3% of revenue.**

"The result", Jack interjected, "is a 'tripling' of *NOP* over the five-year period, from $7 million to $22 million ... and, this is in 'economic' terms".

Exhibit 198	GROWTHSTAR INC.				
	Acquisition Target Financials				
$ Millions	("Economic" Basis)				
	.... "Most Likely" Future Outlook — 5 Years				
"EuroServ" Financials	Yr. #1	Yr. #2	Yr. #3	Yr. #4	Yr. #5
"Most Likely" Scenario					
Profit & Loss					
Service Revenue:					
Growthstar	$54	$65	$78	$94	$113
Other Products	21	30	41	58	81
Total Service Revenue	$75	$95	$119	$152	$194
Operating Costs and Expenses:					
COGS - % to Revenue	20%	20%	22%	22%	22%
- $Millions	15	19	26	33	43
SMS - % to Revenue	44%	44%	44%	44%	44%
- $Millions	33	42	53	67	85
G & A - % Increase/Prior Year (*)	15%	15%	16%	16%	17%
- $Millions	13	14	17	19	23
R & D - % to Revenue	—	3%	3%	3%	3%
- $Millions	3	3	4	5	6
(*) G&A increases @ 60% of Revenue Growth %					
Total Oper. Costs & Exp's	64	78	99	124	156
EBIT / A	12	17	20	28	37
Taxes @ 40%	5	7	8	11	15
NOP	$7	$10	$12	$17	$22

Heads snapped around the table.

"OK, so I've 'come on board'", the Controller said quickly.

Earl looked first at Jonathan, then at Val and Jason. As he did so, he was silently 'pumping his fist' under the table – a sense of exhilaration running through his entire body. Mandy, Frank, Dave and Peter also exchanged looks.

"Let's take a five-minute 'stretch and coffee' break", Jonathan said ... "unless anyone has a question on this exhibit (198)".

After the break, Dave resumed his role. "Next, we've forecasted new investment and invested capital in Exhibit 199".

"We've integrated our working capital assumptions with the outlook for capital expenditures and estimates for new operating lease commitments. The result is an annual level of 'net new investment' ranging from $11 to $16 million, with *ICI* averaging 'forty-seven' cents ($0.47). Thus, nearly 'fifty cents' of *new* capital (in total) is estimated for each *new* revenue dollar. Invested capital should

Exhibit 199	GROWTHSTAR INC.					
$ Millions, except "ICI"	Acquisition Target Financials ("Economic" Basis)					
	.... "Most Likely" Future Outlook — 5 Years					
"EuroServ" Financials	Yr. #1	Yr. #2	Yr. #3	Yr. #4	Yr. #5	
"Most Likely" Scenario Invested Capital						
Memo: Revenue Change	$15	$19	$25	$32	$42	Avg.
New Investment:						"ICI"
Operating Cash	$0.8	$1.0	$1.2	$1.6	$2.1	$0.05
Accounts Receivable	2.5	3.2	4.1	5.4	7.0	$0.17
Inventory ('net' of A/P)	1.5	1.9	2.5	3.2	4.2	$0.10
Other W/C ('net')	0.2	0.2	0.2	0.3	0.4	$0.01
Net Working Capital	4.9	6.3	8.1	10.5	13.7	
Fixed Capital:						
- Gross (CAPEX's)	2.0	4.0	3.0	3.0	3.0	Dep. %
- Depreciation (Cumul.)	(0.2)	(0.6)	(0.9)	(1.2)	(1.5)	10%
- Net Fixed Capital	1.8	3.4	2.1	1.8	1.5	—
Other Capital ('net')	-	-	-	-	-	
Sub-total (Bal. Sheet)	6.7	9.7	10.2	12.3	15.2	—
Operating Leases	4.5	1.0	1.0	1.0	1.0	—
Net New Investment ("I")	$11.2	$10.7	$11.2	$13.3	$16.2	
Memo: "ICI's"						Avg.
Net Working Capital	$0.33	$0.33	$0.33	$0.33	$0.33	$0.33
Net New Investment	$0.74	$0.55	$0.45	$0.41	$0.39	**$0.47**
Invested Capital (IC)						
Current Year - Beginning	$27					
Adjustment - for Year #1 (*)	3					
Balance Forward	$30	$35	$43	$53	$65	
New Invest. - Bal. Sheet	-	7	10	10	12	Avg.
New Invest. - Oper. Leases	5	1	1	1	1	"ICI"
IC (Beginning)	$35	$43	$53	$65	$78	$0.43
(*) Current Year change in "reported" Bal. Sheet						

'more than double' – from \$35 million at the end of the current year (beginning of year #1) to \$78 million by year #5. *ICI* for total invested capital averages 'forty-three cents' (\$0.43) for the five-year outlook period – close to that for net new investment. It's noteworthy that *'EuroServ'* is *more* capital intensive than *Services* in the US".

Jonathan had been looking around the room as Dave commented on Exhibit 199. He noticed that all the heads nodded each time Dave made a point. Therefore, as Dave concluded his remarks on Exhibit 199, Jonathan motioned for him to keep going.

"Exhibits 198 and 199 are then merged into an outlook for Economic Profit (*EP*) and Value Profit Margin (*VPM*). We've analyzed *VPM* on both a 'pre-tax' and 'post-tax' basis, just in case that question might arise".

"You certainly are getting proficient in this subject", Earl chided.

"We're trying to construct the overall *Services* contribution to shareholder value for the company", Dave snapped back ... "and, also, get to *your* level of proficiency, 'Mr Treasurer'".

"Oh, I doubt you'll ever be able to do that", Jack chortled. "Besides, being 'Mr Funny', Earl is also 'Mr Economics' – or, at least he would like us to think that he is!" Jack was in a good mood, and everyone in the room (including Earl) was enjoying the easing of tension between Earl and Jack.

"Moving right along ..." Jonathan interjected.

"Yes, moving right along", Dave resumed ... "Exhibit 200 provides the 'Most Likely' outlook for *EP* and *VPM*".

"Now, this is getting interesting", Val exclaimed. "*EP*, in this 'Most Likely' scenario, increases almost 'fivefold' – that is, from \$3 million in year #1 to \$14 million in year #5. This is in spite of the fact that, Dave, you just indicated that *'EuroServ'* is more capital *intensive than Services*".

"Keep your eyes moving down the page", Dave admonished. "Look at the ('actual') profit margins. The lower COGS and R&D ratios more than offset a higher SMS ratio, and there should be *some* ability to leverage G&A. The result is that the 'pro forma' *NOP* margin for *'EuroServ'* is greater than 10%, beginning in year #2. Compare this to the *NOP* margin for *Services* in year #2/#3 of our 'plan', which is in the '8% range'. This margin differential is over two (2) percentage points and *it is significant*. It also allows for value creation in spite of higher capital intensity. How's that Jason?"

"You're getting to be a 'real pro' at this", Jason chuckled ... winking at Peter and Jonathan. "Now, tell them about *VPM!*"

Dave didn't need any further prodding. "The higher margins offset the higher capital intensity, thus producing positive *VPM* 'spreads'. These *VPM* 'spreads' (*NOP* basis for the total business) increase

Exhibit 200	GROWTHSTAR INC.				
	Acquisition Target Financials				
$ Millions	("Economic" Basis)				
	.... "Most Likely" Future Outlook — 5 Years				
"EuroServ" Financials	**Yr. #1**	**Yr. #2**	**Yr. #3**	**Yr. #4**	**Yr. #5**
"Most Likely" Scenario					
Economic Profit ("EP")					
NOP	$7	$10	$12	$17	$22
CCAP @ 11%	(4)	(5)	(6)	(7)	(9)
"EP"	$3	$5	$6	$9	$14
Value Profit Margin ("VPM")					
EBIT/A Basis					
Actual EBIT/A Margin (%)	15.3%	17.7%	17.0%	18.2%	19.3%
Value Profit Margin ("VPM")	8.5%	8.3%	8.2%	7.8%	7.4%
"Spread" - Actual % vs.VPM	6.8%	9.4%	8.8%	10.3%	11.9%
NOP Basis					
Actual NOP Margin (%)	9.2%	10.6%	10.2%	10.9%	11.6%
Value Profit Margin ("VPM")	5.1%	5.0%	4.9%	4.7%	4.4%
"Spread" - Actual % vs.VPM	4.1%	5.6%	5.3%	6.2%	7.1%
Incremental "VPM"					
NOP Basis					
Actual NOP Margin (%)	12.7%	16.1%	8.5%	13.5%	14.0%
Value Profit Margin ("VPM")	8.2%	6.1%	5.0%	4.6%	4.3%
"Spread" - Actual % vs.VPM	4.5%	10.0%	3.5%	9.0%	9.7%

from approximately 4% in year #1, to over 5% in year #3, and to about 7% by year #5. These 'spreads' are the result of our financial assumptions and the capital expenditure outlook. On an 'incremental' basis, they're really 'snappy'. Cast your eyes on the last row of numbers in Exhibit 200!"

Peter was 'beaming' and not afraid to show his feelings.

Jason was thoroughly pleased by the nature of the discussion. Dave was doing a good job of presenting the most relevant financial aspects of the '*EuroServ*' acquisition. The 'team' members and the others present were asking good questions and focusing on the 'economics'. "One of the advantages of the process we've followed to evaluate this deal, and also the '*Leasing*' acquisition, is that we've established a realistic set of assumptions, without knowing what the outcome would be. Thus, if the assumptions are credible, then so are the results. Before we get overly euphoric, however, remember that there is no 'goodwill' in any of the projected results. With an invested capital at the current year-end of $35 million and an 'asking price' of $85 million ($75 for the equity plus the assumption of $10 million of debt), you will be incurring goodwill in the range of $50 million. Thus, similar to the historical assessment of *Services*, the performance results will be lower that what is shown here. However, as indicated in the last row of numbers that Dave just alluded to – the

Exhibit 201		GROWTHSTAR INC.				
		Acquisition Target Financials				
$ Millions		("Economic" Basis)				
		.... "Most Likely" Future Outlook — 5 Years				
"EuroServ" Financials						*CCAP*
"Most Likely" Scenario						*11.0%*
Valuation						
Free Cash Flow (FCF)		**Yr. #1**	**Yr. #2**	**Yr. #3**	**Yr. #4**	**Yr. #5**
Approach						
Net Operating Profit (NOP) *		$1.9	$5.0	$7.1	$11.5	$17.4
Net New Investment (I)		(11.2)	(10.7)	(11.2)	(13.3)	(16.2)
Free Cash Flow (FCF) - 'Strategy'		$(9.3)	$(5.7)	$(4.1)	$(1.8)	$1.2
*[* Increm'l NOP vs. Current Year 'Base']*						**Residual**
						$158
"Warranted" Market		**"No**				
** Value .... "NPV"**		**Growth"**		**"Growth"**		**"Total"**
Total Market Value ("TMV")		$45		$68		$113
Existing Debt		(10)		███████		(10)
Equity Value		**$35**		**$68**		**$103**
Economic Profit (EP)		**Yr. #1**	**Yr. #2**	**Yr. #3**	**Yr. #4**	**Yr. #5**
Approach						
Net New Investment - 'Cumulative'		$11.2	$21.9	$33.1	$46.4	$62.6
Net Operating Profit (NOP) *		$1.9	$5.0	$7.1	$11.5	$17.4
Capital Charge (CCAP) — @ 11%		(1.2)	(2.4)	(3.6)	(5.1)	(6.9)
Economic Profit ('EP')		$0.7	$2.6	$3.5	$6.4	$10.5
*[* Increm'l NOP vs. Current Year 'Base']*						**Residual**
						$95
"Warranted" Market		**"No**				
Value .... "NPV"		**Growth"**		**"Growth"**		**"Total"**
Total Market Value ("TMV")		$45		$67		$112
Existing Debt		(10)		███████		(10)
Equity Value		**$35**		**$67**		**$102**
ROIC - "Outlook"		**Yr. #1**	**Yr. #2**	**Yr. #3**	**Yr. #4**	**Yr. #5**
ROIC — Total		19.8%	23.5%	22.8%	25.6%	28.7%
ROIC — Incremental		17.0%	22.9%	21.5%	24.8%	27.7%

VPM 'spread' on an 'incremental' basis – there appears to be 'room' to take on goodwill and still create value. I should mention that our objective here is *not* to do a 'pro forma' analysis of '*EuroServ*' under Growthstar ownership. We will do that *just after* the valuation is understood and agreed to. For now, we want to see what '*EuroServ*' is worth and we're building a scenario to arrive at that Net Present Value. Have I set you up adequately for the 'valuation', Dave?"

"Oh, you're a 'dandy', Mr Consultant", Dave quipped. "So, without further ado, here's Exhibit 201, which gives us the 'valuation' that we've all been waiting for".

"Hallelujah ... I thought we'd never get here", Jonathan exclaimed, as Dave clicked on Exhibit 201.

"That is one very impressive schedule", Peter stated – the volume of his voice rising with each successive word in the statement. "Even a 'died in the wool' salesman like me can see that the 'warranted' value exceeds the 'asking price' and that the *ROIC* is above the cost of capital for all years in the outlook period".

"I have to agree with you, Peter", Jonathan sighed ... "and, as Jason said a moment or two ago, if we believe our assumptions, then we accept the results. This is quite a different picture from what we saw with 'Leasing'. Wouldn't you agree, Earl?"

"Absolutely", Earl responded. "And there's no issue of this being a situation of investing in financial transactions that just exceed the cost of capital. This is part of our 'mainstream' business taken to a new geographic region".

"That's an accurate statement", Val chimed in. "Strategically, taking a 'business model' to a new geographic region entails transporting a 'customer/need/solution' framework and establishing the necessary infrastructure in a new region of the world – in this case, Europe. As you all know, one of the important reasons for pursuing this deal in the first place is because we didn't feel that we could establish a complete and effectively functioning infrastructure at a reasonable cost and within a reasonable time frame. Further, we would have to 'compete' with '*EuroServ*' – a company that is established throughout Europe".

"If the investors 'buy off' on our 'plan' for *Services* at the special meeting next week", Mandy added, "they should like this deal – especially if they put the same assumptions into their computer models that we've put into ours".

Jason then interjected ... "This analysis reinforces a concept that we introduced at the beginning of the 'value-based performance' process – that is, when a business is in the '**A**' **Category**, growth is truly profitable and rewarding to the shareholders. '*EuroServ*' is profitable on an 'economic' basis. Further, the assumptions that we all agreed to in our last 'team' meeting have the potential to *enhance* the profitability of '*EuroServ*'. Now, let's make sure we all understand the implications of this analysis. The 'Equity Value' of $102 to $103 million means that the 'difference' (in this case over $25 million – since the 'asking price' is $75 million) is a 'transfer of wealth' to *your* shareholders. As we saw in the '*Leasing*' deal, there was a potential there for just the opposite – that is, a 'wealth transfer' to the *seller's* shareholders. What we now need to do is to look at the 'value-based' performance on a 'pro forma' basis, incorporating the $85 million 'total' purchase price ($75 million for the equity and $10 million for the debt). Then, to 'test' our assumptions and determine how much 'slippage' you may be able to withstand, we'll review the 'Downside' Case".

Peter reacted by saying ... inquisitively ... "You mean, Dave, that you're going to 'spoil' this beautiful situation with a bunch of negative assumptions?"

"Jason made me do it, boss", Dave replied. "You know me – the 'optimist'".

Peter snickered at Jason and, jokingly, said ... "Ian is right – you really do 'rain on our parades'".

"Sorry", Jason snickered back, "it's part of my job ... but, *Jonathan* made *me* do it!"

Jonathan stood up, and as he walked over to the coffeepot to get a refill, said ... "That's right, blame it on the CFO – the 'policeman' ... or is it the 'bad guy'? ... I guess I should just say 'guilty as charged'! Also, I hate to break up the congeniality, but we still have a lot of 'ground to cover' and I have to see Ian before I leave today, so let's move on".

"Always the 'party pooper'", Peter chuckled. "I never realized how dreary your job is, Jonathan".

"You get used to it", the CFO countered. "Now, let's get 'on with it'".

Dave looked at Val, Frank, Jack and Jason and then said ... "I guess that means I'm 'on stage' again. Believe it or not, we have yet another exhibit; this time, it's #202 (Exhibit 202). This one adds $50 million of goodwill to invested capital and re-computes the key financial metrics".

Jonathan studied this schedule very attentively. As far as he was concerned, after seeing that the future financial outlook more than justified the 'asking price', the 'pro forma' highlights for the key value-based performance metrics would be the basis for a 'go/no go' decision. He had become 'wedded' to this way of measuring performance and was particularly interested in how long it would take for measures such as *EP* and the *VPM* 'spread' to turn positive and for *ROIC* to 'beat' the cost of capital. Everyone else in the room noticed how deeply involved in thought Jonathan was, and the room was eerily quiet. There was a respect for the CFO in moments such as this, who everyone knew was formulating his thoughts in terms of the 'message' he was going to take to Ian. No one would even think about speaking until he was through with his mental deliberations and offered the first comment. After several minutes, Jonathan looked at Val and Mandy and then spoke out. "I can live with this, and would think that the shareholders should find this performance acceptable. One year of 'negative' results ... 'break-even' by year #2 ... and a move into 'positive' territory – **Category 'A'** in your terminology, Jason – in

Exhibit 202	GROWTHSTAR INC.				
	Acquisition Target Financials				
$ Millions, except "ICI"	**("Economic" Basis)**				
	... "Pro Forma" Post-Acquisition Outlook — 5 Years ...				
"EuroServ" Financials	**Yr. #1**	**Yr. #2**	**Yr. #3**	**Yr. #4**	**Yr. #5**
"Most Likely" Scenario	.... Value-Based Performance Highlights				
Profit & Loss (No Change)					
Total Service Revenue	$75	$95	$119	$152	$194
Net Operating Profit (NOP)	$7	$10	$12	$17	$22
Invested Capital					
Pre-Acquisition	$35	$43	$53	$65	$78
Goodwill	50	50	50	50	50
Post-Acquisition	$85	$93	$103	$115	$128
"ICI"	$1.13	$0.98	$0.87	$0.76	$0.66
ROIC — Total	**8.2%**	**10.8%**	**11.8%**	**14.4%**	**17.5%**
Economic Profit ("EP")					
NOP	$7	$10	$12	$17	$22
CCAP @ 11%	(9)	(10)	(11)	(13)	(14)
"EP"	**$(2)**	**$(0)**	**$1**	**$4**	**$8**
Value Profit Margin ("VPM")					
[NOP Basis]					
Actual NOP Margin (%)	9.2%	10.6%	10.2%	10.9%	11.6%
Value Profit Margin ("VPM")	12.4%	10.8%	9.5%	8.3%	7.3%
"Spread" - Actual % vs.VPM	-3.2%	-0.2%	0.7%	2.6%	4.3%

year #3 ... followed by what I would characterize as 'solid' economic performance in years #4 and #5 (and, presumably, thereafter). What do you think, Val?"

"Just keep in mind", Val responded, "that as you review and analyze this schedule – and the others – that, even though we have done a credible job of establishing a set of assumptions upon which to base the evaluation, *we do not have a strategic plan* for 'EuroServ'. While I realize this is the situation we're faced with, we *must* understand that there are, potentially, market dynamics which could alter our expectations – and we don't know what they are without actually 'developing' a strategy. One way we can deal with this situation is through the 'Downside' Case, which Dave – or Frank – is going to lead us through".

"It's Frank who's going to do that. Remember, I'm the 'optimist'. Corporate Finance represents the 'negative' side of life".

"Yeah, sure", Jonathan fired back ... "so negative that we risked our capital on *Services* to establish this business. Frank, 'give 'em hell'! And, keep 'educating' Dave". As he spoke, Jonathan flashed a wide grin in Dave's direction. The CFO was truly impressed by the progress that Dave had made in this subject matter and the professional way he had presented the acquisition evaluation. Dave grinned back. He understood the gesture.

Frank blushed. He knew that Dave would probably 'crack' some type of joke, and that Jonathan would 'push back', but he just had such a hard time responding 'on the fly'. Almost everything with Frank was calculated and thought out in advance. And he always blushed when embarrassed. Earl winked at him, as if to say "*don't worry – you'll have your chance to get back!*"

"I always get the 'rewarding' tasks", Frank began. "Our 'Downside' Case reflects the assumptions we made at our last meeting. The major areas affected are revenue growth, G&A and R&D expense, and fixed capital which we held at the 'Most Likely' level for CAPEX's. I'm going to present the same array of exhibits that Dave presented – with different numbers that reflect the results of our 'Downside' assumptions. The first one is Exhibit 203 the '*Downside' Revenue Outlook*".

"The result is a 'top line' that falls short of the 'Most Likely' Scenario by about $45 million in year #5 – $148 million versus $194 million – with lesser shortfalls in the earlier years. The year #5 shortfall is about 23% ($46 million shortfall divided by $194 million 'Most Likely' revenue)".

Exhibit 203	**GROWTHSTAR INC.**				
	Acquisition Target Financials				
$ Millions	("Economic" Basis)				
	.... "Downside" Future Outlook — 5 Years				
"EuroServ" Financials	**Yr. #1**	**Yr. #2**	**Yr. #3**	**Yr. #4**	**Yr. #5**
"Downside" Case - Revenue					
'EuroServ' Revenue					
Growthstar - % Growth	*15%*	*15%*	*15%*	*15%*	*15%*
- $ Millions	*$52*	*$60*	*$69*	*$79*	*$91*
Other Products - $Growth	*$6*	*$8*	*$8*	*$10*	*$10*
Other Products - $Total	$21	$29	$37	$47	$57
'EuroServ' Revenue - $	**$73**	**$89**	**$106**	**$126**	**$148**
Revenue "Tests"					
Growthstar Segment:					
Europe:					
Growthstar - 'EuroServ'	$52	$60	$69	$79	$91
Products-Europe Sales	$81	$95	$110	$125	$140
'EuroServ' - %	64%	63%	63%	63%	65%
U.S.:					
Services - Revenue	$153	$187	$228	$275	$333
Products - U. S. Sales	$253	$285	$320	$352	$388
Services - %	60%	66%	71%	78%	86%
Total Service Revenue - $					
Growth Rates:					
Europe - 'EuroServ'	*21%*	*22%*	*19%*	*19%*	*17%*
U.S. - Services BU	*29%*	*30%*	*32%*	*25%*	*25%*
Difference	*-7%*	*-8%*	*-13%*	*-6%*	*-8%*

"That's a respectable basis for a 'Downside' Case", Jason inter-jected. "If '*EuroServ*' can justify the 'asking price' at this level of revenue shortfall, then you probably have a 'good deal'".

"I would agree with that comment", Jonathan chimed in. "Let's see the *Profit & Loss*".

"We can do that with Exhibit 204", Frank responded.

As the others studied Exhibit 204, Frank went to the flip chart and, on a new sheet, wrote:

NOP Comparison ($MM's)	Yr. #1	Yr. #2	Yr. #3	Yr. #4	Yr. #5
'Most Likely'	7	10	12	17	22
'Downside'	6	9	10	12	14
Difference	1	1	2	5	8

"The *NOP* difference is really significant by year #4", Earl noted.

"I wouldn't even consider this acquisition if I didn't think I could do better than this 'Downside' revenue and profit outlook", Peter retorted. "And, Ian would probably 'fire me' at anything less than this level".

"So, I guess that means we should feel 'safe and secure' at this level", Jonathan chided.

"You can 'count on it'", Peter snapped back. "Let's keep going ... What's next, Frank?"

Exhibit 204	GROWTHSTAR INC.				
	Acquisition Target Financials				
$ Millions	("Economic" Basis)				
	.... "Downside" Future Outlook — 5 Years				
"EuroServ" Financials	Yr. #1	Yr. #2	Yr. #3	Yr. #4	Yr. #5
"Downside" Case					
Profit & Loss					
Service Revenue:					
Growthstar	$52	$60	$69	$79	$91
Other Products	21	29	37	47	57
Total Service Revenue	$73	$89	$106	$126	$148
Operating Costs and Expenses:					
COGS - % to Revenue	20%	20%	22%	22%	22%
- $Millions	15	18	23	28	33
SMS - % to Revenue	44%	44%	44%	44%	44%
- $Millions	32	39	47	56	65
G & A - % Increase/Prior Year (*)	15%	14%	13%	13%	12%
- $Millions	13	14	16	18	20
R & D - % to Revenue	----	----	----	----	----
- $Millions	3	3	4	5	6
(*) G&A increases @ 67% of Revenue Growth %					
Total Oper. Costs & Exp's	62	74	90	106	124
EBIT / A	11	15	16	20	24
Taxes @ 40%	4	6	6	8	10
NOP	$6	$9	$10	$12	$14

Exhibit 205	**GROWTHSTAR INC.**					
	Acquisition Target Financials					
$ Millions, except "ICI"	**("Economic" Basis)**					
	.... **"Downside" Future Outlook — 5 Years**					
"EuroServ" Financials	**Yr. #1**	**Yr. #2**	**Yr. #3**	**Yr. #4**	**Yr. #5**	
"Downside" Case						
Invested Capital						
Memo: Revenue Change	$13	$16	$17	$20	$22	
New Investment:						***"ICI"***
Operating Cash	$0.6	$0.8	$0.8	$1.0	$1.1	$0.05
Accounts Receivable	2.1	2.6	2.8	3.4	3.6	$0.17
Inventory ('net' of A/P)	1.3	1.6	1.7	2.0	2.2	$0.10
Other W/C ('net')	0.1	0.2	0.2	0.2	0.2	$0.01
Net Working Capital	*4.2*	*5.2*	*5.5*	*6.6*	*7.1*	
Fixed Capital:						
- Gross (CAPEX's)	2.0	4.0	3.0	3.0	3.0	Dep. %
- Depreciation (Cumul.)	(0.2)	(0.6)	(0.9)	(1.2)	(1.5)	10%
- Net Fixed Capital	*1.8*	*3.4*	*2.1*	*1.8*	*1.5*	---
Other Capital ('net')	-	-	-	-	-	---
Sub-total (Bal. Sheet)	***6.0***	***8.6***	***7.6***	***8.4***	***8.6***	---
Operating Leases	*4.5*	*1.0*	*1.0*	*1.0*	*1.0*	---
Net New Investment ("I")	**$10.5**	**$9.6**	**$8.6**	**$9.4**	**$9.6**	
Memo: "ICI's"						**Avg.**
Net Working Capital	$0.33	$0.33	$0.33	$0.33	$0.33	$0.33
Net New Investment	$0.82	$0.61	$0.51	$0.46	$0.44	**$0.54**
Invested Capital (IC)						
Current Year - Beginning	$27					
Adjustment - for Year #1 (*)	3					
Balance Forward	$30	$35	$42	$52	$60	
New Invest. - Bal. Sheet	-	6	9	8	8	**Avg.**
New Invest. - Op. Leases	5	1	1	1	1	**"ICI"**
IC (Beginning)	**$35**	**$42**	**$52**	**$60**	**$70**	**$0.48**
(*) Current Year change in "reported" Bal. Sheet						

"Net New Investment and Invested Capital", Frank answered, "shown in Exhibit 205".

Again, as the others reviewed Exhibit 205, Frank went to the flip chart and wrote ... underneath the **'NOP Comparison':**

ICI Comparison: 5-year Avg.	*Incremental ("I")*	*Total ("IC")*
'Most Likely'	*$0.47*	*$0.43*
'Downside'	*0.54*	*0.48*
Difference	*$0.07(15%)*	*$0.05 (12%)*

Jonathan scratched the back of his head as he surveyed Exhibit 205 and the flip chart. "So, the revenue shortfall of 20% or so, when coupled with our assumption to 'hold' CAPEX's at the 'Most Likely' level, results in a significantly higher *ICI* – both for new investment and the balance sheet". He looked at Earl and Jack as he spoke. "OK, let's get to Economic Profit and the Value Profit Margins".

Frank responded by clicking on Exhibit 206.

Exhibit 206	GROWTHSTAR INC.				
	Acquisition Target Financials				
$ Millions	("Economic" Basis)				
	.... "Downside" Future Outlook — 5 Years				
"EuroServ" Financials	**Yr. #1**	**Yr. #2**	**Yr. #3**	**Yr. #4**	**Yr. #5**
"Downside" Case					
Economic Profit ("EP")					
NOP	$6	$9	$10	$12	$14
CCAP @ 11%	(4)	(5)	(6)	(7)	(8)
"EP"	$2	$4	$4	$5	$6
Value Profit Margin ("VPM")					
EBIT/A Basis					
Actual EBIT/A Margin (%)	14.7%	16.6%	15.3%	15.9%	16.3%
Value Profit Margin ("VPM")	8.8%	8.7%	8.9%	8.7%	8.6%
"Spread" - Actual % vs.VPM	5.9%	8.0%	6.4%	7.1%	7.7%
NOP Basis					
Actual NOP Margin (%)	8.8%	10.0%	9.2%	9.5%	9.8%
Value Profit Margin ("VPM")	5.3%	5.2%	5.4%	5.2%	5.2%
"Spread" - Actual % vs.VPM	3.5%	4.8%	3.8%	4.3%	4.6%
Incremental "VPM"					
NOP Basis					
Actual NOP Margin (%)	11.1%	15.4%	5.0%	11.4%	11.1%
Value Profit Margin ("VPM")	9.0%	6.7%	5.6%	5.1%	4.9%
"Spread" - Actual % vs.VPM	2.1%	8.7%	-0.6%	6.3%	6.3%

"So", Mandy reacted, "even with the revenue shortfall and higher *ICI*, the 'incremental' *VPM* 'spread' is positive in all years except year #3, and would appear to be positive on an 'average' basis for the 5-year analytic time frame. In case you're all wondering what I'm talking about, I'm referring to the bottom row of numbers in Exhibit 206. I believe this is one of the factors that the major 'sell side' analysts and institutional investors would focus on".

"In fact, the 'average *NOP* spread' – on an 'incremental' basis for the 5-year period – is very close to 5% (five percentage points)", Frank stated in a 'matter of fact' tone.

"You're amazing, Frank", Dave exclaimed. "Have you also done the 5-year average *VPM* 'spread' (on an *NOP*) basis for the 'Most Likely' Scenario?"

"*That* 'spread' is about 8% (eight percentage points)".

"I don't believe you, Frank", Dave exclaimed. "Is there *any* number or ratio that you haven't calculated?"

Frank looked at Earl and winked. Earl responded with a look of total surprise, because Frank was not one to 'wink' very often – if at all. Earl didn't know what to do, so he simply responded with a wink of his own. That gesture was what Frank was waiting for. He then put his forefinger to the side of his head and said in a 'deadpan' tone ... "The other day, Dave, I tried to compute your total compensation as a percentage of the average for the other financial people in the company with comparable job descriptions. The calculation was so high that it 'blew' my computer and printed 'error'!"

The room erupted in laughter, with Earl, Peter and Jonathan laughing the hardest. Dave realized that he had been 'had' and gave a 'thumbs up' sign to Frank, who started laughing himself, once he saw the reaction of the others.

"Now that we've had our 'afternoon laughs', why don't we take a short break", Jonathan said. "Even though I want to see the 'Downside' valuation, I want to reflect on it in a serious state of mind, which is not the 'current' state of mind. Thank you, Frank, for the humor – as well as the analysis – and thank *you*, Dave, for taking the 'butt' of this joke".

After the group was seated again, Jonathan motioned to Frank to resume his presentation. "We're now at a point at which we can assess a 'warranted value' to the 'Downside' Case", Frank stated. "The results of all our assumptions are captured in Exhibit 207".

"I was afraid of this", Jonathan groaned. "We *cannot* justify the 'asking price' with the 'Downside' Case results. Let's see ... we're about $11 to $12 million below the $75 million 'asking price', even though the 'returns' (*EP* and *ROIC*) are solid. There isn't one year in which *EP* is negative or *ROIC* is below our 11% *CCAP*. In fact, *ROIC* is in the '20% range'. This is a bit of a dilemma".

"You have to remember, boss", Earl interjected, "that you're looking at '*EuroServ*' on its own – that is, before *we* acquire the company and incur $50 million or so of goodwill".

"Of course", Jonathan mused. "I should have remembered. Frank, do you have a 'pro forma' analysis for the 'Downside' Case?"

"Coming right up", Frank answered, as he clicked on Exhibit 208.

"Now, *this* is a *different* picture", Jonathan sighed. "We don't generate a positive 'economic' profit or a 'return' (*ROIC*) above *CCAP* until the fifth year of the future outlook period. Further, *ICI* is over 'one dollar' ($1.00) for two years and remains at a very high level throughout the five-year period". Then, looking at Peter, he said ... in a frustrated tone ... "This picture isn't quite as 'pretty' ... is it?"

"It's not that 'pretty', but I don't believe it's that 'realistic' either. I respect Val's critique about not having a *strategic* plan to support our future projections, and I would encourage and support any effort to develop such a plan, similar to what was done for *Services*. Further, Jonathan, I respect *your* desires to reflect on the potential 'downside' aspects of this deal. With all due respect to *both* of you, however, I feel that one of two conditions exist".

"Can you elaborate ... with *specific* thoughts or perceptions?" Val asked, before Jonathan could respond.

Exhibit 207

GROWTHSTAR INC.
Acquisition Target Financials
("Economic" Basis)

$ Millions

.... "Downside" Future Outlook — 5 Years ....

"EuroServ" Financials
"Downside" Case

	CCAP
	11.0%

Valuation

Free Cash Flow (FCF) Approach	Yr. #1	Yr. #2	Yr. #3	Yr. #4	Yr. #5
Net Operating Profit (NOP) *	$1.4	$3.8	$4.7	$7.0	$9.4
Net New Investment (I)	(10.5)	(9.6)	(8.6)	(9.4)	(9.6)
Free Cash Flow (FCF) - 'Strategy'	$(9.1)	$(5.7)	$(3.9)	$(2.4)	$(0.2)
[* Increm'l NOP vs. Current Year 'Base']					**Residual**
					$86

"Warranted" Market Value .... "NPV"	"No Growth"	"Growth"	"Total"
Total Market Value ("TMV")	$45	$29	$74
Existing Debt	(10)	▆▆▆▆▆	(10)
Equity Value	**$35**	**$29**	**$64**

Economic Profit (EP) Approach	Yr. #1	Yr. #2	Yr. #3	Yr. #4	Yr. #5
Net New Investment - 'Cumulative'	$10.5	$20.0	$28.7	$38.1	$47.8
Net Operating Profit (NOP) *	$1.4	$3.8	$4.7	$7.0	$9.4
Capital Charge (CCAP) — @ 11%	(1.2)	(2.2)	(3.2)	(4.2)	(5.3)
Economic Profit ('EP')	$0.3	$1.6	$1.5	$2.8	$4.2
[* Increm'l NOP vs. Current Year 'Base']					**Residual**
					$38

"Warranted" Market Value .... "NPV"	"No Growth"	"Growth"	"Total"
Total Market Value ("TMV")	$45	$28	$73
Existing Debt	(10)	▆▆▆▆▆	(10)
Equity Value	**$35**	**$28**	**$63**

ROIC - "Outlook"	Yr. #1	Yr. #2	Yr. #3	Yr. #4	Yr. #5
ROIC — Total	18.4%	21.1%	18.9%	20.0%	20.8%
ROIC — Incremental	13.6%	19.2%	16.4%	18.4%	19.8%

Peter looked first at Val and Jonathan, and then at all the others in the room. "My *first* thought is that our performance will be closer to the 'Most Likely' Scenario than the 'Downside' Case. I feel strongly about this and am prepared to take this message to Ian, mainly due to the recent and forecasted performance for *Services*, combined with the opportunities that I see for '*EuroServ*' based on my recent trip. The business has not, in my opinion, been exploited to its potential and I believe there is an opportunity to grow at rates similar to those that we feel are reasonable for *Services*. Specifically, the eastern portion of the European continent is becoming more industrialized and presents a 'golden opportunity' – both for '*NG Euro*' and '*EuroServ*'. Based on what I've been exposed to regarding the '*NG Euro*' evaluation, this potential was probably *not* fully incorporated into *that* analysis.

Exhibit 208	**GROWTHSTAR INC.**				
	Acquisition Target Financials				
$ Millions, except "ICI"	("Economic" Basis)				
	... "Pro Forma" Post-Acquisition Outlook -- 5 Years ...				
"EuroServ" Financials	**Yr. #1**	**Yr. #2**	**Yr. #3**	**Yr. #4**	**Yr. #5**
"Downside" Case	..... **Value-Based Performance Highlights**				
Profit & Loss (No Change)					
Total Service Revenue	$73	$89	$106	$126	$148
Net Operating Profit (NOP)	$6	$9	$10	$12	$14
Invested Capital					
Pre-Acquisition	$35	$42	$52	$60	$70
Goodwill	50	50	50	50	50
Post-Acquisition	$85	$92	$102	$110	$120
"ICI"	$1.16	$1.03	$0.96	$0.87	$0.81
ROIC — Total	**7.6%**	**9.6%**	**9.6%**	**10.9%**	**12.1%**
Economic Profit ("EP")					
NOP	$6	$9	$10	$12	$14
CCAP @ 11%	(9)	(10)	(11)	(12)	(13)
"EP"	$(3)	$(1)	$(1)	$(0)	$1
Value Profit Margin ("VPM")					
[NOP Basis]					
Actual NOP Margin (%)	8.8%	10.0%	9.2%	9.5%	9.8%
Value Profit Margin ("VPM")	12.8%	11.4%	10.6%	9.6%	8.9%
"Spread" - Actual % vs. VPM	**-4.0%**	**-1.4%**	**-1.4%**	**-0.1%**	**0.9%**

Further, the owners stated – very openly – that they have *not* done a good job of penetrating the region of Scandinavia. Therefore, my recent discussions with the owners, along with a review of market data they shared with me on my recent visit, lead me to believe that we have *not* factored in the *full* potential for these geographic segments in the '*EuroServ*' outlook. As Dave mentioned, there should also be some synergism with respect to functions such as G&A and R&D. There may be other 'operating leverage' potential, but we won't know that until we actually develop a *strategy* for this business. Finally, we've 'loaded' the 'Downside' Case with capital expenditures, but the opportunity for savings (that is, lower spending) is limited".

"My *second* thought gets to a perception and line of reasoning that we employed in the internal evaluations for *Products* and *Services*. After we concluded the evaluation of the BU 'plans', we realized that a three-year time frame might be appropriate for strategic target setting and planning, but not necessarily for valuation. I feel that the same situation exists here, in that if growth is slower than the 'Most Likely' Scenario, then the 'time horizon' for purposes of 'valuation' is not necessarily limited to a five-year period. I would suggest that we look at the 'Downside' Case over the same 'seven-year' time frame as we used to establish a 'warranted value' for *Services*. My reasoning is that there are more similarities between Europe and the US than differences and that any growth shortfall in the shortrun (that is, the next three years) is not necessarily lost forever, but rather delayed to later years. We developed all sorts of market data and analyses for our *Services* (US) strategy that, I believe, supports this statement".

Jonathan leaned back in his chair and started thinking.

While the CFO was reflecting on what Peter had just said, Jack spoke up. "We came to the same conclusion regarding the 'time frame' for the evaluation, when we reviewed this situation earlier today. We were unanimous, I believe, in the perception that the time period for 'valuing' this deal should be the same (that is, seven years) as the 'profitable growth horizon' – or 'competitive advantage period' – that we ultimately used for the valuation of *Services*".

Jonathan looked inquisitively at Jack. "That's an interesting comment, coming from *you*, Jack".

"I agree, Jonathan" Jack responded. "I'm starting to surprise myself. Earl had better 'watch out'. Frank, can you show the group the evaluation we prepared using a 'seven-year' time frame?"

"I can handle it", Frank replied ... clicking on Exhibit 209.

Jonathan stared at Exhibit 209 for a moment and then said, "We just about 'make it', in terms of justifying the 'asking price' of $75 million with this extended time horizon".

Earl was poring through his copy of the exhibits. When he found what he was looking for, he came back into the discussion. "One factor that I think is positive is the level of *NOP* in years #6 and #7 – $17 million in year #6 and $20 million in year #7. Take a look at the fourth row down from the top – the one entitled NOP @ Year 5%. Note that the '% sign' designates 'margin'. Thus, year #6 and #7 *NOP* is estimated using the *NOP* 'margin' from year #5 (in the 'Downside' Case) and the revenues projected for those years. These numbers appear to support what Peter was saying about the potential being 'delayed' but not 'lost'".

"I'm sure that this revelation is very noteworthy and potentially 'earthshaking'", Jonathan quipped, as he looked inquisitively at Earl ... "but would you please enlighten us as to the *exact message* that you're trying to communicate".

"Sure, boss", Earl replied, trying to imitate Ian's wry smile. "If you refer back to Exhibit 198 – the *Profit & Loss* for the 'Most Likely' Scenario, you will notice that *NOP* in years #4 and #5 is $17 and $22 million, respectively. So, when I say to 'take a look' at the *fourth row of numbers in Exhibit 209*, that's what I'm talking about. As you can see, the 'Downside' Case delays estimated *NOP* performance by two years. This level of *NOP* ($17 to $20 million) has already proven

Exhibit 209	GROWTHSTAR INC.				
	Acquisition Target Financials				
$ Millions	("Economic" Basis)				
	"Downside" Future Outlook ... +2 Years = 7 Years Total				
"EuroServ" Financials	**Inputs .... Results**		**Yr. #6**	**Yr. #7**	*CCAP*
"Downside" Case	**Revenue** - % Growth		17%	17%	*11.0%*
Valuation	- $Millions		$174	$204	
	Revenue - Increm'l $		$26	$30	
Free Cash Flow	*NOP* @ Year 5 %		$17	$20	
(FCF) Approach					
Net Operating Profit (NOP) *			$11.9	$14.9	
Net New Investment (I)	*[@ 5-year Avg. "ICI"*		(14.0)	(16.4)	
	... higher than year 5]				**Residual**
Free Cash Flow (*FCF*) - 'Strategy'			$(2.0)	$(1.5)	$135
"Warranted" Market	**"No**				**"Total"**
Value .... "*NPV*"	**Growth"**		**"Growth"**		**"Total"**
Total Market Value ("*TMV*")	$45		$40		$85
Existing Debt	(10)		████████		(10)
Equity Value	**$35**		**$40**		**$75**

*[* Increm'l NOP vs. Current Year 'Base']*

Economic Profit (EP) Approach			**Yr. #6**	**Yr. #7**	
Net New Investment - 'Cumulative'			$61.7	$78.1	
Net Operating Profit (*NOP*) *			$11.9	$14.9	
Capital Charge (*CCAP*) — @ 11%			(6.8)	(8.6)	
					Residual
Economic Profit ('*EP*')			$5.2	$6.3	$57

*[* Increm'l NOP vs. Current Year 'Base']*

"Warranted" Market	**"No**	**+2 Years**	**7 - Year**
Value .... "*NPV*"	**Growth"**	**"Growth"**	**"Total"**
Total Market Value ("*TMV*")	$45	$38	$83
Existing Debt	(10)	████████	(10)
Equity Value	**$35**	**$38**	**$73**

ROIC - "Outlook"	**Yr. #6**	**Yr. #7**
ROIC — Total	20.3%	19.9%
ROIC — Incremental	19.3%	19.1%

itself to be 'value creating' – by that, I mean *VPM* 'spreads' in the '6% to 7% range' (*NOP* basis) for years #4 and #5 in the 'Most Likely' Scenario (refer to Exhibit 200). Therefore, Peter's point appears to be justified".

"As I said once before", Peter said energetically – his mood apparent to everyone – "you Corporate Finance folks are alright. Seriously, Earl, I appreciate that insightful comment, because I have no way of 'proving' my contentions, even though I may feel them in my 'gut'. I can't tell you how this Value-Based Performance endeavor has changed my opinion of Corporate Finance and how much of a pleasure it is for me to personally experience operating and staff people working together toward a common objective – getting to 'real value' – or, at least, giving our *best effort* to determine 'real value'".

"I appreciate that comment", Jonathan responded, "and I know that our finance people also appreciate your confidence and support. OK, then, where are we in this process?" The CFO was looking around the conference room as he spoke.

Mandy, who had been listening attentively to the presentation and discussion, felt that there was a 'piece' of the acquisition puzzle that was not clear to her, so she asked ... "Can anyone tell me if the owners have given us *their* rationale supporting the $75 million 'asking price'?"

Dave looked at Val and Peter, who had provided him with input on this issue. Val had discussed the 'asking price' with Dave prior to the first 'team' meeting, based on discussions she had with the owners earlier in the year, and Peter had relayed the input from the owners upon his recent return from Europe. They each motioned to Dave to respond to Mandy, which he did without the need for any further prodding. "There are two formulas that the owners have apprised us of, in terms of how *they* assess and determine equity value. The first is a multiple of revenue and the second is a multiple of after tax profit. In terms of revenue, they claim – without providing any details – that their survey of firms 'comparable' to theirs indicate a multiple of '1.25 times' annual revenue. Applying this year's revenue forecast of $60 million – which '*EuroServ*' will achieve – results in a $75 million 'price tag'. The other formula relates to a 'pro forma' net profit in a format similar to the one we employed in our analysis – that is, adjusting for the excessive owner's compensation". As he was finishing this last sentence, Dave went to the flip chart and wrote:

'EuroServ' – Owners Valuation Formulae/Results

Revenue Multiple: '1.25' times $60 million ... equals $75 million

Net Income Multiple:

	Total	Excess (*)	
Current Year Net Income ...			$1.5 million
Excess Owners Compensation:			
Owners Bonus	$4.0	$2.7	
Tax Impact @ 40%	(1.6)	(1.1)	
After Tax Impact	$2.4	$1.6 ...... 1.6	
Revised Net Income			$3.1 million

[say, $3 million]

'25' times $3 million ... equals $75 million

(*) 'Excess' Owners Compensation @ 67% of Actual Pay-out

Mandy and the others studied the flip chart as Dave was writing. Mandy, who had asked the question leading to the information on the flip chart, followed up with ... "Let's accept, for the moment, their so-called 'survey' leading to the 'revenue multiple'. Have they given us any support for the net income formula?"

Peter looked around the conference table and, with a slight look of sarcasm on his face, said … "When I was with them recently, they told me that … and I quote … '*this is the way that the Americans do it – a Price-to-Earnings (P/E) multiple*'!" Peter snickered at Jason and Earl as he spoke, and winked at Jack.

Jack wasn't about to let this one slip by and retorted … "So, the 'accounting' framework still has some application in the midst of this 'economic' revolution. Isn't that interesting!" Jack was chuckling and also snickering at Earl and Jason as he spoke. Then he cast a look at Jonathan. "Gee, boss, maybe these 'unsophisticated' multi-millionaire Europeans know something that our 'sophisticated' treasurer and consultant don't". Jack was really enjoying himself and wasn't afraid to show it with his facial expression.

Earl and Jason buried their faces in their hands for a moment. Earl was at a loss for words, but Jason had encountered this type of chiding and confrontation before. Jason, thus, responded. "That's good, Jack, and I'm actually glad that you are finally able to have some fun and that we can place this issue of 'accounting-based' valuation formulae 'on the table' for review. Let me respond with a question – what (or who) do you think is the *source* of the 'earnings multiple'?"

Jack thought for a moment and then replied … "A financial institution, or one or more of their people, I guess. Maybe one that had acted as an advisor to them in some capacity".

"OK, that's a reasonable supposition", Jason shot back. "And where do you think that the financial institution – or the person(s) – got *their* 'multiple' from?"

Jack looked down at the file of exhibits lying on the table in front of him, containing the 'economic' evaluations that the group had been developing and analyzing for most of the day. "*Touché*" he uttered … "Case closed … let's 'move on'".

"The case is *not* totally closed", Mandy interjected, "because many of the analysts and portfolio managers will look at revenue and P/E multiples to see if they are within the scope of how they view a particular industry or segment of an industry. These 'rules of thumb' are used by many of the professional investors who determine 'multiples' through 'economic' models similar to those that we have constructed. We need this type of information to be able to engage in a dialogue with the analysts and investors who use 'multiples' in publicizing their valuation work. What we have is a range of values for this deal that we can explain on the basis of both an 'economic' framework and two traditional and widely used 'multiples'. The only item we haven't discussed is the '67% factor' that the owners of '*EuroServ*' used to adjust for their 'excess compensation'".

"My feeling", Dave said quickly, "is if this is what they (the owners) want to use, then let them do it – since it lowers the net income for the 'multiple'".

"It's actually more fundamental", Peter responded. "They feel that a certain level of 'bonus' ... or, 'incentive compensation' ... is what they would be entitled to if they were simply 'employed' in their respective positions within the company. Again, without giving much detail, they feel that about one-third (33%) of the Owners Bonus they have taken over the past two-to-three years represents an appropriate level for a group of 'non-owner' executives. Thus, the '67% factor' equates to the 'excess' compensation. Further, they claim that the 'pro forma' net income calculated under this formula is representative of what the company would have *reported* if it had been publicly owned – even if they had a partial ownership position. Having said all this, they (the owners) took a 'firm stand' on the 'multiples' – almost as though an investment banker or someone in a similar role had implanted them in their minds. We may have some room for negotiation, but I seriously doubt that we can get them below $70 million for the equity plus the $10 million of debt".

"Let me see if I can summarize this deal and our evaluation", Val stated as she leaned forward in her chair. "The total acquisition investment will be in the $80 to $85 million range, including $10 million of debt. This initial acquisition investment, on our part, will generate goodwill in the range of $45 to $50 million, based on invested capital estimated at $35 million by the end of the current year. Revenue will reach a level of $150 to $200 million by year #5. Net new investment will be in the range of $35 to $40+ million during the next five years, with *ICI* in the range of 'forty-seven cents' ($0.47) to 'fifty-four cents' ($0.54). *Before* the allocation of goodwill to '*EuroServ*', returns are well above the cost of capital, economic profits are solidly positive, and *VPM* 'spreads' are significant. This is due mainly to the higher profit margins anticipated for '*EuroServ*' (versus the margins in *Services*) due to the expectation of a lower COGS ratio and the potential to 'leverage' G&A and R&D. The higher profit (*NOP*) margins more than offset higher capital intensity (versus *Services*) to produce 'absolute levels' of *ROIC* and 'spreads' for *VPM* that are very acceptable – even in the 'Downside' Case. *After* a $50 million goodwill allocation, the 'Most Likely' Scenario gets 'into the black' in year #3 and performs well, but the 'Downside' Case stays 'in the red' for most of the five-year outlook period – on an 'economic' basis. The 'Most Likely' Scenario provides a 'transfer of wealth' to our shareholders, based on a 'warranted' equity value (using *only* a five-year future outlook period) of over $100 million, versus the 'asking price' of $75 million. The 'Downside' just barely justifies the 'asking price' if we extend the analytic time horizon to seven years. Finally, the owners – through their own valuation formulae – arrive at a $75 million equity valuation and will probably *not* accept an offer below $70 million".

"I think you've captured the essence of the deal", Peter responded, "and this is the message that we should take to Ian".

"I agree", Jonathan added. "With respect to a meeting with Ian, we need to summarize the information developed to date and discussed today. Ian is very much aware of the 'basics' of this deal and he wants to make this acquisition. Obviously, he doesn't want to overpay, but I agree with Peter in that he will exert the appropriate amount of pressure to get the results needed to justify *more than* the 'asking price'. We also need to develop the 'accounting' impact – EPS, etc. – along with how we plan to finance this transaction".

Mandy then chimed in ... "Now that the 'special' meeting with the major analysts and institutional shareholders is just about upon us, we'll soon have feedback as to their perceptions regarding the future for the *Services* business (in general). This feedback should give us good signals regarding how the major investors will react to an acquisition of this nature".

Val then rose out of her chair, looked around the room and said ... "I think that 'sums it up', unless there are any issues we haven't covered".

"Nothing that I can think of", Jonathan replied. "And, I think we're all 'drained' to the point where we should adjourn this session. Thanks to all for the good work!"

The 'special' investors meeting went extremely well. The attendees were particularly interested in the strategies and future outlooks for the two business units. Ian gave the presentation for *Products*, with Val and Jonathan assisting him. Mandy acted as a moderator and handled the transition from strategy to finance, along with fielding the many questions that were asked. Peter presented the strategy for *Services*, with Dave assisting with the financial highlights. Ian and Jonathan provided a corporate overview to conclude the session.

The attendees seemed especially concerned with the competitive position of the two business units and the strategies/actions that were presented to deal with changing market conditions. Financially, once they understood the historical profile of the two business units (especially *Services*) they were mainly concerned with the rate of growth, along with the margin on incremental revenue and return on new invested capital. One of the major institutional investors actually asked about further growth for *Services* on a global basis. Ian, acting on Mandy's advice, had not planned on making a 'big pitch' on growing *Services* globally through acquisition – à la '*EuroServ*' – but was prepared to discuss the issue should anyone interrogate him. With an opportunity placed before them, Ian and Peter gave a 'high level' overview of the '*EuroServ*' deal. The response was generally favorable, depending on the price that would be paid and the 'pro forma' results. The analysts and institutional investors indicated that they would take the input provided to them and integrate this input into their valuation models – and they would do so quickly.

As the 'special' investors meeting was taking place at a downtown hotel, Jack Earningsly and Jill Debitson were meeting in a small conference room to calculate the important 'accounting' implications of the deal. Jack and Jill were acting on Jonathan's directive to determine the 'pro forma' net earnings and *EPS*. At the same time, Earl D'Mark and Frank Accurato were meeting in Frank's office to lay out financing – debt/equity ... issuance of new shares. The 'game plan' was for them to first work independently and then get together to integrate their respective analyses into a 'pro forma' *EPS* (including accretion/dilution) and capital structure (corporate debt-to-capital ratio).

Jill was experiencing a renewed sense of enthusiasm about her job and responsibilities, in light of Jack's acceptance of the economic framework and his willingness to be a 'proponent' rather than an 'opponent' of the effort to institute value-based performance. The burden and conflict of living in 'two separate worlds' had been lifted. Jack started the dialogue between Jill and himself by saying ... "We need to factor in two major items to calculate the earnings and *EPS* impact of this deal. The first is goodwill amortization. The second is additional interest – the amount that '*EuroServ*' currently carries (which we know) plus the incremental interest related to the new debt financing. We'll either get together with Earl and Frank later today to get a better 'handle' on new debt financing, or they'll send us a copy of their information. To get started, though, they suggested using our existing debt-to-capital ratio, excluding operating leases – which is about 35% – and assume that the total debt related to the acquisition will be determined by this ratio. They also suggested using our existing long-term interest rate of 'nine percent' (9%) to calculate interest expense on new debt related to the acquisition".

"I have a recollection of these ratios", Jill responded. "This information was covered in the Cost of Capital meetings. I have a particularly vivid memory of the Cost of Capital subject and its content because of the practical joke – actually a 'scare tactic' – that Frank and I 'pulled over' on Jason. Now that I think about it, we really 'had him going'".

"I 'pulled one over' on Earl and Jason during the '*Leasing*' acquisition evaluation", Jack shot back. "You should have seen Earl ... he was flabbergasted!"

"So was Jason when I 'pulled off' Dave's prank".

"So" ... Jack exclaimed ... "Dave was behind your prank, also!"

Jack and Jill looked at each other and laughed. It felt good, since both realized that it had been a while since they shared a good laugh.

"So much for the humor", Jack then said. "Let's get to work".

Earl and Frank were laying out the financing for the proposed deal, under a scenario that they had discussed with Jonathan yesterday. They agreed to develop a 'pro forma' financing structure by assuming that Growthstar would pay the 'asking price' – $85 million total. Further, they would finance 35% ($30 million) with debt and the remainder with excess cash and new equity. With regard to excess cash, a 'safety cushion' of about $2 million would be maintained in addition to the 2% 'operating' cash requirement. New shares to be issued would be determined by using the current year's average price of $27.50 per share. Earl and Frank were huddled over Frank's computer and looking at Exhibit 210, which Frank had prepared.

Earl was scratching his chin as he said, "On a consolidated basis, if we add $30 million of 'reported' debt – $10 million inherited from '*EuroServ*' plus $20 million of new debt financing – to the $60 million we currently have, we wind up with $90 million of total debt on a 'pro forma' consolidated basis. This amount translates into a 'book' debt-to-capital ratio of 36%. Our banks will gladly provide this financing, especially when they see the expected results from this acquisition. Let's send this to Jack and Jill".

"Done", Frank exclaimed a moment later and then added ... "We can easily take $10 million of excess cash and use it to help finance this deal. This leaves a $2 million 'safety cushion' in addition to the '2% of revenue' factor for the company's operating cash requirement. I used next year's revenue forecast for the combined entities to calculate the 'operating cash' requirement. Subtracting $20 million of new debt and $10 million of cash availability – $30 million in total – from the 'asking price of $75 million for the equity, leaves a requirement of $45 million for new equity financing. At the average stock price of $27.50 per share this year, the number of new shares is 1.64 million. We would probably 'round up' to 1.65 million shares – entailing an additional 10,000 shares and providing an additional $275,000 of cash. We'll probably need this for attorney and bank fees".

Exhibit 210	**GROWTHSTAR INC.**				
	Acquisition Target Financials				
$Millions, except per share	("Pro Forma")				
	New Financing ... Debt / Equity Capital — Amounts / Ratios				
"EuroServ" Financials	Growthstar	*'EuroServ'*	*'EuroServ'*	*'EuroServ'*	Consol'd
Current Fiscal Year-End	Existing	Existing	Acquisition	Pro Forma	Pro Forma
Total Debt:			[see * Note]		
Short Term	$10	$4	$-	$4	$14
Long Term	50	6	20	26	76
Total Debt	$60	$10	$20	$30	$90
* Note re: Long-term Debt					
Total Acquisition - Maximum			$85		
Total Debt - @ D/TC Ratio =	35%		30		
less existing 'EuroServ' Debt			(10)		
New Acquisition Debt			$20		
Excess Cash					
Total Cash @ Current Year-End			$24		
Oper. Cash @ % to Revenue =	2%	of Next Year			
		Revenue	(12)		
Excess Cash			12		
less: 'Safety' Cushion			(2)		
Excess Cash for Acquisition			$10		
Equity					
Acquisition Cost - "Equity"			$75		
less:					
New Acquisition Debt			(20)		
Excess Cash			(10)		
Existing / New Equity	$116	['Book']	$45	['Market']	$161
Debt-to-Capital (D/TC) Ratio	34%				36%
					Memo: D+E
# New Shares @ Price / Share =	$27.50	(avg. price)	**1.64**	million	$251

"Perhaps more", Earl retorted, "which is why we need the 'safety cushion' of cash. But, you're correct in your supposition, so let's use 1.65 million shares. Call Jill and tell her to use 1.65 million shares".

Jill was working up the 'pro forma' accounting schedule when Frank called with the revised input on the number of new shares. Jill made a note of this and said to Jack ... "We need to develop a schedule that takes revenue and operating income from the two companies for the current fiscal year, and then computes the impact of new debt and equity financing, as well as the goodwill amortization. New debt financing will increase the corporation's interest expense. New equity financing will increase the number of shares outstanding. There are no 'material' asset adjustments to the '*EuroServ*' balance sheet, but I'm not certain as to the exact treatment for the goodwill. Do you know?"

"As a matter of fact, I think that I do", Jack replied. "I researched this issue yesterday after we met with Jonathan. The amortization write-off period for this type of business is twenty-five years. Further,

I do *not* believe there is any opportunity for either a tax deduction for the goodwill expense or an 'up-front' write-off for any portion of the goodwill. So, we're 'stuck' with a constant write-off over twenty-five years that's not tax deductible. How delightful! I have a feeling that this translates into '*EPS* dilution'".

"Now the question is", Jill responded ... "has your *attitude* toward dilution changed?"

"I guess so ... at least a little", the Controller answered. "But, I still don't like it! Earl, the 'cash flow freak', will probably love it!"

Jill decided to ignore this last comment and said ... "I can input the information you gave me and integrate it with what I have already done. Frank gave me a format that he's using, and I have developed the 'P&L' data for the two entities before the acquisition entries". Jill input the goodwill-related information into her computer and then flashed Exhibit 211 on the screen that the small conference room was equipped with.

"Do you want me to call Earl and Frank"? Jill asked.

"Might as well", Jack answered.

As Earl and Frank were entering the small conference room, Jack was writing on the flip chart:

Exhibit 211 — GROWTHSTAR INC.

Acquisition Target Financials ("Pro Forma")

.... Net Earnings and Earnings per Share (EPS) ....

$ Millions, except per share

"EuroServ" Financials — Current Fiscal Year

	Growthstar Existing	'EuroServ' Existing	'EuroServ' Acquisition	'EuroServ' Pro Forma	Consol'd Pro Forma
Revenue	$450	$60	$-	$60	$510
Operating Income	42	3	-	3	45
Financing/Other Expenses:					
Interest Expense	5	1	2	3	8
Interest Income	(0)	-	-	-	(0)
Amortization Expense (*)	1	-	2	2	3
Other - Acquisition Reserve	-	-	-	-	-
Total Financing/Other Expenses	6	1	4	5	11
Net Income Before Taxes	36	2	(4)	(2)	34
Provision for Taxes (**)	13	1	(1)	0	13
Net Income After Taxes	$23	$1	$(3)	$(2)	$21
# Shares Outstanding (millions)	10.00	-	1.65	1.65	11.65
Earnings per Share (*EPS*)	$2.30	-	$(1.85)	-	$1.80

(*) re: Goodwill Amortization

Goodwill Amount	Amortiz'n Period (Years)	Amortiz'n Per Year
$50	25	$2

(**) re: Provision for Taxes ...   'EuroServ' Tax Rate = 40%   Amortization is 'not' tax deductible

'EuroServ' Acquisition – EPS Impact

Growthstar – Current FY Forecast ('close to actual') =	**$2.30**
Growthstar – Current FY 'Pro Forma' Post Acquisition =	**1.80**
EPS Dilution =	**$(0.50)**

Earl looked at the flip chart and then at Jack and Jill. "Does the 'dilution' result mean this deal is 'dead'?"

"I hope not", Jill answered, before Jack had a chance to reply.

Jack sneered at Earl, but the 'nastiness' was gone. "I hope not, either. But, it is an issue we may have to deal with. And, don't be surprised if Jonathan takes a 'hard look' at the potential implication of dilution. Remember, Ian is still motivated by our 'earnings' and *EPS* – especially since part of his annual incentive compensation is tied to it".

"Hopefully that will change next year", Earl retorted.

"Perhaps it will", Jack retorted back. "But, I think that Ian ... and the rest of us – you included – who are on the incentive bonus plan would like to get our 'pay-out' this year, and not be compromised by this acquisition".

"You're right", Earl came back. "This puts the issue of shareholder value creation where we feel it the most – in our 'pocketbooks'. All of us believe that this deal makes sense and that it's in the best interests of the shareholders – especially if we can negotiate a price anywhere below the $75 million 'asking price'. We need to get this issue 'on the table' with Flo Withetide and take a 'hard look' at the overall compensation program".

"Amen", Jack sighed.

"So, what do we do"? Earl asked. "Before you answer that, let me show you the *New Financing* schedule (Exhibit 210)".

Jack and Jill each studied the copy of Exhibit 210 that Frank then gave to them. After a few moments, Jack said ... "We should meet with Jonathan tomorrow. He wants to set a meeting with Ian and these two schedules 'complete the puzzle' for this deal. He'll also have 'fresh' input as to our 'plan' for *Services* from the meeting with the investors ... I wonder how that's going ..."

The following morning just before lunch, Mandy burst into Jonathan's office. "Have you seen today's action on our stock? Our price has 'jumped' by almost 10% – to $30 per share! I called a couple of the analysts, who indicated they were putting a 'buy' recommendation out on Growthstar for the near-to-intermediate term. I also spoke to three of our major institutional shareholders (portfolio managers) who indicated they were going to increase their holdings".

"I was tied up with a risk management issue until about ten minutes ago, and didn't get a chance to check our stock. As a matter of fact, I was about to go 'on line' just as you came in. That's good news. I assume Ian knows".

"He's ecstatic!"

"Well, 'chalk one up' for Mandy Bettertalk's job security. Seriously, I thought the meeting was great yesterday and wanted to congratulate you on the job you did pulling it together and serving as moderator. We really had some probing questions".

"The analysts and portfolio managers want to know what's going on – beyond next quarter's earnings forecast".

"I hope so", Jonathan shot back, "because I have a copy of the '*EPS* dilution' analysis for '*EuroServ*' that Jack and Jill developed yesterday – with input from Earl and Frank. In fact, we're all meeting this afternoon to discuss the financing and earnings impact of this deal. Val is going to be there, and you may want to join us".

"I think that's a good idea. What time?"

"2:00, in the small conference room".

The afternoon meeting was brief. Jonathan noted that the higher stock price ($30 versus $27.50 per share) would reduce the requirement for the number of new shares by approximately 150,000 – to raise $45 million in new equity financing. Jack then pointed out that the impact of this revision would be only a 'few pennies' with respect to *EPS* dilution. In spite of the *EPS* dilution, Mandy was very firm in her statement that the group *not* waver and take a 'go' decision to Ian. Val suggested a 'bid' of $70 million for the equity, based on the 'team' meeting and a follow-up conversation with Peter Uppcomer.

The following Monday afternoon, Peter, Jonathan and the '*EuroServ*' acquisition team met with Ian. Jason did not attend, since the decisions were now 'internal' based on all the evaluations done with his involvement. Further, the end of the year was in sight and the outlining of the capital expenditure and financial reporting systems needed to begin. The discussion was animated and thorough, covering – in graphic form – all the key elements that the 'team' had worked so hard on. Ian sensed the 'completeness' of the work, and asked only a few, albeit penetrating, questions. He was genuinely excited about the high profit margins and understood they were accompanied by a higher capital intensity than that forecasted for *Services* in the US. When the issue of 'what to bid' came up, he went along with the suggestion of Peter and Val to offer $70 million for the equity in the company, plus the assumption of up to $10 million of debt. When the subject of valuation arose, he agreed with the key assumptions in the 'Most Likely' Scenario and with taking the 'Down-side' Case out to seven years as an evaluation time frame. When the issue of *EPS* dilution was, near the end of the session, brought up and 'brushed aside' by Mandy, he was later quoted as saying ... "That 'damn Jason' must be influencing you, Mandy. He's destroying much of what I've believed in – at least financially – for most of my career. But, I have to admit that he's 'on target' in terms of what affects shareholder value". The meeting concluded with Ian directing Val to prepare a 'letter of intent' to acquire '*EuroServ*' according to the terms just discussed.

Five days later, the owners of '*EuroServ*' responded with a counter-offer of $73 million for the equity plus the debt assumption, which both parties agreed would be 'capped' at $10 million. After some negotiating back and forth, a price of $72 million was agreed to, with a closing scheduled for early in the upcoming year.

Mandy immediately scheduled a conference call to announce the acquisition. A press release followed. The day after the press release, the stock rose $2.00 per share. Mandy and Jonathan mentioned to Ian that the 'transfer of wealth' phenomenon was at work, as investors looked beyond the *EPS* dilution and focused on shareholder value creation.

13

Capital investments: planning, evaluation and control

Cathy Casher had been invited to join Earl and Frank in the effort to revise the company's policy and procedure for capital commitments (appropriations) and expenditures. Jonathan had been influenced by Cathy's recently disclosed years of frustration doing – what she considered to be meaningless – capital project evaluations. The CFO felt that Cathy should be part of any revamping of the system for capital spending, since she had been so involved in it. Earl and Frank agreed, as did Jason.

With an 'agreement in principle' having been reached on the '*EuroServ*' acquisition, and Frank now 'freed up', Earl scheduled a morning meeting to be held in the Corporate Finance conference room. Jason would facilitate the group's work effort. He would also be working with Jack and Jill on revisions to the internal financial reporting system.

"There is no rest for the weary", Earl exclaimed to Cathy as he filled his coffee mug. Frank and Jason were entering the conference room as Earl was speaking.

"I understand that you and Frank have been quite busy with the two recent acquisitions", Cathy responded. "And, Frank, I understand that you have now become a practical joker, 'pulling one over' on Dave. Congratulations!"

"That's one for me, versus his many", Frank replied – blushing slightly.

"How should we begin?" Earl then asked, looking at Jason.

"Let's start", Jason answered, "by outlining the major elements of a capital commitment and expenditure system." He walked over to the flip chart and wrote:

Capital Commitments and Expenditures

- **Planning**
- **Evaluation**
- **Control**

"Any effective capital spending system needs to encompass these three elements. You could argue for a fourth element – 'Reporting' – but I like to include this element as part of 'Control'. So, what I'm suggesting is three major components for Growthstar, with the understanding that some firms may want to have four – with 'Reporting' separate."

"Any debate on this?" Earl asked, looking around the table.

"I'm OK with this framework", Cathy stated, "since we have some of these components already. Our problem is that just about *all aspects* of capital spending have been geared toward individual projects rather than major program investments."

Frank nodded, indicating his approval – of what both Jason and Cathy had just said.

Jason resumed speaking. "Our objective should be to develop a summary of policy and procedure revisions during the next few weeks. You should implement these revisions immediately – no later than the beginning of the new year. Give the revised policy and procedure about six months to take hold and be tested. Then, make any final revisions."

"You're too darn logical", Earl snapped. "Can't you give us anything to argue about?"

Cathy chuckled as she said ... "We've had plenty of controversy around here during the past few months. We can probably use a dose of policy revisions that everyone will easily agree to."

"Don't assume that *everyone* will agree to all that we propose", Jason countered.

Frank, thinking as Cathy and Jason spoke, then said ... "We've established at least part of the second element – 'Evaluation' – through the work on the Valuation Hierarchy and the establishment of a Major Program framework for the analysis of capital spending throughout the company."

"Thank goodness", chimed in Cathy. "My workload will be reduced significantly on this aspect of my job. We'll do fewer evaluations, but I have a feeling that the ones we do will have a real impact on the business."

"I hope so", Jason replied ... "because if they don't, then I ... all of us ... haven't done our job!"

"Let's start at the beginning", Earl retorted, "and get into the specifics on the first major element – 'Planning'."

Jason took the cue and said ... "The 'Planning' element integrates the fixed capital segment of value-based outlooks for the BU strategies, value driver programs, and acquisitions. They provide the primary rationale for appropriating and spending capital. The other categories for capital investments are 'non-strategic' replacement of facilities, machinery and equipment, plus administrative needs and legal/safety requirements."

"Please expand on this line of reasoning", Cathy interjected.

"The capital spending forecasted for the BU strategies, value driver programs and acquisitions is what I would call 'growth-oriented' or 'strategic'. If you want to get technical, 'growth-oriented' capital spending is the amount in excess of depreciation. The theory behind this statement is that a firm's (or business unit's) depreciation represents the 'replacement' of assets that wear out over a specified time period (say, a fiscal year). Thus, the primary 'driver' of a capital budget or capital spending plan should be the strategies and growth programs – internal or external – 'bubbling up' from the business units."

"Are you suggesting", Cathy queried, "that we initially break down and categorize our capital investments into 'replacement' and 'growth' groupings? Does this follow the logic and pattern of the 'no-growth' and 'growth' elements of our BU valuations?"

"Not exactly", Jason answered ... "and, before you tell me that I'm confusing you, let me explain my answer. For purposes of developing the annual capital budget (ACB) and a long-range capital plan (LRCP), I prefer to start with a 'strategic' grouping. The theory behind an *ICI* of 'zero' as a 'no-growth' level of net new investment is that, over time, the replacement of the fixed asset base (that is, the reinvestment of depreciation) should allow for sustaining the business at its current level of operation. Most people would agree with this premise for purposes of valuing a business. When we take this 'higher level' analytic framework down a notch to the development of an annual capital budget or long-range capital plan, however, it's often hard to distinguish 'replacement' from 'growth' capital. Both are needed to execute a strategy. Further, many 'replacements' of productive facilities and/or machinery and equipment are made with a goal of improving performance, not just duplicating operations as they were done in the past. Thus, 'strategic' capital investments are all those required to execute a business strategy. This focus also 'drives home' a very important concept of resource allocation – which is that *all investments*, except for administrative and legal/safety expenditures, should be linked to a strategy."

Cathy, Earl and Frank sat back – thinking about what Jason had just said. After a few moments, Earl broke the silence. "So, am I hearing you say that we should 'do away' with our existing categories of 'revenue enhancement', 'cost reduction', 'productivity improvement', and 'replacement' – and group all of these into one 'strategic' category?"

"That's correct", Jason replied, "and *you* should know why."

Earl didn't say anything; thus, silence and reflection again permeated the room. Frank, usually the first one to grasp new concepts, responded with ... "the categories we have in place are 'project oriented'. What we're trying to accomplish now is to align capital spending with business strategies and value driver programs which, by their very nature, are 'strategic'." Cathy and Earl nodded vigorously, to express their understanding and concurrence.

Jason smiled, as could see the acceptance of his logic in their facial expressions.

Earl needed to delve deeper. "So, how do we actually *structure* the annual capital budget and long-range capital plan? Right now, we develop 'lists' of capital projects – under the classifications just mentioned – for the ACB. We had never done any long-range capital planning until this year's BU strategy development effort. Frank, you worked with the business units on their plans. And, Cathy, you spearheaded the effort in *Products*. How were the outlooks for capital spending developed?"

Frank looked at Cathy, who returned the look. She then said ... "We started with the major operational areas – manufacturing and R&D – for each geographic region. Within these areas, we reviewed the major functions with respect to the new capital required to execute the strategic actions under their control. We were able to get reasonably specific for the upcoming year. As we moved out in time, we focused on those regions and functions with the greatest need for new capital and approximately how much."

"That's similar to the approach that was used for *Services*", Frank interjected. "Here, we focused on facilities, testing equipment and vehicles, along with laboratory equipment for R&D – and evaluated capital needs for 'OCS' and 'Growthstar' segments of *Services*."

"So we had similar, but slightly differing focal points for the BUs", Earl commented. "What's your thought on these approaches, Jason?"

"I think they're fine", Jason replied, "since I participated in the planning sessions and probably influenced some of the thinking for the 'capital' portion of the plans. There is no one standardized approach to developing a capital plan. The important point is that capital spending must link to and support strategic actions. Therefore, the structure and output of the 'strategy' – or the 'plan' – dictates how the capital plan is organized and presented. In this way, the 'story' for the business is consistent throughout all of its various elements. The same logic applies to spending for advertising, R&D and so on."

"Here we go again with the logic that's hard to dispute", Earl retorted. "But, I do see your point."

"It really works", Frank chimed in. "I'm convinced that we have credible investment outlooks linked to the BU strategies, and supporting the cash flow and financing analyses. Heck, Earl, I implied this when I led the senior management through 'Sustainable Growth'."

"Yeah, you're right, Frank. Thanks for the reminder."

"What a change for me", Cathy sighed. "I may lose my title as the 'Laundry List Queen'."

Jason wanted to move on. "The 'strategic' element will represent the bulk of both the ACB and LRCP. The structure should be the same for both – 'driven' by strategic actions. The only difference is the level of detail for capital expenditures."

As the others nodded their heads, Jason continued. "The LRCP, which is a component of the strategic plan, establishes the capital commitments. Remember the Value Driver Programs?" Heads nodded. "We determined the total commitments for '*NG Euro*' and '*OCS*', as well as the time period over which the capital would be spent. Thus, the LRCP is a *summary* document – indicating first, the strategies, value driver programs (VDPs) and any acquisitions; second, the total commitment; and third, the estimated timing of the expenditures." He went to the flip chart and wrote:

Long-Range Capital Plan – say, 3 Years

BU	Year 1	Year 2	Year 3	3-Yr. Total	Years 4 + (*)	Total
Strategy #1						
• VDP 'A'						
• VDP 'B'						
Strategy #2						
etc.						
Acquisition(s)						

Total New 'Strategic' Capital . . . total of all Strategies / VDPs / Acquisitions

Administrative . . . Legal/Safety
Prior Capital Funding

Long-Range Capital Plan – say, 3 Years (cont'd)

Capital Funding
  Cancelled or Reduced
Grand Total (Net) Capital

(*) Years 4 + . . . 'optional' . . . if strategy/program has capital spending beyond three (3) years . . . noting that the '3-year' time frame is for 'illustration' only.
Note: 'Total' columns are 'commitments' . . .'Year' columns are 'expenditures' . . . 3-Yr. Total 'commitment' equals sum of annual 'expenditures' (Years 1-3).

"The first year ('Year 1') of the LRCP is the basis for the ACB. The ACB has two components – new commitments and annual expenditures. Commitments approved in prior years should be noted as a 'memo' item. Therefore, the *New Capital* section of the annual capital budget is virtually identical to that in the LRCP – unless a strategy has been altered or the timing of a value driver program/acquisition has changed. The *Expenditure* portion of the ACB is where the 'laundry listing' and detail appears. You need this detail for expenditure control during the upcoming fiscal year. Thus, the Strategy/Value Driver Program/Acquisition totals from 'Year 1' of the LRCP are detailed – by project." Jason again went to the flip chart and wrote:

Annual Capital Budget   FY_____

BU_____   *Total Commitment   Budget Year Expenditure*
Strategy #1
● *VDP 'A'*
  – *Project '1'*
  – *Project '2'*
  – *Project '3'*
● *VDP 'B'*
  – *Project '1'*
Other Strategies . . ..
Acquisition(s)
  – *Details . . ..*
Total New 'Strategic' Capital *. . . total of all Strategies / VDPs / Acquisitions*
Administrative . . . Legal/Safety
Memo: Prior Capital Funding   *ACB Expenditure*
Capital Funding
  Cancelled or Reduced   *[xxxxxx]*   *Expenditure Impact*
Total (Net) Capital   *[xxxxxx]*   **Total Expenditures**

"I see that the administrative and legal/safety expenditures are 'folded in' – to complete the ACB", Earl interjected.

"Right on", Jason shot back, "and you should also make an attempt to incorporate them into the LRCP. For example, if OSHA requirements dictate a multi-year capital program to meet air quality or emission standards, you should 'plan' for this investment. Or, if administrative work stations need to be replaced or upgraded, you should include this type of 'program'."

"OK, I agree", Earl snapped. "Now, just to make sure that I understand another point that you made ... we're including 'productive replacements' as part of 'strategic' capital."

"For the most part", Jason responded. "There may be instances where there are 'straight replacements' with no strategic implications – or, where *some* 'replacement' capital cannot be (or has not been) linked with a business strategy. In these instances, you should add another category – 'replacement' – and treat it similar to the administrative, legal and safety categories."

Earl nodded slightly, indicating his understanding. He then 'shifted gears' and said ... "One *goal* of the 'Planning' element should be to capture *all* of the 'Year 1' capital spending in the LRCP, so that it truly is the basis for the ACB. *Another* is to generate an invested capital intensity (*ICI*) for fixed capital in the future years that is reflective of the strategic direction and action(s) for the business."

Now it was Jason's turn to nod his head in agreement.

Cathy leaned forward and, scratching her chin, said ... "I notice that you've made *no* statements or suggestions about 'approval limits'. Who approves what? What can Larry and Peter approve? What authorization limit does Ian have? At what point does the Board (of Directors) get involved?"

"That's actually part of the 'Control' element", Jason answered, "but I can reply now if you wish."

Earl and Frank shrugged their shoulders. Earl nodded toward Jason, as if to say "*go ahead*".

"What gets approved", Jason stated, "are the strategies, investment programs and acquisitions. Once they're approved, so are all the capital expenditures that are part of them. So, you can eliminate virtually all your existing authorization limits. What you need to do is set a limit for the BU heads and Ian – in terms of what they can approve for the 'non-strategic' programs we just discussed. Since everything under this proposed system is included in the annual capital budget and the Board approves the ACB – in whole and major segments (strategies, acquisitions, non-strategic, etc.) – you have all the necessary approvals. Ian and the Board approve the major strategies for the business units. They also review and approve acquisitions. So, virtually all the approvals are in place. If you add the Long-Range Capital Plan to the information that the Board is exposed to – which you should – you've 'completed the cycle'. The only time you should have to go back for Ian's or the Board's approval is if you exceed authorized amounts by more than, say, 'ten or fifteen percent'. Someone in either Corporate Accounting or Treasury needs to be assigned the responsibility of verifying that requested capital expenditures – during the fiscal year – have been included in the ACB. There should be a space on the 'capital request' form to indicate this. The result is that *commitment approvals* become part of 'strategic' reviews and encompass *significant* amounts of capital – often for a multi-year period. Specific *expenditure approvals* become an administrative function, linked to the cash flow forecast for the fiscal year. Management time and effort is expended at the 'front end' – that is, at the 'strategic' review stage, which eliminates the need for 'back-end' review. This 'back-end' review is a serious weakness in many corporate capital expenditure approval processes, in that it wastes a lot of management time and often causes frustration within the organization."

"Why does this sound so *easy?*" Cathy inquired, her head dropping into her arms that were folded on top of the table.

"Because it *is* easy, if done in a logical and organized manner", Jason replied.

Silence ensued. Earl broke it by asking ... "Can we now move on to the 'Evaluation' component?"

"I'm ready", Cathy sighed, picking up her head, as Frank nodded.

"Let me start this dialogue", Earl responded. "This element should incorporate the analytic framework and valuation techniques that we've established over the past several months. We've evaluated strategies, value driver programs and acquisitions. I don't believe there's anything else, since we do *not* perform financial evaluations for administrative and legal/safety investments. Am I missing something?"

Cathy was a bit uncertain, so she looked at Frank.

Frank thought for a moment and said ... "I don't think so, Earl. We have the formats, techniques, inputs and outputs – through all the 'exhibits' that have been developed – for all of the 'strategic' investments. If we include the 'white paper' on *Present Value* (Exhibit 82) we should be covered."

"You folks are 'catching on' fast", Jason quipped. "You should also include the *Value-Based Analysis ... Valuation Hierarchy* (Exhibit 81). To reiterate ... analysis is done for strategies, value driver programs and acquisitions – *not* individual capital projects. All the 'evaluation' techniques and tools are in place. All that you need to do in the policy and procedure manual is ... *make reference to and provide examples/exhibits of* ... the various analytic routines that are now resident in the company. Finally, don't forget to incorporate 'operating leases' into all the above, since they're part of fixed assets."

"Good point", Frank replied, jotting this on his note pad.

"This is *really* 'coming together' – at last", Cathy sighed. "I can't believe how we could have been so myopic for all these years. This approach is so logical."

"Some people didn't want to listen to new ideas, or were 'too busy' to give them serious consideration", Earl retorted. "But, they're listening now!"

Cathy was fidgeting in her seat. She looked at her notes and burst out with ... "Before we 'wrap up' the 'Evaluation' element, can we discuss 'Lease versus Buy' analysis?"

"Certainly", Jason responded. "What is it that you want to discuss?"

"When do we do it?"

"*You*, Cathy, do *not* do it. Rather, Earl and Frank do it. Further, they do 'lease versus buy' analysis from a *corporate financing* perspective."

"What do you mean by that?"

"What he means", Earl interjected, "is that we'll advise you on the leasing (or purchase) of facilities and machinery/equipment in the context of our overall financing strategy and plan for the company. We'll consider issues such as effective interest rates, tax implications, banking covenants and relationships, capital structure and so on. We'll then instruct you that, for certain types of assets, there will be either a 'mandated' or 'recommended' corporate financing policy. So, you won't have to worry about 'financing' decisions. That's the job of Corporate Treasury. Since all the operating leases are included in your invested capital, everything is captured. 'Pretty cool', huh?"

"You're making me happier by the minute", Cathy snapped back.

The group then sat silent for a moment and, almost as though their minds and bodies were synchronized, rose and headed for the coffee and teapots.

When they returned to their seats, Earl started speaking again. "The first two elements were fairly easy for me to grasp. In fact, much of what you discussed, Jason, had been 'rolling around' in my mind. I'm a bit puzzled, however, by the third element ('Control') which we've agreed will include 'Reporting'."

Cathy added ... "we've always had the 'post-audit' routine in this component, which has been an 'exercise in futility' as far as I'm concerned. Re-computing *IRRs* and *NPVs* on capital projects has been particularly contentious for just about everyone in *Products* – especially when it involves a seemingly endless 'go-around' with the internal auditors within Corporate Accounting."

Jason chuckled. Then, looking empathetically at Cathy, he said ... "I'm sorry for laughing about what is probably *not* a 'laughing matter' for you. Let me say that I spent many years in this environment – when I worked *inside* corporations – and do understand the dilemma. Let's put together a sensible and manageable 'Control' mechanism for Growthstar."

"*Please*, let's do this", Cathy implored.

"The first part of 'Control' – '*Approvals*' – is what we covered just prior to our discussion on 'Evaluation'." The heads nodded. "The second part is '*Reporting*'. We need to start by being specific about exactly what we should report. Any ideas?"

Earl had been giving this subject some thought since the conclusion of the work on the '*Leasing*' acquisition, and had engaged Jason in conversation over a couple of lunches. "I believe there are two (2) aspects to 'Reporting'." As he spoke, Earl went to the flip chart and wrote:

Capital – 'Reporting'

1. Commitments/Expenditures – by 'Strategy'/'Program'
2. Commitments/Expenditures – by BU and TOTAL CO.

Earl then stammered a bit as he said ... "I have the view from '10,000 feet' but not from 'ground level'. You'll have to help me with the specifics, Mr Aradvizer."

As he spoke, Earl looked inquisitively at Frank and Cathy. "Don't look at us for help on this one", they said in unison.

Jason walked to the flip chart and began speaking. "It's actually fairly straightforward. You want to report on a 'running total' for strategies and programs, and the current fiscal year for the business units and total company. Let me be more precise", he said as he wrote beneath what Earl had written on the flip chart:

Capital – 'Reporting'

- **Commitments/Expenditures – by 'Strategy'/'Program'**

Year of Strategy/Program (x)	*#1___*	*#2___*	*#3___*	*Other____*
Total Capital Commitment		$_____ *millions*		
Amount Spent (Cumulative)		$_____ *millions*		
Percent of Authorization Spent		_____ *%*		

    Capital Spending Outlook – within 10% of Authorization yes___ no___
    Memo – re: the Overall Outlook for the 'Strategy'/'Program'
    CSFs (*) within 10% of approved outlook yes___ no___(**)

    (*) CSFs – Critical Success Factors for the Strategy/Program [those 'indicators' judged to be the 'keys' to success]
    (**) Give brief explanation if 'no' – including remedy(ies)

"This (first) report – for each major strategy and value driver program – should be done every six months, and discussed twice each year at your management review meetings. It's a summary of the total 'spent to date' versus the amount planned for and approved." As he finished speaking, Jason realized that he was at the bottom of the flip chart page and had 'run out of room' to write anything further. He 'flipped' the page over and continued writing on a new page.

Capital – 'Reporting' (cont'd)

- **Commitments/Expenditures – by BU and TOTAL CO.**

    BU_____   **FY**_____   **Qtr.**_____

    Total Commitment (Approved ACB)   **$**_____ **millions**

    Total Expenditures:
    Quarter   **$**_____ **millions**
    Year-to-Date   **$**_____ **millions**

    YTD as % to ACB Commitment   _____**%**

    Comparison to ACB:

	Qtr. #1	Qtr. #2	Qtr. #3	Qtr. #4
Actual				
Budget				
Difference		(***)	(***)	(***)

(***) Explain 'cumulative' differences greater than 10% – beginning with Quarter #2.

"This (second) report should be prepared every quarter during the fiscal year. If things are going along according to 'budget', this is all that you need. If *not*, then you can delve into the specifics in greater detail. The combination of the two reports should provide you with a good 'handle' on capital spending without overly burdening management with too much detail."

"That's it?" Cathy asked ... a look of bewilderment covering her face. "We've been reporting on the *individual* projects every quarter."

"It's an antiquated system and we don't even use it", Earl retorted. "Now, we're going to 'kill' it. We have the project detail through the general ledger system, if we ever need it. Except for extraordinary circumstances, however, there's no need to *report* all the detail."

Earl looked around the room for any additional reaction. Seeing none, he continued ... "I think the last item for discussion is the 'post-audit' – or as some people prefer to call it, 'post-evaluation'. And, I think I can sense what the conclusion is going to be." Earl had a sinister smile on his face as he looked first at Jason, and then at Cathy and Frank. "I think 'kill' is, again, going to be the 'operative' word."

"How so?" queried Cathy. "Won't Jack and Jill *kill us*? And, what about Jonathan?"

"Jill and Jonathan won't be opposed", Jason piped in ... "and I don't think Jack will, either ... now that he is, apparently, 'on board' with a value-based performance system. If we structure an approach that deals logically with *how* and *where* post-audits (or, post-evaluations) should occur, I think just about everyone in the company will accept it – since people will be 'freed up' from work that many consider to be unproductive."

"So, then, how does this 'homicide' take place?" Cathy asked. "And, what is the *new* approach?"

"Let's start", Jason continued, "by adopting the term *'Post-Evaluation'*, because this is more reflective of what you should be doing. The optimal approach is to 'track' and 'analyze' the critical success factors (CSFs) for the strategies, value driver programs and acquisitions. The concept is to *post*-evaluate what you *first* evaluated. I believe you will agree that the outcome of the various investment strategies and programs is directly linked to a few 'key factors' of success. These CSFs (some people call them KSFs) may be different for the various strategies and programs – and they will encompass *more than* financial indicators. Whatever they are, the CSFs are the 'keys' for successful future performance. I'm sure that you can see the logic trail. The strategies, value driver programs and acquisitions are the 'building blocks' for the future performance of the business units and the total company. In turn, the CSFs are the 'building blocks' for the major investment strategies and programs. To repeat – you should *post*-evaluate what was *first* evaluated, with a focus on the 'key factors' of success. Further, you should perform this 'CSF Tracking and Analysis' and report on it – probably on an 'exception' basis – at the same six-month intervals as the 'Capital Reports' for the major strategies and programs. Combining this tracking and analysis of CSFs with the recommended capital reporting for the major strategies and programs gives you a 'hands-on' system that is monitored often enough (every six months) without burdening management with unnecessary details. When appropriate, however, you can dig into as much detail as you need to."

"Please remember that, as part of the logic for this recommen-dation, the major investment programs encompass more than *fixed* capital investments. In some cases, *inventory* and/or *receivables* investment may be just as important as *'bricks and mortar'*. I hope these comments justify my conclusion that post-evaluating *any* type of capital *project* is meaningless, just as evaluating the project in the first place is meaningless. Therefore, 'post-audits' – as you have heretofore done them – should be 'killed'."

"If I may add one more comment ... In most cases, 'CSF Tracking and Analysis' is sufficient for '*Post-Evaluation*' – especially if remedies for 'under-performance' of a particular factor, or set of factors, can be established. There may be times when you want to run a revised financial scenario for a strategy, value driver program or acquisition through one of the valuation models to recalculate *NPV* or some other value indicator. However, I would suggest that this type of analysis be the exception and not the rule. Spending the appropriate time and effort in the initial analysis and carefully selecting the CSF's is a better prescription for successful performance, in the long run, than constantly 'second-guessing' yourselves and re-analyzing what you have already done. On the other hand, hindsight is valuable and can be a good learning tool for future investment analysis. What you should *not* do, however, is to build into the policy a 'complete' post-evaluation for every major investment, because then the process becomes a standardized 'post-audit'. Policies *cannot* replace management judgment. They need to be structured to provide a reasonable amount of discipline within the organization, but not so much that they stifle the functioning of the company and its business units by fostering a culture of 'analysis paralysis'."

"*Hallelujah and Amen*", Cathy whispered ... just loud enough so the others could hear it. "Sorry, I don't want this to sound as though I'm in church."

"Well, Cathy, maybe your prayers are finally being answered", Earl chimed in. "Any other comments or inputs? Any disagreements?" Looking around the room and not seeing any reaction, except for Frank giving him a 'thumbs-up' sign, Earl glanced at Jason and said ... "It seems to me that we have all the ingredients. What we need to do is construct a policy document incorporating all that we've discussed today."

"That should be doable", Frank responded.

"It *better* be", Earl quipped ... "since *you're* going to do most of the '*doing*' !"

"I know that you can do it, Frank", Cathy glowed ... "and I'll lend whatever assistance that I can. In fact, I have a couple of ideas based on our discussion today."

"Make the document comprehensive, but keep it concise", Jason concluded.

During the ensuing two weeks, Frank drafted a *Capital Investment Policy*. Cathy, Earl and Jason reviewed and edited the document, which was then sent to Jonathan, Jack and Jill for their review. As a courtesy, copies were also sent to Dave, Val and Mandy. With only a few minor comments from Jonathan and Jack, the policy document's executive summary was then given to Ian for his review. After the CEO's approval, the full *Capital Investment Policy* was printed and distributed throughout the company at the beginning of the new fiscal year.

## 14

Financial reporting and communication: traditional/ modification/ new

For Jason, the transition from 'capital' reporting to 'financial' reporting was swift. Two days after the meeting with Cathy, Earl, and Frank, he was in the small corporate finance conference room with Jack and Jill.

"I never thought we'd be sitting across from each other to revise *my* financial reporting system", Jack stated ... looking at Jason with a cold, hard stare. Then, softening his facial expression and glancing at Jill, he said "But, I have to admit that the concepts and rationale supporting the 'value-based' financial performance system that we're installing do have merit and provide a good template for our operating managers to focus on. The fact that you were able to express a key target in the form of an 'earnings' metric – the *VPM* – was probably the single most important element to bring *me* 'on board'."

"I've sensed that for some time now, Jack", Jason replied. "And, I also want you to know that there was never anything deliberate to 'attack' accounting, except to make the point that the traditional accounting focus and measures do not usually work when trying to get to economic value."

"That point has been made 'abundantly clear' to everyone in this company... and especially to me", Jack quipped.

"Me also", Jill added. "And I look at the 'economic' framework and approach as an 'enhancement' to what we've traditionally done from a financial measurement and reporting perspective."

"That's a good observation and one that we want to communicate to *everyone* – both inside and outside the firm", Jason replied.

"OK ... so, we're all basically on the 'same page' now", Jack stated. "What is it that we need to do specifically to revise our internal reporting? And, are we going to communicate any of this 'economic stuff' – excuse the term – externally?"

"Let's do what we did the other day on the subject of Capital Investments", Jason snapped back, "and take it one element at a time, starting at the beginning."

"So, get us started", Jill admonished.

"Let's begin", Jason replied, "by getting your existing *internal* financial reports 'on the table' for review."

Jill handed out copies of the monthly reporting package. "I think we can focus on the *Financial Summary of Operations* – the 'top page' of the package. The rest (of the package) is detail that we don't need to get into for purposes of what we're trying to accomplish." As she spoke, Jill walked over to the flip chart and wrote:

Growthstar – Monthly Financial Reporting... "Summary"

Fiscal Year_____   Month_____

Income Statement

Revenue and Profit	Current Month ($000's)	YTD ($000's)	YTD % Variance to: AOP	Prior Year
▪ Revenue				
▪ Gross Profit				
▪ Net Income AT				

Profit Margin (%)	Current Month	Year to Date Actual	AOP	Prior Year
▪ Gross Profit				
▪ Net Income AT				

P&L Ratios (%)	Current Month	Year to Date Actual	AOP	Prior Year
▪ COGS				
▪ SMS				
▪ G&A				
▪ R&D				

Note: 'YTD' is year to date... and 'AOP' is annual operating plan

"This is how we report on our Profit & Loss (P&L) statement", Jack was quick to comment. "This is the *Income Statement* 'summary' of our standard internal financial reporting package. It takes up about two-thirds of the 'top page'. By the way, just about everyone in the company uses this term – 'top page' – when referring to this (first) page in the reporting package. I think you know by now that Ian likes to have a 'one-page summary' of just about everything we do. This includes monthly reporting. For the BU managers, there's a set of schedules to provide supporting detail for the 'top page'."

"That point about Ian's desire for a 'one-page summary' is a good one. We need to be sure we incorporate this into the Value-Based Performance report", Jason mused.

Jack and Jason then looked at Jill, since they both knew that Jill had not completed writing the highlights of the 'top page' on the flip chart. Jack motioned for her to continue, and Jill wrote on the flip chart – underneath the *Note* to the *Income Statement*:

Working Capital

Receivables and Inventory

	Current Year Month-End	Prior Year Month-End	Variance
■ **Accounts Receivable**			
– **Amount ($000's)**			
– **Days Outstanding (*)**			
■ **Inventory**			
– **Amount ($000's)**			
– **Turnover (**)**			

Note:
  (*) '360-day' basis – Rolling 12-month average
  (**) 'COGS' basis – Rolling 12-month average

She then spoke again... "This is the other portion of the 'top page' – comprising about one-third of the monthly summary. As you can see, we focus on *Working Capital* management – specifically, receivables and inventory. We report on capital expenditures, but that's a totally separate activity and is done on a 'project-by-project' basis. I'm not even sure if Ian or the BU general managers see anything on capital expenditures."

"Ian does *not*, but the GMs do, along with the BU Financial directors – Cathy and Dave", Jack responded in a serious tone. "We prepare capital expenditure reports quarterly."

"I'm very much aware of that", Jason responded... trying to avoid a wry smile, but not being able to do so.

"You have an expression of *having something up your sleeve*", Jack was quick to snap.

"Guilty", Jason replied, wiping the smile from his mouth with his hand. "We just about 'killed' capital project reporting the other day."

"Well, isn't that just dandy", Jack retorted. "I trust you replaced it with something."

"We did and the new (proposed) reports will have two major thrusts – one for the major business strategies and investment programs, and the other for the business units. In fact, you'll be getting a 'draft' that Frank is working on in about two weeks."

"Well then, rather than debating this issue, why don't we stay focused on the 'financial' reporting task that we're responsible for?" The tone of Jack's remark was conciliatory – a welcome change from the confrontational tone of a few months ago. Jill sensed it and sighed – not afraid to hide her feeling of relief.

"So, what do *you* think we should add or modify to the 'financial' reporting package?" Jason inquired.

Jack thought for a moment and then said... "Well, 'Mr Consultant', you know that I am enamored by the Value Profit Margin (*VPM*)."

"So am I", chuckled Jason. "I don't think that there's any doubt of including this metric in our Value-Based Performance (*VBP*) Reporting. What else?"

"I feel strongly that the growth relationships – revenue, profit and invested capital – are a financial 'driver' that we should focus more attention on", Jill interjected. "I'm just not sure how often we would want to report on these factors. Obviously, we're going to report on Economic Profit (*EP*). We haven't gone through all the effort of the past several months without having this metric as a part of *VBP* Reporting. I would also think that Return on Invested Capital (*ROIC*) would also be a candidate for inclusion."

"These are all fair statements", Jason responded. "*ROIC* can be difficult to compute during the year so we'll want to look at this issue. I'm also wondering if we should enhance your *Working Capital* reporting with comparative growth rates that would go beneath total invested capital and incorporate receivables and inventory. This would be *in addition to*, not *instead of*, the 'days outstanding' and 'turnover' that you currently report on."

"That sounds logical. What about *Fixed Capital* growth"? Jill asked.

"I'm not so sure about that. Fixed capital growth doesn't always 'track' with revenue growth for short periods of time. I believe that it's a good factor to analyze and understand for longer periods of time – especially for strategic plan and acquisition evaluations – but I'm not sure it will be very enlightening for 'one-year' comparisons. In fact, it could cause confusion. Further, I think that the capital reporting framework that we outlined the other day, and which Frank is going to refine, gives management the most relevant information on fixed capital spending."

"OK, I'll accept that for now", Jill responded. "And, if Frank is prepared to develop a policy from work that you, he and Earl have collaborated on, then I would think that what you say is probably the right thing to do."

"What about timing?" Jack asked. "In other words, how often do we report on the 'value-based' performance indicators? I would think that monthly might be too much, based on what I've been able to digest so far."

"I think you've been very perceptive, and I happen to agree with you", Jason replied, "even though not everyone that I have worked with over the years might agree. Some people seem to be 'wedded' to monthly reporting for just about everything. With 'value-based' performance, however, I believe that *quarterly* reporting is optimal."

Jack looked over at Jill, who shrugged her shoulders. "I *think* I concur, but honestly... I haven't really thought about the 'reporting' aspect of this subject very much. Can we 'outline' what a *VBP* Report might look like on the flip chart."

Jason walked to the flip chart – stopping at the coffeepot on the way – and began writing:

'Draft'

Value-Based Performance (VBP) Reporting... Quarterly... by BU

Economic Profit ($000's) Revenue	Current Quarter	Current Year to Date			Prior Year to Date	
		Actual	AOP	% to AOP	Actual	Variance (1)
NOP						
CCAP	(2)	(3)	(3)	–	–	–
EP						
ROIC (%) -?	(4)	(5)	(5)	–	@ Yr.-End	–

Re: Variance –   (1) Current year (YTD) versus the prior year (YTD)
  Re: CCAP –   (2) 25% of AOP Total
          (3) Actual CCAP (capital charge) equals AOP, since the charge is based on prior year-end actual Invested Capital (IC).
  Re: ROIC –   (4) Current Quarter is 'targeted' at 25% of the annual ROIC – aside from any seasonal factor(s)... e.g. if the 'AOP' ROIC is 16%, then each quarter would be 'targeted' at 4%. Alternatively, 25% of the annual IC could be the basis for ROIC calculations.
          (5) Current Year to Date is 'targeted' at 25%, 50%, 75%, or 100% of the annual ROIC – aside from any seasonal factor(s) – depending on the quarter... #1, #2, #3, or #4. Alternatively, the IC basis for the ROIC calculation is 25%, 50%, 75% or 100% of the annual IC, with quarterly comparisons to the AOP's ROIC.

As Jason was writing he said, "you may want to have some of the 'ingredients' included, such as the prior year *IC* and/or the *CCAP* rate." After sipping his coffee, he continued. "The first perspective to focus on with *EP* is how you're progressing toward the achievement of your target for the year. For example, if you're at the end of the second quarter and you're below 50% of *EP* for the AOP, you may have to raise some questions – unless a factor such as 'seasonality' of the business might explain this level of performance. Next, you'll probably want to review this year's *EP* against last year's – on a year to date basis. Under normal conditions, *EP* should increase from year to year. There are situations, however, where the strategy may actually necessitate a *decrease* from one year to the next. That's why it's so important that the financial outlooks be based on business unit strategies and that the AOP is the first year of a strategic plan – or at least the first year of a 'strategically based' financial outlook."

"Jill, you raised the issue of *ROIC*. My feeling is that it's 'questionable' in terms of quarterly reporting. It's good to keep a 'handle' on *ROIC*, and you certainly want to compute and report *ROIC* at the end of each fiscal year, but I believe that *EP* is the more relevant metric *during* the year. The risk with an emphasis on *ROIC* is that it *may* cause managers to avoid good investment programs that are below the *current* level of *ROIC* in 'high *ROIC*' businesses. Further, quarterly-derived 'single-digit' *ROICs* can cause confusion in the operating ranks, regardless of the amount of explanation."

As Jack and Jill nodded, indicating *their* understanding, Jason started writing again.

Financial 'Drivers'	Current Year to Date		
(%'s)	Actual (6)	AOP (6)	Var. to AOP
● **Growth Rates**			
– Revenue			
– NOP	*some firms may want to 'report' EBIT (or, EBITD/A)*		
– IC (Total)	*[quarter-end*	*No quarterly AOP analysis for IC*	
■ A/R	*versus 'prior*	*No quarterly AOP analysis for A/R*	
■ Inventory	*year' qtr-end]*	*No quarterly AOP analysis for Inv.*	
● **Value Profit Margin (VPM)**			
[NOP Basis]	*some firms may want to 'report' on EBIT/DA basis*		
– Actual Margin			
– VPM	*'Actual' equals 'AOP' . . . thus, 'no' variance*		
– 'Spread'			

Note: (6) Revenue and NOP growth rates are current year's 'YTD' versus prior year's 'YTD'. IC growth rate calculations are noted in [brackets].

"What else" . . . Jason mused. "Let's see – you've captured the essence of the working capital *ICIs* with your 'Days Outstanding' and 'Inventory Turnover'. Fixed capital *ICI* isn't all that relevant on a quarterly basis, and neither is total *ICI*. By 'setting' Invested Capital at the prior year-end level, the 'actual' *VPM* equals the

'AOP' in any quarter. For a *Summary Report*, we thus have the key elements – encompassing 'aggregate' and 'surrogate' metrics. What we've outlined will give a good *Summary Report* . . . and you can always 'drill down' into specific problem areas. OK, I think we have it!"

"Will this report enable us to evaluate performance for incentive compensation, should we start 'paying' people on Economic Profit and/or the 'surrogate' metrics?" Jack asked.

"Definitely", Jason answered. "I was thinking about that possibility as I was outlining the items on the flip chart. In fact, Jonathan has scheduled a meeting with Flo to discuss compensation. I think it's in a couple of days. What I'll do now is to prepare this material in a more formal fashion and send it to each of you. Then, we should meet with Jonathan to get his reaction. Then, to the rest of the Corporate staff and the BU heads and finance directors . . . and, finally, to Ian."

"Sounds like a 'winner' to me", Jill exclaimed . . . as Jack nodded, indicating agreement.

Jason wanted to prepare a more formal 'draft' of the report and its contents, so he went back to his office and booted up the computer. As he was starting to format a schedule incorporating all that Jack, Jill and he had worked on, the phone rang. It was Mandy.

"We need to meet as soon as possible, to discuss what we want to communicate and report to the 'external' stakeholders regarding Value-Based Performance", she stated at 'full volume'. Her attitude had become even more enthusiastic after the 'special' meeting with the major investors and Ian's positive reaction, and it was evident by her tone on the telephone. "I think we should go beyond the stockholders and let our lenders know what we're doing. I believe they're going to like it – a lot! I've told this to Jonathan and he agrees. So, tomorrow afternoon at 1:30, we'll meet in Jonathan's office. I have calls in to Val, Earl and Jack. Assume that they'll all be at this meeting."

"OK, I'll be there", Jason replied. After hanging up the telephone, he got back to the computer and the schedule he was preparing – Exhibit 212, the 'quarterly' *VBP Report*.

Satisfied with the 'quarterly' report, he then prepared the summary for the 'annual' *Value-Based Performance Report* – Exhibit 213.

Jason printed out a copy of Exhibit 213 and looked it over. As he reached the bottom of the schedule, he thought . . . *"Well, I've accomplished one objective – to produce a 'one-page' summary that highlights economic profit performance for the year, along with key financial 'drivers'. What's missing, though, is a concise synopsis of invested capital. Ian is going to have to read a second page if he wants to capture what's happened with the balance sheet. On the other hand, he will get a good summary of 'EP', 'ROIC', the 'Growth Drivers' and*

Exhibit 212

Value-Based Performance Report – Quarterly

Fiscal Year _____   **Quarter** ____

Key Data ($000's):

Prior Year-End …	**Invested Capital**	**Receivables** **Inventory**
(same – all quarters) $ _____	$_____	$_____
Cost of Capital (CCAP) _____ %		

Economic Profit	**Current**	**Current Year-to-Date**			**Prior Year-to-Date**	
($000's)	**Quarter**	**Actual**	**AOP**	**% to AOP**	**Actual**	**Variance** [1]
Revenue						
NOP						
minus **CCAP**	_____	Actual = AOP … 100%			_____	_____
equals **EP**	_____	_____	_____	_____	_____	_____

[1] *'Variance': 'Current' year (YTD) versus the 'prior' year (YTD) … ($000's)*

Financial 'Drivers' – %'s   **Current Year-to-Date** [2]

- **Growth Rates**   **Actual**   **AOP**   **Var. to AOP**
  - Revenue
  - NOP

[2] *'Current' YTD versus 'prior' YTD for 'Actual' and 'AOP' Revenue / NOP*

                               Current Year Actual [3]

-    IC (Total)
  - A/R
  - Inventory

[3] *'Current' year quarter-end versus 'prior' year quarter-end for all IC elements.*

- **Value Profit Margin**   **Current Year-to-Date**
  - ('VPM') … NOP Basis   **Actual**   **AOP**   **Var. to AOP**
  - Actual Margin
  - VPM   'Actual' equals 'AOP'   'none'
  - 'Spread'

'VPM' with Exhibit 213. That may be enough for him, and he may want to leave the 'balance sheet' analysis to Jonathan and others. We need an Invested Capital Highlights schedule for the year, however, as part of the year-end report." As he concluded his thoughts, he began to outline Exhibit 214.

"Now, the 'internal reporting' is complete", Jason said to himself as he surveyed the three exhibits (212, 213 and 214) that were laid out on his desk. After giving the three schedules a final review, he sent them to Jack and Jill. He also sent them to Jonathan, which Jack and

---

Exhibit 213

Value-Based Performance Report – Annual

Fiscal Year _____   Cost of Capital (CCAP) _____ %

Summary

Economic Profit ($000's)	4th Quarter	Current Year Total			Prior Year Total	
		Actual	AOP	% to AOP	Actual	Variance [(1)]
Revenue						
NOP						
minus CCAP	_____	Actual = AOP ... 100%			_____	_____
equals EP	_____	_____	_____	_____	_____	_____
ROIC (%)	N / A					

[(1)] *'Variance': 'Current' year total versus the 'prior' year total … ($000's) for 'EP' elements and % points for 'ROIC'. Also, % points for 'VPM' Variance (below).*

Financial 'Drivers' – %'s	Curr. Year Total [(*)] … Year-End [(**)]		
	Actual	AOP	Var. to AOP [(***)]
• **Growth Rates**			
– **Revenue** [(*)]			
– **NOP** [(*)]			
– **IC Total** [(**)]			
▪ **A/R** [(**)]			
▪ **Inventory** [(**)]			

NOTES: [(*)] *'Current' year versus 'prior' year total for Actual and AOP Revenue / NOP.*
[(**)]*'Current' year-end versus 'prior' year-end for all IC elements.*
[(***)] *All 'Var. to AOP' amounts are 'percentage point' variances.*

• Value Profit Margin ('VPM')...NOP Basis	Current Year Total			Prior Year Total	
	Actual	AOP	Var. to AOP	Actual	Variance[(1)]
– Actual Margin					
– VPM	Actual = AOP		'none'	_____	_____
– 'Spread'					

---

he had agreed should be done. Earl could wait until Jonathan had a chance to review and critique. Besides, Earl had already suggested that most of the elements (included in the exhibits) be part of a 'reporting' package. Thus, Earl would *not* be surprised at the type of value-based performance reporting that was being proposed.

The group that Mandy had mentioned to Jason started entering Jonathan's office at 1:25 the next day. After they were all seated around the CFO's conference table, Jonathan glanced at Mandy, who began to speak. "I think we're all aware of why we're meeting. As

---

Exhibit 214

Value-Based Performance Report – Annual

Fiscal Year _____   ($000's) except ICI

Invested Capital Highlights

Total ($000's)	Current Year-End	Prior Year-End	Change $	%
Net Invested Capital	_____	_____	____	____
Receivables				
Inventory				
Net Fixed Capital				
Operating Leases				

'ICI' ($'s)	Total [1]	Incremental [2]
Net Invested Capital	_____	_____
Receivables		
Inventory		
Net Fixed Capital		
Operating Leases		

NOTES: [1] *'Total' ICI based on prior year-end balance sheet and current year revenue.*
[2] *'Incremental' ICI based on balance sheet and revenue changes.*

---

you know, the 'special' meeting with the major institutional analysts and investors was very well received. To keep the momentum going and to take our 'value-based' performance to the external world, Jonathan and I have begun discussing what we should do. So, this is a 'brainstorming' session to generate ideas on what the framework and specifics of our external communication should be, regarding the *Economic Profit* and related system of metrics and financial evaluation approaches that we've put in place over the past several months."

Jonathan started the discussion with … "Let me begin by giving you all a copy of the formats for the 'internal' reports that are 'hot off the press'." As he spoke, Jonathan handed out Exhibits 212, 213 and 214. Everyone took a few moments to read and review the schedules that Jason had prepared the day before. Jonathan had reviewed them this morning and, after speaking to Jack, felt comfortable in sharing them with this group. "As you can see, we have a 'one-page' summary on a quarterly basis and an expanded (two-page) report for year-end. I think we should use the information in these *VBP Reports* to help guide our thoughts as to what we will want to communicate externally."

"I agree and let me offer a suggestion on how to initiate the external communication", Earl said. "I believe that a write-up in the *Annual Report to Shareholders* is the best vehicle to begin publicizing what we are doing with regard to value-based performance and how we are committed to instilling shareholder value enhancement as a 'driving force' for the company. This 'report' reaches all our shareholders and the timing should be right – we're near the end of the fiscal year and the 'report' will be distributed in about three months. This should give us enough time to structure our message to the shareholders. Ian can probably weave in the subject as part of his *Letter to Shareholders*. I'm in favor of a separate section in the *Annual Report* and would gladly take on the responsibility of 'drafting' this section."

Jonathan looked around the table and saw that both Mandy and Val were nodding in agreement. Even Jack gave a slight nod of his head, which always signaled his opinion. "I'm interpreting the 'nodding' of heads as a sign of concurrence", the CFO then stated. The heads nodded again. "OK, Earl, you've got the assignment to 'draft' a section on value-based performance for the *Annual Report*." Now, it was Earl's turn to nod back at Jonathan.

Val had been thinking deeply since the meeting began and said ... "Since we had such a good reaction to the 'special' meeting with the investors, we should consider some type of inclusion of the value-based metrics in our first or second quarter meeting with the analysts during the upcoming year. Perhaps we should wait until we have six months of actual results, which would suggest the *second* quarter. I'm not sure that we should have a 'special' meeting, on this subject alone, when we present the value-based metrics to the analysts for the first time. In fact, it might be preferable to blend a presentation of the 'value-based' measures in with our standard 'quarterly earnings' report and discussion."

"I like that idea", Mandy responded. "These analysts keep telling me that, while there's always a keen interest in the *EPS story*, they also want to be informed about our economic performance. This forum should provide us with a good indication as to how serious they are about the economics of the company. I also agree that we should 'test' the external communication of the economics in the context of a regular quarterly meeting before scheduling another 'special' meeting. Having said that, however, I do feel that we should have *at least one* 'special' meeting each year on an important subject, based on the success we just experienced. In fact, the more that I think about it, a value-based performance session at this time next year may be a very logical follow-on to the 'special' meeting that we just conducted, where the focus was on the future direction and strategies for the company and its major business units. This could be presented as the *linkage of business strategy with value-based financial performance.*"

"That's a powerful combination", Jason chimed in, "and you should get 'good marks' from the investment community for this type of presentation and the discussion that will likely ensue. Mandy, you also mentioned that the *lenders* should be informed about the value-based performance initiative." Jason glanced at Earl as he made this remark.

Earl's reaction was predictable. "The lenders will 'freak out' – and I mean that in a *positive* sense. They're all getting more and more 'tuned in' to the economic framework for measuring performance and many are increasing their focus on 'cash flow' performance in their lending evaluations and their structuring of loans. I'm for arranging a meeting as soon as possible in the first or second quarter of next year – immediately after we get the 'year-end closing' work done. The lenders are important for at least one reason – they are a major funding source for our acquisitions. The more they see that we're focused on economic performance and that cash flow goes beyond *my office*, the more they will be willing to lend at favorable terms – at least that's my opinion based on the discussions I've had during the past few months. I've made the major lenders aware of the value-based performance metrics initiative – in general terms – and it would be very appropriate to now get more specific."

Mandy smiled as she looked around the table. Her intuitions had again proven to be accurate. She had a 'sense' of timing and the time to contact the lenders was 'soon'!

Jonathan quickly grasped the impact of Earl's comments and Mandy's expression. "Earl, it looks as though you may have another assignment. After you 'draft' the section for the *Annual Report*, let's get Frank involved to structure an 'overview' type of presentation for the major lenders. We have so much material that this task shouldn't be too difficult. Further, by the time we meet with the lenders, we'll have our 'final numbers' for this fiscal year. This will enable us to give an accurate historical and current performance profile for the company and the two major business units."

"I think that you're 'on the right track' again", Jason interjected. "The historical assessment, especially showing the steadiness of *Products* and the improvement for *Services* is a good basis to get started with the lenders. I would also give them a 'taste' of the future, since this is where their new lending would be focused. And you have an attractive 'tale' to tell about the future for this company. By doing this, you give them assurances that their past loans are secure and that there is an opportunity for additional lending in the future. After all, that's what they are in business to do – lend money!"

"Are there any more suggestions?" Jonathan asked.

Everyone looked at each other and scratched their chins or the back of their heads. There were, however, no further comments.

Jonathan looked at Mandy, who took the cue and went over to the 'white board' on one of Jonathan's office walls. "Let me try to summarize our conclusions with an 'outline' of the type of external communications that we're proposing." She then wrote:

External communication of VBP – 'framework'

* ***Shareholders / Investors***
  - ***Annual Report – special section on VBP and some mention in the CEO's letter to shareholders .... [Earl to 'draft']***
  - ***2nd Quarter Analyst Meeting – inclusion of 'VBP' measures in presentation, with specifics to be determined during the second quarter ... [Mandy and Jonathan to coordinate]***
  - ***'Special' Meeting with Major Investors later in the upcoming fiscal year ... [specifics and coordinator to be determined by the third quarter].***
* ***Lenders***
  - ***'One-on-one' Presentations to the company's major lending institutions by the second quarter of upcoming fiscal year ... Historical Assessment plus Future Outlook ... [Earl and Frank to coordinate and develop].***

The group reviewed Mandy's outline and the heads began to nod. Jonathan looked at his watch and saw that the time was getting close to when he had to see Ian about the latest forecast for the last quarter of the fiscal year, along with the consolidation of the year in total and a comparison to the annual operating plan. "I think we've accomplished our goal for this meeting, unless anyone has anything to add. I'll have Kay type up what Mandy has written on the 'white board'."

As they were leaving Jonathan's office, Earl grabbed Jason by the arm and asked, "can we meet tomorrow? I'd like to get your thoughts on the contents of the 'VBP' section in the *Annual Report*."

"Certainly", Jason replied. "How about after lunch? Jonathan and I are meeting with Flo Withetide in the morning to discuss incentive compensation."

"That will work. See you then; say, 2:00 – in my office."

Flo and Jason arrived (from different directions) at exactly the same time the next day at Jonathan's office. After coffee and tea mugs had been filled, Jonathan said ... "Yesterday, I got a bit of a surprise from Ian – setting the tone for this meeting." Flo leaned forward, eager to hear what Jonathan was going to say. The CFO continued ... "He wants to put an incentive compensation plan in place during the first quarter of next year, based on the value-based performance metrics. His thought was to place 50% of the incentive bonus in a 'pool' with our traditional *EPS* formula determining the pay-out, and the other 50% in a second 'pool' with *VPM* and the three key 'growth drivers' as the basis for the pay-out."

"Ian mentioned this idea to me last week", Flo responded, "so I'm not too surprised at what you're saying. I was a bit surprised that he had come this far with the *VBP* measures and the underlying framework, and I must admit to doing more listening than interacting with him. He went on at some length to express his opinions of the advantages that he is now seeing with this new approach. Admitting some initial difficulty with the concepts, particularly as Earl and Jason refuted *EPS* as a determinant of value creation, he now believes that he *understands and accepts* the fact that the traditional 'earnings' framework has two major shortcomings – namely, that 'earnings' and *EPS* do not adequately deal with first, 'risk' and second, 'return on capital'."

"And this a major 'leap' for a person who has grown up – at least professionally – on 'earnings growth' as the lifeblood of a business", Jonathan added.

Jason now leaned forward – his hands folded on the top of Jonathan's conference table. "This is gratifying – to say the least – to hear that the CEO appears to now be totally 'on board' ... *along with* the corporate controller. My, we have made progress! I'm concerned, however, with his hypothesis about combining an 'economic' framework with an 'accounting-driven' approach."

"How so?" Flo said inquisitively.

"I think I know", Jonathan answered, "but why don't you explain, Jason?"

"You run the risk of a conflicting set of directional goals. Pursuing an 'earnings' (only) target doesn't place any emphasis on the efficient utilization of invested capital. Pursuing an 'economic profit'-based set of objectives and metrics could undermine *EPS*."

"So, are you saying", Flo broke in, "that we need to make a 'complete break' with the past and move to the 'economic' approach for performance measurement and reward?"

"While I'm *hoping* that you will do just that, I'm *saying* that you need to have an incentive compensation plan that is based on one or the other – not a 'mix' of the two."

"Hmmm", Jonathan muttered. "I had a *feeling* when I left Ian's office yesterday, and this discussion puts it in perspective. You're right, we can't just stick our toe in the water when we're dealing with people's compensation, since it 'drives' their behavior. We either stay with what we now have and continue to 'drive' people toward '*EPS growth*' ... or, we change the incentive compensation plan to 'drive' our managers toward the pursuit of Economic Profit and its related 'goodies'."

"I'll get back to the 'big man' on this topic and express our views", Flo then stated ... "but, Jonathan, I wouldn't mind having you along."

"I'll be there", Jonathan replied, "since there are some compelling financial reasons for 'making a break' – along with the behavioral aspects of the change. This will be a good test to see if Larry and Peter have come 'on board' to the economic way of managing their businesses and measuring their performance. This will really make 'the rubber meet the road' within the two BUs. We'll also need to evaluate what we want to do with the corporate staff in terms of economic performance for the company. I think *you've* got some work to do, Flo."

As Flo looked over at him, Jason said ... "I may be getting near the end of my contributions, since compensation is not my area of expertise."

"I think that I would agree with this observation", Jonathan quipped. "Besides, there are some issues related to compensation that Flo and I should discuss privately." Jason didn't need any further hint that it was time for him to leave, and excused himself. Flo and Jonathan then spent another thirty minutes or so discussing some 'politically charged' matters that had surfaced during the payment of prior year bonuses and that were probably going to re-emerge with this year's payment of incentive bonuses. They also reached a consensus on how they would approach Ian and what they would recommend in terms of a 'process' to move forward on establishing a new management incentive pay plan.

Jason arrived at Earl's office at 2:00. Earl had a page of handwritten notes on his desk, reflecting his thoughts (since the conclusion of yesterday's meeting) on the 'draft' of the section for the *Annual Report*. "Let's talk about the important points to be made in the section on value-based performance", Earl stated. "I've jotted some notes indicating my preliminary thoughts. Without yet prioritizing them, I think the points to be made should include the perspective of producing a return on invested capital above the cost of capital, our choice of *EP* as a basic yardstick for performance measurement, the 'surrogate' measures (financial 'drivers'), and our focus on 'profitable' growth – that is, growing the company while 'beating' the cost of capital."

"That's a good start", Jason responded. "You've got the essence of the contents from a 'technical' perspective. What I would suggest adding is a point or two on the 'behavioral impact' that the economic perspective is expected to bring to the organization, especially since Ian will probably revise the management incentive pay plan. Further, when you discuss 'profitable' growth, you may want to cite that growth is expected to emanate from internal and external sources, and that 'value-based' analytic techniques will be applied to all major new investments. You should make a judgment as to the inclusion of specific Strategies or Value Driver Programs. Finally, keep the write-up to one page."

"Good suggestions", Earl shot back. "You sound like Ian with the 'one-pager'!"

"I'm learning", Jason snipped.

Earl then handed Jason his handwritten page of notes, which Jason looked over. Both of them then sat back in their chairs, closed their eyes and thought for a few moments.

Earl then said ... "I'm a believer in your first thoughts often being your best. With *your* recommendations added to what *I* had noted, I think I have enough to prepare a 'first draft'. I'll probably revise it several times. When I feel it's in good shape, I'll send you a copy."

"Fair enough", Jason replied, as he got up to leave.

On the way back to his office, Jason ran into Dave Dollarby. "It's been a while since we've 'sparred' with each other", Dave snapped. "I've been missing the 'give and take' of the past few months."

"It's been an experience", Jason quipped, "and I hope it's been beneficial."

"Definitely", Dave shot back. "One of my better learning endeavors ... and, one that will have a lot of practical application as time goes on." Dave then gave Jason a 'thumbs-up' sign as the two went in separate directions.

Exhibit 215   *'Final Draft'*

Annual Report Write-Up: Value-Based Performance

*During the past fiscal year, Growthstar's commitment to generating sustainable increases in shareholder value has evolved into a management discipline that is being implemented throughout the company. We have instituted a value-based financial performance system with the **Economic Profit** metric at the 'core'. This measure traces its roots to the basic notion of earning an economic return that is above the cost of all the capital employed in the operations of the company. Complementing this 'core' performance metric is a template of support measures that balance the achievement of growth with the efficient and effective utilization of invested capital. This new economic value management system will enhance and strengthen our traditional focus on growth of revenue and earnings. As we move forward, the balancing of our growth objectives with capital utilization will, we believe, provide the basis for generating an acceptable return on all stakeholder investments.*

The goal of achieving 'profitable' growth will drive our strategies, actions and major new investments, whether they are from internal or external sources. The evaluation of major investment programs is focused on the shareholder value impact they can produce, along with their support of the strategies for the businesses. Examples of such programs are new initiatives in Europe for our major business units, along with a significant thrust to develop the 'non-Growthstar' segment of the US Services business.

*The **Economic Profit** framework provides us with a consistent set of techniques, analytic tools and applications for viewing the company's existing operations and new endeavors. This consistency gives us a 'top-to-bottom' perspective that we believe is in the best long-term interest of the shareholders.*

*Our key operating managers will be compensated on the achievement of a set of **Economic Profit** based financial objectives that are consistent with the overall direction for the company and the strategies for the major business units. By establishing these new pay incentives, we have attempted to put ourselves 'in the shoes of the shareholders'.*

A week later, Jason received Earl's 'final draft' for the *Annual Report* – Exhibit 215.

As Jason reached the end of the *Annual Report* write-up, he leaned back in his chair and said to himself ... *"This 'draft' hardly needs any refinement. 'A Shareholder Value Experience' has occurred, and can now be communicated to the managers and employees who work for this company, along with the key stakeholders in the firm."*

Epilogue

Two days before the annual winter holiday shutdown at Growthstar, Jonathan and Jason met in the CFO's office. Jonathan wanted to briefly recap the efforts of the past several months and identify any 'gaps', along with future tasks.

Jonathan began the conversation by chiding Jason a bit. "We certainly got a 'taste' of Dave's personality during the past few months. I recall that he had 'pulled off' a couple of practical jokes on you and Earl."

"He certainly did", Jason chuckled. "He's quite a character."

"More importantly", Jonathan added, "he progressed professionally. I've been impressed by his grasp of the new concepts and analytic approaches, along with the way he has recently conducted meetings and work sessions."

"I agree", Jason replied. "He grasped the concepts and then put them into action."

"I think Cathy and Jill also gained a lot from this endeavor", Jonathan then stated.

"Cathy really 'opened up' and exhibited some talent on the evaluation of strategies and major investment programs that, frankly, I didn't know she had. Jill showed the type of ability that I've felt has been lying within her and she 'stood her ground' with Jack."

"Frank is a rare talent", Jason chimed in. "He's as smart as anyone I've met in all my years."

"Isn't that the truth", Jonathan sighed. "He's given our Treasury staff a very strong analytic capability. Earl's got a real 'rising star' with him. And, speaking about Earl, he's about as enthusiastic as anyone could be. Sometimes, though, I wish he'd stop talking... just a little!"

"Earl got what he was striving for", Jason said softly... "a comprehensive review of the 'economic value' concepts and framework at the highest level in the company. I think he felt that he had to argue and debate to get a 'full hearing' of the issues."

"Well, he certainly did argue and debate. And, by the way, he wasn't *alone* in wanting a 'full hearing' of the issues. I wanted this also", the CFO stated. "Earl just tends to be emotional... as does Jack."

The two men looked at each other and smiled. Jonathan then shook his head and exclaimed, "I honestly didn't think that Jack would 'come around' as much as he did. He seems to be committed to making this new approach work."

"I think a lot of people were surprised", Jason replied. "Fortunately, a couple of important items 'fell in place'. First, Jack found something that he could 'latch onto' – the Value Profit Margin – especially when he saw that Larry Buildermann and Peter Uppcomer were receptive to *VPM*. Second, you and Jill positioned the economic measures as an 'enhancement' of what Corporate Accounting has been doing for many years. Having his boss and his key aide come out and make this comment 'softened the blow' for Jack."

"Let me add to what you're saying", Jonathan jumped in. "Jack is just as tenacious as Earl. If he truly supports Value-Based Financial Performance, and if Jack and Earl can now agree on performance measurement and evaluation techniques, then this company is moving in the right direction – at least from a Corporate Finance perspective. I'm excited about this prospect."

"The foundation is there", Jason responded. "Now, it's a matter of execution."

"Amen", Jonathan said softly. "OK, so what's left... and are there any 'holes' in what we've done?"

"Let me answer the second question first", Jason replied. "There are no significant 'gaps'. What we've collectively developed is a comprehensive – I would say complete – analytic framework and financial performance measurement system aimed at 'driving' Growthstar's management toward economic value management in a meaningful way. As to what remains to be done, the education and training of the company's managers and supervisors, along with selected non-management employees, will begin during the second week in the new year."

"Yes, I'm aware of this and will be involved in the education and training sessions. Frank and Jill will share the 'corporate' perspective on economic value management. Cathy and Dave will be involved in all the sessions, providing insights and examples for *Products* and *Services* – since we'll be 'mixing up' the training sessions with people from both business units, as well as corporate staff departments. Can you believe it – Mary Frightly, Ian's assistant – has told me that *she* wants to attend a session. Ian must have told her that he has now adopted value-based financial performance and will support its implementation throughout the company. He gave me this message a month ago."

"You and I will kick off the training sessions", Jonathan continued. "You'll provide the generic background – stock market perspectives, overview of the framework of economic value management, transition from 'accounting to economics', etc. I'll give an overview on Growth-star, focusing on how we've progressed as a company in terms of strategic direction and financial performance – in both 'accounting' and 'economic' terms. Then, we'll turn it over to Frank, Jill, Cathy and Dave and let them train their colleagues. I know that you've been working with them and structuring the training sessions during the past week or so."

"That's correct and this process is an example of education and training at its best", Jason reacted... "when the people in an organization internalize the basic concepts and communicate the applications to others."

"We've come a long way", Jonathan stated. "I don't have to tell you that I appreciate what you've done for us – *all of us*! By the way, if you're still interested in working, I've been discussing our endeavor with the CFOs at a couple of other firms – long-time colleagues of mine – who want to embark on an effort similar to ours. They're not totally clear as to how to organize the process, and I mentioned your name. They're interested in talking to you... if you're willing to 'push off' retirement for a while longer."

"Well", Jason sighed... leaning back in his chair and folding his hands... "this experience has had so many positive elements, coupled with a few surprises, that perhaps I ought to pursue one or more future engagements before calling it 'quits'. Why don't you tell your colleagues that I'll meet with them in about a month. By then, we'll be well into the education and training within Growthstar."

"In case I haven't mentioned it", Jason continued, "I'm grateful for the opportunity to have worked here and to have played an advisory role in establishing a 'process' for the development of a value-based financial performance system, along with a 'template' for its implementation. For several years now, I've felt that consciously planning and managing for *shareholder value* can be *a* worthwhile effort within almost every *business*, and I'm delighted that we've begun to *experience* it here."

Index